AMERICAN
DICTIONARY

AMERICAN
BUSINESS
DICTIONARY

edited by
P.H. Collin
Carol Weiland
Derek S. Dohn

PETER COLLIN PUBLISHING

First published in Great Britain 1990
by Peter Collin Publishing Ltd
8, The Causeway, Teddington, Middlesex, TW11 0HE

British Library Cataloguing in Publication Data

American business dictionary.
  1. English language. Business English. American usage
  808.066651021

  ISBN 0-948549-11-4

Computer typeset by Systemset, Hitchin, Herts

Printed and bound in Great Britain by
Butler & Tanner Ltd, Frome and London

Preface

This dictionary has been compiled for the use of students of business. It contains about 4,500 words and phrases which are commonly used in business, covering all aspects of business life from the office clerk to the trader on the stock exchange floor.

Each word and phrase is clearly defined in simple terms. Many further examples are given which show the words used in typical contexts. We also give short grammar notes to remind the user of irregular word-forms and special constructions.

To show how the words are used in real-life situations, we have included quotations from many newspapers and specialist magazines published in the U.S.A. and Canada.

Aa

AAA letters indicating that a bond *or* bank is very reliable; ***these bonds have a AAA rating***
NOTE: you say 'triple A'

Class "A" stock *plural noun* ordinary stock with special advantages relating to voting rights or dividend preferences

A1, A2, A3, A4, A5 *noun* metric international sizes of paper; ***you must xerox the spreadsheet on A3 paper; we must order some more A4 letterhead***

abandon *verb* (a) to give up *or* not to continue; ***we abandoned the idea of setting up a New York office; the development program had to be abandoned when the company ran out of cash; to abandon an action*** = to give up a court case (b) to leave (something); ***the crew abandoned the sinking ship; the store stood next to an abandoned house***

◇ **abandonment** *noun* act of giving something up; **abandonment of a ship** = giving up a ship and cargo to the underwriters against payment for total loss

abatement *noun* act of reducing; **tax abatement** = reduction of tax

> QUOTE Montana state officials were so worried about high unemployment and the depressed economy that the state lent him $5 million and the city came up with tax abatements that cut his taxes from $5 million to $1 million a year
> *Forbes*

abroad *adverb* to or in another country; ***the consignment of cars was shipped abroad last week; the chairman is abroad on business; half of our profit comes from sales abroad***

absence *noun* not being at work *or* at a meeting; **in the absence of** = when someone is not there; ***in the absence of the chairman, his assistant took the chair;*** **leave of absence** = being allowed to be absent from work; ***he asked for a leave of absence to visit his mother in the hospital***

◇ **absent** *adjective* not at work *or* not at a meeting; ***ten of the workers are absent with flu***

◇ **absentee** *noun* person who is away from work, especially for a particular work day; ***the division had six absentees yesterday;*** **absentee owner** = a property owner who lives away from the property

◇ **absenteeism** *noun* staying away from work without authorization; ***absenteeism is high in the week before Christmas; the rate of absenteeism*** *or* ***the absenteeism rate always increases in good weather***

> QUOTE but the reforms still hadn't fundamentally changed conditions on the shop floor: absenteeism was as high as 20% on some days
> *Business Week*

absolute *adjective* total *or* complete *or* whole; **absolute estate** = form of property over which the owner has complete control, possession and total right of disposal

◇ **absolutely** *adverb* completely *or* undoubtedly; ***we are absolutely committed to our suppliers' schedules***

absorb *verb* (a) to take in a small item so as to form part of a larger one; **to absorb a surplus** = to take back surplus stock so that it does not affect a business; **overheads have absorbed all our profits** = all our profits have gone to pay overhead expenses; **to absorb a loss by a subsidiary** = to write a subsidiary company's loss into the main accounts (b) **business which has been absorbed by a competitor** = a small business which has been made part of a larger one

◇ **absorption** *noun* making a smaller business part of a larger one

abstract *noun* short summary of a report *or* document; ***to make an abstract of the proposal***

a/c = ACCOUNT CURRENT

accelerated *adjective* made faster; **accelerated depreciation** = system of depreciation which reduces the value of assets at a more rapid rate in the early years to encourage companies, because of tax advantages, to invest in new equipment

◊ **acceleration** *noun* act *or* state of being speeded up; **acceleration clause** = statement in a contract providing for the immediate payment of the total balance in the event of a breach of the contract

accept *verb* (a) to take something which is being offered; **to accept a bill** = to sign a bill of exchange to indicate that you promise to pay it; **to accept delivery of a shipment** = to take goods into the warehouse officially when they are delivered (b) to say "yes" *or* to agree to something; *she accepted the offer of a job in Australia; he accepted $200 for the car*

◊ **acceptable** *adjective* which can be accepted; *the offer is not acceptable to both parties*

◊ **acceptance** *noun* (a) signing a bill of exchange to show that you agree to pay it; **to present a bill for acceptance** = for payment by the person who has accepted it; **acceptance house** *or* **acceptance bank** = bank or lending institution which assumes responsibility (b) **acceptance of an offer** = agreeing to an offer; **to give an offer a conditional acceptance** = to accept, provided that certain things happen *or* that certain terms apply; **we have his letter of acceptance** = we have received a letter from him accepting the offer; **acceptance sampling** = testing a small part of a batch to see if the whole batch is good enough

◊ **accepting house** *noun* firm which accepts bills of exchange (i.e. promises to pay them) and is paid a commission for this

◊ **acceptor** *noun* person who signs a bill of exchange

access 1 *noun* **to have access to something** = to be able to obtain *or* reach something; *he has access to large amounts of venture capital;* **access time** = time taken by a computer to find data stored in it 2 *verb* to call up (data) which is stored in a computer; *she accessed the address file on the computer*

accident *noun* event which happens by chance and usually results in damage *or* injury (such as the crash of a plane); **industrial accident** = accident which takes place at work; **accident insurance**

= insurance which will pay when an accident takes place

accommodation *noun (usually plural)* place to live; *visitors have difficulty in finding hotel accommodations during the summer*

accompany *verb* to go with; *the chairman asked the new employee to accompany him to the meeting; they sent a formal letter of complaint to accompany an invoice for damage*

accordance *noun* **in accordance with** = in agreement with *or* according to; *in accordance with your instructions we have deposited the money in your account; I am submitting the claim for damages in accordance with the advice of our legal advisers*

◊ **according to** *preposition* as someone says *or* writes; *the computer was installed according to the manufacturer's instructions*

◊ **accordingly** *adverb* in agreement with what has been decided; *we have received your letter and have altered the contract accordingly*

account 1 *noun* (a) record of money paid *or* owed; *please send me your account or a detailed or an itemized account;* **expense account** = money which a businessman is allowed by his company to spend on traveling and/or entertaining clients in connection with his business; *he charged his hotel bill to his expense account* (b) *(in a store)* arrangement which a customer has to buy goods and pay for them at a later date (usually the end of the month); **to have an account** *or* **a charge account** *or* **a credit account with a department store; put it on my account** *or* **charge it to my account;** *(of a customer)* **to open an account** = to ask a shop to supply merchandise which you will pay for at a later date; *(of a store)* **to open an account** *or* **to close an account** = to start *or* to stop supplying a customer on credit; **to settle an account** = to pay all the money owed on an account; **to stop an account** = to stop supplying a customer until he has paid what he owes; **on account** = as part of a total bill; **to pay money on an account** = to pay part of a bill; **advance on account** = money paid on account before final due date (c) customer who does a large amount of business with a firm and has an account; *he is one of our largest accounts; our salesmen call on their best accounts twice a month;* **account executive** = employee who handles all the business with a particular client *or* clients **(d) the accounts of a business** *or* **a company's accounts** = detailed record of a company's financial affairs; **to keep the accounts** = to write each sum of money in the account book; *the accountant's job is to enter all the money received in the accounts;* **annual account** = accounts prepared at the end of a financial year; **management account** = financial information (sales, expenditure, credit, and profitability) prepared for a manager so that he can make decisions; **accounts department** = department in a company which deals with money paid, received, borrowed or owed; **accounts manager** = manager of an accounts department; **accounts payable** = money owed by a company, usually referring to short-term debts for goods and services; **accounts receivable** = money owed to a company for goods or services rendered **(e) bank account** = arrangement to keep money in a bank; *savings bank account; he has an account with Metropolitan Bank; to put money in(to) your account; to take money out of your account or to withdraw money from your account;* **checking account** = account which from which the customer can withdraw money when he wants by writing checks; **frozen account** = account where the money cannot by used or moved because of a court order; **joint account** = account for two people; *most married people have joint accounts so that they can each take money out when they want it;* **overdrawn account** = account where you have taken out more money than you have put in (i.e., where the bank is lending you money); **savings account** = account where you put money in regularly and which pays interest, often at a higher rate than a deposit account; **account number** = number used to name an account; **to open an account** = to start an account by putting money in; *she opened an account at Iowa Federal Savings and Loan;* **to close an account** = to take all money out of a bank account and stop the account; *he closed his account with City Bank* **(f)** notice; **to take account of inflation** *or* **to take inflation into account** = to assume that there will be a certain percentage inflation when making calculations **2** *verb* **to account**

for = to explain and record a money deal; *to account for a loss or a discrepancy; the reps have to account for all their expenses to the sales manager*

◊ **accountability** *noun* making managers responsible for their actions, using objective criteria

◊ **accountant** *noun* person who keeps a company's accounts *or* person who advises a company on its finances *or* person who examines accounts; *the chief accountant of a manufacturing group; I send all my income tax queries to my accountant;* **certified public accountant** = accountant who has earned a professional certificate showing he has met state requirements; **accountant's opinion** = report by a public accountant on the financial statement of a company, after he has carried out the audit; **cost accountant** = accountant who gives managers information about their business costs; **management accountant** = accountant who prepares financial information for managers so that they can make decisions

◊ **accounting** *noun* work of recording money paid, received, borrowed or owed; *accounting machine; accounting methods or accounting procedures; accounting system;* **accounting period** = period usually covered by a company's accounts; **cost accounting** = preparing special accounts of manufacturing and sales costs; **current value accounting** = method of accounting which notes the cost of replacing assets at current prices, rather than valuing assets at their original cost

accredited *adjective* (agent) who is authorized by a company to act on its behalf

accrual *noun* gradual increase by addition; **accrual of interest** = addition of interest to capital

◊ **accrue** *verb* to increase and be due for payment at a later date; *interest accrues from the beginning of the month; accrued interest is added quarterly;* **accrued dividend** = dividend earned since the last dividend was paid

acct = ACCOUNT

accumulate *verb* to grow larger by adding; *to allow dividends to accumulate;* **accumulated profit** =

profit which is not paid as dividend but is taken over into the accounts of the following year

accurate *adjective* correct; *the sales department made an accurate forecast of sales; the designers produced an accurate copy of the plan* ◊ **accurately** *adverb* correctly; *the second quarter's drop in sales was accurately forecast by the computer*

accuse *verb* to say that someone has committed a crime; *she was accused of stealing from the petty cash box; he was accused of industrial espionage* NOTE: you accuse someone **of** a crime or **of** doing something

achieve *verb* to succeed in doing something *or* to do something successfully; *the company has achieved great success in the Far East; we achieved all our objectives in 1990*

acid test *noun* crucial final test that proves the value *or* quality of something

acknowledge *verb* to tell a sender that a letter *or* package *or* shipment has arrived; *he still has not acknowledged my letter of the May 24; we acknowledge receipt of your June shipment*

◊ **acknowledgment,** *noun* act of acknowledging; *she sent an acknowledgment of receipt; they sent a letter of acknowledgment*

acquire *verb* to buy; *to acquire a company*

◊ **acquirer** *noun* person *or* company which buys something

◊ **acquisition** *noun* thing bought; act of getting *or* buying something; *the chocolate factory is his latest acquisition;* data acquisition *or* acquisition of data = obtaining and classifying data

acre *noun* measure of the area of land equal to 43,560 square feet NOTE: the plural is used with figures, except before a noun: **he has bought a farm of 250 acres** *or* **he has bought a 250-acre farm**

acronym *noun* word formed from the first letters of a series of words (such as Amex)

across-the-board *adjective* applying to everything *or* everyone; *an across-the-board price increase*

act 1 *noun* **(a)** law passed by a legislative body; *an Act of Congress;* **Equal Employment Opportunity Act** = law that gives the Equal Employment Opportunity Commission power to take court action against discriminatory organizations; **Fair Labor Standards Act** = federal law requiring employers to pay a minimum hourly wage and overtime pay beyond 40 hours a week **(b) act of God** = something you do not expect to happen, and which cannot be avoided (such as storms *or* floods) **2** *verb* **(a)** to work; *to act as an agent for a British company; to act for someone or to act on someone's behalf* **(b)** to do something; *the board will have to act quickly if the company's losses are going to be reduced; the lawyers are acting on our instructions;* **to act on a letter** = to do what a letter asks to be done

◊ **acting** *adjective* working in place of someone for a short time; *acting manager; the Acting Chairman*

◊ **action** *noun* **(a)** thing which has been done; **to take action** = to do something; *you must take action if you want to prevent further shoplifting* **(b)** case in a law court where a person *or* company sues another person *or* company; **to take legal action** = to sue someone; *action for damages; action for libel;* **to bring an action for damages against someone;** **civil action** = case brought by a person *or* company against someone who has done them civil wrong; **criminal action** = case brought by the state against someone who is charged with a crime

◊ **active** *adjective* busy; *an active demand for oil shares; oil shares are very active; an active day on the Stock Exchange; business is active;* **active partner** = partner who presently works in the company;

◊ **actively** *adverb* presently working on; *the company is actively recruiting new personnel*

◊ **activity** *noun* state of being active *or* busy; *a low level of business activity; there was a lot of activity on the Stock Exchange;* **activity chart** = plan showing work which has been done so that it can be compared to the plan of work to be done; **monthly activity report** = report by a department on what has been done during the past month

actual 1 *adjective* accurate *or* correct; *what is the actual cost of one unit?* **the actual figures for board members' expenses are not shown to the shareholders 2** *plural noun* **(a)** real figures; *these figures are the actuals for 1989* **(b)** real commodities traded on a commodity exchange (as opposed to commodity futures)

actuary *noun* person employed by an insurance company to calculate premiums

◊ **actuarial** *adjective* relating to the mathematics and statistics of insurance; *the premiums are worked out according to actuarial calculations;* **actuarial tables =** lists showing how long people of certain ages are likely to live, used to calculate life insurance premiums

ad *noun* = ADVERTISEMENT

add *verb* **(a)** to put figures together to make a total; *to add interest to the capital; interest is added monthly* **(b)** to put things together to make a large group; *we are adding to the sales force; they have added two new products to their line;* this all adds to the **company's costs =** this makes the company's costs higher

◊ **add up** *verb* to put several figures together to make a total; *to add up a column of figures;* **the figures do not add up =** the total given is not correct

◊ **add up to** *verb* to make a total; *the total expenditure adds up to more than $1,000*

◊ **adding** *noun* which adds *or* which makes additions; *an adding machine*

◊ **addition** *noun* **(a)** thing or person added; *the management is planning further additions to the staff; we are exhibiting several additions to our product line; a bank vice-president is the latest addition to the board; they have constructed an addition to the west wing* **(b)** **in addition to =** added to *or* as well as; *there are twelve registered letters to be sent in addition to this packet* **(c)** putting numbers together; *you don't need a calculator to do simple addition*

◊ **additional** *adjective* extra *or* which is added; *additional costs; additional charges; additional clauses to a*

contract; additional duty will have to be paid

address 1 *noun* details of number, street and town where an office is or a person lives; *address list; address book; my business address and phone number are printed on the card;* **cable address =** short address for sending cables; **forwarding address =** address to which a person's mail can be sent on; **home address =** address of a house or apartment where someone lives; *please send the documents to my home address;* **mailing address =** location where mail is sent to **2** *verb* **(a)** to write the details of an address on an envelope, etc.; *to address a letter or a parcel; please address your enquiries to the manager; a letter addressed to the executive director; an incorrectly addressed package* **(b)** to speak; *to address a meeting* **(c)** to deal with; to speak about; *he addressed the issue of absenteeism*

◊ **addressee** *noun* person to whom a letter *or* package is addressed

◊ **addressing machine** *noun* machine which puts addresses on envelopes automatically

adequate *adjective* **(a)** sufficient *or* enough; **to operate without adequate cover =** to act without being completely protected by insurance **(b)** satisfactory *or* acceptable; *her test results were adequate*

ad hoc *adjective* for one particular purpose; *an ad hoc committee was formed to study the problem*

adjourn *verb* to stop a meeting for a period; *to adjourn a meeting; the chairman adjourned the meeting until three o'clock; the meeting adjourned at noon*

◊ **adjournment** *noun* act of adjourning; *he proposed the adjournment of the meeting*

adjudicate *verb* to give a judgment between two parties in law; to decide a legal problem; *to adjudicate a claim; to adjudicate in a dispute*

◊ **adjudication** *noun* act of giving a judgment *or* of deciding a legal problem; **adjudication of bankruptcy =** decree *or* process of determining the status of the bankrupt

◇ **adjudicator** *noun* person who gives a decision on a problem; *an adjudicator in an industrial dispute*

adjust *verb* to change something to fit new conditions; *to adjust prices to take account of inflation; prices are adjusted for inflation; (on federal income tax return)* **adjusted gross income** = an individual's gross income, minus allowable expenses and deductions

◇ **adjuster** *noun* person who calculates losses for an insurance company; **insurance adjuster** = person who calculates how much insurance is to be paid

◇ **adjustment** *noun* act of adjusting; slight change; *tax adjustment; wage adjustment; to make an adjustment to salaries; adjustment of prices to take account of rising costs;* **average adjustment** = calculation of the cost of damage or loss

◇ **adjustor** *noun* = ADJUSTER

QUOTE inflation-adjusted GNP moved up at a 1.3% annual rate
Fortune
QUOTE on a seasonally-adjusted basis, output of trucks, electric power, steel and paper decreased
Business Week

admin = ADMINISTRATION

administer *verb* to organize *or* to manage; *he administers a large pension fund;* **administered price** = price established under situations of competition, where one company has some degree of control

◇ **administration** *noun* (a) organization *or* control *or* management of a company; *the expenses of the administration or* **administration expenses** = costs of management, not including production, marketing or distribution costs (b) management and settlement of the estate of a person who has died (c) **the Administration** = group that makes up the executive branch of a presidential government; *business benefited under the last Administration*

◇ **administrative** *adjective* referring to administration; *administrative details; administrative expenses*

◇ **administrator** *noun* (a) person who directs the work of other employees in a business (b) person appointed by a court to manage the estate of someone who dies without leaving a will

admission *noun* (a) permission for someone to go in; *there is a $1 admission charge; admission is free on presentation of this card; free admission on Sundays* (b) revealing that something really happened; *he had to resign after his admission that he had passed information to the rival company*

admit *verb* (a) to allow someone to go in; *children are not admitted to the bank vaults; senior citizens are admitted at half price* (b) to say that something really happened; *the chairman admitted he had taken the cash from the company's safe*
NOTE: **admitting - admitted**

◇ **admittance** *noun* allowing someone to go in; *no admittance except on business*

adopt *verb* to agree to (something) *or* to accept (something); *to adopt a resolution; the proposals were adopted unanimously*

ad valorem *phrase* showing that a tax is calculated according to the value of the goods taxed; *ad valorem duty; ad valorem tax*

advance 1 *noun* (a) money paid as a loan or as a part of a payment to be made later; *a cash advance; to receive an advance from the bank; an advance on account; to make an advance of $100 to someone; to pay someone an advance against a security; can I have an advance of $50 against next month's salary?* (b) **in advance** = early *or* before something happens; *to pay in advance; freight payable in advance; price fixed in advance* (c) increase; *advance in trade; advance in prices* **2** *adjective* early; *advance booking; advance payment; you must give seven days' advance notice of withdrawals from the account* **3** *verb* (a) to lend; *the bank advanced him $10,000 against the security of his house* (b) to increase; *prices generally advanced on the stock market* (c) to make something happen earlier; *the date of the annual meeting has been advanced to May 10; the meeting with the German distributors has been advanced from 11:00 to 09:30*

◇ **advancement** *noun* promotion; *she is looking for a company in which rapid advancement is possible*

advantage *noun* something useful which may help you to be successful; *fast typing is an advantage in a secretary; knowledge of two foreign languages is an advantage; there is no advantage in arriving at the fair before it opens;* to take advantage of something = to use something to help you; *the larger company has the advantage* = it is doing better than its smaller competitor

adverse *adjective* bad *or* not helpful; **adverse balance of trade** = situation when a country imports more than it exports; **adverse trading conditions** = bad conditions for trade

advertise *verb* to announce that something is for sale *or* that a job is vacant *or* that a service is offered; *to advertise a job opening or a vacancy; to advertise for a secretary; to advertise a new product*

◊ **ad** *noun informal* = ADVERTISEMENT *we put an ad in the paper; she answered an ad in the paper; he found his job through an ad in the paper;* **classified ads** *or* **want ads** = advertisements listed in a newspaper under special headings (like "property for sale","help wanted"); *look in the ads to see if anyone has a computer for sale;* **coupon ad** = advertisement with a form attached, which is to be cut out and returned to the advertiser with your name and address for further information; **display ad** = advertisement which is designed to attract attention

◊ **advertisement** *noun* notice which shows that something is for sale *or* that a service is offered *or* that someone wants something *or* that a job is vacant, etc.; *to put an advertisement in the paper; to answer an advertisement in the paper;* **classified advertisements** = advertisements listed in a newspaper under special headings (such as "property for sale" or "jobs wanted"); **display advertisement** = advertisement which is designed to attract attention

◊ **advertiser** *noun* person *or* company which advertises; *the catalog gives a list of advertisers*

◊ **advertising** *noun* business of announcing that something is for sale *or* of trying to persuade customers to buy a product or service; *she works in advertising; he has a job in advertising;* **advertising agent;**

advertising budget; advertising campaign; advertising agency = office which plans, designs and manages advertising for other companies; **advertising rates** = amount of money charged for advertising space in a newspaper *or* advertising time on TV; **advertising space** = space in a newspaper set aside for advertisements; **to buy advertising space in a paper** = to put an advertisement in a newspaper

advice *noun* **(a) advice note** = written notice to a customer giving details of goods ordered and shipped but not yet delivered; **as per advice** = according to what is written on the advice note **(b)** opinion as to what action to take; **to take legal advice** = to ask a lawyer what should be done; *the accountant's advice was to send the documents to the police; we sent the documents to the police on the advice of the accountant or we took the accountant's advice and sent the documents to the police*

advise *verb* **(a)** to tell someone what has happened; *we are advised that the shipment will arrive next week* **(b)** to suggest to someone what should be done; *we are advised to take the shipping company to court; the accountant advised us to send the documents to the police*

◊ **advise against** *verb* to suggest that something should not be done; *the bank manager advised against closing the account; my broker has advised against buying these bonds*

◊ **adviser** *or* **advisor** *noun* person who suggests what should be done; *he is consulting the company's legal adviser;* **financial adviser** = person *or* company which gives advice on financial problems for a fee

◊ **advisory** *adjective* as an adviser; *he is acting in an advisory capacity;* **an advisory board** = a group of advisers

aerogram *or* **aerogramme** *noun* sheet of thin blue paper which when folded can be sent by airmail without an envelope

affair *noun* business dealing; *his business affairs were so difficult to understand that the lawyers had to ask accountants for advice*

affect *verb* to change *or* to have an effect on (something); *the new government* regulations *do not affect us; the company's sales in the Far East were seriously affected by the embargo*

affiliate *noun* company that is owned *or* controlled by another company; *Circus Toys is an affiliate of the MYA Corporation*
◊ **affiliated** *adjective* connected with *or* owned by another company; *one of our affiliated companies*

affirmative *adjective* meaning "yes"; *the answer was in the affirmative* = the answer was yes; **affirmative action program** = program to remedy and to avoid discrimination in employment

affluent *adjective* wealthy; *we live in an affluent society*

afford *verb* to be able to pay *or* buy; *we could not afford the cost of two telephones; the company cannot afford the time to train new staff*

AFL-CIO = AMERICAN FEDERATION OF LABOR - CONGRESS OF INDUSTRIAL ORGANIZATIONS an organization linking US labor unions

after-hours *adjective* **after-hours buying** *or* **selling** *or* **dealing** = buying *or* selling *or* dealing in shares after the Stock Exchange has officially closed for the day
◊ **after-sales service** *noun* service of a machine carried out by the seller for some time after the machine has been bought
◊ **after-tax profit** *noun* profit remaining after tax has been deducted

against *preposition* relating to *or* next to; *to pay an advance against a security; can I have an advance against next month's salary? the bank advanced him $10,000 against the security of his house*

agency *noun* **(a)** office *or* job representing a company in some area; *they signed an agency agreement or an agency contract;* **sole agency** = situation where only one person *or* firm, etc., is empowered to act as an agent; *he has the sole agency for Ford cars* **(b)** office *or* business which arranges things for other companies; **advertising agency** = office which plans *or* designs and manages advertising for companies; **employment agency** = office which

finds jobs for individuals *or* finds qualified people to fill vacancies in various companies; **real estate agency** = office which deals in the sale of properties; **news agency** = office which distributes news to newspapers and television stations; **travel agency** = office which arranges travel for customers **(c) agency shop** = contract arrangement making it mandatory for workers who refuse to join a union to pay the union a fee

agenda *noun* list of things to be discussed at a meeting; *the conference agenda* or *the agenda of the conference; after two hours we were still discussing the first item on the agenda; the secretary put finance at the top of the agenda; the chairman wants two items removed from the agenda*

agent *noun* **(a)** person who represents a company *or* another person in an area; *the author's agent is negotiating for higher royalties;* **sole agent** = person who has the sole agency for a company in an area; *he is the sole agent for Ford cars;* **agent's commission** = money (often a percentage of sales) paid to an agent **(b)** person in charge of an agency; *advertising agent; real estate agent; travel agent;* **commission agent** = agent who is paid by commission, not by fee; **forwarding agent** = person *or* company which collects and ships; **insurance agent** = person who arranges insurance for clients **(c) business agent** = official of a local union who is responsible for settling grievances and negotiating contracts

aggregate *adjective* total *or* with everything added together; *aggregate output*

aging (schedule) *noun* list of debts, showing the credit terms, the due dates, and how many months late the payments are

agio *noun* charge made for changing money of one currency into another

agree *verb* **(a)** to affirm *or* say yes *or* accept; *it has been agreed that the lease will run for 25 years; after some discussion he agreed to our plan; the bank will never agree to lend the company $250,000; we all agreed on the plan* (NOTE: to agree **to** *or* **on** a plan) **(b) to agree to do something** = to say that you will do something; *she agreed to be chairman; will the finance director agree to resign?* (c) to the same as; *the two sets of calculations do not agree*

◊ **agree with** *verb* (a) to say that your opinions are the same as someone else's; *I agree with the chairman that the figures are lower than normal* (b) to be the same as; *the auditors' figures do not agree with those of the accounts department*

◊ **agreed** *adjective* which has been accepted by everyone; *an agreed amount; on agreed terms*

◊ **agreement** *noun* contract between two parties which explains how they will act; *written agreement; unwritten or verbal agreement; to draw up or to draft an agreement; to break an agreement; to sign an agreement; to witness an agreement; an agreement has been reached or concluded or signed; to reach an agreement or to come to an agreement on prices or salaries; an international agreement on trade; an agency agreement; a marketing agreement;* **blanket agreement** = agreement which covers many different items; **gentleman's agreement** = verbal agreement between two parties who trust each other

QUOTE after three days of tough negotiations the company has reached agreement with its 1,200 unionized workers
Toronto Star

agribusiness *noun* farming as a business *or* as part of the economy, including growing and marketing crops and making products used by farmers

agriculture *noun* use of land for growing crops *or* raising animals

◊ **agricultural** *adjective* referring to agriculture *or* referring to farms; **agricultural co-operative** = farm run by groups of workers who are the owners and share the profits; **agricultural economist** = person who specializes in the study of finance and investment in agriculture

ahead *adverb* in front of *or* better than; *we are already ahead of our sales forecast; the company has a lot of work ahead of it if it wants to increase its share of the market*

aim 1 *noun* something which you try to do; *one of our aims is to increase the quality of our products;* **the company has achieved all its aims** = the

company has done all the things it had hoped to do **2** *verb* to try to do something; *we aim to be No. 1 in the market in two years' time; each salesman must aim to double his previous year's sales*

air 1 *noun* method of traveling *or* sending goods using aircraft; *to send a letter or a shipment by air;* **air carrier** = company which sends cargo *or* passengers by air; **air forwarding** = arranging for goods to be shipped by air; **air letter** = airmail letter *or* special sheet of thin blue paper which when folded can be sent by airmail without an envelope **2** *verb* **to air a grievance** = to talk about *or* to discuss a grievance; *the management committee is useful because it allows the workers' representatives to air their grievances*

◊ **air cargo** *noun* goods *or* mail sent by air

◊ **aircraft** *noun* machine which flies in the air, carrying passengers or cargo; *the airline has a fleet of ten commercial aircraft; the company is one of the most important American aircraft manufacturers;* **to charter an aircraft** = to hire an aircraft for a special purpose
NOTE: no plural: **one aircraft, two aircraft**

◊ **airfreight 1** *noun* **(a)** method of shipping goods in an aircraft; *to send a shipment by airfreight;* **airfreight charges** *or* **rates (b)** charge to ship goods by air; *the airfreight totaled $800* **2** *verb* to send goods by air; *to airfreight a consignment to Mexico; we airfreighted the shipment because our agent ran out of stock*

◊ **airline** *noun* company which carries passengers or cargo by air

◊ **airmail 1** *noun* way of sending letters *or* parcels by air; *to send a package by airmail; airmail charges have risen by 15%;* **airmail envelope** = very light envelope for sending airmail letters; **airmail sticker** = blue sticker with the words "by air mail" which can be stuck to an envelope or packet to show it is being sent by air **2** *verb* to send letters *or* parcels by air; *to airmail a document to London*

◊ **airport** *noun* place where planes land and take off; *O'Hare Airport is the main airport for Chicago;* **airport bus** = bus which takes passengers to and from an airport; **airport tax** = tax included in the price of the air ticket to cover the cost of running an airport; **airport terminal** = main building at an airport where passengers arrive and depart

◊ **airtight** *adjective* which does not allow air to get in; *the goods are packed in airtight containers*

a.k.a. = ALSO KNOWN AS *John Charles Smith, a.k.a. J.C. Smith*

all *adjective & pronoun* everything *or* everyone; *all (of) the managers attended the meeting; a salesman should know the prices of all the products he is selling*

allocate *verb* to divide (a sum of money) in various ways and share it out; *we allocate 10% of revenue to publicity; $2,500 was allocated to office furniture*

◊ **allocation** *noun* dividing a sum of money in various ways; *allocation of capital; allocation of funds to a project*

allot *verb* to give *or* assign as a share; *to allot shares* = to give a certain number of shares to underwriters in a syndicate NOTE: **allotting - allotted**

◊ **allotment** *noun* **(a)** sharing out funds by giving money to various departments; *allotment of funds to a project* **(b)** giving shares in a new company to underwriters who have underwritten the issue; *share allotment; payment in full on allotment*

all-out *adjective* complete *or* full-scale; *the union called for an all-out strike; the personnel manager has launched an all-out campaign to get the staff to work on Friday afternoons*

allow *verb* **(a)** to say that someone can do something; *junior members of the staff are not allowed to use the executive lunch room; the company allows all employees to take six days' vacation at Christmas* **(b)** to give; *to allow someone a discount; to allow 5% discount to members of staff; to allow 10% interest on large sums of money* **(c)** to agree *or* to accept legally; *to allow a claim or an appeal*

◊ **allow for** *verb* to give a discount for *or* to add an extra sum to cover something; *to allow for money paid in advance; to allow 10% for packing; allow 28 days for delivery* = calculate that delivery will take at least 28 days

◊ **allowable** *adjective* legally accepted; *allowable expenses* = expenses which can be claimed against tax

◊ **allowance** *noun* **(a)** money which is given for a special reason; *travel allowance or traveling allowance; foreign currency allowance; cost-of-living allowance* = addition to normal salary to cover increases in the cost of living; *entertainment allowance* = money which a manager is allowed to spend each month on meals with clients or potential clients **(b)** part of an income which is not taxed; *allowances against tax or tax allowances; personal allowances* **(c)** money removed in the form of a discount; *allowance for depreciation; allowance for exchange loss*

◊ **allowed time** *noun* paid time which the management agrees a worker can spend on rest *or* cleaning *or* meals, not working

QUOTE the compensation plan includes base, incentive and car allowance totaling $50,000+
Globe and Mail (Toronto)

all-risks policy *noun* insurance policy which covers risks of any kind, except those specifically excluded in the policy

all-time *adjective* **all-time high** *or* **all-time low** = highest or lowest point ever reached; *sales have fallen from their all-time high of last year*

alphabet *noun* the 26 letters used to make words

◊ **alphabetical order** *noun* arrangement of records (such as files, index cards) in the order of the letters of the alphabet (A,B,C,D, etc.)

alter *verb* to change; *to alter the terms of a contract*

◊ **alteration** *noun* change which has been made; *he made some alterations to the terms of a contract; the agreement was signed without any alterations*

alternative 1 *noun* thing which can be done instead of another; *what is the alternative to firing half the staff?;* **we have no alternative** = there is nothing else we can do **2** *adjective* other *or* which can take the place of something; *to find someone alternative employment* = to find someone another job

altogether *adverb* putting everything together; *the employees of the three companies in the group number 2,500 altogether; the company lost $2m last year and $4m this year, making $6m altogether for the two years*

a.m. *adverb* in the morning *or* before 12 noon; *the flight leaves at 9:20 a.m.; telephone calls before 6 a.m. are charged at the discount rate*

amend *verb* to change and make more correct *or* acceptable; *please amend your copy of the contract accordingly*
◊ **amendment** *noun* change to a document; *to propose an amendment to the constitution; to make amendments to a contract*

Amex *noun informal* = AMERICAN STOCK EXCHANGE

amortize *verb* to pay off (a debt) by putting money aside regularly over a period of time; *the capital cost is amortized over five years*
◊ **amortizable** *adjective* which can be amortized; *the capital cost is amortizable over a period of ten years*
◊ **amortization** *noun* act of amortizing; *amortization of a debt*

amount 1 *noun* quantity of money; *amount paid; amount deducted; amount owing; amount written off; what is the amount outstanding? a small amount invested in blue-chip stocks* **2** *verb* **to amount to** = to make a total of; *their debts amount to over $1m*

analog computer *noun* computer which works on the basis of electrical impulses representing numbers

analyze *verb* to examine in detail; *to analyze a statement of account; to analyze the market potential*
◊ **analysis** *noun* detailed examination and report; *job analysis; market analysis; sales analysis; to carry out an analysis of the market potential; to write an analysis of the economic situation; cost analysis* = examination in advance of the costs of a new product; *systems analysis* = using a computer to examine how a company can work more efficiently by analyzing the way it works currently
NOTE: plural is **analyses**

◊ **analyst** *noun* person who analyses; *market analyst; systems analyst*

announce *verb* to tell something to the public; *to announce the sales for 1989; to announce a program of investment*
◊ **announcement** *noun* telling something in public; *announcement of a cutback in spending; announcement of the appointment of a new company president; the manager made an announcement to the staff*

annual *adjective* for one year; *annual statement of income; he has six weeks' annual leave; the annual accounts; annual growth of 5%;* **annual percentage rate (APR)** = rate of interest (such as on a loan) shown on an annual compound basis; **annual report** = report of a company's financial situation at the end of a year, sent to all the shareholders; **on an annual basis** = each year; *the figures are revised on an annual basis*
◊ **annual meeting** *noun* yearly meeting of all the shareholders, when the company's financial situation is discussed
◊ **annually** *adverb* each year; *the figures are updated annually*

QUOTE real wages have risen at an annual rate of only 1% in the last two years
Sunday Times

annuity *noun* series of periodic payments, such as money paid each year to a retired person; *he has a government annuity or an annuity from the government; to buy or to take out an annuity; annuity for life or life annuity* = annual payments made to someone as long as he is alive
NOTE: plural is **annuities**
◊ **annuitant** *noun* person who receives an annuity

annul *verb* to cancel *or* to make something invalid; *the contract was annulled by the court*
NOTE: **annulling - annulled**
◊ **annullable** *adjective* which can be canceled
◊ **annulling 1** *adjective* which cancels; *annulling clause* **2** *noun* act of canceling; *the annulling of a contract*
◊ **annulment** *noun* act of canceling; *annulment of a contract*

annum *see* PER ANNUM

answer 1 *noun* reply, letter or conversation coming after someone has written or spoken; *I am writing in answer to your letter of October 6; my letter got no answer or there was no answer to my letter; I tried to phone his office but there was no answer* 2 *verb* to speak or write after someone has spoken or written to you; **to answer a letter** = to write a letter in reply to a letter which you have received; **to answer the telephone** = to lift the telephone when it rings and greet the caller

◊ **answering** *noun* **answering machine** = machine which answers the telephone automatically when someone is not in the office; **answering service** = office which answers the telephone and takes messages for someone *or* for a company

antedate *verb* to put an earlier date on a document; *the invoice was antedated to January 1*

anti- *prefix* against

◊ **antidumping** *adjective* which protects a country against dumping; *antidumping legislation*

◊ **anti-inflationary** *adjective* which tries to restrict inflation; *anti-inflationary measures*

◊ **antitrust** *adjective* which attacks monopolies and encourages competition; *anti trust laws or legislation*

apologize *verb* to say you are sorry; *to apologize for the delay in answering; she apologized for being late*

◊ **apology** *noun* saying you are sorry; *to write a letter of apology; I enclose a check for $10 with apologies for the delay in answering your letter*

appeal 1 *noun* (a) being attractive; **customer appeal** = being attractive to customers; **sales appeal** = quality which makes customers want to buy (b) asking a court *or* a government department to change its decision; *the appeal against the planning decision will be heard next month; he lost his appeal for damages against the company;* she won her case on appeal = her case was lost in the first court, but the appeal court said that she was right NOTE: no plural for (a) 2 *verb* (a) to attract; *this record appeals to the under-25 market; the idea of working in Hawaii for six months appealed to her* (b) to ask a government department *or* a law court to alter its decision; *the company*

appealed against the decision of the planning committee NOTE: you appeal **to** a court or a person **against** a decision

appear *verb* to seem; *the company appeared to be doing well; the chairman appears to be in control*

apply *verb* (a) to ask for something, usually in writing; *to apply for a job; to apply in writing; to apply in person* (b) to affect *or* to touch; *this clause applies only to international deals*

◊ **applicant** *noun* person who applies for something; *applicant for a job or job applicant; there were thousands of applicants for shares in the new company*

◊ **application** *noun* (a) asking for something, usually in writing; *application for shares; shares payable on application; attach the check to the share application form; application for a job or job application;* **application form** = form to be filled out when applying; *to fill out an application (form) for a job or a job application (form);* **letter of application** = letter in which someone applies for a job (b) use to which a thing is put; *computer applications in business are endless*

◊ **applied** *adjective* put to use to solve practical problems; *applied economics; applied research*

appoint *verb* to choose someone for a job; *to appoint James Smith (to the post of) manager; we have appointed a new distribution manager* NOTE: you appoint a person **to** a job

◊ **appointee** *noun* person who is appointed to a job

◊ **appointment** *noun* (a) arrangement to meet; *to make an appointment for two o'clock; to make an appointment with someone for two o'clock; he was late for his appointment; she had to cancel her appointment;* **appointments book** = desk diary in which appointments are noted (b) being appointed to a job; **on his appointment as manager** = when he was made manager; **letter of appointment** = letter in which someone is appointed to a job (c) job; *she has a new appointment as vice-president for research*

apportion *verb* to divide up; *costs are apportioned according to projected revenue*

◊ **apportionment** *noun* dividing something up

appraise *verb* to assess *or* to calculate the value of something; *he asked the jeweler to appraise the diamond*

◊ **appraisal** *noun* calculation of the value of someone *or* something; **performance appraisals =** reports on how well each employee is working

appreciate *verb* (a) to notice how good something is; *the customer always appreciates efficient service; tourists do not appreciate long delays at banks* (b) to increase in value; *the dollar has appreciated in terms of the yen; these shares have appreciated by 5%*

◊ **appreciation** *noun* (a) increase in value; *these shares show an appreciation of 10%; the appreciation of the dollar against the peseta* (b) valuing something highly; *he was given a raise in appreciation of his excellent work*

apprentice 1 *noun* young person who works under contract with a skilled workman to learn from him **2** *verb* **to be apprenticed to someone =** to work with a skilled workman to learn from him

◊ **apprenticeship** *noun* time spent learning a skilled trade; *he served a six-year apprenticeship in the steelworks*

approach 1 *noun* getting in touch with someone with a proposal; *the company made an approach to the supermarket chain; the board turned down all approaches on the subject of mergers; we have had an approach from a Japanese company to buy our car division* **2** *verb* to get in touch with someone with a proposal; *he approached the bank with a request for a loan; the company was approached by a Canadian publisher with the suggestion of a merger; we have been approached several times but have turned down all offers*

appropriate 1 *verb* to put a sum of money aside for a special purpose; *to appropriate a sum of money for a capital project* **2** *adjective* fitting; *an appropriate use of company funds*

◊ **appropriation** *noun* act of putting money aside for a special purpose; *appropriation of funds to the reserve;* **appropriation statement =** part of a profit and loss statement which shows

how the profit has been allocated (i.e., how much has been given to the shareholders as dividends, how much is being put into the reserves, etc.)

approve *verb* (a) **to approve of =** to think something is good; *the president approves of the new company letterhead; the sales reps do not approve of interference from the accounts division* (b) to agree to something officially; **to approve the terms of a contract;** *the proposal was approved by the board*

◊ **approval** *noun* (a) agreement; *to submit a budget for approval; the new retirement policy met with her approval* (b) **on approval =** sale where the buyer only pays for goods if they are satisfactory; *to buy a photocopier on approval*

approximate *adjective* not exact, but almost correct; *the sales division has made an approximate forecast of expenditures*

◊ **approximately** *adverb* almost correctly; *expenditure is approximately 10% down on the previous quarter*

◊ **approximation** *noun* rough calculation; *approximation of tax owed; the final figure is only an approximation*

APR = ANNUAL PERCENTAGE RATE

arbitrage *noun* (a) selling on one market and buying on another at almost the same time to profit from different exchange rates (b) buying shares in companies which are likely to be taken over and so rise in price

◊ **arbitrager** *or* **arbitrageur** *noun* person whose business is arbitrage

arbitrate *verb* *(of an outside party)* to be chosen by both sides to try to settle an industrial dispute; *to arbitrate in a dispute*

◊ **arbitration** *noun* settling of a dispute by an outside person, chosen by both sides; *to submit a dispute to arbitration; to refer a question to arbitration; to take a dispute to arbitration; to go to arbitration;* **arbitration board =** group which arbitrates; *to accept the ruling of the arbitration board;* **arbitration clause =** part of a contract that requires disputes about the contract to be settled by an outside person

◇ **arbitrator** *noun* person not concerned with a dispute who is chosen by both sides to try to settle it; *industrial arbitrator; to accept or to reject the arbitrator's ruling*

area *noun* (a) measurement of the space taken up by something; *the area of this office is 3,400 square feet; we are looking for a shop with a sales area of about 100 square yards* (b) region of the world; *free trade area =* group of countries practicing free trade; *sterling area =* areas of the world where the pound is the main trading currency (c) subject; *a problem area or an area for concern* (d) district *or* part of a town; *the office is in the commercial area of the town; their factory is in a very good area for getting to the freeways and airports* (e) part of a country, a division for commercial purposes; *his sales area is the Northwest; he finds it difficult to cover all his area in a week*

◇ **area code** *noun* special telephone number which is given to a particular area; *the area code for Cleveland is 216*

argue *verb* to discuss something about which you do not agree; *they argued over or about the price; we spent hours arguing with the chairman about the site for the new factory; the union officials argued among themselves over the best way to deal with the ultimatum from management* NOTE: you argue **with** someone **about** *or* **over** something

◇ **argument** *noun* discussing something without agreeing; *they got into an argument with the customs officials over the documents; he was fired after an argument with the executive director*

around *preposition* approximately *or* nearly; *the office costs around $2,000 a year to heat; his salary is around $85,000*

arrange *verb* (a) to put in order; *the office is arranged as an open-plan area with small separate rooms for meetings; the files are arranged in alphabetical order; arrange the invoices in order of their dates* (b) to organize; *we arranged to have the meeting in their offices; she arranged for a staff member to meet him at the airport*

NOTE: you arrange **for** someone to do something; you arrange **for** something to be done; or you arrange **to** do something

◇ **arrangement** *noun* (a) way in which something is organized; *the company secretary is making all the arrangements for the meeting* (b) settling of a financial dispute; *to come to an arrangement with the creditors*

arrears *plural noun* money which is owed, but which has not been paid at the right time; *arrears of interest; to allow the payments to fall into arrears; salary with arrears effective from January 1; in arrears =* owing money which should have been paid earlier; *the payments are six months in arrears; he is six weeks in arrears with his rent*

arrive *noun* (a) to reach a place; *the consignment has still not arrived; the shipment arrived without any documentation; the plane arrives in Sydney at 4:00; the train leaves Paris at 9:20 and arrives at Bordeaux two hours later* NOTE: you arrive **at** *or* **in** a place or town, but only **in** a country (b) **to arrive at =** to calculate and agree; *to arrive at a price; after some discussion we arrived at a compromise*

◇ **arrival** *noun* reaching a place; *we are waiting for the arrival of a consignment of spare parts*

article *noun* (a) product *or* thing for sale; *to launch a new article on the market; a black market in luxury articles* (b) section of a legal agreement; *see article 8 of the contract* (c) **articles of incorporation =** document which sets up a corporation and says what work it will do; *director appointed under the articles of the corporation; this procedure is not allowed under the articles of incorporation*

artificial intelligence *noun* capability of a mechanical device to perform functions such as reasoning and learning, which are usually associated with human intelligence

asap = AS SOON AS POSSIBLE

aside *adverb* to one side *or* out of the way; *to put aside or to set aside =* to save (money); *he is putting $50 aside each week to pay for his car*

ask *verb* (a) to put a question to someone; *he asked the information*

office for details on the companies exhibiting at the show; ask the salesgirl if the bill includes sales tax **(b)** to tell someone to do something; *he asked the switchboard operator to get him a number in Germany; she asked her secretary to get a file from the director's office; the customs officials asked him to open his case*
◊ **ask for** *verb* **(a)** to say that you want *or* need something; *he asked for the file on 1984 debtors; they asked for more time to repay the loan; there is a man in reception asking for Mr. Smith* **(b)** to put a price on something for sale; *they are asking $24,000 for the car*
◊ **asking price** *noun* price which the seller asks for the goods being sold; *the asking price is $24,000*

assay *noun* determining the percentage of gold or silver in coin or bullion

assemble *verb* to put a product together from various parts; *the engines are made in Japan and the bodies in Detroit, and the cars are assembled in Iowa*
◊ **assembly** *noun* **(a)** putting an item together from various parts; *there are no assembly instructions to show you how to put the computer together;* car assembly plant = factory where cars are put together from parts made in other factories **(b)** meeting
◊ **assembly line** *noun* production system where the product (such as a car) moves slowly through the factory with new sections added to it as it goes along; *he works on an assembly line* or *he is an assembly line worker*

assess *verb* to calculate the value of something; *to assess damages at $1,000; to assess a property for the purposes of insurance*
◊ **assessment** *noun* calculation of value; *assessment of damages; assessment of property; tax assessment*

asset *noun* thing which belongs to company or person, and which has a value; *he has an excess of assets over liabilities; her assets are only $640 as against liabilities of $24,000;* **capital assets** *or* **fixed assets** = property *or* machinery which a company owns and uses; **current assets** = assets used by a company in its ordinary work (such as materials, finished goods, cash); **frozen assets** = assets of a company which

cannot be sold because someone has a claim against them; **intangible assets** = assets which have a value, but which cannot be seen (such as goodwill. or a patent, or a trademark); **liquid assets** = cash, or bills which can be quickly converted into cash; **tangible assets** = assets which are solid (such as furniture or jewels or cash); **asset value** = total value of assets after deducting liabilities

QUOTE many companies are discovering that a well-recognized brand name can be a priceless asset that lessens the risk of introducing a new product
Duns Business Month

assign *verb* **(a)** to give legally; *to assign a right to someone; to assign shares to someone* **(b)** to give someone a job or task; *he was assigned the job of checking the sales figures; we assigned her to the marketing department*
◊ **assignation** *noun* legal transfer; *assignation of shares to someone; assignation of a patent*
◊ **assignee** *noun* person who receives something which has been assigned
◊ **assignment** *noun* **(a)** legal transfer of a property *or* of a right; *assignment of a patent or of a copyright; to sign a deed of assignment* **(b)** particular job of work; *he was appointed sales director with the assignment to improve the company's profits; the oil team is on an assignment in the Pacific*
◊ **assigner** *or* **assignor** *noun* person who assigns something to someone

assist *verb* to help; *can you assist the stock controller in taking the inventory? he assists me with my income tax returns*
NOTE: you assist someone **in** doing something or **with** something
◊ **assistance** *noun* help; **financial assistance** = help in the form of money
◊ **assistant** *noun* person who helps, a clerical employee; **administrative assistant** = secretary who also performs some administrative duties; **assistant manager** = person who helps a manager

associate 1 *adjective* linked; **associate company** = company which is partly owned by another; **associate director** = director who attends board meetings, but has not been elected by the shareholders **2** *noun* person who works in the same business as someone; *she is a business associate of mine*

◇ **associated** *adjective* linked; *Smith Inc. and its associated company, Jones Brothers*

◇ **association** *noun* **(a)** group of people *or* of companies with the same interest; *trade association; employers' association; manufacturers' association* **(b)** relationship; *the two companies' association is a close one*

assume *verb* to take on; *to assume all risks; he has assumed responsibility for marketing*

◇ **assumable** *adjective* (something) that can be assigned by one person to another without changing the terms; *an assumable mortgage*

◇ **assumption** *noun* taking; *assumption of risks*

assurance *noun (in Britain, Canada)* insurance *or* agreement that in return for regular payments, a company will pay compensation for loss of life

ATM = AUTOMATED TELLER MACHINE

at par *phrase* **share at par** = share whose value on the stock market is the same as its face value

attach *verb* to fasten *or* to link; *I am attaching a copy of my previous letter; please find attached a copy of my letter of June 24; the machine is attached to the floor so it cannot be moved; the bank attaches great importance to the deal*

◇ **attaché** *noun* junior diplomat who does special work; **commercial attaché** = diplomat whose job is to promote the commercial interests of his country; **attache case** = small case for carrying papers and documents

◇ **attachment** *noun* holding a debtor's property to prevent it from being sold until debts are paid

attempt **1** *noun* trying to do something; *the company made an attempt to break into the American market; the takeover attempt was turned down by the board; all his attempts to get a job have failed* **2** *verb* to try; *the company is attempting to get into the tourist market; we are attempting the takeover of a manufacturing company; he attempted to have the sales director fired*

attend *verb* to be present at; *the chairman has asked all managers to attend the meeting; none of the shareholders attended the annual meeting*

◇ **attend to** *verb* to give careful thought to (something) and deal with it; *the vice-president will attend to your complaint personally; we have brought in experts to attend to the problem of installing the new computer*

◇ **attention** *noun* giving careful thought; *for the attention of the Executive Director;* **has this been called to your attention?** = have you been informed of this?

attorney *noun* person who is legally qualified to act on behalf of someone else; **attorney-at-law** = individual who has a state license to practice in a court of law; **power of attorney** = legal document giving someone the right to act on someone's behalf in legal matters; *his lawyer was granted power of attorney*

attract *verb* to make something or someone join *or* come in; *the company is offering free trips to Spain to attract buyers; we have difficulty in attracting skilled employees to this part of the country*

◇ **attractive** *adjective* which attracts; **attractive prices** = prices which are low enough to make buyers want to buy; **attractive salary** = good salary to induce high-quality applicants to apply for the job

> QUOTE airlines offer special stopover rates and hotel packages to attract customers and to encourage customer loyalty
> *Business Traveler*

attribute 1 *noun* characteristic **2** *verb* to assign; *the remark was attributed to the Chairman*

attrition *noun* decrease in the work force of a company through retirement, resignation or death

auction 1 *noun* selling of goods where people offer bids, and the item is sold to the person who makes the highest offer; *sale by auction; auction rooms; to sell goods by auction or at auction;* **to put something up for auction** = to offer an item for sale at an auction; **Dutch auction** = auction where the auctioneer offers an item for sale at a high price and gradually reduces the price until someone makes a bid **2** *verb* to sell at an auction; *the factory was closed and the machinery was auctioned off*

◊ **auctioneer** *noun* person who conducts an auction

audit 1 *noun* examination of the books and accounts of a company; *to carry out the annual audit;* **external audit** *or* **independent audit** = audit carried out by an independent auditor; **internal audit** = audit carried out by a department inside the company; *he is the manager of the internal audit department* **2** *verb* to examine the books and accounts of a company; *to audit the accounts; the books have not yet been audited*

◊ **auditing** *noun* action of examining the books and accounts

◊ **auditor** *noun* person who audits; *the board appoints the company's auditors;* **external auditor** = independent person who audits the company's accounts; **internal auditor** = member of staff who audits a company's accounts

authenticate *verb* to say that something is true

authority *noun* **(a)** power to do something; *he has no authority to act on our behalf* **(b) local authority** = elected section of government which runs a small area of a country; **the authorities** = the government *or* the people in control

authorize *verb* **(a)** to give permission for something to be done; *to authorize payment of $10,000* **(b)** to give someone permission to do something; *to authorize someone to act on the company's behalf*

◊ **authorization** *noun* permission *or* power to do something; *do you have authorization for this expenditure? he has no authorization to act on our behalf*

◊ **authorized** *adjective* permitted; **authorized capital stock** = amount of stock capital which a company is allowed to issue, as stated in the articles of incorporation; **authorized dealer** = person *or* company with a franchise to sell another company's products

QUOTE in 1934 Congress authorized President Franklin D. Roosevelt to seek lower tariffs with any country willing to reciprocate
Duns Business Month

auto *see* AUTOMOBILE

automated *adjective* worked automatically by machines; *fully automated car assembly plant;* **automated teller machine** = machine which gives out money when a special card is inserted and special instructions given

◊ **automation** *noun* use of machines to do work with very little supervision by people

automatic *adjective* which works *or* takes place without any person making it happen; *there is an automatic increase in salaries on January 1;* **automatic data processing** = data processing done by a computer

◊ **automatically** *adverb* working without a person giving instructions; *the invoices are sent out automatically; addresses are typed in automatically; a demand note is sent automatically when the invoice is overdue*

automobile *noun* motor vehicle for carrying people; **automobile insurance** = insurance of an automobile against accident

available *adjective* which can be obtained *or* bought; *available in all branches; item no longer available; items available to order only; funds which are made available for investment in small businesses;* **available capital** = capital which is ready to be used

◊ **availability** *noun* being easily obtained; **offer subject to availability** = the offer is valid only if the goods are available

average 1 *noun* **(a)** number calculated by adding together several figures and dividing by the number of figures added; *the average for the last three months or the last three months' average; sales average or average of sales;* **weighted average** = average in which different values are assigned to the items to be averaged; **on average** = in general; *on average, $15 worth of goods are stolen every day* **(b)** index of stock exchange prices, showing average percentage rises or falls calculated over a range of securities; *see also* DOW JONES **(c)** sharing of the cost of damage or loss between the insurers and the owners; **average adjuster** = person who calculates how much insurance is to be paid; **general average** = sharing of the cost of the lost goods by all parties to an insurance; **particular average** = situation where part of a shipment is lost or damaged and the insurance costs are borne by the owner of the lost goods and not shared among all the owners of the shipment **2** *adjective* **(a)** middle (figure); *average cost per unit; average price; average sales per representative; the average figures for the last three months; the average increase in prices* **(b)** not very good; *the company's performance has been only average; he is an average worker* **3** *verb* to produce as an average figure; *price increases have averaged 10% per annum; days lost through sickness have averaged twenty-two over the last four years*

◊ **average due date** *noun* date when several payments (due at different dates) are settled in one payment

◊ **average out** *verb* to come to a figure as an average; *it averages out at 10% per annum; sales increases have averaged-out at 15%*

◊ **average-sized** *adjective* not large or small; *they are an average-sized company; he has an average-sized office*

◊ **averaging** *noun* buying shares at different times and at different prices to give an average price

QUOTE averaged over the three months ended February, the merchandise goods deficit was over 5% worse than for the preceding three months

Forbes Magazine

avoid *verb* to try not to do something; *the company is trying to avoid bankruptcy; my aim is to avoid paying too much tax; we want to avoid direct competition with Smith Company* NOTE: you avoid something or avoid **doing** something

◊ **avoidance** *noun* trying not to do something; *avoidance of an agreement or of a contract;* **tax avoidance** = trying (legally) to pay as little tax as possible

await *verb* to wait for; *we are awaiting the decision of the planning department; they are awaiting a decision of the court; the agent is awaiting our instructions*

award 1 *noun* decision or judgment; *the arbitrator's award was set aside on appeal* **2** *verb* to decide or judge, often relating to money; *to award someone a salary increase; to award damages;*

the judge awarded costs to the defendant; **to award a contract to someone** = to decide that someone will have the contract to do work

away *adverb* not here or somewhere else; *the executive director is away on business; the company is moving away from its down-market image*

ax or **axe 1** *noun* **the project got the ax** = the project was stopped **2** *verb* to cut or to stop; *to ax expenditures; several thousand jobs are to be axed*

Bb

Class "B" stock *plural noun* ordinary stock with limited voting rights

baby bonds *plural noun* bonds in small denominations ($100 or less)

back 1 *noun* opposite side to the front; *write your address on the back of the envelope; the conditions of sale are printed on the back of the invoice; please endorse the check on the back* **2** *adjective* referring to the past; **back interest** = interest not yet paid; **back orders** = orders received in the past and not fulfilled (usually because the item is out of stock); *after the strike it took the factory six weeks to clear all the accumulated back orders;* **back pay** = salary which has not been paid; *I am owed $500 in back pay;* **back payment** = paying money which is owed; *the salesmen are claiming for back payment of unpaid commission;* **back payments** = payments which are due; **back rent** = rent owed; *the company owes $100,000 in back rent* **3** *adverb* as things were before; *he will pay back the money in monthly installments; the store sent back the check because the date was wrong; the company went back on its agreement to supply at $1.50 a unit* **4** *verb* **(a) to back someone** = to help someone financially; *the bank is backing him to the tune of $10,000; he is looking for someone to back his project* **(b) to back a bill** = to promise to pay a bill if the person it is addressed to is not able to do so

◊ **backdate** *verb* to put an earlier date on a check or an invoice; *backdate your*

invoice to April 1; the pay increase is
backdated to January 1

◊ **backer** noun (a) person who sponsors
someone; he has an Australian backer;
one of the company's backers has
withdrawn (b) backer of a bill = person
who backs a bill

◊ **background** noun (a) past work or
experience; his background is in the
steel industry; the company is looking
for someone with a background of
success in the electronics industry;
she has a publishing background; what
is his background or do you know
anything about his background? (b)
past details; he explained the
background of the claim; I know the
contractual situation as it stands now,
but can you fill in the background
details?

◊ **backing** noun (a) financial support; he
has the backing of an Australian bank;
the company will succeed only if it has
sufficient backing; who is providing
the backing for the project or where
does the backing for the project come
from? (b) currency backing = gold or
government securities which give value
to a currency

◊ **backlog** noun work (such as orders or
letters) which has piled up waiting to be
done; the warehouse is trying to cope
with a backlog of orders; my secretary
can't deal with the backlog of
paperwork

◊ **back out** verb to stop being part of a
deal or an agreement; the bank backed
out of the contract; we had to cancel
the project when our German partners
backed out

◊ **back up** verb to support or to help; he
brought along a file of documents to
back up his claim; the finance
manager said the executive director
had refused to back him up in his
argument with the IRS

◊ **backup** adjective supporting or
helping; we offer a free backup service
to customers; backup copy = copy of a
computer disk to be kept in case the
original disk is damaged

◊ **backwardation** noun arrangement in
the commodity markets in which prices
in future delivery months are
progressively lower than in the nearest
delivery months

bad adjective not good; bad bargain =
item which is not worth the price asked;
bad buy = thing bought which was not
worth the money paid for it; bad debt =
debt which will not be paid; the

company has written off $30,000 in
bad debts

bag noun thing made of paper, cloth, or
plastic for carrying items; he brought
his files in a Macy's bag; we gave away
5,000 plastic bags at the trade fair;
shopping bag = bag used for carrying
goods you have bought

baggage noun suitcases or bags for
carrying clothes when traveling; free
baggage allowance = amount of
baggage which a passenger can take with
him free on a plane; baggage room =
room where cases can be left while
passengers are waiting for a plane or
train
NOTE: no plural; to show one suitcase, etc., you can
say **a piece of baggage**

bail noun payment made to a court as
guarantee that a prisoner will return for
trial after being released; to stand bail or
to post bail of $3,000 for someone; he
was released on bail of $3,000 or he was
released on payment of $3,000 bail; to
jump bail = not to appear in court after
having been released on bail

◊ **bail out** verb (a) to rescue a company
which is in financial difficulties (b) to
bail someone out = to pay money to a
court as a guarantee that someone will
return to face charges; she paid $3,000
to bail him out

◊ **bail-out** noun rescue of a company in
financial difficulties

balance 1 noun (a) amount in an account
which makes the total debits and credits
equal; credit balance = balance in an
account showing that more money has
been received than is owed; debit
balance = balance in an account
showing that more money is owed than
has been received; the account has a
credit balance of $100; because of
large payments to suppliers, the
account has a debit balance of $1,000;
balance brought down = amount
entered in an account at the end of a
period to balance income and
expenditure; balance brought forward
or balance carried forward = amount
entered in an account at the end of a
period to balance the expenditure and
income which is then taken forward to
start the new period (b) rest of an
amount owed; you can pay $100 deposit
and the balance within 60 days;
balance due to us = amount owed to us
which is due to be paid (c) balance of
payments = net amount of money paid

or received by a country, resulting from its imports and exports; **balance of trade** *or* **trade balance** = the difference between the amount of goods a country exports and imports; **adverse** *or* **unfavorable balance of trade** = situation where a country imports more than it exports; **favorable trade balance** = situation where a country exports more than it imports; *the country has had an adverse balance of trade for the second month running* **(d) bank balance** = state of an account at a bank at a particular time **2** *verb* **(a)** to calculate the amount needed to make the two sides of an account equal; *I have finished balancing the accounts for March;* **the February accounts do not balance** = the two sides are not equal **(b)** to plan a budget so that expenditure and income are equal; *the president is planning for a balanced budget*

◊ **balance sheet** *noun* statement of the financial position of a company at a particular time, such as the end of the financial year or the end of a quarter; *the company balance sheet for 1989 shows a substantial loss; the accountant has prepared the balance sheet for the first half-year*

bale 1 *noun* large pack of wool *or* paper *or* cotton,etc.; *a bale of cotton; 2,520 bales of wool were destroyed in the fire* **2** *verb* to tie wool *or* paper *or* cotton to make a bale

balloon *noun* large final payment on a loan, after a number of periodic smaller loans; *balloon loan; balloon mortgage*

ballot 1 *noun* **(a)** election where people vote for someone by marking a paper with a list of names **(b)** paper which the voter marks to show who he wants to vote for; **ballot box** = sealed box into which ballots are put; **secret ballot** = election where the voters vote in secret **2** *verb* to take a vote by ballot; *the union is balloting for the office of president*

ban 1 *noun* order which forbids someone from doing something; *a government ban on the import of weapons; a ban on the export of computer software;* **overtime ban** = order by a labor union which forbids overtime work by its members; **to impose a ban on smoking** = to make an order which forbids smoking; **to lift the ban on smoking** = to allow people to smoke; **to beat the ban on something** = to do something which is forbidden - usually by doing it

rapidly before a ban is imposed, or by finding a legal way to avoid a ban **2** *verb* to forbid something *or* to make something illegal; *the government has banned the sale of alcohol*
NOTE: **banning - banned**

band *noun* **rubber band** = thin ring of rubber for attaching things together; *put a band around the file cards to keep them in order*

bank 1 *noun* **(a)** business which holds money for its clients, which lends money at interest, and trades generally in money; *The First National Bank; he put all his earnings into the bank; I have received a letter from my bank telling me my account is overdrawn;* **bank loan** *or* **bank advance** = loan from a bank; *he asked for a bank loan to start his business;* **bank deposits** = all money placed in banks **(b)** **central bank** = main government-controlled bank in a country, which controls the financial affairs of the country by fixing main interest rates, issuing currency and controlling the foreign exchange rate; **the Federal Reserve Banks** = central banks in the US which are owned by the government, and directed by the Federal Reserve Board; **the Bank of England** = central British bank, owned by the state, which, together with the Treasury, regulates the nation's finances; **the World Bank** = central bank, controlled by the United Nations, whose funds come from the member states of the UN and which lends money to member states **(c)** **savings bank** = bank where you can deposit money and receive interest on it; **commercial bank** = bank that specializes in demand deposits and loans to businesses **(d)** **data bank** = store of information in a computer **2** *verb* to deposit money into a bank or to have an account with a bank; *he banked the check as soon as he received it;* **where do you bank?** = where do you have a bank account?; *I bank at or with First Federal*

◊ **bankable** *adjective* which a bank will accept; *a bankable paper*

◊ **bank account** *noun* account which a customer has with a bank, where the customer can deposit and withdraw money; *to open a bank account; to close a bank account; how much money do you have in your bank account? she has $100 in her savings bank account; if you let the balance in your bank account fall below $100, you have to pay bank charges*

◊ **bank balance** *noun* amount of a bank account at any particular time; *our bank balance went into the red last month*

◊ **bankbook** *noun* book, given by a bank, which shows amounts that you deposit or withdraw from your savings account

◊ **bank charges** *plural noun* charges which a bank makes for carrying out work for a customer

◊ **bank draft** *noun* order by one bank telling another bank to pay money to someone

◊ **banker** *noun* (a) person who is in an important position in a bank; **commercial banker** = person who has a high position in a commercial bank (b) generally, a bank; **banker's bill** = order by one bank telling another bank (usually in another country) to pay money to someone; **investment banker** = business which buys a new issue of stock and sells it to the general public

◊ **bank holiday** *noun* a weekday which is a public holiday when the banks are closed; *New Year's Day is a bank holiday*

◊ **banking** *noun* the business of banks; *he is studying banking; she has gone into banking;* **banking account** = account which a customer has with a bank; **a banking crisis** = crisis affecting the banks; **banking hours** = hours when a bank is open for its customers; *you cannot get money out of the bank after banking hours*

◊ **bank manager** *noun* person in charge of a branch of a bank; *he asked the bank manager for a loan*

◊ **bank note** *noun* promissory note of a bank that is payable to the bearer on demand and is acceptable as money

◊ **bank on** *verb* to be sure something will happen; *he is banking on getting a loan from his father to set up a business; do not bank on the sale of your house*

◊ **bankroll** *verb informal* to pay for *or* to finance (a project)

◊ **bank statement** *noun* statement from a bank showing the balance of an account and deposits and withdrawals made within a given period

bankrupt 1 *adjective & noun* (person *or* company) which has been declared by a court not to be capable of paying its debts and whose affairs are put into the hands of a receiver; *he was declared bankrupt; a bankrupt property developer; he went bankrupt after two years in business;* **discharged**

bankrupt = person who has been released from being bankrupt because he has paid his debts; **undischarged bankrupt** = person who has been declared bankrupt and has not been released from that state **2** *verb* to make someone become bankrupt; *the recession bankrupted my father*

◊ **bankruptcy** *noun* state of being bankrupt; *the recession has caused thousands of bankruptcies;* **adjudication of bankruptcy** *or* **declaration of bankruptcy** = legal order making someone bankrupt; **discharge of bankruptcy** = being released from bankruptcy after paying debts; **to file a petition in bankruptcy** = to apply officially to be made bankrupt *or* to ask officially for someone else to be made bankrupt

bar *noun* (a) place where you can buy and drink alcohol; *the sales reps met in the bar of the hotel* (b) small shop; **sandwich bar** = small shop where you can buy sandwiches; **snack bar** = small restaurant where you can get simple meals (c) thing which stops you from doing something; *government legislation is a bar to foreign trade* (d) the profession of lawyer; **to be called to the bar** = to become a lawyer

◊ **bar chart** *noun* chart where values *or* quantities are shown as thick columns of different heights

◊ **bar code** *noun* system of lines printed on a product which when read by a computer give a reference number or price

barely *adverb* almost not; *there is barely enough money left to pay the staff; she barely had time to call her lawyer*

bargain 1 *noun* (a) agreement on the price of something; **to make a bargain;** **to drive a hard bargain** = to be a difficult negotiator; **to strike a hard bargain** = to arrange a deal which is favorable to you; **it is a bad bargain** = it is not worth the price (b) thing which is cheaper than usual; *that car is a (real) bargain at $500;* **bargain hunter** = person who looks for cheap deals **2** *verb* to discuss a price for something; *you will have to bargain with the dealer if you want a discount; they spent two hours bargaining about* or *over the price*

NOTE: you bargain **with** someone **over** *or* **about** *or* **for** something

◊ **bargain basement** *noun* basement floor in a store where goods are sold cheaply; **I'm selling this at a bargain basement price** = I'm selling this very cheaply

◊ **bargain counter** *noun* counter in a store where goods are sold cheaply

◊ **bargain offer** *noun* sale of a particular type of goods at a cheap price; *this week's bargain offer - 30% off all carpet prices*

◊ **bargain price** *noun* cheap price; *these carpets are for sale at a bargain price*

◊ **bargaining** *noun* act of discussing a price, usually wage increases for workers; **collective bargaining** = negotiations between employers and workers' representatives over wage increases and conditions; **bargaining power** = strength of one person or group when discussing prices *or* wage settlements; **bargaining position** = statement of position by one group during negotiations

barometer *noun* way of calculating a change; *oil price rises are a useful barometer of political stability in the Middle East*

barrel *noun* (a) large round container for liquids; *he bought twenty-five barrels of wine; to sell wine by the barrel* (b) amount of liquid contained in a barrel; *the price of oil has reached $20 a barrel*

barrier *noun* thing which stops someone from doing something, especially sending goods from one place to another; **customs barriers** *or* **tariff barriers** = customs duty intended to make trade more difficult; **to impose trade barriers on certain goods** = to restrict the import of certain goods by charging high duty; *autoworkers' unions have asked the government to impose trade barriers on foreign cars;* **to lift trade barriers from imports** = to remove restrictions on imports; *the government has lifted trade barriers on foreign cars*

barrister *noun GB* lawyer (especially in England) who can speak *or* argue a case in one of the higher courts

barter 1 *noun* system where goods are exchanged for other goods and not sold for money; **barter agreement** *or* **barter arrangement** *or* **barter deal** = agreement to exchange goods by barter; *the company has agreed to a barter deal with Bulgaria* **2** *verb* to exchange goods for other goods, but not buy them for money; *they agreed to barter tractors for barrels of wine*

◊ **bartering** *noun* act of exchanging goods and not for money

QUOTE under the barter agreements, Nigeria will export 175,000 barrels a day of crude oil in exchange for trucks, food, planes and chemicals
Wall Street Journal

base 1 *noun* (a) lowest or first position; *turnover increased by 200%, but starting from a low base;* **base year** = first year of an index, against which later years' changes are measured; **base pay** *or* **base rate** = basic rate of pay for a job, not including such extras as overtime, bonuses or commissions (b) place where a company has its main office or factory *or* place where a businessman has his office; *the company has its base in London and branches in all European countries; he has an office in Madrid which he uses as a base while he is traveling in Southern Europe* **2** *verb* (a) to start to calculate *or* to negotiate from a position; *we based our calculations on the forecast turnover;* **based on** = calculating from; *based on last year's figures; based on population forecasts* (b) to set up a company *or* a person in a place; *the East Coast manager is based in our New York office; our overseas branch is based in the Bahamas; a Los Angeles-based sales executive*

◊ **basement** *noun* section of a building *or* store which is underground; **bargain basement** = basement floor in a store where goods are sold cheaply; *I am selling this at a bargain basement price*

QUOTE the base lending rate, or prime rate, is the rate at which banks lend to their top corporate borrowers
Wall Street Journal

basic 1 *adjective* (a) normal; **basic pay** *or* **basic salary** *or* **basic wage** = normal salary without extra payments; **basic discount** = normal discount without extra percentages; *our basic discount is 20%, but we offer 5% extra for a cash payment* (b) essential; **basic commodities** = most important farm produce, produced in large quantities (such as corn, rice, sugar, etc.) (c) simple *or* from which everything starts; *he has a basic knowledge of the market; to work at the cash desk, you need a basic education in math*

◊ **basics** *plural noun* simple and important facts; *he has studied the*

basics of foreign exchange dealing; to get back to basics = to consider the fundamental facts again

◇ **basically** *adverb* seen from the point from which everything starts

◇ **BASIC** *noun* = BEGINNER'S ALL-PURPOSE SYMBOLIC INSTRUCTION CODE simple language for computer programming

basis *noun* (a) base *or* number from which calculations are made; *we forecast the turnover on the basis of a 6% price increase;* **basis point =** one hundredth of one percentage point (a measure of small changes in interest rates, yields, etc.) (b) general terms of agreement; **on a short-term** *or* **long-term basis =** for a short *or* long period; *he has been appointed on a short-term basis; we have three people working on a volunteer basis*
NOTE: the plural is **bases**

basket *noun* container made of thin pieces of wood *or* metal *or* plastic; *a basket of apples;* **filing basket =** container kept on a desk for documents which have to be filed; **market basket =** group of commonly purchased household items, chosen to calculate the increase in inflation; **shopping basket =** basket used for carrying items which you wish to buy in a self-service store; **waste basket =** container into which paper or pieces of garbage can be thrown

batch 1 *noun* (a) group of items which are made at one time; *this batch of shoes has the serial number 25-02* (b) group of items which are processed at the same time; *a batch of invoices; today's batch of orders; the accountant signed a batch of checks; we deal with the orders in batches of fifty;* **batch processing =** system of data processing where information is collected into batches before being loaded into the computer **2** *verb* to put items together in groups; *to batch invoices or checks*

◇ **batch number** *noun* number attached to a batch; *when making a complaint always quote the batch number on the package*

battery *noun* (a) object that contains and provides electric power; *the calculator needs a new battery; a battery-powered calculator* (b) series; *she had to pass a battery of tests to qualify for the job*

battle *noun* fight; **boardroom battles =** arguments between board members; **circulation battle =** fight between two newspapers to sell more copies in the same section of the market

bay *noun* **loading bay =** section of road in a warehouse, where trucks can drive in to load or unload

bear 1 *noun (stock exchange)* dealer who sells stocks because he thinks the price will fall and he will be able to buy them again more cheaply later; **bear market =** period when stock prices fall because shareholders are selling; *compare* BULL **2** *verb* (a) to give interest; *government bonds which bear 5% interest* (b) to have (a name) *or* to have something written on it; *the check bears the signature of the company secretary; envelope which bears a Chicago postmark; a letter bearing yesterday's date; the stock certificate bears his name* (c) to pay costs; *the costs of the exhibition will be borne by the company; the company bore the legal costs of both parties*
NOTE: **bearing - bore - has borne**

◇ **bearer** *noun* person who holds a check *or* certificate; **the check is payable to bearer =** is paid to the person who holds it, not to any particular name written on it

◇ **bearer bond** *noun* bond which is payable to the bearer and does not have a name written on it

◇ **bearing** *adjective* which bears *or* which produces; *certificate bearing interest at 5%; interest-bearing deposits*

> QUOTE bearish sentiment about gold has been deepening for some time, though gold prices have occasionally revived
> *Business Week*

beat *verb* (a) to win *or* conquer; *they have beaten their rivals into second place in the computer market;* **to beat down a price =** to bargain hard so that a price is lowered (b) **to beat a ban =** to do something which is generally forbidden
NOTE: **beating - beat - has beaten**

become *verb* to pass from one state to another; *the export market has become very difficult since the rise in the dollar; the company became very profitable in a short time*
NOTE: **becoming - became - has become**

beep *verb* **(a)** to make a short high-pitched sound **(b)** to call someone on a beeper

◊ **beeper** *noun* device which makes a short high-pitched sound when called by radio

begin *verb* to start; *the company began to lose its share of the market; he began the report which the shareholders had asked for; the auditors' report began with a description of the general principles adopted*
NOTE: you begin something *or* begin **to do** something *or* begin **with** something. Note also: **beginning - began - has begun**

◊ **beginning** *noun* first part; *the beginning of the report is a list of the directors and their stockholdings*

behalf *noun* **on behalf of** = acting for (someone *or* a company); *I am writing on behalf of the minority stockholders; she is acting on my behalf; lawyers acting on behalf of the Canadian company*

behind **1** *preposition* at the back *or* after; *the company is No. 2 in the market, about $4m behind their rivals* **2** *adverb* after; *we have fallen behind our rivals* = we have fewer sales *or* make less profit than our rivals; *the company has fallen behind with its deliveries* = it is late with its deliveries

believe *verb* to think that something is true; *we believe he has offered to buy 25% of the common stock; the CEO is believed to be in South America on business*

belong *verb* **(a) to belong to** = to be the property of; *the company belongs to an old American banking family; the patent belongs to the inventor's son* **(b) to belong with** = to be related *or* connected with; *those documents belong with the sales reports*

below *preposition* under *or* less than; *we sold the property at below the market price; you can get a television at below $75 from a discount store*

◊ **below-the-line** *adjective* **below-the-line expenditure** = exceptional payments which are separated from a company's normal accounts

benchmark *noun* point in an index which is important, and can be used to compare with other figures

beneficial *adjective* **beneficial owner** = person who is the real owner of a property; **beneficial interest** = interest which allows someone to occupy or receive rent from a property, but not to own it

◊ **beneficiary** *noun* person who gains money from something; *the beneficiaries of a will*

benefit **1** *noun* **(a)** payments which are made to someone under a public or private insurance scheme; *she receives $50 a week in unemployment benefits; the sickness benefit is paid monthly; the insurance office sends out benefit checks each week;* **death benefit** = money paid to the beneficiary of an insurance policy when the insured dies **(b) fringe benefits** = extra items given by a company to workers in addition to their salaries (such as company cars, group health insurance) **2** *verb* **(a)** to make better *or* to improve; *a fall in inflation benefits the exchange rate* **(b) to benefit from** *or* **by something** = to be improved by something *or* to gain more money because of something; *exports have benefited from the fall in the exchange rate; the employees have benefited from the profit-sharing plan*

bequest *noun* property, money, etc., given to someone in a will; *he made several bequests to his staff*

best **1** *adjective* very good *or* better than all others; *his best price is still higher than all the other suppliers; 1985 was the company's best year ever* **2** *noun* very good effort; *the salesmen are doing their best, but the stock simply will not sell at that price*

◊ **best-seller** *noun* item (especially a book) which sells very well

◊ **best-selling** *adjective* which sells very well; *these computer disks are our best-selling line*

bet 1 *noun* amount deposited when you risk money on the result of a race *or* of a game **2** *verb* to risk money on the result of something; *he bet $100 on the result of the election; I bet you $25 the dollar will rise against the pound*
NOTE: betting - bet - has bet

better *adjective* more desirable compared with something else; *this year's figures are better than last year's; we will shop around to see if we can get a better price*

◊ **Better Business Bureau** *noun* organization of local business executives to promote ethical business practices

◊ **betterment** *noun* improvement which adds value to a property

beware *verb* to be cautious; **beware of imitations** = be careful not to buy cheap low-quality items which are made to look like more expensive items

bi- *prefix* two; **bimonthly** = (i) once every two months; (ii) twice a month; **biannually** = twice a year

bid 1 *noun* **(a)** offer to buy something at a certain price; **to make a bid for something** = to offer to buy something; *he made a bid for the house; the company made a bid for its rival;* **to make a cash bid** = to offer to pay cash for something; **to put in a bid for something** *or* **to enter a bid for something** = to offer (usually in writing) to buy something; *(at an auction)* **opening bid** = first bid; **closing bid** = last bid at an auction *or* the bid which is successful **(b)** offer to do some work at a certain price; *he made the lowest bid for the job* **(c)** offer to sell something at a certain price; *they asked for bids for the supply of spare parts* **(d)** takeover **bid** = offer to buy all or a majority of shares in a company so as to control it; *to make a takeover bid for a company; to withdraw a takeover bid;* the company **rejected the takeover bid** = the directors recommended that the shareholders should not accept it **2** *verb (at an auction)* **to bid for something** = to offer to buy something; *he bid $1,000 for the jewels* = he offered to pay $1,000 for the jewels

NOTE: bidding - bid - has bid

◊ **bidder** *noun* person who makes a bid (usually at an auction); *several bidders made offers for the house;* **the property was sold to the highest bidder** = to the person who had made the highest bid *or* who offered the most money; **the contract will go to the lowest bidder** = to the person who offers the best terms *or* the lowest price for services

◊ **bidding** *noun* action of making offers to buy (usually at an auction); **the bidding started at $1,000** = the first and lowest bid was $1,000; **the bidding stopped at $250,000** = the last bid (and the successful bid) was for $250,000; **the auctioneer started the bidding at $100** = he suggested that the first bid should be $100

Big Board *noun informal* = NEW YORK STOCK EXCHANGE

bilateral *adjective* between two parties *or* countries; *the president signed a bilateral trade agreement*

bilk *verb (informal)* to defraud someone

bill 1 *noun* **(a)** written list of charges to be paid; *the salesman wrote out the bill; does the bill include sales tax? the bill is made out to Smith Co.; the builder sent in his bill; he left the country without paying his bills;* **to foot the bill** = to pay the costs **(b)** written paper promising to pay money; **bill of exchange** = document which tells a bank to pay a person (usually used in payments in foreign currency); **demand bill** *or* **sight bill** = bill of exchange which must be paid when payment is asked for; **to accept a bill** = to sign a bill of exchange to show that you promise to pay it; **bills payable** = bills which a debtor will have to pay; **bills receivable** = bills which a creditor will receive in the end **(c) bill of lading** = list of goods being shipped, which the transporter gives to the person sending the goods to show that the goods have been loaded **(d)** piece of paper money; *a $5 bill* **(e) bill of sale** = document which the seller gives to the buyer to show that the sale has taken place **(f)** draft of a new law which will be discussed in a legislature; *he has just introduced a bill in Congress* **2** *verb* to present a bill to someone so that it can be paid; *the builders billed him for the repairs to his neighbor's house*

◊ **billing** *noun* writing of invoices or bills; *the payment will be processed before the next billing*

billion number one thousand million
NOTE: written **bn** after figures: **$25bn**

bin *noun* container or section of warehousing space where inventory is kept (in a two-bin system, the first bin contains the working inventory, and the second bin is the backup)

bind *verb* to tie *or* to attach; *the company is bound by its articles of incorporation; he does not consider himself bound by the agreement which was signed by his predecessor*
NOTE: **binding - bound**
◊ **binder** *noun* **(a)** stiff cardboard cover for papers; **ring binder =** cover with rings in it which fit into special holes made in sheets of paper **(b)** temporary agreement for insurance sent before the insurance policy is issued **(c)** money paid as part of an initial agreement to purchase property
◊ **binding** *adjective* which legally forces someone to do something; *a binding contract; this document is not legally binding;* **the agreement is binding on all parties =** all parties signing it must do what is agreed

bit *noun* smallest unit of computer information, usually represented by the figure 0 or 1

black *adjective* **(a) black market =** buying and selling goods in a way which is not allowed by law (as in a time of rationing); *there is a flourishing black market in spare parts for cars; you can buy stolen goods on the black market;* **to pay black market prices =** to pay high prices to get items which are not easily available **(b) black economy =** system in which work which is paid for in cash, and therefore not declared for tax **(c) in the black =** in credit; *the company has moved into the black; my bank account is still in the black*
◊ **blacklist 1** *noun* list of goods *or* people *or* companies which are considered undesirable **2** *verb* to put goods *or* people *or* a company on a blacklist; *his firm was blacklisted by the government*

blame 1 *noun* saying that someone has done something wrong *or* that someone is responsible; *the sales reps got the blame for the poor sales figures* **2** *verb* to say that someone has done something wrong *or* is responsible for a mistake; *the CEO blamed the head accountant for not warning him of the loss; the union is blaming the management for poor industrial relations*

blank 1 *adjective* not written on *or* unmarked; **a blank check =** a check with no amount of money or name written on it, but signed by the drawer **2** *noun* space on a form which has to be completed; *fill in the blanks and return the form to your local office*

blanket *noun* **blanket agreement =** agreement which covers many items; **blanket insurance =** insurance which covers various items (such as a house and its contents); **blanket order** *or* **standing order =** order for goods which are supplied in the same amounts on a regular basis; **blanket refusal =** refusal to accept many different items

blister pack *noun* type of packing where the item for sale is covered with a stiff plastic sheet sealed to a card backing

block 1 *noun* **(a)** series of items grouped together; *he purchased a block of 10,000 shares* **(b)** piece of land in a city *or* town; buildings on such a piece of land; *they bought up all the buildings on the block; drive six blocks south, then turn right* **2** *verb* to stop something from taking place; *he used his casting vote to block the motion; the planning committee blocked the redevelopment plan;* **blocked currency =** currency which cannot be converted into another because of exchange controls; *the company has a large account in blocked rubles*

blue *adjective* **blue-chip investments** *or* **blue-chip stocks =** shares in well-established companies, normally with a long positive dividend record and all the characteristics of a safe investment; **blue-collar worker =** manual worker in a factory; **blue-collar union =** labor union formed mainly of blue-collar workers; **blue law =** law regulating business activity on Sunday; **blue-sky law =** law which protects investors against unscrupulous dealers in new issues

blurb   *noun*   piece   of   advertising, especially an advertisement written by a publisher for a book

bn = BILLION

board 1 *noun* **(a) board of directors =** group of people elected by the stockholders to draw up company policy and to appoint the president and other executive officers who are responsible for managing the company; *the bank has two representatives on the board; he sits on the board as a representative of the bank; two directors were removed from the board at the annual meeting;* **she was asked to join the board =** she was asked to become a director; **board meeting =** meeting of the directors of a company **(b)** group of people who run a trust *or* a society; **advisory board =** group of advisers; **editorial board =** group of editors **(c) on board =** on a ship *or* plane *or* train; **free on board (f.o.b.) =** term used in shipping, meaning that the responsibility and liability of the seller do not end until the goods are placed aboard a ship **(d)** regular unit of trade on a stock exchange; *the board lot on the New York stock exchange is 100 shares* **2** *verb* to go on to a ship *or* plane *or* train; *customs officials boarded the ship in the harbor*

◇ **boarding card** *or* **boarding pass** *noun* card given to passengers who have checked in for a flight to allow them to board the plane

◇ **boardroom** *noun* room where the directors of a company meet; **boardroom battles =** arguments between directors

bona fide *adjective* trustworthy *or* which can be trusted; **a bona fide offer =** an offer which is made honestly

bonanza *noun* great wealth; very profitable business; *the oil well was a bonanza for the company; 1984 was a bonanza year for the computer industry*

bond 1 *noun* **(a)** contract document promising to repay money borrowed by a company *or* by the government; *government bonds or treasury bonds;* **municipal bond =** bond issued by a town or district **(b)** contract document promising to repay money borrowed by a person; **bearer bond =** bond which is payable to the bearer and does not have a name written on it; **debenture bond =** bond secured only by the integrity of the owner; **mortgage bond =** certificate showing that a mortgage exists and that property is security for it; **U.S. Savings Bond =** small nonnegotiable bond issued by the federal government **(c) goods (held) in bond =** goods held by customs until duty has been paid; **entry of goods under bond =** bringing goods into a country in bond; **to take goods out of bond =** to pay duty on goods so that they can be released by the customs **2** *verb* to become a surety for another; *the firm bonded the new employee*

◇ **bonded** *adjective* held in bond; **bonded warehouse =** warehouse where goods are stored in bond until duty is paid

◇ **bondholder** *noun* person who holds government bonds

bonus *noun* extra payment; **Christmas bonus =** extra payment made to employees at Christmas; **incentive bonus =** extra pay offered to a worker to encourage him to work harder; **productivity bonus =** extra payment made because of increased productivity; **bonus stock =** extra stock given to an existing stockholder
NOTE: plural is **bonuses**

book 1 *noun* set of sheets of paper attached together; **a company's books =** the financial records of a company; **account book =** book which records sales and purchases; **order book =** record of orders; **the company has a full order book =** it has sufficient orders to keep the workforce occupied; **book value =** value as recorded in the company's books; **phone book** *or* **telephone book =** book which lists names of people or companies with their addresses and telephone numbers **2** *verb* to order *or* to reserve something; *to book a room in a hotel ; to book someone*

into a hotel *or* **onto a flight** = to order a room *or* a plane ticket for someone; **the hotel** *or* **the flight is fully booked** *or* **is booked up** = all the rooms *or* seats are reserved; *the show is booked up over the Christmas season*

◊ **booking** *noun* act of ordering a room *or* a seat; **to confirm a booking** = to say that a booking is certain; **double booking** = booking by mistake of two people into the same hotel room *or* the same seat on a plane

◊ **bookkeeper** *noun* person who keeps the financial records of a company

◊ **bookkeeping** *noun* keeping of the financial records of a company *or* an organization; **single-entry bookkeeping** = noting a deal with only one entry; **double-entry bookkeeping** = noting of both credit and debit sides of an account

◊ **booklet** *noun* small book with a paper cover

◊ **bookseller** *noun* person who sells books

◊ **bookstore** *noun* store which sells books

◊ **bookstall** *noun* small open bookstore (as in a train station)

boom 1 *noun* time when sales *or* production *or* business activity are increasing; *a period of economic boom; the boom of the 1970s;* **boom industry** = industry which is expanding rapidly; **a boom share** = share in a company which is expanding; **the boom years** = years when there is an economic boom **2** *verb* to expand *or* to become prosperous; *business is booming; sales are booming*

◊ **booming** *adjective* which is expanding *or* becoming prosperous; *a booming industry or company; technology is a booming sector of the economy*

boost 1 *noun* help to increase; *this publicity will give sales a boost; the government hopes to give a boost to industrial development* **2** *verb* to make something increase; *we expect our publicity campaign to boost sales by 25%; the company hopes to boost its profits; incentive schemes are boosting production*

booth *noun* (a) small place for one person to stand or sit; **telephone booth** = public box with a telephone; **ticket booth** = place outdoors where a person sells tickets (b) section of a commercial fair where a company exhibits its products or services

bootstrap *noun* method of loading a computer program, using a brief set of instructions

bore, borne *see* BEAR

borrow *verb* to use money from someone for a time, possibly paying interest for it, and repaying it at the end of the period; *he borrowed $1,000 from the bank; the company had to borrow heavily to repay its debts; they borrowed $25,000 against the security of the factory*

◊ **borrower** *noun* person who borrows; *borrowers from the bank pay 12% interest*

◊ **borrowing** *noun* action of borrowing money; **borrowing power** = amount of money which a company can borrow

boss *noun informal* employer *or* person in charge of a company *or* an office; *if you want a pay raise, go and talk to your boss; he became a manager when he married the boss's daughter*

bottleneck *noun* position when business activity is slowed down because one section of the operation cannot cope with the amount of work; *a bottleneck in the supply system; there are serious bottlenecks in the production line*

bottom 1 *noun* lowest part *or* point; **sales have reached rock bottom** = the very lowest point of all; **the bottom has fallen out of the market** = sales have fallen below what previously seemed to be the lowest point; **bottom price** = lowest price; **rock-bottom price** = lowest price of all; **bottom line** = last line on a balance sheet indicating profit or loss; **the boss is interested only in the bottom line** = he is only interested in the final profit **2** *verb* **to bottom (out)** = to reach the lowest point; **the market has bottomed out** = has reached the lowest point and does not seem likely to fall further

bought *see* BUY

bounce *verb (of a check)* to be returned to the person who has tried to cash it, because there is not enough money in the payer's account to pay it; *he paid for the car with a check that bounced*

bounty *noun* government subsidy made to help an industry

boutique *noun* small specialized shop, especially for up-to-date clothes; section of a department store selling up-to-date clothes; *a jeans boutique; a ski boutique*

box *noun* **(a)** cardboard *or* wood *or* plastic container; *the merchandise was sent in thin cardboard boxes; the watches are prepacked in plastic display boxes; paperclips come in boxes of two hundred =* packed two hundred to a box; **box file =** file (for papers) made like a box **(b) box number =** reference number used in a post office or an advertisement to avoid giving an address; *please reply to Box No. 209; our address is: P.O. Box 74209, San Diego*

◊ **boxed** *adjective* put in a box *or* sold in a box; **boxed set =** set of items sold together in a box

boycott 1 *noun* refusal to buy *or* to deal in certain products; *the union organized a boycott against *or* of imported cars* **2** *verb* to refuse to buy *or* to deal in a certain product; *we are boycotting all imports from that country;* the management has *boycotted the meeting =* has refused to attend the meeting

bracket 1 *noun* group of items *or* people taken together; **people in the middle-income bracket =** people with average incomes, not high or low; **he is in the top tax bracket =** he pays the highest level of tax **2** *verb* **to bracket together =** to treat several items together in the same way; *in the sales reports, all the European countries are bracketed together*

branch 1 *noun* local office of a bank or large business; local store of a large chain of stores; *the bank *or* the store has branches in most towns in the South; the insurance company has closed its branches in South America; he is the manager of our local branch of First National; we have decided to open a branch office in Chicago; the manager of our branch in Lagos *or* of our Lagos branch;* **branch manager =** manager of a branch **2** *verb* **to branch out =** to start a new (but usually related) type of business; *from car retailing, the*

company branched out into car leasing

brand *noun* make of product, which can be recognized by a name *or* by a design; *the top-selling brands of toothpaste; the company is launching a new brand of soap;* **brand name =** name of a brand; **brand loyalty =** loyalty by the customer who always buys the same brand; **own brand =** name of a store which is used on products which are specially packed for that store

◊ **brand-new** *adjective* quite new *or* very new

breach *noun* failure to carry out the terms of an agreement; **breach of contract =** failing to do something which is in a contract; **the company is in breach of contract =** it has failed to carry out the duties of the contract; **breach of warranty =** failure to fulfill a warranty contract

break 1 *noun* short space of time, when you can rest; *she typed for two hours without a break;* **coffee break =** rest time during work; *he went on a coffee break; she's having a coffee break* **2** *verb* **(a)** to fail to carry out the duties of a contract; *the company has broken the contract *or* the agreement;* **to break an engagement to do something =** not to do what has been agreed **(b)** to cancel (a contract); *the company is hoping to be able to break the contract*
NOTE: **breaking - broke - has broken**

◊ **breakages** *plural noun* items broken; *customers are expected to pay for breakages*

◊ **break down** *verb* **(a)** to stop working because of mechanical failure; *the telex machine has broken down; what do you do when your photocopier breaks down?* **(b)** to stop; *negotiations broke down after six hours* **(c)** to show all the items in a total list of costs *or* expenditure; *we broke the expenditure down into fixed and variable costs; can you break down this invoice into spare parts and labor?*

◊ **breakdown** *noun* (a) stopping work because of mechanical failure; *we cannot communicate with our Manila office because of the breakdown of the telex lines* (b) stopping talking; *a breakdown in wage negotiations* (c) showing details item by item; *give me a breakdown of investment costs*

◊ **break even** *verb* to balance costs and receipts, but not make a profit; *last year the company only just broke even; we broke even in our first two months of trading*

◊ **break-even point** *noun* point at which sales cover costs, but do not show a profit

◊ **break off** *verb* to stop; *we broke off the discussion at midnight; management broke off negotiations with the union*

◊ **break up** *verb* (a) to split something large into small sections; *the company was broken up and separate divisions sold off* (b) to come to an end; *the meeting broke up at 12:30*

bribe 1 *noun* money given to someone in authority to get him to help; *the councilman was dismissed for taking bribes* **2** *verb* to pay someone money to get him to do something for you; *we had to bribe the vice-president's secretary before she would let us see her boss*

bridge loan *noun* short-term loan to help someone buy a new house when he has not yet sold his old one

brief *verb* to explain to someone in detail; *the salesmen were briefed on the new product; the company president briefed the board on the progress of the negotiations*

◊ **briefcase** *noun* case with a handle for carrying papers and documents; *he put all the files into his briefcase*

◊ **briefing** *noun* telling someone details; *all salesmen have to attend a sales briefing on the new product*

bring *verb* to come to a place with someone or something; *he brought his documents with him; the financial director brought his secretary to take notes at the meeting; to bring a lawsuit against someone =* to tell someone to appear in court to settle an argument

NOTE: **bringing - brought**

◊ **bring down** *verb* (a) to reduce; *gasoline companies have brought down the price of oil* (b) to add a figure

to an account at the end of a period to balance expenditure and income; *balance brought down: $365.15*

◊ **bring forward** *verb* (a) to make earlier; *to bring forward the date of repayment; the date of the next meeting has been brought forward to March* (b) to take a balance brought down as the starting point for the next period in a balance sheet; *balance brought forward: $365.15*

◊ **bring in** *verb* to earn (an interest); *the shares bring in a small amount*

◊ **bring out** *verb* to introduce something new; *they are bringing out a new model of the car for the Motor Show*

◊ **bring up** *verb* to refer to something for the first time; *the chairman brought up the question of insurance payments*

brisk *adjective* selling actively; *sales are brisk; the market in oil shares is particularly brisk; a brisk market in oil shares*

broadside *noun* large format publicity leaflet

brochure *noun* publicity booklet; *we sent off for a brochure about vacations in Greece* or *about postal services*

broke *adjective informal* having no money; *the company is broke; he cannot pay for the new car because he is broke; to go broke =* to become bankrupt; *the company went broke last month*

broker *noun* (a) dealer; **foreign exchange broker =** person who buys and sells foreign currency on behalf of other people; **insurance broker =** person who sells insurance to clients; **ship broker =** person who sells shipping or transport of goods to clients (b) person who buys or sells securities for clients

◊ **brokerage** or **broker's commission** *noun* payment to a broker for a deal carried out; **brokerage house =** firm which buys or sells securities for clients

buck 1 *noun informal* dollar **2** *verb* **to buck the trend =** to go against the trend

bucket shop *noun* dishonest brokerage firm where customers' orders to buy and sell stock are treated as bets on the rise and fall of prices

QUOTE at last something is being done about the thousands of bucket shops across the nation that sell investment scams by phone
Forbes Magazine

budget 1 *noun* **(a)** plan of expected spending and income for a business or government (usually for one year); *to draw up a budget; we have agreed on the budget for next year; the President proposed a budget aimed at boosting the economy;* **to balance the budget =** to plan income and expenditure so that they balance; *the governor is planning for a balanced budget;* **advertising budget =** money planned for spending on advertising; **cash budget =** plan of cash income and expenditure; **overhead budget =** plan of probable overhead costs; **publicity budget =** money allowed for expected expenditure on publicity; **sales budget =** plan of probable sales **(b)** *(in stores)* cheap; **budget department =** cheaper department; **budget prices =** low prices **2** *verb* to plan probable income and expenditure; *we are budgeting for $10,000 of sales next year*

◊ **budgetary** *adjective* referring to a budget; **budgetary policy =** policy of planning income and expenditure; **budgetary control =** keeping check on spending; **budgetary requirements =** spending or income required to meet the budget forecasts

◊ **budgeting** *noun* preparing of schedules to help plan expenditure and income

build *verb* to construct; *to build a sales structure; to build on past experience* = to use experience as a base on which to act in the future
NOTE: **building - built**

◊ **building** *noun* house *or* factory *or* office structure; *they have redeveloped the site of the old office building;* **the Shell Building =** the structure where the head office of Shell is

◊ **build up** *verb* **(a)** to create something by adding pieces together; *he bought several shoe stores and gradually built up a chain* **(b)** to expand something gradually; *to build up a profitable business; to build up a team of salesmen*

◊ **buildup** *noun* gradual increase; *a buildup in sales* or *a sales buildup; there will be a big publicity buildup before the launch of the new model*

◊ **built-in** *adjective* forming part of the system *or* of a machine; *the computer has a built-in clock; the accounting system has a series of built-in checks*

bulk *noun* large quantity of goods; **in bulk =** in large quantities; *to buy rice in bulk;* **bulk buying** *or* **bulk purchase =** buying large quantities of goods at a lower price; **bulk carrier =** ship which carries large quantities of loose goods (such as coal); **bulk rate =** special lower price rate applied to large orders; **bulk shipments =** shipments of large quantities of goods

◊ **bulky** *adjective* large and awkward; *the Post Office does not accept bulky packages*

bull *noun Stock Exchange* dealer who believes the market will rise, and therefore buys securities to sell at a higher price later; **bull market =** period when stock market prices rise because people are optimistic and buy shares; *see* BEAR

bulletin *noun* public notice *or* announcement, generally of news recently received

bullion *noun* gold or silver bars; *gold bullion; the price of bullion is fixed daily; to fix the bullion price for silver*

bumper *noun* very large crop; *a bumper crop of corn;* **1984 was a bumper year for computer sales =** 1984 was an excellent year for sales

bumping *noun* **(a)** situation where a senior employee takes the place of a junior during a period of layoffs **(b)** passing passengers to other flights when a plane is overbooked

bureau *noun* office which specializes, especially a government office; *Bureau of the Census; Bureau of Labor Statistics;* **clipping bureau =** firm which cuts out references to a client from newspapers and magazines and sends them on to him; **employment bureau =** office which finds jobs for people; **information bureau =** office which gives information; **trade bureau =** office which specializes in commercial enquiries; **visitors' bureau =** office which deals with visitors' questions
NOTE: the plural is **bureaus** *or* **bureaux**

burn *verb* to destroy by fire; *the chief accountant burnt the documents before the police arrived*

NOTE: **burning - burnt**

◊ **burn down** *verb* to destroy completely in a fire; *the warehouse burnt down and all the stock was destroyed; the company records were all lost when the offices were burnt down*

burster *noun* machine for separating continuous forms printed out by a computer printer

bus *noun* motor vehicle for carrying passengers; *he goes to work by bus; she took the bus to go to her office;* **bus company** = company which runs the buses in a town

bushel *noun* measure of dry goods, such as corn (= 32 quarts)

business *noun* (a) work in buying or selling; *business is expanding; business is slow; he does a thriving business in repairing cars; what's your line of business?;* **business call** = visit to talk to someone on business; **business center** = part of a town where the main banks, stores and offices are located; **business class** = type of airline travel which is less expensive than first class but more comfortable than tourist class; **business college** *or* **business school** = place where commercial studies are taught; **business correspondence** = letters concerned with a business; **business equipment** = machines used in an office; **business expenses** = money spent on running a business, not on stock or assets; **business day** *or* **business hours** = time (usually 9 a.m. to 5 p.m.) when a business is open; **business letter** = letter about commercial matters; **business lunch** = lunch to discuss business matters; **business trip** = trip to discuss business matters with clients; **to be in business** = to be in a commercial firm; **to go into business** = to start a commercial firm; *he went into business as a car dealer;* **to go out of business** = to stop trading; *the firm went out of business during the recession;* **on business** = on commercial work; *he had to go abroad on business; the chairman is in Holland on business* (b) commercial company; *he owns a small car repair business; she runs a business from her home; he set up in business as an insurance broker;* **business address** = details of number, street and town where a company is located; **business card** = card showing a businessman's name and the name and address of the company he works for;

big business = very large commercial firms (c) affairs discussed; *the main business of the meeting was finished by 3 p.m.;* **any other business** = item at the end of an agenda, where any matter can be raised

◊ **business agent** *noun* official of a local union who is responsible for settling grievances and negotiating contracts

◊ **businessman** *or* **businesswoman** *noun* man *or* woman engaged in business; *she's a good businesswoman* = she is good at commercial deals; **a small businessman** = man who owns a small business

bust *adjective informal* **to go bust** = to become bankrupt

busy *adjective* occupied in doing something or in working; *he is busy preparing the annual report; the manager is busy at the moment, but he will be free in about fifteen minutes; the busiest time of year for stores is the week before Christmas; summer is the busy season for hotels;* **the line is busy** = the telephone line is being used

buy 1 *verb* to get something by paying money; *he bought 10,000 shares; the company has been bought by its leading supplier;* **to buy wholesale and sell retail; to buy for cash; to buy forward** = to buy foreign currency before you need it, in order to be sure of the exchange rate NOTE: **buying - bought 2** *noun* **good buy** *or* **bad buy** = thing bought which is *or* is not worth the money paid for it; *that watch was a good buy; this car was a bad buy*

◊ **buy back** *verb* to buy something which you have sold; *he sold the store last year and is now trying to buy it back*

◊ **buyer** *noun* (a) person who buys; **there were no buyers** = no one wanted to buy; **a buyers' market** = market where products are sold cheaply because there are few buyers; **cash buyer** = buyer who pays cash or uses a charge card; **impulse buyer** = person who buys something when he sees it, not because he was planning to buy it (b) person who buys a certain type of goods wholesale, which are then stocked by a large store; **head buyer** = most important buyer in a store; *she is the shoe buyer for a New York department store*

◊ **buying** *noun* getting something for money; **bulk buying** = getting large quantities of goods at low prices;

forward buying *or* **buying forward** = buying shares *or* commodities *or* currency for delivery at a later date; **impulse buying** = buying items which you have just seen, not because you had planned to buy them; **panic buying** = rush to buy something at any price because stocks may run out; **buying department** = department in a company which buys raw materials or goods for use in the company; **buying power** = ability to buy; *the buying power of the dollar has fallen over the last several years*

◊ **buyout** *noun* takeover of a company by a group of employees or managers; **leveraged buyout** = buying all the shares in a company by borrowing money against the security of the shares to be bought

> QUOTE in a normal leveraged buyout, the acquirer raises money by borrowing against the assets or cash flow of the target company
> *Fortune*

by-product *noun* product made as a result of manufacturing a main product; *soap is a useful by-product of oil*

bylaw *noun* rule accepted by an organization for its own government; *the board discussed an amendment to the company's bylaws*

byte *noun* storage unit in a computer, equal to one character

Cc

cab *noun* car which takes people from one place to another for money; *he took a cab to the airport; cab fares are very high in New York*

cabinet *noun* piece of furniture for storing records or display; *last year's correspondence is in the bottom drawer of the filing cabinet;* **display cabinet** = piece of furniture with a glass top or glass doors for showing goods for sale

cablegram *noun* telegram *or* message sent by telegraph

cafeteria *noun* self-service restaurant in an organization, where employees can buy meals cheaply

calculate *verb* (a) to find the answer to a problem using numbers; *the bank clerk calculated the rate of exchange for the dollar* (b) to estimate; *I calculate that we have six months' stock left*

◊ **calculating machine** *noun* machine which calculates

◊ **calculation** *noun* answer to a problem in mathematics; **rough calculation** = approximate answer; *I made some rough calculations on the back of an envelope; according to my calculations, we have six months' stock left; we are $20,000 off in our calculations* = we have $20,000 too much or too little

◊ **calculator** *noun* electronic machine which works out the answers to problems in mathematics; *my pocket calculator needs a new battery; he worked out the discount on his calculator*

calendar *noun* (a) book *or* set of sheets of paper showing the days and months in a year, often attached to pictures; *the garage sent me a calendar with photographs of old cars;* **desk calendar** *or* **wall calendar** = calendar which stands on a desk *or* can hang on a wall; **calendar month** = a whole month as on a calendar, from the first day to the last day; **calendar year** = year from January 1 to December 31 (b) list of days, with blanks to write in appointments; *my calendar is full, but I shall try to fit you in tomorrow afternoon*

call 1 *noun* (a) conversation on the telephone; **local call** = call to a number on the same exchange; **long-distance call** = call to a number in a different zone *or* area; **overseas call** *or* **international call** = call to another country; **person-to-person call** = call where you ask the operator to connect you with a named person; **collect call** = call where the person receiving the call agrees to pay for it; **to make a call** = to dial and speak to someone on the telephone; **to take a call** = to answer the telephone; **to log calls** = to note all details of telephone calls made (b) demand for repayment of a loan by a lender; **call money** = money loaned for which repayment can be demanded without notice (c) *(Stock Exchange)* demand to pay for new shares; **call**

option = option to buy shares at a certain price **(d)** visit; *the salesmen make six calls a day;* **business call =** visit to talk to someone on business; **cold call =** sales visit where the salesman has no appointment and the client is not an established customer **2** *verb* **(a)** to telephone to someone; *I'll call you at your office tomorrow* **(b)** to call on someone = to visit; *our salesmen call on their best accounts twice a month* **(c)** to ask someone to do something; **the union called a strike =** the union told its members to go on strike

◊ **callable bond** *noun* bond which must be repaid at notice

◊ **callback pay** *noun* pay given to a worker who has been called back to work after his normal working hours

◊ **caller** *noun* **(a)** person who telephones **(b)** person who visits

◊ **call in** *verb* **(a)** to telephone to make contact; *we ask the reps to call in every Friday to report the weeks' sales* **(b)** to ask for a debt to be paid

◊ **call off** *verb* to ask for something not to take place; *the union has called off the strike; the deal was called off at the last moment*

calm *adjective* quiet *or* not excited; *the markets were calmer after the White House statement on the exchange rate*

campaign *noun* planned method of working; **sales campaign =** planned work to achieve higher sales; **publicity campaign** *or* **advertising campaign =** planned period when publicity takes place; *they are working on a campaign to launch a new brand of soap*

cancel *verb* **(a)** to stop something which has been signed *or* planned; *to cancel an appointment or a meeting; to cancel a contract; the government has canceled the order for a fleet of buses* **(b) to cancel a check =** to stop payment of a check which you have signed

◊ **cancellation** *noun* stopping something which has been signed *or* planned; *cancellation of an appointment or of an agreement or of an insurance;* **cancellation clause =** clause in a contract which states the terms on which the contract may be canceled

◊ **cancel out** *verb* to balance and so make invalid *or* even; *the two clauses cancel each other out; costs have canceled out the sales revenue*

candidate *noun* person who applies for a job; *there are six candidates for the post of assistant manager*

canvass *verb* to visit people to ask them to buy goods *or* to vote *or* to say what they think; *he's canvassing for customers for his hairdresser's shop; we have canvassed the office about raising the prices in the employee restaurant*

◊ **canvasser** *noun* person who canvasses

◊ **canvassing** *noun* action of asking people to buy *or* to vote *or* to say what they think; *canvassing techniques; door-to-door canvassing*

capable *adjective* **(a) capable of =** able *or* clever enough to do something; *she is capable of very fast typing speeds; the sales force must be capable of selling all the stock in the warehouse* **(b)** efficient; *she is a very capable departmental manager*
NOTE: you are capable **of** something or **of doing** something

capacity *noun* **(a)** amount which can be produced *or* amount of work which can be done; *industrial or manufacturing or production capacity;* **to work at full capacity =** to do as much work as possible; **to use up spare** *or* **excess capacity =** to make use of time *or* space which is not fully used **(b)** amount of space; **storage capacity =** space available for storage; **warehouse capacity =** space available in a warehouse **(c)** ability; *he has a particular capacity for business;* **earning capacity =** amount of money someone is able to earn **(d) in a capacity =** acting as; *in his capacity as chairman;* **speaking in an official capacity =** speaking officially

QUOTE analysts are increasingly convinced that the industry simply has too much capacity
Fortune

capita see PER CAPITA

capital *noun* **(a)** money, property and assets used in a business; *company with $10,000 capital* *or* *with a capital of $10,000;* **authorized capital =** maximum capital which is permitted by a company's articles of incorporation; **capital account =** account of dealings (money invested in the company, or taken out of the company) by the owners of a company; **capital assets =** property *or* machines, etc. which a company owns and uses; **capital equipment** = equipment which a factory or office uses to work; **capital expenditure** or **investment** or **outlay** = money spent on fixed assets (property, machines, furniture); **capital gains** = money made by selling a fixed asset or by selling shares; **capital gains tax** = tax paid on capital gains; **capital goods** = goods used to manufacture other goods (i.e. machinery); **capital levy** = tax on the value of a person's or a company's property and possessions; **capital loss** = loss made by selling assets; **capital reserves** = part of capital used to supplement cash flow when needed; **capital structure of a company** = way in which a company's capital is set up; **capital transfer tax** = tax on gifts or bequests of money or property; **circulating capital** = capital used in the day-to-day operations of a business; **equity capital** = amount of a company's capital which is owned by the shareholders; **fixed capital** = capital in the form of buildings and machinery; **issued capital** = amount of capital issued as shares to the shareholders; **paid-in capital** = amount of money paid for the issued capital shares; **risk capital** or **venture capital** = capital for investment which may easily be lost in risky projects; **working capital** = excess amount of current assets over current liabilities which is immediately available **(b)** money for investment; **movements of capital** = changes of investments from one place to another; **flight of capital** = rapid movement of capital from one place to another to make a gain or to avoid a loss; **capital market** = places where companies can look for investment capital **(c) capital letters** = letters written as in A, B, C, D, etc., and not a, b, c, d; *write your name in capital letters at the top of the form*

◊ **capitalism** *noun* economic system where each person has the right to invest money, to work in business, to buy and sell, with no restriction from the state

◊ **capitalist 1** *noun* person who invests money in a business **2** *adjective* working according to the principles of capitalism; *a capitalist economy; the capitalist system; the capitalist countries* or *world*

◊ **capitalize** *verb* to invest money in a working company; **company capitalized at $10,000** = company with a working capital of $10,000

◊ **capitalize on** *verb* to make a profit from; *to capitalize on one's market position*

◊ **capitalization** *noun* **market capitalization** = value of a company calculated by multiplying the price of its shares on the stock exchange by the number of shares issued; *company with a $1m capitalization;* **capitalization of reserves** = issuing free bonus shares to shareholders

> QUOTE to prevent capital from crossing the Atlantic in search of high US interest rates and exchange-rate capital gains
> *Duns Business Month*
> QUOTE Canadians' principal residences have always been exempt from capital gains tax
> *Toronto Star*

captive market *noun* market where one supplier has a monopoly and the buyer has no choice over the product which he must purchase

capture *verb* to take or to get control of something; **to capture 10% of the market** = to sell hard, and so take a 10% market share; **to capture 20% of a company's shares** = to buy shares in a company rapidly and so own 20% of it

car *noun* small motor vehicle for carrying people; **company car** = car owned by a company and lent to an employee to use as if it were his own

carat *noun* **(a)** measure of the quality of gold (pure gold being 24 carat); *a 22-carat gold ring* **(b)** measure of the weight of precious stones; *a 5-carat diamond*

carbon *noun* **(a)** carbon paper; *you forgot to put a carbon in the typewriter* **(b)** carbon copy; *make an original and two carbons*

◊ **carbon copy** *noun* copy made with carbon paper; *give me the original, and file the carbon copy*

◊ **carbonless** *adjective* which makes a copy without using carbon paper; *our reps use carbonless order pads*

◊ **carbon paper** *noun* sheet of paper with a black material on one side, used in a typewriter to make a copy; *you put the carbon paper in the wrong way round*

card *noun* **(a)** stiff paper; *we have printed the instructions on thick white card* **(b)** small piece of stiff paper or plastic; **business card** = card showing a person's name, title, and the address of the company he works for; **cash card** = plastic card used to obtain money from an automated teller machine; **charge card** = plastic card which allows you to buy goods and pay for them later; **credit card** = plastic card which allows you to borrow money or to buy goods without paying for them immediately; **file card** = card with information written on it, used to classify information in correct order; **index card** = card used to make a card file; **punch card** = card with holes punched in it which a computer can read (c) postcard (d) **to get one's cards** = to be dismissed

◊ **cardboard** *noun* thick stiff brown paper; **cardboard box** = box made of cardboard

◊ **card file** *noun* series of cards with information written on them, kept in special order so that the information can be found easily

care of *phrase (in an address)* words to show that the person lives at the address, but only as a visitor; *Herr Schmidt, care of Mr. W. Brown*
NOTE: abbreviated as **c/o**

career *noun* job which you are trained for, and which you expect to do all your life; *he made his career in electronics; she has had a successful career in advertising;* **they are a two-career couple** = both husband and wife work in business or in the professions

cargo *noun* load of goods which are sent in a ship *or* plane, etc.; **the ship was taking on cargo** = was being loaded with goods; **to load cargo** = to put cargo on a ship; **air cargo** = goods sent by air; **cargo ship** *or* **cargo plane** = ship *or* plane which carries only cargo and not passengers
NOTE: plural is **cargoes**

carnet *noun* international document which allows dutiable goods to cross several European countries by road without paying duty until the goods reach their final destination

carriage *noun* transporting goods from one place to another; cost of transport of goods; *to pay for carriage; to allow 10% for carriage; carriage is 15% of the total cost;* **carriage free** = deal where the customer does not pay for the shipping; **carriage paid** = deal where the seller has paid for the shipping; **carriage forward** = deal where the customer will pay for the shipping when the goods arrive

carrier *noun* (a) company which transports goods; *we only use reputable carriers;* **air carrier** = company which sends cargo *or* passengers by air (b) vehicle *or* ship which transports goods; **bulk carrier** = ship which carries large quantities of loose goods (such as corn)

carry *verb* (a) to take from one place to another; *to carry goods; a tanker carrying oil from the Gulf; the train was carrying a consignment of cars for export* (b) to vote to approve; **the motion was carried** = the motion was accepted after a vote (c) to produce; *the bonds carry interest at 10%* (d) to keep in stock; *to carry a line of goods; we do not carry pens*

◊ **carryback** *noun* taking past tax losses to offset current taxable profits

◊ **carry forward** *verb* to take a balance brought down as the starting point for the next period or page; **balance carried forward** = amount entered in an account at the end of a period to balance the income and expenditure which is then taken forward to start the next period

◊ **carrying** *noun* transporting from one place to another; **carrying charges; carrying cost**

◊ **carry on** *verb* to continue *or* to go on doing something; *the staff carried on with their work in spite of the fire;* **to carry on a business** = to be active in running a business

◊ **carry over** *verb* (a) **to carry over a balance** = to take a balance from the end of one page or period to the beginning of the next (b) **to carry over stock** = to hold stock from the end of one stocktaking period to the beginning of the next

cart *noun* **shopping cart** = metal basket with wheels used by shoppers to carry goods in a supermarket

cartage *noun* charge for pickup and delivery of goods

cartel *noun* group of companies which try to fix the price *or* to regulate the supply of a product because they can then profit from this situation

carton *noun* cardboard box; *a carton of cigarettes*

case 1 *noun* (a) suitcase, box with a handle for carrying clothes and personal belongings when traveling; *the customs officer made him open his case; she had a small case which she carried onto the plane* (b) cardboard or wooden box for packing and carrying goods; **six cases of wine** = six boxes, each containing twelve bottles; **a packing case** = large wooden box for carrying items which can be easily broken (c) **display case** = table or counter with a glass top or sides, used for displaying items for sale (d) **court case** = legal action or trial; **the case is being heard next week** = the case is coming to court **2** *verb* to pack in a case

cash 1 *noun* (a) money in coins or notes; **cash in hand** = money and notes in the till, kept to pay small debts; **hard cash** = money in notes and coins, as opposed to checks or credit cards; **petty cash** = small amounts of money; **ready cash** = money which is immediately available for payment; **cash account** = account which records the money which is received and spent; **cash advance** = loan in cash against a future payment; **cash balance** = balance in cash, as opposed to amounts owed; **cash box** = metal box for keeping cash; **cash budget** = plan of cash income and expenditure; **cash card** = card used to obtain money from a cash machine; **cash desk** = place in a store where you pay for the goods bought; **cash float** = cash put into the cash box at the beginning of the day or week to allow business to start; **cash machine** = machine which gives out money when a special card is inserted and instructions given; **cash offer** = offer to pay in cash; **cash payment** = payment in cash; **cash purchases** = purchases made in cash; **cash register** = machine which shows and adds the prices of items bought, with a drawer for keeping the cash received; **cash reserves** = a company's reserves in cash, deposits or bills, kept in case of urgent need (b) using money in coins or notes; **to pay cash down** = to pay a cash deposit; **cash price** *or* **cash terms** = lower price *or* terms which apply if the customer pays cash; **settlement in cash** *or* **cash settlement** = paying a bill in cash; **cash sale** *or* **cash transaction** = transaction paid for in cash; **terms: cash with order** = terms of sale showing the payment has to be made in cash when the order is placed; **cash on delivery (COD)** = payment in cash when goods are delivered; **cash discount** *or* **discount for cash** = discount given for payment in cash **2** *verb* **to cash a check** = to exchange a check for cash

◇ **cashable** *adjective* which can be cashed; *an unsigned check is not cashable at any bank*

◇ **cash and carry** *noun* large store, selling goods at low prices, where the customer pays cash and has to take the goods away himself; *cash and carry warehouse*

◇ **cashbook** *noun* book in which cash transactions are entered

◇ **cash flow** *noun* cash which comes into a company from sales less the money which goes out in purchases or overhead expenditure; **cash flow forecast** = forecast of when cash will be received or paid out; **cash flow statement** = report which shows cash sales and purchases; **net cash flow** = difference between the money coming in and the money going out during a specific period, not including non-cash items such as depreciation; **negative cash flow** = situation where more money is going out of a company than is coming in; **positive cash flow** = situation where more money is coming into a company than is going out; **the company is suffering from cash flow problems** = cash income is not coming in fast enough to pay the expenditure going out

◇ **cashier** *noun* person who takes money from customers in a store; person who deals with customers' money in a bank; **cashier's check** = a bank's own check, drawn on itself and signed by the cashier or other bank official

◇ **cash in** *verb* to sell (shares) for cash

◇ **cash in on** *verb* to profit from; *the company is cashing in on the interest in computer games*

◇ **cash out** *verb* to count the cash at the end of the day

cassette *noun* small plastic box with a magnetic tape on which words or information can be recorded; *copy the information from the computer onto a cassette*

casting vote *noun* vote used by the chairman in the case where the votes for and against a proposal are equal; *the chairman has the casting vote; he used his casting vote to block the motion*

casual *adjective* not permanent *or* not regular; **casual labor** = workers who are hired for a short period; **casual work** = work where the workers are hired for a short period; **casual laborer** *or* **casual worker** = worker who can be hired for a short period

catalog 1 *noun* list of items for sale, usually with prices; *an office equipment catalog; they sent us a catalog of their new line of desks;* **mail order catalog** = catalog from which a customer orders items to be sent by mail; **catalog price** = price as marked in a catalog **2** *verb* to put an item into a catalog

cause 1 *noun* thing which makes something happen; *what was the cause of the bank's collapse? the police tried to find the cause of the fire* **2** *verb* to make something happen; *the recession caused hundreds of bankruptcies*

caveat *noun* warning; **to enter a caveat** = to warn legally that you have an interest in a case, and that no steps can be taken without your permission
◊ **caveat emptor** = LET THE BUYER BEWARE phrase meaning that the buyer is himself responsible for checking what he buys is of good quality

cc = COPIES
NOTE: **cc** is put on a letter to show who has received a copy of it

CD = CERTIFICATE OF DEPOSIT

ceiling *noun* (a) top part which covers a room; **ceiling light** = electric light attached to the ceiling (b) highest point; *output has reached a ceiling; to fix a ceiling to a budget;* **ceiling price** *or* **price ceiling** = highest price that can be reached

cent (a) *noun* small coin, one hundredth of a dollar; *the stores are only a 25-cent bus ride away; they sell oranges at 99 cents each* NOTE: **cent** is usually written ¢ in prices: 25¢, but not when a dollar price is mentioned: $1.25 **(b)** *see also* PERCENT

centimeter *noun* measurement of length (one hundredth of a meter); *the paper is fifteen centimeters wide*
NOTE: **centimeter** is usually written **cm** after figures: **260cm**

central *adjective* organized by one main point; **central bank** = main government-controlled bank in a country, which controls the financial affairs of the country by fixing main interest rates, issuing currency and controlling the foreign exchange rate; **central office** = main office which controls all smaller offices; **central purchasing** =

purchasing organized by a central office for all branches of a company
◊ **centralization** *noun* organization of everything from a central point
◊ **centralize** *verb* to organize from a central point; *all purchasing has been centralized in our main office; the group benefits from a highly centralized organizational structure*

> QUOTE central bankers in Europe and Japan are reassessing their intervention policy
> *Duns Business Month*

center *noun* (a) **business center** = part of a town where the main banks, stores and offices are (b) important town; *industrial center; manufacturing center; the center for the shoe industry* (c) **shopping center** = group of stores linked together and having a large parking lot (d) group of items in an account; **cost center** = person or group whose costs can be itemized; **profit center** = part of a business which is responsible for both revenues and expenses

CEO = CHIEF EXECUTIVE OFFICER

certain *adjective* (a) sure; *the chairman is certain we will pass last year's total sales* (b) **a certain** = one particular; **a certain number** *or* **a certain quantity** = some

certificate *noun* official document which shows that something is true; **stock certificate** = document proving that you own shares; **certificate of approval** = document showing that an item has been officially approved; **certificate of deposit (CD)** = document from a bank showing that money has been deposited in an account for a given period of time at a specified interest; **certificate of origin** = document showing where goods were made; **certificate of registration** = document showing that an item has been registered

certify *verb* to make an official declaration in writing; *I certify that this is a true copy; the document is certified as a true copy;* **certified public accountant** = accountant who has received a certificate showing he has met state requirements; **certified check** = check which a bank says is good and will be paid out of money put aside from the bank account

cession *noun* giving up property to someone (especially a creditor)

CFO = CHIEF FINANCIAL OFFICER

chain *noun* series of stores belonging to the same company; *a chain of hotels or a hotel chain; the chairman of a large hardware chain; he runs a chain of shoe stores; she bought several shoe stores and gradually built up a chain* ◊ **chain store** *noun* one store in a chain

chair 1 *noun* position of the chairman, presiding over a meeting; *to be in the chair; she was voted into the chair;* Mr. Jones took the chair = Mr. Jones presided over the meeting; **to address the chair =** in a meeting, to speak to the chairman and not to the rest of the people at the meeting; *please address your remarks to the chair* **2** *verb* to preside over a meeting; *the meeting was chaired by Mrs. Smith*
◊ **chairman** *noun* **(a)** person who is in charge of a meeting; *Mr. Howard was chairman or acted as chairman;* Mr. Chairman *or* Madam Chairman = way of speaking to the chairman **(b)** person who presides over the board meetings of a company; **the chairman of the board** = the highest ranking executive in a company; **the chairman's report** = report from the chairman of a company to the board of directors
◊ **chairmanship** *noun* being a chairman; *the committee met under the chairmanship of Mr. Jones*
◊ **chairperson** *noun* person who is in charge of a meeting
NOTE: the plurals are **chairmen, chairpersons**

> QUOTE the corporation's entrepreneurial chairman seeks a dedicated but part-time president. The new president will work a three-day week
>
> *Globe and Mail (Toronto)*

Chamber of Commerce *noun* group of local businessmen who meet to discuss problems which they have in common and to promote commerce in their town; *the Denver Chamber of Commerce*

chance *noun* **(a)** being possible; *the company has a good chance of winning the contract; his promotion chances are small* **(b)** opportunity to do something; *she is waiting for a chance to see the vice-president; he had his chance of promotion when the financial director's assistant resigned*

NOTE: you have a chance **of doing** something or **to do** something

change 1 *noun* **(a)** money in coins or small notes; **small change =** coins; **to give someone change for $10 =** to give someone coins or notes in exchange for a ten dollar bill; **change machine =** machine which gives small change for a larger coin or bill **(b)** money given back by the seller, when the buyer can pay only with a larger bill *or* coin than the amount asked; *he gave me the wrong change; you paid me $5.75 bill with a $10 bill, so you should have $4.25 change;* **keep the change =** keep it as a tip (said to waiters, etc.) **2** *verb* **(a)** to change a $10 bill = to give change in smaller bills or coins for a $10 bill **(b)** to give one type of currency for another; *to change $1,000 into pesetas; we want to change some traveler's checks* **(c)** to change hands = to be sold to a new owner; *the store changed hands for $100,000*

channel *noun* way in which information or goods are passed from one place to another; **to go through the official channels =** to deal with government officials (especially when making a request); **to open up new channels of communication =** to find new ways of communicating with someone; **distribution channels** *or* **channels of distribution =** ways of sending goods from the manufacturer to the customer

chapter 11 *noun* bankruptcy where a company, instead of selling off assets and folding, continues to trade in a reorganized form

> QUOTE the company filed under Chapter 11 of the federal bankruptcy code, the largest failure ever in the steel industry
>
> *Fortune*

charge 1 *noun* **(a)** money which must be paid *or* price of a service; *to make no charge for delivery; to make a small charge for rental; there is no charge for parking;* **admission charge** *or* **entry charge =** price to be paid before going into an exhibition, etc.; **handling charge =** money to be paid for packing *or* invoicing *or* dealing with goods which are being shipped; **inclusive charge =** charge which includes all items; **interest charges =** money paid as interest on a loan; **scale of charges =** list showing various prices; **service charge =** (i) charge made by a bank for services to a customer; (ii) charge added to a bill in a restaurant to pay for service; **the bank adds a monthly service charge to your statement; does the bill include a service charge?**; **charge account** = arrangement which a customer has with a store to buy goods and to pay for them at a later date, usually when the invoice is sent at the end of the month; **charge card** *or* **charge plate** = plastic card with the customer's name and account number, used to charge purchases; **charges forward** = charges which will be paid by the customer; **a token charge is made for heating** = a small charge is made which does not cover the real costs at all; **free of charge** = free *or* with no payment to be made **(b)** debit on an account; **it appears as a charge in the books of account (c)** being formally accused in a court; **he appeared in court on a charge of embezzling** *or* **on an embezzlement charge 2** *verb* **(a)** to ask someone to pay for services later; **to charge the packing to the customer** *or* **to charge the customer with the packing** = the customer has to pay for packing **(b)** to ask for money to be paid; **to charge $5 for delivery; how much does he charge?**; he charges $6 an hour = he asks to be paid $6 for an hour's work **(c)** to pay for something by putting it on your charge account; **he charged the pair of slacks and three sweaters (d)** *(in a court)* to accuse someone formally of having committed a crime; **he was charged with embezzling his clients' money**

◇ **chargeable** *adjective* which can be charged; **repairs chargeable to the occupier; sums chargeable to the reserve** = sums which can be debited to a company's reserves

chart *noun* diagram showing information as a series of lines *or* blocks, etc.; **bar chart** = diagram where quantities and values are shown as thick columns of different heights *or* lengths; **flow chart** = diagram showing the arrangement of various work processes in a series; **organization chart** = diagram showing how a company *or* an office is organized; **pie chart** = diagram where information is shown as a circle cut up into sections of different sizes; **sales chart** = diagram showing how sales vary from month to month

charter 1 *noun* **(a) bank charter** = official government document allowing the incorporation of a bank **(b)** hiring transport for a special purpose; **charter flight** = flight in an aircraft which has

been hired for a specific purpose; **charter plane** = plane which has been chartered **(c) charter member** = one of the original members of an organization *or* corporation **2** *verb* to hire for a special purpose; **to charter a plane** *or* **a boat** *or* **a bus**

◇ **chartered** *adjective* **(a)** established by an official written document; *GB* **chartered accountant** = accountant who has passed the professional examinations and is a member of the Institute of Chartered Accountants **(b) chartered ship** *or* **bus** *or* **plane** = ship *or* bus *or* plane which has been hired for a special purpose

◇ **charterer** *noun* person who hires a ship, etc., for a special purpose

◇ **chartering** *noun* act of hiring transportation for a special purpose

chase *verb* **(a)** to run after someone *or* something to try to catch them **(b) to chase down** = to try to find; **we will chase down your order with the production department**

chattel *noun* movable property; **real chattel** = property connected with real estate; **personal chattel** = item of personal property such as a car or piece of furniture

cheap *adjective & adverb* not costing a lot of money *or* not expensive; **cheap labor** = workforce which does not earn much money; **we have opened a factory in the Far East because of the cheap labor** *or* **because labor is cheap; cheap money** = money which can be borrowed at low interest; **to buy something cheap** = at a low price; **he bought two companies cheap and sold them again at a profit; they work out cheaper by the box** = these items are less expensive per unit if you buy a box of them

◇ **cheaply** *adverb* without paying much money; **the salesman was living cheaply at home and claiming a high hotel bill on his expenses**

cheat *verb* to trick someone so that they lose money; **he cheated the IRS out of thousands of dollars; she was accused of cheating clients who came to ask her for advice**

check 1 *noun* **(a)** note to a bank asking them to pay money from your account to the account of the person whose name is written on the note; **a check for $10** *or* **a $10 check; blank check** = check with the amount of money and the payee left blank, but signed by the drawer; **personal check** = check written by a person, as opposed to a check from an organization or government service; **traveler's checks** = checks taken by a traveler, which can be cashed in a foreign country; **bouncing check** *or* **check which bounces** *or* **rubber check** = check which cannot be cashed because the person writing it has too little money in the account to pay it **(b) to cash a check** = to exchange a check for cash; **to endorse a check** = to sign a check on the back to show that you accept it; **to make out a check to someone** = to write someone's name on a check; *who shall I make the check out to?;* **to pay by check** = to pay by writing a check, and not using cash or a credit card; **to pay a check into your account** = to deposit a check; **the bank referred the check to drawer** = returned the check to the person who wrote it because there was not enough money in the account to pay it; **to sign a check** = to sign on the front of a check to show that you authorize the bank to pay the money from your account; **to stop a check** *or* **to stop payment on a check** = to ask a bank not to pay a check which you have written **(c)** sudden stop; **to put a check on imports** = to stop some imports **(d) check sample** = sample to be used to see if a consignment is acceptable **(e)** investigation *or* examination; *the auditors carried out checks on the petty cash book; a routine check of the fire equipment;* **baggage check** = examination of passengers' baggage to see if it contains bombs **(f)** *(in restaurant)* paper showing the charge **(g)** mark on paper to indicate something; *make a check in the box marked "R"* **2** *verb* **(a)** to stop *or* to delay; *to check the entry of contraband into the country* **(b)** to examine *or* to investigate; *to check that an invoice is correct; to check and sign for goods; he checked the computer printout against the invoices* = he examined the printout and the invoices to see if the figures were the same **(c)** to mark with a sign to show that something is correct; *check the box marked "R"*

◊ **checkbook** *noun* booklet with new checks

◊ **check in** *verb* **(a)** *(at a hotel)* to arrive at a hotel and sign for a room; *he checked in at 12:15* **(b)** *(at an airport)* to present your ticket to show you are ready to take the flight **(c) to check**

baggage in = to pass your baggage to the airline to put it on the plane for you

◊ **check-in** *noun* place where passengers present their tickets for a flight; *the check-in is on the first floor;* **check-in counter** = counter where passengers check in; **check-in time** = time at which passengers should check in

◊ **checking** *noun* **(a)** examination *or* investigation; *the inspectors found some defects during their checking of the building* **(b)** checking account = bank account on which you can write checks

◊ **check out** *verb (at a hotel)* to leave and pay for a room; *we will check out before breakfast*

◊ **checkout** *noun* **(a)** *(in a supermarket)* checkout counter = place where you pay for the goods you have decided to purchase **(b)** *(in a hotel)* checkout time is 12:00 = time by which you have to leave your room

◊ **checkroom** *noun* place where you leave your coat *or* luggage, etc.

cheque *GB* = CHECK

chief *adjective* most important; *he is the chief accountant of an industrial group;* chief executive officer (CEO) = executive in charge of a company, responsible to the board of directors for its profits and operations; **chief financial officer (CFO)** = executive in charge of a company's financial operations, reporting to the CEO

chip *noun* **(a)** a computer chip = a small piece of silicon able to store data, used in computers **(b)** blue chips = shares in well-established companies, normally with a long positive dividend record and all the characteristics of a safe investment

choice 1 *noun* **(a)** decision between various alternatives; *you must give the customer time to make his choice* **(b)** range of items to choose from; *we have only a limited choice of suppliers;* the store carries a good choice of paper = the store carries many types of paper to choose from **2** *adjective* specially selected (food); *choice meat; choice wines*

choose *verb* to decide to do a particular thing *or* to buy a particular item (as opposed to something else); *there were several good candidates to choose from; they chose the only woman*

applicant as sales manager; you must give the customers plenty of time to choose
NOTE: **choosing - chose - chosen**

chronic *adjective* perpetual *or* which exists all the time; *the company has chronic cash flow problems; we have a chronic shortage of skilled employees;* **chronic unemployment** = being unemployed for more than six months

chronological *adjective* system of arrangement of records (files, invoices, etc.) in order of dates

c.i.f. *or* **CIF** = COST, INSURANCE AND FREIGHT

circular 1 *adjective* in the shape of a circle; **circular file** = wastebasket **2** *noun* leaflet *or* letter sent to many people; *they sent out a circular offering a 10% discount*
◊ **circularize** *verb* to send a circular to; *the committee has agreed to circularize the members; they circularized all their customers with a new list of prices*
◊ **circulate** *verb* (**a**) *(of money)* **to circulate freely** = to move about without restriction by the government (**b**) to send *or* to give out without restrictions; **to circulate money** = to issue money *or* to make money available to the public and industry (**c**) to send information to; *they circulated a new list of prices to all their customers*
◊ **circulating** *adjective* which is moving about freely; **circulating capital** = capital used in the day-to-day operations of a business
◊ **circulation** *noun* (**a**) movement; *the company is trying to improve the circulation of information between departments;* **circulation of capital** = movement of capital from one investment to another (**b**) **to put money into circulation** = to issue new money to business and the public; *the amount of money in circulation increased more than was expected* (**c**) *(of newspapers)* number of copies sold; *the audited circulation of a newspaper; the new editor hopes to improve the circulation;* **a circulation battle** = competition between two papers to try to sell more copies in the same market

city *noun* large town with its own government; *the largest cities in Europe are linked by hourly flights;* **capital city** = main town in a country, where the government is located; **inter-city** = between cities; *inter-city train services are often quicker than going by air;* **city council** = governing body of a city; **city editor** = newspaper editor in charge of local news and reporters' assignments
◊ **city hall** *noun* (i) main government building in a city; (ii) the city government; *he was battling city hall over a zoning law*

civil *adjective* referring to ordinary people; **civil action** = court case brought by a person *or* a company against someone who has done them civil wrong; **civil law** = laws relating to people's rights and agreements between individuals; **civil rights** = rights of personal freedom for each citizen
◊ **civil service** *noun* organization and personnel which administer a country; *you have to pass an examination to get a job in the civil service or to get a civil service job*
◊ **civil servant** *noun* person who works in the civil service

claim 1 *noun* (**a**) demand for something which is said to be due; **wage claim** = asking for an increase in wages; *the union put in a 6% wage claim* = the union asked for a 6% increase in wages for its members (**b**) **legal claim** = statement that you think you own something legally; *he has no legal claim to the property* (**c**) **insurance claim** = asking an insurance company to pay for damages *or* for loss; **claims department** = department of an insurance company which deals with claims; **claim form** = form to be filled in when making a claim; **to put in a claim** = to ask the insurance company officially to pay damages; *to put in a claim for repairs to the car; she put in a claim for $250,000 damages against the driver of the other car;* **to settle a claim** = to agree to pay what is asked for; *the insurance company refused to settle his claim for storm damage* (**d**) **small claims court** = court which deals with claims for small amounts of money **2** *verb* (**a**) to ask for money; *he claimed $100,000 damages against the cleaning firm; she claimed for repairs to the car against her insurance* (**b**) to say that something is your property; *he is claiming possession of the house; no one claimed the umbrella found in my office* (**c**) to state that something is a fact; *he claims he never received the* *goods; she claims that the securities are her property*

◇ **claimant** *noun* person who claims; **rightful claimant** = person who has a legal claim to something

◇ **claimer** *noun* = CLAIMANT

◇ **claiming** *noun* act of making a claim

class *noun* group into which things are classified; **Class A stock** = stock that carries certain advantages relating to voting rights *or* dividend preferences; **Class B stock** = ordinary stock with limited voting rights; **class action** = legal action taken by one or more persons on behalf of all those suffering the same wrong; **first-class** = top quality *or* most expensive; *he is a first-class accountant;* **economy class** *or* **tourist class** = lower quality *or* less expensive way of traveling; *I travel economy class because it is cheaper; tourist class travel is less comfortable than first class; he always travels first class because tourist class is too uncomfortable;* **first-class mail** = mail that includes letters, postcards, and sealed matter; **second-class mail** = mail that includes newspapers and periodicals

classify *verb* to put into classes; **classified advertising** = advertisements listed in a newspaper under special headings (such as "real estate" or "help wanted"); **classified directory** = book which lists businesses grouped under various headings (such as computer stores *or* banks)

◇ **classification** *noun* way of putting into classes; **job classification** = describing jobs listed in various groups

clause *noun* provision of a formal *or* legal document; *there are ten clauses in the contract; according to clause six, payments will not be due until next year;* **exclusion clause** = clause in an insurance policy *or* warranty which says which items are not covered by the policy; **penalty clause** = clause which lists the penalties which will result if the contract is not fulfilled; **termination clause** = clause which explains how and when a contract can be terminated

clear 1 *adjective* (a) easily understood; *he made it clear that he wanted the manager to resign; you will have to make it clear to the staff that productivity is falling* (b) **clear profit** = profit after all expenses have been paid;

we made $6,000 clear profit on the sale **2** *verb* (a) to sell cheaply in order to get rid of stock; *"demonstration models to clear"* (b) **to clear goods through customs** = to have all documentation passed by the customs so that goods can leave the country (c) **to clear 10%** *or* **$5,000 on the deal** = to make 10% *or* $5,000 clear profit; **we cleared only our expenses** = the sales revenue only paid for the expenses without making any profit (d) **to clear a check** = to pass a check through the banking system, so that the money is transferred from the payer's account to another; *the check took ten days to clear* or *the bank took ten days to clear the check*

◇ **clearance** *noun* (a) approval; **customs clearance** = passing goods through customs so that they can enter or leave the country; **clearance paper** = certificate showing that goods have been passed by customs (b) **clearance sale** = sale of items at low prices to get rid of stock (c) **clearance of a check** = passing of a check through the banking system, transferring money from one account to another; *you should allow six days for check clearance*

◇ **clearing** *noun* (a) clearing of goods through customs = passing of goods through customs (b) **clearing of a debt** = paying all of a debt

◇ **clearinghouse** *noun* central office where a group of banks exchange checks drawn against one another

◇ **clear up** *verb* to clear up a debt = to pay all of a debt

clerical *adjective* (work) done in an office *or* done by a clerk; **clerical error** = mistake made when writing *or* copying something; **clerical staff** = support staff of an office; **clerical work** = paperwork done in an office; **clerical worker** = person who works in an office performing support duties

clerk 1 *noun* (a) person who works in an office; **chief clerk** *or* **head clerk** = most important clerk; **file clerk** = clerk who files documents; **invoice clerk** = clerk who deals with invoices; **shipping clerk** = clerk who deals with shipping documents (b) **desk clerk** = person who works at the reception desk in a hotel; **sales clerk** = person who sells in a store **2** *verb* to work as a clerk

clever *adjective* intelligent *or* able to learn quickly; *he is very clever at spotting a bargain; clever investors* *have made a lot of money on the share deal*

client *noun* person *or* company with whom business is done *or* person who pays for a service
◊ **clientele** *noun* all the clients of a business; all the customers of a store

climb *verb* to go up; *the company has climbed to the No. 1 position in the market; profits climbed rapidly as the new management cut costs*

QUOTE more recently, the company climbed back to 10, for a market value of $30 million: this for a company that lost $3 million on $4 million of sales in the last nine months
Forbes Magazine

clinch *verb* to settle (a business deal) *or* to come to an agreement; *he offered an extra 5% to clinch the deal; they need approval from the board before they can clinch the deal*

clipping *noun* small piece of paper clipped out of a newspaper; **press clipping bureau =** company which clips our references to a client from newspapers and magazines and sends them on to him; *we have a file of press clippings on our rivals' products*

clock *noun* machine which shows the time; *the office clock is fast; the computer has a built-in clock;* **digital clock =** clock which shows the time using numbers (as 12:05)
◊ **clock in** *or* **clock on** *verb (of worker)* to record the time of arriving for work by putting a card into a special timing machine
◊ **clock out** *or* **clock off** *verb (of worker)* to record the time of leaving work by putting a card into a special timing machine

close 1 *noun* end; *at the close of the day's trading the shares had fallen 20%* **2** *adjective* **close to =** very near *or* almost; *the company was close to bankruptcy; we are close to meeting our sales targets* **3** *verb* to end **(a)** to stop doing business for the day; *the office closes at 5:30; we close early on Saturdays* **(b) to close the accounts =** to come to the end of an accounting period and make up the profit and loss account **(c) to close an account =** (i) to stop supplying a customer on credit; (ii) to take all the money out of a bank account and stop the account; **he closed**

his credit union account = he took all the money out and stopped using the account **(d) the shares closed at $15 =** at the end of the day's trading the price of the shares was $15 **(e) to close a deal =** to complete a deal; *they closed on their new house last Friday*
◊ **closed corporation** *noun* company where the stock is owned by only a few people
◊ **closed** *adjective* **(a)** shut *or* not open *or* not doing business; *the office is closed on Mondays; all the banks are closed on the holiday* **(b)** restricted; **closed shop =** system where a company agrees to employ only union members in certain jobs; *a closed shop agreement; the union is asking the management to agree to a closed shop;* **closed market =** market where a supplier deals only with one agent *or* distributor and does not supply any others direct; *they signed a closed market agreement with an Egyptian company*
◊ **close down** *verb* to shut a store *or* factory for a long period or forever; *the company is closing down its London office; the strike closed down the railway system*
◊ **close out** *verb* to sell all the stock *or* to sell a business; **close-out sale =** sale of goods at very low prices to get rid of them
◊ **closing 1** *adjective* **(a)** final *or* coming at the end; **closing bid =** last bid at an auction *or* the bid which is successful; **closing costs =** costs involved in the sale of property; **closing date =** last date; *the closing date for applications to be received is May 1;* **closing price =** price of a share at the end of a day's trading **(b)** at the end of an accounting period; *closing balance; closing inventory* **2** *noun* **(a)** shutting of a store *or* other business; **closing time =** time when a store or office stops work **(b) closing of an account =** act of stopping supply to a customer on credit
◊ **closure** *noun* act of closing

QUOTE the best thing would be to have a few more plants close down and bring supply more in line with current demand
Fortune

club *noun* group of people who have the same interest; place where these people meet; *the manager has joined a local businessman's club; he has applied to join the health club;* **club membership =** all the members of a club; **club dues =** money paid to belong to a club

cm = CENTIMETER

c/o = CARE OF

Co. = COMPANY *J. Smith & Co.*

co- *prefix* working *or* acting together
◊ **co-creditor** *noun* person who is a creditor of the same company as you are
◊ **co-director** *noun* person who is a director of the same company as you
◊ **coinsurance** *noun* insurance policy where the risk is shared among several insurers
◊ **co-worker** *noun* person who works in the same department *or* company as you

coach class *noun* cheapest class of airline ticket

COD *or* **c.o.d.** = CASH ON DELIVERY, COLLECT ON DELIVERY

code *noun* **(a)** system of symbols *or* numbers *or* letters which mean something; **area code** = numbers which indicate an area for telephoning; **bar code** = system of lines printed on a product which can be read by a computer to give a reference number *or* price; **international dialing code** = numbers used for dialing to another country; **machine-readable codes** = sets of signs or letters (such as bar codes *or* ZIP codes) which can be read by computers; **ZIP code** = series of numbers used to represent the region in a city or town where an address is situated; *the company's ZIP code is 60614;* **stock code** = numbers and letters which refer to an item of stock **(b)** set of rules; **code of practice** = rules drawn up by an association which the members must follow when doing business
◊ **coding** *noun* act of putting a code on something; *the coding of invoices*

coin *noun* piece of metal money; *he gave me two 10-franc coins in my change; I need some coins for the telephone*
◊ **coinage** *noun* system of metal money used in a country

cold *adjective* **(a)** not hot; *the machines work badly in cold weather; the office was so cold that the staff started complaining; the coffee machine also sells cold drinks* **(b)** without being prepared; **cold call** = sales call where the salesman has no appointment and the client is not an established customer

collaborate *verb* to work together; *to collaborate with a French firm on a building project; they collaborated on the new aircraft*
NOTE: you collaborate **with** someone **on** some venture
◊ **collaboration** *noun* working together; *their collaboration on the project was very profitable*

collapse 1 *noun* **(a)** sudden fall in price; *the collapse of the market in silver; the collapse of the dollar on the foreign exchange markets* **(b)** sudden failure of a company; *investors lost thousands of dollars in the collapse of the company* **2** *verb* **(a)** to fall suddenly; *the market collapsed; the yen collapsed on the foreign exchange markets* **(b)** to fail suddenly; *the company collapsed with $25,000 in debts*

collar *noun* part of a coat *or* shirt which goes around the neck; **blue-collar worker** = manual worker in a factory; **white-collar worker** = office worker; *he has a white-collar job* = he works in an office

collate *verb* to put separate pieces together in proper order; *the copies will automatically collate your documents*

collateral *adjective & noun* (security) used to provide a guarantee for a loan

> QUOTE examiners have come to inspect the collateral that thrifts may use in borrowing from the Fed
> *Wall Street Journal*

collect 1 *verb* **(a)** to receive payment *or* to force someone to pay; **to collect a debt** = to go and make someone pay a debt; **collect on delivery (COD)** = payment in cash when the goods purchased are delivered **(b)** to take things away from a place; *we have to collect the stock from the warehouse; letters are collected twice a day* = the post office workers take them from the letter box to the post office for dispatch **2** *adverb & adjective* (phone call) where the person receiving the call agrees to pay for it; *to make a collect call; he called his office collect*
◊ **collection** *noun* **(a)** getting money together *or* making someone pay money which is owed; **tax collection**; **debt collection** = collecting money which is owed; **collection agency** = company which collects debts for other companies

for a commission; **bills for collection** = bills where payment is due **(b)** group of objects which have been gathered together for keeping; *he has a collection of early toy trains in his office* **(c)** taking of letters from a mailbox to the post office for dispatch; *there are six collections a day from this mailbox*

◇ **collective** *adjective* working together; **collective bargaining** = negotiations about wage increases and working conditions between management and labor unions; **collective farm** = state-owned farm which is run by the workers; **collective ownership** = ownership of a business by the workers who work in it; *they signed a collective wage agreement* = an agreement was signed between management and the union about wages

◇ **collector** *noun* person who makes people pay money which is owed; *collector of taxes or tax collector; debt collector*

college *noun* place where people study after they have graduated from high school; **business college** *or* **commercial college** = college which teaches general business methods; **secretarial college** = college which teaches shorthand, typing and word-processing

column *noun* **(a)** series of numbers, one under the other; *to add up a column of figures; put the total at the bottom of the column;* **credit column** = right-hand side in an account book showing money received; **debit column** = left-hand side in an account book showing money paid or owed **(b)** section of printed words in a newspaper *or* magazine; **column-inch** = space in inches in a newspaper column, used for calculating charges for advertising

combine 1 *noun* large financial or commercial group; *a German industrial combine* **2** *verb* to join together; *the workforce and management combined to fight the takeover bid*

◇ **combination** *noun* **(a)** several things which are joined together; *a combination of cash flow problems and difficult trading conditions caused the company's collapse* **(b)** series of numbers which open a special lock; *I have forgotten the combination of the lock on my briefcase; the office safe has a combination lock*

commerce *noun* business *or* buying and selling of goods and services; **Chamber of Commerce** = group of local businessmen who meet to discuss problems which they have in common and to promote business in their town; **Department of Commerce** = US federal department which enforces regulations and encourages trade; **Commerce Secretary** = official of the US government in charge of the Commerce Department

◇ **commercial 1** *adjective* **(a)** referring to business; **commercial aircraft** = aircraft used to carry cargo *or* passengers for payment; **commercial artist** = artist who designs advertisements *or* posters, etc. for payment; **commercial attaché** = diplomat who represents and tries to promote his country's business interests; **commercial bank** = bank that specializes in demand deposits and loans to businesses; **commercial college** = college which teaches business studies; **commercial course** = course where business skills are studied; *he took a commercial course by correspondence;* **commercial directory** = book which lists all the businesses and business people in a town; **commercial district** = part of a town where offices and stores are; **commercial law** = laws regarding business; **commercial load** = amount of goods *or* number of passengers which a bus *or* train *or* plane must carry to make a profit; **commercial port** = port which has only goods traffic; **commercial property** = property zoned for business use; **commercial traveler** = salesman who travels around an area visiting customers on behalf of his company; **commercial vehicle** = van *or* truck, etc. used for business purposes; **sample only - of no commercial value** = not worth anything if sold **(b)** profitable; **not a commercial proposition** = not likely to make a profit **2** *noun* message advertising a product *or* service on television or radio; **commercial break** = time between programs or between sections of programs when commercials are shown

◇ **commercialization** *noun* making something into a business proposition; *the commercialization of museums*

◇ **commercialize** *verb* to make something into a business; *the resort town has become so commercialized that it is unpleasant*

◇ **commercially** *adverb* in a business way; **not commercially viable** = not likely to make a profit

commission *noun* **(a)** money paid to a salesman *or* an agent, usually a percentage of the sales made; *she gets 10% commission on everything she sells;* he charges 10% commission = he asks for 10% of sales as his payment; **commission agent** = agent who is paid a percentage of sales; **commission merchant** = person who buys or sells goods for others for a commission; **commission sale** *or* **sale on commission** = sale where the salesman is paid a commission **(b)** group of people officially appointed to examine some problem; *the federal government has appointed a commission of inquiry to look into the problems of small exporters; he is the chairman of the federal commission on export subsidies*
◊ **commissionable** *adjective* (sales *or* service) on which a commission is paid to an agent

commit *verb* **(a)** to carry out (a crime) **(b)** to bind oneself to do something; *the company has committed itself to paying an extra 5%*
NOTE: **committing - committed**

committee *noun* official group of people who organize or plan for a larger group; *to be a member of a committee or to sit on a committee; he was elected to the planning committee of the ski club; the new plans have to be approved by the committee members; to chair a committee* = to be the chairman of a committee; *he is the chairman of the planning committee; she is the secretary of the finance committee*

commodity *noun* thing sold in very large quantities, especially raw materials and food such as metals or corn; **primary** *or* **basic commodities** = farm produce grown in large quantities, such as corn, rice, cotton, soybeans; **staple commodities** = basic food or raw material which is most important in a country's economy; **commodity market** *or* **commodity exchange** = place where people buy and sell commodities; **commodity futures** = trading in commodities for delivery at a later date; *silver rose 5% on the commodity futures market yesterday;* **commodity trader** = person whose business is buying and selling commodities

common *adjective* **(a)** ordinary *or* frequent; *putting the carbon paper in the wrong way is a common mistake; being unemployed is very common these days* **(b)** belonging to several different people or to everyone; **common carrier** = firm which carries goods or passengers, and which anyone can use; **common ownership** = ownership of a company *or* a property by a group of people; **common pricing** = illegal fixing of prices by several businesses so that they all charge the same price; **common stock** = ordinary shares in a corporation, giving shareholders a right to vote at meetings and to receive dividends; **common stockholder** = person who owns common stock in a corporation
◊ **Common Market** *noun* the European Common Market = the European Economic Community, an organization which links several European countries for the purposes of trade

communicate *verb* to pass information to someone; *he finds it impossible to communicate with his staff; communicating with the head office has been quicker since we installed the telex*
◊ **communication** *noun* **(a)** passing of information; *communication with the head office has been made easier by the telex;* to enter into communication with someone = to start discussing something with someone, usually in writing; *we have entered into communication with the relevant government department in Washington* **(b)** official message; *we have had a communication from the state tax office* **(c)** communications = being able to contact people *or* to pass messages; *after the flood all communications with the outside world were broken*

community *noun* **(a)** group of people living or working in the same place; **community property** = property owned by both husband and wife; **the local business community** = the business people living and working in the area **(b)** **the European Economic Community** = the Common Market

commute *verb* **(a)** to travel to work from home each day; *he commutes from the country to his office in the center of town* **(b)** to change a payment into a different form; *he decided to commute part of his pension into a lump sum payment*
◊ **commuter** *noun* person who commutes to work; **commuter train** =

train which commuters take in the morning and evening

> QUOTE Commuting is never business use. A trip to work is personal and not deductible. And making a business phone call or holding a business meeting in your car while you drive will not change that fact
> *Nation's Business*
>
> QUOTE In recent years, more than one third of new homeowners in north San Diego County are commuting to Orange County
> *American City & County*

company *noun* business *or* group of people organized to buy, sell or provide a service **(a) to put a company into liquidation =** to close a company by selling its assets for cash; **to set up a company =** to start a company legally; **family company =** company where most of the shares are owned by members of a family; **holding company =** company which exists only to own shares in subsidiary companies; **joint-stock company =** company whose stock is held by many people who are together responsible for the debts of the company; **limited (liability) company =** British company where a shareholder is responsible for repaying the company's debts only to the face value of the shares he owns; **listed company =** company whose shares can be bought or sold on a Stock Exchange; **parent company =** company which owns more than half of another company's shares; **private company =** company with a small number of shareholders, whose shares are not traded on a Stock Exchange; **subsidiary company =** company which is owned by a parent company **(b) finance company =** company which loans money to consumers and to businesses; **insurance company =** company whose business is insurance; **shipping company =** company whose business is in transporting goods; **a tractor** *or* **aircraft** *or* **chocolate company =** company which makes tractors *or* aircraft *or* chocolate **(c) company car =** car which belongs to a company and is lent to an employee to use; **company store =** store set up by a company to sell goods to its employees; **company town =** community in which most of the property and stores are owned by a large company that employs the residents

compare *verb* to look at several things to see how they differ; *the financial manager compared the figures for the first and second quarters*

◇ **compare with** *verb* to put two things together to see how they differ; *how do the sales this year compare with last year's? compared with 1982, last year was a boom year*

◇ **comparable** *adjective* able to be compared; *the two sets of figures are not comparable; which is the nearest company comparable to this one in size? =* which company is of a similar size and can be compared with this one?; *the two investments have comparable worth =* the two investments have similar value

◇ **comparison** *noun* way of comparing; *sales are down in comparison with last year; there is no comparison between foreign and domestic sales =* foreign and domestic sales are so different they cannot be compared

compensate *verb* to pay for damage done; *to compensate a manager for loss of commission*
NOTE: you compensate someone **for** something

◇ **compensation** *noun* **(a) compensation for damage =** payment for damage done; **workers' compensation =** system of insurance, varying among states, for paying workers who are injured or disabled on the job **(b)** salary; **compensation package =** salary, pension and other benefits offered with a job

> QUOTE golden parachutes are liberal compensation packages given to executives leaving a company
> *Publishers Weekly*
>
> QUOTE last year he paid $22,000 for workers' compensation insurance, a sum that equaled about one-fourth of the total payroll for his small band of employees
> *Nation's Business*

compete *verb* to **compete with someone** *or* **with a company =** to try to do better than another person *or* another company; *we have to compete with cheap imports from the Far East; they were competing unsuccessfully with local companies on their home territory; the two companies are competing for a better share of the market* **or** *for a contract =* each company is trying to win a larger part of the market *or* to win the contract

◇ **competing** *adjective* which competes; **competing firms =** firms which compete with each other; **competing products =** products from different companies which have the same use and are sold in the same markets at similar prices

◊ **competition** *noun* **(a)** trying to do better than another person *or* organization; **free competition** = being free to compete without government interference; **keen competition** = strong competition; *we are facing keen competition from European manufacturers* **(b) the competition** = companies which are trying to compete with your product; *we have lowered our prices to beat the competition; the competition have brought out a new range of products*
NOTE: singular, but can take a plural verb

◊ **competitive** *adjective* which competes fairly; **competitive price** = low price aimed at competing with that of a rival product; **competitive pricing** = putting low prices on goods so as to compete with other products; **competitive products** = products made to compete with existing products

◊ **competitively** *adverb* **competitively priced** = sold at a low price which competes with the price of similar products from other companies

◊ **competitor** *noun* person *or* company which competes; *two German firms are our main competitors*

> QUOTE competition is steadily increasing and could affect profit margins as the company tries to retain its market share
> *Citizen (Ottawa)*
> QUOTE the company blamed fiercely competitive market conditions in Europe for a $14m operating loss last year
> *Financial Times*
> QUOTE farmers are increasingly worried by the growing lack of competitiveness for their products on world markets
> *Australian Financial Review*

competence *or* **competency** *noun* **the case falls within the competence of the court** = the court is legally able to deal with the case

◊ **competent** *adjective* **(a)** capable *or* qualified; *she is a competent secretary or a competent manager* **(b) the court is not competent to deal with this case** = the court is not legally able to deal with the case

complain *verb* **to complain about something** = to express dissatisfaction with something; *the office is so cold the employees have started complaining; she complained about the service; they are complaining that our prices are too high; if you want to complain, write to the manager*

◊ **complaint** *noun* statement of dissatisfaction about something; *when*

making a complaint, always quote the reference number; she sent her letter of complaint to the president of the company;* **to make** *or* **lodge a complaint against someone** = to write and send an official complaint to someone's superior; **complaints department** = department which deals with complaints from customers; **complaints procedure** = established method for submitting a complaint

complete **1** *adjective* whole *or* with nothing missing; *the order is complete and ready for sending; the order should be delivered only if it is complete* **2** *verb* to finish; *the factory completed the order in two weeks; how long will it take you to complete the job?*

◊ **completely** *adverb* all *or* totally; *the cargo was completely ruined by water; the warehouse was completely destroyed by fire*

◊ **completion** *noun* act of finishing something; **completion date** = date when something will be finished; **completion of a contract** = signing of a contract for the sale of a property when the buyer pays and the seller transfers ownership to the buyer

complex **1** *noun* series of large buildings; *a large industrial complex*
NOTE: plural is **complexes** **2** *adjective* with many different parts; *a complex system of import controls; the specifications for the machine are very complex*

compliment **1** *noun* remark in praise *or* admiration of something; *the bank received many compliments on its remodeling of the lobby* **2** *verb* to praise *or* admire something; *the manager complimented the rep on his outstanding sales record*

◊ **complimentary** *adjective* **complimentary ticket** = free ticket, given as a present

comply *verb* to yield; **to comply with a court order** = to obey an order given by a court

◊ **compliance** *noun* act of complying *or* yielding

component *noun* one of the parts of a whole *or* section which will be put into a final product; *the assembly line stopped because delivery of a component was delayed;* **components factory** = factory which makes parts to be used in other factories to make finished products

composition *noun* agreement between a debtor and creditors to settle a debt by repaying only part of it

compound 1 *adjective* **compound interest** = interest which is added to the capital and then earns interest itself 2 *verb* (a) to add to; *the interest is compounded daily* (b) to agree to settle something, such as a debt

comprehensive *adjective* which includes everything; **comprehensive insurance** = insurance policy which covers you against all risks which are likely to happen

compromise 1 *noun* agreement between two sides, where each side makes concessions; *management offered $5 an hour, the union asked for $9, and a compromise of $7.50 was reached* 2 *verb* to reach an agreement by giving way a little; *he asked $15 for it, I offered $7 and we compromised on $10*

comptroller *noun* financial controller; **Comptroller General** = federal official appointed by the President to supervise the use of public funds and to audit federal agencies

compulsory *adjective* obligatory *or* ordered; **compulsory insurance** = insurance coverage required by law, as auto insurance in many states; **compulsory liquidation** = liquidation which is ordered by a court

compute *verb* to calculate *or* to do calculations
◊ **computable** *adjective* which can be calculated
◊ **computation** *noun* calculation
◊ **computational error** *noun* mistake made in calculating
◊ **computer** *noun* electronic machine which calculates *or* stores information and processes it automatically; **computer department** = department in a company which manages the company's computers; **computer error** = mistake made by a computer; **computer file** = section of information on a computer (such as the payroll, list of addresses, customer accounts); **computer language** = system of signs, letters and words used to instruct a computer; **computer listing** = printout

of a list of items taken from data stored in a computer; **computer manager** = person in charge of a computer department; **computer program** = instructions to a computer, telling it to do a particular piece of work; **computer programmer** = person who writes computer programs; **computer time** = time when a computer is being used (paid for at an hourly rate); *running all those sales reports costs a lot in computer time;* **business computer** = powerful small computer which is programmed for special business uses; **personal computer** *or* **home computer** = small computer which can be used in the home
◊ **computerize** *verb* to change from a manual system to one using computers; *our inventory control has been completely computerized*
◊ **computerized** *adjective* worked by computers; *a computerized invoicing system*
◊ **computer-readable** *adjective* which can be read and understood by a computer; *computer-readable codes*
◊ **computing** *noun* referring to computers; **computing speed** = speed at which a computer calculates

con 1 *noun informal* trick done to try to get money from someone; *trying to get us to pay him for ten hours' overtime was just a con* 2 *verb informal* to trick someone to try to get money; *they conned the bank into lending them $25,000 with no security; he conned the finance company out of $100,000* NOTE: **con - conning - conned**

concealment *noun* hiding for criminal purposes; **concealment of assets** = hiding assets so that creditors do not know they exist

concern 1 *noun* (a) business *or* company; *his business is a going concern* = the company is working (and making a profit); **sold as a going concern** = sold as an actively trading company (b) being worried about a problem; *the management showed no concern at all for the workers' safety* 2 *verb* to deal with *or* to be connected with; *he filled in a questionnaire concerning computer utilization*

concession *noun* (a) right to use someone else's property for business purposes; **mining concession** = right to dig a mine on a piece of land (b) right to be the only seller of a product in a place;

she runs a jewelry concession in a department store **(c)** small booth *or* vending machine in an office building, stadium, etc.; *he runs a hot dog concession at the arena*

◊ **concessionaire** *noun* person who operates a small booth *or* has the right to be the only seller of a product in a place

conciliation *noun* bringing together the parties in a dispute so that the dispute can be settled

conclude *verb* **(a)** to complete successfully; *to conclude an agreement with someone* **(b)** to believe from evidence; *the police concluded that the thief had got into the building through the main entrance*

condition *noun* **(a)** term of a contract *or* duties which have to be carried out as part of a contract *or* something which has to be agreed upon before a contract becomes valid; **conditions of employment** = terms of a contract of employment; **conditions of sale** = agreed ways in which a sale takes place (such as discounts *or* credit terms); **on condition that** = provided that; *they were granted the lease on condition that they paid the legal costs* **(b)** general state; *the union has complained of the bad working conditions in the factory; item sold in good condition; what was the condition of the car when it was sold? adverse trading conditions*

◊ **conditional** *adjective* provided that certain things take place; **to give a conditional acceptance** = to accept, provided that certain things happen *or* certain terms apply; **the offer is conditional on the board's acceptance** = provided the board accepts; *he made a conditional offer* = he offered to buy, provided that certain terms applied

condominium *noun* system of ownership, where each person owns an apartment in a building, together with a share of the land, stairs, elevator, roof, etc., and pays a management charge for the upkeep of the common areas

conduct *verb* to direct *or* manage; *to conduct negotiations; the chairman conducted the negotiations very efficiently*

conference *noun* **(a)** meeting of people to discuss problems; **to be in conference**

= to be in a meeting; **conference call** = telephone call in which three or more people on different lines can participate; **conference phone** = telephone so arranged that several people can speak into it from around a table; **conference room** = room where small meetings can take place; **press conference** = meeting where newspaper and TV reporters are invited to hear news of a new product *or* a takeover bid, etc.; **sales conference** = meeting of sales managers, representatives, marketing staff, etc., to discuss future sales plans **(b)** meeting of an association *or* a society *or* a union; *the annual conference of the Electricians' Union; the conference of the Booksellers' Association; the conference agenda or the agenda of the conference was drawn up by the secretary*

confidence *noun* **(a)** feeling sure *or* being certain; *the sales teams do not have much confidence in their manager; the board has total confidence in the company president* **(b)** in confidence = in secret; *I will show you the report in confidence*

◊ **confidence game** *noun* business deal where someone gains another person's confidence and then tricks him

◊ **confidence man** *noun* person who carries out a confidence game on someone

◊ **confident** *adjective* certain *or* sure; *I am confident the turnover will increase rapidly; are you confident the sales team is capable of handling this product?*

◊ **confidential** *adjective* secret *or* not to be told or shown to other people; *he sent a confidential report to the chairman; please mark the letter "Private and Confidential"*

◊ **confidentiality** *noun* being secret; *he broke the confidentiality of the discussions* = he told someone about the secret discussions

confirm *verb* to say that something is certain; *to confirm a hotel reservation or a ticket or an agreement; to confirm someone in a job* = to say that someone is now permanently in the job

◊ **confirmation** *noun* **(a)** being certain; **confirmation of a reservation** = checking that a reservation is certain **(b)** document which confirms something; *he received confirmation from the bank that the deeds had been deposited*

conflict *noun* **conflict of interest** = situation where a person may profit personally from decisions which he makes in his official capacity

confuse *verb* to make it difficult for someone to understand something *or* to make something difficult; *the chairman was confused by all the reporters' questions; to introduce the problem of a sales tax will only confuse the issue*

conglomerate *noun* group of subsidiary companies linked together and forming a group making very different types of products

congratulate *verb* to express your pleasure to someone for having done something well; *the sales manager congratulated the salesmen on doubling sales; I want to congratulate you on your promotion*
◊ **congratulations** *plural noun* good wishes; *the staff sent him their congratulations on his promotion*

conman *noun informal* = CONFIDENCE MAN NOTE: plural is **conmen**

connect *verb* (a) to link *or* to join; *the company is connected to the government because the chairman's father is a senator* (b) the flight from New York connects with a flight to Athens = the plane from New York arrives in time for passengers to catch the plane to Athens
◊ **connecting flight** *noun* plane which a passenger will be on time to catch and which will take him to his final destination; *check at the helicopter desk for connecting flights to the downtown area*
◊ **connection** *noun* (a) link *or* something which joins; *is there a connection between his argument with the personnel director and his sudden promotion to warehouse manager?;* in connection with = referring to; *I want to speak to the CEO in connection with the sales forecasts* (b) connections = people you know *or* customers *or* contacts; *he has useful connections in industry*

conservative *adjective* careful *or* not overestimating; *a conservative estimate of sales; his forecast of expenditure is very conservative;* a conservative estimate = calculation which probably underestimates the final

figure; *their turnover has risen by at least 20% in the last year, and that is probably a conservative estimate*
◊ **conservatively** *adverb* not overestimating; *the total sales are conservatively estimated at $2.3m*

consider *verb* to think seriously about something; **to consider the terms of a contract** = to examine and discuss if the terms are acceptable
◊ **consideration** *noun* (a) serious thought; *we are giving consideration to moving our headquarters to Atlanta* (b) something valuable exchanged as part of a contract; **for a small consideration** = for a small fee *or* payment

considerable *adjective* large; *we sell considerable quantities of our products to Africa; they lost a considerable amount of money on the commodity market*
◊ **considerably** *adverb* quite a bit; *sales are considerably higher than they were last year*

consign *verb* to consign goods to someone = to send goods to someone for him to use or to sell for you
◊ **consignation** *noun* act of consigning
◊ **consignee** *noun* person who receives goods from someone for his own use or to sell for the sender
◊ **consignment** *noun* (a) sending of goods to someone who will sell them for you; **goods on consignment** = goods kept for another company to be sold on their behalf (payment is made when the goods are sold, or if made in advance, can be refunded if the goods are not sold) (b) group of goods sent for sale; *a consignment of goods has arrived; we are expecting a consignment of cars from Japan*
◊ **consignor** *noun* person who consigns goods to someone

consist of *verb* to be made up of; *the trade mission consists of the sales managers of ten major companies; the package tour consists of air travel, six nights in a luxury hotel, all meals and visits to places of interest*

consolidate *verb* (a) to incorporate smaller accounts into one larger account (b) to group together
◊ **consolidated** *adjective* (a) **consolidated balance sheet** = where

the balance sheets of subsidiary companies are grouped together into the balance sheet of the parent company **(b) consolidated shipment =** goods from different companies grouped together into a single shipment

◊ **consolidation** *noun* grouping together

consortium *noun* group of companies which work together; *a consortium of Canadian companies or a Canadian consortium; a consortium of French and British companies is planning to construct the new aircraft*

constitution *noun* set of written rules *or* regulations of a society *or* association *or* club *or* state; *under the society's constitution, the chairman is elected for a two-year period; payments to officers of the association are not allowed by the constitution*

◊ **constitutional** *adjective* according to a constitution; *the reelection of the chairman is not constitutional*

construct *verb* to build; *the company has bid for the contract to construct the new airport*

◊ **construction** *noun* building; **construction company =** company which specializes in building; **under construction =** being built; *the airport is under construction*

◊ **constructive** *adjective* which helps in the making of something; *she made some constructive suggestions for improving management-worker relations; we had a constructive proposal from a distribution company in Italy*

◊ **constructor** *noun* person *or* company which constructs

consult *verb* to ask an expert for advice; *he consulted his accountant about his taxes*

◊ **consultancy** *noun* act of giving specialist advice; *a consultancy firm; he offers a consultancy service*

◊ **consultant** *noun* specialist who gives advice; *engineering consultant; management consultant; tax consultant*

◊ **consulting** *adjective* person who gives specialist advice; *consulting engineer*

consumer *noun* person *or* company which buys and uses goods and services; *gas consumers are protesting at the increase in prices; the factory is a heavy consumer of water;* **consumer council =** group representing the interests of consumers; **consumer credit** = credit given by stores, banks and other financial institutions to consumers so that they can buy goods; **consumer durables** = items such as washing machines *or* refrigerators *or* stoves which are bought and used by the public, and which last some time; **consumer goods** = goods bought by consumers *or* by members of the public; **consumer panel** = group of consumers who report on products they have used so that the manufacturers can improve them or use what the panel says about them in advertising; **Consumer Price Index (CPI) =** index showing how prices of consumer goods have changed over a period of time, used as a way of measuring inflation and the cost of living; **consumer protection** = protecting consumers against unfair *or* illegal selling practices; **consumer research** = research into why consumers buy goods and what goods they really want to buy; **consumer resistance** = lack of interest by consumers in buying a product; *the latest price increases have produced considerable consumer resistance;* **consumer society =** type of society where consumers are encouraged to buy goods; **consumer spending =** spending by consumers

QUOTE analysis of the consumer price index for the first half of 1985 shows that the rate of inflation went down by about 12.9 per cent
Business Times (Lagos)

consumption *noun* buying or using goods or services; *a car with low gas consumption; the factory has a heavy consumption of coal;* **home consumption** *or* **domestic consumption** = use of something in the home

contact 1 *noun* **(a)** person you know *or* person you can ask for help or advice; *he has many contacts in the city; who is your contact in the legislature?* **(b)** act of getting in touch with someone; *I have lost contact with them =* I do not communicate with them any longer; *he put me in contact with a good lawyer =* he told me how to get in touch with a good lawyer **2** *verb* to get in touch with someone *or* to communicate with someone; *he tried to contact his office by phone; can you contact the vice-president at his home?*

contain *verb* to hold something inside; *each crate contains two computers and their peripherals; a barrel contains 42 gallons; we have lost a file containing important documents*

◊ **container** *noun* (a) box *or* bottle *or* can, etc., which can hold goods; *the gas is shipped in strong metal containers; the container burst during shipping* (b) very large metal case of a standard size for loading and transporting goods on trucks, trains and ships; *container ship; container terminal; to ship goods in containers; a container-load of spare parts* = a shipment of spare parts sent in a container

◊ **containerization** *noun* putting into containers; shipping in containers

◊ **containerize** *verb* to put goods into containers; to ship goods in containers

contango *noun* extra payments added to the price of futures, to cover interest and other charges

content *noun* the ideas inside a letter, etc.; **the content of the letter** = the real meaning of the letter

◊ **contents** *plural noun* things contained *or* what is inside something; *the contents of the bottle poured out onto the floor; the customs officials inspected the contents of the crate;* **the contents of the letter** = the words written in the letter

contingency *noun* possible state of emergency when decisions will have to be made quickly; **contingency fund** *or* **contingency reserve** = money set aside in case it is needed urgently; **contingency plans** = plans which will be put into action if something happens which no one expects; **to add on 10% to provide for contingencies** = to provide for further expenditures which may be incurred; *we have built 10% for contingencies into our cost forecast*

◊ **contingent** *adjective* (a) **contingent expenditures** = expenditures which will be incurred only if something happens (b) **contingent policy** = policy which pays out only if something happens (as if the person named in the policy dies before the person due to benefit)

continue *verb* to go on doing something *or* to do something which you were doing earlier; *the chairman continued speaking in spite of the noise from the shareholders; the meeting started at*

10:00 a.m. and continued until 6:00 p.m.; negotiations will continue next Monday

◊ **continual** *adjective* which happens again and again; *production was slow because of continual breakdowns*

◊ **continually** *adverb* again and again; *the photocopier is continually breaking down*

◊ **continuation** *noun* act of continuing

◊ **continuous** *adjective* with no end *or* with no breaks; **continuous audit; continuous production line; continuous forms** = computer stationery in the form of a single long piece of paper, with perforations to allow each sheet to be separated

contra 1 *noun* **contra account** = account which offsets another account; **contra entry** = entry made in the opposite side of an account to make an earlier entry worthless (i.e. a debit against a credit) **2** *verb* **to contra an entry** = to enter a similar amount in the opposite side of an account

contraband *noun* **contraband (goods)** = goods brought into a country illegally, without paying customs duty

contract 1 *noun* (a) legal agreement between two parties; **to draw up a contract; to draft a contract; to sign a contract; the contract is binding on both parties** = both parties signing the contract must do what is agreed; **under contract** = bound by the terms of a contract; *the firm is under contract to deliver the goods by November;* **to void a contract** = to make a contract invalid; **contract of employment** = contract between management and employee showing all conditions of work; **service contract** = contract between a company and a director showing all conditions of work (b) **contract law** *or* **law of contract** = laws relating to agreements; **by private contract** = by private legal agreement (c) agreement for supply of a service or goods; *contract for the supply of spare parts; to enter into a contract to supply spare parts; to sign a contract for $10,000 worth of spare parts;* **to put work out to contract** = to decide that work should be done by another company on a contract, rather than employing members of staff to do it; **to award a contract to a company** *or* **to place a contract with a company** = to decide that a company shall have the contract to do work for you; **to bid for a contract** = to put forward an estimate of cost for work under contract; *conditions of contract* or *contract conditions;* **breach of contract** = breaking the terms of a contract; **the company is in breach of contract** = the company has failed to do what was agreed in the contract; **contract work** = work done according to a written agreement **2** *verb* to agree to do some work by contract; *to contract to supply spare parts* or *to contract for the supply of spare parts; the supply of spare parts was contracted out to Smith Co.* = Smith Co. was given the contract for supplying spare parts; **to contract out of an agreement** = to withdraw from an agreement with written permission of the other party

◊ **contracting** *adjective* **contracting party** = person or company which signs a contract

◊ **contractor** *noun* person or company which does work according to a written agreement; **general contractor** or **prime contractor** = company which contracts to do a job and subcontracts some of the work to other companies; **government contractor** = company which supplies the government with goods by contract

◊ **contractual** *adjective* according to a contract; **contractual liability** = legal responsibility for something as stated in a contract; **to fulfill your contractual obligations** = to do what you have agreed to do in a contract; **he is under no contractual obligation to buy** = he has signed no agreement to buy

◊ **contractually** *adverb* according to a contract; *the company is contractually bound to pay his expenses*

contrary *noun* opposite; **unless we receive instructions to the contrary** = unless different instructions are given; **on the contrary** = quite the opposite; *the chairman was not annoyed with his assistant - on the contrary, he promoted him*

contribute *verb* to give or to add to; *to contribute 10% of the profits; he contributed to the pension fund for 10 years*

◊ **contribution** *noun* money paid to add to a sum; **contribution of capital** = money paid to a company as additional capital; **employer's contribution** = money paid by an employer towards a worker's pension; **pension**

contributions = money paid by a company or worker into a pension fund

◊ **contributor** *noun* **contributor of capital** = person who contributes capital

◊ **contributory** *adjective* **(a)** **contributory pension plan** = pension plan where the employee has to contribute a percentage of salary **(b)** which helps to cause; *falling exchange rates have been a contributory factor in* or *to the company's loss of profits*

control 1 *noun* **(a)** power or being able to direct something; *the company is under the control of three shareholders; the family lost control of its business; to gain control of a business* = to buy more than 50% of the shares so that you can direct the business; **to lose control of a business** = to find that you have less than 50% of the shares in a company, and so are no longer able to direct it **(b)** restricting or checking something or making sure that something is kept in check; **under control** = kept in check; *expenses are kept under tight control; the company is trying to bring its overheads back under control;* **out of control** = not kept in check; *costs have got out of control;* **budgetary control** = keeping check on spending; **credit control** = checking that customers pay on time and do not exceed their credit limits; **inventory control** = maintaining inventory by using a system; **quality control** = making sure that the quality of a product is good **(c)** **exchange controls** = government restrictions on changing the local currency into foreign currency; *the government has imposed exchange controls; they say the government is going to lift exchange controls;* **price controls** = legal measures to prevent prices from rising too fast **(d)** **control group** = small group which is used to check a sample group **2** *verb* **(a)** **to control a business** = to direct a business; *the business is controlled by a company based in Luxembourg; the company is controlled by the majority shareholder* **(b)** to make sure that something is kept in check or is not allowed to develop; *the government is fighting to control inflation* or *to control the rise in the cost of living* NOTE: **controlling - controlled**

◊ **controlled** *adjective* regulated or kept in check; **government-controlled** = ruled by a government; **controlled economy** = economy where the most business activity is directed by orders from the government

◊ **controller** *noun* chief accountant in a company

◊ **controlling** *adjective* **to have a controlling interest in a company** = to own more than 50% of the shares so that you can direct how the company is run

convene *verb* (**a**) to come together for a meeting; *the board of directors convened Thursday morning at nine o'clock* (**b**) to ask people to come together; *to convene a meeting of shareholders*

convenience *noun* **at your earliest convenience** = as soon as you find it possible; **convenience foods** = food which is already prepared before it is sold, so that it needs only heating to be made ready to eat; **convenience store** = small store selling foods and household goods, open late at night or 24 hours; **ship sailing under a flag of convenience** = flying the flag of a country which may have no ships of its own but allows ships of other countries to be registered in its ports

◊ **convenient** *adjective* suitable *or* handy; *a bank draft is a convenient way of sending money abroad; is 9:30 a convenient time for the meeting?*

convention *noun* assembly, often periodical, of delegates *or* representatives of various businesses

conversion *noun* change (**a**) **conversion of funds** = using money which does not belong to you for a purpose for which it is not supposed to be used (**b**) **conversion price** *or* **conversion rate** = rate at which a currency is changed into a foreign currency; price at which preferred stock is converted into common stock

◊ **convert** *verb* to change money of one country for money of another; *we converted our pounds into Swiss francs;* **to convert funds to one's own use** = to use someone else's money for yourself

◊ **convertibility** *noun* ability to exchange one currency for another easily

◊ **convertible** *adjective* **convertible debenture** = corporate bond that can be converted into common stock; **convertible term insurance** = term insurance that can be converted into permanent insurance without a further medical exam

convey *verb* to pass along *or* to move something from one place to another; *he conveyed the information to the personnel manager*

◊ **conveyor** *noun* mechanism, as an endless belt, for transferring packages or other items from one place to another

conveyance *noun* legal document which transfers a property from the seller to the buyer

◊ **conveyancer** *noun* lawyer who draws up a conveyance

◊ **conveyancing** *noun* legally transferring a property from a seller to a buyer; **do-it-yourself conveyancing** = drawing up a legal conveyance without the help of a lawyer

cooling off period *noun* during an industrial dispute, a period when negotiations have to be carried on and no action can be taken by either side

coop *noun* = COOPERATIVE 2

◊ **cooperate** *verb* to work together; *the governments are cooperating in the fight against piracy; the two firms have cooperated on the computer project*

◊ **cooperation** *noun* working together; *the project was completed ahead of schedule with the cooperation of the workforce*

◊ **cooperative 1** *adjective* willing to work together; *the workforce has not been cooperative over the management's productivity plan;* **cooperative society** = society where the customers and workers are partners and share the profits **2** *noun* business run by a group of workers who are the owners and who share the profits; **agricultural cooperative** = group of farmers who joint together to buy expensive machinery or to sell their produce more effectively

co-opt *verb* (**a**) **to co-opt someone onto a committee** = to ask someone to join a committee without being elected (**b**) to take over; *they co-opted the secretary's office for their meeting*

co-owner *noun* person who owns something with another person; *the two sisters are co-owners of the property*

◊ **co-ownership** *noun* arrangement where something is owned by more than one person

copartner *noun* person who is a partner in a business with another person

◊ **copartnership** *noun* arrangement where partners *or* workers have shares in the company

cope *verb* to manage to do something; *the new assistant manager coped very well when the manager was on vacation; the warehouse is trying to cope with the backlog of orders*

copier *noun* = COPYING MACHINE, PHOTOCOPIER

copy 1 *noun* (a) document which is made to look the same as another; **carbon copy** = copy made with carbon paper; **certified copy** = document which is certified as being the same as another; **file copy** = copy of a document which is filed in an office for reference (b) document; **fair copy** *or* **final copy** = document which is written or typed with no changes or mistakes; **hard copy** = printout of a text which is on a computer *or* printed copy of something which is on microfilm; **rough copy** = draft of a document which, it is expected, will have changes made to it; **top copy** = first or top sheet of a document which is typed with carbon copies (c) a book *or* a newspaper; *have you kept yesterday's copy of the "New York Times"? I read it in the office copy of "Fortune" ; where is my copy of the telephone directory?* (d) text of an advertisement (as opposed to an illustration) **2** *verb* to make a second document which is like the first; *he copied the company report at night and took it home*

◊ **copier** *or* **copy machine** *noun* machine which makes copies of documents

◊ **copyright 1** *noun* legal right (lasting for fifty years after the death of a writer) which a writer has to publish his own work and not to have it copied; **copyright law** = laws concerning copyright; **work which is out of copyright** = work by a writer who has been dead for fifty years; **work still in copyright** = work by a living writer, or by a writer who has not been dead for fifty years; **infringement of copyright** *or* **copyright infringement** = act of illegally copying a work which is in copyright; **copyright notice** = note in a book showing who owns the copyright and the date of ownership **2** *verb* to confirm the copyright of a written work by inserting a copyright notice and publishing the work **3** *adjective* covered by the laws of copyright; *it is illegal to photocopy a copyright work*

◊ **copyrighted** *adjective* in copyright

copywriter *noun* person who writes the texts of advertisements

corner 1 *noun* (a) place where two streets *or* two walls join; *the Post Office is on the corner of Main Street and Fremont Road;* **corner store** = small general store in a town on a street corner (b) place where two sides join; *the box has to have especially strong corners; the corner of the crate was damaged* (c) situation where one person or a group controls the supply of a certain commodity **2** *verb* to **corner the market** = to own most or all of the supply of a certain commodity and so control the price; *the syndicate tried to corner the market in silver*

corp = CORPORATION

corporate *adjective* referring to a whole company; **corporate bond** = document promising to repay money borrowed by a corporation; **corporate charter** = document by which a corporation is officially incorporated; **corporate image** = idea which a company would like the public to have of it; **corporate income tax** = tax on the earnings of a corporation; **corporate plan** = plan for the future work of a whole company; **corporate planning** = planning the future work of a whole company; **corporate profits** = profits of a corporation; **corporate secretary** = administrative officer who keeps the official records of a corporation

◊ **corporation** *noun* large company, which is incorporated in the U.S.; **finance corporation** = company whose business is to make loans to individuals or other companies; **corporation income tax** = tax on net earnings of incorporated companies; **corporation tax** = tax on profits made by corporations

> QUOTE the prime rate is the rate at which banks lend to their top corporate borrowers
> *Wall Street Journal*
> QUOTE if corporate forecasts are met, sales will exceed $50 million in 1985
> *Citizen (Ottawa)*

correct 1 *adjective* accurate *or* right; *the published balance sheet does not give a correct picture of the company's financial position* **2** *verb* to remove mistakes from something; *the accounts* department has corrected the invoice; you will have to correct all these typing errors before you send the letter

◊ **correction** *noun* **(a)** making something correct; change which makes something correct; *he made some corrections to the text of the speech* **(b)** reverse movement in the price of a stock or bond, usually a decline in an upward trend

correspond *verb* **(a) to correspond with someone =** to write letters to someone **(b) to correspond with something =** to fit *or* to match something
◊ **correspondence** *noun* letters which are exchanged; **business correspondence =** letters concerned with a business; **to be in correspondence with someone =** to write letters to someone and receive letters back; **correspondence school =** school that offers courses that can be completed at home, with books and tests exchanged by mail
◊ **correspondent** *noun* **(a)** person who writes letters **(b)** journalist who writes articles for a newspaper on specialized subjects; *a financial correspondent; the "Times" business correspondent; he is the Paris correspondent of the "Post"*

cost 1 *noun* **(a)** amount of money which has to be paid for something; *what is the cost of a first-class ticket to New York? computer costs are falling each year; we cannot afford the cost of two telephones;* **to cover costs =** to produce enough money in sales to pay for the costs of production; *the sales revenue barely covers the costs of advertising or the manufacturing costs;* **to sell at cost =** to sell at a price which is the same as the cost of manufacture or the wholesale cost; **fixed costs =** business costs which do not change with the quantity of the product made; **labor costs =** cost of hourly-paid workers employed to make a product; **manufacturing costs** *or* **production costs =** costs of making a product; **operating costs** *or* **running costs =** cost of the day-to-day organization of a company; **variable costs =** production costs which increase with the quantity of the product made (such as wages, raw materials); **cost accountant =** accountant who gives managers information about their business costs; **cost accounting =** specially prepared accounts of manufacturing and sales costs and their analysis; **cost analysis =**

calculating in advance what a new product will cost; **cost center =** group *or* machine whose costs can be itemized and to which fixed costs can be allocated; **cost, insurance and freight (c.i.f.) =** estimate of a price, which includes the cost of the goods, the insurance and the transport charges; **cost price =** selling price which is the same as the price which the seller paid for the item (i.e. either the manufacturing cost or the wholesale price); **cost of sales** *or* **cost of goods sold =** all the costs of a product sold, including manufacturing costs and the staff costs of the production department **(b) costs =** expenses involved in a court case; **to pay costs =** to pay the expenses of a court case; *the judge awarded costs to the defendant; costs of the case will be borne by the prosecution* **2** *verb* **(a)** to have a price; *how much does the machine cost? this cloth costs $10 a yard* **(b) to cost a product =** to calculate how much money will be needed to make a product, and so work out its selling price
◊ **cost-benefit** *noun* **cost-benefit analysis =** examining the ratio between costs and benefits, especially in comparing different production processes
◊ **cost-cutting** *noun* reducing costs; *we have taken out the air-conditioner as a cost-cutting measure*
◊ **cost-effective** *adjective* which gives value for the money spent, especially when compared with something else; *we find advertising in the Sunday newspapers very cost-effective*
◊ **cost-effectiveness** *noun* being cost-effective; *can we calculate the cost-effectiveness of air freight against shipping by sea?*
◊ **costing** *noun* calculation of the manufacturing costs, and so the selling price of a product; *the costings give us a retail price of $2.95; we cannot do the costing until we have details of all the production expenditures*
◊ **costly** *adjective* expensive *or* costing a lot of money
◊ **cost of living** *noun* money which has to be paid for food, heating, rent, etc.; *to allow for the cost of living in the salaries;* **cost-of-living adjustment** *or* **cost-of-living allowance =** addition to normal salary to cover increases in the cost of living; **cost-of-living bonus =** extra money paid to meet the increase in the cost of living; **cost-of-living increase =** increase in salary to allow it to keep up with the increased cost of

living; **cost-of-living index** = measure of the average changes in the cost of goods purchased by consumers at any time against the cost during the base period

◇ **cost plus** *noun* system of charging, where the buyer pays the costs plus a percentage commission to the seller; *we are charging for the work on a cost plus basis*

◇ **cost-push inflation** *noun* inflation caused by increased wage demands which lead to higher prices and in turn lead to further wage demands

council *noun* official group chosen to run something *or* to advise on a problem; **consumer council** = group representing the interests of consumers; **city council** = representatives elected to run a city; **Council of Economic Advisers** = group which advises the President on economic matters

counsel *noun* lawyer acting for one of the parties in a legal action; *defense counsel; prosecution counsel*

count *verb* **(a)** to add figures together to make a total; *he counted up the sales for the six months to December* **(b)** to include; *did you count my trip to New York as part of my sales expenses?*

◇ **count on** *verb* to expect something to happen; *they are counting on getting a good response from the TV advertising; do not count on a bank loan to start your business*

counter *noun* **(a)** long flat surface in a store for displaying and selling goods; **goods sold over the counter** = retail sales of goods in stores; *some drugs are sold over the counter, but others need to be prescribed by a doctor;* **under the counter** = illegally; **under-the-counter sales** = black market sales; **bargain counter** = counter where things are sold cheaply; **check-in counter** = place where plane passengers have to check in; **ticket counter** = place where tickets are sold **(b)** *(Stock Exchange)* **over-the-counter sales** = legal selling of shares which are not listed on a stock exchange; **over the counter stock** = unlisted security

counter- *prefix* against

◇ **counterbid** *noun* higher bid in reply to a previous bid; *when I bid $20 he put in a counterbid of $25*

◇ **counterclaim 1** *noun* claim for damages made in reply to a previous claim; *Jones claimed $25,000 in damages against Smith, and Smith entered a counterclaim of $50,000 for loss of income* **2** *verb* to put in a counterclaim; *Jones claimed $25,000 in damages and Smith counterclaimed $50,000 for loss of income*

◇ **counterfeit 1** *adjective* false *or* imitation (money) **2** *verb* to make imitation money

◇ **counterfoil** *noun* slip of paper kept after writing a check *or* an invoice *or* a receipt, as a record of the deal which has taken place

◇ **countermand** *verb* **to countermand an order** = to say that an order must not be carried out

◇ **counteroffer** *noun* more attractive offer made in reply to another offer; *Smith Co. made an offer of $1m for the property, and Blacks replied with a counteroffer of $1.4m*

◇ **counterpart** *noun* person who has a similar position in another company; *John is my counterpart at Smith's* = he has the same post as I have here

◇ **countersign** *verb* to sign a document which has already been signed by someone else; *all checks have to be countersigned by the finance director; the sales manager countersigns all my orders*

country *noun* **(a)** land which is separate and governs itself; *the contract covers distribution in the countries of the Common Market; some African countries export oil; the Organization of Petroleum Exporting Countries;* the executive director is out of the **country** = he is on a business trip abroad **(b)** land which is not near a city; *distribution is difficult in country areas; his territory is mainly the country, but he is based in the city*

couple *noun* two things or people associated together; *we only have enough stock for a couple of weeks; a couple of the board members were ill, so the meeting was canceled;* the negotiations lasted a couple of hours = the negotiations went on for about two hours

coupon *noun* **(a)** piece of paper used in place of money; *the magazine contained a coupon for a free bottle of shampoo* **(b)** piece of paper which replaces an order form; **coupon ad** =

advertisement with a form attached, which is to be cut out and returned to the advertiser with your name and address if you want further information about the product advertised; **reply coupon =** form attached to a coupon ad, which must be filled in and returned to the advertiser **(c) coupon bond =** bond with detachable coupons attached, which can be presented to collect the interest; **interest coupon =** slip of paper attached to a government bond certificate which can be cashed to provide the periodic interest; **cum coupon =** with a coupon attached; **ex coupon =** without the interest coupons

courier *noun* **(a)** messenger who takes packages or letters from one place to another by car, van or motorcycle **(b)** person who goes with a party of tourists to guide them on a package tour

course *noun* **(a) in the course of =** during *or* while something is happening; *in the course of the discussion, the vice-president explained the company's expansion plans; sales have risen sharply in the course of the last few months* **(b)** series of classes; *she has finished her secretarial course; the company has paid for her to attend a course for trainee sales managers* **(c) of course =** naturally; *of course the company is interested in profits; are you willing to go on a sales trip to Australia? - of course!*

court *noun* place where a judge listens to a case and decides legally which of the parties in the argument is right; **court case =** legal action *or* trial; **to take someone to court =** to tell someone to appear in court to settle an argument; **a settlement was reached out of court** *or* **the two parties reached an out-of-court settlement =** the dispute was settled between the two parties privately without continuing the court case

cover 1 *noun* **(a)** thing put over a machine, etc. to keep it clean; *put the cover over your calculator when you leave the office; always keep a cover over the typewriter* **(b)** security to guarantee a loan; *do you have sufficient cover for this loan?* **(c)** *(in restaurant or night-club)* **cover charge =** charge in addition to the charge for food **(d) under cover =** in an envelope; **to send something under separate cover =** in a separate envelope; **to send**

a magazine under plain cover = in an ordinary envelope with no company name printed on it; **cover letter =** letter sent with documents to say why you are sending them **2** *verb* **(a)** to put something over a machine, etc. to keep it clean; *don't forget to cover your typewriter before you go home* **(b) to cover a risk =** to be protected by insurance against a risk; **to be fully covered =** to have insurance against all risks; *the insurance covers fire, theft and loss of work* **(c)** to have enough money to pay; to ask for security against a loan which you are making; **the damage was covered by the insurance =** the insurance company paid for the damage **(d)** to earn enough money to pay for costs, expenses etc.; *we do not make enough sales to cover the expense of running the store; break-even point is reached when sales cover all costs;* **the dividend is covered four times =** profits are four times the dividend paid out

◊ **coverage** *noun* **(a) press coverage** *or* **media coverage =** reports about something in the newspapers *or* on TV, etc.; *the company had good media coverage for the launch of its new model* **(b)** protection guaranteed by insurance; *do you have coverage against fire damage or against theft?;* **to operate without adequate coverage =** without being protected by insurance; **to ask for additional coverage =** to ask the insurance company to increase the amount for which you are insured; **full coverage =** insurance against all risks **(c)** asset value of a bond or share

◊ **covering letter** *or* **covering note** *noun* letter or note sent with documents to say why you are sending them

QUOTE When reviewing coverage, agencies should do more than just examine what buildings and structures are covered. Not many governments have loss-of-use coverage for damaged facilities, computer systems or structures such as toll bridges
American City & County

CPA = CERTIFIED PUBLIC ACCOUNTANT

CPI = CONSUMER PRICE INDEX

crane *noun* machine for lifting heavy objects; *the container slipped as the crane was lifting it onto the ship; they had to hire a crane to get the machine into the factory*

crash 1 *noun* **(a)** accident to a car *or* plane *or* train; *the car was damaged in the crash; the plane crash killed all the* *passengers or all the passengers were killed in the plane crash* **(b)** financial collapse; *he lost all his money in the crash of 1929* **2** *verb* **(a)** to hit something and be damaged; *the plane crashed into the mountain; the truck crashed into the post office* **(b)** to collapse financially; *the company crashed with debts of over $1 million*

crate 1 *noun* large wooden box; *a crate of oranges* **2** *verb* to put goods into crates

create *verb* to make something new; *by acquiring small unprofitable companies he soon created a large manufacturing group; the government program aims at creating new jobs for young people*
◊ **creation** *noun* making; **job creation program** = program to create jobs for unemployed workers

> QUOTE he insisted that the tax advantages he directed towards small businesses will help create jobs and reduce the unemployment rate
> *Toronto Star*

credere *see* DEL CREDERE

credit 1 *noun* **(a)** time given to a customer before he has to pay; *to give someone six months' credit; to sell on good credit terms;* **extended credit** = credit on very long repayment terms; **interest-free credit** = arrangement to borrow money without paying interest on the loan; **long credit** = terms allowing the borrower a long time to pay; **open credit** = bank credit given to good customers without security; **short credit** = terms allowing the customer only a short time to pay; **credit account** = account which a customer has with a store which allows him to buy goods and pay for them later; *to open a credit account;* **credit bureau** = company which reports on the creditworthiness of customers to show whether they should be allowed credit; **credit check** = check on someone's credit status; **credit control** = check that customers pay on time and do not owe more than their credit limit; **credit facilities** = arrangement with a bank or supplier to have credit so as to buy goods; **credit crunch** *or* **credit freeze** *or* **credit squeeze** = period when lending by banks is restricted by the government; **letter of credit** = letter from a bank, allowing someone credit and promising to repay at a later date; **irrevocable letter of credit** = letter of credit which cannot be

canceled; **credit limit** = fixed amount which is the most a customer can owe on credit; *he has exceeded his credit limit* = he has borrowed more money than he is allowed; **to open a line of credit** *or* a **credit line** = to make credit available to someone; **credit status** *or* **credit rating** = evaluation of a customer's ability to repay a loan; **on credit** = without paying immediately; *to live on credit; we buy everything on sixty days credit; the company exists on credit from its suppliers* **(b)** money received by a person *or* company and recorded in the account books; *to enter $100 to someone's credit; to pay $100 to the credit of Mr. Smith;* **debit and credit** = money which a company owes and which it receives; **credit balance** = balance in an account showing that more money has been received than is owed by the company; *the account has a credit balance of $1,000;* **credit column** = right-hand column in books of account showing money received; **credit entry** = entry on the credit side of an account; **credit note** = note showing that money is owed to a customer; *the company sent the wrong order and had to issue a credit note;* **credit side** = right-hand side of books of account showing money received; **account in credit** = account where the credits are higher than the debits; **bank credit** = loans or overdrafts from a bank to a customer; **tax credits** = direct reduction in the amount of tax owed **2** *verb* to put money into someone's account; to note money received in an account; *to credit an account with $100 or to credit $100 to an account*
◊ **credit card** *noun* plastic card which allows you to borrow money and to buy goods without paying for them immediately
◊ **creditor** *noun* person who is owed money; **creditors' meeting** = meeting of all persons to whom a bankrupt company owes money, to decide how to obtain the money owed
◊ **credit union** *noun* financial institution set up by and for members of a group, such as state employees or a labor union
◊ **creditworthy** *adjective* able to buy goods on credit
◊ **creditworthiness** *noun* ability of a customer to pay for goods bought on credit

crew *noun* group of people who work together; *the ship carries a crew of 250*

crime *noun* act which is against the law; *crimes in supermarkets have risen by 25%*

◇ **criminal**   *adjective*   illegal; *misappropriation of funds is a criminal act;* **criminal action =** court case brought by the state against someone who is charged with a crime

crisis *noun* serious economic situation where decisions have to be made rapidly; *international crisis; banking crisis; financial crisis*
NOTE: plural is **crises**

criterion *noun* standard on which to make a judgment; *what criteria are you using in choosing someone to fill the position?*
NOTE: plural is **criteria**

criticize *verb* to say that something *or* someone is wrong *or* is working badly, etc.; *the CEO criticized the sales manager for not improving the volume of sales; the design of the new catalog has been criticized*

cross *verb* to go across; *Concorde only takes three hours to cross the Atlantic; to get to the bank, you turn left and cross the street at the post office*

◇ **cross off** *verb* to remove something from a list; *he crossed my name off his list; you can cross him off our mailing list*

◇ **cross out** *verb* to put a line through something which has been written; *she crossed out $250 and put in $500*

◇ **cross rate** *noun* exchange rate between two currencies expressed in a third currency

crown jewels *noun* most important and valuable asset of a corporation, to try to acquire which other corporations may mount takeover bids

crude (oil) *noun* raw petroleum, taken from the ground; *the price for Arabian crude has slipped*

cubic *adjective* measured in volume by multiplying length, depth and width; *the crate holds six cubic meters;* **cubic measure =** volume measured in cubic feet or meters
NOTE: cubic is written in figures as ³: **10ft³ =** ten cubic feet; **6m³ =** six cubic meters

cum *preposition* with; **cum dividend =** price of a share including the next dividend still to be paid; **cum coupon =** with a coupon attached

cumulative *adjective* which is added automatically each year; **cumulative interest =** interest which is added to the capital each year; **cumulative preferred stock =** stock which will have the dividend paid at a later date even if the company is not able to pay a dividend in the current year

currency *noun* money in coins and notes which is used in a particular country; **convertible currency =** currency which can easily be exchanged for another; **foreign currency =** currency of another country; **foreign currency account =** bank account in the currency of another country (e.g. a Swiss franc account); **foreign currency reserves =** a country's reserves in currencies of other countries; **hard currency =** currency of a country which has a strong economy and which can be changed into other currencies easily; *to pay for imports in hard currency; to sell raw materials to earn hard currency;* **legal currency =** money which is legally used in a country; **soft currency =** currency of a country with a weak economy, which is cheap to buy and difficult to exchange for other currencies; **currency backing =** gold *or* securities which maintain the international strength of a currency; **currency note =** piece of paper money
NOTE: currency has no plural when it refers to the money of one country: **he was arrested trying to take currency out of the country**

> QUOTE the strong dollar's inflationary impact on European economies, as national governments struggle to support their sinking currencies and push up interest rates
> *Duns Business Month*

current *adjective* referring to the present time; **current assets =** assets used by a company in its ordinary work (such as materials, finished products, cash); **current cost accounting =** method of accounting which notes the cost of replacing assets at current prices, rather than valuing assets at their original cost; **current liabilities =** debts which a company has to pay within the next accounting period; **current market value =** value of stock held by an investor, at today's market price; **current price =** today's price; **current rate of exchange =** today's rate of exchange; **current yield =** dividend calculated as a percentage of the price paid per share

◊ **currently** *adverb* at the present time; *we are currently negotiating with the bank for a loan*

QUOTE crude oil output plunged during the past month and is likely to remain at its current level for the near future
Wall Street Journal
QUOTE customers' current deposit and current accounts also rose to $655.31 million at the end of December
Hongkong Standard

curve *noun* line which bends around; *the graph shows an upward curve;* **sales curve** = graph showing how sales increase or decrease

custom *noun* (a) usual practice; *it is a custom for the store to decorate a large tree at Christmastime* (b) **custom-built** *or* **custom-made** = made specially for one customer; *he drives a custom-built Rolls Royce*

◊ **customer** *noun* person *or* company which buys goods; *the store was full of customers; can you help this customer first please? he is a regular customer of ours;* **customer appeal** = what attracts customers to a product; **customer list** = mailing list of addresses of customers; **customer service department** = department which deals with customers and their complaints and inquiries

◊ **customize** *verb* to change something to fit the special needs of a customer; *we used customized computer terminals*

◊ **customs** *plural noun* U.S. Customs Service = federal government department which organizes the collection of taxes on imports; office of this department at a port *or* airport; **to go through customs** = to pass through the area of a port or airport where customs officials examine goods; **to take something through customs** = to carry something illegal through the customs area without declaring it; *he was stopped at customs; her car was searched by the customs;* **customs broker** = person *or* company which takes goods through the customs for a shipping company; **customs clearance** = document given by customs to a shipper to show that customs duty has been paid and the goods can be shipped; *to wait for customs clearance;* **customs declaration** = statement showing goods being imported on which duty will have to be paid; *to fill in a customs (declaration) form;* **customs duty** =

tax paid on goods brought into or taken out of a country; **the crates had to go through a customs examination** = the crates had to be examined by customs officials; **customs officers** *or* **customs officials** = people working for customs; **customs tariff** = list of duties to be paid on imported goods; **customs union** = agreement between several countries that goods can travel between them, without paying duty, while goods from other countries have to pay special duties

cut 1 *noun* (a) sudden lowering of a price *or* salary *or* numbers of jobs; **price cuts** *or* **cuts in prices; salary cuts** *or* **cuts in salaries; job cuts** = reductions in the number of jobs; **he took a cut in salary** = he accepted a lower salary (b) share in a payment; *he introduces new customers and gets a cut of the salesman's commission* **2** *verb* (a) to lower suddenly; *we are cutting prices on all our models;* **to cut (back) production** = to reduce the quantity of products made; *the company has cut back its sales force; we have taken out the air-conditioner in order to try to cut costs* (b) to stop *or* to reduce the number of something; **to cut jobs** = to reduce the number of jobs by laying off employees and not rehiring them; **he cut his losses** = he stopped doing something which was creating a loss
NOTE: **cutting - cut - has cut**

◊ **cutback** *noun* reduction; **cutbacks in government spending**

◊ **cut down (on)** *verb* to reduce suddenly the amount of something used; *the government is cutting down on welfare payments; the office is trying to cut down on electricity consumption; we have installed a word processor to cut down on paperwork*

◊ **cut in** *verb informal* **to cut someone in on a deal** = to give someone a share in the profits of a deal

◊ **cutthroat** *adjective* **cutthroat competition** = sharp competition by reducing prices and offering high discounts

◊ **cutting** *noun* **cost cutting** = reducing costs; *we have eliminated three secretarial positions as part of our cost-cutting program;* **price cutting** = sudden lowering of prices; **price-cutting war** = competition between companies to get a larger market share by cutting prices

cwt = HUNDREDWEIGHT

cycle *noun* period of time when something leaves its original position and then returns to it; **economic cycle** *or* **trade cycle** *or* **business cycle** = period during which trade expands, then slows down and then expands again
◊ **cyclical** *adjective* which happens in cycles; **cyclical factors** = way in which a trade cycle affects businesses

Dd

daily *adjective* done every day; **daily consumption** = amount used each day; **daily production of cars** = number of cars produced each day; **daily sales returns** = reports of sales made each day; **a daily newspaper** *or* **a daily** = newspaper which is produced every day

damage 1 *noun* (a) harm done to things; **fire damage** = damage caused by a fire; **storm damage** = damage caused by a storm; **to suffer damage** = to be harmed; *we are trying to assess the damage which the shipment suffered in transit;* **to cause damage** = to harm something; *the fire caused damage estimated at $100,000;* **damage survey** = survey of damage done (b) **damages** = money claimed as compensation for harm done; *to claim $1000 in damages; to be liable for damages; to pay $25,000 in damages;* **to bring an action for damages against someone** = to take someone to court and claim damages **2** *verb* to harm; *the storm damaged the cargo; stock which has been damaged by water*
◊ **damaged** *adjective* which has suffered damage *or* which has been harmed; *goods damaged in transit;* **fire-damaged goods** = goods harmed in a fire

danger *noun* possibility of being harmed or killed; *the old machinery presents a danger to the workforce;* **there is no danger of the sales manager leaving** = it is not likely that the sales manager will leave; **in danger of** = which may easily happen; *the company is in danger of being taken over; she is in danger of being fired*
◊ **dangerous** *adjective* which can be harmful; **dangerous job** = job where the workers may be killed or hurt

data *noun* information (in the form of letters or figures) available on computer; **data acquisition** *or* **data capture** = getting information; **data bank** *or* **bank of data** = store of information held by an organization in its computer; **data processing** = selecting and examining data in a computer to produce special information
◊ **database** *noun* store of information in a large computer; *we can extract the lists of potential customers from our database*

date 1 *noun* (a) number of day, month and year; *please include today's date at the top of the letter;* **date stamp** = rubber stamp for marking the date on letters received; **date of receipt** = date when something is received (b) **up to date** = current *or* recent *or* modern; *an up-to-date computer system;* **to bring something up to date** = to add the latest information to something; **to keep something up to date** = to keep adding information to something so that it is always current; *we spend a lot of time keeping our mailing list up to date* (c) **to date** = up to now; **interest to date** = interest up to the present time (d) **out of date** = old-fashioned; *their computer system is years out of date; they are still using out-of-date machinery* (e) **maturity date** = date when a loan becomes due *or* when a certificate of deposit matures; **date of bill** = date when a bill will mature **2** *verb* to put a date on a document; *the check was dated March 24; you forgot to date the check;* **to date a check forward** = to put a later date than the present one on a check
◊ **dated** *adjective* (a) with a date written on it; *thank you for your letter dated June 15* (b) out of date; *the company's brochure is dated*

day *noun* (a) period of 24 hours; *there are thirty days in June; the first day of the month is a public holiday;* **settlement day** = day when stock that has been bought must be paid for and transferred to the buyer (b) period of work from morning to night; *she took* **two days off** = she did not come to work for two days; *he works* **three days on,**

two days off = he works for three days, then has two days off; **to work an eighthour day** = to spend eight hours at work each day; **day shift** = shift which works during the daylight hours such as from 8 a.m. to 5:30 p.m.; *there are 150 men on the day shift; he works the day shift*

◊ **daybook** *noun* book with an account of sales and purchases made each day

◊ **day-to-day** *adjective* ordinary *or* which goes on all the time; *he organizes the day-to-day running of the company; sales only just cover the day-to-day expenses*

◊ **day worker** *noun* person who works the day shift

dead *adjective* (a) not alive; *six people were dead as a result of the accident; the founders of the company are all dead* (b) not working; **dead account** = account which is no longer used; **the line went dead** = the telephone line suddenly stopped working; **dead money** = money which is not invested to make a profit; **dead season** = time of year when there are few tourists about

◊ **deadline** *noun* date by which something has to be done; **to meet a deadline** = to finish something in time; *we've missed our October 1 deadline*

◊ **deadlock 1** *noun* point where two sides in a dispute cannot agree; *the negotiations have reached a deadlock;* **to break a deadlock** = to find a way to start discussions again **2** *verb* to be unable to agree to continue discussing; **talks have been deadlocked for ten days** = after ten days the talks have not produced any agreement

◊ **deadweight** *noun* heavy goods like coal, iron or sand; **deadweight cargo** = heavy cargo which is charged by weight, not by volume; **deadweight capacity** *or* **deadweight tonnage** = largest amount of cargo which a ship can carry safely

deal 1 *noun* (a) business agreement *or* affair *or* contract; *to arrange a deal or to set up a deal or to do a deal; to sign a deal; the sales director set up a deal with a Russian bank; the deal will be signed tomorrow; they closed a deal with a British airline;* **to call off a deal** = to stop an agreement; *when the chairman heard about the deal he called it off;* **cash deal** = sale done for cash; **package deal** = agreement *or* offer that includes several different items; *they agreed on a package deal, which involves the construction of the factory, training of staff and purchase*

of the product (b) **a great deal** *or* **a good deal of something** = a large quantity of something; *he has made a good deal of money in futures trading; the company lost a great deal of time asking for expert advice* **2** *verb* (a) **to deal with** = to organize; *leave it to the mail clerk - he'll deal with it;* **to deal with an order** = to process an order (b) to trade *or* to buy and sell; **to deal with someone** = to do business with someone; **to deal in leather** *or* **to deal in options** = to buy and sell leather *or* options; *he deals on the Stock Exchange* = his work involves buying and selling shares on the Stock Exchange for clients

◊ **dealer** *noun* person who buys and sells; *dealer in tobacco or tobacco dealer;* **foreign exchange dealer** = person who buys and sells foreign currencies; **retail dealer** = person who sells to the general public; **wholesale dealer** = person who sells in bulk to retailers; **dealer brand** = product sold under the brand name of the store that sells it

◊ **dealing** *noun* (a) buying and selling; **foreign exchange dealing** = buying and selling foreign currencies; **forward dealings** = buying or selling commodities forward; **insider dealing** = illegal buying and selling of shares by staff of a company who have secret information about the company's plans; **option dealing** = buying and selling share options (b) buying and selling goods; **to have dealings with someone** = to do business with someone

dear *adjective* (a) way of starting a letter; **Dear Sir** *or* **Dear Madam** = addressing a man or woman whom you do not know, or addressing a company; **Dear Sirs** = addressing a firm; **Dear Mr. Smith** *or* **Dear Mrs. Smith** *or* **Dear Miss Smith** = addressing a man or woman whom you know; **Dear James** *or* **Dear Julia** = addressing a friend *or* a person you do business with (b) expensive *or* costing a lot of money; *property is very dear in this area;* **dear money** = money borrowed at a high rate of interest

death *noun* act of dying; **death benefit** = insurance benefit paid to the beneficiary when the insured person dies; **death tax** = tax paid on the property left by a dead person

debenture *noun* agreement to repay a debt with fixed interest backed only by general credit or the firm's integrity; *the bank holds a debenture on the*

company; mortgage debenture = debenture where the lender can be repaid by selling the company's property; **debenture issue** or **issue of debentures** = borrowing money against the security of the company's assets; **debenture bond** = unsecured interest-bearing bond; **debenture capital** or **debenture stock** = capital borrowed by a company, using its fixed assets as security; **debenture holder** = person who holds a debenture for money lent; **debenture register** or **register of debentures** = list of debenture holders of a company

debit 1 noun money which a company owes; **debits and credits** = money which a company owes and money it receives; **debit balance** = balance in an account, showing that the company owes more money than it has received; **debit column** = left-hand column in books of account showing the money paid or owed to others; **debit entry** = entry on the debit side of an account; **debit side** = left-hand side of an account showing the money paid or owed to others; **debit note** = note showing that a customer owes money; *we undercharged Mr. Smith and had to send him a debit check for the extra amount* **2** verb to **debit an account** = to charge an account with a cost; *his account was debited for the sum of $25*

◇ **debitable** adjective which can be debited

debt noun (a) money owed for goods or services; *the company stopped trading with debts of over $1 million;* **to be in debt** = to owe money; *he is $250 in debt* = he owes $250; **to get into debt** = to start to borrow more money than you can pay back; **the company is out of debt** = the company does not owe money any more; **to pay back a debt** = to pay all the money owed; **to pay off a debt** = to finish paying money owed; **to service a debt** = to pay interest on a debt; *the company is having problems in servicing its debts;* **bad debt** = money owed which will never be paid back; *the company has written off $30,000 in bad debts;* **secured debts** or **unsecured debts** = debts which are guaranteed or not guaranteed by assets; **debt collection** = collecting money which is owed; **debt collection agency** = company which collects debts for a commission; **debt collector** = person who collects debts; **debts due** = money

owed which is due for repayment **(b) funded debt** = debt formalized by bonds or notes and ordinarily maturing in more than one year; **the national debt** = money borrowed by a government

◇ **debtor** noun person who owes money; **debtor side** = debit side of an account; **debtor nation** = country whose foreign debts are larger than money owed to it by other countries

> QUOTE the United States is now a debtor nation for the first time since 1914, owing more to foreigners than it is owed itself
> *Economist*

decal noun = STICKER

deceit or **deception** noun misleading someone in order to trick him into paying money; *he obtained $10,000 by deception*

decentralize verb to organize from various points, away from the center; *the group has a policy of decentralized purchasing where each division is responsible for its own purchasing*

◇ **decentralization** noun organization from various points, away from the center; *the decentralization of the buying departments*

decide verb to make up your mind to do something; *to decide on a course of action; to decide to appoint a new chief accountant*

◇ **deciding** adjective **deciding factor** = most important factor which influences a decision

decimal noun **decimal system** = system of measuring based on the number 10; **correct to three decimal places** = correct to three figures after the decimal point (e.g. 3.485); **decimal point** = dot which indicates the division between the whole unit and its smaller parts (such as 4.75)

◇ **decimalization** noun act of changing to a decimal system

◇ **decimalize** verb to change to a decimal system

decision noun conclusion; *to come to a decision* or *to reach a decision* or *to make a decision;* **decision making** = act of coming to a decision; **decision-making processes** = ways in which decisions are reached; **decision maker** = person who has to decide

deck *noun* flat floor in a ship; **deck cargo** = cargo carried on the open top deck of a ship

◊ **deckhand** *noun* ordinary sailor on a cargo ship

declaration *noun* official statement; **declaration of bankruptcy** = official statement that someone is bankrupt; **customs declaration** = statement declaring goods brought into a country on which customs duty should be paid

◊ **declare** *verb* to make an official statement *or* to announce to the public; *to declare someone bankrupt; to declare a dividend of 10%;* **to declare goods to customs** = to state that you are importing goods which are liable to duty; *the customs officials asked him if he had anything to declare;* **to declare an interest** = to state in public that you own shares in a company being investigated *or* that you are related to someone who can benefit from your contacts, etc.

◊ **declared** *adjective* which has been made public or officially stated; **declared value** = value of goods entered on a customs declaration

decline 1 *noun* gradual fall; *the decline in the value of the franc; a decline in buying power; the last year has seen a decline in real wages* **2** *verb* to fall slowly; *shares declined in a weak market; imports have declined over the last year; the economy declined during the last administration*

decontrol *verb* to free something from control; **to decontrol the price of gasoline** = to stop controlling the price of gasoline so that it can be reached freely by the market; **to decontrol wages** = to allow wage fluctuations to occur freely
NOTE: **decontrolling - decontrolled**

decrease 1 *noun* fall *or* reduction; *decrease in price; decrease in value; decrease in imports; exports have registered a decrease; sales show a 10% decrease on last year* **2** *verb* to fall *or* to reduce; *imports are decreasing; the value of the dollar has decreased by 5%*

dedicated *adjective* used for a special purpose only; **dedicated keyboard** = keyboard used for one type of work only; **dedicated line** = telephone line used for a single use, such as transferring information from one computer to another

deduct *verb* to subtract money from a total; *to deduct $3 from the price; to deduct a sum for expenses; you can deduct your moving expenses from your taxable income; after deducting costs the gross margin is only 23%; expenses are still to be deducted;* **tax deducted at source** = tax which is removed from a salary, interest payment *or* dividend payment on shares before the money is paid

◊ **deductible 1** *adjective* which can be deducted; **tax-deductible** = which can be deducted from an income before tax is paid; **these expenses are not tax-deductible** = tax has to be paid on these expenses **2** *noun* amount that the insured has agreed to pay per claim on an insurance policy; *the deductible on this auto policy is $250*

◊ **deduction** *noun* removing of money from a total *or* money removed from a total; *net salary is amount after deduction of tax and social security;* **deductions from salary** *or* **salary deductions** *or* **deductions at source** = money which a company subtracts from salaries to pay to the government as tax, social security contributions, etc.; **tax deductions** = business expenses which can be claimed against tax

deed *noun* legal document *or* written agreement; **deed of assignment** = document which legally transfers a property from a debtor to a creditor; **deed of partnership** = agreement which sets up a partnership; **deed of transfer** = document which transfers the ownership of shares; **deed of trust** = conveyance of property to one person to be held in trust for another; **title deeds** = document showing who owns a property; *we have deposited the deeds of the house in the bank*

deep discount *noun* high discount offered by a manufacturer to a wholesaler

defalcation *noun* illegal use of money by someone who is not the owner but who has been trusted to look after it

default 1 *noun* failure to carry out the terms of a contract, especially failure to pay back a debt; **in default of payment** = with no payment made; **the company is in default** = the company has failed to carry out the terms of the contract; **by default** = because no one else will act; **he was elected by default** = he was elected because all the other candidates withdrew **2** *verb* to fail to carry out the terms of a contract, especially to fail to pay back a debt; **to default on payments** = not to make payments which are due under the terms of a contract
◊ **defaulter** *noun* person who defaults

defeat 1 *noun* loss of a vote; *the chairman offered to resign after the defeat of the proposal at the stockholders' meeting* **2** *verb* to beat someone *or* something in a vote; *the proposal was defeated by 10 votes to 23; he was heavily defeated in the election*

defect *noun* imperfection *or* something which is wrong *or* which stops a machine from working properly; *a computer defect or a defect in the computer*
◊ **defective** *adjective* (a) faulty *or* not working properly; *the machine broke down because of a defective cooling system* (b) not legally valid; *his title to the property is defective*

defense *noun* (a) protecting someone *or* something against attack; *the bank is organizing the company's defense against the takeover bid* (b) argument in a lawsuit on behalf of a defendant; **defense counsel** = lawyer who represents the defendant in a lawsuit
◊ **defend** *verb* to protect someone *or* something which is being attacked; *the company is defending itself against the takeover bid; he hired the best lawyers to defend him against the IRS;* **to defend a lawsuit** = to appear in court to state your case when accused of something
◊ **defendant** *noun* person who is sued *or* accused

defer *verb* to put back to a later date *or* to postpone; *to defer payment; the decision has been deferred until the next meeting*
NOTE: **deferring - deferred**
◊ **deferment** *noun* postponement *or* putting back to a later date; *deferment of payment; deferment of a decision*

◊ **deferred** *adjective* put back to a later date; **deferred payment** = payment for goods by installments over a long period; **deferred annuity** = annuity which does not begin payments until some years in the future

deficiency *noun* lack; money lacking; *there is a $10 deficiency in the petty cash;* **to make up a deficiency** = to put money into an account to balance it

deficit *noun* amount by which spending is higher than income; **the account shows a deficit** = the account shows a loss; **to make good a deficit** = to put money into an account to balance it; **balance of payments deficit** *or* **trade deficit** = situation when a country imports more than it exports; **deficit financing** = planning by a government to borrow money to cover the shortfall between tax income and expenditure

deflate *verb* **to deflate the economy** = to reduce activity in the economy by cutting the supply of money
◊ **deflation** *noun* reduction in economic activity
◊ **deflationary** *adjective* which can cause deflation; *the federal government has introduced some deflationary measures in the budget*

QUOTE the strong dollar's deflationary impact on European economies as national governments push up interest rates
Duns Business Month

defray *verb* to provide money to pay (costs); *the city council agreed to defray the costs of the trade fair*

delay 1 *noun* time when someone *or* something is later than planned; *there was a delay of thirty minutes before the meeting started or the meeting started after a thirty minute delay; we are sorry for the delay in supplying your order or in replying to your letter* **2** *verb* to put off; to make someone late; *he was delayed because his taxi had an accident; the company has delayed payment of all invoices*

del credere *noun* **del credere agent** = agent who receives a high commission because he guarantees payment by customers

delegate 1 *noun* person who represents others at a meeting; *the management refused to meet the union delegates* **2**

verb to pass authority or responsibility to someone else; *to delegate authority; he cannot delegate =* he wants to control everything himself and refuses to give up any of his responsibilities to his subordinates

◊ **delegation** *noun* (a) group of delegates; *a Chinese trade delegation; the management met a union delegation* (b) act of passing authority or responsibility to someone else

delete *verb* to remove words printed in a document; *they want to delete all references to credit terms from the contract; the lawyers have deleted clause two*

delinquent *adjective* (account *or* payment of tax) which is overdue

◊ **delinquency** *noun* being overdue in payment of an account

delisting *noun* removing a corporation's stock from the list of securities traded on a Stock Exchange

deliver *verb* to transport to a customer; *goods delivered on board =* goods transported free to the ship *or* plane but not to the customer's warehouse; *delivered price =* price which includes packing and transport

◊ **delivery** *noun* (a) delivery of goods = transport of goods to a customer's address; *parcels awaiting delivery; free delivery or delivery free; delivery date; delivery within 28 days; allow 28 days for delivery; delivery is not included;* delivery note = list of goods being delivered, given to the customer with the goods; **delivery order =** instructions given by the customer to the person holding his goods, to tell him to deliver them; *the store has a delivery service to all parts of the city =* the store will deliver goods to all parts of the city; delivery time = number of days before something will be delivered; delivery truck = truck for delivering goods to retail customers; **express delivery =** very fast delivery; **cash** *or* **collect on delivery (COD) =** payment in cash when the goods are delivered; *to take delivery of goods =* to accept goods when they are delivered; *we took delivery of the inventory into our warehouse on May 25* (b) goods being delivered; *we take in three deliveries a day; there were four items missing in the last delivery* (c) *(in trading)* passing of securities from a seller to a

buyer; transportation to the purchaser of commodities purchased on the futures market; *(in law)* irrevocable transfer of a deed

demand 1 *noun* (a) asking for payment; **payable on demand =** which must be paid when payment is asked for; **demand deposit =** money in a bank account which can be taken out when you want it by writing a check; **final demand =** last reminder from a supplier, after which he will sue for payment (b) need for goods at a certain price; *there was an active demand for oil stocks on the stock exchange;* to meet a demand *or* to fill a demand = to supply what is needed; *the factory had to increase production to meet the extra demand; the factory cut production when demand slackened; the office cleaning company cannot keep up with the demand for its services;* there is not much demand for this item = not many people want to buy it; this book is in great demand *or* there is a great demand for this book = many people want to buy it; **effective demand =** actual demand for a product which can be paid for; **demand price =** price at which a certain quantity of goods will be bought; **supply and demand =** amount of a product which is available and the amount which is wanted by customers; **law of supply and demand =** general rule that the amount of a product which is available is related to the needs of potential customers **2** *verb* to ask for something and expect to get it; *she demanded a refund; the suppliers are demanding immediate payment of their outstanding invoices*

QUOTE spot prices are now relatively stable in the run-up to the winter's peak demand
Economist

demise *noun* (a) death; *on his demise the estate passed to his daughter* (b) granting of a property on a lease

demonetize *verb* to stop using a coin or note as money

◊ **demonetization** *noun* stopping a coin or note from being used as money

demonstrate *verb* to show how something works; *he was demonstrating a new tractor when he was killed; the managers saw the new inventory control system being demonstrated*

◊ **demonstration** *noun* showing how something works; *we went to a demonstration of new computer equipment;* in-store demonstration = demonstration of a device or product inside a department store or supermarket; **demonstration model** = piece of equipment used in demonstrations and later sold off cheaply
◊ **demonstrator** *noun* person who demonstrates pieces of equipment

demote *verb* to give someone a less important job; *he was demoted from manager to salesman; her salary was reduced when she was demoted*
◊ **demotion** *noun* reassigning someone to a less important job; *he was very angry at his demotion*

demurrage *noun* money paid to a customer when a shipment is delayed at a port or by customs

denomination *noun* naming the unit of money (on a coin, paper currency or stamp); *coins of all denominations; small denomination bills*

depart *verb* (a) to leave; *the plane departs from Paris at 11:15* (b) to **depart from normal practice** = to act in a different way from the normal practice
◊ **department** *noun* (a) specialized section of a large company; *complaints department; design department; dispatch department; export department; legal department;* **accounts department** = section which deals with money paid or received; **personnel department** = section of a company dealing with the employees; **head of a department** or **department head** or **department manager** = person in charge of a department (b) section of a large store selling one type of product; *you will find beds in the furniture department;* **budget department** = department in a large store which sells cheaper goods (c) section of a government dealing with a certain area; *the U.S. Department of Agriculture*
◊ **department store** *noun* large store with sections for different types of goods
◊ **departmental** *adjective* referring to a department; **departmental manager** = manager of a department

departure *noun* (a) going away; *the plane's departure was delayed by two* hours; **departure lounge** = room in an airport where passengers wait to get on their planes (b) new venture or a new type of business; *selling records will be a departure for the local bookstore*

depend *verb* (a) **to depend on** = to need someone or something to exist; *the company depends on efficient service from its suppliers; we depend on government grants to pay our salaries* (b) to happen because of something; *the success of the launch will depend on the publicity;* **depending on** = which varies according to something; *depending on the advertising budget, the new product will be launched on radio or on TV*

deposit 1 *noun* (a) money placed in a bank for safekeeping or to earn interest; **certificate of deposit** = fixed-income debt security issued by chartered banks for terms of normally one to six years; **bank deposits** = all the money placed in banks; *bank deposits are at an all-time high;* **deposit slip** = piece of paper stamped by the cashier to prove that you have paid money into your account (b) **safe deposit** = bank safe where you can leave jewelry or documents; **safe deposit box** = small box which you can rent, in which you can keep jewelry or documents in a bank's safe (c) money given in advance so that the thing which you want to buy will not be sold to someone else; *to pay a deposit on a watch; to leave $10 as deposit* **2** *verb* (a) to put documents somewhere for safekeeping; *to deposit shares with a bank; we have deposited the deeds of the house with the bank; he deposited his will with his lawyer* (b) to put money into a bank account; *to deposit $100 in a savings account*
◊ **depositary** *noun* person or company with whom money or documents can be deposited
◊ **depositor** *noun* person who deposits money in a bank
◊ **depository** *noun* person or company with whom money or documents can be deposited; warehousing facility where personal property (such as furniture) can be stored

depot *noun* central warehouse for goods; center for transport; *bus depot; freight depot; oil storage depot*

depreciate *verb* (a) to reduce the value of assets in books of account; *we*

depreciate our company cars over three years (b) to lose value; *share which has depreciated by 10% over the year; the pound has depreciated by 5% against the dollar*

◊ **depreciation** *noun* **(a)** reduction in value of an asset; **depreciation rate =** rate at which an asset is depreciated each year in the books of account; **accelerated depreciation =** system of depreciation which reduces the value of assets at a high rate in the early years to encourage companies, as a result of tax advantages, to invest in new equipment; **annual depreciation =** reduction in the book value of an asset at a certain rate per year; **straight line depreciation =** depreciation calculated by dividing the cost of an asset by the number of years it is likely to be used **(b)** loss of value; *this stock has shown a depreciation of 10% over the year; the depreciation of the pound against the dollar*

depress *verb* to reduce; *reducing the money supply has the effect of depressing demand for consumer goods*

◊ **depressed** *adjective* **depressed area =** part of a country suffering from depression; **depressed market =** market where there are more goods than customers

◊ **depression** *noun* period of economic crisis with high unemployment and loss of trade; *an economic depression;* **the Great Depression =** the world economic crisis of 1929-1933

dept = DEPARTMENT

deputy *noun* person who acts for *or* in place of another; *to act as deputy for someone or* **to act as someone's deputy;** *deputy chairman; deputy manager*

◊ **deputize** *verb* to empower someone to act for another

deregulate *verb* to reduce the level of government control over an industry; *banks were deregulated under the previous Administration*

◊ **deregulation** *noun* reducing government control over an industry; *the deregulation of the airlines*

describe *verb* to say what someone *or* something is like; *the leaflet describes the services the company can offer; the CEO described the company's difficulties with cash flow*

◊ **description** *noun* words which show what something is like; **job description =** official document which says what a job involves; **trade description =** description of a product to attract customers

design 1 *noun* planning *or* drawing of a product before it is built or manufactured; **industrial design =** design of products made by machines (such as cars and refrigerators); **product design =** design of consumer products; **design department =** department in a large company which designs the company's products or its advertising; **design studio =** independent firm which specializes in creating designs **2** *verb* to plan *or* to draw something before it is built or manufactured; *he designed a new car factory; she designs garden furniture*

◊ **designer** *noun* person who designs; *she is the designer of the new computer*

designate *adjective* person who has been appointed to a job but who has not yet started work; *the chairman designate*
NOTE: always follows a noun

desk *noun* **(a)** writing table in an office, usually with drawers for stationery; *desk calendar; desk drawer; desk light;* a three-drawer **desk =** desk with three drawers; **desk pad =** pad of paper kept on a desk for writing notes **(b)** place in a store where you pay for goods bought; *please pay at the desk* **(c)** department of a newspaper office; **the city desk =** the department which deals with local news

◊ **desktop publishing** *noun* use of a small computer and printer to produce newsletters, brochures, etc.

despatch = DISPATCH

destination *noun* place to which something is sent *or* to which something is going; *the ship will take ten weeks to reach its destination;* **final destination** *or* **ultimate destination =** place reached at the end of a journey after stopping at several places en route

detail 1 *noun* small part of a description; *the catalog gives all the details of our product range; we are worried by some of the details in the contract;* **in detail =** giving many particulars; *the catalog* lists all the products in detail 2 *verb* to list in detail; **the catalog details the payment arrangements for overseas buyers; the terms of the license are detailed in the contract**

◇ **detailed** *adjective* in detail; **detailed account** = account which lists every item

determine *verb* to fix *or* to arrange *or* to decide; **to determine prices** *or* **quantities; conditions are still to be determined**

Deutschmark *noun* unit of money used in Germany
NOTE: also called a **mark;** when used with a figure, usually written **DM** before the figure: **DM250** (say "two hundred and fifty Deutschmarks")

devalue *verb* to reduce the value of a currency against other currencies; **the peso has been devalued by 7%; the government has devalued the franc by 7%**

◇ **devaluation** *noun* reduction in value of a currency against other currencies; **the devaluation of the lira**

develop *verb* **(a)** to plan and produce; **to develop a new product (b)** to plan and build an area; **to develop an industrial estate**

◇ **developer** *noun* **property developer** = person who plans and builds a group of new houses *or* new factories *or* shopping facilities on a piece of land

◇ **developing country** *or* **developing nation** *noun* country which is not fully industrialized

◇ **development** *noun* **(a)** planning the production of a new product; **research and development (b)** planning to use a piece of land in a profitable way; **development property** = piece of land which is suitable for commercial development; **housing development** = group of houses built and sold or rented by one company; **industrial development** = planning and building of new industries in special areas

device *noun* small useful machine; **he invented a device for screwing tops on bottles**

diagram *noun* drawing which shows something as a plan or a map; **diagram showing sales locations; he drew a diagram to show how the decision-making processes work; the paper** gives a diagram of the company's organizational structure

◇ **diagrammatic** *adjective* **in diagrammatic form** = in the form of a diagram; **the chart showed the sales pattern in diagrammatic form**

◇ **diagrammatically** *adverb* using a diagram; **the chart shows the sales pattern diagrammatically**

dial *verb* to call a telephone number on a telephone; **to dial a number; to dial the operator; to dial direct** = to contact a phone number without asking the operator to do it for you; **you can dial London direct from New York; dial tone** = noise made by a telephone to show that it is ready for you to dial a number

◇ **dialing** *noun* act of calling a telephone number; **international direct dialing** = calling telephone numbers in other countries direct without the operator's assistance

Dictaphone *noun* trademark for a brand ⌐f dicting machine

dictate *verb* to say something to someone who then writes down your words; **to dictate a letter to a secretary; he was dictating instructions into his pocket dictating machine; dictating machine** = machine which records what someone dictates, which a secretary can play back in order to type the text

◇ **dictation** *noun* act of dictating; **to take dictation** = to write down what someone is saying; **the secretary was taking dictation from the vice-president; dictation speed** = number of words per minute which a secretary can write down in shorthand

differ *verb* not to be the same as something else; **the two products differ considerably - one has an electric motor, the other runs on oil**

◇ **difference** *noun* way in which two things are not the same; **what is the difference between these two products? differences in price** *or* **price differences**

◇ **different** *adjective* not the same; **our product range is quite different in design from that of our rivals; we offer ten models each in six different colors**

◇ **differential 1** *adjective* which shows a difference; **differential tariffs** = different tariffs for different classes of goods **2** *noun* **price differential** = difference in price between products in a range; **wage differentials** = differences in salary between workers in similar types of jobs; **to erode wage differentials** = to reduce differences in salary gradually

difficult *adjective* not easy; *the company found it difficult to sell into the European market; she had the difficult choice of leaving the company or staying with a lower salary*
◊ **difficulty** *noun* problem *or* thing which is not easy; *they had a lot of difficulty selling into the European market; we have had some difficulties with customs over the export of computers*

digit *noun* single number; *a seven-digit phone number*
◊ **digital** *adjective* **digital clock** = clock which shows the time as a series of figures (such as 12:05:23); **digital computer** = computer which calculates on the basis of integers

dilution *noun* **dilution of equity** *or* **of stockholding** = situation where the ordinary share capital of a company has been increased but without an increase in the assets, so that each share is worth less than before

dime *noun* ten-cent coin; **dime store** = store selling cheap goods

diminish *verb* to become smaller; *our share of the market has diminished over the last few years;* **law of diminishing returns** = general rule that as more factors of production (land, labor and capital) are added to the existing factors, so the amount they produce is proportionally smaller

dip 1 *noun* sudden small fall; *last year saw a dip in the company's performance* **2** *verb* to fall in price; *shares dipped sharply in yesterday's trading*
NOTE: **dipping - dipped**

diplomat *noun* person (such as an ambassador) who is the official representative of his country in another country
◊ **diplomatic** *adjective* referring to diplomats; **diplomatic immunity** = being outside the control of the laws of the country you are in because of being a

diplomat; *he claimed diplomatic immunity to avoid being arrested;* **to grant someone diplomatic status** = to give someone the rights of a diplomat

direct 1 *verb* **(a)** to manage *or* to organize; *he directs our Southeast Asian operations; she was directing the development unit until last year* **(b)** to pass on; *may I direct your call to another department?* **2** *adjective* straight *or* with no interference; **direct cost** = production cost of a product; **direct marketing** = marketing a product or service direct to potential customers; **direct selling** = selling a product direct to the customer without going through a store; **direct taxation** = tax, such as income tax, which is paid direct to the government; *the government raises more money by direct taxation than by indirect* **3** *adverb* straight *or* with no third party involved; *we pay income tax direct to the government;* **to dial direct** = to call a phone number yourself without the operator's assistance; *you can dial London direct from New York if you want*
◊ **direction** *noun* **(a)** organizing *or* managing; *he took over the direction of a multinational group* **(b)** **directions for use** = instructions showing how to use something
◊ **directly** *adverb* **(a)** straight *or* with no third party involved; *we deal directly with the manufacturer, without using a wholesaler* **(b)** immediately; *he left for the airport directly after receiving the telephone message*
◊ **direct mail** *noun* selling a product by sending publicity material to possible buyers through the mail; *these calculators are only sold by direct mail; the company runs a successful direct-mail operation;* **direct-mail advertising** = advertising by sending leaflets to people through the mail
◊ **director** *noun* **(a)** member of a company's board of directors; **board of directors** = group of people elected by the shareholders to draw up company policy and to appoint the president and other executive officers responsible for managing the company; **associate director** = director who attends board meetings but has not been elected by the shareholders; **inside directors** = directors who are executive officers of a company; **outside directors** = directors who are not executive officers of the company, but are appointed because of their experience and contacts as board

members of other companies **(b)** person who is in charge of a project, an official institute, etc.; *the director of the government research institute; she was appointed director of the organization*

◊ **directorate** *noun* group of directors

◊ **directorship** *noun* post of director; *he was offered a directorship with Smith Inc.*

> QUOTE what benefits does the executive derive from his directorship? In the first place compensation has increased sharply in recent years
> *Duns Business Month*

directory *noun* list of people *or* businesses with information about their addresses and telephone numbers; **classified directory =** list of businesses grouped under various headings, such as computer stores *or* restaurants; **commercial directory** *or* **trade directory =** book which lists all the businesses and business people in a city; **street directory =** part of a city map which lists all the streets in alphabetical order in an index; **telephone directory =** book which lists all people and businesses in alphabetical order with their phone numbers; *to look up a number in the telephone directory; his number is in the Toronto directory*

disallow *verb* not to accept a claim for insurance; *he claimed $2,000 for fire damage, but the claim was disallowed*

disaster *noun* **(a)** very bad accident; *ten people died in the air disaster* **(b)** financial collapse; **the company is heading for disaster** *or* **is on a disaster course =** the company is going to collapse; **the advertising campaign was a disaster =** the advertising campaign was very bad *or* did not have the required effect **(c)** accident in nature; *a storm disaster on the Florida coast*

◊ **disastrous** *adjective* very bad; *the company suffered a disastrous drop in sales*

disburse *verb* to pay money

◊ **disbursement** *noun* payment of money

discharge 1 *noun* **(a) discharge of bankruptcy =** being released from bankruptcy after paying one's debts **(b)** payment of debt; **in full discharge of a debt =** paying a debt completely; **final discharge =** final payment of what is

left of a debt **(c) in discharge of his duties as director =** carrying out his duties as director **2** *verb* **(a) to discharge a bankrupt =** to release someone from bankruptcy because he has paid his debts **(b) to discharge a debt** *or* **to discharge one's liabilities =** to pay a debt *or* one's liabilities in full **(c)** to dismiss *or* to fire; *to discharge an employee*

disciplinary *adjective* referring to discipline; **disciplinary procedure =** way of warning a worker officially that he is breaking rules *or* that he is working incorrectly

disclaimer *noun* legal refusal to accept responsibility

disclose *verb* to reveal *or* to make known; *the bank has no right to disclose details of my account to my employer*

◊ **disclosure** *noun* act of telling details; *the disclosure of the takeover bid raised the price of the shares*

discontinue *verb* to stop stocking *or* selling *or* making (a product); *these carpets are a discontinued line*

discount 1 *noun* **(a)** percentage by which a full price is reduced to a buyer by the seller; *to give a discount on bulk purchases;* to sell goods at a discount *or* at a discount price = to sell goods below the normal price; **basic discount =** normal discount without extra percentages; *we give 25% as a basic discount, but can add 5% for cash payment;* **deep discount =** discount offered by a manufacturer to a wholesaler, which may be higher than a wholesaler's discount to a retailer; **quantity discount =** discount given to people who buy large quantities; **10% discount for quantity purchases =** you pay 10% less if you buy a large quantity; **10% discount for cash** *or* **10% cash discount =** you pay 10% less if you pay in cash; **trade discount =** discount offered to all customers of a certain class, such as wholesalers and retailers **(b) discount house =** (i) financial company which specializes in discounting bills; (ii) store which specializes in selling cheap goods bought at a high discount; **discount rate =** percentage taken when a bank buys bills; **discount store =** store which specializes in cheap goods bought at a high discount **(c) shares which stand at a discount =**

shares which are lower in price than their face value **2** *verb* to reduce prices; **to discount bills of exchange =** to sell bills of exchange for less than the value written on them; **discounted cash flow =** calculating the forecast return on capital investment in current terms, including reductions for current interest rates; **discounted value =** difference between the face value of a share and its lower market price

◊ **discountable** *adjective* which can be discounted; *these bills are not discountable*

◊ **discounter** *noun* person *or* company which discounts bills or sells goods at a discount

QUOTE a 100,000 square-foot warehouse generates ten times the volume of a discount retailer; it can turn its inventory over 18 times a year, more than triple a big discounter's turnover
Duns Business Month

discover *verb* to find something new; *we discovered that our agent was selling our rival's products at the same price as ours; the auditors discovered some errors in the books of account*

discrepancy *noun* situation where totals do not add up correctly in accounts; **there is a discrepancy in the accounts =** there is an error; **statistical discrepancy =** amount by which sets of figures differ

discretion *noun* good judgment *or* prudence; **I leave it to your discretion =** I leave it for you to decide what to do; **at the discretion of someone =** if someone decides; *membership is at the discretion of the committee*

◊ **discretionary** *adjective* which can be done if someone wants; **discretionary account =** special account where the client allows a broker to act on his behalf without asking for permission for his actions; **discretionary income =** personal income left after payment of taxes and the purchase of essential items such as food, rent, heating, etc.; **the president's discretionary powers =** powers which the president could use if he thought he should do so

discrimination *noun* treating people in different ways because of class, religion, race, language, color or sex; **sexual discrimination** *or* **sex discrimination** *or* **discrimination on grounds of sex =** treating men and women in different ways

discuss *verb* to talk about a problem; *they spent two hours discussing the details of the contract; the committee discussed the question of import duties on automobiles; the board will discuss wage increases at its next meeting; we discussed delivery schedules with our suppliers*

◊ **discussion** *noun* talking about a problem; *after ten minutes' discussion the board agreed on the salary increases; we spent the whole day in discussions with our suppliers*

disenfranchise *verb* to take away someone's right to vote; *the company has tried to disenfranchise the ordinary shareholders*

dishonor *verb* **to dishonor a bill =** not to pay a bill; **dishonored check =** check which the bank will not pay because there is not enough money in the account to pay it

disk *noun* round flat object, used to store information in computers; **floppy disk =** small disk for storing information through a computer; **hard disk =** solid disk which will store a large amount of computer information in a sealed case, usually fixed inside a computer; **disk drive =** part of a computer which makes a disk spin around in order to read it or store information on it

◊ **diskette** *noun* very small floppy disk

dismiss *verb* **to dismiss an employee =** to remove an employee from a job; *he was dismissed for being late*

◊ **dismissal** *noun* removal of an employee from a job; **constructive dismissal =** situation where an employee leaves his job voluntarily, but because of pressure from the management; **unfair dismissal =** removing someone from a job for reasons which are not fair; **wrongful dismissal =** removing someone from a job for reasons which are wrong; **dismissal procedures =** correct way of dismissing someone according to company policy

dispatch 1 *noun* **(a)** sending of goods to a customer; *the strike held up dispatch for several weeks* **(b)** goods which have been sent; *the weekly dispatch went off yesterday* **2** *verb* to send goods *or* messages

◊ **dispatcher** *noun* **(a)** person who sends goods or messages **(b)** person responsible for the route schedules of cab drivers, bus drivers, etc.

dispenser *noun* machine which automatically provides something (an object *or* a drink *or* some food), often when money is put in; *automatic dispenser; towel dispenser*

display 1 *noun* showing of goods for sale; *the showroom has several car models on display; an attractive display of kitchen equipment;* **window display** = the display of goods in the window of a store; **display advertisement** = advertisement which is well designed to attract attention; **display bin** = container formed of a large box with an open top, in which goods are placed for sale; **display cabinet** *or* **display case** = piece of furniture with a glass top or glass doors for showing goods for sale; **display card** = card which advertises a product or service and is placed where potential clients can easily see it; **display material** = posters, photographs, etc., to be used to attract attention to goods which are for sale; **display pack** *or* **display box** = special box for showing goods for sale; *the watches are prepacked in plastic display boxes;* **display stand** *or* **display unit** = special stand for showing goods for sale; **visual display unit** *or* **visual display terminal** = screen attached to a computer which shows the information as it is typed in **2** *verb* to show; *the company was displaying three new car models at the show*

dispose *verb* **to dispose of** = to get rid of *or* to sell cheaply; *to dispose of excess stock; to dispose of one's business*

◊ **disposable** *adjective* **(a)** which can be used and then thrown away; *disposable cups* **(b) disposable income** = personal income left after tax and other payments to government have been deducted

dispute *noun* **industrial disputes** *or* **labor disputes** = arguments between management and workers; **to adjudicate** *or* **to mediate in a dispute** = to try to settle a dispute between other parties

dissolve *verb* to bring to an end; *to dissolve a partnership or a company*

◊ **dissolution** *noun* ending (of a partnership)

distress merchandise *noun* goods sold cheaply to pay a company's debts

distribute *verb* **(a)** to share out dividends; *profits were distributed among the shareholders* **(b)** to send out goods from a manufacturer's warehouse to retail stores; *Smith Co. distributes for several smaller companies*

◊ **distribution** *noun* **(a)** act of sending goods from the manufacturer to the wholesaler and then to retailers; *distribution costs; distribution manager;* **channels of distribution** *or* **distribution channels** = ways of sending goods from the manufacturer to the retailer; **distribution network** = series of points *or* small warehouses from which goods are sent all over a country **(b) distribution slip** = paper attached to a document *or* a magazine showing all the people in an office who should read it

◊ **distributor** *noun* company which sells goods for other companies which make them; **sole distributor** = retailer who is the only one in an area who is allowed by the manufacturer to sell a certain product; **a network of distributors** = a series of distributors spread all over a country

◊ **distributorship** *noun* position of being a distributor for a company

district *noun* section of a country *or* of a city; *district manager;* **the commercial district** *or* **the business district** = part of a city where offices and stores are located

diversification *noun* adding another, quite different type of business to a firm's existing trade; **product diversification** *or* **diversification into new products** = adding new types of products to the range already made

◊ **diversify** *verb* **(a)** to add new types of business to existing ones; *to diversify into new products* **(b)** to invest in different types of shares or savings so as to spread the risk of loss

divest *verb* **to divest oneself of something** = to get rid of something; *the company had divested itself of its French interests*

◊ **divestiture** *noun* action of selling an asset, especially a subsidiary company

divide *verb* to cut into separate sections; *the country is divided into six representative's areas; the two companies agreed to divide the market between them*

dividend *noun* percentage of profits paid to shareholders; **to raise** *or* **to increase the dividend =** to pay out a higher dividend than in the previous year; **to maintain the dividend =** to keep the same dividend as in the previous year; **to pass the dividend =** to pay no dividend; **final dividend =** dividend paid at the end of a year; **interim dividend =** dividend paid at the end of a half-year; **stock dividend =** dividend paid in the form of new stock; **dividend cover =** the ratio of profits to dividend; **dividend warrant =** check which makes payment of a dividend; **dividend yield =** dividend expressed as a percentage of the price of a share; **cum dividend =** share sold with the dividend still to be paid; **ex dividend =** share sold after the dividend has been paid; **the stock is quoted ex dividend =** the price does not include the right to the dividend

division *noun* (**a**) major section of a large company; *marketing division; production division; retail division; the paints division of Dupont; the hotel division of Marriott; he is in charge of one of the major divisions of the company* (**b**) company which is part of a large group; *Smith's is now a division of the Brown group of companies*
◊ **divisional** *adjective* referring to a division; *a divisional director; the divisional headquarters*

DM = DEUTSCHMARK *or* MARK

dock 1 *noun* harbor *or* place where ships can load or unload; *loading dock; a dock worker; the dock manager;* **the docks =** part of a town where the harbor is; **dock dues =** fees paid by a ship going into or out of a dock **2** *verb* (**a**) to go into dock; *the ship docked at 10:00* (**b**) to deduct money from someone's wages; *we will have to dock his pay if he is late for work again; he had $20 docked from his pay for being late*
◊ **dockyard** *noun* place where ships are built

doctor *noun* specialist who examines people when they are sick to see how they can be made well; *the employees*

are all sent to see the company doctor once a year; **company doctor =** doctor who works for a company and looks after sick workers

document *noun* paper with writing on it that is relied upon as record or proof; *legal document*
◊ **documentary** *adjective* in the form of documents; *documentary evidence; documentary proof*
◊ **documentation** *noun* all documents referring to something; *please send me the complete documentation concerning the sale*

do-it-yourself *adjective* done by an ordinary person, not by a skilled worker; **do-it-yourself magazine =** magazine with articles on work which the average person can do to repair or paint his house

dole *noun* money given by the government to unemployed people; *he is on the dole =* he is receiving unemployment benefits

dollar *noun* (**a**) money used in the U.S. and other countries; *the U.S. dollar rose 2%; fifty Canadian dollars; it costs six Australian dollars;* **five-dollar bill =** piece of paper money representing five dollars (**b**) the currency used in the U.S.A.; **dollar crisis =** fall in the exchange rate for the U.S. dollar; **dollar gap** *or* **dollar shortage =** situation where the supply of dollars is not enough to satisfy the demand for them from overseas buyers
NOTE: usually written $ before a figure: **$250.** The currencies used in different countries can be shown by the initial letter of the country: **C$** (Canadian dollar) **A$** (Australian dollar), etc.

domestic *adjective* referring to the home market *or* the market of the country where the business is situated; **domestic consumption =** consumption on the home market; *domestic consumption of oil has fallen sharply;* **domestic market =** market in the country where a company is based; *they produce goods for the domestic market;* **domestic production =** production of goods for domestic consumption

domicile 1 *noun* place where someone lives *or* where a company's office is registered **2** *verb* **he is domiciled in Denmark =** he lives in Denmark officially

door *noun* piece of wood *or* metal, etc. which closes the entrance to a building *or* room; *the finance director knocked on the chairman's door and walked in; the sales manager's name is on his door; the store opened its doors on June 1 =* the store started in business on June 1

◊ **door-to-door** *adjective* going from one house to the next, asking the occupants to buy something or to vote for someone; *door-to-door canvassing; door-to-door salesman; door-to-door selling*

dot *noun* small round spot; *three dots indicate that part of the report has been omitted*

◊ **dot-matrix printer** *noun* printer which makes letters by printing many small dots

◊ **dotted line** *noun* line made of a series of dots; *please sign on the dotted line; do not write anything below the dotted line*

double 1 *adjective* **(a)** twice as large *or* two times the size; *their sales volume is double ours; to be on double time =* to earn twice the usual wages for working on Sundays or other holidays; **double-entry bookkeeping** = system of bookkeeping where both credit and debit sides of an account are noted; **double taxation** = taxing the same income twice (as when corporate earnings are taxed and then a shareholder pays money on the same money paid to him in the form of dividend); **double taxation agreement** = agreement between two countries that a person living in one country shall not be taxed in both countries on the income earned in the other country **(b) in double figures** = with two figures, from 10 through 99; *inflation is in double figures; we have had double-figure inflation for some years* **2** *verb* to become twice as big; *to make something twice as big; we have doubled our profits this year or our profits have doubled this year*

◊ **double-book** *verb* to reserve the same hotel room *or* plane seat, etc., to more than one person at a time; *we had to change our flight as we were double-booked*

◊ **double-booking** *noun* reservation made by a travel agent for the same hotel room *or* the same plane seat to more than one person at a time

Dow Jones Industrial Average *noun* index of share prices on the New York Stock Exchange, based on a group of major companies; *the Dow Jones Average rose ten points; general optimism showed in the rise on the Dow Jones Average*

down *adverb & preposition* in a lower position *or* to a lower position; *the inflation rate is gradually coming down; utilities are slightly down; the price of gasoline has gone down; to pay money down =* to make a deposit; *he paid $50 down and the rest in monthly installments*

◊ **downgrade** *verb* to reduce the importance of someone *or* of a job; *his job was downgraded in the company reorganization*

◊ **down market** *adverb & adjective* cheaper *or* appealing to a less wealthy section of the population; *the company has adopted a down-market image; the company has decided to go down market =* the company has decided to make products which appeal to a wider section of the public

◊ **down payment** *noun* part of a total payment made in advance; *he made a down payment of $100*

◊ **downside** *noun* **downside factor** = possibility of making a loss (in an investment); *the sales force has been asked to give downside forecasts =* they have been asked for pessimistic forecasts

◊ **downtime** *noun* time when a machine is not working because it is broken *or* being fixed, etc.; time when a worker cannot work because machines have broken down, because components are not available, etc.

◊ **downtown** *noun & adverb* the central business district of a city; *his office is in downtown Baltimore; a downtown store; they established a business downtown*

◊ **downturn** *noun* movement towards lower prices *or* sales *or* profits; *a downturn in the market price; the last quarter saw a downturn in the economy*

◊ **downward 1** *adjective* toward a lower position **2** *adverb (also downwards)* toward a lower position; *the company's profits have moved downward over the last few years*

dozen *noun* twelve; *to sell in sets of one dozen; cheaper by the dozen =* the product is cheaper if you buy twelve at a time

draft 1 *noun* **(a)** order for money to be paid by a bank; *bank draft ;* **to make a draft on a bank =** to ask a bank to pay money for you; **sight draft =** bill of exchange which is payable when it is presented **(b)** first rough plan *or* document which has not been finished; *draft of a contract or* **draft contract;** *he drew up the draft agreement on the back of an envelope; the first draft of the contract was corrected by the executive vice-president; the finance department has passed the final draft of the financial statement;* **rough draft =** plan of a document which may have changes made to it before it is complete **2** *verb* to make a first rough plan of a document; *to draft a letter; to draft a contract; the contract is still being drafted or is still in the drafting stage*

◊ **drafter** *noun* person who makes a draft; *the drafter of the agreement*

◊ **drafting** *noun* act of preparing the draft of a document; *the drafting of the contract took six weeks*

drain 1 *noun* **(a)** pipe for taking dirty water from a house **(b)** gradual loss of money flowing away; *the costs of the New York office are a continual drain on our resources* **2** *verb* to remove something gradually; *the expansion plan has drained all our profits; the company's capital resources have drained away*

draw *verb* **(a)** to take money away; *to draw money out of an account;* to draw **a salary =** to have a salary paid by the company; *the chairman does not draw a salary* **(b)** to write a check; *he paid the invoice with a check drawn on an Egyptian bank*
NOTE: **drawing - drew - has drawn**

◊ **drawback** *noun* **(a)** thing which is not convenient *or* likely to cause problems; *one of the main drawbacks of the scheme is that it will take six years to complete* **(b)** paying back customs duty when imported goods are then reexported

◊ **drawee** *noun* person or bank asked to make a payment by a drawer

◊ **drawer** *noun* person who writes a check *or* a bill asking a drawee to pay money to a payee; *the bank returned the check to drawer =* the bank would not pay the check because the person who wrote it did not have enough money in the account to pay it

◊ **drawing** *noun* **drawing account =** account on which salesmen or other employees can draw to pay expenses

◊ **draw up** *verb* to write a legal document; *to draw up a contract or an agreement; to draw up a company's articles of incorporation*

drift *verb* to move slowly; *shares drifted lower in a dull market; strikers are drifting back to work*

drive 1 *noun* **(a)** energy *or* energetic way of working; **economy drive =** vigorous effort to save money or materials; **sales drive =** vigorous effort to increase sales; *he has a lot of drive =* he is very energetic **(b)** part of a machine which moves other parts; **disk drive =** part of a computer which makes the disk spin around in order to store information on it **2** *verb* **(a)** to make a car *or* truck, etc. go in a certain direction; *he was driving to work when he heard the news on the car radio; she drives a leased car* **(b)** he drives a hard bargain = he is a difficult negotiator
NOTE: **driving - drove - has driven**

◊ **drive-in** *noun* business where customers drive their cars into the business premises and stay in their cars to do business; **drive-in bank =** bank where the customer drives his car up to a teller window

drop 1 *noun* **(a)** fall; *drop in sales; sales show a drop of 10%; a drop in prices* **(b)** **drop shipment =** delivery of an order from the manufacturer direct to a retailer's store or warehouse without going through an agent or wholesaler **2** *verb* to fall; *sales have dropped by 10% or have dropped 10%; the pound dropped three points against the dollar*
NOTE: **dropping - dropped**

◊ **drop ship** *verb* to deliver an order direct to a retailer or another customer

dry *adjective* not wet; **dry goods =** cloth, clothes and household goods; **dry measure =** way of calculating loose dry produce (such as corn)

DTP = DESKTOP PUBLISHING

duck *see* LAME DUCK

dud *adjective & noun informal* not good (coin or bank bill); *the $50 note was a dud;* **dud check =** check which the bank refuses to pay because the person writing it has not enough money in his account to pay it

due *adjective* **(a)** owed; *sum due from a debtor; bond due for repayment;* **to fall due** *or* **to become due** = to be ready for payment; **bill due on May 1** = bill which has to be paid on May 1; **balance due to us** = amount owed to us which should be paid; **due date** = date when an amount must be paid; *you must pay this amount by due date* **(b)** expected to arrive; *the plane is due to arrive at 10:30 or is due at 10:30* **(c)** in due form = written in the correct legal form; *receipt in due form; contract drawn up in due form;* **after due consideration of the problem** = after thinking seriously about the problem **(d)** caused by; *supplies have been delayed due to a strike at the manufacturers; the company pays the wages of employees who are absent due to illness*

◊ **dues** *plural noun* fee paid at regular intervals to retain membership in a union or other organization

dull *adjective* not interesting *or* not exciting; **dull market** = market where little business is done

◊ **dullness** *noun* being dull; *the dullness of the market*

duly *adverb* **(a)** properly; *duly authorized representative* **(b)** as was expected; *we duly received his letter of October 21*

dump *verb* **to dump goods on a market** = to get rid of large quantities of excess goods cheaply in an overseas market

◊ **dump bin** = DISPLAY BIN

◊ **dumping** *noun* act of getting rid of excess goods cheaply in an overseas market; *the government has passed anti-dumping legislation; dumping of goods on the European market;* **panic dumping of sterling** = rush to sell sterling at any price because of possible devaluation

duplicate 1 *noun* copy; *he sent me the duplicate of the contract;* **duplicate receipt** *or* **duplicate of a receipt** = copy of a receipt; **in duplicate** = with a copy; **receipt in duplicate** = two copies of a receipt; *to print an invoice in duplicate* **2** *verb* **to duplicate a letter** = to make a copy of a letter

◊ **duplicating** *noun* copying; **duplicating machine** = machine which makes copies of documents; **duplicating paper** = special paper to be used in a duplicating machine

◊ **duplication** *noun* copying of documents; **duplication of work** = work which is done twice without being necessary

◊ **duplicator** *noun* machine which makes copies of documents

durable 1 *adjective* **durable goods** = goods which will be used for some years (such as washing machines or refrigerators); **durable effects** = effects which will be felt for a long time; *the strike will have durable effects on the economy* **2** *noun* **consumer durables** = goods bought by the public which will be used for some years (such as washing machines or refrigerators)

Dutch *adjective* **Dutch auction** = auction where the auctioneer offers an item for sale at a high price and then gradually reduces the price until someone makes a bid; **to go Dutch** = to pay each his share in a restaurant

dutiable *adjective* **dutiable goods** *or* **dutiable items** = goods on which a customs duty has to be paid

◊ **duty** *noun* import or export tax on goods; *to take the duty off alcohol; to put a duty on cigarettes;* **ad valorem duty** = tax calculated on the basis of the value of the goods; **customs duty** *or* **import duty** = tax on goods imported into a country; **goods which are liable to duty** = goods on which customs or excise tax has to be paid; **duty-paid goods** = goods where the duty has been paid

◊ **duty-free** *adjective & adverb* sold with no duty to be paid; *he bought a duty-free watch at the airport or he bought the watch duty-free;* **duty-free store** = store at an airport *or* on a ship where goods can be bought without paying duty

QUOTE Canadian and European negotiators agreed to a deal under which Canada could lower its import duties on $150 million worth of European goods

Globe and Mail (Toronto)

Ee

EA = EXPENSE ACCOUNT

eager *adjective* wanting to do something; *the management is eager to get into the Far Eastern markets; our salesmen are eager to see the new product range*

early *adjective & adverb* (a) before a certain time; *the mail arrived early;* **at your earliest convenience** = as soon as possible; **at an early date** = very soon; **early retirement** = leaving a job before the usual retirement age (b) at the beginning of a period of time; *he took an early flight to Chicago;* **we hope for an early resumption of negotiations** = we hope negotiations will start again soon

earmark *verb* to reserve for a special purpose; *to earmark funds for a project; the money is earmarked for computer systems development*

earn *verb* (a) to be paid money for working; *to earn $50 a week; our agent in Paris certainly does not earn his commission;* **earned income** = for tax purposes, income from wages or salary (b) to produce interest *or* dividends; *what level of dividend do these shares earn? account which earns interest at 10%*

◊ **earning** *noun* **earning capacity** *or* **earning power** = amount of money someone is able to earn; *he is such a fine dress designer that his earning power is very large;* **earning potential** = (i) amount of money a person should be able to earn; (ii) amount of dividend a share should produce

◊ **earnings** *plural noun* (a) salary *or* wages received by a person; **compensation for loss of earnings** = payment to someone who has stopped earning money *or* who is not able to earn money (b) profits of a corporation; **earnings before tax** = profits before taxes are paid; **earnings per share** *or* **earnings yield** *or* **earnings-price ratio** = money earned in dividends per share, shown as a percentage of the market price of one share; **gross earnings** = earnings before tax and other deductions; **price/earnings ratio (P/E)** = the market price of a unit of stock divided by the current profit it produces; *these shares sell at a P/E of 7;* **retained earnings** = profits which are not paid out to shareholders as dividend (c) **invisible earnings** = foreign currency earned by a country in providing services (such as banking, tourism), not in selling goods

QUOTE if corporate forecasts are met, sales will exceed $50 million in 1985 and net earnings could exceed $7 million
Citizen (Ottawa)
QUOTE the US now accounts for more than half of our world-wide sales. It has made a huge contribution to our earnings turnaround
Duns Business Month
QUOTE last fiscal year the chain reported a 116% jump in earnings, to $6.4 million or $1.10 a share
Barrons

earnest *noun* money paid as a down payment

ease *verb* to fall a little; *the share index eased slightly today*

easement *noun* right which someone has to use land belonging to someone else (such as for a path to a garage)

easy *adjective* not difficult; **easy terms** = terms which are not difficult to accept *or* price which is not difficult to pay; *the store is leased on very easy terms; the loan is repayable in easy payments* = with very small sums paid back regularly; **easy money** = (i) money which can be earned with no difficulty; (ii) money available on easy repayment terms; **easy money policy** = government policy of expanding the economy by making money more easily available

◊ **easily** *adverb* (a) without any difficulty; *we passed through customs easily* (b) much *or* a lot (compared to something else); *he is easily our best salesman; the firm is easily the biggest in the market*

EC = EUROPEAN COMMUNITY *EC ministers met today in Brussels; the US is increasing its trade with the EC*

echelon *noun* group of people of a certain grade in an organization; *the upper echelons of industry*

econometrics *plural noun* study of the statistics of economics, using computers
NOTE: takes a singular verb

economic *adjective* (a) which provides enough money; *the apartment is let at an economic rent; it is hardly economic for the company to run its own warehousing facility* (b) referring to the financial state of a country; *economic planner; economic planning; the government's economic policy; the economic situation; the country's economic system; economic trends; economic crisis or economic depression* = state where a country is in financial collapse; *the government has introduced import controls to solve the current economic crisis; economic cycle* = period during which trade expands, then slows down, then expands again; **economic development** = expansion of the commercial and financial situation; *the economic development of the region has totally changed since oil was discovered there;* economic growth = increase in the national income; *the country enjoyed a period of economic growth in the 1960s;* economic indicators = statistics which show how the economy is going to perform in the short or long term; **economic sanctions** = restrictions on trade with a country in order to make its government change policy; *the western nations imposed economic sanctions on the country;* the European Economic Community = the Common Market

◇ **economical** *adjective* which saves money or materials *or* which is cheap; **economical car** = car which does not use much gasoline; **economical use of resources** = using resources as carefully as possible

◇ **economics** *plural noun* (a) study of production, distribution, selling and use of goods and services (b) study of financial structures to show how a product or service is costed and what returns it produces; *the economics of town planning; I do not understand the economics of the coal industry*
NOTE: takes a singular verb

◇ **economist** *noun* person who specializes in the study of economics; **agricultural economist**

◇ **economize** *verb* **to economize on gasoline** = to save gasoline

◇ **economy** *noun* (a) being careful not to waste money or materials; **an economy measure** = an action to save money or materials; **to introduce economies** *or* **economy measures into the system** = to start using methods to save money or materials; **economy of scale** = making a product at a lower unit cost by manufacturing it or buying it in larger quantities; **economy car** = car which does not use much gasoline; **economy class** = cheapest class on a plane; *to travel economy class;* **economy drive** = campaign to save money or materials; **economy size** = large size *or* large packet which is a bargain (b) financial state of a country *or* way in which a country makes and uses its money; *the country's economy is in ruins;* **black market economy** = work which is paid for in cash or goods, but not declared to the tax authorities; **capitalist economy** = system where each person has the right to invest money, to work in business, to buy and sell with no restrictions from the state; **controlled economy** = system where business activity is controlled by orders from the government; **free market economy** = system where the government does not interfere in business activity in any way; **mixed economy** = system which contains both private enterprise and some government control of business; **planned economy** = system where the government plans all business activity

QUOTE the European economies are being held back by rigid labor markets and wage structures, huge expenditures on social welfare programs and restrictions on the free movement of goods within the Common Market
Duns Business Month

edge 1 *noun* (a) side of a flat surface; *he sat on the edge of the president's desk; the printer has printed the figures right to the edge of the printout* (b) advantage; **to have the edge on a rival company** = to be slightly more profitable *or* to have a slightly larger share of the market than a rival; *having a local office gives us a competitive edge over Smith Co.* 2 *verb* to move a little; *prices on the stock market edged upward today; sales figures edged downward in January*

QUOTE the leading index edged down slightly for the week ended May 13, its first drop in six weeks
Business Week
QUOTE the evidence suggests that U.S. companies have not lost their competitive edge over the last 20 years
Harvard Business Review

editor *noun* person in charge of a newspaper or a section of a newspaper;

the editor of the "Post" ; the city **editor** = editor in charge of local news and reporters' assignments

◊ **editorial 1** *adjective* referring to an editor; **editorial board** = group of editors (on a newspaper, etc.) **2** *noun* main article in a newspaper, written by the editor

EDP = ELECTRONIC DATA PROCESSING

EEC = EUROPEAN ECONOMIC COMMUNITY

effect 1 *noun* **(a)** result; *the effect of the pay increase was to raise productivity levels;* **terms of a contract which take effect** *or* **come into effect from January 1** = terms which start to operate on January 1; **prices are increased 10% with effect from January 1** = new prices will apply from January 1; **to remain in effect** = to continue to be applied **(b)** meaning; **clause to the effect that** = clause which means that; **we have made provision to this effect** = we have put into the contract terms which will make this work **(c)** *personal effects* = personal belongings **2** *verb* to carry out; **to effect a payment** = to make a payment; **to effect customs clearance** = to clear something through customs; **to effect a settlement between two parties** = to bring two parties together and make them agree to a settlement

◊ **effective** *adjective* **(a)** **effective demand** = actual demand for a product which can be paid for; **effective interest rate** = the actual annual interest rate when buying an item on installment purchase; **effective yield** = actual yield shown as a percentage **(b)** **effective date** = date on which a rule *or* a contract starts to be applied; **clause effective as of January 1** = clause which starts to be applied on January 1 **(c)** which works *or* which produces results; *advertising in the Sunday papers is the most effective way of selling;* see COST-EFFECTIVE

◊ **effectiveness** *noun* working *or* producing results; *I doubt the effectiveness of television advertising;* see COST-EFFECTIVENESS

◊ **effectual** *adjective* which produces a correct result

efficiency *noun* ability to work well *or* to produce the right result or the right work quickly; *with a high degree of*

efficiency; *a business efficiency exhibition; an efficiency expert*

◊ **efficient** *adjective* able to work well *or* to produce the right result quickly; *the efficient working of a system; he needs an efficient secretary to look after him; efficient machine*

◊ **efficiently** *adverb* in an efficient way; *she organized the sales conference very efficiently*

QUOTE increased control means improved efficiency in purchasing, shipping, sales and delivery
Duns Business Month

efflux *noun* flowing out; *efflux of European capital to North America*

effort *noun* using the mind or body to do something; *the salesmen made great efforts to increase sales; thanks to the efforts of the finance department, the overhead has been reduced; if we make one more effort, we should clear the backlog of orders*

EFT = ELECTRONIC FUNDS TRANSFER

e.g. for example *or* such as; *the contract is valid in some countries (e.g., France and Belgium) but not in others*

EI = EMPLOYEE INVOLVEMENT

800 numbers toll-free numbers, telephone numbers beginning with the digits 800, by which calls can be made free of charge (the supplier pays for them, not the caller)

elastic *adjective* which can expand or contract easily because of small changes in price

◊ **elasticity** *noun* ability to change easily; **elasticity of supply and demand** = changes in supply and demand of an item depending on its market price

elect *verb* **(a)** to choose someone by a vote; *to elect the officers of an association; she was elected president* **(b)** to choose to do something

◊ **-elect** *suffix* person who has been elected but has not yet started the term of office; *she is the president-elect*
NOTE: the plural is **presidents-elect**

◊ **election** *noun* act of electing; *the election of officers of an association; the election of board members by the shareholders*

electricity *noun* force used to make light *or* heat *or* power; *the electricity was cut off this morning, so the computers could not work; our electricity bill has increased considerably this quarter; electricity costs are an important factor in our overhead*

◊ **electric** *adjective* operated by electricity; *an electric typewriter*

◊ **electrical** *adjective* referring to electricity; *the engineers are trying to repair an electrical fault*

electronic *adjective* **electronic data processing (EDP)** = selecting and examining data stored in a computer to produce information; **electronic engineer** = engineer who specializes in electronic machines; **electronic funds transfer (EFT)** = movement of funds from one account to another, using a computer terminal such as an automated teller machine; **electronic mail** = system of sending messages from one computer terminal to another, via telephone lines

◊ **electronics** *plural noun* applying the scientific study of electrons to produce manufactured products, such as computers, calculators or telephones; *the electronics industry; an electronics specialist or expert; electronics engineer*
NOTE: takes a singular verb

element *noun* basic part; *the elements of a settlement*

elevator *noun* machine which takes people or goods from one floor to another in a building; *take the elevator to the 26th floor of the building*

eligible *adjective* person who can be chosen; *she is eligible for reelection*

◊ **eligibility** *noun* being eligible; *the chairman questioned her eligibility to stand for reelection*

eliminate *verb* to remove; *to eliminate defects in the system; using a computer should eliminate all possibility of error*

embargo **1** *noun* government order which stops a type of trade; **to lay** *or* **put an embargo on trade with a country** = to say that trade with a country must not take place; *the government has put an embargo on the export of computer equipment;* **to lift an embargo** = to

allow trade to start again; *the government has lifted the embargo on the export of computers;* **to be under an embargo** = to be forbidden (NOTE: plural is **embargoes**) **2** *verb* to stop trade *or* not to allow trade; *the government has embargoed trade with the Eastern countries*

QUOTE the Commerce Department is planning to loosen export controls for products that have been embargoed but are readily available elsewhere in the West
Duns Business Month

embark *verb* (a) to go on a ship; *the passengers embarked at Boston* (b) **to embark on** = to start; *the company has embarked on an expansion program*

◊ **embarkation** *noun* going on to a ship or plane; **port of embarkation** = port at which you get on to a ship; **embarkation card** = card given to passengers getting on to a plane or ship

embezzle *verb* to use illegally money which is not yours, but which you are custodian of for someone; *he was sent to prison for six months for embezzling his clients' money*

◊ **embezzlement** *noun* act of embezzling; *he was sent to prison for six months for embezzlement*

◊ **embezzler** *noun* person who embezzles

emergency *noun* dangerous situation where decisions have to be made quickly; **the government declared a state of emergency** = the government decided that the situation was so dangerous that the police or army had to intervene; **to take emergency measures** = to take action rapidly to stop a crisis from developing; *the company had to take emergency measures to stop losing money;* **emergency reserves** = ready cash held in case it is needed suddenly

emolument *noun* pay, salary or fee for a service

employ *verb* to give someone regular paid work; **to employ twenty workers** = to have twenty people working for you; **to employ twenty new workers** = to hire twenty new people

◊ **employed** **1** *adjective* (a) in regular paid work; *he is not gainfully employed* = he has no regular paid work; **self-employed** = working for yourself; *he worked in a bank for ten* *years but now is self-employed* **(b)** (money) used profitably; *return against capital employed* **2** *plural noun* people who are working; *the employers and the employed;* the self-employed = people who work for themselves

◊ **employee** *noun* worker *or* person employed by a company; *employees of the firm are eligible to join a profit-sharing plan; relations between management and employees have improved; the company has decided to hire new employees;* **employee involvement (EI)** = program to encourage participation of workers in management decisions; **employee stock purchase plan** *or* **employee stock ownership plan (ESOP)** = system whereby employees can purchase stock in the company for which they work, at a lower price than the current market price

◊ **employer** *noun* person *or* company which has regular workers and pays them; **employer's contribution** = money paid by an employer towards a worker's pension or insurance; **employer identification number** = number given to each employer, used for social security contributions, etc.

◊ **employment** *noun* regular paid work; **full employment** = situation where everyone in a country who can work has a job; **full-time employment** = work for all of a working day; *to be in full-time employment;* **part-time employment** = work for part of a working day; **temporary employment** = work which is not permanent; **to be without employment** = to have no work; **to find someone alternative employment** = to find another job for someone; **conditions of employment** = terms of a contract where someone is employed; **contract of employment** *or* **employment contract** = contract between management and an employee showing all the conditions of work; **employment security** = feeling by a worker that he has the right to keep his job until he retires; **employment office** *or* **agency** = office which finds jobs for people; **employment tax** = tax paid by an employer on the salaries of people employed by him

emporium *noun* large store
NOTE: plural is **emporia**

empower *verb* to give someone the power to do something; *she was empowered by the company to sign the contract*

empty 1 *adjective* with nothing inside; *the envelope is empty; you can take that filing cabinet back to the storeroom as it is empty; start the computer file with an empty workspace* **2** *verb* to take the contents out of something; *she emptied the filing cabinet and put the files in boxes; he emptied the petty cash box into his briefcase*

◊ **empties** *plural noun* empty bottles *or* cases; **returned empties** = empty bottles which are taken back to a store to get back a deposit paid on them

EMS = EUROPEAN MONETARY SYSTEM

enc *or* **encl** = ENCLOSURE note put on a letter to show that a document is enclosed with it

enclose *verb* to put something inside an envelope with a letter; *to enclose an invoice with a letter; I am enclosing a copy of the contract; letter enclosing a check; please find the check enclosed*

◊ **enclosure** *noun* document (leaflet, subscription form, xerox, etc.) enclosed with a letter; *letter with enclosures*

encourage *verb* **(a)** to make it easier for something to happen; *the general rise in wages encourages consumer spending; leaving your credit cards on your desk encourages people to steal* *or* *encourages stealing; the company is trying to encourage sales by giving large discounts* **(b)** to help someone to do something by giving advice; *he encouraged me to apply for the job*

◊ **encouragement** *noun* giving advice to someone to help him to succeed; *the designers produced a very marketable product, thanks to the encouragement of the sales manager*

end 1 *noun* final point *or* last part; *at the end of the contract period;* **at the end of six months** = after six months have passed; **end product** = manufactured product, made at the end of a production process; *after six months' trial production, the end product is still not acceptable;* **in the end** = at last *or* after a lot of problems; *in the end the company had to pull out of the US market; in the end they signed the contract at the airport; in the end the company had to send for the police;* **on end** = for a long time *or* with no breaks; *the discussions continued for hours on end; the production department* *worked at top speed for weeks on end to finish the order on time;* to come to an end = to finish; *our distribution agreement comes to an end next month* **2** *verb* to finish; *the distribution agreement ends in July; the chairman ended the discussion by getting up and walking out of the meeting*

◊ **end up** *verb* to finish; *we ended up with a bill for $10,000*

endorse *verb* **to endorse a bill** *or* **a check =** to sign a bill *or* a check on the back to show that you accept it

◊ **endorsee** *noun* person whose name is written on a bill *or* a check as having the right to cash it

◊ **endorsement** *noun* **(a)** act of endorsing; signature on a document which endorses it (as on the back of a check) **(b)** note on an insurance policy which adds conditions to the policy

◊ **endorser** *noun* person who endorses a bill which is then paid to him

endowment *noun* giving money to provide a regular income; **endowment insurance** *or* **endowment policy =** insurance policy where a sum of money is paid to the insured person on a certain date, or to his heirs if he dies earlier

energy *noun* **(a)** force *or* strength; *he hasn't the energy to be a good salesman; they wasted their energies on trying to sell cars in the German market* **(b)** power from electricity *or* gas, etc.; *we try to save energy by switching off the lights when the rooms are empty; if you reduce the room temperature to sixty-five degrees, you will save energy*

◊ **energetic** *adjective* with a lot of energy; *the salesmen have made energetic attempts to sell the product*

◊ **energy-saving** *adjective* which saves energy; *the company is introducing energy-saving measures*

enforce *verb* to make sure something is done *or* is obeyed; *to enforce the terms of a contract*

◊ **enforcement** *noun* making sure that something is obeyed; *enforcement of the terms of a contract*

engage *verb* **(a)** to employ; *we have engaged the best commercial lawyer to represent us; the company has engaged twenty new salesmen* **(b)** to be engaged in = to be busy with; *he is engaged in work on computers; the company is engaged in trade with Africa*

engine *noun* machine which drives something; *a car with a small engine is more economic than a car with a large one; the elevator engine has broken down again - we shall just have to walk up to the fourth floor*

◊ **engineer** *noun* person who looks after technical equipment; **civil engineer =** person who specializes in the construction of roads, bridges, railways, etc.; **consulting engineer =** engineer who gives specialist advice; **product engineer =** engineer in charge of the equipment for making a product; **project engineer =** engineer in charge of a project

◊ **engineering** *noun* science of technical equipment; **civil engineering =** construction of roads, bridges, railways, etc.; **the engineering department =** section of a company dealing with equipment; **an engineering consultant =** an engineer who gives specialist advice

enquire = INQUIRE

◊ **enquiry** = INQUIRY

en route *adverb* on the way; *the tanker sank when she was en route to the Gulf*

entail 1 *noun* legal condition which passes ownership of a property only to certain persons **2** *verb* to involve; *itemizing the sales figures will entail about ten days' work*

enter *verb* **(a)** to go in; *they all stood up when the chairman entered the room; the company has spent millions trying to enter the do-it-yourself market* **(b)** to write; *to enter a name on a list; the clerk entered the interest in my bank book; to enter an item in a ledger;* **to enter a bid for something =** to offer (usually in writing) to buy something **(c)** **to enter into =** to begin; *to enter into relations with someone; to enter into negotiations with a foreign government; to enter into a partnership with a legal friend; to enter into an agreement* or *a contract*

◊ **entering** *noun* act of writing items in a record

enterprise *noun* **(a)** system of carrying on a business; **free enterprise =** system of business free from government interference; **private enterprise** = businesses which are owned privately, not by the government; *the project is completely funded by private enterprise* (b) a business; **a small-scale enterprise** = a small business; **a state enterprise** = a state-controlled company; *bosses of state enterprises are appointed by the government*

entertain *verb* (a) to offer meals *or* hotel accommodation *or* theater tickets, etc. to (business) visitors (b) to be ready to consider (a proposal); *the management will not entertain any suggestions from the union representatives*

◊ **entertainment** *noun* offering meals, etc. to business visitors; **entertainment allowance** = money which a manager is allowed by his company to spend on meals with visitors; **entertainment expenses** = money spent on meals for business visitors

entitle *verb* to give the right to something; **he is entitled to a discount** = he has the right to be given a discount

entrance *noun* way in *or* going in; *the taxi will drop you at the main entrance; deliveries should be made to the Maple Road entrance;* **entrance (charge)** = money which you have to pay to go in; *entrance is $1.50 for adults and $1 for children*

entrepot *noun* **entrepot port** = town with a large international commercial port dealing in reexports

entrepreneur *noun* person who starts a company and takes commercial risks

◊ **entrepreneurial** *adjective* taking commercial risks; *an entrepreneurial decision*

entrust *verb* **to entrust someone with something** *or* **to entrust something to someone** = to give someone the responsibility for looking after something; *he was entrusted with the keys to the office safe*

entry *noun* (a) written information put in an account ledger; **credit entry** *or* **debit entry** = entry on the credit *or* debit side of an account; **single-entry bookkeeping** = noting a deal with only one entry; **double-entry bookkeeping** = noting of both debit and credit sides of an account; **to make an entry in a**

ledger = to write in details of a deal; **contra entry** = entry made in the opposite side of an account to make an earlier entry worthless (such as a debit entry against a credit) (b) act of going in; place where you can go in; **to pass a customs entry point; entry of goods under bond; entry charge** = money which you have to pay before you go in; **entry-level position** = position with low pay for someone starting his career; **entry visa** = visa allowing someone to go into a country; **multiple entry visa** = entry visa which allows someone to enter a country as often as he likes

envelope *noun* flat paper cover for sending letters; **airmail envelope** = very light envelope for airmail letters; **window envelope** = envelope with a hole covered with film so that the address on the letter inside can be seen; **sealed** *or* **unsealed envelope** = envelope where the flap has been stuck down to close it *or* envelope where the flap has been pushed into the back of the envelope; *to send the information in a sealed envelope;* **a stamped addressed envelope** = an envelope with your own address written on it and a stamp stuck on it to pay for return postage; *please send a stamped addressed envelope for further details and our latest catalog;* **envelope stuffer** = advertising paper put into an envelope for mailing

EOE = EQUAL OPPORTUNITY EMPLOYER

equal 1 *adjective* exactly the same; *male and female workers have equal pay;* **equal opportunity program** = program to avoid discrimination in employment **2** *verb* to be the same as; *production this month has equaled our best month ever*

◊ **equalize** *verb* to make equal; *to equalize dividends*

◊ **equalization** *noun* the process of making equal

◊ **equally** *adverb* in the same way; *costs will be shared equally between the two parties; they were both equally responsible for the disastrous launch*

equip *verb* to provide with machinery; *to equip a factory with new machinery; the office is fully equipped with word processors*

◊ **equipment** *noun* machinery and furniture required to make a factory or office work; *office equipment or*

business equipment; office equipment supplier; office equipment catalog; capital equipment = equipment which a factory *or* office uses to work; **heavy equipment** = large machines, such as for making cars or for printing

equity *noun* **(a)** right to receive dividends as part of the profit of a company in which you own shares **(b) shareholders' equity** *or* **equity capital** = amount of a company's capital which is owned by its shareholders **(c)** value of a property beyond any debt

◊ **equities** *plural noun* common stocks

equivalence *noun* being equivalent

◊ **equivalent** *adjective* **to be equivalent to** = to have the same value as *or* to be the same as; *the total dividend paid is equivalent to one quarter of the pretax profits*

ergonomics *plural noun* study of people at work and their working conditions
NOTE: takes a singular verb

◊ **ergonomist** *noun* scientist who studies people at work and tries to improve their working conditions

erode *verb* to wear away gradually; **to erode wage differentials** = to reduce gradually differences in salary between similar types of job

error *noun* mistake; *he made an error in calculating the total; the secretary must have made a typing error;* **clerical error** = mistake made in an office; **computer error** = mistake made by a computer; **margin of error** = number of mistakes which are accepted in a document *or* in a calculation; **errors and omissions** = disclaimer written on an invoice to show that the company has no responsibility for mistakes in the invoice; **error rate** = number of mistakes per thousand entries *or* per page; **in error** *or* **by error** = by mistake; *the letter was sent to the Chicago office in error*

escalate *verb* to increase steadily

◊ **escalation** *noun* **escalation of prices** = steady increase in prices; **escalation clause** = ESCALATOR CLAUSE

◊ **escalator clause** *noun* clause in a contract allowing for regular price increases because of increased costs

escape *noun* getting away from a difficult situation; **escape clause** = clause in a contract which allows either party to avoid carrying out the terms of the contract under certain conditions

escrow *noun* **in escrow** = held in safe keeping by a third party; **document held in escrow** = document given to a third party to keep and to pass on to someone when money has been paid; **escrow account** = account where money is held in escrow until a contract is signed *or* until goods are delivered, etc.

ESOP = EMPLOYEE STOCK OWNERSHIP PLAN

espionage *noun* **industrial espionage** = trying to find out the secrets of a competitor's work or products, usually by illegal means

essential *adjective* very important; *it is essential that an agreement be reached before the end of the month; the factory is lacking essential spare parts*

◊ **essentials** *plural noun* goods *or* products which are very important

establish *verb* to set up *or* to make *or* to open; *the company has established a branch in Australia; the business was established in Pennsylvania in 1823; it is a young company - it has been established for only four years;* **to establish oneself in business** = to become successful in a new business

◊ **establishment** *noun* commercial business; *he runs an important printing establishment*

estate *noun* **(a) real estate** = property (land or buildings) **(b) industrial estate** = area of land near a town for factories and warehouses **(c)** property left by a dead person; **estate tax** = federal tax on property left by a dead person

estimate **1** *noun* **(a)** calculation of probable cost *or* size *or* time of something; **rough estimate** = approximate calculation; **at a conservative estimate** = calculation which probably underestimates the final figure; *their sales volume has risen by at least 20% in the last year, and that is a conservative estimate;* **these figures are only an estimate** = these are not the final accurate figures; *can you give me an estimate of how much time was* *spent on the job?* **(b)** calculation of how much something is likely to cost in the future, given to a client so as to get him to make an order; *estimate of costs* or *of expenditure; before we can give the grant we must have an estimate of the total costs involved; to ask a builder for an estimate for building the warehouse; to put in an estimate =* to give someone a written calculation of the probable costs of carrying out a job; *three firms put in estimates for the job* **2** *verb* **(a)** to calculate the probable cost or size or time of something; *to estimate that it will cost $1m* or *to estimate costs at $1m; we estimate current sales at only 60% of last year* **(b) to estimate for a job =** to state in writing the future costs of carrying out a piece of work so that a client can make an order; *three firms estimated for the remodeling of the offices*

◊ **estimated** *adjective* calculated approximately; *estimated sales; estimated figure*

◊ **estimation** *noun* approximate calculation

◊ **estimator** *noun* person whose job is to calculate estimates for carrying out work

etc. and so on; *the import duty is to be paid on luxury items including cars, watches, etc.*

Euro- *prefix* referring to Europe or the European Community

◊ **Eurobond** *noun* bond issued by an international corporation or government outside its country of origin and sold to Europeans who pay in Eurodollars; *the Eurobond market*

◊ **Eurocurrency** *noun* European currencies used for trade within Europe but outside their countries of origin; *a Eurocurrency loan; the Eurocurrency market*

◊ **Eurodollar** *noun* dollar in a European bank, used for trade within Europe; *a Eurodollar loan; the Eurodollar market*

◊ **Europe** *noun* group of countries to the West of Asia and the North of Africa; *most of the countries of Western Europe are members of the Common Market; Canadian exports to Europe have risen by 25%*

◊ **European** *adjective* referring to Europe; **the European Economic Community =** the Common Market; **the European Monetary System =** system of controlled exchange rates between some member countries of the Common Market

evade *verb* to try to avoid something; **to evade tax =** to try illegally to avoid paying tax

evaluate *verb* to calculate a value; *to evaluate costs*

◊ **evaluation** *noun* calculation of value; **performance evaluation =** examination of how well an employee is doing his job

evasion *noun* avoidance; **tax evasion =** illegally trying not to pay tax

evidence *noun* written or spoken report at a trial; **documentary evidence =** evidence in the form of documents; **the secretary gave evidence for** or **against her former employer =** the secretary was a witness, and her report suggested that her former employer was or was not guilty

ex- *preposition* **(a)** out of or exclusive of; **price ex warehouse =** price for a product which is to be collected from the manufacturer's or agent's warehouse and so does not include delivery; **price ex works** or **ex factory =** price not including transport from the maker's factory **(b) ex coupon =** bond without the interest coupon; **share quoted ex dividend =** share price not including the right to receive the next dividend; *the shares went ex dividend yesterday* **(c)** formerly; *Mr. Smith, the ex-chairman of the company*

exact *adjective* precise; *the exact time is 10:27; the salesgirl asked me if I had the exact amount, since the store had no change*

◊ **exactly** *adverb* precisely; *the total cost was exactly $6,502*

examine *verb* to look at someone or something very carefully to see if it can be accepted; *the customs officials asked to examine the inside of the car; the police are examining the papers from the vice-president's safe*

◊ **examination** *noun* **(a)** looking at something very carefully to see if it is acceptable; **customs examination =** looking at goods or baggage by customs officials **(b)** test to see if someone has passed a course; *he passed his accounting examinations; she came first in the final examination for the* course; *he failed his proficiency examination and so had to leave his job*

example *noun* something chosen to show; *the auto show has many examples of energy-saving cars on display;* **for example** = to show one thing out of many; *the government wants to encourage exports, and, for example, it gives free credit to exporters*

exceed *verb* to be more than; *discount not exceeding 15%; last year costs exceeded 20% of income for the first time;* **he has exceeded his credit limit** = he has borrowed more money than he is allowed

excellent *adjective* very good; *the quality of the firm's products is excellent, but its sales force is not large enough*

except *preposition & conjunction* not including; *sales tax is charged on all goods and services except groceries; sales are rising in all markets except the Far East*

◊ **excepted** *adverb* not included; *past employees are excepted from the new insurance plan*

◊ **exceptional** *adjective* not usual *or* different; **exceptional items** = items in a balance sheet which do not appear there each year

excess *noun* amount which is more than what is allowed; *an excess of expenditure over revenue;* **excess baggage** = extra payment at an airport for taking baggage which is heavier than the normal passenger's allowance; **excess capacity** = spare capacity which is not being used; **in excess of** = above *or* more than; *quantities in excess of twenty-five pounds;* **excess profits** = profit which is more than what is thought to be normal; **excess profits tax** = tax on excess profits

◊ **excessive** *adjective* too large; **excessive costs**

QUOTE most airlines give business class the same baggage allowance as first class, which can save large sums in excess baggage
Business Traveler
QUOTE control of materials provides manufacturers with an opportunity to reduce the amount of money tied up in excess materials
Duns Business Month

exchange 1 *noun* (a) giving of one thing for another; **part exchange** = giving an old product as part of the payment for a new one; *to take a car in part exchange;* **exchange of contracts** = point in the sale of property when the buyer and the seller both sign the contract of sale which then becomes binding (b) **foreign exchange** = (i) exchanging the money of one country for that of another; (ii) money of another country; *the company has more than $1m in foreign exchange;* **foreign exchange broker** = person who buys and sells foreign currency on behalf of other people; **foreign exchange market** = dealings in foreign currencies; *he trades on the foreign exchange market; foreign exchange markets were very active after the dollar devalued;* **rate of exchange** *or* **exchange rate** = price at which one currency is exchanged for another; *the current rate of exchange is 1.75 yen to the dollar;* **exchange control** = control by a government of the way in which its currency may be exchanged for foreign currencies; *the government had to impose exchange controls to stop the rush to buy dollars;* **exchange dealer** = person who buys and sells foreign currency; **exchange dealings** = buying and selling foreign currency; **exchange premium** = extra cost above the normal rate for buying a foreign currency (c) **Stock Exchange** = place where securities and bonds are bought and sold; *the company's shares are traded on the New York Stock Exchange; he works on the Stock Exchange;* **commodity exchange** = place where commodities are bought and sold **2** *verb* (a) to exchange one article for another = to give one thing in place of something else; *he exchanged his motorcycle for a car; if the gloves are too small you can take them back and exchange them for a larger pair; goods can be exchanged only on production of the sales slip* (b) **to exchange contracts** = to sign a contract when buying a property (done by both buyer and seller at the same time) (c) to change money of one country for money of another; *to exchange yen for dollars*

◊ **exchangeable** *adjective* which can be exchanged

◊ **exchanger** *noun* person who buys and sells foreign currency

QUOTE under the barter agreements, Nigeria will export crude oil in exchange for trucks, food, planes and chemicals

Wall Street Journal

QUOTE can free trade be reconciled with a strong dollar resulting from floating exchange rates

Duns Business Month

QUOTE a draft report on changes in the international monetary system casts doubt on any return to fixed exchange-rate parities

Wall Street Journal

excise 1 *noun* **excise tax =** tax on certain goods produced in a country *or* certain occupations or privileges; *to pay excise on wine* **2** *verb* to cut out; *please excise all references to the strike in the minutes*

QUOTE excise taxes account for a sizable 45% of liquor prices but only about 10% of wine and beer prices

Business Week

exclude *verb* to keep out *or* not to include; *the interest charges have been excluded from the document; damage by fire is excluded from the policy*

◊ **excluding** *preposition* not including; *all salesmen, excluding those living in New York, can claim expenses for attending the sales conference*

◊ **exclusion** *noun* act of not including; **exclusion clause =** clause in an insurance policy *or* warranty saying which items are not covered

◊ **exclusive** *adjective* **(a) exclusive agreement =** agreement where a person is made sole agent for a product in a market; **exclusive right to market a product =** right to be the only person to market the product **(b) exclusive of =** not including; *all payments are exclusive of tax; the invoice is exclusive of sales tax*

◊ **exclusivity** *noun* exclusive right to market a product

excuse 1 *noun* reason for doing something wrong; *his excuse for not coming to the meeting was that he had been told about it only the day before; the CEO refused to accept the sales manager's excuses for the poor sales =* he refused to believe that there was a good reason for the poor sales **2** *verb* to forgive a small mistake; *she can be excused for not knowing the French word for "photocopier"*

execute *verb* to carry out (an order)

◊ **execution** *noun* carrying out of an order; **stay of execution =** temporary stopping of a legal order; *the court granted the company a two-week stay of execution*

◊ **executive 1** *adjective* which puts decisions into action; **executive committee =** committee which runs an organization; **executive director =** director who is a working officer of an organization; **executive powers =** right to put decisions into actions **2** *noun* manager *or* director *or* person in a business who makes decisions; *sales executive; senior or junior executive; account executive =* employee who is the link between his company and certain customers; **chief executive officer =** executive in charge of a company; **executive assistant** *or* **executive secretary =** secretary to a senior member of an organization

executor *noun* person who sees that the terms of a will are carried out; *he was named executor of his brother's will*

exempt 1 *adjective* not covered by a law; not forced to obey a law; **exempt from tax** *or* **tax-exempt =** not required to pay tax; *as a non-profit organization we are exempt from tax* **2** *verb* to free something from having tax paid on it or from having to pay tax; *non-profit organizations are exempted from tax; food is exempted from sales tax; the government exempted trusts from tax*

◊ **exemption** *noun* act of exempting something from a contract *or* from a tax; **exemption from tax** *or* **tax exemption =** being free from having to pay tax; *as a non-profit organization you can claim tax exemption*

QUOTE it increases to $500,000, from the present $345,000, the annual sales-level threshold at which the law takes effect. Companies with sales under $500,000 a year will be exempt from the minimum-wage requirements

Nation's Business

exercise 1 *noun* use of something; **exercise of an option =** using an option *or* putting an option into action **2** *verb* to use; **to exercise an option =** to put an option into action; *he exercised his option to acquire sole marketing rights for the product; the chairperson exercised her veto to block the motion*

ex gratia *adjective* **an ex gratia payment =** payment made as a gift, with no other obligations

exhibit 92 experience

exhibit 1 *noun* **(a)** thing which is shown; *the buyers admired the exhibits at our booth* **(b)** single section of a trade fair; *the U.S. Trade Exhibit at the International Computer Fair* **2** *verb* **to exhibit at the Auto Show** = to display new models of cars

◊ **exhibition** *noun* showing goods so that buyers can look at them and decide what to buy; *the government has sponsored an exhibition of good design; we have a booth at the Ideal Home Exhibition; the agricultural exhibition grounds;* **exhibition room** *or* **hall** = place where goods are shown so that buyers can look at them and decide what to buy; **exhibition booth** = separate section of an exhibition where a company exhibits its products or services

◊ **exhibitor** *noun* person *or* company which shows products at an exhibition

exist *verb* to be; *I do not believe the document exists - I think it has been shredded*

exit *noun* way out of a building; *the customers all rushed towards the exits;* **fire exit** = door which leads to a way out of a building if there is a fire

ex officio *adjective & adverb* because of an office held; *the treasurer is ex officio a member* *or* *an ex officio member of the finance committee*

expand *verb* to increase *or* to get bigger *or* to make something bigger; *an expanding economy; the company is expanding fast; we have had to expand our sales force*

◊ **expansion** *noun* increase in size; *the expansion of the domestic market; the company had difficulty in financing its current expansion program*

> QUOTE inflation-adjusted GNP moved up at a 1.3% annual rate, its worst performance since the economic expansion began
>
> *Fortune*

expect *verb* to hope that something is going to happen; *we are expecting him to arrive at 10:45; they are expecting a check from their agent next week; the house was sold for more than the expected price*

◊ **expectancy** *noun* **life expectancy** = number of years a person is likely to live

expenditure *noun* amounts of money spent; **below-the-line expenditure** = exceptional payments which are separated from a company's normal expenditures in the annual report; **capital expenditure** = money spent on fixed assets (such as property or machinery); **the company's current expenditure program** = the company's spending according to the current plan; **heavy expenditure on equipment** = spending large sums of money on equipment

◊ **expense** *noun* **(a)** money spent; *it is not worth the expense; the expense is too much for my bank balance;* **at great expense** = having spent a lot of money; *he furnished the office regardless of expense* = without thinking how much it cost **(b)** **expense account** = money which a businessman is allowed by his company to spend on traveling and entertaining clients in connection with his business; *I'll put this lunch on my expense account; expense account lunches form a large part of our current expenditure*

◊ **expenses** *plural noun* money paid for doing something; *the salary offered is $10,000 plus expenses;* **all expenses paid** = with all costs paid by the company; *the company sent him to San Francisco all expenses paid;* **to cut down on expenses** = to try to reduce spending; **allowable expenses** = business expenses which are allowed against tax; **business expenses** = money spent on running a business, not on stock or assets; **entertainment expenses** = money spent on meals for business visitors; **fixed expenses** = operating expenses which do not change in relation to sales *or* production variations; **incidental expenses** = small amounts of money spent at various times, in addition to larger amounts; **legal expenses** = money spent on fees paid to lawyers; **overhead expenses** *or* **general expenses** *or* **running expenses** = money spent on the day-to-day cost of a business; **traveling expenses** = money spent on traveling and hotels for business purposes

◊ **expensive** *adjective* which costs a lot of money; *first-class air travel is becoming more and more expensive*

experience 1 *noun* having lived through various situations and therefore knowing how to make decisions; *he is a man of considerable experience; she has a lot of experience in dealing with German companies; he gained most of his experience in the Far East; some experience is required for this job* **2**

verb to live through a situation; *the company experienced a period of falling sales*

◊ **experienced** *adjective* person who has lived through many situations and has learned from them; *he is the most experienced negotiator I know; we have appointed a very experienced woman as sales director*

expert *noun* person who knows a lot about something; *an expert in the field of electronics or an electronics expert; the company asked a financial expert for advice or asked for expert financial advice*

◊ **expertise** *noun* specialist knowledge; *we hired Mr. Smith because of his financial expertise or because of his expertise in the African market*

expiration *noun* coming to an end; *expiration of an insurance policy; to repay before the expiration of the stated period; on expiration of the lease* = when the lease comes to an end

◊ **expire** *verb* to come to an end; *the lease expires in 1998; his passport has expired* = his passport is no longer valid

◊ **expiry** *noun* coming to an end; *expiry of an insurance policy; expiry date* = date when something will end

explain *verb* to give reasons for something; *he explained to the customs officials that the two computers were presents from friends; can you explain why the sales in the first quarter are so high? the sales manager tried to explain the sudden drop in unit sales*

◊ **explanation** *noun* reason for something; *the auditor asked for an explanation of the invoices; at the stockholders' meeting, the chairman gave an explanation for the high level of interest payments*

exploit *verb* to use something to make a profit; *the company is exploiting its contacts in the State Department; we hope to exploit the oil resources in the China Sea*

explore *verb* to examine carefully; *we are exploring the possibility of opening an office in Los Angeles*

export 1 *noun* **(a) exports** = goods sent to a foreign country to be sold; *exports to Africa have increased by 25%* **(b)**

action of sending goods to a foreign country to be sold; *the export trade or the export market;* **export department** = section of a company which deals in sales to foreign countries; **export duty** = tax paid on goods sent out of a country for sale; **export house** = company which specializes in the export of goods made by other manufacturers; **export license** = government permit allowing something to be exported; *the government has refused an export license for computer parts;* **export manager** = person in charge of an export department in a company (NOTE: usually used in the plural, but the singular form is used before a noun) **2** *verb* to send goods to foreign countries for sale; *50% of our production is exported; the company imports raw materials and exports the finished products*

◊ **exportation** *noun* act of sending goods to foreign countries for sale

◊ **exporter** *noun* person *or* company *or* country which sells goods in foreign countries; *a major furniture exporter; Canada is an important exporter of oil or an important oil exporter*

◊ **exporting** *adjective* which exports; **oil exporting countries** = countries which produce oil and sell it to other countries

exposition *noun* fair where goods are shown so that buyers can look at them and decide what to buy; *the agricultural exposition grounds*

exposure *noun* **(a)** amount of risk which a lender runs; *he is trying to cover his exposure in the property market* **(b)** advertising; *the company is getting a great deal of exposure in the media*

express 1 *adjective* **(a)** rapid *or* very fast; *express letter; express delivery;* **express mail service** = very fast mail service offered by the USPS **(b)** clearly shown in words; *the contract has an express condition forbidding sales in Africa* **2** *verb* **(a)** to put into words or diagrams; *this chart shows home sales expressed as a percentage of total sales volume* **(b)** to send very fast; *we expressed the order to the customer's warehouse*

◊ **expressly** *adverb* clearly in words; *the contract expressly forbids sales to the United States*

ext = EXTENSION

extend *verb* **(a)** to make available *or* to give; *to extend credit to a customer* **(b)** to make longer; *to extend a contract for two years*

◊ **extended credit** *noun* credit allowing the borrower a very long time to pay; *we sell to Australia on extended credit*

◊ **extension** *noun* **(a)** allowing longer time; *to get an extension of credit* = to get more time to pay back; **extension of a contract** = continuing the contract for a further period **(b)** *(in an office)* individual telephone linked to the main switchboard; *can you get me extension 21? extension 21 is busy; the sales manager is on extension 53*

◊ **extensive** *adjective* very large *or* covering a wide area; *an extensive network of sales outlets*

QUOTE the White House refusal to ask for an extension of the auto import quotas
Duns Business Month

external *adjective* **(a)** outside a country; **external trade** = trade with foreign countries **(b)** outside a company; **external audit** = audit carried out by an independent auditor

extra 1 *adjective* which is added *or* which is more than usual; *there is no extra charge for heating; to charge 10% extra for postage; he had $25 extra pay for working on Sunday; service is extra* **2** *plural noun* **extras** = items which are not included in a price; *packing and postage are extras*

extract *noun* printed document which is part of a larger document; *he sent me an extract of the accounts*

extraordinary *adjective* different from normal; **extraordinary items** = items in an annual report which do not appear each year and need to be noted; *the auditors noted several extraordinary items in the report*

extremely *adverb* very much; *it is extremely difficult to break into the European market; their management team is extremely efficient*

Ff

face value *noun* value written on a coin *or* bill *or* stock certificate; *travelers checks cost 1% of their face value - some banks charge more for small amounts*

facility *noun* **(a)** being able to do something easily; *he has a facility for negotiating* **(b)** total amount of credit which a lender will allow a borrower; **credit facilities** = arrangement with a bank *or* supplier *or* lender to have credit *or* to borrow funds; **overdraft facility** = arrangement with a bank to have an overdraft paid through a line of credit associated with the person's account **(c)** **facilities** = equipment *or* buildings which make it easy to do something; *storage facilities; harbor facilities; recreational facilities; there are no facilities for passengers; there are no facilities for unloading or there are no unloading facilities* **(d)** single large building; *we have opened our new warehouse facility in Texas*

QUOTE What is new is that American-owned multinationals are beginning to rely on foreign facilities to do many of their most technologically complex activities and are beginning to export from their foreign facilities - including bringing products back to the United States
Harvard Business Review

facsimile *noun* exact copy; *he presented a facsimile of the letter as evidence ; see also* FAX

fact *noun* something which is true and real; *the chairman asked to see all the facts on the tax claim; the sales manager can give you the facts and figures about the African operation ; the fact of the matter is* = what is true is that; *the fact of the matter is that the product does not fit the market;* **in fact** = really; *the chairman blamed the finance staff for the loss when in fact he was responsible for it himself*

◊ **fact-finding** *adjective* looking for information; *a fact-finding mission* = visit, usually by a group of people, to search for information about a problem; *the senator went on a fact-finding tour of the region*

factor 1 *noun* **(a)** thing which is important *or* which influences; *the drop in sales is an important factor in the company's lower profits;* **cost factor =** cost as a variable in factor analysis; **cyclical factors =** way in which a trade cycle affects businesses; **deciding factor =** most important factor which influences a decision; **load factor =** figure which represents a firm's manufacturing capacity; **factors of production =** resources needed to produce a product (land, labor and capital) **(b) by a factor of ten =** ten times **(c)** person or company which is responsible for collecting debts for companies, by buying debts at a discount on their face value **2** *verb* to buy debts from a company at a discount

◊ **factoring** *noun* business of buying debts at a discount; **factoring charges =** cost of selling debts to a factor for a commission

factory *noun* building where products are manufactured; *car factory; shoe factory;* **factory hand** *or* **factory worker =** person who works in a factory; **factory cost =** manufacturing cost, not including transportation or distribution; **factory price** *or* **price ex factory =** price not including transport from the maker's factory; **factory unit =** single building on an industrial estate

fail *verb* **(a)** not to do something which you were trying to do; *the company failed to notify the IRS of its change of address; the prototype failed its first test* **(b)** to be unsuccessful commercially; **the company failed =** the company went bankrupt; *he lost all his savings when the bank failed*

◊ **failing 1** *noun* weakness; *the chairman has one failing - he goes to sleep at board meetings* **2** *preposition* if something does not happen; **failing prompt payment =** if the payment is not made on time; **failing that =** if that does not work; *try the vice-president, or, failing that, the chairman*

◊ **failure** *noun* **(a)** breakdown *or* stop; *the failure of the negotiations* **(b) failure to pay a bill =** not having paid the bill **(c) commercial failure =** financial collapse *or* bankruptcy; *he lost all his money in the bank failure*

fair 1 *noun* **trade fair =** large exhibition and meeting for advertising and selling a certain type of product; *to organize or to run a trade fair; the fair is open from 9 a.m. to 5 p.m.; the computer fair runs from April 1 to 6; there are two trade fairs running in Chicago at the same time - the carpet manufacturers' and the computer dealers'* **2** *adjective* **(a)** honest *or* correct; **fair deal =** arrangement where both parties are treated equally; *the workers feel they did not get a fair deal from the management;* **fair dealing =** legal buying and selling of shares; **fair price =** good price for both buyer and seller; **fair trade =** (i) international business system where countries agree not to charge import duties on certain items imported from their trading partners; (ii) = RESALE PRICE MAINTENANCE; **fair trading** *or* **fair dealing =** way of doing business which is reasonable and does not harm the consumer **(b) fair copy =** document which is written or typed with no changes or mistakes

◊ **fairly** *adverb* quite; *the company is fairly close to financial collapse; she is a fairly fast keyboarder*

faith *noun* **to have faith in something** *or* **someone =** to believe that something *or* a person is good or will work well; *the salesmen have great faith in the product; the sales teams do not have much faith in their manager; the board has faith in the CEO's judgment;* **to buy something in good faith =** to buy something thinking that it is of good quality *or* that it has not been stolen *or* that it is not an imitation

fake 1 *noun* imitation *or* copy made for criminal purposes; *the shipment came with fake documentation* **2** *verb* to make an imitation for criminal purposes; *faked documents; he faked the results of the test*

fall 1 *noun* sudden drop *or* suddenly becoming smaller *or* loss of value; *a fall in the exchange rate; fall in the price of gold; a fall on the Stock Exchange; profits showed a 10% fall* **2** *verb* **(a)** to drop suddenly to a lower price; *shares* fell on the market today; gold shares fell 10% or fell 45 cents on the New York Stock Exchange; the price of gold fell for the second day running; the pound fell against other European currencies (b) to happen or to take place; the legal holiday falls on a Tuesday; payments which fall due = payments which are now due to be made NOTE: falling - fell - has fallen

◊ **fall back** verb to become lower or cheaper after rising in price; stocks fell back in light trading

◊ **fall back on** verb to have to use money kept for emergencies; to fall back on cash reserves

◊ **fall behind** verb to be late in doing something; he fell behind with his mortgage payments

◊ **falling** adjective which is growing smaller or dropping in price; a falling market = market where prices are coming down; the falling dollar = the dollar which is losing its value against other currencies

◊ **fall off** verb to become lower or cheaper or less; sales have fallen off since the tourist season ended

◊ **fall out** verb the bottom has fallen out of the market = sales have fallen below what previously seemed to be their lowest point

◊ **fall through** verb not to happen or not to take place; the plan fell through at the last moment

QUOTE for the first time since mortgage rates began falling in March a financial institution has raised charges on homeowner loans
Globe and Mail (Toronto)

false adjective not true or not correct; to make a false entry in the balance sheet; false advertising = misrepresentation in advertising; false pretenses = doing or saying something to cheat someone; he was sent to prison for obtaining money under false pretenses; false weight = (i) weight on store scales which is wrong and so cheats customers; (ii) informal falsification of billing

◊ **falsify** verb to change something to make it wrong; to falsify the accounts

◊ **falsification** noun action of making false entries in accounts

famous adjective very well known; the company owns a famous department store in New York City

Fannie Mae informal = FEDERAL NATIONAL MORTGAGE ASSOCIATION

fare noun (a) price to be paid for a ticket to travel; train fares have gone up by 5%; the government is asking the airlines to keep air fares down; discount fare = reduced fare for certain types of passengers (such as employees of the transportation or travel company); full fare = ticket sold at a price which is not discounted; half fare = half-price ticket for a child; one-way fare = fare for a journey from one place to another; round-trip fare = fare for a journey from one place to another and back again (b) paying rider in a cab; he picked up his last fare of the night (c) food served at table

farm 1 noun property in the country where crops are grown or where animals are raised for sale; collective farm = state-owned farm which is run by the workers; fish farm = place where fish are grown for food; mixed farm = farm which has both animals and crops 2 verb to own a farm; he farms 150 acres

◊ **farming** noun job of working on a farm or of raising animals for sale or of growing crops for food; chicken farming; dairy farming; mixed farming

◊ **farm out** verb to farm out work = to hand over work for another person or company to do for you; she farms out the office typing to various secretarial services

fast adjective & adverb quick or quickly; the train is the fastest way of getting to our supplier's factory; home computers sell fast in the preChristmas period

◊ **fast-moving** or **fast-selling** adjective fast-selling items = items which sell fast; dictionaries are not fast-moving stock

◊ **fast track** noun path to rapid promotion within a corporation

fault noun (a) being to blame for something which is wrong; it is the stock controller's fault if the warehouse runs out of stock; the chairman said the lower sales figures were the fault of a badly motivated sales force (b) error; the technicians are trying to correct a programming fault; we think there is a basic fault in the product design

◊ **faulty** *adjective* which does not work properly; *faulty equipment; they installed faulty computer programs*

favor 1 *noun* (a) as a favor = to help *or* to be kind to someone; *he asked the secretary for a loan as a favor* (b) favor of = in agreement with *or* feeling that something is right; *six members of the board are in favor of the proposal, and three are against it* 2 *verb* to agree that something is right *or* to vote for something; *the board members all favor Smith Inc. as partners in the project*

◊ **favorable** *adjective* which gives an advantage; *favorable balance of trade* = situation where a country's exports are more than the imports; *on favorable terms* = on specially good terms; *the store is let on very favorable terms*

◊ **favorite** *adjective* which is liked best; *this brand of chocolate is a favorite with the children's market*

fax 1 *noun* (a) system for sending facsimile copies of documents via the telephone lines; *the fax machine has an automatic dialing facility; we need more fax paper* (b) a copy of a document sent via the telephone lines; *we have received your fax of June 24* 2 *verb* to send a copy of a document using a fax machine; *we will fax the report to you tomorrow; the details of the offer were faxed to his Boston office*

FDA = FOOD AND DRUG ADMINISTRATION

feasibility *noun* ability to be done; *to report on the feasibility of a project; feasibility report* = report saying if something can be done; *to carry out a feasibility study on a project* = to carry out an examination of costs and profits to see if the project should be started

federal *adjective* referring to a system of government where a group of states are linked together in a federation; especially the central government of the United States; *most federal offices are in Washington; federal debt* = the national debt of the government of the U.S.A.; *federal deficit* = deficit incurred by the federal government when it spends more than it receives in tax revenue; *federal funds* = deposits by commercial banks with the Federal Reserve Banks, which can be used for short-term loans to other banks

◊ **the Fed** *noun informal* = FEDERAL RESERVE BOARD

◊ **Federal National Mortgage Association** *noun* organization which regulates mortgages and helps offer mortgages backed by federal funds

◊ **Federal Reserve** *noun* system of federal government control of the U.S. banks, where the Federal Reserve Board regulates money supply and issues government bonds

◊ **Federal Reserve Bank** *noun* one of the twelve U.S. central banks which are owned by the state and directed by the Federal Reserve Board

◊ **Federal Reserve Board** *noun* board which runs the central banks in the U.S.

◊ **Federal Trade Commission** *noun* federal agency established to keep business competition free and fair

◊ **federation** *noun* group of societies *or* companies *or* organizations *or* states, which have a central organization which represents them and looks after their common interests; *federation of labor unions; an employers' federation*

QUOTE examiners have come to inspect the collateral that thrifts may use in borrowing from the Fed
Wall Street Journal
QUOTE federal examiners will determine which of the privately-insured savings and loans qualify for federal insurance
Wall Street Journal
QUOTE pressure on the Federal Reserve Board to ease monetary policy mounted yesterday with the release of a set of pessimistic economic statistics
Financial Times

fee *noun* (a) money paid for work carried out by a professional person (such as an accountant *or* a doctor *or* a lawyer); *we charge a small fee for our services; attorney's fees; consultant's fee* (b) money paid for something; *entrance fee or admission fee; registration fee*

feed 1 *noun* device which puts paper into a printer *or* into a photocopier; *the paper feed has jammed; continuous feed* = device which feeds in continuous computer stationery into a printer; *sheet feed* = device which puts one sheet at a time into a printer **2** *verb* to put information into a computer
NOTE: **feeding - fed**

◊ **feedback** *noun* information, especially about people's reactions; *have you had any feedback from the sales* *force about the customers' reaction to the new model?*

ferry *noun* boat which takes passengers or goods across water; *we are going to take the night ferry to Vancouver;* **car ferry** = ferry which carries cars; **passenger ferry** = ferry which only carries passengers

fetch *verb* (a) to go to bring something; *we have to fetch the goods from the warehouse* (b) to be sold for a certain price; *to fetch a high price; these computers fetch very high prices on the black market*

few *adjective & noun* (a) not many; *we sold so few of this item that we have discontinued the line; few of the staff stay with us more than six months* (b) a **few** = some; *a few of our salesmen drive Cadillacs; we get only a few orders during the week after Christmas*

fiat *noun* **fiat money** = coins or notes which are not worth much as paper or metal, but are said by the government to have a value

fictitious *adjective* false *or* which does not exist; **fictitious asset entry** = entry showing ownership of assets which do not really exist; **fictitious payee** = payee named on a check, but clearly nonexistent (such as John Doe), making the check payable to bearer; **fictitious person** = treatment by law of a group as an imaginary person distinct from the group's members

fide *see* BONA FIDE

fiduciary *adjective & noun* (person) acting as trustee for someone else

field *noun* **in the field** = outside the office *or* among the customers; *we have sixteen reps in the field;* **field staff** = employees who work in the field, visiting customers, and not in the company's offices; **first in the field** = first company to introduce a product *or* to start a service; *Smith Inc. has a great advantage in being first in the field with a reliable electric car*
◊ **fieldwork** *noun* work *or* information gathering done in the field, such as polling done for market research; *he had to do a lot of fieldwork to find the right market for the product*

FIFO = FIRST IN FIRST OUT

fifty-fifty *adjective & adverb* half; **to go fifty-fifty** = to share the costs equally; *he has a fifty-fifty chance of making a profit* = he has an equal chance of making a profit or a loss

figure *noun* (a) number *or* cost written in numbers; *the figure in the books for heating is very high; he put a very low figure on the value of the lease* = he calculated the value of the lease as very low (b) **figures** = written numbers; **sales figures** = total sales; **to work out the figures** = to calculate; *his income runs into six figures* *or* *he has a six-figure income* = his income is at least $100,000; **in round figures** = not totally accurate, but correct to the nearest 10 or 100; *they have a workforce of 2,500 in round figures* (c) **figures** = numerical summary of a firm's performance; *the figures for last year* *or* *last year's figures*

file 1 *noun* (a) cardboard holder for documents, which can fit in the drawer of a filing cabinet; *put these letters in the customer file; look in the file marked "monthly sales"* ; **box file** = cardboard box for holding documents (b) documents kept for reference; **to place something on file** = to keep a record of something; **to keep someone's name on file** = to keep someone's name on a list for reference; **file card** = card with information written on it, used to classify information in a certain order; **file clerk** = clerk who files documents; **file copy** = copy of a document which is kept for reference in an office; **card file** = information kept on file cards (c) section of data on a computer (such as payroll, address list, customer accounts); *how can we protect our computer files?* **2** *verb* (a) to **file documents** = to put documents in order so that they can be found easily; *the correspondence is filed under "complaints"* (b) to make an official request; **to file a petition in bankruptcy** = to ask officially to be made bankrupt *or* to ask officially for someone else to be made bankrupt (c) to register something officially; *to file an application for a patent; to file an income tax return*
◊ **filing** *noun* (a) act of registering something officially; *a bankruptcy filing* (b) documents which have to be put in order; *there is so much filing to do at the end of the week; the manager*

looked through the week's filing to see what letters had been sent; filing **basket** *or* **filing tray** = container kept on a desk for documents which have to be filed; **filing cabinet** = metal box with several drawers for keeping files; **filing system** = way of putting documents in order for reference

> QUOTE the company filed under Chapter 11 of the federal bankruptcy code, the largest failure ever in the steel industry
> *Fortune*
> QUOTE the bankruptcy filing raises questions about the future of the company's pension plan
> *Fortune*

fill 1 *verb* **(a)** to make something full; *we have filled our order book with orders for Africa; the production department has filled the warehouse with defective products* **(b) to fill a gap** = to provide a product *or* service which is needed, but which no one has provided before; *the new range of small cars fills a gap in the market* **(c) to fill a position** *or* **a vacancy** = to find someone to do a job; *your application arrived too late - the position has already been filled*

◊ **filler** *noun* something which fills a space; substance added to a product to increase the bulk; *these hot dogs contain a lot of filler*

◊ **fill in** *verb* to write in the blank spaces in a form; *fill in your name and address in block capitals*

◊ **filling station** *noun* place where you can buy gasoline; *he stopped at the filling station before getting back on the freeway*

◊ **fill out** *verb* to write the required information in the blank spaces on a form; *to get customs clearance you must fill out three forms*

◊ **fill up** *verb* to make something completely full; *he filled up the car with gasoline; my appointments book is completely filled up*

final *adjective* last *or* coming at the end of a period; *to pay the final installment; to make the final payment; to put the final details on a document;* **final date for payment** = last date by which payment should be made; **final demand** = last reminder from a supplier, after which he will sue for payment; **final discharge** = last payment of what is left of a debt; **final dividend** = dividend paid at the end of the year; **final product** = manufactured product, made at the end of a production process

◊ **finalize** *verb* to give final approval to; *we hope to finalize the agreement tomorrow; after six weeks of negotiations the loan was finalized yesterday*

◊ **finally** *adverb* in the end; *the contract was finally signed yesterday; after weeks of trials the company finally accepted the computer system*

finance 1 *noun* **(a)** system of money, credit and capital; *he is studying finance;* **finance charge** = the cost of credit, the interest paid on money borrowed; **finance company** *or* **finance corporation** = company which loans money to individuals *or* businesses; **finance market** = place where large sums of money can be lent or borrowed; **high finance** = lending, investing and borrowing of very large sums of money organized by financiers **(b)** money (of a club, etc.); *she is the secretary of the library's finance committee* **(c) finances** = money *or* cash which is available; *the bad state of the company's finances* **2** *verb* to provide money to pay for something; *to finance an operation*

◊ **financial** *adjective* concerning money; **financial adviser** = person *or* company which gives advice on financial matters for a fee; **financial assistance** = help in the form of money; **financial correspondent** = journalist who writes articles on money matters for a newspaper; **financial position** = state of a person's *or* a company's bank balance (assets and debts); *he must think of his financial position;* **financial resources** = money which is available for investment; *a company with strong financial resources;* **financial risk** = possibility of losing money; *there is no financial risk in selling to East European countries on credit;* **financial statement** = document which shows the financial situation of a company; *the accounts department has prepared a financial statement for the stockholders*

◊ **financially** *adverb* regarding money; **company which is financially sound** = company which is profitable and has strong assets

◊ **financier** *noun* person who lends large amounts of money to companies

◊ **financing** *noun* providing money; *the financing of the project was done by two international banks;* **deficit financing** = planning by a government to borrow money to cover the shortfall between expenditure and income from taxation

QUOTE he was sued for allegedly financing his stake by borrowing more than the Federal Reserve Board margin rules allow
Fortune

QUOTE an official said that the company began to experience a sharp increase in demand for longer-term mortgages at a time when the flow of money used to finance these loans diminished
Globe and Mail

find *verb* (a) to get something which was not there before; *to find backing for a project;* found money = profit which is easy to make (b) to make a legal decision in court; *the tribunal found that both parties were at fault;* the judge found for the defendant = the judge decided that the defendant was right
NOTE: **finding - found**

◊ **findings** *plural noun* the findings of the parks commission = the recommendations of the commission

◊ **find time** *verb* to make enough time to do something; *we must find time to visit the new employees' health club; the chairman never finds enough time to play golf*

fine 1 *noun* money paid because of something wrong which has been done; *he was asked to pay a $25,000 fine; we had to pay a $10 parking fine* **2** *verb* to punish someone by making him pay money; *to fine someone $2,500 for obtaining money under false pretenses* **3** *adverb & adjective* very thin *or* very small; *we are cutting our margins very fine* = we are reducing our margins to the smallest possible; fine print = part of a contract describing restrictions *or* exceptions; *be sure to read the fine print before signing the lease*

finish 1 *noun* (a) surface; *the product has an attractive finish* (b) end of a day's trading on the Stock Exchange; *oil stocks rallied at the finish* **2** *verb* (a) to do something *or* to make something completely; *the order was finished in time; she finished the test before all the other candidates* (b) to come to an end; *the construction is due to finish next month*

◊ **finished** *adjective* finished goods = manufactured goods which are ready to be sold

QUOTE control of materials, from purchased parts to finished goods, provides manufacturers with an opportunity to reduce the amount of money tied up in excess materials
Duns Business Month

fink *noun* worker hired to replace a striking worker

fire 1 *noun* thing which burns; *the shipment was damaged in the fire on board the cargo boat; half the stock was destroyed in the warehouse fire;* to catch fire = to start to burn; *the papers in the wastepaper basket caught fire;* fire damage = damage caused by fire; *he claimed $250 for fire damage;* fire-damaged goods = goods which have been damaged in a fire; fire door = special door to prevent fire going from one part of a building to another; fire escape = door *or* stairs which allow people to get out of a building which is on fire; fire hazard *or* fire risk = situation *or* goods which could start a fire; *that warehouse full of paper is a fire hazard;* fire insurance = insurance against damage by fire **2** *verb* to fire someone = to dismiss someone from a job; *the new CEO fired half the sales force*

◊ **fireproof** *adjective* which cannot be damaged by fire; *we packed the papers in a fireproof safe; it is impossible to make the office completely fireproof*

firm 1 *noun* business *or* partnership; *he is a partner in a law firm; a manufacturing firm; an important publishing firm* **2** *adjective* (a) which cannot be changed; *to make a firm offer for something; to place a firm offer for two aircraft; they are quoting a firm price of $1.22 per unit* (b) not dropping in price, and possibly going to rise; *sterling was more firm on the foreign exchange markets; stocks remained firm*

◊ **firmness** *noun* being steady at a price *or* being likely to rise; *the firmness of the dollar*

◊ **firm up** *verb* to finalize *or* to agree on final details; *we expect to firm up the deal at the next trade fair*

first *noun* person *or* thing which is there at the beginning *or* earlier than others; *our company was one of the first to reach the European market;* first quarter = three months' period from January to the end of March; first half *or* first half-year = six months' period from January to the end of June; first in

first out (FIFO) = accounting policy where inventory sold is valued at the price of the oldest purchases

◊ **first-class** *adjective & noun* **(a)** top quality *or* most expensive; *he is a first-class accountant* **(b)** most expensive and comfortable type of travel *or* type of hotel; *to travel first-class; first-class travel provides the best service; a first-class ticket; to stay in first-class hotels* **(c)** first-class mail = rapid mail service for sealed letters and postcards; *a first-class letter should get to Chicago in a day*

◊ **first-line** *adjective* **first-line management** = the managers who have immediate contact with the workers

QUOTE fill huge warehouses with large quantities of first-quality merchandise and sell the goods at rock-bottom prices
Duns Business Month

fiscal *adjective* referring to tax *or* to government revenues; *the government's fiscal policies; fiscal measures* = tax changes made by a government to improve the working of the economy; *fiscal year* = twelve-month period on which taxes or annual statements are based (not always the same as the calendar year)

QUOTE last fiscal year the chain reported a 116% jump in earnings
Barrons

fit *verb* to be the right size for something; *the paper doesn't fit the typewriter*
NOTE: **fitting - fitted**

◊ **fit in** *verb* to make something go into a space; *will the computer fit into that little room? the chairman tries to fit in a game of golf every afternoon; my calendar is full, but I shall try to fit you in tomorrow afternoon*

◊ **fit out** *verb* to provide equipment *or* furniture for a business; *they fitted out the factory with computers; the store was fitted out at a cost of $10,000*

◊ **fittings** *plural noun* items in a property which are sold with it but are not permanently fixed (such as carpets or shelves); *the electrical fittings need replacing*

five and ten (cent) store *noun* store selling cheap household items

fix *verb* **(a)** to arrange *or* to agree; *to fix a meeting for 3 p.m.; we will have to fix a date for the conference; the price of*
gold was fixed at $300; the mortgage rate has been fixed at 11% **(b)** to repair; *the technicians are coming to fix the telephone switchboard; can you fix the photocopier?*

◊ **fixed** *adjective* permanent *or* which cannot be removed; **fixed assets** = property *or* machinery which a company owns and uses; **fixed capital** = capital in the form of buildings and machinery; **fixed costs** = money paid in producing a product which does not increase with the amount of product made (such as rent); **fixed deposit** = deposit which pays a stated interest over a set period; **fixed expenses** = money which is spent regularly (such as rent, electricity, telephone); **fixed income** = income which does not change (as from an annuity); **fixed-income** *or* **fixed-interest investments** = investments producing an interest which does not change; **fixed-price agreement** = agreement where a company provides a service *or* a product at a price which stays the same for the whole period of the agreement; **fixed scale of charges** = rate of charging which cannot be altered

◊ **fixer** *noun informal* person who has a reputation for arranging business deals (often illegally)

◊ **fixing** *noun* **(a)** arranging; *fixing of charges; fixing of a mortgage rate* **(b)** **price fixing** = illegal agreement between companies to charge the same price for competing products **(c)** the **London gold fixing** = system where the world price for gold is set each day in London

QUOTE a draft report on changes in the international monetary system casts doubt about any return to fixed exchange rate parities
Wall Street Journal

◊ **fixture** *noun* item in a property which is permanently attached to it (such as a sink or toilet); *most of the fixtures in the house are very old*

flag 1 *noun* **(a)** piece of cloth with a design on it which shows which country it belongs to; *a ship flying a Canadian flag;* **ship sailing under a flag of convenience** = ship flying the flag of a country which may have no ships of its own, but allows ships of other countries to be registered in its ports **(b)** something used to attract attention, such as a mark which is attached to information in a computer so that the information can be found easily **2** *verb* to mark with a flag so that information can be found easily
NOTE: **flagging - flagged**

flat *adjective* (a) falling because of low demand; *the market was flat today* (b) fixed *or* not changing; **flat rate** = charge which always stays the same; *we pay a flat rate for electricity each quarter; he is paid a flat rate of $2 per thousand*

◊ **flat out** *adverb* in a blunt *or* direct way; *he refused the offer flat out*

flea market *noun* market, usually in the open air, for selling secondhand goods

fleet *noun* group of cars belonging to a company and used by its staff; *a company's fleet of representatives' cars;* a **fleet car** = car which is one of a fleet of cars; **fleet discount** = specially cheap price for purchase or rental of a company's cars; **fleet rental** = renting all a company's cars at a special price

flexible *adjective* which can be altered *or* changed; *flexible budget; flexible prices; flexible pricing policy ;* flexible **working hours** = system where workers can start or stop work at different hours of the morning or evening provided that they work a certain number of hours per day or week; *we work flexible hours*

◊ **flexibility** *noun* being easily changed; *there is no flexibility in the company's pricing policy*

◊ **flextime** *or* **flexitime** *noun* work system where workers can start or stop work at different hours of the morning or evening, provided that they work a certain number of hours per day or week; *we work flextime; the company introduced flextime working two years ago*

flier *noun* small advertising leaflet designed to encourage customers to ask for more information about the product for sale; *see also* FLYER

flight *noun* (a) journey by an aircraft, leaving at a regular time; *flight AC 267 is leaving from Gate 46; he missed his flight; I always take the afternoon flight to Boston; if you hurry you will catch the six o'clock flight to Paris* (b) rapid movement of money out of a country because of a lack of confidence in the country's economic future; *the flight of capital from Europe into the U.S.; the flight from the franc into the dollar* (c) series of steps; **top-flight** = the most important position *or* very efficient; *top-flight managers can earn very high salaries*

flip chart *noun* way of showing information to a group of people by writing on large sheets of paper which can then be turned over to show the next sheet

float 1 *noun* (a) cash taken from a central supply and used for running expenses; *the sales reps have a float of $100 each;* **cash float** = cash put into the cash box at the beginning of the day to allow business to start; *we start the day with a $20 float in the cash desk* (b) starting a new company by selling shares in it on the Stock Exchange; *the float of the new company was a complete failure* (c) number of shares in a company which are available for trade on a Stock Exchange **2** *verb* (a) **to float an issue** = to start a new company by selling shares in it on a Stock Exchange; **to float a loan** = to raise a loan on the financial market by asking banks and companies to subscribe to it (b) to let a currency find its own exchange rate on the international markets and not be fixed; *the government has decided to float the dollar*

◊ **floating 1** *noun* (a) floating of a new **issue** = starting a new company by selling shares in it on a Stock Exchange (b) **the floating of the dollar** = letting the dollar find its own exchange rate on the international market **2** *adjective* which is not fixed; *floating exchange rates; the floating pound;* **floating-rate mortgage** = mortgage where the interest rate is not fixed, but can move up or down according to the current market rates

QUOTE in a world of floating exchange rates the dollar is strong because of capital inflows rather than weak because of the nation's trade deficit
Duns Business Month

flood 1 *noun* great flow *or* large quantity; *we received a flood of orders; floods of tourists filled the hotels* **2** *verb* to fill with a large quantity of something; *the market was flooded with cheap imitations; the sales department is flooded with orders or with complaints*

floor *noun* (a) part of the room which you walk on; **floor space** = area of floor in an office *or* warehouse; *we have 3,500 square feet of floor space to rent;* the **factory floor** = main works of a factory; **on the shop floor** = in the factory *or* among the ordinary workers; *the feeling on the shop floor is that the manager does not know his job* (b) all rooms on one level in a building; **the shoe department is on the first floor; her office is on the 26th floor;** floor **manager** = person in charge of the sales staff in a department store **(c)** main trading area of a Stock Exchange; **floor trader** = member of a Stock Exchange who buys and sells securities on his own account

◊ **floorwalker** *noun* employee of a department store who advises the customers, and supervises the sales assistants in a department

flop 1 *noun* failure *or* not being a success; **the new design was a flop 2** *verb* to fail *or* not to be a success; **the flotation of the new company flopped badly**
NOTE: **flopping - flopped**

◊ **floppy 1** *adjective* **floppy disk** = small disk for storing information in a computer **2** *noun* small disk for storing computer information; **the data is on 5¼-inch floppies**

flotation *noun* **the flotation of a new issue** = starting a new company by selling shares in it

flotsam *noun* **flotsam and jetsam** = rubbish floating in the water after a ship has been wrecked and rubbish washed on to the land

flourish *verb* to be prosperous *or* to do well in business; **the company is flourishing; trade with Nigeria flourished**

◊ **flourishing** *adjective* profitable; **flourishing trade** = trade which is profitable; **he runs a flourishing shoe business**

flow 1 *noun* **(a)** movement; **the flow of capital into a country; the flow of investments into Japan (b) cash flow** = cash which comes into a company from sales and goes out in purchases or overhead expenditure; **discounted cash flow** = calculation of forecast sales of a product in current terms with reductions for current interest rates; **the company is suffering from cash flow problems** = cash income is not coming in fast enough to pay for the expenditure going out **(c) flow diagram** = FLOWCHART **2** *verb* to move smoothly; **production is now flowing normally after the strike**

◊ **flowchart** *noun* chart which shows the arrangement of work processes in a series

fluctuate *verb* to move up and down; **prices fluctuate between $1.10 and $1.25; the dollar fluctuated all day on the foreign exchange markets**

◊ **fluctuating** *adjective* moving up and down; **fluctuating dollar prices**

◊ **fluctuation** *noun* up and down movement; **the fluctuations of the franc; the fluctuations of the exchange rate**

fly *verb* to move through the air in an aircraft; **the chairman is flying to Germany on business; the overseas sales manager flies about 100,000 miles a year visiting the agents**

◊ **fly-by-night** *adjective* company which is not reliable *or* which might disappear to avoid paying debts; **I want a reputable builder, not one of these fly-by-night outfits**

◊ **flyer** *noun* **high flyer** = (i) person who is very successful *or* who is likely to rise to a very important position; (ii) share whose market price is rising rapidly; *see also* FLIER

FOB *or* **f.o.b.** = FREE ON BOARD

fold *verb* **(a)** to bend a flat thing, so that part of it is on top of the rest; **she folded the letter so that the address was clearly visible (b)** *informal* to fold (up) = to stop trading; **the business folded up last December; the company folded with debts of over $1m**

◊ **-fold** *suffix* times; **four-fold** = four times over

QUOTE the company's sales have nearly tripled and its profits have risen seven-fold since 1982
Barrons

◊ **folder** *noun* **(a)** cardboard envelope for carrying papers; **put all the documents in a folder for the chairman (b)** advertising material made of a folded sheet of paper

folio 1 *noun* page with a number, especially two facing pages in an account book which have the same number **2** *verb* to put a number on a page

follow *verb* to come behind *or* to come afterwards; **the samples will follow by surface mail; we will pay $10,000 down, with the balance to follow in six months' time**

◊ **follow up** *verb* to examine something further; **I'll follow up your idea of putting our address list onto the computer; to follow up an initiative** =

to take further action on a plan which is already in progress

◇ **follow-up letter** *noun* letter sent to someone who has not acted on the instructions in a previous letter, or to discuss in more detail points which were raised earlier, or to answer an inquiry

food *noun* things which are eaten; *he is very fond of Indian food; the food in the company cafeteria is excellent*

◇ **Food and Drug Administration (FDA)** *noun* federal agency established to ensure safety of food products, cosmetics and medicines

◇ **food stamp** *noun* coupon issued by the federal government and used by low-income people to buy food at a discount; *this supermarket accepts food stamps*

foot 1 *noun* **(a)** part of the body at the end of the leg; **on foot** = walking; *the reps make most of their central New York calls on foot; the rush hour traffic is so bad that it is quicker to go to the office on foot* **(b) on one's feet** = (i) in a stable financial position; *since taking up the new job, he's getting back on his feet;* (ii) quickly; *good managers must be able to think on their feet* **(c)** bottom part; *he signed his name at the foot of the invoice* **(d)** measurement of length (= 12 inches); *the table is six feet long; my office is ten feet by twelve* NOTE: the plural is **feet** for (a) and (c); there is no plural for (b). In measurements, **foot** is usually written **ft** or ' after figures: **10 ft; 10' 2** *verb* **(a) to foot the bill** = to pay the bill; *the director footed the bill for the department's Christmas party* **(b) to foot up an account** = to add up a column of numbers

forbid *verb* to tell someone not to do something *or* to say that something must not be done; *the contract forbids resale of the goods to Japan; employees are forbidden to use the front entrance* NOTE: **forbidding - forbade - forbidden**

force 1 *noun* **(a)** strength; **to be in force** = to be operating *or* working; *the rules have been in force since 1946;* **to come into force** = to start to operate *or* work; *the new regulations will come into force on January 1* **(b)** group of people; **labor force** *or* **workforce** = all the workers in a company *or* in an area; *the management has made an increased offer to the labor force; we are opening a new factory in the Far East because of the cheap local labor force;*

sales force = group of salesmen **(c)** **force majeure** = something which happens which is out of the control of the parties who have signed a contract (such as strike, war, storm) **2** *verb* to make someone do something; *competition has forced the company to lower its prices*

◇ **forced** *adjective* **forced sale** = sale which takes place because a court orders it *or* because it is the only way to avoid a financial crisis

◇ **force down** *verb* to make something become lower; **to force prices down** = to make prices come down; *competition has forced prices down*

◇ **force up** *verb* to make something become higher; **to force prices up** = to make prices go up; *the war forced up the price of oil*

forecast 1 *noun* description *or* calculation of what will probably happen in the future; *the chairman did not believe the sales manager's forecast of higher sales volume;* **cash flow forecast** = forecast of when cash will be received or paid out; **population forecast** = calculation of how many people will be living in a country *or* in a city at some point in the future; **sales forecast** = calculation of future sales **2** *verb* to calculate *or* to say what will probably happen in the future; *he is forecasting sales of $2m; economists have forecast a fall in the exchange rate* NOTE: **forecasting - forecast**

◇ **forecasting** *noun* calculating what will probably happen in the future; **manpower forecasting** = calculating how many workers will be needed in the future, and how many will actually be available NOTE: no plural

QUOTE if corporate forecasts are met, sales will exceed $50 million in 1986
Citizen, Ottawa

foreclose *verb* to sell a property because the owner cannot repay money which he has borrowed (using the property as security); **to foreclose on a mortgaged property**

◇ **foreclosure** *noun* act of foreclosing

QUOTE bad loans and foreclosed real estate rose to $175 million by last March
Barrons

foreign *adjective* not of one's own country; *foreign cars have flooded our market; we are increasing our trade* *with foreign countries* ; **foreign currency** = money of another country; **foreign goods** = goods manufactured in other countries; **foreign investments** = money invested in other countries; **foreign money order** = money order in a foreign currency which is payable to someone living in a foreign country; **foreign trade** = trade with other countries

◊ **foreign exchange** *noun* **(a)** exchanging the money of one country for that of another; **foreign exchange broker** *or* **dealer** = person who deals on the foreign exchange market; **foreign exchange dealing** = buying and selling foreign currencies; **foreign exchange market** = market where people buy and sell foreign currencies; **foreign exchange rates** = prices of world currencies in relation to each other; **foreign exchange reserves** = foreign money held by a government to support its own currency and pay its debts; **foreign exchange transfer** = sending of money from one country to another

◊ **foreigner** *noun* person from another country

QUOTE news that gross national product increased only 1.3% in the first quarter of the year sent the dollar into a tail-spin in foreign exchange markets
Fortune

QUOTE a sharp setback in foreign trade accounted for most of the winter slowdown
Fortune

foreman *or* **forewoman** *noun* skilled worker in charge of several other workers
NOTE: plural is **foremen** *or* **forewomen**

forex *or* **Forex** = FOREIGN EXCHANGE

QUOTE the amount of reserves sold by the authorities were not sufficient to move the $200 billion Forex market permanently
Duns Business Month

forfeit 1 *noun* taking something away as a punishment; **forfeit clause** = clause in a contract which says that goods *or* deposit will be taken away if the contract is not obeyed; **the goods were declared forfeit** = the court said that the goods had to be taken away from their owner **2** *verb* to have something taken away as a punishment; **to forfeit a patent** = to lose a patent because payments have not been made; **to forfeit a deposit** = to lose a deposit which was left for an item because you have decided not to buy that item

◊ **forfeiture** *noun* act of forfeiting a property

forge *verb* to copy money or a signature illegally *or* to make a document which looks like a real one; *he tried to enter the country with forged documents*

◊ **forgery** *noun* **(a)** making an illegal copy; *he was sent to prison for forgery* **(b)** illegal copy; *the signature was proved to be a forgery*

forget *verb* to fail to remember; *she forgot to put a stamp on the envelope; don't forget we're having lunch together tomorrow*
NOTE: **forgetting - forgot - forgotten**

forklift *noun* type of small tractor with two metal arms in front, used for lifting and moving heavy objects

form 1 *noun* **(a) legal form** = words correctly laid out for a legal document; **receipt in due form** = correctly written receipt **(b)** official printed paper with blank spaces which have to be filled in with information; *you have to fill out form A20; customs declaration form; a pad of order forms;* **application form** = form which has to be filled out to apply for something; **claim form** = form which has to be filled out when making an insurance claim; **contract form** = legal form for a given contract; **form contract** = contract following a given form without variation **2** *verb* to start *or* to organize; *the brothers have formed a new company*

◊ **formation** *or* **forming** *noun* act of organizing; *the formation of a new company*

forma *see* PRO FORMA

formal *adjective* **(a)** clearly and legally written; *to make a formal application; to send a formal order* **(b)** following established procedure; *staff members are invited to a formal dinner*

◊ **formality** *noun* something which has to be done to obey the law; **customs formalities** = declaration of goods by the shipper and examination of them by the customs

◊ **formally** *adverb* in a formal way; *we have formally applied for planning permission for the new shopping district*

former *adjective* before *or* at an earlier time; *the former chairman has taken a job with the rival company*

◊ **formerly** *adverb* at an earlier time; *he is currently executive vice-president of Smith Co., but formerly he worked for Jones*

formula investing *noun* investing according to a set plan, balancing investments in bonds and securities to produce a steady income and capital growth

fortune *noun* large amount of money; *he made a fortune from investing in oil; she left her fortune to her three children*

Fortune 500 list of the 500 largest companies, published each year by Fortune magazine

forward 1 *adjective* in advance *or* to be paid at a later date; **forward buying** *or* **buying forward =** buying securities *or* currency *or* commodities at today's price for delivery at a later date; **forward contract =** agreement to buy foreign currency *or* securities *or* commodities for delivery at a later date at a certain price; **forward market =** market for purchasing foreign currency *or* oil *or* commodities for delivery at a later date; **forward (exchange) rate =** rate for purchase of foreign currency at a fixed price for delivery at a later date; *what are the forward rates for the dollar?;* **forward sales =** sales for delivery at a later date **2** *adverb* **(a) to date a check forward =** to put a later date than the present one on a check; **carriage forward** *or* **freight forward =** deal where the customer pays for transporting the goods; **charges forward =** charges which will be paid by the customer **(b) to buy forward =** to buy foreign currency before you need it, in order to be certain of the exchange rate; **to sell forward =** to sell foreign currency for delivery at a later date **(c) balance brought forward** *or* **carried forward =** balance which is entered in an account at the end of a period and is then taken to be the starting point of the next period **3** *verb* **to forward something to someone =** to send something to someone; *to forward a consignment to Nigeria;* **please forward** *or* **to be forwarded =** words written on an envelope, asking the person receiving it to send it on to the person whose name is written on it

◊ **forwarder** *see* FREIGHT FORWARDER

◊ **forwarding** *noun* **(a)** arranging shipping and customs documents; **air forwarding =** arranging for goods to be shipped by air; **forwarding agent =** FREIGHT FORWARDER; **forwarding instructions** *or* **instructions for forwarding =** instructions showing how the goods are to be shipped and delivered **(b) forwarding address =** address to which a person's mail can be sent on

foul *adjective* **foul bill of lading =** bill of lading which says that the goods were in bad condition when received by the shipper

founder *noun* person who starts a company; **founder's shares =** special shares issued to the person who starts a company

fourth *adjective* coming after third; **fourth class =** mail service for heavy packets; **fourth quarter =** period of three months from October to the end of the year

Fr = FRANC

fraction *noun* very small amount; *only a fraction of the new share issue was subscribed*

◊ **fractional** *adjective* very small; **fractional certificate =** certificate for part of a share

fragile *adjective* which can be easily broken; *there is an extra premium for insuring fragile goods in shipment*

franc *noun* money used in France, Belgium, Switzerland and many other countries; **franc account =** bank account in francs

NOTE: in English usually written **Fr** before the figure: **Fr2,500** (say: "two thousand, five hundred francs"). Currencies of different countries can be shown by the initial letters of the countries: **FFr** (French francs); **SwFr** (Swiss francs); **BFr** (Belgian francs)

franchise 1 *noun* license to trade using a brand name and paying a royalty for it; *he has bought a printing franchise or a hot dog franchise* **2** *verb* to sell licenses for people to trade using a brand name and paying a royalty; *his sandwich bar was so successful that he decided to franchise it*

◊ **franchisee** *noun* person who runs a franchise

◊ **franchiser** *noun* person who licenses a franchise

◊ **franchising** *noun* act of selling a license to trade as a franchise; *he runs his sandwich chain as a franchising operation*

◊ **franchisor** *noun* = FRANCHISER

QUOTE a fast-growing trend among packaged goods producers: using franchise extension to diversify into new product lines
Duns Business Month
QUOTE they will be converted to restaurants in the family-style chain that the company operates and franchises throughout most parts of the U.S.
Fortune
QUOTE many new types of franchised businesses will join the ranks of the giant chains of fast-food restaurants, hotels and motels and rental car agencies
Franchising Opportunities

franco *adverb & adjective* free *or* at a price including all risks and charges; *the cost franco is $255; see also* FREE ON BOARD, FREE ON RAIL

frank *verb* to stamp the date and postage on a letter; **franking machine** = machine which marks the date and postage on letters so that the sender does not need to use stamps

fraud *noun* making money by making people believe something which is not true; *he got possession of the property by fraud; he was accused of frauds relating to foreign currency ; to obtain money by fraud* = to obtain money by saying or doing something to cheat someone; **fraud squad** = special police department which investigates frauds

◊ **fraudulent** *adjective* not honest *or* aiming to cheat people; *a fraudulent transaction*

◊ **fraudulently** *adverb* not honestly; *goods imported fraudulently*

Freddie Mac *(informal)* = FEDERAL HOME LOAN MORTGAGE CORPORATION

free 1 *adjective & adverb* **(a)** not costing any money; *exhibitors are given two free tickets to the trade fair; the price includes free delivery; goods are delivered free; catalog sent free on request; carriage free* = the customer does not pay for the shipping; **free gift** = present given by a retailer to a customer who buys a certain amount of goods; *there is a free gift worth $25 to any customer buying a washing machine;* **free sample** = sample given free to advertise a product; **free trial** = testing

of a machine with no payment involved; *to send a piece of equipment for two weeks' free trial ;* **free of charge** = with no payment to be made; **free on board (f.o.b.)** = price including all the seller's costs until the goods are delivered to a certain place; *they are sending the shipment f.o.b. St. Louis;* **free on rail** = price including all the seller's costs until the goods are delivered to the railway for shipment **(b)** with no restrictions; **free collective bargaining** = negotiations over wage increases and working conditions between the management and the unions; **free competition** = being free to compete without government interference; **free currency** = currency which is allowed by the government to be bought and sold without restriction; **free enterprise** = system of business with no interference from the government; **free market economy** = system where the government does not interfere in business activity in any way; **free port** *or* **free trade zone** = port *or* area where there are no customs duties; **free of tax** *or* **tax-free** = with no tax having to be paid; *he was given a tax-free sum of $25,000 when his job was terminated; interest free of tax* *or* **tax-free interest; interest-free credit** *or* **loan** = credit *or* loan where no interest is paid by the borrower; **free of duty** *or* **duty-free** = with no duty to be paid; *to import wine free of duty* *or* *duty-free;* **free trade** = system where goods can go from one country to another without any restrictions; *the government adopted a free trade policy;* **free trade area** = group of countries practicing free trade; **free trader** = person who is in favor of free trade **(c)** not busy *or* not occupied; *are there any free tables in the restaurant? I shall be free in a few minutes; the chairman always keeps Friday afternoon free for a game of bridge* **2** *verb* to make something available *or* easy; *the government's decision has freed millions of dollars for investment*

QUOTE in 1934 Congress authorized President Roosevelt to seek lower tariffs with any country willing to reciprocate, and that started the U.S. down a path toward free trade it has followed ever since
Duns Business Month
QUOTE can free trade be reconciled with a strong dollar resulting from floating exchange rates?
Duns Business Month
QUOTE free traders hold that the strong dollar is the primary cause of the nation's trade problems
Duns Business Month

◊ **freehold** *noun* **freehold property** = property which the owner holds forever and on which no rent is paid

◊ **freeholder** *noun* person who owns a freehold property

◊ **freelance** **1** *adjective* & *noun* independent worker who works for several different companies but is not employed by any of them; *we have about twenty freelances working for us or about twenty people working for us on a freelance basis; she is a freelance journalist* **2** *adverb* selling one's work to various firms, but not being employed by any of them; *he works freelance as a designer* **3** *verb* **(a)** to do work for several firms but not be employed by any of them; *she freelances for the local newspapers* **(b)** to send work out to be done by a freelancer; *we freelance work out to several specialists*

◊ **freelancer** *noun* freelance worker

◊ **freely** *adverb* with no restrictions; *money should circulate freely within the Common Market*

◊ **freeway** *noun* main highway

freeze **1** *noun* **credit freeze** = period when lending by banks is restricted by the government; **wage-price freeze** *or* a **freeze on wages and prices** = period when wages and prices are not allowed to be increased **2** *verb* to keep money *or* costs, etc. at their present level and not allow them to rise; *we have frozen expenditures at last year's levels; to freeze wages and prices; to freeze credits; to freeze company dividends* NOTE: **freezing - froze - has frozen**

◊ **freeze out** *verb* **to freeze out competition** = to trade successfully and cheaply and so prevent competitors from operating

> QUOTE the company agreed to freeze earnings at the current rate for four years rather than ask for an immediate pay cut
> *Business Week*

freight **1** *noun* **(a)** cost of transporting goods by air, sea or land; *rail freight; truck freight; at an auction, the buyer pays the freight* ; **freight charges** *or* **freight rates** = money charged for transporting goods; *freight charges have gone up sharply this year;* **freight costs** = money paid to transport goods; **freight collect** = deal where the customer pays for transporting the goods **(b) air freight** = shipping of goods in an aircraft; *to send a shipment by air freight;* **air freight charges** *or* **rates** =

money charged for sending goods by air **(c)** goods which are transported; **to take on freight** = to load goods onto a ship, train or truck; **freight car** = railway car for carrying goods; **freight depot** = central point where goods are collected before being shipped; **freight elevator** = strong elevator for carrying goods; **freight plane** = aircraft which carries goods, not passengers; **freight train** = train used for carrying goods **2** *verb* **to freight goods** = to send goods; *we freight goods to all parts of the U.S.*

◊ **freightage** *noun* cost of transporting goods

◊ **freighter** *noun* **(a)** aircraft or ship which carries goods **(b)** person *or* company which organizes the transport of goods

◊ **freight forwarder** *noun* person *or* company which arranges shipping and customs documents for several shipments from different companies, putting them together to form one large shipment

frequent *adjective* which comes *or* goes *or* takes place often; *there is a frequent ferry service to France; we send frequent messages to New York; how frequent are the planes to Atlanta?*

◊ **frequently** *adverb* often; *the photocopier is frequently out of use; we telex our New York office very frequently - at least four times a day*

fringe benefits *plural noun* extra items given by a company to workers in addition to a salary (such as company cars, health insurance)

> QUOTE What benefits does the executive derive from his directorship? Compensation has increased sharply in recent years, and fringe benefits for directors have proliferated
> *Duns Business Month*

front *noun* **(a)** part of something which faces away from the back; *the front of the office building is on Main Street; the front page of the company report has a photograph of the chief executive officer; our ad appeared on the front page of the newspaper* **(b)** in **front of** = before *or* on the front side of something; *they put up a "for sale" sign in front of the factory; the chairman's name is in front of all the others on the staff list* **(c)** business or person used to hide an illegal trade; *his restaurant is a front for a drug organization* **(d)** money **up front** = payment in advance; *they are asking* for $10,000 up front before they will consider the deal; he had to put money up front before he could clinch the deal

◇ **front-line** *adjective* front-line **management** = managers who have immediate contact with the workers

◇ **front man** *noun* person who seems honest but is hiding an illegal trade

frozen *adjective* not allowed to be changed or used; **frozen account** = bank account where the money cannot be changed or used because of a court order; **frozen assets** = a company's assets which by law cannot be sold because someone has a claim against them; **his assets have been frozen by the court** = the court does not allow him to sell his assets; **frozen credits** = credit in an account which cannot be moved; *see also* FREEZE

ft = FOOT

fuel 1 *noun* material (like oil, coal, gas) used to give power; *the annual fuel bill for the plant has doubled over the last five years; he has bought a car with low fuel consumption* **2** *verb* to add to; *market worries were fueled by news of an increase in electricity charges; the rise in the market price of the stock was fueled by rumors of a merger bid*

fulfill *verb* to complete something in a satisfactory way; *the clause regarding payments has not been fulfilled;* to **fulfill an order** = to supply the items which have been ordered; *we are so understaffed that we cannot fulfill any more orders before Christmas;* to **fulfill the terms of an agreement**

◇ **fulfillment** *noun* carrying something out in a satisfactory way; **contract fulfillment** = following the terms of a contract

full *adjective* **(a)** with as much inside it as possible; *the train was full of commuters; is the container full yet? we sent a truck full of spare parts to our warehouse; when the disk is full, don't forget to make a backup copy* **(b)** complete *or* including everything; **we are working at full capacity** = we are doing as much work as possible; **full costs** = all the costs of manufacturing a product, including both fixed and variable costs; **full coverage** = insurance coverage against all risks; **in full discharge of a**

debt = paying a debt completely; **full employment** = situation where all the people who can work have jobs; **full fare** = ticket for a journey by an adult at full price; **full price** = price with no discount; *he bought a full-price ticket* **(c) in full** = completely; *give your full name and address or your name and address in full; he accepted all our conditions in full; full refund or refund paid in full; he got a full refund when he complained about the service;* **full payment** *or* **payment in full** = paying all money owed

◇ **full-scale** *adjective* complete *or* very thorough; *the CEO ordered a full-scale review of credit terms*

◇ **full-service** *adjective* providing a complete range of services; *full-service banking; full-service gas station*

◇ **full-time** *adjective & adverb* working all the normal working time (i.e., about eight hours a day, five days a week); *she is in full-time work or she works full-time or she is employed full-time; he is one of our full-time accountants*

◇ **full-timer** *noun* person who works full-time

◇ **fully** *adverb* completely; **fully-paid shares** = shares where the full face value has been paid; **fully paid-up capital** = all money paid for the issued capital shares

> QUOTE the administration launched a full-scale investigation into maintenance procedures
> *Fortune*

function 1 *noun* duty *or* job; **management function** *or* **function of management** = the duties of being a manager **2** *verb* to work; *the advertising campaign is functioning smoothly; the new management structure does not seem to be functioning very well*

fund 1 *noun* money set aside for a special purpose; **contingency fund** = money set aside in case it is needed urgently; **pension fund** = money which provides pensions for retired employees; **the International Monetary Fund** = (part of the United Nations) a type of bank which helps member states in financial difficulties, gives financial advice to members and encourages world trade **2** *plural noun* money which is available for spending; *the company has no funds to pay for the research program ; the company called for extra funds* = the company asked for more money; **to run out of funds** = to come to the end of the money available;

public funds = government money available for expenditure; *the park was paid for out of public funds;* **conversion of funds** = using money which does not belong to you for a purpose for which it is not supposed to be used; **to convert funds to another purpose** = to use money for a wrong purpose; **to convert funds to one's own use** = to use someone else's money for yourself **3** *verb* to provide money for a purpose; **to fund a company** = to provide money for a company to operate; *the company does not have enough resources to fund its expansion program*

◊ **funded** *adjective* backed by long-term loans; *long-term funded capital;* **funded debt** = the debt of a business in the form of such long-term instruments as bonds

◊ **funding** *noun* (a) providing money for spending; *the bank is providing the funding for the new product launch* (b) changing a short-term debt into a long-term loan; *the capital expenditure program requires long-term funding*

QUOTE the S&L funded all borrowers' development costs, including accrued interest
Barrons

furnish *verb* (a) to supply *or* to provide (b) to put furniture into an office *or* room; *he furnished his office with secondhand chairs and desks; the company spent $10,000 on furnishing the chairman's office ;* **furnished accommodation** = apartment *or* house, etc., which is rented with furniture in it

furniture *noun* chairs, tables, beds, etc.; **office furniture** = chairs, desks, filing cabinets used in an office; *he deals in secondhand office furniture; an office furniture store*

further 1 *adjective* (a) at a greater distance away; *the office is further down Main Street; the flight from Paris terminates in New York - for further destinations you must change to internal flights* (b) additional *or* extra; *further orders will be dealt with by our London office; nothing can be done while we are awaiting further instructions;* **to ask for further details;** *he had borrowed $100,000 and then tried to borrow a further $25,000; the company is asking for further credit; he asked for a further six weeks to pay* (c) **further to** = referring to something in addition; **further to our letter of June 21** = in addition to what

we said in our letter; **further to your letter of June 21** = here is information which you asked for in your letter; **further to our telephone conversation** = here is some information which we discussed **2** *verb* to help *or* to promote; *he was accused of using his membership on the council to further his own interests*

future 1 *adjective* referring to time to come *or* to something which has not yet happened; **future delivery** = delivery at a later date **2** *noun* time which has not yet happened; *try to be more careful in the future; in the future all reports must be sent to Australia by air*

◊ **futures** *plural noun* trading in bonds or commodities for delivery at a later date; *cotton rose 5% on the commodity futures market yesterday*

Gg

g = GRAM

gain 1 *noun* (a) increase *or* becoming larger; **gain in experience** = getting more experience; **gain in profitability** = becoming more profitable (b) increase in profit *or* price *or* value; *oil stocks showed gains on the Stock Exchange; the property sector put on gains of 10%-15%;* **capital gains** = profit made by selling a fixed asset for more than it cost; **capital gains tax** = specific tax paid on capital gains; **short-term gains** = increase in price made over a short period **2** *verb* (a) to get *or* to obtain; *he gained some useful experience working in a bank;* **to gain control of a business** = to buy more than 50% of the shares so that you can direct the business (b) to rise in value; *the dollar gained six points on the foreign exchange markets*

◊ **gainful** *adjective* **gainful employment** = employment which pays money

◊ **gainfully** *adverb* **gainfully employed** = working and earning money

gallon *noun* measure of liquids (= 4 quarts); *the car goes twenty-five miles per gallon or the car goes twenty-five miles to the gallon* = the car uses one gallon of gasoline in traveling twenty-five miles

NOTE: usually written **gal** after figures: **25gal**

galloping inflation *noun* very rapid inflation which is almost impossible to reduce

gap *noun* empty space; **gap in the market** = opportunity to make a product which is needed but which no one has sold before; *to look for or to find a gap in the market; this computer has filled a real gap in the market;* **trade gap** = difference in value between a country's imports and exports

> QUOTE these savings are still not great enough to overcome the price gap between American products and those of other nations
> *Duns Business Month*

gate *noun* door leading to an aircraft at an airport; *flight AZ270 is now boarding at Gate 23*

gather *verb* (a) to collect together *or* to put together; *he gathered his papers together before the meeting started; she has been gathering information on import controls from various sources* (b) to understand *or* to find out; *I gather he has left the office; did you gather who will be at the meeting?*

GATT = GENERAL AGREEMENT ON TARIFFS AND TRADE

gear *verb* to link to *or* to orient to; *bank interest rates are geared to the prime rate;* salary geared to the cost of living = salary which rises as the cost of living increases

◊ **gear up** *verb* to get ready; **to gear up for a sales drive** = to make all the plans and get ready for a sales drive; *the company is gearing itself up for expansion into the African market*

general *adjective* (a) overall *or* ordinary *or* not specific; **general expenses** = all kinds of minor expenses *or* money spent on the day-to-day costs of running a business; **general manager** = manager in charge of the administration of a company; **general office** = main administrative office of a company; **General Post Office** = main post office in a city (b) dealing with everything *or* with everybody; **general audit** = examining all the books of account of a company; **general average** = sharing of the cost of lost goods between all parties

to an insurance; **general meeting** = meeting of all the shareholders of a company; **general strike** = strike of all the workers in a country (c) **the General Agreement on Tariffs and Trade** = international organization which aims to try to reduce restrictions in trade between countries (d) **general trading** = dealing in all types of goods; **general store** = small country store which sells a large range of goods

◊ **generally** *adverb* normally *or* usually; *the office is generally closed between Christmas and New Year's Day; we generally offer a 25% discount for bulk purchases*

generous *adjective* (person) who is glad to give money; *the staff contributed a generous amount for the retirement present for the manager*

gentleman *noun* (a) "gentlemen" = way of starting to talk to a group of men; *"good morning, gentlemen; if everyone is here, the meeting can start"; "well, gentlemen, we have all read the report from our Australian office"; "ladies and gentlemen"* = way of starting to talk to a group of women and men (b) man; **gentlemen's agreement** = verbal agreement between two parties who respect each other; *they have a gentleman's agreement not to trade in each other's area*

genuine *adjective* true *or* real; *this old table is genuine; a genuine leather purse;* **the genuine article** = real article, not an imitation

◊ **genuineness** *noun* being real *or* not being an imitation

get *verb* (a) to receive; *we got a letter from the attorney this morning; when do you expect to get more stock? he gets $250 a week for doing nothing; she got $5,000 for her car* (b) to arrive at a place; *the shipment got to Canada six weeks late; she finally got to the office at 10:30*

NOTE: **getting - got - has got** *or* **gotten**

◊ **get across** *verb* to make someone understand something; *the manager tried to get across to the workforce why some people were being laid off*

◊ **get along** *verb* (a) to manage; *we are getting along quite well with only half the staff* (b) to be friendly *or* to work well with someone; *do you get along with your boss?*

◊ **get around** *verb* to avoid; *we tried to get around the embargo by shipping from Canada*

◊ **get back** *verb* to receive something which you had before; *I got my money back after I had complained to the manager; he got his initial investment back in two months*

◊ **get on with** *verb* (a) to be friendly *or* to work well with someone; *she does not get on with her new boss* (b) to go on doing work; *the staff got on with the work and finished the order on time*

◊ **get out** *verb* (a) to produce something (on time); *the accounts department got out the draft financial statement in time for the meeting* (b) to sell an investment; *he didn't like the annual report, so he got out before the company collapsed*

◊ **get out of** *verb* to stop trading in (a product *or* an area); *the company is getting out of computers; we got out of the South American market*

◊ **get through** *verb* (a) to speak to someone on the phone; *I tried to get through to the complaints department* (b) to finish *or* complete; *he got through his exams, so he is now a qualified engineer* (c) to try to make someone understand; *I could not get through to her that I had to be at the airport by 2:15*

gift *noun* thing given to someone; **gift certificate** = card, bought in a store, which is given as a present and which must be exchanged in that store for goods; *we gave her a gift certificate for her birthday;* **gift shop** = store selling small items which are given as presents; **gift tax** = tax on large gifts, especially on gifts of money made to avoid estate tax; **free gift** = present given by a store to a customer to attract business

◊ **gift-wrap** 1 *noun* gift-wrapping service for wrapping purchases in attractive wrapping paper 2 *verb* to wrap a present in attractive paper; *do you want this book gift-wrapped?*

◊ **gift-wrapping** *noun* (a) service in a store for wrapping purchases for customers to give as presents (b) attractive paper for wrapping presents

gilt-edged *adjective* investment which is very safe; **gilt-edged bond**

gimmick *noun* clever idea *or* trick; *a publicity gimmick; the PR men thought up this new advertising gimmick*

Ginnie Mae *(informal)* = GOVERNMENT NATIONAL MORTGAGE ASSOCIATION

give *verb* (a) to pass something to someone as a present; *the office gave him a clock when he retired* (b) to pass something to someone; *she gave the documents to the accountant; can you give me some information about the new computer system?* do not give any details to the police (c) to organize; *the company gave a party on a boat to publicize its new discount system*
NOTE: giving - gave - has given

◊ **give away** *verb* to give something as a free present; *we are giving away a pocket calculator with each $10 purchase*

◊ **giveaway** 1 *adjective* to sell at giveaway prices = to sell at very cheap prices 2 *noun* thing which is given as a free gift when another item is bought

glue 1 *noun* substance which sticks items together; *she put some glue on the back of the poster to fix it to the wall; the glue on the envelope does not stick very well* 2 *verb* to stick things together with glue; *he glued the label to the box*

glut 1 *noun* a glut of produce = too much produce, which is then difficult to sell; *a coffee glut or a glut of coffee;* **glut of money** = situation where there is too much money available to borrowers 2 *verb* to fill the market with something which is then difficult to sell; *the market is glutted with cheap cameras*
NOTE: glutting - glutted

gm = GRAM

gnome *noun informal* **the gnomes of Zurich** = important Swiss international bankers

GNP = GROSS NATIONAL PRODUCT

go *verb* (a) to move from one place to another; *the check went to your bank yesterday; the plane goes to Frankfurt, then to Rome; he is going to our Detroit office* (b) to be placed; *the date goes at the top of the letter*
NOTE: going - went - has gone

◊ **go-ahead** 1 *noun* **to give something the go-ahead** = to approve something *or* to say that something can be done; *his project got a government go-ahead; the board refused to give the go-ahead to the expansion plan* 2 *adjective* energetic or eager to do well; *he is a very go-ahead type; she works for a go-ahead clothing company*

◊ **go back on** *verb* not to do what has been promised; *two months later they went back on the agreement*

◊ **going** *adjective* **(a)** active or busy; **to sell a business as a going concern** = to sell a business as an actively trading company; **it is a going concern** = the company is working (and making a profit); **going-concern value** = value of a company as a going concern, as opposed to its value if its assets are liquidated **(b) the going price** = the usual or current price or the price which is being charged now; *what is the going price for secondhand 1975 Volkswagens?;* **the going rate** = the usual or current rate of payment; *we pay the going rate for typists; the going rate for offices is $10 per square foot*

◊ **going to** *verb* **to be going to do something** = to be just about to start doing something; *the firm is going to open an office in New York next year; when are you going to answer my letter?*

◊ **go into** *verb* **(a) to go into business** = to start in business; *he went into business as a car dealer; she went into business in partnership with her son* **(b)** to examine carefully; *the bank wants to go into the details of the inter-company loans*

◊ **go on** *verb* **(a)** to continue; *the staff went on working in spite of the fire; the chairman went on speaking for two hours* **(b)** to work with; *the figures for 1982 are all he has to go on; we have to go on the assumption that sales will not double next year*
NOTE: you go on **doing** something

◊ **go out** *verb* **to go out of business** = to stop trading; *the firm went out of business last week*

◊ **go public** *verb* (of a private company) to offer shares to the general investor by selling them on a Stock Exchange for the first time

goal *noun* aim or something which you try to do; *our goal is to break even within twelve months; the company achieved all its goals*

godown *noun* warehouse (in the Far East)

gofer *noun* person who does all types of work in an office for low wages

gold *noun* **(a)** very valuable yellow metal; *to buy gold; to deal in gold; gold coins;* **gold bullion** = bars of gold **(b) the country's gold reserves** = the country's store of gold kept to pay international debts; **the gold standard** = linking of the value of a currency to the value of a quantity of gold; **the dollar abandoned the gold standard in 1934** = the dollar stopped being linked to the value of gold **(c) gold point** = amount by which a currency which is linked to gold can vary in price **(d) gold card** = special charge card for people with high salaries, offering special advantages; **gold shares** or **golds** = shares in gold mines

◊ **golden** *adjective* looking as though made of gold; **golden handcuffs** = contract which offers a large sum of money or other benefits to a top executive provided he stays with the company; **golden parachute** = contract which provides a large sum of money or other benefits to a top executive when the company he is working for merges with another firm and he loses his job; *when the company was taken over, the sales director received a golden parachute of $250,000*

◊ **goldmine** *noun* mine which produces gold; *that store is a little goldmine* = that store is a very profitable business

good *adjective* **(a)** not bad; **a good buy** = excellent item which has been bought cheaply; **to buy something in good faith** = to buy something thinking it is of good quality or that it has not been stolen or that it is not an imitation **(b) a good deal of** = a large quantity of; *we wasted a good deal of time discussing the arrangements for the meeting; the company had to pay a good deal for the building site;* **a good many** = very many; *a good many staff members have joined the union*

◊ **goods** *plural noun* **(a) goods and chattels** = movable personal possessions **(b)** items which can be moved and are for sale; **goods in bond** = imported goods held by the customs until duty is paid; **capital goods** = machinery, buildings and raw materials which are used to make other goods; **consumer goods** = goods bought by the general public and not by businesses; **dry goods** = cloth and clothes; **finished goods** = manufactured goods which are ready to be sold; **household goods** = items which are used in the home; **luxury goods** = expensive items which are not basic necessities; **manufactured**

goods = items which are made by machine

◊ **goodwill** *noun* good reputation of a business; *he paid $10,000 for the goodwill of the store and $4,000 for the stock*

govern *verb* to rule; *the country is governed by a group of military leaders*

◊ **government** *noun* **(a)** organization which administers a country; **federal government =** main organization dealing with the affairs of the whole of the U.S.A.; **local government =** organizations dealing with the affairs of a city *or* town *or* county; **provincial government** *or* **state government =** organization dealing with the affairs of a province *or* of a state **(b)** coming from the government *or* referring to the government; *government employees; government intervention or intervention by the government; a government ban on the import of arms; a government investigation into organized crime; government officials prevented him from leaving the country; government policy is outlined in the booklet; government regulations state that import duty has to be paid on luxury items; he invested all his savings in government securities;* **government aid =** money paid by the government; **government contractor =** company which supplies goods or services to the government on contract; **government support =** financial help given by the government; *the computer industry relies on government support*

◊ **governmental** *adjective* referring to a government

◊ **government-backed** *adjective* supported by the government

◊ **government-controlled** *adjective* under the direction of the government; *advertisements cannot be placed in government-controlled newspapers*

◊ **Government National Mortgage Association** *noun* federal organization which provides backing for mortgages

◊ **government-regulated** *adjective* regulated by the government

◊ **government-sponsored** *adjective* encouraged by the government and backed by government money; *he is working in a government-sponsored program to help small businesses*

grace *noun* favor shown by granting a delay; *to give a creditor a period of*

grace *or* **two weeks' grace; taxpayers have a period of grace before the IRS starts chasing them for not filing tax returns**

grade 1 *noun* level *or* rank; *to reach the top grade in the civil service;* **high-grade =** of very good quality; *high-grade gasoline;* **a high-grade trade delegation =** a delegation made up of important people; **low-grade =** not very important *or* not of very good quality; *the car runs well on low-grade gasoline;* **top-grade =** most important *or* of the best quality; **a top-grade official 2** *verb* **(a)** to sort something into different levels of quality; *to grade coal* **(b)** to make something rise in steps according to quantity; **graded tax =** local tax structure in which taxes are higher for unimproved property

gradual *adjective* slow *or* step by step; *1984 saw a gradual return to profits; his resume describes his gradual rise to the position of CEO*

◊ **gradually** *adverb* slowly *or* step by step; *the company has gradually become more profitable; she gradually learned the details of the import-export business*

graduate *noun* person who has a degree *or* diploma; *high school graduate; college graduate; he is a graduate of Boston University*

◊ **graduated** *adjective* rising in steps according to quantity; **graduated payment mortgage =** mortgage with lower payments in the early years than in the later years; **graduated wage =** wage structure in an organization where the various wage levels are determined by seniority, experience or performance

gram *or* **gramme** *noun* metric measure of weight (one thousandth of a kilo) NOTE: usually written **g** or **gm** with figures: **25g**

grand 1 *adjective* important; **grand plan =** major plan; *he explained his grand plan for redeveloping the factory site;* **grand total =** final total made by adding several subtotals **2** *noun informal* one thousand dollars; *they offered him fifty grand for the information*

grant 1 *noun* money given by the government *or* a private foundation to help pay for something; *the laboratory has a government grant to cover the* *cost of the development program; she is applying for a grant to study aspects of international trade* **2** *verb* to agree to give someone something; *to grant someone a loan* or *a subsidy; the local government granted the company an interest-free loan to start up the new factory*

QUOTE the budget grants a tax exemption for $500,000 in capital gains
Toronto Star

graph *noun* diagram which shows statistics as a drawing; *to set out the results in a graph; to draw a graph showing the rising profitability; the sales graph shows a steady rise;* graph **paper** = special paper divided by lines into many little squares, used for drawing graphs

gratia see EX GRATIA

gratis *adverb* free or not costing anything; *we got into the computer show gratis*

gratuity *noun* money given to someone who has helped you; *the employees are instructed not to accept gratuities*

gray market *noun* trading in commodities or securities outside the usual markets, but not illegally done

great *adjective* large; **a great deal of** = very much; *he made a great deal of money on the Stock Exchange; there is a great deal of work to be done before the company can be made really profitable*

greenback *noun informal* dollar bill

◊ **green card** *noun* work permit for a person who is not a U.S. citizen coming to live in the U.S.A.

◊ **greenmail** *noun* making a profit by buying a quantity of a company's shares, threatening to take the company over, and then selling the shares back to the company at a higher price

QUOTE gold's drop this year is of the same magnitude as the greenback's 8.5% rise
Business Week
QUOTE proposes that there should be a limit on greenmail, perhaps permitting payment of a 20% premium on a maximum of 8% of the stock
Duns Business Month

grid *noun* system of numbered squares; **grid structure** = structure based on a grid

grievance *noun* complaint made by a union or a worker to the management; **grievance procedure** = official way of presenting complaints from a union to the management

gross 1 *noun* twelve dozen (144); *he ordered four gross of pens* **2** *adjective* (a) total or with no deductions; **gross earnings** = total earnings before tax and other deductions; **gross income** or **gross salary** = salary before tax is deducted; **gross margin** = percentage difference between sales income and the cost of goods sold; **gross profit** = profit calculated as sales revenue less expenses, not including taxes; **gross revenues** = total amount of money received before any expenses are deducted; **gross yield** = profit from investments before the deduction of tax (b) **gross national product** = annual value of goods and services traded in a country including income from other countries (c) **gross tonnage** = total amount of space in a ship; **gross weight** = weight of both the container and its contents **3** *adverb* with no deductions; *his salary is paid gross* **4** *verb* to make a gross profit; *the group grossed $25m in 1989*

QUOTE news that gross national product increased only 1.3% in the first quarter of the year sent the dollar down on foreign exchange markets
Fortune
QUOTE accurate gross sales figures for merchandise are impossible, since this is still primarily a cash business
Forbes Magazine

ground *noun* (a) soil or earth; **the factory was burned to the ground** = the factory was completely destroyed in a fire; **ground landlord** = person or company which owns the freehold of a property which is then leased and subleased; **ground lease** = first lease on land on which a building is then constructed; **ground rent** = rent paid by a lessee to the ground landlord (b) **grounds** = basic reasons; *does he have good grounds for complaint? there are no grounds on which we can be sued; what are the grounds for the wage increase demand?*

group 1 *noun* (a) several things or people together; *a group of the employees sent a memo to the chairman complaining about noise in the office;* **group insurance** = health or life insurance plan under which a group of employees are covered by one policy (b) several companies linked together in the same organization; *the group chairman or the chairman of the group; group sales forecast* 2 *verb* to **group together** = to put several items together; *sales from six different agencies are grouped together under the heading "European sales"*

◊ **Group of Seven** *or* **G7** group of seven major industrialized countries (U.S.A., Canada, Great Britain, France, Germany, Japan, Italy) whose finance ministers meet regularly to discuss international financial problems

◊ **Group of Ten** *or* **G10** group of ten major countries who lend to the International Monetary Fund (U.S.A., Canada, Great Britain, Germany, France, Japan, Italy, Belgium, the Netherlands, Sweden)

grow *verb* to become larger; *the company has grown from a small repair shop to a multinational electronics business; sales volume is growing at a rate of 15% per annum; the computer industry grew fast in the 1980s*
NOTE: growing - grew - has grown

◊ **growth** *noun* increase in size; *the company is aiming for growth* = is aiming to expand rapidly; **economic growth** = rate at which a country's national income grows; **a growth area** *or* **a growth market** = an area where sales are increasing rapidly; **growth fund** = fund which is invested in growth stocks; **a growth industry** = industry which is expanding rapidly; **growth rate** = speed at which something grows; **growth share** *or* **growth stock** = stock which people think is likely to rise in value

QUOTE a general price freeze succeeded in slowing the growth in consumer prices *Financial Times* QUOTE the thrift had grown from $4.7 million in assets in 1980 to $1.5 billion *Barrons* QUOTE our number one priority is to make the investment in our basic business to get the kind of growth and earnings and cash flow we want over the next four or five years *Forbes Magazine*

guarantee 1 *noun* **(a)** legal document which promises that a machine will work properly or that an item is of good quality; *the guarantee lasts for two years; it is sold with a twelve-month guarantee; the car is still under guarantee* = is still covered by the maker's guarantee **(b)** promise that someone will pay another person's debts **(c)** thing given as a security; *to leave*

share certificates as a guarantee **2** *verb* to give a promise that something will happen; **to guarantee for someone** = to act as security for someone's debts; **to guarantee a debt** = to promise that you will pay a debt made by someone else; **to guarantee an associate company** = to promise that an associate company will pay its debts; **to guarantee a bill of exchange** = to promise that the bill will be paid; **the product is guaranteed for twelve months** = the manufacturer says that the product will work properly for twelve months, and will repair it free of charge if it breaks down; **guaranteed wage** = wage which a company promises will not fall below a certain figure

◊ **guarantor** *noun* person who promises to pay someone's debts; *he stood guarantor for his brother*

guess 1 *noun* calculation made without any real information; *the forecast of sales is only a guess;* he made a guess **at the earnings before tax** = he tried to calculate roughly what the earnings would be; **it is anyone's guess** = no one really knows what is the right answer **2** *verb* to **guess (at)** something = to try to calculate something without any information; *they could only guess at the total loss; the sales director tried to guess the sales achieved by the Far East division*

◊ **guesstimate** *noun & verb informal* (to make) a rough calculation

QUOTE a senior economist guesstimates that the number could reach 3 million to 4 million by 1995 *Washington Post*

guideline *noun* unofficial suggestion as to how something should be done; *the government has issued guidelines on increases in incomes and prices; the increase in retail price breaks or goes against the government guidelines*

guild *noun* association of merchants; *trade guild; the guild of master bakers*

guilty *adjective* (person) who has done something wrong; *he was found guilty of libel; the company was guilty of not reporting the sales to the auditors*

gum *noun* glue; *he stuck the label to the box with gum*

◊ **gummed** *adjective* with glue on it; **gummed label** = label with dry glue on it, which has to be made wet to make it stick

Hh

ha = HECTARE

haggle *verb* to discuss prices and terms and try to reduce them; *to haggle about or over the details of a contract*

half 1 *noun* one of two parts into which something is divided; *the first half of the agreement is acceptable;* **the first half** *or* **the second half of the year** = the periods from January 1 to June 30 *or* from June 30 to December 31; **we share the profits half and half** = we share the profits equally NOTE: plural is **halves 2** *adjective* divided into two parts; **half a percent** *or* **a half percent** = 0.5%; *his commission on the deal is twelve and a half percent* = 12.5%; **half a dozen** *or* **a half-dozen** = six; **to sell goods at half price** = at 50% of the price for which they were sold before; **a half-price sale** = sale of all goods at half the price

◊ **half-dollar** *noun* fifty cents

◊ **half-life** *noun* period when half the principal borrowed on a mortgage has been repaid NOTE: plural is **half-lives**

◊ **half-year** *noun* six months of an accounting period; **first half-year** *or* **second half-year** = first six months *or* second six months of a company's accounting year; **to announce the sales for the half-year to June 30** *or* **the first half-year's results** = results for the period January 1 to June 30; *we look forward to improvements in the second half-year*

◊ **half-yearly 1** *adjective* happening every six months *or* referring to a period of six months; *half-yearly report; half-yearly payment; half-yearly statement; a half-yearly meeting* **2** *adverb* every six months; *we pay the account half-yearly*

hallmark 1 *noun* mark put on gold or silver items to show that the metal is of the correct quality **2** *verb* to put a hallmark on a piece of gold or silver; *a hallmarked spoon*

hammer 1 *noun* tool used to hit something; **auctioneer's hammer** = wooden hammer used by an auctioneer to hit his desk, showing that an item has been sold; **to go under the hammer** = to be sold by auction; **all the stock went under the hammer** = all the stock was sold by auction **2** *verb* to hit hard; **to hammer the competition** = to attack and defeat the competition; **to hammer prices** = to reduce prices sharply

◊ **hammering** *noun* beating; *the company took a hammering in Europe* = the company had large losses in Europe *or* lost parts of its European markets; **we gave them a hammering** = we beat them

◊ **hammer out** *verb* to hammer out an agreement = to agree on something after long and difficult negotiations; *the contract was finally hammered out*

hand *noun* **(a) to shake hands** = to grasp someone's hand when meeting to show you are pleased to meet him or to show that an agreement has been reached; *the two negotiating teams shook hands and sat down at the conference table;* **to shake hands on a deal** = to shake hands to show that an agreement has been made **(b) by hand** = using the hands, not a machine; *these shoes are made by hand;* **to send a letter by hand** = to ask someone to carry and deliver a letter personally, not sending it through the mail **(c) in hand** = kept in reserve; **balance in hand** *or* **cash in hand** = cash held to pay small debts and running costs; *we have $10,000 in hand;* **work in hand** = work which is in progress but not finished **(d) goods left on hand** = unsold goods left with the retailer or manufacturer; *they were left with half the stock on their hands* **(e) show of hands** = vote where people show how they vote by raising their hands; *the motion was carried on a show of hands* **(f) to change hands** = to be sold to a new owner; *the store changed hands for $100,000* **(g) note of hand** = document where someone promises to pay money at a stated time without conditions **(h)** worker; *to take on ten more hands;* **factory hand** = worker in a factory

◊ **handbill** *noun* sheet of printed paper handed out to members of the public as an advertisement

◊ **handbook** *noun* book which gives instructions on how something is to be used; *the handbook does not say how you open the photocopier; look in the handbook to see if it tells you how to* clean the typewriter; service **handbook** = book which shows how to service a machine

◇ **hand in** *verb* to deliver (a letter) by hand; **he handed in his notice** *or* **he handed in his resignation** = he resigned

◇ **hand luggage** *noun* small cases which passengers can carry themselves (and so can take with them onto a plane)

◇ **handmade** *adjective* made by hand, not by machine; *he writes all his letters on handmade paper*

◇ **hand-operated** *adjective* worked by hand, not automatically; *a hand-operated machine*

◇ **handout** *noun* (a) **publicity handout** = information sheet which is given to members of the public (b) free gift; *the company exists on handouts from the state government*

◇ **hand over** *verb* to pass something to someone; *she handed over the documents to the lawyer*

◇ **handshake** *noun* grasping someone's hand to show you are pleased to meet him *or* that an agreement has been reached; *he has a firm handshake*

◇ **handwriting** *noun* writing done by hand; **send a letter of application in your own handwriting** = written by you with a pen, and not typed

◇ **handwritten** *adjective* written by hand, not typed; *it is more professional to send in a typed rather than a handwritten letter of application*

handle *verb* (a) to deal with something *or* to organize something; *the accounts department handles all the cash; we can handle orders for up to 15,000 units; they handle all our overseas orders* (b) to sell *or* to trade in (a type of product); *we do not handle foreign cars; they will not handle goods produced by other firms*

◇ **handling** *noun* moving something by hand *or* dealing with something; **handling charges** = money to be paid for packing and invoicing *or* for dealing with something in general *or* for moving goods from one place to another; *the bank adds on a 5% handling charge for changing travelers' checks*

handy *adjective* useful *or* convenient; *they are sold in handy-sized packs; this small case is handy for use when traveling*

hang *verb* to attach something to a hook, nail, etc.; *hang your coat on the hook behind the door; he hung his umbrella over the back of his chair*
NOTE: **hanging - hung**

◇ **hang on** *verb* to wait (while phoning); *if you hang on one moment, the chairman will be off the other line soon*

◇ **hang up** *verb* to stop a telephone conversation by putting the telephone back on its hook; *when I asked him about the invoice, he hung up*

happen *verb* (i) to take place by chance; (ii) to occur; *the contract happened to arrive when the manager was away on vacation; he happened to be in the store when the customer placed the order;* **what has happened to** = what went wrong with *or* what is the matter with *or* where is; *what has happened to that order for Japan?*

happy *adjective* very pleased; *we will be happy to supply you at a 25% discount; the CEO was not at all happy when the sales figures came in*

harbor *noun* port *or* place where ships come to load or unload; **harbor dues** = payment which a ship makes to the harbor authorities for the right to use the harbor; **harbor installations** *or* **harbor facilities** = buildings *or* equipment in a harbor

hard 1 *adjective* (a) strong *or* not weak; **to take a hard line in union negotiations** = to refuse to accept any proposal from the other side (b) difficult; *these typewriters are hard to sell; it is hard to get good people to work for low salaries* (c) solid; **hard cash** = money in notes and coins which is ready at hand; *he paid out $100 in hard cash for the chair;* **hard copy** = printout of a text which is on a computer *or* printed copy of a document which is on microfilm; *he made the presentation with diagrams and ten pages of hard copy;* **hard disk** = computer disk which has a sealed case and can store large quantities of information; **hard goods** = solid goods for use in the home, such as pans or hammers (d) **hard bargain** = bargain with difficult terms; **to drive a hard bargain** = to be a difficult negotiator; **to strike a hard bargain** = to agree on a deal where the terms are especially favorable to you; **after weeks of hard bargaining** = after weeks of difficult discussions **(e) hard currency =** currency of a country which has a strong economy and which can be changed into other currencies easily; *exports which can earn hard currency for the Soviet Union; these goods must be paid for in hard currency; a hard currency deal* 2 *adverb* with a lot of effort; *if everyone works hard, the order should be completed on time*

◊ **harden** *verb* prices are hardening = are settling at a higher price

◊ **hardening** *noun* **a hardening of prices** = becoming settled at a higher level

◊ **hardness** *noun* **hardness of the market** = being strong *or* not being likely to fall

◊ **hard sell** *noun* **to give a product the hard sell** = to make great efforts to persuade people to buy it; **he tried to give me the hard sell** = he put a lot of effort into trying to make me buy

◊ **hard selling** *noun* act of selling by using great efforts; *a lot of hard selling went into that deal*

◊ **hardware** *noun* **(a) computer hardware** = machines used in data processing, including the computers and printers, but not the programs; *hardware maintenance contract* **(b) military hardware** = guns *or* rockets *or* tanks, etc. **(c)** solid goods for use in the home (such as pans or hammers); *a hardware store*

harm 1 *noun* damage done; *the recession has done a lot of harm to export sales* 2 *verb* to damage; *the bad publicity has harmed the company's reputation*

haul *noun* distance traveled with a load of cargo; *it is a long haul from Birmingham to Nashville;* **short-haul flight** = flight over a short distance (up to 1000 km); **long-haul flight** = long-distance flight, especially between continents

haven *noun* safe place; **tax haven** = country where taxes are low, which encourages companies to set up their main offices there

hawk *verb* to sell goods from door to door or in the street; *to hawk newspapers on the corner*

◊ **hawker** *noun* person who sells goods from door to door or in the street

hazard *noun* situation which is dangerous; **fire hazard** = situation *or* goods which could start a fire; *that warehouse full of wood and paper is a fire hazard*

head 1 *noun* **(a)** most important person; **head of department** *or* **department head** = person in charge of a department **(b)** most important *or* main; *head clerk; head salesman;* **head buyer** = most important buyer in a department store; **head office** = main office of a company **(c)** top part *or* first part; *write the name of the company at the head of the list* **(d)** person; *representatives cost on average $25,000 per head per annum* 2 *verb* **(a)** to be the manager *or* to be the most important person; *to head a department; he is heading a buying mission to China* **(b)** to be first; *the two largest oil companies head the list of stock market leaders*

◊ **headed** *adjective* **headed paper** = stationery with the name of the company and its address printed on it

◊ **head for** *verb* to go towards; **the company is heading for disaster** = the company is going to collapse

◊ **headhunt** *verb* to look for managers and offer them jobs in other companies; **he was headhunted** = he was approached by a headhunter and offered a new job

◊ **headhunter** *noun* person *or* company which looks for top managers and offers them jobs in other companies

◊ **heading** *noun* **(a)** words at the top of a piece of text; *items are listed under several headings; look at the figure under the heading "Costs 85-86"* **(b) letter heading** *or* **heading on stationery** = name and address of a company printed at the top of a piece of stationery

◊ **headquarters** *plural noun* main office of a company; *the company's headquarters are in New York;* **divisional headquarters** = main office of a division of a company

◊ **head up** *verb* to be in charge of; *he has been appointed to head up our European organization*

health *noun* **(a)** being fit and well, not ill; **health insurance** = insurance which pays the cost of treatment for illness **(b) to give a company a clean bill of health** = to report that a company is trading profitably

◊ **healthy** *adjective* **a healthy balance sheet** = balance sheet which shows a good profit; **the company made some**

very healthy profits or **a very healthy profit** = made a large profit

hear verb (a) to sense a sound with the ears; **you can hear the printer in the next office; the traffic makes so much noise that I cannot hear my phone ringing** (b) to have a letter or a phone call from someone; **we have not heard from them for some time; we hope to hear from the lawyers within a few days**
NOTE: **hearing - heard**

heavy adjective (a) large or in large quantities; **a program of heavy investment overseas; he had heavy losses on the Stock Exchange; the company is a heavy user of steel** or **a heavy consumer of electricity; the government imposed a heavy tax on luxury goods; heavy costs** or **heavy expenditure** = spending large sums of money (b) which weighs a lot; **the Post Office refused to handle the package because it was too heavy; heavy industry** = industry which makes large products (such as steel bars, ships or machinery); **heavy machinery** = large machines

◇ **heavily** adverb **he is heavily in debt** = he has many debts; **they are heavily into property** = they have large investments in property; **the company has had to borrow heavily to repay its debts** = the company has had to borrow large sums of money

QUOTE the steel company had spent heavily on new equipment
Fortune

hectare noun measurement of area of land (= 2.47 acres)
NOTE: usually written **ha** after figures: **16ha**

hectic adjective busy or very active; **a hectic day on the Stock Exchange; after last week's hectic trading, this week has been very calm**

hedge 1 noun protection; **a hedge against inflation** = investment which should increase in value more than the increase in the rate of inflation; **he bought gold as a hedge against exchange losses 2** verb **to hedge one's bets** = to make investments in several areas so as to be protected against loss in one of them; **to hedge against inflation** = to buy investments which will rise in value faster than the increase in the rate of inflation

◇ **hedging** noun buying investments at a fixed price for delivery later, so as to protect oneself against possible loss

QUOTE gold and silver, the usual hedges against inflation and a weak dollar, have been on the wane
Business Week
QUOTE hedgers might move into currency and interest-rate options
Business Week

height noun (a) measurement of how tall or high something is; **what is the height of the desk from the floor? he measured the height of the room from floor to ceiling** (b) highest point; **it is difficult to find hotel accommodations at the height of the tourist season**

heir noun person who will receive property when someone dies; **his heirs split the estate between them**

helicopter noun aircraft with a large propeller on top which allows it to lift straight off the ground; **he took the helicopter from the airport to the center of town; it is only a short helicopter flight from the center of town to the factory site**

help 1 noun thing which makes it easy to do something; **she finds the word processor a great help in writing letters; the company was set up with financial help from the government; her assistant is not much help in the office - he cannot type or drive 2** verb to make it easy for something to be done; **he helped the salesman carry his case of samples; the computer helps in the rapid processing of orders** or **helps us to process orders rapidly; the government helps exporting companies with easy credit**
NOTE: you help someone or something **to do** something

hereafter adverb from this time on

◇ **hereby** adverb in this way or by this letter; **we hereby revoke the agreement of January 1, 1982**

◇ **herewith** adverb together with this letter; **please find the check enclosed herewith**

hereditament noun property which can be inherited

hesitate verb not to be sure what to do next; **the company is hesitating about**

starting up a new computer factory; she hesitated for some time before accepting the job

hidden *adjective* which cannot be seen; **hidden asset** = asset which is valued much less in the company's books of account than its true market value; **hidden discount** = extra discount given on some items in a bulk purchase when other items must be sold at a fixed price; **hidden reserves** = illegal reserves which are not declared in the company's balance sheet; **hidden defect in the program** = defect which was not noticed when the program was tested

high 1 *adjective* **(a)** tall; *the shelves are 15 in. high; the door is not high enough to let us get the machines into the building; they are planning a 30-story high office block* **(b)** large *or* not low; *high overhead costs increase the unit price; high prices put customers off; they are budgeting for a high level of expenditure; investments which bring in a high rate of return; high interest rates are killing small businesses;* **high finance** = lending, investing and borrowing of very large sums of money organized by financiers; **high flyer** = person who is very successful *or* who is likely to get a very important job; share whose market price is rising rapidly; **high sales** = large amount of revenue produced by sales; **high taxation** = taxation which imposes large taxes on incomes *or* profits; **highest tax bracket** = the group which pays the most tax; **high volume (of sales)** = large number of items sold **(c) highest bidder** = person who offers the most money at an auction; *the property was sold to the highest bidder; a decision made at the highest level* = decision made by the most important person or group **2** *adverb* **prices are running high** = prices are above their usual level **3** *noun* point where prices *or* sales are very large; *share prices have dropped by 10% since the high of January 2;* **the highs and lows on the Stock Exchange** = stocks that have reached new high or low points on the market; **sales volume has reached an all-time high** = has reached the highest point it has ever been at

◊ **high-grade** *adjective* of very good quality; *high-grade gasoline; a high-grade trade delegation* = a delegation made up of very important people

◊ **high-income** *adjective* which yields large earnings; *high-income shares; a high-income portfolio*

◊ **high-level** *adjective* **(a)** very important; **a high-level meeting** *or* **delegation** = meeting *or* delegation of the most important people (such as executives, board members); **a high-level decision** = decision made by the most important person or group **(b) high-level computer language** = programming language which uses normal words and figures

◊ **highly** *adverb* very; **highly-paid** = earning a large salary; **highly-priced** = with a large price; **she is highly thought of by the CEO** = the CEO thinks she is very competent

◊ **high pressure** *noun* strong influence by other people to do something; **working under high pressure** = working with a manager telling you what to do and to do it quickly *or* with customers asking for supplies urgently; **high-pressure salesman** = salesman who forces the customer to buy something he does not really need; **high-pressure sales techniques** *or* **high-pressure selling** = forcing a customer to buy something he does not really want

◊ **high-quality** *adjective* of very good quality; *high-quality goods; high-quality steel*

◊ **high technology** *or* **high tech** *noun* new developments in advanced fields of technology, such as computers, electronics and robotics; *he works for a high technology firm; high tech stocks are popular but risky*

QUOTE the accepted wisdom built upon for well over 100 years that government and high-grade corporate bonds were almost riskless
Forbes Magazine
QUOTE in a leveraged buyout the acquirer raises money by selling high-yielding debentures to private investors
Fortune

hike 1 *noun* increase; **pay hike** = increase in salary **2** *verb* to increase; *the union hiked its demand to $3 an hour*

hire 1 *noun* **(a)** paying money to rent a car *or* boat *or* piece of equipment for a time; *car hire; equipment hire* **(b) "for hire"** = sign on a taxi showing it is empty **(c) for hire contract** = freelance contract; **to work for hire** = to work freelance **2** *verb* **(a) to hire employees** = to employ new people; **to hire and fire** = to employ new workers and dismiss existing workers frequently; *we have hired the best lawyers to represent us;*

they hired a small company to paint the offices **(b) to hire a car** *or* **a crane =** to pay money to use a car *or* a crane for a time; *he hired a truck to move his furniture* **(c) to hire out cars** *or* **equipment =** to lend cars *or* equipment to customers who pay for their use

◊ **hiring** *noun* employing; *hiring of new personnel has been stopped; the company has a hiring freeze*

historic *or* **historical** *adjective* which goes back over a period of time; **historic(al) cost =** actual cost of an item purchased which was made some time ago; **historical figures =** figures which were current in the past

hit *verb* **(a)** to knock against something; *he hit his head against the table; we have hit our export targets =* we have reached our targets **(b)** to hurt *or* to damage; *the company was badly hit by the falling exchange rate; our sales of summer clothes have been hit by the bad weather; the new legislation has hit the small companies hardest*
NOTE: **hitting - hit**

hive off *verb* to split off part of a large company to form a smaller subsidiary; *the new owners hived off the retail sections of the company*

hoard *verb* to buy and store food in case of need *or* to keep cash instead of investing it

◊ **hoarder** *noun* person who buys and stores food in case of need

◊ **hoarding** *noun* **(a)** **hoarding of supplies =** buying large quantities of money *or* food to keep in case of need **(b)** temporary board fence put round a construction site

hold *verb* **(a)** to own *or* to keep; *he holds 10% of the company's shares; you should hold these shares - they seem likely to rise =* you should keep these shares and not sell them **(b)** to contain; *the carton holds twenty packets; each box holds 250 sheets of paper; a bag can hold twenty pounds of sugar* **(c)** to make something happen; *to hold a meeting or a discussion; the computer show will be held in St. Louis next month; board meetings are held in the boardroom; the conference will be held on March 24; the receiver will hold an auction of the company's assets; the accountants held a review of the company's accounting practices*

(d) *(on telephone)* **hold the line please =** please wait; *the chairman is on the other line - will you hold?*
NOTE: **holding - held**

◊ **hold back** *verb* to wait *or* not to go forward; *investors are holding back until after the election =* investors are waiting until they hear the results of the election before they decide whether to buy or sell; *he held back from signing the lease until he had checked the details =* he delayed signing the lease until he had checked the details; *payment will be held back until the contract has been signed =* payment will not be made until the contract has been signed

◊ **hold down** *verb* **(a)** to keep at a low level; *we are cutting margins to hold our prices down* **(b) to hold down a job =** to manage to keep a job

◊ **holder** *noun* **(a)** person who owns *or* keeps something; **holders of government bonds** *or* **bondholders; holder of stock** *or* **of shares in a company; holder of an insurance policy** *or* **policy holder; credit card holder =** person who has a credit card; **debenture holder =** person who holds a debenture for money lent **(b)** thing which keeps something *or* which protects something; **card holder** *or* **message holder =** frame which protects a card *or* a message; **credit card holder =** plastic wallet for keeping credit cards

◊ **holding** *noun* **(a)** group of shares owned; *he has sold all his holdings in the Far East; the company has holdings in German manufacturing companies* **(b) cross holdings =** situation where two companies own shares in each other in order to stop each from being taken over; *the two companies have protected themselves from takeover by a system of cross holdings*

◊ **holding company** *noun* company which exists only to own shares in subsidiary companies

◊ **hold on** *verb* to wait *or* not to change; *the company's shareholders should hold on and wait for a better offer =* they should keep their shares and not sell them

◊ **hold out for** *verb* to wait and ask for; *you should hold out for a 10% pay raise =* do not agree to a pay raise of less than 10%

◊ **hold over** *verb* to postpone *or* to put back to a later date; *discussion of item 4 was held over until the next meeting*

◇ **hold to** *verb* not to allow something to change; **we will try to hold him to the contract** = we will try to stop him from going against the contract; **the government hopes to hold wage increases to 5%** = the government hopes that wage increases will not be more than 5%

◇ **hold up** *verb* (a) to stay at a high level; *share prices have held up well; sales held up during the tourist season* (b) to delay; *the shipment has been held up at customs; payment will be held up until the contract has been signed; the strike will hold up deliveries for some weeks*

◇ **hold-up** *noun* delay; *the strike caused hold-ups in deliveries*

holiday *noun* day when most businesses are closed, and people celebrate a certain event; **New Year's Day is one of our official holidays** = one of the days when we are excused from work; **legal holiday** = holiday which is fixed by law; *the office is closed for the Thanksgiving holiday;* **holiday pay** = salary which is still paid during a holiday; *did you get holiday pay for the Fourth of July?*

home *noun* (a) place where a person lives; *please send the letter to my home address, not my office;* **home office** = office based in a person's home (mainly used by people working as freelancers) (b) **home country** = country where a company is based; **home sales** *or* **sales in the home market** = sales in the country where a company is based; **home-produced products** = products manufactured in the country where the company is based (c) house; **new home sales** = sales of new houses; **home equity credit** *or* **home loan** = loan by a bank *or* a mortgage company to a person buying a house

◇ **homegrown** *adjective* which has been developed in a local area *or* in a country where the company is based; *a homegrown computer industry; India's homegrown car industry*

◇ **homemade** *adjective* made in a home; *homemade jam*

◇ **homeowner** *noun* person who owns a private house; **homeowner's insurance policy** = insurance policy covering a house and its contents and the personal liability of the people living in it

hon = HONORABLE, HONORARY

honest *adjective* respected *or* saying what is right; **to play the honest broker** = to act for the parties in a negotiation to try to make them agree to a solution

◇ **honestly** *adverb* truthfully *or* not cheating

honor *verb* to pay something because it is owed and is correct; **to honor a bill; to honor a signature** = to pay something because the signature is valid

honorable *adjective* honest *or* correct

honorarium *noun* money paid to a professional person, such as an accountant *or* a lawyer, when he does not ask for a fee
NOTE: plural is **honoraria**

◇ **honorary** *adjective* person who is not paid a salary; **honorary secretary; honorary president;** **honorary member** = member who does not have to pay dues

hope *verb* to expect *or* to want something to happen; *we hope to be able to dispatch the order next week; he is hoping to break into the U.S. market; they had hoped the TV commercials would help sales*

horizontal *adjective* level *or* going from side to side, not up and down; **horizontal integration** = joining similar companies *or* taking over a company in the same line of business; **horizontal communication** = communication between workers at the same level

horse trading *noun* hard bargaining which ends with someone giving something in return for a concession from the other side

hostess *noun* woman who looks after passengers *or* clients; **airline hostess** = woman who looks after passengers in a plane

hot *adjective* (a) very warm; *the staff complains that the office is too hot in the summer and too cold in the winter; the vending machine sells coffee, tea and hot soup; switch off the machine if it gets too hot* (b) not safe *or* very bad; **to make things hot for someone** = to make it difficult for someone to work *or* to trade; *customs officials are making things hot for the drug smugglers* (c) stolen; *a hot car*

hotel *noun* building where you can rent a room for a night, or eat in a restaurant; *hotel bill; hotel expenses; hotel manager; hotel staff;* **hotel accommodation** = rooms available in hotels; *all hotel accommodation has been booked up for the convention;* **hotel chain** *or* **chain of hotels** = group of hotels owned by the same company; **the hotel trade** = business of running hotels

◊ **hotelier** *noun* person who owns *or* manages a hotel

hour *noun* **(a)** period of time lasting sixty minutes; **to work a thirty-five hour week** = to work seven hours a day each weekday; **we work an eight-hour day** = we work for eight hours a day, e.g. from 8:30 to 5:30 with one hour for lunch **(b)** sixty minutes of work; *he earns $4 an hour; we pay $6 an hour;* **to pay by the hour** = to pay people a fixed amount of money for each hour worked **(c)** **banking hours** = time when a bank is open for its customers; *you cannot get money out of the bank outside banking hours;* **office hours** = time when an office is open; *do not telephone during office hours; the shares rose in after-hours trading* = in trading after the Stock Exchange had closed

◊ **hourly** *adverb* per hour; **hourly-paid workers** = workers paid at a fixed rate for each hour worked; **hourly rate** = amount of money paid for an hour worked

house *noun* **(a)** place (building *or* apartment) in which someone lives **(b)** company; *the largest Wall Street finance house; he works for a brokerage house or a publishing house;* **discount house** = (i) financial company which specializes in discounting bills; (ii) store which specializes in selling cheap goods bought at a high discount; **export house** = company which specializes in the export of goods manufactured by other companies; **house brand** = product sold under the brand name of the store that sells it; **house organ** = magazine produced for the employees of a company to give them news about the company; **house telephone** = internal telephone for calling from one office to another **(c)** legislative body; *the U.S. House of Representatives*

◊ **household** *noun* people living in a house; **household expenses** = money spent on running a private house; **household goods** = goods which are used in a house

◊ **householder** *noun* person who lives in a house or apartment alone or as head of the household

◊ **housing** *noun* apartments *or* houses for people; *the city has a housing shortage;* **housing starts** = number of new private houses or apartments of which the construction has begun during a certain period

◊ **house-to-house** *adjective* going from one house to the next, asking people to buy something *or* to vote for someone; *house-to-house canvassing; house-to-house salesman; house-to-house selling*

human resources (HR) *noun* department in a large corporation which deals with the employees

hundredweight *noun* weight of 100 pounds
NOTE: usually written **cwt** after figures: **20cwt**

hurry 1 *noun* doing things fast; *there is no hurry for the figures, we do not need them until next week;* **in a hurry** = very fast; *the sales manager wants the report in a hurry* **2** *verb* to do something *or* to make something *or* to go very fast; *the production team tried to hurry the order through the factory; the chairman does not want to be hurried into making a decision; the directors hurried into the meeting*

◊ **hurry up** *verb* to make something go faster; *can you hurry up that order? - the customer wants it immediately*

hurt *verb* to harm *or* to damage; *the bad publicity did not hurt our sales; sales of summer clothes were hurt by the bad weather; the company has not been hurt by the recession*
NOTE: **hurting - hurt**

hype 1 *noun* excessive claims made in advertising; *all the hype surrounding the launch of the new soap* **2** *verb* to make excessive claims in advertising

hyper- *prefix meaning* very large
◊ **hyperinflation** *noun* inflation which is so rapid that it is almost impossible to reduce
◊ **hypermarket** *noun* very large supermarket, usually on the outside of a large town

hypothecation *noun* using a property as security for a loan, as with a mortgage

Ii

IC = INDEPENDENT CONTRACTOR

ICC = INTERSTATE COMMERCE COMMISSION

idea *noun* thing which you think of; *one of the salesman had the idea of changing the product color; the chairman thinks it would be a good idea to ask all managers to itemize their expenses*

ideal *adjective* perfect *or* very good for something; *this is the ideal site for a new shopping mall*

idle *adjective* **(a)** not working; *2,000 employees were made idle by the recession* **(b) idle capacity** *or* **idle machinery** *or* **machines lying idle** = work time *or* machinery not being used **(c) idle capital** = capital not being used productively; **money lying idle** *or* **idle money** = money which is not being used to produce interest *or* which is not invested in business

i.e. that is; *the largest companies, i.e., Smith's and Brown's, had a very good first quarter; the import restrictions apply to expensive items, i.e., items costing more than $2,500*

illegal *adjective* not legal *or* against the law
◇ **illegality** *noun* being illegal
◇ **illegally** *adverb* against the law; *he was accused of illegally importing arms into the country*

illicit *adjective* not legal *or* not permitted; *illicit sale of alcohol; trade in illicit alcohol*

illiquid *adjective* (asset, such as a bond) which cannot easily be sold for cash

ILO = INTERNATIONAL LABOR ORGANIZATION

image *noun* general idea which the public has of a product *or* a company; *they are spending a lot of advertising money to improve the company's image; the company has adopted a down-market image* ; **brand image** = picture which people have in their minds of a product associated with the brand name; **corporate image** = idea which a company would like the public to have of it; **to promote a corporate image** = to publicize a company so that its reputation is improved

IMF = INTERNATIONAL MONETARY FUND

imitate *verb* to do what someone else does; *they imitate all our sales gimmicks*
◇ **imitation** *noun* copy of something that is original; **beware of imitations** = be careful not to buy low-quality goods which are made to look like other more expensive items

immediate *adjective* happening at once; *he wrote an immediate letter of complaint; your order will receive immediate attention*
◇ **immediately** *adverb* at once; *he immediately placed an order for 2,000 boxes; as soon as he heard the news he immediately faxed his office*

immovable *adjective* which cannot be moved; **immovable property** = houses and other buildings on land

immunity *noun* protection against arrest; **diplomatic immunity** = being outside a country's laws because of being a diplomat; *he was granted immunity from prosecution* = he was told he would not be prosecuted

impact *noun* shock *or* strong effect; *the impact of new technology on the cotton trade; the new design has made little impact on the buying public*

> QUOTE the strong dollar's deflationary impact on European economies as governments push up interest rates to support their sinking currencies
> *Duns Business Month*

imperfect *adjective* not perfect; *sale of imperfect items; to check a batch for imperfect products*
◇ **imperfection** *noun* part of an item which is not perfect; *to check a batch for imperfections*

impersonal *adjective* without any personal touch *or* as if done by machines; *an impersonal style of management*

implement 1 *noun* tool *or* instrument used to do some work **2** *verb* to put into action; *to implement an agreement*

◊ **implementation** *noun* putting into action; *the implementation of new rules*

import 1 *noun* **(a) imports** = goods brought into a country from abroad for sale; *imports from Poland have risen to $1m a year;* **invisible imports** = services (such as banking, tourism) which are paid for in foreign currency; **visible imports** = real goods which are imported **(b) import ban** = forbidding imports; *the government has imposed an import ban on arms;* **import duty** = tax on goods imported into a country; **import license** *or* **import permit** = government license *or* permit which allows goods to be imported; **import quota** = fixed quantity of a particular type of goods which the government allows to be imported; *the government has imposed an import quota on cars;* **import surcharge** = extra duty charged on imported goods, to try to prevent them from being imported and to encourage local manufacture (NOTE: usually used in the plural, but the singular form is used before a noun) **2** *verb* to bring goods from abroad into a country for sale; *the company imports television sets from Japan; this car was imported from France; the union organized a boycott of imported cars*

QUOTE European manufacturers rely heavily on imported raw materials which are mostly priced in dollars
Duns Business Month

◊ **importation** *noun* act of importing; *the importation of arms is forbidden*

◊ **importer** *noun* person *or* company which imports goods; *a cigar importer; the company is a big importer of foreign cars*

◊ **import-export** *adjective* dealing with both bringing foreign goods into a country and sending locally made goods abroad; *import-export trade; he is in import-export*

◊ **importing 1** *adjective* which imports; *oil-importing countries; an importing company* **2** *noun* act of bringing foreign goods into a country for sale; *the importing of arms into the country is illegal*

importance *noun* having a value *or* mattering a lot; *the bank attaches great importance to the deal*

◊ **important** *adjective* which matters a lot; *he left a pile of important papers in the taxi; she has an important meeting at 10:30; he was promoted to a more important job*

impose *verb* to make a tax *or* a duty on goods mandatory; *to impose a tax on bicycles; they tried to impose a ban on smoking; the government imposed a special duty on oil; the customs office has imposed a 10% tax increase on luxury items; the unions have asked the government to impose trade barriers on foreign cars*

◊ **imposition** *noun* putting a tax on goods or services

impossible *adjective* which cannot be done; *getting skilled staff is becoming impossible; government regulations make it impossible for us to export*

impound *verb* to take something away and keep it until a tax is paid; *the customs officials impounded the whole cargo*

◊ **impounding** *noun* act of taking something and keeping it until a tax *or* fee is paid

imprest *noun* the **imprest system** = system of controlling petty cash, where cash is paid out against a written receipt and the receipt is used to get more cash to bring the float to the original level

improve *verb* to make something better *or* to become better; *we are trying to improve our image with a series of TV commercials; they hope to improve the company's cash flow position; we hope the cash flow position will improve or we will have difficulty in paying our bills;* **export trade has improved sharply during the first quarter** = export trade has increased

◊ **improved** *adjective* better; *the union rejected the management's improved offer*

◊ **improvement** *noun* **(a)** getting better; *there is no improvement in the cash flow situation; sales are showing a sharp improvement over last year* **(b)** thing which is better; **improvement on an offer** = making a better offer

◊ **improve on** *verb* to do better than; **he refused to improve on his previous offer =** he refused to make a better offer

impulse *noun* sudden decision; **impulse buying =** buying things which you have just seen, not because you had planned to buy them; *the store puts racks of candies by the checkout counter to attract the impulse buyer* ; impulse **buy** *or* **impulse purchase =** thing bought as soon as it is seen; **to do something on impulse =** to do something because you have just thought of it, not because it was planned

in = INCH

inactive *adjective* not active *or* not busy; **inactive market =** stock market with few buyers or sellers

Inc = INCORPORATED

incentive *noun* thing which encourages someone; **staff incentives =** pay and better conditions offered to workers to make them work better; **wage incentive** *or* **incentive bonus** *or* **incentive payment =** extra pay offered to a worker to make him work better; **wage incentive plan =** plan to encourage better work by paying higher commission or bonuses; *wage incentive plans are boosting production*

inch *noun* measurement of length (= one twelfth of a foot)
NOTE: usually written **in** or " after figures: **2in** or **2"**

incidental 1 *adjective* which is not important, but connected with something else; **incidental expenses =** small amounts of money spent at various times in addition to larger amounts **2** *noun* **incidentals =** incidental expenses

include *verb* to count something along with other things; *the charge includes sales tax; the total comes to $1,000 including freight; the total is $140 not including insurance and freight; the account covers services up to and including the month of June*
◊ **inclusive** *adjective* which counts something in with other things; *inclusive of tax; not inclusive of interest; inclusive sum* or **inclusive charge =** charge which includes all costs

income *noun* **(a)** money which a person receives as salary or dividends; **annual**

income = money received during a calendar year; **disposable income =** income left after tax and social security have been deducted; **earned income =** money received as a salary or wages; **fixed income =** portion of income which does not change from year to year; **gross income =** income before tax has been deducted; **net income =** income left after tax has been deducted; **personal income =** income received by an individual person; **unearned income =** money received from interest or dividends; **lower** *or* **upper income bracket =** groups of people who earn low or high salaries considered for tax purposes; **he is in the higher income bracket =** he is in a group of people earning high incomes and therefore paying more tax; **personal income tax =** tax on a person's income; **income tax form** *or* **income tax return =** statement declaring income to the tax office **(b)** money which a company receives over a period from sales, investments, etc.; **gross income =** total income received by a business before costs, taxes and other items are deducted; **net income =** income received by a business, less the cost of goods sold and other expenses; **income statement =** financial statement for a company which shows expenditure and sales balanced to give a final profit or loss; **corporate** *or* **corporation income tax =** tax paid on the income of a business **(c)** money which an organization receives as gifts or from investments; *the hospital has a large income from gifts*

> QUOTE the company will be paying income tax at the higher rate in 1985
> *Citizen (Ottawa)*

incoming *adjective* **(a) incoming call =** phone call coming into the office from someone outside; **incoming mail =** mail which comes into an office **(b)** which have recently been elected *or* appointed; **the incoming board of directors =** the new board which is about to start working; *the incoming chairman or president*

incompetent *adjective* (person) who lacks ability to work well; *the sales manager is quite incompetent; the company has an incompetent chairman*

inconvertible *adjective* (currency) which cannot be converted into precious metal

incorporate *verb* (a) to bring something in to form part of a main group; *income from the 1989 acquisition is incorporated into the accounts* (b) to form a registered company; *a company incorporated in the U.S.; an incorporated company; J. Doe Incorporated*

◊ **incorporation** *noun* act of incorporating a company

incorrect *adjective* wrong *or* not correct; *the minutes of the meeting were incorrect and had to be changed*

◊ **incorrectly** *adverb* wrongly *or* not correctly; *the package was incorrectly addressed*

increase 1 *noun* (a) growth *or* becoming larger; *increase in tax or tax increase; increase in price or price increase; profits showed a 10% increase or an increase of 10% on last year;* increase in the cost of living = rise in the annual cost of living (b) higher salary; *increase in pay or pay increase; increase in salary or salary increase; the government hopes to hold salary increases to 3% ;* he had two increases last year = his salary went up twice; cost-of-living increase = increase in salary to allow it to keep up with higher cost of living; **merit increase** = increase in pay given to a worker whose work is good (c) **on the increase** = growing larger *or* becoming more frequent; *shoplifting is on the increase 2 verb* (a) to grow bigger *or* higher; *profits have increased faster than the increase in the rate of inflation; exports to Africa have increased by more than 25%; the price of oil has increased twice in the past week;* to increase in price = to cost more; to increase in size *or* in value = to become larger *or* more valuable (b) *the company increased his salary to $20,000* = the company gave him a raise in salary to $20,000

◊ **increasing** *adjective* which is growing bigger; *increasing profits; the company has an increasing share of the market*

◊ **increasingly** *adverb* more and more; *the company has to depend increasingly on the export market*

> QUOTE competition is steadily increasing and could affect profit margins as the company tries to retain its market share
> *Citizen (Ottawa)*

increment *noun* regular automatic increase in salary; *annual increment;*

salary which rises in annual increments of $500 = each year the salary is increased by $500

◊ **incremental** *adjective* which rises automatically in stages; **incremental cost** = cost of making a single extra unit above the number already planned; **incremental increase** = increase in salary according to an agreed annual increment; **incremental scale** = salary scale with regular annual salary increases

incur *verb* to make yourself liable to; **to incur the risk of a penalty** = to make it possible that you risk paying a penalty; **to incur debts** *or* **costs** = to do something which means that you owe money *or* that you will have to pay costs; *the company has incurred heavy costs to implement the expansion program* = the company has had to pay large sums of money

NOTE: **incurring - incurred**

indebted *adjective* owing money to someone; *to be indebted to a mortgage company*

◊ **indebtedness** *noun* state of indebtedness = being in debt *or* owing money

indemnification *noun* payment for damage

◊ **indemnify** *verb* to pay for damage; *to indemnify someone for a loss*

◊ **indemnity** *noun* guarantee of payment after a loss; *he had to pay an indemnity of $100;* letter of indemnity = letter promising payment as compensation for a loss

indent 1 *noun* (a) line of typing which starts several spaces from the left-hand margin (b) purchase order to an overseas supplier for a range of goods **2** *verb* to start a line of typing several spaces from the left-hand margin; *indent the first line three spaces*

indenture *noun* formal agreement stating the terms of a bond issue

independent *adjective* free *or* not controlled by anyone; **independent company** = company which is not controlled by another company; **independent contractor** = self-employed worker; **independent seller** *or* **independent store** = store which is owned by an individual proprietor, not by a chain; **the independents** = stores or companies which are owned by private individuals

index *noun* (**a**) list of items classified into groups or put in alphabetical order; **index card** = small card used for filing (**b**) regular statistical report which shows rises and falls in prices, etc.; **growth index** = index showing how something has grown; **cost-of-living index** = measure of the average changes in the cost of goods purchased by consumers at any time, against the cost during the base period; **consumer price index** = index showing how prices of consumer goods have risen over a period of time, used as a way of measuring inflation and the cost of living; **wholesale price index** = index showing rises and falls of prices of manufactured goods as they leave the factory; **index number** = number which shows the percentage rise of something over a period of time
NOTE: plural is **indexes** or **indices**

◊ **indexation** *or* **indexing** *noun* linking of something to an index; **indexation of wage increases** = linking of wage increases to the percentage rise in consumer prices

◊ **index-linked** *adjective* which rises automatically by the percentage increase in the consumer price index; *index-linked pensions; his pension is index-linked; index-linked government bonds*

indicate *verb* to show; *the latest figures indicate a fall in the inflation rate; our sales for 1985 indicate a move from the domestic market to exports*

◊ **indicator** *noun* thing which indicates; **economic indicators** = statistics which show how the country's economy is going to perform in the short or long term; **leading indicator** = indicator which forecasts changes in a country's economy some months before they actually occur

indicia *noun* stamp printed on an envelope to show that postage has been paid by the sender

indirect *adjective* not direct; **indirect expenses** *or* **costs** = costs which are not directly attached to the making of a product (such as cleaning, rent, administration); **indirect labor costs** = costs of paying workers who are not directly involved in making a product

(such as secretaries, inspectors, cleaners); **indirect taxation** = taxes (such as sales tax) which are not paid directly to the government; *the government raises more money by indirect taxation than by direct*

individual **1** *noun* one single person; *savings plan made to suit the requirements of the private individual* **2** *adjective* single *or* belonging to one person; *a pension plan designed to meet each person's individual requirements; we sell individual portions of ice cream;* **Individual Retirement Account (IRA)** = private pension plan, where persons can make contributions separate from a company pension plan

inducement *noun* thing which helps to persuade someone to do something; *they offered him a company car as an inducement to stay*

industry *noun* (**a**) all factories *or* companies *or* processes involved in the manufacturing of products; *all sectors of industry have shown rises in output;* **basic industry** = most important industry of a country (such as coal, steel, agriculture); **a boom industry** *or* **a growth industry** = industry which is expanding rapidly; **heavy industry** = industry which deals in heavy raw materials (such as coal) or makes large products (such as ships or engines); **light industry** = industry making small products (such as clothes, books, calculators); **primary industry** = industry dealing with basic raw materials (such as coal, wood, farm produce); **secondary industry** = industry which uses basic raw materials to produce manufactured goods; **service industry** *or* **tertiary industry** = industry which does not produce raw materials or manufacture products but offers a service (such as banking, retailing, accounting) (**b**) group of companies making the same type of product; *the aircraft industry; the building industry; the car industry; the food processing industry; the mining industry; the petroleum industry*

◊ **industrial** **1** *adjective* referring to manufacturing work; **industrial accident** = accident which takes place at work; **to take industrial action** = to go on strike; **industrial average** = index of market prices of industrial stocks on a Stock Exchange; **industrial**

capacity = amount of work which can be done in a factory or several factories; **industrial center** = large town with many industries; **industrial consumer** or **industrial user** = manufacturing company which purchases a certain product (as opposed to a personal or commercial purchaser); **industrial design** = design of products made by machines (such as cars, refrigerators); **industrial disputes** = arguments between management and workers; **industrial espionage** = trying to find out the secrets of a competitor's work or products, usually by illegal means; **industrial park** = area of land near a town specially for factories and warehouses; **industrial expansion** = growth of industries in a country or a region; **industrial injuries** = injuries which happen to workers at work; **industrial processes** = processes involved in manufacturing products in factories; **industrial relations** = relations between management and workers; **good industrial relations** = situation where management and workers understand each others' problems and work together for the good of the company; **industrial training** = training of new workers to work in an industry; **land zoned for light industrial use** = land where planning permission has been given to build small factories for light industry **2** noun **industrials** = (i) manufacturing companies; (ii) shares in manufacturing companies

◊ **industrialist** noun owner or director of a factory

◊ **industrialization** noun changing of an economy from being based on agriculture to industry

◊ **industrialize** verb to set up industries in a country which had none before; **industrialized societies** = countries which have many industries

> QUOTE central bank and finance ministry officials of the industrialized countries will continue work on the report
> *Wall Street Journal*

inefficiency noun lack of efficiency; *the report criticized the inefficiency of the sales staff*

◊ **inefficient** adjective not efficient or not doing a job well; *an inefficient sales director*

inertia noun being lazy; **inertia selling** = method of selling items by sending

them when they have not been ordered and assuming that if the items are not returned, the person who has received them is willing to buy them

inexpensive adjective cheap or not expensive

◊ **inexpensively** adverb without spending much money

inferior adjective not as good as others; *inferior products* or *products of inferior quality*

inflate verb **(a)** to inflate prices = to increase prices; *tourists don't want to pay inflated New York prices* **(b)** to inflate the economy = to make the economy more active by increasing the money supply

◊ **inflated** adjective **(a)** inflated prices = prices which have been increased **(b)** inflated currency = currency which is too high in relation to other currencies

◊ **inflation** noun situation where prices rise to keep up with increased production costs; **we have 15% inflation** or **inflation is running at 15%** = prices are 15% higher than at the same time last year; **to take measures to reduce inflation; high interest rates tend to increase inflation; rate of inflation** or **inflation rate** = percentage increase in prices over a twelve-month period; **galloping inflation** or **runaway inflation** = very rapid inflation which it is almost impossible to reduce; **spiraling inflation** = inflation where price rises make workers ask for higher wages which then increase prices again

◊ **inflationary** adjective which tends to increase inflation; *inflationary trends in the economy;* **the economy is in an inflationary spiral** = in a situation where price rises encourage higher wage demands which in turn make prices rise; **anti-inflationary measures** = measures to reduce inflation

> QUOTE for now, inflation signals are mixed. The consumer price index jumped 0.7% in April after average monthly gains had speeded up to 0.5% during the first quarter. The core rate of inflation, which excludes food and energy, has stayed steady during the past six months at a 4.5% annual rate
> *Business Week*

inflow noun flowing in; **inflow of capital into the country** = capital which is coming into a country by way of international purchases or investments

QUOTE the dollar is strong because of capital inflows rather than weak because of the trade deficit

Duns Business Month

influence 1 *noun* effect which is had on someone *or* something; *the price of oil has a marked influence on the price of manufactured goods; we are suffering from the influence of a high exchange rate* **2** *verb* to have an effect on someone *or* something; *the board was influenced in its decision by the memo from the managers; the price of oil has influenced the price of manufactured goods; high inflation is influencing our profitability*
NOTE: you influence someone **to do** something

influx *noun* rushing in; *an influx of foreign currency into the country; an influx of cheap labor into the cities*
NOTE: plural is **influxes**

inform *verb* to tell someone officially; *I regret to inform you that your bid was not acceptable; we are pleased to inform you that your offer has been accepted; we have been informed by the Department of Commerce that new tariffs are coming into force*

◊ **information** *noun* **(a)** details which explain something; *please send me information on or about vacations in Alaska; have you any information on or about savings accounts? I enclose this leaflet for your information; to disclose a piece of information; to answer a request for information; for further information, please write to Department 27; disclosure of confidential information* = telling someone information which should be secret; **flight information** = information about flight times and conditions; **tourist information** = information for tourists **(b) information technology** = working with computer data; **information retrieval** = storing and then finding data in a computer **(c) information bureau** *or* **information office** = office which gives information to tourists *or* visitors; **information officer** = person whose job is to give information about a company *or* an organization *or* a government department to the public; person whose job is to give information to other departments in the same organization
NOTE: no plural; for one item say **a piece of information**

infrastructure *noun* **(a)** basic structure; **the company's infrastructure** = how the company is organized **(b)** basic services of a community *or* state, etc.; **a country's infrastructure** = the road and rail systems, education and legal systems, etc.

QUOTE buildings should be seen as an essential portion of the national infrastructure

American City & County

infringe *verb* to break a law *or* to deny a right; **to infringe a copyright** = to copy a copyright text illegally; **to infringe a patent** = to make a product which works in the same way as a patented product and not pay a royalty to the patent holder

◊ **infringement** *noun* breaking a law *or* denying a right; **infringement of copyright** *or* **copyright infringement** = act of illegally copying a work which is in copyright; **infringement of patent** *or* **patent infringement**

ingot *noun* bar of gold or silver

inherit *verb* to get something from a person who has died; *when her father died she inherited the store; he inherited $10,000 from his grandfather*

◊ **inheritance** *noun* property which was bequeathed by a person before his death; **inheritance tax** = state tax on the right to inherit property

in-house *adverb & adjective* working inside a company's building; *the in-house staff; we do all our data processing in-house;* **in-house training** = training given to staff at their place of work

initial 1 *adjective* first *or* starting; **initial capital** = capital which is used to start a business; *he started the business with an initial expenditure or initial investment of $500;* **initial sales** = first sales of a new product; *the initial response to the TV advertising has been very good* **2** *noun* **initials** = first letters of the words in a name; *what do the initials IMF stand for? the chairman wrote his initials by each alteration in the contract he was signing* **3** *verb* to write your initials on a document to show you have read it and approved; *to initial an amendment to a contract; please initial the agreement at the place marked with an X*

initiate *verb* to start; *to initiate discussions*

◇ **initiative** *noun* (i) motivation; (ii) decision to start something; **to take the initiative =** to decide to do something; **to follow up an initiative =** to take action once someone else has decided to do something

inject *verb* **to inject capital into a business =** to put money into a business

◇ **injection** *noun* **a capital injection of $100,000** *or* **an injection of $100,000 capital =** putting $100,000 into an existing business

injunction *noun* court order telling someone not to do something; *he got an injunction preventing the company from selling his car; the company applied for an injunction to stop their rival from marketing a similar product*

injure *verb* to hurt (someone); *two workers were injured in the fire*

◇ **injured party** *noun* party in a legal dispute which has been harmed by another party

◇ **injury** *noun* hurt caused to a person; **injury benefit =** money paid to a worker who has been hurt at work; **industrial injuries =** injuries caused to workers at work

ink pad *noun* small pad with ink on it, used for putting ink on a rubber stamp

inland *adjective* inside a country; the interior of a country *or* region; **inland carrier =** company that transports goods from a port to points inside a country

innovate *verb* to bring in new ideas *or* new methods

◇ **innovation** *noun* new idea *or* new method *or* new product

◇ **innovative** *adjective* (person or thing) which is new and makes changes

◇ **innovator** *noun* person who brings in new ideas and methods

input 1 *noun* **computer input =** data fed into a computer; **input lead =** lead for connecting the electric current to the machine **2** *verb* **to input information =** to put data into a computer
NOTE: **inputting - inputted** *or* **input**

inquire *verb* to ask questions about something; *he inquired if anything was wrong; she inquired about the mortgage rate;* **"inquire within" =** ask for more details inside the office *or* store

◇ **inquire into** *verb* to investigate *or* to try to find out about something; *we are inquiring into the background of the new supplier*

◇ **inquiry** *noun* official question; asking for information about a product or service; *I refer to your inquiry of May 25; all inquiries should be addressed to this department*

insert 1 *noun* thing which is put inside something; **an insert in a magazine mailing** *or* **a magazine insert =** advertising sheet put into a magazine when it is mailed **2** *verb* to put something in; *to insert a clause into a contract; to insert a publicity piece into a magazine mailing*

inside 1 *adjective & adverb* in, especially in a company's office or building; *we do all our design work inside;* **inside information =** information about a business which is known by its employees, and which may be valuable if passed to a rival company; **inside directors =** directors who are also executive officers of a company; **inside worker =** worker who works in the office or factory (not in the open air, not a salesman) **2** *preposition* in; *there was nothing inside the container; we have a contact inside our rival's production department who gives us very useful information*

◇ **insider** *noun* person who works in an organization and therefore knows its secrets; **insider dealings** *or* **insider trading =** illegal buying or selling of shares by employees of a company who have secret information about the company's plans

insolvent *adjective* not able to pay debts; **he was declared insolvent =** he was officially stated to be insolvent

◇ **insolvency** *noun* not being able to pay debts; **he was in a state of insolvency =** he could not pay his debts

inspect *verb* to examine in detail; *to inspect a machine or an installation; to inspect the accounts;* **to inspect products for defects =** to look at products in detail to see if they have any defects

◇ **inspection** *noun* close examination of something; *to make an inspection or to carry out an inspection of a machine or* an installation; inspection of a product for defects; customs inspection; quality control inspection

◊ **inspector** *noun* official who inspects; **factory inspector** = government official who inspects factories to see if they are safely run

◊ **inspectorate** *noun* all inspectors

instability *noun* being unstable *or* moving up and down; **period of instability in the money markets** = period when currencies fluctuate rapidly

install *verb* to put (a machine) into an office *or* into a factory; *to install new machinery; to install a new data processing system*

◊ **installation** *noun* (a) machines, equipment and buildings; *harbor installations; the fire seriously damaged the oil installations* (b) putting new machines into an office *or* a factory; *to supervise the installation of new equipment*

◊ **installment** *noun* part of a payment which is paid regularly until the total amount is paid; *the first installment is payable on signature of the agreement;* **the final installment is now due** = the last of a series of payments should be paid now; **to pay $25 down and monthly installments of $20** = to pay a first payment of $25 and the rest in payments of $20 each month; **to miss an installment** = not to pay an installment at the right time

◊ **installment sales** *or* **installment buying** *noun* system of buying something by paying a sum regularly each month; *to buy a car on an installment plan*

instance *noun* particular example *or* case; *in this instance we will overlook the delay*

instant *adjective* immediately available; *instant credit*

institute 1 *noun* official organization; **research institute** = organization set up to do research **2** *verb* to start; *to institute proceedings against someone*

◊ **institution** *noun* organization *or* society set up for a particular purpose; **financial institution** = bank *or* insurance company whose work involves lending or investing large sums of money

◊ **institutional** *adjective* referring to a financial institution; **institutional**

buying *or* **selling** = buying or selling shares by financial institutions; **institutional investors** = financial institutions that invest money in securities

instruct *verb* to give an order to someone; **to instruct someone to do something** = to tell someone officially to do something; *he instructed the credit manager to take action*

◊ **instruction** *noun* order which tells what should be done *or* how something is to be used; *he gave instructions to his stockbroker to sell the shares immediately;* **to await instructions** = to wait for someone to tell you what to do; **to issue instructions** = to tell everyone what to do; **in accordance with** *or* **according to instructions** = as the instructions show; **failing instructions to the contrary** = unless someone tells you to do otherwise; **forwarding instructions** *or* **shipping instructions** = details of how goods are to be shipped and delivered

◊ **instructor** *noun* person who shows how something is to be done

instrument *noun* (a) tool *or* piece of equipment; *the technician brought instruments to measure the output of electricity* (b) legal document; **negotiable instrument** = document (such as a bill of exchange *or* a check) which can be exchanged for cash

insufficient *adjective* not enough; **insufficient funds** = not enough money in a checking account to pay a check that has been presented

insure *verb* to have a contract with a company where, if regular small payments are made, the company will pay compensation for loss, damage, injury or death; *to insure a house against fire; to insure someone's life; he was insured for $100,000; to insure baggage against loss; to insure against bad weather; to insure against loss of earnings;* **the life insured** = the person whose life is covered by life insurance

◊ **insurable** *adjective* which can be insured

◊ **insurance** *noun* (a) agreement that in return for regular small payments, a company will pay compensation for loss, damage, injury or death; **to take out insurance against fire** = to pay a premium, so that if a fire happens, compensation will be paid; **to take out**

insurance on the house = to pay a premium, so that if the house is damaged compensation will be paid; **the damage is covered by the insurance** = the insurance company will pay for the damage; *repairs will be paid for by the insurance;* **to pay the insurance on a car** = to pay premiums to insure a car **(b) accident insurance** = insurance which will pay if an accident takes place; **car insurance** *or* **auto insurance** = insuring a car, the driver and passengers in case of accident; **comprehensive insurance** = insurance which covers against all risks which are likely to happen; **endowment insurance** = situation where a sum of money is paid to the insured person on a certain date or to his heir if he dies before that date; **fire insurance** = insurance against damage by fire; **home insurance** = insuring a home and its contents against damage; **life insurance** = insurance which pays a sum of money when someone dies; **medical insurance** = insurance which pays the cost of medical treatment; **term insurance** = life insurance which covers a person's life for a fixed period of time; **third-party insurance** = insurance which pays compensation if someone who is not the insured person incurs loss or injury; **whole life insurance** = insurance where the insured person pays premiums for all his life and the insurance company pays a sum when he dies **(c) insurance agent** *or* **insurance broker** = person who arranges insurance for clients; **insurance claim** = asking an insurance company to pay for damage; **insurance company** = company whose business is to receive payments and pay compensation for loss or damage; **insurance contract** = agreement by an insurance company to insure; **insurance coverage** = protection guaranteed by an insurance policy; **insurance policy** = document which shows the conditions of an insurance agreement; **insurance premium** = payment made by the insured person to the insurer

◊ **insurer** *noun* company which insures

intangible *adjective* which cannot be touched; **intangible assets** = assets which have a value, but which cannot be seen (such as goodwill, patent or a trademark)

integrate *verb* to link things together to form one whole group

◊ **integration** *noun* bringing several businesses together under a central control; **horizontal integration** = joining similar companies *or* merging with a company in the same line of business; **vertical integration** = joining two businesses together which deal with different stages in the production or sale of a product

intend *verb* to plan *or* to expect to do something; *the company intends to open an office in New York next year; we intend to offer jobs to 250 unemployed young people*

intensive *adjective* **intensive farming** = farming small areas of expensive land, using machines and fertilizers to obtain high crops; **capital-intensive industry** = industry which needs a large amount of capital investment in plant to make it work; **labor-intensive industry** = industry which needs large numbers of workers *or* where labor costs are high in relation to capital investment

intent *noun* what is meant *or* planned; **letter of intent** = letter which states what a company *or* individual intends to do about a business matter

inter- *prefix* between; **inter-bank loan** = loan from one bank to another; **the inter-city rail services are good** = train services between cities are good; **inter-company dealings** = dealings between two companies in the same group; **inter-company comparisons** = comparing the results of one company with those of another in the same product area; **inter-industry competition** = competition between different industries (as between the oil and electricity industries)

interest 1 *noun* **(a)** special attention; *the CEO takes no interest in the employees' problems; the buyers showed a lot of interest in our new product range* **(b)** payment made by a borrower for the use of money, calculated as a percentage of the capital borrowed; **simple interest** = interest calculated on the capital only, and not added to it; **compound interest** = interest which is added to the capital and then earns interest itself; **accrual of interest** = automatic addition of interest to capital; **accrued interest** = interest which has accumulated; **back interest** = interest which has not yet been paid; **fixed interest** = interest which is paid at a set rate; **high** *or* **low interest** = interest at a high or low percentage; **interest charges** = cost of paying interest; **interest rate** *or* **rate of interest =** (i) percentage charge for borrowing money; (ii) percentage paid on an investment; **interest-free credit** *or* **loan =** credit or loan where no interest is paid by the borrower; *the company gives its staff interest-free loans* **(c)** money paid as income on investments or loans; *the bank pays 10% interest on deposits; to receive interest at 5%; the loan pays 5% interest; deposit which yields* **or** *gives* **or** *bears 5% interest; account which earns interest at 10%* **or** *which earns 10% interest;* **interest-bearing deposits =** deposits which produce interest **(d)** money invested in a business *or* financial share in a business; **beneficial interest =** situation where someone is allowed to occupy or receive rent from a house without owning it; *he has a controlling interest in the company =* he owns more than 50% of the stock and so can direct how the company is run; **lifetime interest =** situation in which an individual maintains a stake in something for life; **majority interest** *or* **minority interest =** situation where someone owns a majority *or* a minority of shares in a company; *he has a majority interest in a supermarket chain; to acquire a substantial interest in a business =* to buy a large number of shares in a business; **to declare an interest =** to announce formally and openly your stake in something **2** *verb* to attract someone's attention; *he tried to interest several companies in his new invention;* **interested in =** paying attention to; *the CEO is interested only in increasing profitability;* **interested party =** person *or* company with a financial interest in a company

◊ **interesting** *adjective* which attracts attention; *they made us a very interesting offer for the factory*

interface 1 *noun* link between two different computer systems or pieces of hardware **2** *verb* to meet and act with; *the office computers interface with the mainframe computer at the office*

interfere *verb* to get involved *or* to try to change something which is not your concern

◊ **interference** *noun* the act of interfering; *the sales department complained of continual interference from the accounts department*

interim *noun* intermediate period; **interim dividend =** dividend paid at the

end of a half-year; **interim payment =** payment of part of a dividend; **interim report =** report given sometime during the middle of a period of time; **in the interim =** in the meantime *or* for the time being

intermediary *noun* person who is the link between parties who do not agree or who are negotiating; *he refused to act as an intermediary between the two managers*

internal *adjective* **(a)** inside a company; *we decided to make an internal appointment =* we decided to appoint an existing member of the staff to the position, and not bring someone in from outside the company; **internal audit =** audit carried out by a department within the company; **internal audit department** *or* **internal auditor =** department *or* member of staff who audits the books of the company he works for; **internal telephone =** telephone which is linked to other phones in an office **(b)** inside a country; **an internal flight =** flight to a town inside the same country; **Internal Revenue Service (IRS) =** federal government department which deals with tax; **internal trade =** trade between various parts of a country

◊ **internally** *adverb* inside a company; *the job was advertised internally*

international *adjective* working between countries; **international call =** telephone call to another country; **international dialing code =** sequence of numbers used to make a telephone call to another country; **International Labor Organization (ILO) =** section of the United Nations, an organization which tries to improve working conditions and workers' pay in member countries; **international law =** laws governing relations between countries; **the International Monetary Fund (IMF) =** (part of the United Nations) a type of bank which helps member states in financial difficulties, gives financial advice to members and encourages world trade; **international trade =** trade between different countries

interpret *verb* to translate what someone has said into another language; *my assistant knows Greek, so he will interpret for us*

◊ **interpreter** *noun* person who translates what someone has said into another language; *my secretary will act as interpreter*

interstate *adjective* between two or more states; *interstate highways;* **Interstate Commerce Commission (ICC) =** federal agency which regulates business activity involving two or more states

intervene *verb* to come in to modify *or* influence; **to intervene in a dispute =** to try to settle a dispute
◊ **intervention** *noun* acting to make a change in a system; *the government's intervention in the foreign exchange markets; the central bank's intervention in the banking crisis; the government's intervention in the labor dispute*

interview 1 *noun* (a) formal meeting with a person who is applying for a job; *we called six people for interviews; I have an interview next week or I am going for an interview next week* (b) asking a person questions as part of an opinion poll **2** *verb* to talk to a person applying for a job to see if he is suitable; *we interviewed ten candidates, but did not find anyone suitable*
◊ **interviewee** *noun* person who is being interviewed
◊ **interviewer** *noun* person who is conducting the interview

inter vivos *Latin phrase meaning* between living persons; **inter vivos trust =** trust that becomes operative during the lifetime of the person who creates it

intestate *adjective* **to die intestate =** to die without having made a will

in transit *adverb* **goods in transit =** goods being transported

intrastate *adjective* within one state; *intrastate regulations*

in tray *noun* basket on a desk for letters *or* memos which have been received and are waiting to be dealt with

introduce *verb* to make someone meet with and get to know a new person; **to introduce a client =** to bring in a new client and make him known to someone; **to introduce a new product on the**

market **=** to produce a new product and launch it on the market
◊ **introduction** *noun* (a) letter presenting someone to another person; *I'll give you an introduction to the vice-president - he is an old friend of mine* (b) bringing into use; **the introduction of new technology =** putting new machines (usually computers) into a business or industry
◊ **introductory** *adjective* **introductory offer =** special price or free gift offered with a new product to attract customers

invalid *adjective* not valid *or* not legal; *permit that is invalid; claim which has been declared invalid*
◊ **invalidate** *verb* to make something invalid; *because the company has been taken over, the contract has been invalidated*
◊ **invalidation** *noun* making invalid
◊ **invalidity** *noun* being invalid; *the invalidity of the contract*

invent *verb* to make something which has never been made before; *she invented a new type of computer terminal; who invented shorthand? the chief accountant has invented a new system of customer filing*
◊ **invention** *noun* thing which has been invented; *he tried to sell his latest invention to a Japanese car manufacturer*
◊ **inventor** *noun* person who invents something; *he is the inventor of the all-plastic car*

inventory 1 *noun* (a) supply of goods in a warehouse or store; *to carry a high inventory; to aim to reduce inventory ;* **inventory control =** system of checking that there is not too much stock in a warehouse, but just enough to meet requirements; **to take inventory =** to count and record the number of each different item in stock; **inventory turnover =** number of times the inventory of a business is sold during a period of twelve months (b) list of the contents of a house for sale, of an office for rent, etc.; *to draw up an inventory of fixtures* **2** *verb* to make a list of stock or contents

QUOTE a warehouse needs to tie up less capital in inventory and with its huge volume spreads out costs over bigger sales
Duns Business Month

invest *verb* **(a)** to put money into stocks, bonds, or property, hoping that it will produce interest and increase in value; *he invested all his money in an engineering business; she was advised to invest in real estate or in government bonds;* **to invest abroad** = to put money into stocks *or* bonds in other countries **(b)** to spend money on something which you believe will be useful; *to invest money in new machinery; to invest capital in a new factory*

◊ **investment** *noun* **(a)** placing of money so that it will increase in value and produce interest; *they called for more government investment in new industries; investment in real estate; to make investments in oil companies;* **return on investment (ROI)** = interest or dividends shown as a percentage of the money invested **(b)** shares, bonds, deposits bought with invested money; **long-term investment** *or* **short-term investment** = shares, etc., which are likely to increase in value over a long or short period; **safe investment** = shares, etc. which are not likely to fall in value; **blue-chip investments** = shares of well-established companies, normally with a long positive dividend record, which form a safe investment; **he is trying to protect his investments** = he is trying to make sure that the money he has invested is not lost **(c) investment adviser** = person who advises people on what investments to make; **investment banker** = business which buys a new issue of stock and sells it to the general investors; **investment company** *or* **investment trust** = company specializing in the business service of investing; **investment income** = income (such as interest and dividends) from investments

◊ **investor** *noun* person who invests money; **the small investor** *or* **the private investor** = person with a small sum of money to invest; **the institutional investor** = organization (like a pension fund or insurance company) with large sums of money to invest

investigate *verb* to examine something which may be wrong

◊ **investigation** *noun* examination to find out what is wrong; *to conduct an investigation into irregularities in share dealings*

◊ **investigator** *noun* person who investigates; *government investigator*

invisible 1 *adjective* **invisible assets** = assets which have a value but which cannot be seen (such as goodwill or patents); **invisible earnings** = foreign currency earned by a country by providing services, not selling goods; **invisible items** = services which are paid for in foreign currency or earn foreign currency without actually selling a physical product (e.g. banking or tourism) **2** *plural noun* **invisibles** = invisible imports and exports

invite *verb* to ask someone to do something *or* to ask for something; *to invite someone to an interview; to invite someone to join the board; to invite bids for a contract*

◊ **invitation** *noun* asking someone to do something; *to issue an invitation to someone to join the board; invitation to bid for a contract*

invoice 1 *noun* **(a)** note asking for payment for goods or services supplied; *your invoice dated November 10; they sent in their invoice six weeks late; to make out an invoice for $250; to settle or to pay an invoice;* **the total is payable within thirty days of invoice** = the total sum has to be paid within thirty days of the date on the invoice **(b) invoice clerk** = office worker who processes invoices; **invoice price** = price as stated on an invoice; **total invoice value** = total amount on an invoice, including transportation and tax expenses **2** *verb* to send an invoice to someone; *to invoice a customer;* **we invoiced you on November 10** = we sent you the invoice on November 10

◊ **invoicing** *noun* sending of an invoice; *our invoicing is done by the computer;* **invoicing in triplicate** = preparing three copies of invoices

IOU *noun* = I OWE YOU signed document promising that you will pay back money borrowed; *to pay off all your IOUs*

IRA = INDIVIDUAL RETIREMENT ACCOUNT

irrecoverable *adjective* which cannot be recovered; **irrecoverable debt** = debt which will never be paid

irredeemable *adjective* which cannot be redeemed

irregular *adjective* not according to common form or rule *or* not done in the

correct way; *irregular documentation; this procedure is highly irregular*
◊ **irregularity** *noun* **(a)** not being regular *or* not being on time; *the irregularity of the postal deliveries* **(b) irregularities** = things which are not done in the correct way and which are possibly illegal; *to investigate irregularities in the share dealings*

irrevocable *adjective* which cannot be changed *or* withdrawn; **irrevocable acceptance** = acceptance which cannot be withdrawn; **irrevocable letter of credit** = letter of credit which cannot be canceled or changed

IRS = INTERNAL REVENUE SERVICE

QUOTE if you a driving a company car, the IRS wants to know if your employer allows you to use the automobile to commute
Nation's Business

island *noun* display of merchandise in a store, which can be approached from all sides by customers

issue 1 *noun* sale of new shares; **bonus issue** = new shares given free to shareholders; **issue of debentures** *or* **debenture issue** = borrowing money by giving lenders debentures; **issue of new shares** *or* **share issue** = selling new shares in a company to the public; **rights issue** = giving shareholders the right to buy more shares at a lower price; **new issues department** = section of a bank which deals with issues of new shares in companies; **issue price** = price of shares when they are offered for sale for the first time **2** *verb* to put out *or* to give out; *to issue a letter of credit; to issue shares in a new company; to issue a writ against someone; the government issued a report on traffic in Washington, D.C.*
◊ **issued** *adjective* **issued capital** = amount of capital which is given out as shares to shareholders
◊ **issuing** *noun* which organizes a sale of shares; **issuing bank** *or* **issuing house** = bank which organizes the selling of shares in a new company

item *noun* **(a)** thing for sale; **cash items** = goods sold for cash; *we are holding orders for out-of-stock items* = for goods which are not in stock; *please find enclosed an order for the following items from your catalog* **(b)** piece of information; *items on a balance sheet; extraordinary items* = items in an

annual report which do not appear each year and need to be noted; **item of expenditure** = goods or services which have been paid for and appear in the accounts **(c)** point on a list; *we will now take item four on the agenda* = we will now discuss the fourth point on the agenda
◊ **itemize** *verb* to make a detailed list of things; *itemizing the sales figures will take about two days;* **itemized account** = detailed record of money paid or owed; **itemized deductions** = specific deductions from taxable income listed on a tax return; **itemized invoice** = invoice which lists each item purchased

itinerary *noun* list of places to be visited on one journey; *a salesman's itinerary*

Jj

jam 1 *noun* blocking; **traffic jam** = situation where there is so much traffic on the road that it moves only very slowly **2** *verb* to stop working *or* to be blocked; *the paper feed has jammed; the switchboard was jammed with calls*
NOTE: **jamming - jammed**

janitor *noun* person who looks after a building
◊ **janitorial services** *noun* cleaning of a commercial building, such as an office

jetsam *noun* **flotsam and jetsam** = rubbish floating in the water after a ship has been wrecked and rubbish washed on to the land

jettison *verb* to throw cargo from a ship into the sea to make the ship lighter

jingle *noun* short and easily remembered tune used to advertise a product on television, etc.

job *noun* **(a)** piece of work; **to do a job** = to complete a piece of work; **to do odd jobs** = to do various pieces of work; *he does odd jobs for us around the house;* **to be paid by the job** = to be paid for each piece of work done; **job printer** = printer who does small printing jobs, such a letterheads, business cards, leaflets, etc. **(b)** order being worked on; *we are working on six jobs at this time; the shipyard has a big job starting in August* **(c)** regular paid work; *he is looking for a job in the computer industry; he lost his job when the factory closed; she got a job in a factory; to apply for a job in an office;* office job *or* white-collar job = job in an office; **to give up one's job** = to resign from one's work; **to look for a job** = to try to find work; **to retire from one's job** = to leave work and live on social security, pension and savings; **to be out of a job** = to have no work **(d)** job analysis = detailed examination and report on the duties of a job; **job application** *or* **application for a job** = asking for a job in writing; *you have to fill in a job application form;* job classification = setting up various classifications for a range of jobs, comparing their requirements and pay scales; **job description** = official document from the management which says what a job involves; **job evaluation** = examining different jobs within an organization to see what skills and qualifications are needed to carry them out; **job satisfaction** = a worker's feeling that he is happy in his place of work and pleased with the work he does; **job security** = feeling which a worker has that he has a right to keep his job, or that his job will never end; **job specification** = very detailed description of what is involved in a job; **job title** = name given to a person in a certain job; *her job title is "Chief Buyer"* ; **on-the-job training** = training given to workers at their place of work; **off-the-job training** = training given to workers away from their place of work (e.g., at a college) **(e) job lot** = group of miscellaneous items sold together; *he sold the household furniture as a job lot* **(f)** difficulty; *finding a qualified secretary was a big job*

◊ **jobber** *noun* wholesaler, person who buys goods in quantity from manufacturers or importers and sells them to dealers

◊ **jobbing** *noun* buying and selling goods from manufacturers

◊ **jobless** *noun* **the jobless** = people with no jobs *or* the unemployed

◊ **job-sharing** *noun* system where part-time workers share one job

join *verb* **(a)** to put things together; *the offices were joined together by making a door in the wall; if the paper is too short to take all the accounts, you can join an extra piece on the bottom* **(b) to join a firm** = to start work with a company; *he joined on January 1* = he started work on January 1 **(c) to join an association** *or* **a group** = to become a member of an association *or* a group; *all the employees have joined the company pension plan; he was asked to join the board; Smith Co. has applied to join the trade association*

joint *adjective* **(a)** combined *or* with two or more organizations linked together; **joint commission of inquiry** *or* **joint committee** = commission *or* committee with representatives of various organizations on it; **joint discussions** = discussions between management and workers before something is done; **joint management** = management done by two or more people; **joint venture** = single business undertaking entered into by two or more businesses *or* partners **(b) joint account** = bank account for two people; **joint-stock company** = company whose stock is held by many people who are together responsible for all the debts of the company **(c)** one of two or more people who work together *or* who are linked; *joint beneficiary; joint manager; joint owner; joint signatory;* **joint ownership** = owning of a property by several owners

◊ **jointly** *adverb* together with one or more other people; *to own a property jointly; to manage a company jointly; they are jointly liable for damages*

journal *noun* **(a)** book with the account of sales and purchases made each day **(b)** magazine; **trade journal** = magazine produced for people or companies in a certain trade

◊ **journalist** *noun* person who writes for a newspaper

journey *noun* long trip

◊ **journeyman** *noun* skilled craftsman who has completed his apprenticeship

judge 1 *noun* person who decides in a legal case; *the judge sent him to prison for embezzlement* **2** *verb* to decide; *he judged it was time to call an end to the discussions*

◊ **judgment** *or* **judgement** *noun* legal decision *or* official decision; **to pronounce judgment** *or* **to give one's judgment on something** = to give an official or legal decision about something; **judgment debtor** = debtor who has been ordered by a court to pay a debt

NOTE: the spelling **judgment** is more common

judicial *adjective* referring to the law; **judicial processes** = the ways in which the law works

jump 1 *noun* sudden rise; *jump in prices; jump in unemployment figures* **2** *verb* **(a)** to go up suddenly; *oil prices have jumped since the war started; share values jumped on the Stock Exchange* **(b)** to go away suddenly; **to jump bail** = not to appear in court after having been released on bail; **to jump the gun** = to start to do something too early *or* before you should; **to jump ship** = (i) to leave a ship where you work as a sailor and not to go back; (ii) to abandon a job before it is completed

◊ **jumpy** *adjective* nervous *or* excited; **the market is jumpy** = the stock market is nervous and prices are likely to fluctuate

junior 1 *adjective* younger *or* lower in rank; **junior executive** *or* **junior manager** = young manager in a company; **junior partner** = person who has been made a partner more recently than others; **John Smith, Junior** = the younger John Smith (i.e., the son of John Smith, Senior) **2** *noun* person occupying a position which is lower than others in an organization

junk *noun* rubbish *or* useless items; *you should throw away all that junk;* junk **bonds** = bonds raised as debentures on the security of a company which is the subject of a takeover bid; **junk dealer** = person who buys useless items for scrap; **junk mail** = advertising material sent through the mail

jurisdiction *noun* **within the jurisdiction of the court** = in the legal power of a court

Kk

K *abbreviation* one thousand; **"salary: $15K+ "** = salary more than $15,000 per annum; *they only offered $60K for the company*

keen *adjective* eager *or* active; **keen competition** = strong competition; *we are facing some keen competition from European manufacturers;* **keen demand** = wide demand; *there is a keen demand for home computers*

keep *verb* **(a)** to go on doing something; *they kept working, even when the boss told them to stop; the other secretaries complain that she keeps singing when she is typing* **(b)** to do what is necessary; **to keep an appointment** = to be there when you said you would be; **to keep the books of a company** *or* **to keep a company's books** = to note the accounts of a company accurately **(c)** to hold items for sale *or* for information; **we always keep this item in stock** = we always have this item in our warehouse *or* store; **to keep someone's name on file** = to have someone's name on a list for reference **(d)** to hold things at a certain level; *we must keep our mailing list up to date; to keep spending to a minimum; the price of oil has kept the dollar at a high level; the government is encouraging industry to keep prices low; lack of demand for typewriters has kept prices down*

NOTE: **keeping - kept**

◊ **keep back** *verb* to hold on to something which you could give to someone; *to keep back information or to keep something back from someone; to keep $100 back from someone's salary*

◊ **keep on** *verb* to continue to do something; *the factory kept on working in spite of the fire; we keep on receiving orders for this item although it was discontinued two years ago*

◊ **keep up** *verb* (i) to hold at a certain high level; (ii) to prevent something from falling; *we must keep up the sales volume in spite of the recession; she* *kept up a rate of sixty words per minute for several hours*

Keogh plan *noun* private pension program allowing self-employed businessmen and professionals to set up pension and retirement plans for themselves

key *noun* (a) piece of metal used to open a lock; *we have lost the keys to the computer room* (b) part of a computer *or* typewriter which you press with your fingers; *there are sixty-four keys on the keyboard;* control key = key on a computer which works part of a program; shift key = key which makes a typewriter *or* computer move to capital letters (c) important; *key factor; key industry; key personnel; key post; key staff*

◊ **keyboard 1** *noun* part of a typewriter or computer with keys which are pressed to make a letter or figure; qwerty keyboard = English language keyboard, where the first letters are Q-W-E-R-T-Y; *the computer has a normal qwerty keyboard* **2** *verb* to press the keys on a keyboard to type something; *he is keyboarding our address list*

◊ **keyboarder** *noun* person who types information into a computer

◊ **keyboarding** *noun* act of typing on a keyboard; *keyboarding costs have risen sharply*

◊ **key in** *verb* to press the keys on a computer to input information; *she keyed in the address*

◊ **keypad** *noun* small keyboard; numeric keypad = part of a computer keyboard which is a programmable set of numbered keys

kg = KILOGRAM

kickback *noun* illegal commission paid to someone (especially a government official) who helps in a business deal

killing *noun informal* very large profit; *he made a killing on the stock market*

kilo *or* **kilogram** *noun* measure of weight (= one thousand grams)

◊ **kilobyte** *noun* unit of storage in a computer (= 1,024 bytes)

◊ **kilometer** *noun* measure of length (= one thousand meters)

kind *noun* sort *or* type; *the printer produces two kinds of printout; our*

vending machine has three kinds of soups; payment in kind = payment made by giving goods or food, but not money

kiosk *noun* small wooden shelter, for selling goods out of doors; *a newspaper kiosk;* telephone kiosk = shelter with a public telephone in it

kite *verb* to get money *or* credit by using bad checks (the person writes the check when there is no money in his account to pay it, and cashes it at another branch, so getting cash while the check is being cleared through the system)

kitty *noun* money which has been collected by a group of people to be used later (such as for an office party)

km = KILOMETER

knock *verb* (a) to hit something; *he knocked on the door and went in; she knocked her head on the filing cabinet* (b) to knock the competition = to point out the negative characteristics of the competition

◊ **knock down** *verb* to knock something down to a bidder = to sell something at an auction; *the stock was knocked down to him for $10,000*

◊ **knockdown** *noun* knockdown prices = very low prices; *he sold me the car at a knockdown price*

◊ **knock off** *verb* (a) to stop work (b) to reduce a price by an amount; *he knocked $10 off the price for cash*

know *verb* (a) to learn *or* to have information about something; *I do not know how a computer works; does he know how long it takes to get to the airport? the executive director's secretary does not know where he is* (b) to have met someone; *do you know Mr. Jones, our new sales director? he knows the African market very well* NOTE: knowing - known

◊ **know-how** *noun* knowledge about how something works *or* how something is made; *electronic know-how; to acquire computer know-how*

◊ **knowledge** *noun* what is known; *he had no knowledge of the contract* = he did not know that the contract existed

kraft paper *noun* cheap brown paper used to make envelopes and paper bags

Ll

l = LITER

L measurement of money supply, calculated as M3, plus Treasury bills, bonds and commercial paper

label 1 *noun* **(a)** piece of paper *or* card attached to something to show its price *or* an address *or* instructions for use; **gummed label =** label which you wet to make it stick on the item; **peel-off label =** gummed label which is removed from backing paper and stuck on an envelope; **self-sticking label =** sticky label, ready to stick on an item; **tie-on label =** label with a piece of string attached so that it can be tied on to an item **(b) address label** *or* **mailing label =** label with an address on it; **price label =** label showing a price; **quality label =** label which states the quality of something **(c) own label goods =** goods specially produced for a store with the store's name on them **2** *verb* to attach a label to something; **incorrectly labeled parcel =** parcel with the wrong information on the label
◊ **labeling** *noun* putting a label on something; **labeling department =** section of a factory where labels are attached to the product

laboratory *noun* place where scientific research is carried out; *the product was developed in the company's laboratories; all products are tested in our own laboratories*

labor *noun* **(a)** heavy work; **manual labor =** work done by hand; **to charge for materials and labor =** to charge for both the materials used in a job and also the hours of work involved; **labor costs** *or* **labor charges =** cost of the workers employed to make a product (not including materials or overhead); **indirect labor costs =** cost of wages of workers who are not directly involved in making the product (such as secretaries, inspectors, cleaners); **labor is charged at $5 an hour =** each hour of work costs $5 **(b)** workers *or* the workforce; **casual labor =** workers who are hired for a short period; **cheap labor =** workers

who do not earn much money; **local labor =** workers recruited near a factory, not brought in from somewhere else; **organized labor =** workers who are members of labor unions; **skilled labor =** workers who have special knowledge or qualifications; **labor force =** all workers; *the management has made an increased offer to the labor force; we are setting up a factory in the Far East because of the cheap labor available;* **labor market =** number of workers who are available for work; **25,000 young people have finished school and have come on to the labor market =** 25,000 people have left school and become available for work; **labor shortage** *or* **shortage of labor =** situation where there are not enough workers to fill jobs; **labor-intensive industry =** industry which needs large numbers of workers *or* where labor costs are high in relation to capital investment **(c) labor disputes =** arguments between management and workers; **labor laws** *or* **labor legislation =** laws relating to the employment of workers; **labor relations =** relations between management and workers; **labor union =** organization which represents workers who are its members in discussions about wages and conditions of work with management **(d) Department of Labor =** U.S. federal department which supervises relations between employers and labor, and enforces labor regulations; **International Labor Organization =** section of the United Nations which tries to improve working conditions and workers' pay in member countries
◊ **laborer** *noun* person who does manual labor; **agricultural laborer =** person who does heavy work on a farm; **casual laborer =** worker who can be hired for a short period; **manual laborer =** person who does heavy work with his hands
◊ **labor-saving** *adjective* which saves you from doing hard work; *a labor-saving device*

QUOTE European economies are being held back by rigid labor markets and wage structures
Duns Business Month

lack 1 *noun* not having enough; **lack of data** *or* **lack of information =** not having enough information; *the decision has been put back for lack of up-to-date information;* **lack of funds =** not enough money; *the project was canceled because of lack of funds* **2** *verb* not to have enough of something; *the company lacks capital;* **the sales**

reps lack motivation = the sales reps are not motivated enough

ladder *noun* (a) series of steps made of wood or metal which can be moved about, and which you can climb; *you will need a ladder to look into the machine* (b) **corporate ladder** = path for promotion within a corporation; **promotion ladder** = established method *or* path by which people can be promoted; *by being appointed sales manager, he moved several steps up the promotion ladder*

laden *adjective* loaded; **fully-laden ship** = ship with a full cargo; **ship laden in bulk** = ship which has a loose cargo (such as corn) which is not packed in containers

lading *noun* loading *or* putting goods on a ship; **bill of lading** = list of goods being shipped, which the transporter gives to the person sending the goods to show that they have been loaded

laissez-faire economy *noun* economy where the government does not interfere because it believes it is right to let the economy run itself

lame *adjective* walking badly because of a bad leg

◊ **lame duck** *noun & adjective* (a) speculator who has failed in a venture (b) official who has been defeated for reelection, but is finishing his term of office; *a lame duck president* (c) business which is in financial difficulties; *the government has refused to help lame duck companies*

land 1 *noun* area of earth; **land grant** = land given by the government for roads, railroads or agricultural colleges; **land office** = government office where land sales are registered; **land registry** = government office where land is registered; **land taxes** = taxes on the amount of land someone owns **2** *verb* (a) to put goods *or* passengers on to land after a voyage by sea *or* by air; *to land goods at a port; to land passengers at an airport;* **landed costs** = costs of goods which have been delivered to a port, unloaded and passed through customs; *what were the landed costs of the most recent shipment?* (b) to come down to earth after a flight; *the plane landed ten minutes late*

◊ **landing** *noun* **landing card** = card given to passengers who have passed customs and can land from a ship *or* an aircraft; **landing charges** = payment for putting goods on land and the customs duties; **landing order** = permit which allows goods to be unloaded into a bonded warehouse without paying customs duty

◊ **landlady** *noun* woman who owns a property which she lets

◊ **landlord** *noun* person *or* company which owns a property which is let; **ground landlord** = person *or* company which owns the freehold of a property which is then let and sublet; *our ground landlord is an insurance company*

◊ **landowner** *noun* person who owns large areas of land

language *noun* form of selecting and communicating words which are characteristic of people in a certain country; *the chief executive officer conducted the negotiations in three languages;* **programming language** = system of signs, letters and words used to instruct a computer; *what language does the program run on?*

lapse 1 *noun* **a lapse of time** = a period of time which has passed **2** *verb* to stop being valid *or* to stop being active; *the guarantee has lapsed;* **to let an offer lapse** = to allow time to pass so that an offer is no longer valid

large *adjective* very big *or* important; *our company is one of the largest suppliers of computers to the government; he is our largest customer; why does she have an office which is larger than mine?*

◊ **largely** *adverb* mainly *or* mostly; *our sales are largely in the domestic market; they have largely pulled out of the European market*

◊ **large-scale** *adjective* working in a large way, with large numbers of people *or* large amounts of money involved; *large-scale investment in new technology; large-scale layoffs in the construction industry*

laser printer *noun* printing machine attached to a computer, which prints text and graphics using a laser beam

last 1 *adjective & adverb* (a) coming at the end of a series; *out of a line of twenty people, I was served last; this is our last board meeting before we* move to our new offices; we finished the last items in the order just two days before the promised delivery date; **last quarter** = period of three months to the end of the financial year **(b)** most recent *or* most recently; *where is the last batch of orders?* the last ten orders were only for small quantities; **last week** *or* **last month** *or* **last year** = the week *or* month *or* year before this one; *last week's sales were the best we have ever had; the sales managers have been asked to report on last month's drop in unit sales; last year's accounts have to be ready before the annual meeting* **(c) the week** *or* **month** *or* **year before last** = the week *or* month *or* year before the one before this; *last year's figures were bad, but they were an improvement on those of the year before last* 2 *verb* to go on *or* to continue; *the boom started in the 1970s and lasted until the early 1980s; the discussions over layoffs lasted all day*

◊ **last in first out (LIFO)** *noun* **(a)** layoff policy, where the people who have been most recently appointed are the first to be laid off **(b)** accounting method where inventory sold is valued at the price of the latest purchases

late 1 *adjective* **(a)** after the time stated or agreed on; *we apologize for the late arrival of the plane from Montreal; there is a penalty for late delivery* = if delivery is later than the agreed date, the supplier has to pay a fine **(b)** at the end of a period of time; **latest date for signature of the contract** = the last acceptable date for signing the contract **(c) latest** = most recent; *he always drives the latest model of car; here are the latest sales figures* **2** *adverb* after the time stated or agreed on; *the shipment was landed late; the plane was two hours late*

◊ **late-night** *adjective* happening late at night; *he had a late-night meeting at the airport; their late-night negotiations ended in an agreement which was signed at 3 a.m.*

launch 1 *verb* to put a new product on the market (usually spending money on advertising it); *they launched their new car model at the auto show; the company is spending thousands of dollars to launch a new brand of soap* **2** *noun* act of putting a new product on the market; *the launch of the new model has been put back three months; the company is geared up for the launch of the new brand of soap;*

the management has decided on a September launch date

◊ **launching** *noun* act of putting a new product on the market; **launching costs** = costs of publicity for a new product; **launching date** = date when a new product is officially shown to the public for the first time

launder *verb* to pass illegal profits *or* money which has not been taxed, etc. into the normal banking system; *to launder money through a foreign bank*

law *noun* **(a) laws** = rules by which a country is governed and the activities of people and organizations controlled; **labor laws** = laws concerning the employment of workers **(b)** all the laws of a country taken together; **civil law** = laws relating to arguments between individuals and the rights of individuals; **commercial law** = laws regarding business; **corporate law** = laws which refer to the way companies work; **contract law** *or* **the law of contract** = laws relating to private agreements; **copyright law** = laws concerning the protection of copyright; **criminal law** = laws relating to crime; **international law** = laws referring to the way countries deal with each other; **maritime law** *or* **the law of the sea** = laws referring to ships, ports, etc.; **law courts** = place where a judge listens to cases and decides questions of law; **inside the law** *or* **within the law** = obeying the laws of a country; **against** *or* **outside the law** = not according to the laws of a country; *the company is operating outside the law;* **to break the law** = to do something which is not allowed by law; *he is breaking the law by selling goods on Sunday; you will be breaking the law if you try to take that computer out of the country without an export license* **(c)** general rule; **law of supply and demand** = general rule that the amount of a product which is available is related to the needs of the possible customers; **law of diminishing returns** = general rule that as more factors of production (land, labor and capital) are added to the existing factors, so the amount they produce is proportionately smaller

◊ **lawful** *adjective* acting within the law; **lawful practice** = action which is permitted by the law; **lawful trade** = trade which is allowed by law

◊ **lawfully** *adverb* acting within the law

◊ **lawsuit** *noun* case brought to a court; **to bring a lawsuit against someone** =

to tell someone to appear in court to settle an argument; **to defend a lawsuit** = to appear in court to state your case

◇ **lawyer** *noun* person who has studied law and can act for people on legal business; **commercial lawyer** *or* **corporate lawyer** = person who specializes in company law *or* who advises companies on legal problems; **international lawyer** = person who specializes in international law; **maritime lawyer** = person who specializes in laws concerning ships

lay *verb* to put; **to lay an embargo on trade with a country** = to forbid trade with a country
NOTE: **laying - laid**

◇ **lay off** *verb* **(a)** to reduce a possible future risk by buying forward **(b) to lay off workers** = to dismiss workers for a time (until more work is available); *the factory laid off half its workers because of lack of orders*

◇ **layoff** *noun* action of dismissing a worker for a time; *the recession has caused hundreds of layoffs in the car industry*

◇ **lay out** *verb* to spend money; *we had to lay out half our cash budget on equipping the new factory*

◇ **layout** *noun* arrangement of the inside of a building; design of an advertisement, a page of a catalog, etc.; *they have altered the layout of the offices; the design manager approved the layout of the catalog*

◇ **lay up** *verb* **(a)** to stop using a ship because there is no work; *half the shipping fleet is laid up by the recession* **(b)** to stop working because of an illness *or* injury; *nearly half of the employees were laid up with the flu*

QUOTE the company lost $52 million last year, and has laid off close to 2,000 employees
Toronto Star

lazy *adjective* (person) who does not want to work; *she is too lazy to do any overtime; he is so lazy he does not even send in his expense claims on time*

lb = pound

LBO = LEVERAGED BUYOUT

L/C = LETTER OF CREDIT

lead *verb* **(a)** to be the first *or* to be in front; *the company leads the market in low-priced computers* **(b)** to be the main person in a group; *she will lead the trade mission to Nigeria; the tour of Japanese factories will be led by a trade official* **(c)** to guide someone; *she will lead you through the office procedures until you are more familiar with them*
NOTE: **leading - led**

◇ **leader** *noun* **(a)** person who manages *or* directs others; *the leader of the construction workers' union* *or* *the construction workers' leader; she is the leader of the trade mission to Nigeria; the minister was the leader of the party of industrialists on a tour of American factories* **(b)** product which sells best; **a market leader** = product which sells most in a market *or* company which has the largest share of a market; **loss leader** = article which is sold very cheaply to attract customers **(c)** important stock which is often bought or sold on the Stock Exchange

◇ **leading** *adjective* most important; *leading industrialists feel the end of the recession is near; leading securities rose on the Stock Exchange; leading shareholders in the company forced a change in management policy; they are the leading company in the field;* **leading indicators** = indicators which forecast changes in the economy some months before they actually occur

◇ **lead time** *noun* time between deciding to begin a process and completing the process; *the lead time for developing a new ad campaign is four weeks*

◇ **lead (up) to** *verb* to be the cause of; *the discussions led to a big argument between the management and the union; we received a series of approaches leading up to the takeover bid*

leaflet *noun* sheet of paper giving information, used to advertise something; **to mail leaflets** *or* **to hand out leaflets describing services;** *they did a leaflet mailing to 20,000 addresses*

leak *verb* to pass on a secret; *information on the contract was leaked to the press; they discovered the head of finance was leaking information to a rival company*

◇ **leakage** *noun* amount of goods lost in storage (by going bad *or* by being stolen *or* by escaping from the container)

lease 1 *noun* **(a)** written contract for letting or renting of a building *or* a piece of land *or* a piece of equipment for a period against payment of a fee; **long lease** *or* **short lease =** lease which runs for fifty years or more *or* for up to two or three years; **to take an office building on a long lease; we have a short lease on our current premises; to rent office space on a twenty-year lease; sublease =** lease from a tenant to another tenant; **the lease expires** *or* **runs out in 1999 =** the lease comes to an end in 1999; **on expiration of the lease =** when the lease comes to an end **(b) to hold an oil lease in the Gulf =** to have a lease on a section of the Gulf to explore for oil **2** *verb* **(a)** to let or rent offices *or* land *or* machinery for a period; **to lease offices to small firms; to lease equipment (b)** to use an office *or* land *or* machinery for a time and pay a fee; **to lease an office from an insurance company; all our company cars are leased**

◊ **lease back** *verb* to sell a property *or* machinery to a company and then take it back on a lease; **they sold the office building to raise cash, and then leased it back for twenty-five years**

◊ **leaseback** *noun* arrangement where property is sold and then taken back on a lease; **they sold the office building and then took it back under a leaseback arrangement**

◊ **leasehold** *noun & adjective* holding property on a lease; **leasehold property; the company has some valuable leaseholds; to buy a property leasehold**

◊ **leaseholder** *noun* person who holds a property on a lease

◊ **leasing** *noun* which leases *or* working under a lease; **the company has branched out into car leasing; an equipment-leasing company; to run a copier under a leasing arrangement;** *see also* LESSEE

leave 1 *noun* permission to be away from work; **six weeks' annual leave =** six weeks' vacation each year; **leave of absence =** being allowed to be away from work; **maternity leave =** permission given to a woman to be away from work to have a baby; **sick leave =** period when a worker is away from work because of illness; **to go on leave** *or* **to be on leave =** to be away from work; **she is away on sick leave** *or* **on maternity leave 2** *verb* **(a)** to go away from; **he left his office early to go to the meeting;**

the next plane leaves at 10:20 (b) to resign; **he left his job and bought a farm**
NOTE: leaving - left

◊ **leave out** *verb* not to include; **she left out the date on the letter; the contract leaves out all details of marketing arrangements**

ledger *noun* book in which accounts are written; **purchase ledger =** book in which expenditure is noted; **sales ledger clerk =** office worker who deals with the bought ledger *or* the sales ledger; **payroll ledger =** list of staff and their salaries; **sales ledger =** book in which sales are recorded

left *adjective* opposite of right; **the numbers run down the left side of the page; put the debits in the left column;** *see also* LEAVE

◊ **left-hand** *adjective* belonging to the left side; **the debits are in the left-hand column in the accounts; he keeps the personnel files in the left-hand drawer of his desk**

legacy *noun* property *or* money given by someone to someone else at his death

legal *adjective* **(a)** according to the law *or* allowed by the law; **the company's action was completely legal (b)** referring to the law; **to take legal action =** to sue someone *or* to take someone to court; **to get legal advice =** to ask a lawyer to advise about a legal problem; **legal adviser =** person who advises clients about the law; **legal aid =** legal help provided to those who are unable to pay for it; **legal claim =** statement that someone owns something legally; **he has no legal claim to the property; legal costs** *or* **legal charges** *or* **legal expenses =** money spent on fees to lawyers; **legal currency =** money which is legally used in a country; **legal department** *or* **legal section =** section of a company dealing with legal matters; **legal expert =** person who knows a lot about the law; **legal folder =** very large size folder which can take long pieces of paper; **legal holiday =** day when banks and other businesses are closed; **legal list =** list of blue-chip securities in which banks and financial institutions are allowed to invest by the state in which they are based; **legal tender =** coins or notes which can be legally used to pay a debt

◊ **legality** *noun* being allowed by law; *there is doubt about the legality of the company's action in dismissing him*

◊ **legalize** *verb* to make something legal

◊ **legalization** *noun* making something legal

◊ **legally** *adverb* according to the law; *the contract is legally binding* = according to the law, the contract has to be obeyed; *the directors are legally responsible* = the law says that the directors are responsible

legatee *noun* person to whom a legacy is left

legislation *noun* laws; *labor legislation* = laws concerning the employment of workers

lend *verb* to allow someone to use something for a period; *to lend something to someone* or *to lend someone something; he lent the company money* or *he lent money to the company; to lend money against security; the bank lent him $50,000 to start his business*
NOTE: **lending - lent**

◊ **lender** *noun* person who lends money; **lender of last resort** = central bank which lends money to commercial banks (in the U.S.A., this is the Federal Reserve Bank)

◊ **lending** *noun* act of letting someone use money for a time; **lending limit** = limit on the amount of money a bank can lend

length *noun* (a) measurement of how long something is; *the boardroom table is twelve feet in length; inches and centimeters are measurements of length* (b) **to go to great lengths to get something** = to do anything right (even commit a crime) to get something; *they went to considerable lengths to keep the merger secret*

less 1 *adjective* smaller than or of a smaller size or of a smaller value; *we do not grant credit for sums of less than $100; he sold it for less than he had paid for it* **2** *preposition* minus or with a sum removed; *purchase price less 15% discount; interest less service charges*

lessee *noun* person who has a lease or who pays money for a property he leases

◊ **lessor** *noun* person who grants a lease on a property

let *verb* to rent or lease a house or an office or a farm to someone for a payment; **to let an office** = to allow someone to use an office for a time in return for payment of rent; **offices to let** = offices which are available to be rented by companies
NOTE: **letting - let**

letter *noun* (a) piece of writing sent from one person or company to another to give information; **business letter** = letter which deals with business matters; **circular letter** = letter sent from employee to employee throughout a particular office; **cover letter** = letter sent with documents to say why they are being sent; **follow-up letter** = letter sent to someone after a previous letter or after a visit; **form letter** = letter which is sent without change to various correspondents; **private letter** = letter which deals with personal matters; **letter carrier** = mailman, an employee of the USPS who delivers mail (b) **letter of acknowledgment** = letter which says that something has been received; **letters of administration** = letter given by a court to allow someone to deal with the estate of someone who has died; **letter of application** = letter in which someone applies for a job; **letter of appointment** = letter in which someone is appointed to a job; **letter of complaint** = letter in which someone complains; **letter of credit (L/C)** = letter from a bank allowing someone credit and promising to repay at a later date; **letter of indemnity** = letter promising payment of compensation for a loss; **letter of intent** = letter which states what a company or individual intends to do about a business matter; **letters patent** = official document which gives someone the exclusive right to make and sell something which he has invented; **letter of reference** = letter in which an employer recommends someone for a new job (c) **air letter** = special thin blue paper which when folded can be sent by air without an envelope; **airmail letter** = letter sent by air; **express letter** = letter sent very fast; **registered letter** = letter which is noted by the post office before it is sent, so that compensation can be claimed if it is lost (d) **to acknowledge receipt by letter** = to write a letter to say that something has been received (e) written or printed sign (such as A, B, C, etc.); *write your name and address in capital letters*

◊ **letterhead** *noun* **(a)** sheet of stationery with the name and address of a company printed at the top **(b)** name and address of a company printed at the top of a piece of stationery

◊ **lettershop** *noun* company which organizes mailings

level 1 *noun* position where high is large and low is small; *low level of productivity* or *low productivity levels; to raise the level of employee benefits; to lower the level of borrowing;* high level of investment = large amount of money invested; **a decision made at the highest level** = decision made by the most important person or group; **low-level** = not very important; *a low-level delegation;* high-level = very important; *a high-level meeting* or *decision;* decisions made at managerial level = decisions made by managers; **staffing levels** = number of people required in each department of a company to do the work efficiently **2** *verb* **to level off** or **to level out** = to stop rising or falling; *profits have leveled off over the last few years; prices are leveling out*

leverage *noun* **(a)** influence which you can use to achieve an aim; *he has no leverage over the chairman* **(b)** relation between a company's capital borrowed at a fixed interest and the value of its ordinary shares **(c)** borrowing money at fixed interest which is then used to produce more money than the interest paid

◊ **leveraged** *adjective* involving borrowing; **leveraged buyout (LBO)** = buying all the shares in a company by borrowing money against the security of the shares to be bought; **leveraged lease** = lease where a bank lends the lessor money to buy the property on mortgage against the security of the lease, the rent being paid by the lessee

> QUOTE the offer came after management had offered to take the company private through a leveraged buyout for $825 million
> *Fortune*

levy 1 *noun* money which is demanded and collected by the government; **capital levy** = tax on the value of a person's property and possessions; **import levy** = tax on imports; **levies on luxury items** = taxes on luxury items **2** *verb* to demand payment of a tax or an extra payment and to collect it; *the government has decided to levy a tax on imported cars;*

to levy a duty on the import of luxury items

liability *noun* **(a)** being legally responsible for damage or loss, etc.; **to accept liability for something** = to agree that you are responsible for something; **to refuse liability for something** = to refuse to agree that you are responsible for something; **contractual liability** = legal responsibility for something as stated in a contract; **employers' liability insurance** = insurance to cover accidents which may happen at work, and for which the company may be responsible; **limited liability** = situation where someone's liability for debt is limited by law; **limited liability company** = British company where a shareholder is responsible for repaying the company's debts only to the face value of the shares he owns **(b)** **liabilities** = debts of a business; *the balance sheet shows the company's assets and liabilities;* **current liabilities** = debts which a company should pay within the next accounting period; **long-term liabilities** = debts which are not due to be paid for some time; **he was not able to meet his liabilities** = he could not pay his debts; **to discharge one's liabilities in full** = to pay everything which one owes

◊ **liable** *adjective* **(a)** **liable for** = legally responsible for; *the customer is liable for breakages; the chairman was personally liable for the company's debts* **(b)** **liable to** = which is officially due to be paid; *goods which are liable to import duty*

libel 1 *noun* untrue written statement which damages someone's character; **action for libel** or **libel action** = case in a law court where someone says that another person has written a libel **2** *verb* **to libel someone** = to damage someone's character in writing; *Compare* SLANDER

license 1 *noun* **(a)** official document which allows someone to do something; **driver's license** = document which allows someone to drive a car or a truck, etc.; *applicants should hold a valid driver's license;* **import license** or **export license** = documents which allow goods to be exported or imported; **liquor license** = government document allowing someone to sell alcohol **(b)** **goods manufactured under license** = goods made with the permission of the owner of the copyright or patent **2** *verb* to give someone official permission to do something; *licensed to sell beers, wines and spirits; to license a company to manufacture spare parts; she is licensed to run an employment agency* ◊ **licensee** *noun* person who has a license

◊ **licensing** *noun* which refers to licenses; *a licensing agreement; licensing laws*

lien *noun* legal right to hold someone's goods and keep them until a debt has been paid

lieu *noun* in lieu of = instead of; *she was given two months' salary in lieu of notice* = she was given the salary and asked to leave immediately

life *noun* **(a)** time when a person is alive; **for life** = for as long as someone is alive; *his pension gives him a comfortable income for life;* life annuity *or* annuity **for life** = annual payments made to someone as long as he is alive; **life insurance** = insurance which pays a sum of money when someone dies, or at a certain date if he is still alive; **life expectancy** = number of years a person is likely to live; **life interest** = interest in something which stops when a person dies **(b)** period of time something exists; *the life of a loan; during the life of the agreement;* **shelf life of a product** = length of time during which a product can stay in the store and still be good to use

◊ **lifeboat** *noun* boat used to rescue passengers from sinking ships; **lifeboat operation** = rescue of a company (especially of a bank) which is in difficulties

LIFO = LAST IN FIRST OUT

lift 1 *noun* GB elevator **2** *verb* to take away *or* to remove; *the government has lifted the ban on imports from Japan; to lift trade barriers; Congress has lifted the embargo on the export of computers to East European countries*

light *adjective* not heavy; **shares fell back in light trading** = shares lost value on a day when there was little business done on the Stock Exchange; **light industry** = industry which makes small products (such as clothes, books, calculators)

limit 1 *noun* constraint, point at which something ends *or* point where you can go no further; **to set limits to imports** *or* **to impose import limits** = to allow only a certain amount of imports; **age limit** = top age at which you are allowed to do something; *there is an age limit of thirty-five on the position of buyer;* **credit limit** = largest amount of money which a customer can borrow; **he has exceeded his credit limit** = he has borrowed more money than he is allowed; **lending limit** = restriction on the amount of money a bank can lend; **time limit** = maximum time which can be taken to do something; *to set a time limit for acceptance of the offer;* **weight limit** = maximum weight **2** *verb* to stop something from going beyond a certain point; **the banks have limited their credit** = the banks have allowed their customers only a certain amount of credit; **each agent is limited to twenty-five units** = each agent is allowed only twenty-five units to sell

◊ **limitation** *noun* **(a)** act of allowing only a certain quantity of something; **limitation of liability** = making someone liable for only a part of the damage or loss; **time limitation** = amount of time available; *the contract imposes limitations on the number of cars which can be imported* **(b)** **statute of limitations** = law which allows only a certain amount of time (a few years) for someone to claim damages or property

◊ **limited** *adjective* restricted *or* not open; **limited market** = market which can take only a certain quantity of goods; **limited (liability) company** = British company where a shareholder is responsible for the company's debts only to the face value of his shares

◊ **limiting** *adjective* which limits; *a limiting clause in a contract; the short tourist season is a limiting factor on the hotel trade*

line *noun* **(a)** long mark; *paper with thin blue lines; I prefer notepaper without any lines; he drew a thick line across the bottom of the column to show which figure was the total* **(b)** shipping line *or* **airline** = large shipping or aircraft company which carries passengers or cargo; *profits of major airlines have been affected by the rise in fuel prices* **(c)** line of business *or* line **of work** = type of business or work; *what is his line?;* **line of product** *or* **product line** = series of different products which form a group, all made by the same company; *we do not stock that line;* **computers are not one of our best-selling lines (d)** row of letters *or* figures on a page; **bottom line** = last line in accounts, showing the net profit; *the boss is interested only in the bottom line;* **to open a line of credit** *or* **a credit line** = to make credit available to someone; *his charge card has a line of credit of $3000* = he can use his card for purchases up to a limit of $3000 **(e) assembly line** *or* **production line** = production system where the product (such as a car) moves slowly through a factory with new sections added to it as it goes along; *he works on the production line* or *he is a production line worker in the car factory* **(f) line chart** *or* **line graph** = chart or graph using lines to indicate values; **line printer** = fast machine which prints information from a computer one line at a time **(g) line of command** *or* **line management** *or* **line organization** = organization of a business where each manager is responsible for doing what his superior tells him to do **(h) telephone line** = wire along which telephone messages travel; **the line is bad** = it is difficult to hear clearly what someone is saying; **a crossed line** = when two telephone conversations get mixed; **the line is busy** = the person is already speaking on the phone; **the chairman is on the other line** = the chairman is using the other telephone; **outside line** = line from an internal office telephone system to the main telephone exchange

◊ **lined** *adjective* with lines; *he prefers lined paper for writing notes*

◊ **liner** *noun* large passenger ship

> QUOTE the best thing would be to have a few more plants close down and bring supply more in line with current demand
>
> *Fortune*

link *verb* to join *or* to attach to something else; *to link pensions to inflation; his salary is linked to the cost of living; to link bonus payments to productivity*

liquid *adjective* **liquid assets** = cash, or bills which can easily be changed into cash; **to go liquid** = to convert as many assets as possible into cash

◊ **liquidate** *verb* **to liquidate a company** = to close a company and sell its assets; **to liquidate a debt** = to pay a debt in full; **to liquidate stock** = to sell stock to raise cash

◊ **liquidation** *noun* **(a) liquidation of a debt** = payment of a debt **(b)** closing of a

company and selling of its assets; **the company went into liquidation** = the company was closed and its assets sold; **compulsory liquidation** = liquidation which is ordered by a court; **voluntary liquidation** = situation where a company itself decides it must close

◊ **liquidator** *noun* person named to supervise the closing of a company which is in liquidation

◊ **liquidity** *noun* having cash or assets which can be changed into cash; **liquidity crisis** = time when someone is having difficulty liquidating their assets

lira *noun* money used in Italy; *the book cost 2,700 lira* or *L2,700*
NOTE: **lira** is usually written **L** before figures: **L2,700**

list 1 *noun* **(a)** several items written one after the other; *list of products* or *product list; stock list; to add an item to a list; to cross an item off a list;* **address list** *or* **mailing list** = list of names and addresses of people and companies; **list rental** = purchase of a list of addresses to be used once only **(b)** catalog; **list price** = price as given in a catalog; **price list** = sheet giving prices of goods for sale **2** *verb* **(a)** to write a series of items one after the other; *to list products by size; to list representatives by area; to list products in a catalog; the catalog lists twenty-three models of washing machines* **(b)** **listed company** = business whose shares can be bought or sold on a Stock Exchange; **listed securities** = securities which can be bought or sold on a stock exchange *or* securities which appear on the official stock exchange list

◊ **listing** *noun* **(a)** **stock exchange listing** = being on the official list of shares which can be bought or sold on stock exchange; *the company is planning to obtain a New York Stock Exchange listing;* **listing requirements** = conditions which a company must meet to be listed on a Stock Exchange (such as minimum number of shares, minimum annual net income, etc.) **(b)** **computer listing** = printout of a list of items taken from the data stored in a computer

liter *noun* measure of liquids; *the wine is sold by the liter*
NOTE: usually written **l** after figures: **25l**

literature *noun* written information about something; *please send me* *literature about your new product range*

litigation *noun* the bringing of a lawsuit against someone

lively *adjective* **lively market** = active stock market, with many shares being traded

living *noun* **cost of living** = money which a person has to pay for rent, food, heating, etc.; **he does not earn a living wage** = he does not earn enough to pay for essentials (food, heat, rent); **standard of living** *or* **living standards** = quality of personal home life (amount of food, clothes bought, size of the family car, etc.); *living standards fell as unemployment rose*

load 1 *noun* (a) goods which are transported; **load of a truck** *or* **of a container** = goods carried by a truck or container; **container-load** = amount of goods carried in a container; *a container-load of spare parts is missing;* **commercial load** = amount of goods *or* number of passengers which a bus *or* train *or* plane has to carry to make a profit; **maximum load** = largest weight of goods which a truck *or* plane can carry; **load-carrying capacity** = amount of goods which a truck is capable of carrying (b) **workload** = amount of work which a person has to do; *he has difficulty in coping with his heavy workload* **2** *verb* (a) **to load a truck** *or* a **ship** = to put goods into a truck *or* a ship for transporting; *to load cargo onto a ship; a truck loaded with boxes; a ship loaded with iron;* **fully loaded ship** = ship which is full of cargo (b) *(of ship)* to take on cargo; *the ship is loading a cargo of wood* (c) to put a program into a computer; *load the word processing program before you start keyboarding*

◇ **loading** *noun* **loading bay** = section of road in a warehouse where trucks can drive in to be loaded; **loading dock** = (i) part of a harbor where ships can load or unload; (ii) raised platform which makes it easier to load goods onto a truck

◇ **load line** *noun* line painted on the side of a ship to show where the water should reach for maximum safety if the ship is fully loaded

loan 1 *noun* money which has been lent; **loan capital** = part of a company's capital which is a loan to be repaid at a later date; **loan stock** = money lent to a

company at a fixed rate of interest; **convertible loan stock** = money which can be exchanged for shares at a later date; **bank loan** = money lent by a bank; **bridge loan** = a loan given for a short period of time to someone who expects to receive funds shortly; **government loan** = money lent by the government; **home loan** = loan by a bank or mortgage company to help someone buy a house; **short-term loan** *or* **long-term loan** = loans which have to be repaid within a few weeks or some years; **soft loan** = loan (from a company to an employee *or* from one government to another) with little or no interest payable; **unsecured loan** = loan made with no security **2** *verb* to lend

lobby 1 *noun* group of people who try to influence members of a legislature to pass laws favorable to their interests; **the energy conservation lobby** = people who try to persuade members of a legislature to pass laws to save energy **2** *verb* to try to influence members of a legislature; *the group lobbied the chairmen of all the committees*

local 1 *adjective* referring to a particular area, especially one near where a factory *or* an office is based; **local call** = telephone call to a number in the same area as the person making the call; **local government** = elected administrative bodies which run cities, counties and towns; **local labor** = workers who are recruited near a factory, and are not brought there from a distance; **local media** = newspapers and TV and radio stations serving a local community **2** *noun* branch of a labor union

◇ **locally** *adverb* in the area near where an office or factory is based; *we recruit all our staff locally*

locate *verb* **to be located** = to be in a certain place; *the warehouse is located near the freeway*

◇ **location** *noun* place where something is; **the company has moved to a new location** = the company has moved to a new office or a different town

lock 1 *noun* device for closing a door *or* box so that it can be opened only with a key; *the lock is broken on the petty* *cash box; I have forgotten the combination of the lock on my briefcase* **2** *verb* to close a door with a key, so that it cannot be opened; *the manager forgot to lock the door of the computer room; the petty cash box was not locked*

◊ **lockbox** *noun* **(a)** box at a post office which can be rented and can be opened only the person or company renting it **(b)** system where checks sent to a Post Office box are picked up and deposited in a bank account

◊ **lock out** *verb* to lock out workers = to close the factory so that workers cannot get in and so force them not to work until the conditions imposed by the management are met

◊ **lockout** *noun* industrial dispute where the management will not let the workers into the factory until they have agreed to the management's conditions

◊ **lock up** *verb* to lock up a store *or* an office = to close and lock the door at the end of the day's work; **to lock up capital** = to have capital invested in such a way that it cannot be used for other investments

◊ **locking up** *noun* the locking up of money in stock = investing money in stock so that it cannot be used for other, possibly more profitable, investments

lodge *verb* to lodge a complaint against someone = to make an official complaint about someone; **to lodge money with someone** = to deposit money with someone; **to lodge securities as collateral** = to put securities into a bank to be used as collateral for a loan

log *verb* to write down all that happens; **to log phone calls** = to note all details of phone calls made
NOTE: **logging - logged**

logo *noun* symbol *or* design *or* group of letters used by a company as a mark on its products and in advertising

long *adjective* for a great period of time; **long bond** = bond which matures in more than ten years' time; **long credit** = credit terms which allow the borrower a long time to pay; **in the long term** = over a long period of time; **to take the long view** = to plan for a long period before current investment becomes profitable

◊ **long-dated** *adjective* long-dated bills = bills which are payable in more than three months' time

◊ **long-distance** *adjective & adverb* to make a long-distance call *or* to call long-distance = to make a telephone call to a number which is out of the area; **long-distance flight** = flight to a destination which is a long way away

◊ **longhand** *noun* handwriting where the words are written out in full and not typed or in shorthand; *applications should be written in longhand and sent to the personnel officer*

◊ **long-haul** *adjective* transportation over a long distance; **long-haul flight** = long-distance flight especially between continents

◊ **long-range** *adjective* for a long period of time in the future; **long-range economic forecast** = forecast which covers a period of several years

◊ **long-standing** *adjective* which has been arranged for a long time; *long-standing agreement;* long-standing customer *or* customer of long standing = person who has been a customer for many years

◊ **long-term** *adjective* on a long-term basis = for a long period of time; **long-term debts** = debts which will be repaid many years later; **long-term forecast** = forecast for a period of over three years; **long-term loan** = loan to be repaid many years later; **long-term objectives** = aims which will take years to achieve

QUOTE the company began to experience a demand for longer-term mortgages when the flow of money used to finance these loans diminished
Globe and Mail (Toronto)

loophole *noun* to find a loophole in the law = to find a means of legally avoiding the law; **to find a tax loophole** = to find a means of legally not paying tax

QUOTE because capital gains are not taxed but money taken out in profits is taxed, owners of businesses will be using accountants and tax experts to find loopholes in the law
Toronto Star

loose *adjective* not packed together; **loose change** = money in coins; **to sell loose sugar** *or* to sell sugar loose = to sell sugar in separately weighed quantities, not in packages

◊ **loose-leaf notebook** *noun* book with loose pages which can be taken out and fixed back in again on rings

lose *verb* **(a)** not to have something any more; **to lose an order** = not to get an order which you were hoping to get; *during the strike, the company lost six*

orders to Japanese competitors; **to lose control of a company** = to find that you have less than 50% of the shares and so are no longer able to direct the company; **to lose customers** = to have fewer customers; *their service is so slow that they have been losing customers; she lost her job when the factory closed* **(b)** to have less money; *he lost $25,000 in his father's computer company;* **the dollar has lost value** = the dollar is worth less **(c)** to drop to a lower price; *the dollar lost two cents against the yen; gold shares lost 5% on the market yesterday*
NOTE: **losing - lost**

◊ **lose out** *verb* to suffer as a result of something; *the company has lost out in the rush to make cheap computers*

loss *noun* **(a) loss of customers** = not keeping customers because of bad service *or* high prices, etc.; **loss of an order** = not getting an order which was expected; **the company suffered a loss of market penetration** = the company found it had a smaller share of the market; **compensation for loss of earnings** = payment to someone who has stopped earning money *or* who is not able to earn money **(b)** having less money than before *or* not making a profit; **the business suffered a loss** = the business did not make a profit; **to report a loss** = not to show a profit in the annual report; *the company reported a loss of $1m on the first year's trading ;* **capital loss** = loss made by selling assets; **the car was written off as a total loss** = the car was so badly damaged that the insurers said it had no value; **paper loss** = loss made when an asset has fallen in value but has not been sold; **trading loss** = situation where the company's receipts are less than its expenditure; **at a loss** = making a loss *or* not making any profit; *the company is trading at a loss; he sold the store at a loss;* **to cut one's losses** = to stop doing something which was losing money **(c)** being worth less *or* having a lower value; *shares showed losses of up to 5% on the Stock Exchange* **(d) loss in weight** = goods which weigh less than when they were packed

◊ **loss leader** *noun* article which is sold at a loss to attract customers; *we use these cheap films as a loss leader*

lot *noun* **(a)** large quantity; *a lot of people or lots of people are out of work* **(b)** group of items sold together at an auction; *to bid for lot 23; at the end of*

the auction half the lots were unsold **(c)** group of shares which are sold; *to sell a lot of shares; to sell shares in small lots* **(d)** piece of land, especially one to be used for redevelopment; **parking lot** = area for parking cars

lottery *noun* game where numbered tickets are sold and prizes given for some of the numbers

lounge *noun* comfortable room; **departure lounge** = room in an airport where passengers wait to board their planes; **airport lounge** = room in an airport where passengers wait for connecting flights

low 1 *adjective* small *or* not high; *low overhead costs keep the unit cost low; we try to keep our wages bill low; the company offered him a mortgage at a low rate of interest; the pound is at a very low rate of exchange against the dollar; our aim is to buy at the lowest price possible; shares are at their lowest in two years;* **low sales** = small amount of money produced by sales; **low volume of sales** = small number of items sold; **the contract will go to the lowest bidder** = the contract will be awarded to the person who offers the best terms **2** *noun* point where prices *or* sales are very small; *sales have reached a new low; the highs and lows on the stock market;* **shares have hit an all-time low** = shares have reached their lowest price ever

◊ **lower 1** *adjective* smaller *or* less high; *a lower rate of interest; sales were lower in December than in November* **2** *verb* to make smaller *or* less expensive; *to lower prices to secure a larger market share; to lower the interest rate*

◊ **lowering** *noun* making smaller *or* less expensive; *lowering of prices; we hope to achieve low prices with no lowering of quality*

◊ **low-grade** *adjective* not very important *or* not of very good quality; *a low-grade official from the State Department; the car runs best on low-grade gasoline*

◊ **low-level** *adjective* **(a)** not very important; *a low-level delegation visited the department; a low-level committee decided to put off making a decision* **(b)** **low-level computer language** = programming language similar to machine code

◊ **low-pressure** *adjective* **low-pressure sales** = sales where the salesman does

not force someone to buy, but only
encourages him to do so

◊ **low-quality** *adjective* not of good
quality; *they tried to sell us some low-
quality steel*

> QUOTE the pound which had been as low as
> $1.02 earlier this year, rose to $1.30
> *Fortune*
> QUOTE Canadian and European negotiators
> agreed to a deal under which Canada could
> keep its quotas but lower its import duties
> *Globe and Mail (Toronto)*

loyalty *noun* **brand loyalty** = feeling of
a customer who always buys the same
brand of product; **customer loyalty** =
feeling of customers who always shop at
the same store

Ltd = LIMITED

luggage *noun* suitcases *or* bags for
carrying clothes when traveling; **hand
luggage** *or* **cabin luggage** = small cases
which passengers can take with them
into the cabin of a plane *or* ship; **free
luggage allowance** = amount of luggage
which a passenger can take with him
free of charge
NOTE: no plural; to show one suitcase, etc., say **a
piece of luggage**

lull *noun* quiet *or* inactive period; *after
last week's hectic trading this week's
lull was welcome*

lump *noun* **lump sum** = money paid in
one single amount, not in several small
sums; *when he retired he was given a
lump-sum bonus; she sold her house
and invested the money as a lump sum;*
lump sum settlement = settlement of a
debt in one single payment, not in
installments

lunch *noun* meal eaten in the middle of
the day; *the hours of work are from
9:30 to 5:30 with an hour off for lunch;
the chairman is out to lunch;* **business
lunch** = meeting between businessmen
where they have lunch together to
discuss business deals

◊ **lunch hour** *or* **lunchtime** *noun* time
when people have lunch; *the office is
closed during the lunch hour or at
lunchtime*

luxury *noun* expensive thing which is
not necessary but which is nice to have;
*luxury items or luxury goods; a black
market in luxury articles*

Mm

m = METER, MILE, MILLION

M = ONE THOUSAND

M measurements of money supply
◊ **M1** currency, banks deposits and
savings bank deposits
◊ **M2** M1 plus savings accounts and time
deposits of less than $100,000
◊ **M3** M2 plus time deposits of over
$100,000; *see also* L

machine *noun* **(a)** device which works
with power from a motor; **adding
machine** = machine which adds
numbers; **copy machine** *or* **duplicating
machine** = machine which makes copies
of documents; **dictating machine** =
machine which records what someone
dictates, which a typist can then play
back and type out; **automatic vending
machine** = machine which provides
food or drink when money is put in it;
machine shop = place where working
machines are serviced; **machine tools** =
tools worked by motors, used to work on
wood or metal **(b)** **machine-made** *or*
machine-produced = manufactured by
a machine, not by people **(c)** **machine
code** *or* **machine language** =
instructions and information shown as a
series of figures (0 and 1) which can be
read by a computer; **machine-readable
codes** = sets of signs or letters (such as
bar codes, post codes) which a computer
can read

◊ **machinery** *noun* **(a)** machines; **idle
machinery** *or* **machinery lying idle** =
machines not being used; **machinery
guards** = pieces of metal to prevent
workers from getting hurt by the moving
parts of a machine **(b)** organization *or*
system; *the government machinery;
the machinery of local government;
administrative machinery; the
machinery for awarding government
contracts*

◊ **machinist** *noun* person who works a
machine

macro- *prefix* very large, covering a
wide area; **macroeconomics** = study of
the economics of a whole area *or* whole

industry *or* whole group of the population *or* whole country

Madam *noun* formal way of addressing a woman, especially one whom you do not know; **Dear Madam** = beginning of a letter to a woman whom you do not know; **Madam Chairman** = formal way of addressing a woman who is the chairperson at a meeting

made *adjective* produced *or* manufactured; *made in Japan or Japanese made; see also* MAKE

Madison Avenue the advertising business (from the name of the avenue in New York where many advertising agencies are based)

magazine *noun* publication, usually with pictures, which comes out regularly, every month or every week; **computer magazine** = magazine with articles on computers and programs; **do-it-yourself magazine** = magazine with articles on work which the average person can do to repair or decorate the house; **trade magazine** = magazine produced for people or companies in certain trades; **travel magazine** = magazine with articles on vacations and travel; **women's magazine** = magazine aimed at the women's market; **magazine insert** = advertising sheet put into a magazine when it is mailed or sold; **insert a leaflet in a magazine** = to put an advertising leaflet into a magazine before it is mailed or sold; **magazine mailing** = sending of copies of a magazine by mail to subscribers

magnate *noun* important *or* influential businessman; *a shipping magnate*

magnetic ink *noun* special ink used for printing numbers on checks so that they can be recognized by special reading devices in banks

◊ **magnetic tape** *or* **mag tape** *noun* plastic tape for recording information on a large computer

mail 1 *noun* **(a)** system of sending letters and parcels from one place to another; *to put a letter in the mail; the check was lost in the mail; the invoice was put in the mail yesterday; mail to some of the islands in the Pacific can take six weeks;* **by mail** = using the postal services, not sending something by hand or by messenger; **to send a package by** **surface mail** = to send a package by land or sea, not by air; **to receive a sample by air mail** = by mail using a plane; **first-class mail** = mail service for sealed letters and cards; **second-class mail** = mail service for newspapers and magazines; **third-class mail** = mail service for unsealed letters and advertising material; **fourth-class mail** = mail service for parcels; *we sent the order by first-class mail; a first-class letter should reach Chicago tomorrow;* **electronic mail** = system of sending messages from one computer to another, using the telephone lines **(b)** letters sent or received; *has the mail arrived yet? to open the mail; your check arrived in yesterday's mail; my secretary opens my mail as soon as it arrives; the receipt was in this morning's mail;* **incoming mail** = mail which arrives; **outgoing mail** = mail which is sent out; **mail room** = room in an office where incoming letters are sorted and sent to each department, and where outgoing mail is collected for sending **(c)** **direct mail** = selling a product by sending publicity material to possible buyers through the mail; *the company runs a successful direct-mail operation; these calculators are sold only by direct mail;* **direct-mail advertising** = advertising by sending leaflets to people by mail **2** *verb* to send something through the postal system; *to mail a letter; we mailed our order last Wednesday*

◊ **mailbox** *noun* (i) box outside a house *or* one of several boxes in a large building where incoming mail is put; (ii) box for putting letters, etc., which you want to send

◊ **mailer** *noun* leaflet suitable for sending by mail

◊ **mailing** *noun* sending something through the postal system; *the mailing of publicity material;* **direct mailing** = sending of publicity material by mail to possible buyers; **mailing list** = list of names and addresses of people who might be interested in a product *or* list of names and addresses of members of a society; *his name is on our mailing list; to build up a mailing list; to buy a mailing list* = to pay a society, etc. money to buy the list of members so that you can use it to mail publicity material; **mailing piece** = leaflet suitable for sending by direct mail

◊ **mailman** *noun* employee of the USPS who delivers mail

mail 156 make

◇ **mail order** *noun* system of buying and selling from a catalog, placing orders and sending goods by mail

◇ **mail-order** *adjective* referring to a system of buying and selling from a catalog; **mail-order business** *or* **mail-order firm** *or* **mail-order house** = company which sells a product by mail; **mail-order catalog** = catalog from which a customer can order items to be sent by mail

main *adjective* most important; *main office; main building; one of our main customers;* **Main Street** = often, most important street in a town, where the stores and banks are

◇ **mainframe** *noun* large computer; *the office computer interfaces with the mainframe in the head office*

◇ **mainly** *adverb* mostly *or* usually; *their sales are mainly in the home market; we are interested mainly in buying children's gift items*

maintain *verb* (a) to keep something going *or* working; *to maintain good relations with one's customers; to maintain contact with an overseas market* (b) to keep something working at the same level; *the company has maintained the same volume of business in spite of the recession; to maintain an interest rate at 5%;* **to maintain a dividend** = to pay the same dividend as the previous year

◇ **maintenance** *noun* (a) keeping things going *or* working; *maintenance of contacts; maintenance of supplies* (b) keeping a machine in good working order; *we offer a full maintenance service;* **maintenance contract** = contract by which a company keeps a piece of equipment in good working order

QUOTE the federal administration launched a full-scale investigation into the airline's maintenance procedures
Fortune

majeure *see* FORCE MAJEURE

major *adjective* important; **major shareholder** = shareholder with a large number of shares

◇ **majority** *noun* larger group than all others; **majority of the shareholders** = more than 50% of the shareholders; *the board accepted the proposal by a majority of three to two* = three members of the board voted to accept and two voted against; **majority vote** *or*

majority decision = decision made after a vote according to the wishes of the largest group; **majority holding** *or* **majority interest** = group of more than half of all the shares in a company; **a majority shareholder** = person who owns more than half the shares in a company

QUOTE monetary officials have reasoned that coordinated greenback sales would be able to drive the dollar down against other major currencies
Duns Business Month

make **1** *noun* type of product manufactured; *Japanese makes of cars; a standard make of equipment; what make is the new computer system or what is the make of the new computer system?* **2** *verb* (a) to produce *or* to manufacture; *to make a car or to make a computer; the workmen spent ten weeks making the table; the factory makes three hundred cars a day* (b) to sign *or* to agree; *to make a deal or to make an agreement;* **to make a bid for something** = to offer to buy something; **to make a payment** = to pay; **to make a deposit** = to pay money as a deposit (c) to earn *or* to increase in value; *he makes $50,000 a year or $25 an hour; the stock made $2.92 in today's trading* (d) to make a decision = to decide to act in a certain way; **to make a market** = to be prepared to buy or sell a certain security (used of dealers on a Stock Exchange); **to make a profit** *or* **to make a loss** = to have more money *or* less money after a deal; **to make a killing** = to make a very large profit
NOTE: **making - made**

◇ **make good** *verb* (a) to repair *or* to compensate; *the company will make good the damage; to make good a loss* (b) to be a success; **a local boy made good** = local person who became successful

◇ **make out** *verb* to write; *to make out an invoice; the invoice is made out to Smith Inc.;* **to make out a check to someone** = to write someone's name on a check

◇ **make over** *verb* to transfer property legally; *to make over the house to one's children*

◇ **make up** *verb* (a) to compensate for something; **to make up a loss** *or* **to make up the difference** = to pay extra so that the loss or difference is covered (b) **to make up accounts** = to complete the accounts

◇ **make up for** *verb* to compensate for something; *to make up for a short* *payment or to make up for a late payment*

◊ **maker** *noun* company *or* person who makes something; *a major car maker; a furniture maker;* **decision maker** = person who decides *or* who makes decisions

◊ **making** *noun* production of an item; *ten tons of concrete were used in the making of the wall;* **decision making** = act of coming to a decision

maladministration *noun* incompetent administration

mall *noun* **shopping mall** = enclosed covered area for shopping, with stores, restaurants, banks and other facilities

man 1 *noun* person *or* ordinary worker; *all the men went back to work yesterday* **2** *verb* to provide the workforce for something; *to man a shift; to man an exhibition; the exhibit booth was manned by three salesgirls;* see also MANNED, MANNING

manage *verb* **(a)** to direct *or* to be in charge of; *to manage a department; to manage a branch office* **(b) managed account** *or* **managed fund** = account or fund where investment decisions are handled by the managers and not by the client; **managed price** = price established under conditions of competition, where one company has some degree of control; **to manage property** = to look after rented property for the owner **(c) to manage to** = to be able to do something; *did you manage to see the buyer? she managed to write six orders and take three phone calls all in two minutes*

◊ **manageable** *adjective* which can be dealt with easily; *difficulties which are still manageable; the problems are too large to be manageable*

◊ **management** *noun* **(a)** directing *or* running a business; *to study management; good management* or *efficient management; bad management* or *inefficient management; a management graduate* or *a graduate in management;* **line management** = organization of a business where each manager is responsible for doing what his superior tells him to do; **portfolio management** = buying and selling shares by a person or by a specialist on behalf of a client; **product management** = directing the making and selling of a product as an

independent item; **management accountant** = accountant who prepares specialized information for managers so that they can make decisions; **management accounts** = financial information (on sales, costs, credit, profitability) prepared for a manager; **management committee** = committee which manages a club, a pension fund, etc.; **management consultant** = person who gives advice on how to manage a business; **management course** = training course for managers; **management fee** = charge paid to a mutual fund to cover the costs of managing the fund; **management by objectives (MBO)** = way of managing a business by planning work for the managers and testing to see if it is completed correctly and on time; **management team** = a group of managers working together; **management techniques** = ways of managing a business; **management training** = training managers by making them study problems and work out ways of solving them; **management trainee** = young person being trained to be a manager **(b)** group of managers or directors; *the management has decided to give an overall pay increase;* **top management** = the main executives of a company; **middle management** = the department managers of a company who carry out the policy set by the directors and organize the work of a group of workers

◊ **manager** *noun* **(a)** head of a department in a company; *a department manager; personnel manager; production manager; sales manager;* **accounts manager** = head of the accounts department; **area manager** = manager who is responsible for the company's work (usually sales) in an area; **general manager** = manager in charge of the administration in a large company **(b)** person in charge of a branch or store; *Mr. Smith is the manager of our local First National Bank; the manager of our British branch is in Washington for a series of meetings;* **bank manager** = person in charge of a branch of a bank; **branch manager** = person in charge of a branch of a company

◊ **managerial** *adjective* referring to managers; *managerial staff; to be appointed to a managerial position* = to be appointed a manager; **decisions made at managerial level** = decisions made by managers

◊ **managership** *noun* job of being a manager; *after six years, he was offered the managership of a branch in Houston*

> QUOTE the No. 1 managerial productivity problem in America is managers who are out of touch with their people and out of touch with their customers
>
> *Fortune*

mandate *noun* command *or* authorization; *he received a clear mandate from the vice-president to proceed with the negotiations;* **bank mandate** = written order allowing someone to sign checks on behalf of a company

mandatory *adjective* **mandatory meeting** = meeting which all members have to attend

man-hour *noun* work done by one man in one hour; *one million man-hours were lost through industrial action*

manifest *noun* list of goods in a shipment; **passenger manifest** = list of passengers on a ship or plane

manila *or* **manilla** *noun* thick brown paper; *a manila envelope*

manipulate *verb* **to manipulate the accounts** = to make false accounts so that the company seems profitable; **to manipulate the market** = to work to influence stock market prices in your favor
◊ **manipulation** *noun* **stock market manipulation** = trying to influence the price of securities
◊ **manipulator** *noun* **stock market manipulator** = person who tries to influence the price of securities in his own favor

manned *adjective* with someone working on it; *the switchboard is manned twenty-four hours a day; the booth was manned by our sales staff*
◊ **manning** *noun* people who are needed to do a work process; **manning levels** = number of people required in each department of a company to do the work efficiently; **manning agreement** = agreement between the company and the workers about how many workers are needed for a certain job

manpower *noun* number of workers; **manpower forecasting** = forecasting how many workers will be needed, and how many will be available; **manpower planning** = planning to obtain the right number of workers in each job; **manpower requirements** = number of workers needed; **manpower shortage** *or* **shortage of manpower** = lack of workers

manual 1 *adjective* done by hand *or* done without the aid of machinery; **manual labor** *or* **manual work** = heavy work done by hand; **manual laborer** = person who does heavy work with his hands; **manual worker** = person who works with his hands **2** *noun* book of instructions; **operating manual** = book showing how to operate a machine; **service manual** = book showing how to service a machine
◊ **manually** *adverb* done by hand, not by a machine; *invoices have had to be made manually because the computer has broken down*

manufacture 1 *verb* to make a product for sale, using machines; *manufactured goods; the company manufactures spare parts for cars* **2** *noun* making a product for sale, using machines; **products of foreign manufacture** = products made in foreign countries
◊ **manufacturer** *noun* person *or* company which produces machine-made products; *foreign manufacturers; cotton manufacturer; sports car manufacturer;* **manufacturer's brand** = product with a brand name which belongs to the manufacturer, not to the retailer; **manufacturer's recommended price** = price at which the manufacturer suggests the product should be sold on the retail market, though often reduced by the retailer; *all typewriters - 20% off the manufacturer's recommended price*
◊ **manufacturing** *noun* producing machine-made products for sale; **manufacturing capacity** = amount of a product which a factory is capable of making; **manufacturing costs** = costs of making a product; **manufacturing industries** = industries which take raw materials and make them into finished products; **manufacturing overhead** = costs incurred in making a product

margin *noun* **(a)** difference between the money received when selling a product and the money paid for it; **gross margin** = sales minus the cost of goods sold, which may be shown as a percentage of net sales; **net margin** = percentage difference between received price and all costs, including overhead; **we are cutting our margins very narrow** = we are reducing our margins to the smallest possible to be competitive; **our margins have been squeezed** = profits have been reduced because our margins have to be smaller to stay competitive **(b)** extra space *or* time allowed; **margin of error** = number of mistakes which are accepted in a document *or* in a calculation; **safety margin** = time *or* space allowed for something to be safe; **margin of safety** = sales which are above the break-even point

◊ **marginal** *adjective* **(a) marginal cost** = cost of making a single extra unit above the number already planned; **marginal pricing** = making the selling price the same as the marginal cost; **marginal rate of tax** = tax rate applied to the next dollar earned; **marginal revenue** = income from selling a single extra unit above the number already sold **(b)** not very profitable *or* hardly worth the money paid; **marginal return on investment; marginal land** = land which is almost not worth farming; **marginal purchase** = thing which a buyer feels is barely worth buying

marine 1 *adjective* referring to the sea; **marine insurance** = insurance of ships and their cargoes; **marine underwriter** = person who insures ships and their cargoes **2** *noun* **the merchant marine** = all the commercial ships of a country

◊ **maritime** *adjective* referring to the sea; **maritime law** = laws governing ships, ports, etc.; **maritime lawyer** = lawyer who specializes in legal matters concerning ships and cargoes; **maritime trade** = transporting commercial goods by sea

mark 1 *noun* **(a)** sign put on an item to show something; **assay mark** = hallmark *or* mark put on gold or silver items to show that the metal is of the correct quality **(b)** money used in Germany; **the price is twenty-five marks; the mark rose against the dollar** (NOTE: usually written **DM** after a figure: **25DM**. Also called **Deutschmark, D-Mark) 2** *verb* to put a sign on something; **to mark a product "for export only"** ; **article marked at $1.50; to mark the price on something**

◊ **mark down** *verb* to make lower; **to mark down a price** = to lower the price of something; **this range has been marked down to $24.99; we have**

marked all prices down by 30% for the sale

◊ **markdown** *noun* **(a)** reduction of the price of something to less than its usual price **(b)** percentage amount by which a price has been lowered; **we have used a 30% markdown to fix the sale price**

◊ **marker pen** *noun* felt pen which makes a wide colored mark

◊ **mark up** *verb* to increase; **to mark up prices** = to increase prices; **these prices have been marked up by 10%**

◊ **markup** *noun* **(a)** increase in price; **we put into effect a 10% markup of all prices in June (b)** amount added to the cost price to give the selling price; **we work to a 3.5 times markup** *or* **to a 350% markup** = we take the unit cost and multiply by 3.5 to obtain the selling price

market 1 *noun* **(a)** (i) place (often in the open air) where farm produce is sold; (ii) store where a certain type of produce is sold; **fish market; flower market; open-air market; here are this week's market prices for lamb; flea market** = market for secondhand goods; **market day** = day when a market is regularly held; **Tuesday is market day, so the streets are closed to traffic (b)** place where a product might be sold *or* group of people who might buy a product; **domestic market** = market in the country where the selling company is based; **sales in the home market rose by 22% (c)** possible sales of a certain type of product *or* demand for a certain type of product; **the market for home computers has fallen sharply; we have 20% of the U.S. car market; there is no market for electric typewriters; a growth market** = market where sales are likely to rise rapidly; **the labor market** = number of workers available for work; **25,000 graduates have come on to the labor market** = they have become available for work because they have graduated from college; **the property market** = sales of real estate **(d) the Common Market** = the European Economic Community; **the Common Market agricultural policy** *or* **the Common Market ministers (e) the black market** = buying and selling goods in a way which is not allowed by law; **there is a flourishing black market in spare parts for cars; to pay black market prices** = to pay high prices to get items which are not easily available **(f) a buyer's market** = market where goods are sold cheaply because there is little demand; **a seller's market** = market where the seller can ask high prices because there is a large demand for the product **(g) closed market =** market where a supplier deals with only one agent or distributor and does not supply any others direct; **free market economy =** system where the government does not interfere in business activity in any way; **open market =** market where anyone can buy and sell **(h) capital market =** place where businesses can look for investment capital; **the foreign exchange markets =** places where currencies are bought or sold; **forward markets =** places where foreign currency or commodities can be bought or sold for delivery at a later date; **money market** or **finance market =** place where large sums of money are lent or borrowed **(i) commodity market =** place where commodities are bought or sold; **stock market** ≃ place where securities are bought and sold; *the market in oil stocks was very active or there was a brisk market in oil stocks;* **to buy securities in the open market =** to buy securities on the stock exchange, not privately; **over-the-counter market =** secondary market in securities which are not listed on a stock exchange; **gray market =** market in commodities or securities which are traded outside the normal markets, but not illegally **(j) market analysis =** detailed examination and evaluation of a market; **market capitalization =** value of a corporation calculated by multiplying the price one of its shares on the stock exchange by the number of shares issued; **market economist =** person who specializes in the study of financial structures and the return on investments in the stock market; **market forces =** influences on the sales of a product; **market forecast =** forecast of prices on the stock market; **market leader =** company with the largest market share; *we are the market leader in home computers;* **market maker =** dealer who makes a market in the stock of a certain corporation; **market opportunities =** possibility of finding new sales in a market; **market penetration** or **market share =** percentage of a total market which the sales of a company cover; *we hope our new product range will increase our market share;* **market price =** (i) price at which a product can be sold; (ii) price of a share on a Stock Exchange; **market rate =** normal price in the market; *we pay the market rate for secretaries* or *we pay secretaries the market rate;* **market research =** examining the

possible sales of a product before it is put on the market; **market trends =** gradual changes taking place in a market; **market value =** value of a product or of a company if sold today **(k) up market** or **down market =** more expensive or less expensive; **to go up market** or **to go down market =** to make products which appeal to a wealthy section of the market or to a wider, less wealthy, section of the market **(l) to be in the market for secondhand cars =** to look for secondhand cars to buy; **to come onto the market =** to start to be sold; *this soap has just come onto the market;* **to put something on the market =** to start to offer something for sale; *they put their house on the market; I hear the company has been put on the market;* the company has **priced itself out of the market =** the company has raised its prices so high that its products do not sell **2** *verb* to arrange to sell products using various techniques; *this product is being marketed in all European countries*

◊ **marketable** *adjective* which can be sold easily

◊ **marketing** *noun* techniques used in selling a product (such as packaging, advertising, etc.); **marketing agreement =** contract by which one company will market another company's products; **marketing department =** department in a company which specializes in using marketing techniques to sell a product; **marketing director =** person in charge of a marketing department; **marketing policy** or **marketing plans** or **marketing strategy =** ideas of how the company's products are going to be marketed; *to plan the marketing of a new product*

◊ **marketplace** *noun* **(a)** open space in the middle of a town where a market is held **(b)** place where goods are sold; *our salesmen find life difficult in the marketplace; what is the reaction to the new model in the marketplace?* or *what is the marketplace reaction to the new model?*

mart *noun* market or place where things are sold; *car mart;* **auction mart =** auction rooms

mass *noun* **(a)** large group of people; **mass marketing =** marketing which aims at reaching large numbers of people; **mass media =** means of communication which reach large numbers of people (such as radio, television, newspapers); **mass**

unemployment = unemployment of large numbers of workers **(b)** large number; *we have a mass of letters to write*

◇ **mass-produce** *verb* to manufacture in large quantities; *to mass-produce cars*

◇ **mass production** *noun* making large quantities of products

master *noun* main *or* original; **master copy of a file =** main copy of a computer file, kept for security purposes

material *noun* **(a)** substance which can be used to make a finished product; **building materials =** bricks, cement, etc., used in building; **raw materials =** substances which have not been manufactured (such as wool, wood, sand); **synthetic materials =** substances made as products of a chemical process; **materials handling =** moving materials from one part of a factory to another in an efficient way; **materials management =** organization of the purchase, moving and using of materials **(b)** **display material =** posters, photographs, etc., which can be used to attract attention to goods which are for sale

maternity *noun* becoming a mother; **maternity leave =** permission for a woman to be away from work to have a baby

matter 1 *noun* **(a)** problem; *it is a matter of concern to the members of the committee =* the members of the committee are worried about it **(b)** **printed matter =** printed books, newspapers, publicity sheets, etc.; **publicity matter =** sheets *or* posters *or* leaflets used for publicity **(c)** question *or* problem to be discussed; *the most important matter on the agenda; we shall consider first the matter of last month's fall in prices* **2** *verb* to be important; *does it matter if one month's sales are down?*

mature 1 *adjective* **mature economy =** fully developed economy **2** *verb* **bills which mature in three weeks' time =** bills which will be due for payment in three weeks

◇ **maturity** *noun* **date of maturity** *or* **maturity date =** date when a government stock *or* an insurance policy *or* a debenture will become due for payment; **amount payable on maturity** = amount received by the insured person when the policy becomes mature

maximization *noun* making as large as possible; *profit maximization or maximization of profit*

◇ **maximize** *verb* to make as large as possible; *to maximize profits*

maximum 1 *noun* largest possible number *or* price *or* quantity; **up to a maximum of $10 =** no more than $10; **to increase exports to the maximum =** as much as possible; *it is the maximum the insurance company will pay* (NOTE: plural is **maxima** *or* **maximums**) **2** *adjective* largest possible; *maximum income tax rate or maximum rate of tax; maximum load; maximum production levels; maximum price;* **to increase production to the maximum level =** as much as possible; **maximum weekly benefit (MWB) =** highest possible benefit payment a person may receive per week

mayor *noun* leading elected representative in a city, the head of the city council

Mb = MEGABYTE

M.B.A. = MASTER OF BUSINESS ADMINISTRATION

M.B.O. = MANAGEMENT BY OBJECTIVES

mean 1 *adjective* average; *mean annual increase ;* **mean price =** average price of a stock in a day's trading **2** *noun* average *or* number calculated by adding several figures together and dividing by the number of figures added; *unit sales are over the mean for the first quarter or above the first quarter mean*

◇ **means** *plural noun* **(a)** way of doing something; *air freight is the fastest means of getting stock to South America; do we have any means of copying all these documents quickly?* **(b)** money *or* resources; *the company has the means to launch the new product; such a level of investment is beyond the means of a small private company;* **means test =** inquiry into how much money someone earns to see if he is eligible for public assistance; **he has private means =** he has income from dividends *or* interest *or* rent which is not part of his salary

measure 1 *noun* **(a)** way of calculating size *or* quantity; **cubic measure =** volume in cubic feet or meters, calculated by multiplying height, width and length; **dry measure =** way of calculating the quantity of loose dry goods (such as corn); **square measure =** area in square feet or meters, calculated by multiplying width and length; **inspector of weights and measures =** government inspector who inspects weighing machines and goods sold in stores to see if the quantities and weights are correct; **as a measure of the company's performance =** as a way of judging if the company's business has been good or bad **(b) made to measure =** made specially to fit; *he has his clothes made to measure* **(c) tape measure =** long tape with inches or centimeters marked on it, used to measure how long something is **(d)** type of action; **to take measures to prevent something from happening =** to act to stop something from happening; **to take crisis** *or* **emergency measures =** to act rapidly to stop a crisis from developing; **an economy measure =** an action to save money; **fiscal measures =** tax changes made by the government to improve the working of the economy; **as a precautionary measure =** to prevent something from taking place; **safety measures =** actions to make sure that something is safe **2** *verb* **(a)** to find out the size *or* quantity of something; to be of a certain size *or* quantity; *to measure the size of a package; a package which measures 10in. by 25in. or a package measuring 10in. by 25in.* **(b)** to measure the government's performance = to judge how well the government is doing

◊ **measurement** *noun* **(a) measurements =** size (in inches, centimeters, etc.); *to write down the measurements of a package* **(b)** way of judging something; **performance measurement** *or* **measurement of performance; measurement of profitability =** way of calculating how profitable something is

◊ **measuring tape** *noun* long tape with inches or centimeters marked on it, used to measure how long something is

mechanic *noun* person who works with engines *or* machines; *car mechanic*

◊ **mechanical** *adjective* worked by a machine; *a mechanical pump*

◊ **mechanism** *noun* way in which something works; *a mechanism to slow down inflation; the company's discount mechanism*

◊ **mechanize** *verb* to use machines in place of workers; *the country is aiming to mechanize its farming industry*

◊ **mechanization** *noun* using machines in place of workers; *farm mechanization or the mechanization of farms*

media *noun* **the media** *or* **the mass media =** means of communicating information to the public (such as television, radio, newspapers); *the product attracted a lot of interest in the media or a lot of media interest;* **media analysis** *or* **media research =** examining different types of media (such as the readers of newspapers, television viewers) to see which is best for promoting a certain type of product; **media coverage =** reports about something in the media; *we had good media coverage for the launch of the new model*
NOTE: **media** is followed by a plural verb

median *noun* the very middle of a list of numbers

mediate *verb* to try to make the two sides in an argument come to an agreement; *to mediate between the manager and his staff; the government offered to mediate in the dispute*

◊ **mediation** *noun* attempt by a third party to make the two sides in an argument agree; *the employers refused an offer of government mediation; the dispute was ended through the mediation of union officials*

◊ **mediator** *noun* person who tries to make the two sides in a dispute agree

medical *noun* referring to the study or treatment of illness; **medical insurance =** insurance which pays the cost of medical treatment; **he resigned for medical reasons =** he resigned because he was too ill to work

◊ **Medicare** *noun* federal system of medical insurance for older citizens

medium 1 *adjective* middle *or* average; *the company is of medium size* **2** *noun* way of doing something *or* means of doing something; **advertising medium =** type of advertisement (such as a TV commercial); *the product was advertised through the medium of the trade press*
NOTE: plural is **media**

◊ **medium-sized** *adjective* a **medium-sized engineering company** = company which is neither very large nor very small

◊ **medium-term** *adjective* referring to a point between short term and long term; **medium-term forecast** = forecast for two or three years

meet *verb* **(a)** to come together with someone; *to meet a negotiating committee; to meet an agent at his hotel; the two sides met in the lawyer's office* **(b)** to be satisfactory for; *to meet a customer's requirements; to meet a sales forecast* = to sell as many units as was forecast; **to meet the demand for a new product** = to fill the demand for a product; **we will try to meet your price** = we will try to offer a price which is acceptable to you; *they failed to meet the deadline* = they were not able to complete in time **(c)** to pay for; *the company will meet your expenses; he was unable to meet his mortgage payments*
NOTE: **meeting - met**

◊ **meet with** *verb* **(a)** to come together with someone; *I hope to meet with him in New York* **(b)** his request met with a **refusal** = his request was refused

◊ **meeting** *noun* **(a)** coming together of a group of people; *management meeting; staff meeting; board meeting* = meeting of the directors of a company; **general meeting** *or* **meeting of shareholders** *or* **shareholders' meeting** = meeting of all the shareholders of a company *or* meeting of all the members of a society **(b) to hold a meeting** = to organize a meeting of a group of people; *the meeting will be held in the committee room; to open a meeting* = to start a meeting; **to conduct a meeting** = to be the chairperson for a meeting; **to close a meeting** = to end a meeting; **to address a meeting** = to speak to a meeting

QUOTE if corporate forecasts are met, sales will exceed $50 million in 1985
Citizen (Ottawa)

megabyte (Mb) *noun* storage unit in computers, equal to 1,048,576 bytes

member *noun* **(a)** person who belongs to a group *or* a society; *members of a committee* *or* *committee members; they were elected members of the board;* **ordinary member** = person who pays dues to belong to a group; **honorary member** = special person who does not

have to pay dues **(b)** organization which belongs to a society; *the member countries of the EC; the members of the United Nations; the member companies of a trade association; the member banks of the Federal Reserve; the member firms of the Stock Exchange*

◊ **membership** *noun* **(a)** belonging to a group; *membership qualifications; conditions of membership; membership card; to pay your membership fees* **(b)** all the members of a group; *the membership was asked to vote for the new president;* **the club's membership secretary** = committee member who deals with the ordinary members of a society; **the club has a membership of five hundred** = the club has five hundred members

QUOTE the bargaining committee will recommend that its membership ratify the agreement at a meeting called for June
Toronto Star
QUOTE in 1984 exports to Canada from the member-states of the European Community jumped 38 per cent
Globe and Mail (Toronto)

memo *noun* short message sent from one person to another in the same organization; *to write a memo to the finance director; to send a memo to all the sales representatives; according to your memo about debtors; I sent the CEO a memo about your complaint*

◊ **memo pad** *noun* pad of paper for writing short notes

◊ **memorandum** *noun* short message; *he received an official memorandum from the vice-president*

memory *noun* facility for storing of data in a computer

mention *verb* to talk about something for a short time; *the chairman mentioned the work of the retiring president; can you mention to the secretary that the date of the next meeting has been changed?*

mercantile *adjective* commercial; **mercantile country** = country which earns income from trade; **mercantile law** = laws relating to business

merchandise 1 *noun* goods which are for sale *or* which have been sold; *the merchandise is shipped through two ports* **2** *verb* to sell goods by a wide variety of means, including display,

advertising, sending samples, etc.; *to merchandise a product*
◇ **merchandiser** *noun* person *or* company which organizes the display and promotion of goods
◇ **merchandising** *noun* organizing the display and promotion of goods for sale; *merchandising of a product; merchandising department*

QUOTE fill huge warehouses with large quantities but limited assortments of top-brand, first-quality merchandise and sell the goods at rock-bottom prices
Duns Business Month
QUOTE what's made them grow, is their dedication to buying better and better merchandise, concentrating on clothes that can't be bought in major department stores, and developing a more sophisticated clientele
Nation's Business

merchant *noun* (a) businessman who buys and sells goods (especially imported goods) for retail sale; *coal merchant; tobacco merchant; wine merchant* (b) **merchant bank** = European bank which lends money to companies and deals in international finance; **merchant navy** *or* **merchant marine** = all the commercial ships of a country; **merchant ship** *or* **merchant vessel** = commercial ship *or* ship which carries a cargo
◇ **merchantman** *noun* commercial ship

merge *verb* to join together; *the two companies have merged; the firm merged with its main competitor*
◇ **merger** *noun* joining together of two or more companies; *as a result of the merger, the company is the largest in the field*

merit *noun* being good or efficient; **merit award** *or* **merit bonus** = extra money given to a worker because he has worked well; **merit increase** = increase in pay given to someone because his work is good; **merit rating** = judging how well a worker does his work, so that he can be paid according to merit

message *noun* piece of news which is sent to someone; *to send a message; I will leave a message with his secretary; can you give the manager a message from his wife? he says he never received the message*

messenger *noun* person who brings a message; *he sent the package by special messenger;* **office messenger** = person who carries messages from one

person to another in a large office; **messenger boy** = young man who delivers messages

Messrs. *noun* plural form of Mr.; *Messrs. White and Smith*

method *noun* way of doing something; *a new method of making something or of doing something; what is the best method of payment? his organizing methods are out of date; their manufacturing methods or production methods are among the most modern in the country*

meter *noun* measure of length (= 3.4 feet)
NOTE: usually written **m** after figures: **the case is 2m wide by 3m long**
◇ **metric** *adjective* using the meter as a basic measurement; **metric ton** = 1000 kilograms; **the metric system** = system of measuring, using meters, liters and grams

metro area *noun* central part of a city

mg = MILLIGRAM

mi = MILE

micro- *prefix* very small
◇ **microcomputer** *noun* small computer for general use in the home or office
◇ **microeconomics** *noun* study of the economics of persons or single companies
◇ **microfiche** *noun* index sheet, made of several microfilm photographs; *we hold our records on microfiche*
◇ **microfilm 1** *noun* roll of film on which a document is photographed in very small scale; *we hold our records on microfilm* **2** *verb* to make a very small scale photograph; *send the 1980 correspondence to be microfilmed or for microfilming*
◇ **microprocessor** *noun* small computer processing unit

mid- *prefix* middle; *from mid-1982* = from the middle of 1982; *the factory is closed until mid-July*
◇ **mid-month** *adjective* taking place in the middle of the month; *mid-month accounts*
◇ **midweek** *adjective* which happens in the middle of a week; *the midweek lull in sales*

middle *adjective* in the center *or* between two points; **middle management** = department managers in a company, who carry out the policy set by the directors and organize the work of a group of workers

◊ **middle-income** *adjective* **people in the middle-income bracket** = people with average incomes, not very high or very low

◊ **middleman** *noun* businessman who buys from the manufacturer and sells to the public; *we sell direct from the factory to the customer and cut out the middleman*
NOTE: plural is **middlemen**

◊ **middle-sized** *adjective* neither small nor large; *a middle-sized company*

migrant *or* **migratory** *adjective* moving from place to place; **migrant laborer** = farm laborer who moves from one job to another

mile *noun* measure of length (= 5,280 feet); **the car goes twenty-five miles to the gallon** *or* **twenty-five miles per gallon** = the car uses one gallon of gasoline to travel twenty-five miles
NOTE: miles per gallon is usually written **mpg** after figures: **the car goes 25 mpg**

◊ **mileage** *noun* distance traveled in miles; **mileage allowance** = money allowed as expenses to someone who uses his own car for business travel; **the salesman's average annual mileage** = the number of miles which a salesman drives in a year

mill *noun* **(a)** building where a certain type of material is processed or made; *after lunch the visitors were shown around the mill;* **cotton mill** = factory where raw cotton is processed; **paper mill** = factory where wood is made into paper **(b)** one-tenth of a cent, used in calculating property taxes

milligram *noun* one thousandth of a gram
NOTE: usually written **mg** after figures

◊ **milliliter** *noun* one thousandth of a liter
NOTE: usually written **ml** after figures

◊ **millimeter** *noun* one thousandth of a meter
NOTE: usually written **mm** after figures

million number 1,000,000; *the company lost $10 million in the African market; our sales have risen to $13.4 million*

NOTE: can be written **m** after figures: **$5m** (say "five million dollars")

◊ **millionaire** *noun* person who has more than one million dollars; **paper millionaire** = person who owns securities or bonds which, if sold, would be worth one million dollars

min = MINUTE, MINIMUM

mine 1 *noun* hole in the ground for digging out coal, gold, iron etc.; *the mines have been closed by a strike* **2** *verb* to dig and bring out coal, gold, etc.; *the company is mining coal in the south of the country;* **mining concession** = right to use a piece of land for mining

mini- *prefix* very small

◊ **minicomputer** *noun* computer which is larger than a microcomputer but smaller than a mainframe

◊ **minicontainer** *noun* small container

◊ **minimarket** *noun* very small self-service store

minimal *adjective* the smallest possible; *there was a minimal quantity of imperfections in the batch; the head office exercises minimal control over the branch offices*

◊ **minimize** *verb* to make something seem to be very small and not very important; *do not minimize the risks involved; he tends to minimize the difficulty of the project*

◊ **minimum 1** *noun* smallest possible quantity *or* price *or* number; *to keep expenses to a minimum; to reduce the risk of a loss to a minimum* (NOTE: plural is **minima** or **minimums**) **2** *adjective* smallest possible; **minimum charge** = charge made for a service, even if the service is not carried out; **minimum dividend** = smallest dividend which is guaranteed to the shareholders; **minimum payment** = smallest payment necessary; **minimum quantity** = smallest quantity which is acceptable; **minimum wage** = lowest hourly wage which a business can legally pay its workers

minister *noun (in Britain, and many other countries)* member of a government who is in charge of a ministry; *the Minister of Trade or the Trade Minister*

◊ **ministry** *noun* department in a government; *he works in the Ministry of Finance*

minor *adjective* less important; *minor expenditure; minor shareholders; a loss of minor importance* = not a very serious loss

◊ **minority** *noun* number *or* quantity which is less than half of the total; *a minority of board members opposed the chairman;* **minority holding** *or* **minority interest** = group of shares which are less than one half of the shares in a corporation; **minority shareholder** = person who owns a group of shares but less than half of the shares in a corporation; **in the minority** = being fewer than half; *good salesmen are in the minority in our sales team*

mint 1 *noun* factory where coins are made **2** *verb* to make coins

minus 1 *adverb* less *or* without; *net salary is gross salary minus tax and social security deductions; gross profit is sales minus production costs* **2** *adjective* **the accounts show a minus figure** = show that more has been spent than has been received; **minus factor** = unfavorable factor; *to have lost sales in the best quarter of the year is a minus factor for the sales team*

minute 1 *noun* (a) one sixtieth part of an hour; *I can see you for ten minutes only; if you do not mind waiting, Mr. Smith will be free in about twenty minutes* (b) **the minutes of the meeting** = notes of what happened at a meeting, written by the secretary; **to take the minutes** = to write notes of what happened at a meeting; **the chairman signed the minutes of the last meeting** = he signed them to show that they are a correct record of what was said and what decisions were made; **this will not appear in the minutes of the meeting** = this is unofficial and will not be noted as having been said **2** *verb* to put something into the minutes of a meeting; *the chairman's remarks about the auditors were minuted;* **I do not want that to be minuted** *or* **I want that not to be minuted** = do not put that comment into the minutes of the meeting

◊ **minute book** *noun* book in which the minutes of a meeting are kept

misappropriate *verb* to use illegally money which is not yours, but with which you have been trusted

◊ **misappropriation** *noun* illegal use of money by someone who is not the owner but who has been trusted to look after it

misc = MISCELLANEOUS

miscalculate *verb* to calculate wrongly; *the salesman miscalculated the discount, so we barely broke even on the deal*

◊ **miscalculation** *noun* mistake in calculating

miscellaneous *adjective* various *or* mixed *or* not all of the same sort; *miscellaneous items; a box of miscellaneous pieces of equipment; miscellaneous expenditure*

miscount 1 *noun* mistake in counting **2** *verb* to count wrongly; *the sales clerk miscounted, so we got twenty-five bars of chocolate instead of two dozen*

misdirect *verb* to give wrong directions

mismanage *verb* to manage badly

◊ **mismanagement** *noun* bad management; *the company failed because of the officers' mismanagement*

misrepresent *verb* to report facts wrongly

◊ **misrepresentation** *noun* wrongly reporting facts; **fraudulent misrepresentation** = giving someone wrong information in order to cheat him

Miss *noun* title given to a woman who is not married; *Miss Smith is our sales manager*

miss *verb* (a) not to hit; *the company has missed its profit forecast again; the sales team has missed its sales targets* (b) not to meet; *I arrived late, so missed most of the discussion;* **he missed the chairman by ten minutes** = he left ten minutes before the chairman arrived

mission *noun* group of people going on a journey for a special purpose; **trade mission** = visit by a group of businessmen to discuss trade; *he led a trade mission to China;* **a fact-finding mission** = visit to an area to search for information about a problem

mistake *noun* wrong action *or* wrong decision; **to make a mistake** = to do something wrong; *the store made a mistake and sent the wrong items; there was a mistake in the address;*

she made a mistake in addressing the letter; **by mistake** = in error *or* wrongly; *they sent the wrong items by mistake; she put my letter into an envelope for the chairman by mistake*

misunderstanding *noun* lack of agreement *or* mistake; *there was a misunderstanding over my tickets*

misuse *noun* wrong use; *misuse of funds or of assets*

mix 1 *noun* things put together; **product mix** = range of different products which a company has for sale; **sales mix** = sales and profitability of a wide range of different products **2** *verb* to put different things together; *I like to mix business with pleasure - why don't we discuss the deal over lunch?*
◊ **mixed** *adjective* **(a)** of different sorts *or* of different types together; **mixed economy** = system which contains both nationalized industries and private enterprise; **mixed farm** = farm which has both animals and crops **(b)** neither good nor bad

ml = MILLILITER

mm = MILLIMETER

mobile *adjective* which can move about; **mobile home** = dwelling made in a factory, to be transported to a site and connected to utilities; **mobile workforce** = workers who move from place to place to get work
◊ **mobility** *noun* being able to move from one place to another; **mobility of labor** = situation when workers agree to move from one place to another to get work
◊ **mobilize** *verb* to bring together, especially to fight; **to mobilize capital** = to collect capital to support something; **to mobilize resources to defend a merger bid** = to get the support of shareholders, etc., to stop a company from merging with another

mock-up *noun* model of a new product for testing or to show to possible buyers

mode *noun* way of doing something; **mode of payment** = way in which payment is made (such as cash or check)

model 1 *noun* **(a)** small copy of something to show what it will look like when finished; *he showed us a model of the new office building* **(b)** style *or* type of product; *this is the latest model; the model on display is last year's; he drives a 1985 model Ford;* **demonstration model** = piece of equipment used in demonstrations and then sold cheaply **(c)** person whose job is to wear new clothes to show them to possible buyers **(d) economic model** = theory describing a possible plan for an economic system **2** *adjective* which is a perfect example to be copied; *a model agreement* **3** *verb* to wear new clothes to show them to possible buyers

modem *noun* device which links a computer to the telephone line, allowing data to be sent from one computer to another

moderate 1 *adjective* not too large; *the union made a moderate claim; the government proposed a moderate increase in the tax rate* **2** *verb* to make less strong *or* less large; *the union was forced to moderate its claim*

modern *adjective* referring to the recent past or the present time; *it is a fairly modern invention - it was patented only in the 1960s*
◊ **modernize** *verb* to make modern; *he modernized the whole product line*
◊ **modernization** *noun* making modern; *the modernization of the workshop*

modest *adjective* small; *oil shares showed modest gains over the week's trading*

modify *verb* to change *or* to make something fit a different use; *the management modified its proposals; this is the new modified agreement; the car will have to be modified to pass the government tests; the refrigerator was considerably modified before it went into production*
◊ **modification** *noun* change; *to make or to carry out modifications to the plan; the new model has had several important modifications; we asked for modifications to the contract*

modular *adjective* made of various sections

momentum *noun* movement forwards; **to gain** *or* **to lose momentum** = to move faster or more slowly; *the strike is*

gaining momentum = more workers are joining the strike

monetary *adjective* referring to money or currency; **monetary policy** = Federal Reserve Board plan or course of action relating to the money supply; **monetary standard** = established units of coinage or currency of a country; **the international monetary system** = methods of controlling and exchanging currencies between countries; **The International Monetary Fund** = (part of the United Nations) a type of bank which helps member states in financial difficulties, gives financial advice to members and encourages world trade; **monetary unit** = standard currency in a country (the dollar, the pound, the yen, etc.)

◊ **monetarism** *noun* idea that inflation can be controlled by regulating the money supply (i.e., the amount of money available in the economy)

◊ **monetarist 1** *noun* person who believes in monetarism and acts accordingly **2** *adjective* according to monetarism; *monetarist theories*

> QUOTE a draft report on changes in the international monetary system
> *Wall Street Journal*

money *noun* **(a)** coins and notes used for buying and selling; **to earn money** = to be paid for working at a job; **to earn good money** = to have a large salary *or* paycheck; **to lose money** = to make a loss *or* not to make a profit; **the company has been losing money for months** = the company has been working at a loss; **to get your money back** = to earn enough to cover your original investment; **to make money** = to make a profit; **to put money into the bank** = to deposit money into a bank account; **to put money into a business** = to invest money in a business; *he put all his investment money into opening a store*; **to put money down** = to pay cash, especially as a deposit; *he put $25 down and paid the rest in installments*; **cheap money** = money which can be borrowed at a low rate of interest; **dear money** = money which has to be borrowed at a high rate of interest; **easy money** = (i) money which can be earned with no difficulty; (ii) loan money available on easy repayment terms; *selling insurance is easy money*; **paper money** = money in notes, not coins; **ready money** = cash *or* money which is immediately available; **money lying idle** = money not being used to produce interest; **they are worth a lot of money** = they are valuable **(b) money supply** = amount of money which exists in a country; **money markets** = markets for buying and selling short-term loans; *the international money markets are nervous;* **money rates** = rates of interest for borrowers or lenders **(c) money order** = document which can be bought, usually by a person without a checking account, for sending money through the mail; **foreign money order** *or* **international money order** *or* **overseas money order** = money order in a foreign currency which is payable to someone living in a foreign country **(d) monies** = sums of money; *monies owing to the company; to collect monies due*

◊ **moneylender** *noun* person who lends money at interest

◊ **money-making** *adjective* which makes money; *a money-making plan*

monitor 1 *noun* screen (like a TV screen) on a computer **2** *verb* to check *or* to examine how something is working; *he is monitoring the progress of sales; how do you monitor the performance of the sales force?*

monopoly *noun* situation where one person or company controls the entire market in the supply of a product; *to have a monopoly of alcohol sales or to have an alcohol monopoly; to be in a monopoly situation; the company has an absolute monopoly of imports of French wine; the factory has an absolute monopoly of jobs in the town;* **public monopoly** *or* **state monopoly** = situation where the state is the only suppliers of a product or service (such as the postal service)

◊ **monopolize** *verb* to create a monopoly *or* to get control of the entire supply of a product

◊ **monopolization** *noun* making a monopoly

month *noun* one of twelve periods which make a year; *the company pays him $100 a month; he earns $2,000 a month; bills due at the end of the current month;* **calendar month** = whole month as on a calendar; **paid by the month** = paid once each month; **to give a customer two months' credit** = to allow a customer to pay not immediately, but after two months

◊ **month end** *noun* the end of a calendar month, when accounts have to be balanced; *month-end accounts*

◇ **monthly 1** *adjective* happening every month *or* which is received every month; **monthly statement; monthly payments; he is paying for his car by monthly installments; my monthly salary check is late; monthly pass =** ticket for travel which is good for travel throughout one month **2** *adverb* every month; **to pay monthly; the account is credited monthly**

moonlight *verb informal* to do a second job for cash (often in the evening) as well as a regular job

◇ **moonlighter** *noun* person who moonlights

◇ **moonlighting** *noun* doing a second job; **he makes thousands of dollars a year from moonlighting**

mooring *noun* place where boats can be tied up in a harbor

moratorium *noun* temporary stop to repayments of money owed; **the banks called for a moratorium on payments** NOTE: plural is **moratoria**

mortality tables *plural noun* chart, used by insurers, which shows how long a person of a certain age can be expected to live on average

mortgage 1 *noun* agreement where someone lends money to another person so that he can buy a property, the property being the security; money lent in this way; **to take out a mortgage on a house; to buy a house with a $20,000 mortgage; mortgage payments =** money paid each month as interest on a mortgage, plus repayment of a small part of the capital borrowed; **first mortgage =** main mortgage on a property; **second mortgage =** further mortgage on a property which is already mortgaged; **to foreclose on a mortgaged property =** to sell a property because the owner cannot repay money which he has borrowed, using the property as security; **to pay off a mortgage =** to pay back the principal and all the interest on a loan to buy a property; **mortgage bond =** certificate showing that a mortgage exists and that property is security for it; **mortgage debenture =** debenture where the lender can be repaid by selling the company's property; **mortgage famine =** situation where there is not enough money available to offer mortgages to house buyers **2** *verb* to accept a loan with a property as

security; **the house is mortgaged; he mortgaged his house to set up in business**

◇ **mortgagee** *noun* person or company which lends money for someone to buy a property

◇ **mortgager** *or* **mortgagor** *noun* person who borrows money to buy a property

QUOTE for the first time since mortgage rates began falling a financial institution has raised charges on homeowner loans
Globe and Mail (Toronto)

most 1 *noun* a majority *or* very large amount *or* quantity; **most of the staff are graduates; most of our customers live near the factory; most of the orders come in the early part of the year 2** *adverb* to the greatest extent; **she is the most successful manager I know; he is the most pleasant employee we have on our staff**

◇ **most favored nation** *noun* country which has the best trade terms; **most-favored-nation clause =** agreement between two countries that each will offer the best possible terms in commercial contracts

◇ **mostly** *adverb* mainly *or* generally; **the staff are mostly women of twenty to thirty years of age; he works mostly in the Chicago office**

motion *noun* **(a)** moving about; **time and motion study =** study in an office *or* factory of the time taken to do certain jobs and the movements workers have to make to do them **(b)** proposal which will be put to a meeting to vote on; **to propose** *or* **to move a motion; the meeting voted on the motion; to speak against** *or* **for a motion; the motion was carried** *or* **was defeated by 220 votes to 196; to table a motion =** to remove a proposal from consideration for an indefinite period

motivated *adjective* **highly motivated sales reps =** sales reps who are very eager to sell

◇ **motivation** *noun* encouragement *or* being eager to sell; **the sales reps lack motivation =** the sales reps are not motivated enough

QUOTE creative people aren't necessarily motivated by money or titles, they may not want a larger office or more work, they don't often want more responsibility. They want to see their ideas implemented
Nation's Business

mountain *noun* pile *or* large heap; *I have mountains of typing to do; there is a mountain of invoices on the sales manager's desk*

mounting *adjective* increasing; *he resigned in the face of mounting pressure from the shareholders; the company is faced with mounting debts*
◊ **mount up** *verb* to increase rapidly; *costs are mounting up*

move *verb* (a) to go from one place to another; *the company is moving from the suburbs to the center of town; we have decided to move our factory to a site near the airport* (b) to be sold *or* to sell; *the stock is starting to move; the salesmen will have to work hard if they want to move all that stock by the end of the month* (c) to propose formally that a motion be accepted by a meeting; *he moved that the accounts be approved; I move that the meeting should adjourn for ten minutes*
◊ **movable** *or* **moveable** 1 *adjective* which can be moved; *movable property* 2 *plural noun* **movables** = movable property
◊ **movement** *noun* (a) changing position *or* going up or down; *movements in the money markets; cyclical movements of trade;* **movements of capital** = changes in a company's present capital structure; **stock movements** = passing of stock into *or* out of the warehouse; *all stock movements are logged by the computer* (b) group of people working toward the same aim; *the labor movement; the free trade movement*
◊ **mover** *noun* person who proposes a motion

mpg = MILES PER GALLON

Mr. *noun* title given to a man; *Mr. Smith is the Executive Vice-President*

MRP = MANUFACTURER'S RECOMMENDED PRICE

Mrs. *noun* title given to a married woman; *the chair was taken by Mrs. Smith*

Ms. *noun* title given to a woman where it is not known if she is married, or where she does not wish to indicate if she is married or not; *Ms. Smith is the personnel officer*

multi- *prefix* referring to many things
◊ **multilateral** *adjective* between several parties; *a multilateral agreement;* **multilateral trade** = trade between several countries
◊ **multimedia advertising** *noun* advertising which uses several different media
◊ **multimillion** *adjective* referring to several million dollars; *they signed a multimillion dollar deal*
◊ **multimillionaire** *noun* person who owns several million dollars
◊ **multinational** *noun* company which has branches *or* subsidiary companies in several countries; *the company has been bought by one of the big multinationals*

QUOTE factory automation is a multi-billion-dollar business
Duns Business Month
QUOTE what is new is that American-owned multinationals are beginning to employ large numbers of foreigners relative to their American work forces
Harvard Business Review

multiple 1 *adjective* many; **multiple listing** = listing of a company that appears more than once in the same directory; **multiple ownership** = situation where something is owned by several parties jointly 2 *noun* company with stores in several different towns

multiply *verb* (a) to calculate the sum of various numbers repeated a certain number of times; *to multiply twelve by three; square measurements are calculated by multiplying length by width* (b) to grow *or* to increase; *profits multiplied in the boom years*
◊ **multiplication** *noun* act of multiplying; **multiplication sign** = sign used to show that a number is being multiplied by another

municipal *adjective* referring to a town; *municipal taxes; municipal offices;* **municipal bond** = bond issued by a town, city or county

Murphy's law *noun* law, based on wide experience, which says that in commercial life if something can go wrong it will go wrong

mutual *adjective* belonging to two or more people; **mutual (insurance) company** = company which belongs to insurance policy holders; **mutual funds** = organizations which receive money

from investors and invest it in
diversified securities for them, the
investment being in the form of shares in
the fund

MWB = MAXIMUM WEEKLY BENEFIT

Nn

name *noun* word used to identify a thing
or a person; *I cannot remember the
name of the president of Smith Corp.;
his first name is John, but I am not
sure of his last name;* **brand name** =
name of a particular make of product;
corporate name = name of a large
corporation; **under the name of** = using
a particular name; **trading under the
name of** "Best Foods" = using the name
"Best Foods" as a commercial name, but
not the name of the corporation

◊ **named** *adjective* **person named in
the policy** = person whose name is given
on an insurance policy as the person
insured

NASDAQ NATIONAL ASSOCIATION OF
SECURITIES DEALERS AUTOMATED
QUOTATIONS computer system which
gives current information about prices of
securities

nation *noun* country and the people
living in it; **most favored nation** =
country which has the best trade terms;
most-favored-nation clause =
agreement between two countries that
each will give the other the best possible
trade terms in commercial contracts; **the
United Nations** = organization linking
almost all countries in the world

◊ **national** *adjective* referring to a
particular country; **national
advertising** = advertising in every part
of a country, not just in one city; *we took
national advertising to promote our
new 24-hour delivery service;* **national
bank** = commercial bank, a member of
the Federal Reserve, established with
the approval of the U.S. Comptroller of
the Currency; **national campaign** =
sales or publicity campaign in every part
of a country; **the national debt** = money
borrowed by a government; **national
income** = value of income from the sales
of goods and services in a country;
national newspapers *or* **the national**

press = newspapers which sell in all
parts of a country; **gross national
product** = annual value of goods and
services traded in a country including
income from other countries

◊ **nationality** *noun* **he is of British
nationality** = he is a British citizen

◊ **nationalize** *verb* to put a privately-
owned industry under state ownership
and control; *the government is
planning to nationalize the banking
system*

◊ **nationalized** *adjective* **nationalized
industry** = industry which was
privately owned, but is now owned by
the state

◊ **nationalization** *noun* taking over of
private industry by the state

◊ **nationwide** *adjective* all over a
country; *the union called for a
nationwide strike; we offer a
nationwide delivery service; the new
car is being launched with a
nationwide sales campaign*

nature *noun* kind *or* type; *what is the
nature of the contents of the parcel?
the nature of his business is not
known*

◊ **natural** *adjective* **(a)** found in the
earth; *natural gas;* **natural resources** =
raw materials (such as coal, gas, iron)
which are found in the earth **(b)** not made
by people; *natural fibers* **(c)** normal; *it
was natural for the storekeeper to
feel annoyed when the supermarket
was set up close to his small store ;*
natural attrition = losing workers
because they resign or retire, not
through layoffs or dismissals; *the
company is hoping to avoid layoffs
and reduce its staff by natural
attrition*

NB = NOTE

necessary *adjective* which has to be
done *or* which is needed; *it is necessary
to fill in the form correctly if you are
to avoid delays at customs; is it really
necessary for the chairman to have six
executive assistants? you must have
all the necessary documentation
before you apply for a subsidy*

◊ **necessity** *noun* thing which is
absolutely important, without which
nothing can be done; *being unemployed
makes it difficult to afford even the
basic necessities*

negative *adjective* meaning "no"; **the
answer was in the negative** = the

answer was "no"; **negative cash flow =** situation where a business is spending more money than it receives

neglected *adjective* ignored *or* not well looked after; **neglected shares =** shares which are not bought or sold often; *bank shares have been a neglected sector of the market this week;* **neglected business =** business which has not been actively run by its owners and could therefore do better

negligence *noun* lack of proper care *or* not doing a duty; **criminal negligence =** not doing a duty with the result that harm is done to the interests of people

◊ **negligent** *adjective* not taking proper care *or* not doing one's duty

◊ **negligible** *adjective* very small *or* not worth bothering about; *his contribution to the problem was negligible;* **not negligible =** quite large *or* significant

> QUOTE negligent practices in hiring, retaining, and supervising employees now represent three of the hottest issues in current employment law
> *Nation's Business*

negotiable *adjective* **not negotiable =** which cannot be exchanged for cash; **"not negotiable" =** words written on a check to show that it can be paid only to a certain person; **negotiable check =** check made payable to bearer (i.e., to anyone who holds it); **negotiable instrument =** document (such as a bill of exchange, or check) which can be exchanged for cash *see also* NOW

◊ **negotiate** *verb* **to negotiate with someone =** to discuss a problem formally with someone, so as to reach an agreement; *the management refused to negotiate with the union;* **to negotiate terms and conditions** *or* **to negotiate a contract =** to discuss and agree on terms of a contract; **he negotiated a $250,000 loan with the bank =** he came to an agreement with the bank for a loan of $250,000; **negotiating committee =** group of representatives of management or unions who negotiate a settlement

◊ **negotiation** *noun* discussion of terms and conditions to reach an agreement; **contract under negotiation =** contract which is being discussed; **a matter for negotiation =** something which must be discussed before a decision is reached; **to enter into negotiations** *or* **to start negotiations =** to start discussing a problem; **to resume negotiations =** to start discussing a problem again, after talks have stopped for a time; **to break off negotiations =** to refuse to go on discussing a problem; **to conduct negotiations =** to negotiate; **negotiations broke down after six hours =** discussions stopped because no agreement was possible; **pay negotiations** *or* **wage negotiations =** discussions between management and workers about pay

◊ **negotiator** *noun* person who discusses with the aim of reaching an agreement; **an experienced union negotiator =** member of a labor union who has experience of discussing terms of employment with management

> QUOTE after three days of tough negotiations, the company reached agreement with its 1,200 unionized workers
> *Toronto Star*
> QUOTE many of the large travel agency chains are able to negotiate even greater discounts
> *Duns Business Month*

nest egg *noun* money saved (usually for retirement)

net 1 *adjective* **(a)** price *or* weight *or* pay, etc., after all deductions have been made; **net assets** *or* **net worth =** value of all the property of a company after taking away what the company owes; **net cash flow =** difference between money coming in and money going out of a business; **net earnings** *or* **net income =** total earnings of a business after tax and other deductions; **net income** *or* **net salary =** person's income which is left after taking away tax and other deductions; **net loss =** actual loss, after deducting overhead; **net margin =** net profit shown as a percentage of sales; **net price =** price paid, after discounts; **net profit =** amount of income from sales after all expenditures are subtracted; **net receipts =** receipts after deducting commission *or* tax *or* discounts, etc.; **net sales =** sales less damaged or returned items; **net weight =** weight of goods after deducting the weight of packaging material and container; **net yield =** profit from investments after deduction of costs **(b) terms strictly net =** payment has to be the full price, with no discount allowed **2** *verb* to make a true profit; *to net $10,000 after taxes* NOTE: **netting - netted**

network 1 *noun* system which links different points together; **a network of distributors** *or* **a distribution network =** series of points *or* warehouses from which goods are sent all over a country; **computer network =** computer system where several microcomputers are linked so that they all draw on the same database; **television network** = system of linked television stations covering the whole country **2** *verb* **(a)** to link together in a network; **to network a television program** = to send out the same television program through several TV stations; **networked system** = computer system where several microcomputers are linked together so that they all draw on the same database **(b)** to make use of all available business contacts

new *adjective* recent *or* not old; **under new management** = with a new owner; **new issue** = sale of stock of a corporation to the public for the first time; **new issues department** = section of a bank which deals with issues of new shares; **new technology** = electronic instruments which have recently been invented

◊ **New York Stock Exchange (NYSE)** *noun* largest and oldest stock exchange in the U.S.

◊ **news** *noun* information about things which have happened; *business news; financial news; financial markets were shocked by the news of the devaluation;* news agency = office which distributes news to newspapers and television companies; **news release** = sheet giving information about a new event which is sent to newspapers and TV and radio stations so that they can use it; *the company sent out a news release about the new president*

◊ **newsletter** *noun* **company newsletter** = printed sheet or small newspaper giving news about a business or group

◊ **newsstand** *noun* small kiosk selling newspapers and magazines

niche *noun* special place in a market, occupied by one company

nickel *noun* five cent coin; **nickel and dime store** = store selling cheap goods

night *noun* period of time from evening to morning; **night safe** = safe in the outside wall of a bank where money and documents can be deposited at night using a special door; **night shift** = shift which works at night; *there are thirty men on the night shift; he works nights or he works the night shift*

nil *noun* zero *or* nothing; *to make a nil return; the advertising budget has been cut to nil*

No. = NUMBER

no-load fund *noun* mutual fund that charges no sales fee to shareholders

nominal *adjective* **(a)** very small (payment); *we make a nominal charge for our services; they are paying a nominal rent* **(b)** **nominal account** = general statement of account showing income and expenditure, closed out at the end of the year; **nominal capital** = the total of the face value of all the shares in a company; **nominal value** = face value *or* value written on a stock certificate *or* a coin *or* a bill

nominate *verb* to suggest someone *or* to name someone for a job; **to nominate someone to a post** = to appoint someone to a post without an election; **to nominate someone as proxy** = to name someone as your proxy

◊ **nomination** *noun* act of nominating

◊ **nominee** *noun* person who is nominated, especially someone who is appointed to deal with financial matters on your behalf; **nominee account** = account held on behalf of someone

non- *prefix* not

◊ **nonacceptance** *noun* situation where the person who is to pay a bill of exchange does not accept it

◊ **noncontributory** *adjective* **noncontributory pension plan** = pension plan where the employee does not make any contributions and the company pays everything; *the company pension plan is noncontributory*

◊ **nondelivery** *noun* situation where something is not delivered

◊ **nondurable goods** *or* **nondurables** *plural noun* goods which are used up soon after they have been bought (such as food, newspapers)

◊ **nonfeasance** *noun* not doing something which should be done by law

◊ **nonnegotiable** *adjective* **nonnegotiable instrument** = document (such as an unsigned check) which cannot be exchanged for cash

◊ **nonpayment** *noun* **nonpayment of a debt** = not paying a debt due

◊ **nonprofit organization** *or* **nonprofit corporation** *noun* organization (such as a club or charity) which is not allowed by law to make a profit; **nonprofit organizations are exempted from corporation income tax**

◊ **nonrecurring** *adjective* nonrecurring charge *or* nonrecurring items = special items in a corporation's financial statement which appear only once

◊ **nonrefundable** *adjective* which will not be refunded; **nonrefundable deposit**

◊ **nonresident** *noun* person who is not considered a resident of a country for tax purposes; **he has a nonresident bank account**

◊ **nonreturnable** *adjective* which cannot be returned; **nonreturnable merchandise** = goods which cannot be returned to the seller after purchase; **nonreturnable packing** = packing which is to be thrown away when it has been used and not returned to the sender

◊ **nonstop** *adjective & adverb* without stopping; **they worked nonstop to finish the audit on time**

◊ **nonsufficient** *adjective* nonsufficient funds = not enough money in a checking account to pay a check that has been presented

◊ **nontaxable** *adjective* which is not subject to tax; **nontaxable income**

◊ **nonunion** *adjective* company using nonunion labor = company employing workers who do not belong to labor unions

◊ **nonvoting** *adjective* nonvoting shares = shares which do not allow the shareholder to vote at meetings

norm *noun* the usual quantity *or* the usual rate; **the output from this factory is well above the norm for the industry** *or* **well above the industry norm**

◊ **normal** *adjective* usual *or* which happens regularly; **normal deliveries are made on Tuesdays and Fridays; now that the strike is over we hope to resume normal service as soon as possible;** under normal conditions = if things work in the usual way; **under normal conditions a package takes two days to get to San Francisco; normal wear and tear** = acceptable damage caused by normal use

no-strike clause *noun* clause in an agreement in which the workers say that they will never strike

notary public *noun* public officer who has the authority to witness documents

and spoken statements, making them official
NOTE: plural is **notaries public**

note 1 *noun* (a) short document *or* short piece of information; **advice note** = written notice to a customer giving details of goods ordered and shipped but not yet delivered; **cover note** = letter from an insurance company giving details of an insurance policy and confirming that the policy exists; **credit note** = note showing that money is owed to a customer; **debit note** = note showing that a customer owes money; **we undercharged Mr. Smith and had to send him a debit note for the extra amount; delivery note** = list of goods being delivered, given to the customer with the goods; **dispatch note** = note saying that goods have been sent; **note of hand** *or* **promissory note** = document stating that someone promises to pay an amount of money on a certain date (b) short letter *or* short piece of information; **to send someone a note; I left a note on his desk; she left a note for the sales manager with his secretary 2** *verb* to write down details of something and remember them; **we note that the goods were delivered in bad condition; your order has been noted and will be dispatched as soon as we have stock; your complaint has been noted**

◊ **notebook** *noun* book for writing notes in

◊ **notepad** *noun* pad of paper for writing short notes

◊ **notepaper** *noun* writing paper for notes

notice *noun* (a) piece of written information; **the secretary pinned up a notice about the pension plan; copyright notice** = note in a book showing who owns the copyright and the date of ownership (b) official warning that a contract is going to end *or* that terms are going to be changed; **until further notice** = until different instructions are given; **you must pay $200 on the last day of each month until further notice** (c) written announcement that a worker is leaving his job on a certain date; **period of notice** = time stated in the contract of employment which the worker or company has to allow between resigning or being fired and the worker actually leaving his job; **we require three months' notice; he gave six months' notice; we gave him three months' wages in lieu of notice; she handed in**

her notice = she resigned **(d)** time allowed before something takes place; **at short notice =** with very little warning; *the bank manager will not see anyone at short notice;* **you must give seven days' notice of withdrawal =** you must ask to take money out of the account seven days before you want it **(e)** legal document (such as telling a tenant to leave property which he is occupying); *to give a tenant notice to quit;* **to serve notice on someone =** to give someone a legal notice

notify *verb* **to notify someone of something =** to tell someone something formally; *they were notified of the arrival of the shipment*

◊ **notification** *noun* informing someone

NOW account *noun* NEGOTIABLE ORDER OF WITHDRAWAL ACCOUNT an interest-bearing checking account in which a minimum of $500 has to be kept at all times

nsf = NONSUFFICIENT FUNDS

null *adjective* with no meaning *or* which cannot legally be enforced; **the contract was declared null and void =** the contract was said to be not valid; **to render a decision null =** to make a decision useless *or* to cancel a decision

◊ **nullification** *noun* act of making something invalid

◊ **nullify** *verb* to make something invalid *or* to cancel something

number 1 *noun* **(a)** quantity of things *or* people; *the number of persons on the payroll has increased over the last year; the number of days lost through strikes has fallen; the number of shares sold;* **a number of =** some; *a number of the staff will be retiring this year* **(b)** written figure; *account number; batch number; check number; invoice number; order number; page number; serial number; phone number or telephone number;* **number account** = bank account (usually in Switzerland) which is referred to only by a number, the name of the person holding it being kept secret; **box number =** reference number used when asking for mail to be sent to a post office or when asking for replies to an advertisement to be sent to the newspaper's offices; *please reply to Box No. 209;* **index number =** (i) number of something in an index; (ii) number showing the percentage rise of

something over a period NOTE: often written **No.** with figures; also indicated by the **#** sign **2** *verb* to put a figure on a document; *to number an order; I refer to your invoice numbered 1234*

◊ **numeric** *or* **numerical** *adjective* referring to numbers; **in numerical order =** in the order of figures (such as 1 before 2, 33 before 34); *file these invoices in numerical order;* **numeric data =** data in the form of figures; **numeric keypad =** part of a computer keyboard which is a programmable set of numbered keys

NYSE = NEW YORK STOCK EXCHANGE

Oo

oath *noun* legal promise stating that something is true; **he was under oath =** he had promised in court to say what was true

object *verb* to refuse to do something *or* to say that you do not accept something; *to object to a clause in a contract* NOTE: you object **to** something

◊ **objection** *noun* **to raise an objection to something =** to object to something; *the union delegates raised an objection to the wording of the agreement*

objective 1 *noun* something which you try to do; *the company has achieved its objectives; we set the sales forces certain objectives;* **long-term objective** *or* **short-term objective =** aim which you hope to achieve within a few years or a few months; **management by objectives =** way of managing a business by planning work for the managers to do and testing if it is completed correctly and on time **2** *adjective* considered from a general point of view, not from that of the person involved; *you must be objective in assessing the performance of the staff; to carry out an objective survey of the market*

obligate *verb* **to be obligated to do something =** to have a legal duty to do something

◊ **obligation** *noun* **(a)** duty to do something; **to be under an obligation to do something** = to feel it is your duty to do something; *there is no obligation to buy; to be under no obligation to do something;* **he is under no contractual obligation to buy** = he has signed no contract which forces him to buy; **to fulfill one's contractual obligations** = to do what is stated in a contract; **two weeks' free trial without obligation** = the customer can try the item at home for two weeks without having to buy it at the end of the test **(b)** debt; **to meet one's obligations** = to pay one's debts

◊ **obligatory** *adjective* necessary according to the law or rules; *each person has to pass an obligatory medical examination*

◊ **oblige** *verb* **to oblige someone to do something** = to make someone feel he must do something; *he felt obliged to cancel the contract*

o.b.o. = OR BEST OFFER

obsolescence *noun* act of going out of date, and therefore becoming less useful and valuable; **built-in obsolescence** *or* **planned obsolescence** = situation where the manufacturer designs his products to become out-of-date so that the customers can be persuaded to replace them with new models

◊ **obsolescent** *adjective* out of date

◊ **obsolete** *adjective* no longer used; *when the office was equipped with word processors the typewriters became obsolete*

obtain *verb* to get; *to obtain supplies from abroad; we find these items very difficult to obtain; to obtain an injunction against a company; he obtained control by buying the founder's shares*

◊ **obtainable** *adjective* which can be got; *prices fall when raw materials are easily obtainable; our products are obtainable in all computer stores*

occasional *adjective* which happens from time to time

occupancy *noun* act of occupying a property (such as a house, an office, a room in a hotel); **with immediate occupancy** = empty and available to be occupied immediately; **occupancy rate** = average number of units occupied in a hotel, apartment building or office building over a period of time shown as a percentage of the total number of units; *during the winter months the occupancy rate was down to 50%*

◊ **occupant** *noun* person or company which occupies a property

occupation *noun* **(a) occupation of a building** = act of occupying a building **(b)** job *or* work; *what is her occupation? his main occupation is house building* **(c) occupations** = types of work; *people in professional occupations*

◊ **occupational** *adjective* referring to a job; **occupational accident** = accident which takes place at work; **occupational disease** = disease which affects people in certain jobs; **occupational hazards** = dangers which apply to certain jobs; *heart attacks are one of the occupational hazards of executives;* **Occupational Safety and Health Act** = federal law that rules on the conditions at places of work

◊ **occupier** *noun* person who lives in a property; **owner-occupier** = person who owns the property in which he lives

◊ **occupy** *verb* **(a)** to live or work in a property (such as a house, an office, a hotel room); *all the rooms in the hotel are occupied; the company occupies three floors of an office building* **(b)** to fill; *looking for a job occupied most of his time*

odd *adjective* **(a) odd numbers** = numbers (like 17 or 33) which cannot be divided by two into whole numbers; *odd-numbered buildings or buildings with odd numbers are on the south side of the street* **(b) a hundred odd** = approximately one hundred; **keep the odd change** = keep the small change which is left over **(c)** one of a group; **an odd shoe** = one shoe of a pair; **we have a few odd boxes left** = we have a few boxes left out of the total shipment; **odd lot** = (i) group of stocks *or* bonds that includes less than 100 shares; (ii) less than the normal quantity of any item sold (such as 19 instead of 20); **to do odd jobs** = to do various pieces of work **(d) odd sizes** = strange sizes which are not usual

off 1 *adverb* **(a)** not working *or* not in operation; *the agreement is off; they called the strike off* **(b)** deducted from a price; *these carpets are sold at $25 off the marked price; we give 5% off for early payment* 2 *preposition* (a) away from a price; *to take $25 off the price; we give 10% off our normal prices* (b) away from work; *to take time off work; we give the staff four days off at Christmas; it is my secretary's day off tomorrow*

off-board *adjective* (security) which is not listed on a main Stock Exchange, but which is traded over the counter

offer 1 *noun* (a) statement that you are willing to pay a certain amount of money to buy something; *to make an offer for a company; he made an offer of $10 a share; we made a written offer for the house; $1,000 is the best offer I can make; to accept an offer of $1,000 for the car;* the house is under offer = someone has made an offer to buy the house and the offer has been accepted provisionally; we are open to offers = we are ready to discuss the price which we are asking; cash offer = being ready to pay in cash; best offer *or* nearest offer = an offer of a price which is slightly less than the price asked; *the car is for sale at $2,000 or best offer* (NOTE: often shortened to o.b.o., o.n.o.) (b) statement that you are willing to sell something; offer for sale = situation where a company advertises that a product *or* new shares are available for sale; offer price = price at which new shares are put on sale (c) he received six offers of jobs *or* six job offers = six companies told him he could have a job with them (d) bargain offer = sale of a particular type of good at a cheap price; *this week's bargain offer - 30% off all carpet prices;* introductory offer = special price offered on a new product to attract customers; special offer = goods put on sale at a specially low price; *we have a special offer on men's shirts* 2 *verb* (a) to offer someone a job = to tell someone that he can have a job in your company; *he was offered a sales position with Smith Corporation* (b) to say that you are willing to pay a certain amount of money for something; *to offer someone $100,000 for his house; he offered $10 a share* (c) to say that you are willing to sell something; *we offered the house for sale*

◊ **offering** *noun* making new stock in a corporation available for sale to the public

office *noun* (a) set of rooms where a company works *or* where business is done; **branch office** = less important office, usually in a different town or country from the main office; **head office** *or* **main office** = administrative center of a company (b) **office building** = building which contains only offices; **office boy** = young man who works in an office, usually taking messages from one department to another; **office equipment** = furniture and machines needed to make an office work; **office hours** = time when an office is open; *open during normal office hours; do not telephone during office hours; the manager can be reached at home after office hours;* **office space** *or* **office accommodation** = space available for offices or occupied by offices; *we are looking for extra office space;* **office staff** = people who work in offices; **office supplies** = stationery and furniture used in an office; **an office supplies firm** = company which sells office supplies; **for office use only** = something which must only be used in an office; **office worker** = person who works in an office (c) room where someone works and does business; *come into my office; the manager's office is on the third floor* (d) **box office** = office at a theater where tickets can be bought; **employment office** = office which finds jobs for people; **general office** = main administrative office in a company; **information office** = office which gives information to tourists *or* visitors; **ticket office** = office where you can buy tickets for a performance *or* for travel (e) post *or* position; *he holds or performs the office of treasurer;* **high office** = important position or job

officer *noun* (a) person who has an official position; **customs officer** = person working for the customs department; **fire safety officer** = person responsible for fire safety in a building; **information officer** = person who gives information about a company *or* about a government department to the public; **personnel officer** = person who deals with the employees of a company, especially interviewing new workers; **training officer** = person who deals with the training of staff; **the company officers** *or* **the officers of a company** = the main executives *or* directors of a company (b) official (usually unpaid) of a club *or* society, etc.; *the election of officers of an association*

official 1 *adjective* **(a)** from a government department or organization; *on official business; he left official documents in his car; she received an official letter of explanation;* **speaking in an official capacity** = speaking officially; **to go through official channels** = to deal with officials, especially when making a request; **the official exchange rate** = exchange rate which is imposed by the government; *the official exchange rate is ten to the dollar, but you can get twice that on the black market* **(b)** done or approved by a director *or* by a person in authority; *this must be an official order - it is written on the company's stationery;* **the strike was made official** = the local strike was approved by the main labor union officials 2 *noun* person working in a government department; *airport officials inspected the shipment; government officials stopped the import license;* **customs official** = person working for the customs; **high official** = important person in a government department; **minor official** = person in a low position in a government department; *some minor official tried to stop my request for building permission;* **top official** = very important person in a government department; **union officials** = paid organizers in a labor union

◊ **officialese** *noun* language used in government documents which can be difficult to understand

◊ **officially** *adverb* in an official way; *officially he knows nothing about the problem, but unofficially he has given us advice about it*

officio *see* EX OFFICIO

off-peak *adjective* not during the most busy time; **during the off-peak period** = at the time when business is less busy; **off-peak rate** = lower fees charged when the service is not busy

off-season 1 *adjective* **off-season rate** = cheaper fares *or* fees which are charged in a season when there is less business 2 *noun* less busy season for travel (usually during the winter); *to travel in the off-season; air fares are cheaper in the off-season*

offset *verb* to balance one thing against another so that they cancel each other out; *to offset losses against tax;*

foreign exchange losses more than offset profits in the domestic market NOTE: **offsetting - offset**

offshore *adjective & adverb* **(a)** on an island *or* in the sea near to land; *offshore oil field; offshore oil platform* **(b)** in a place outside the U.S.; *offshore fund*

oil *noun* natural liquid found in the ground, used to burn to give power; **oil-exporting countries** = countries which produce oil and sell it to others; **oil field** = area of land or sea under which oil is found; *the North Sea oil fields;* **oil-importing countries** = countries which import oil; **oil-producing countries** = countries which produce oil; **oil platform** *or* **oil rig** = large structure with equipment for drilling wells to find oil; **oil well** = hole in the ground from which oil is pumped

old *adjective* having existed for a long time; *the company is 125 years old next year; we have decided to get rid of our old computer system and install a new one*

◊ **old-fashioned** *adjective* out of date *or* not modern; *he still uses an old-fashioned typewriter*

ombudsman *noun* official who investigates complaints by the public against government departments NOTE: plural is **ombudsmen**

omit *verb* **(a)** to leave something out *or* not to put something in; *the secretary omitted the date when typing the contract* **(b)** not to do something; *he omitted to tell the vice-president that he had lost the documents* NOTE: **omitting - omitted**

◊ **omission** *noun* thing which has been omitted; **errors and omissions excepted** = words written on an invoice to show that the company has no responsibility for mistakes in the invoice

omnibus *noun* **omnibus agreement** = agreement which covers many different items

on *preposition* **(a)** being a member of a group; *to sit on a committee; she is on the boards of two companies; we have 250 people on the payroll; she is on our full-time staff* **(b)** in a certain way; *on a commercial basis; to buy something on approval; to buy a car on the installment plan; to get a mortgage on* *easy terms* (c) at a time; *on weekdays; the store is closed on Wednesday afternoons; on May 24* (d) doing something; *the director is on vacation; she is in Germany on business; the switchboard operator is on duty from 6 to 9*

◊ **on-board security** = LISTED SECURITY

one-man *adjective* **one-man business** *or* **firm** *or* **company** *or* **operation** = business run by one person alone with no staff or partners

◊ **one-sided** *adjective* which favors one side and not the other; *one-sided agreement*

◊ **one-way** *adjective* **one-way ticket** = ticket for a journey from one place to another; **one-way fare** = fare for a journey from one place to another; **one-way trade** = situation where one country sells to another, but does not buy anything in return

◊ **one-way street** *noun* street where the traffic is allowed to go only in one direction; *the store is on a one-way street, which makes it very difficult for parking*

onerous *adjective* heavy; *the repayment terms are particularly onerous* = the loan is particularly difficult to pay back

on-line *or* **online** *adverb* linked directly to a mainframe computer; *the sales office is on-line to the warehouse; we get our data on-line from the stock control department*

o.n.o. = OR NEAR OFFER

on-the-job *adjective* **on-the-job training** = training given to workers at their place of work

OPEC = ORGANIZATION OF PETROLEUM EXPORTING COUNTRIES

open 1 *adjective* (a) at work *or* not closed; *the store is open on Sunday mornings; our offices are open from 9 to 6; they are open for business every day of the week* (b) ready to accept something; *the job is open to all applicants* = anyone can apply for the job; *we will keep the job open for you until you have passed your driving test* = we will not give the job to anyone else, and will wait until you have obtained a valid driver's license; **open to**

offers = ready to accept a reasonable offer; **the company is open to offers for the empty factory** = the company is ready to discuss an offer which is lower than the suggested price (c) **open account** = unsecured credit *or* amount owed with no security; **open credit** = credit given to good customers without security up to a certain maximum sum; **open market** = market where anyone can buy or sell; **to buy shares on the open market** = to buy shares on the Stock Exchange, not privately; **open ticket** = ticket which can be used on any date **2** *verb* (a) to start a new business; *she has opened a store on Main Street; we have opened an office in Los Angeles* (b) to start work *or* to be at work; *the office opens at 9 a.m.; we open for business on Sundays* (c) to begin; **to open negotiations** = to begin negotiating; *he opened the discussions with a description of the product; the chairman opened the meeting at 10:30* (d) to start *or* to allow something to start; *to open a bank account; to open a line of credit* (e) **the shares opened lower** = share prices were lower at the beginning of the day's trading

◊ **open-end** *or* **open-ended** *adjective* with no fixed limit *or* with some items not specified; **open-end agreement; open-end mortgage** = mortgage in which the borrower may increase the amount of the loan

◊ **opening 1** *noun* (a) act of starting a new business; *the opening of a new branch; the opening of a new market or of a new distribution network* (b) **opening hours** = hours when a store or business is open (c) **job openings** = jobs which are empty and need filling; *we have openings for secretaries;* **a market opening** = possibility of starting to do business in a new market **2** *adjective* at the beginning *or* first; **opening balance** = balance at the beginning of an accounting period; **opening bid** = first bid at an auction; **opening entry** = first entry in an account; **opening price** = price at the start of the day's trading; **opening inventory** = inventory at the beginning of the accounting period

◊ **open-plan** *adjective* **open-plan office** = large room divided into smaller working spaces with no fixed divisions between them

◊ **open up** *verb* **to open up new markets** = to work to start business in markets where such business has not been done before

operate *verb* **(a)** to work; *the new terms of service will operate from January 1; the office operates on flextime* **(b)** to **operate a machine** = to make a machine work; *he is learning to operate the new telephone switchboard*

◊ **operating** *noun* general running of a business *or* of a machine; **operating budget** = forecast of income and expenditure over a period of time; **operating cash flow** = the cash flow generated by the day-to-day operation of a business; **operating costs** *or* **operating expenses** = costs of the day-to-day organization of a company; **operating manual** = book which shows how to work a machine; **operating profit** *or* **operating loss** = profit or loss made by a company in its usual business; **operating system** = the main program which operates a computer

QUOTE selling companies must defer recognizing the gain and the income from the sale until the new company's operating cash flow covers its interest charges and dividends
Forbes Magazine
QUOTE shares are trading at about seven times operating cash flow, or half the normal multiple
Business Week

operation *noun* **(a)** business organization and work; *the company's operations in West Africa; he heads up the operations in the Southwest;* **operations review** = examining the way in which a company or department works to see how it can be made more efficient and profitable; **a franchising operation** = selling licenses to trade as a franchise **(b) Stock Exchange operation** = buying or selling of shares on the Stock Exchange **(c) in operation** = working *or* being used; *the system will be in operation by June; the new system came into operation on June 1*

◊ **operational** *adjective* **(a)** referring to how something works; **operational budget** = forecast of expenditure on running a business; **operational costs** = costs of running a business; **operational planning** = planning how a business is to be run; **operational research** = study of a company's way of working to see if it can be made more efficient and profitable **(b) the system became operational on June 1** = the system began working on June 1

◊ **operative** **1** *adjective* **to become operative** = to start working; *the new system has been operative since June 2* **noun** person who operates a machine which makes a product

◊ **operator** *noun* **(a)** person who works a machine; *a keyboard operator; a telex operator* **(b)** person who works a telephone switchboard; *switchboard operator; to call the operator or to dial the operator; to place a call through or via the operator* **(c)** *(on a stock exchange)* person who buys and sells shares hoping to make a quick profit **(d) tour operator** = person *or* company which organizes package tours

QUOTE a leading manufacturer of business, industrial and commercial products requires a branch manager to head up its mid-western Canada operations based in Winnipeg
Globe and Mail (Toronto)
QUOTE the company gets valuable restaurant locations which will be converted to the family-style restaurant chain that it operates and franchises throughout most parts of the US
Fortune

opinion *noun* **(a) public opinion** = what people think about something; **opinion poll** *or* **opinion research** = asking a sample group of people what their opinion is, so as to estimate the opinion of the whole population; *opinion polls showed that the public preferred butter to margarine; before starting the new service, the company carried out nationwide opinion polls* **(b)** piece of expert advice; *the lawyers gave their opinion; to ask an adviser for his opinion on a case*

OPM = OTHER PEOPLE'S MONEY money which a business "borrows" , such as by not paying invoices on schedule, and so avoids risking its own funds

opportunity *noun* situation where you can do something successfully; **investment opportunities** *or* **sales opportunities** = possibilities for making investments or sales which will be profitable; **a market opportunity** = possibility of going into a market for the first time; **employment opportunities** *or* **job opportunities** = new jobs being available; *the increase in export orders has created hundreds of job opportunities*

oppose *verb* to try to stop something from happening; to vote against something; *a minority of board members opposed the motion; we are all opposed to the takeover*

opposite *noun* **opposite number** = person who has a similar job in another company; **Jack is my opposite number**

at Smith's = Jack has the same job at Smith's as I have here

optimal *adjective* best

◊ **optimism** *noun* being sure that everything will work out well; *he has considerable optimism about sales possibilities in the Far East;* **market optimism =** feeling that the stock market will rise

◊ **optimistic** *adjective* feeling sure that everything will work out well; **he takes an optimistic view of the exchange rate =** he expects the exchange rate will go in his favor

◊ **optimum** *adjective* best; *the market offers optimum conditions for sales*

option *noun* **(a)** option to purchase *or* to sell = giving someone the possibility to buy or sell something within a period of time; **first option =** allowing someone to be the first to be able to take advantage of an opportunity; **to grant someone a six-month option on a product =** to allow someone six months to decide if he wants to be the agent *or* if he wants to manufacture the product; **to take up an option** *or* **to exercise an option =** to accept the option which has been offered and to put it into action; *he exercised his option* **or** *he took up his option to acquire sole marketing rights to the product;* **I want to leave my options open =** I want to be able to decide what to do when the time is right; **to take the soft option =** to decide to do something which involves the least risk, effort or problems **(b)** *(stock exchange)* **call option =** option to buy shares at a certain price; **put option =** option to sell shares at a certain price; **stock option =** (i) right to buy or sell securities at a certain price at a time in the future; (ii) right to buy shares at a cheap price given by a corporation to its employees; **option contract =** right to buy or sell shares at a fixed price; **option dealing** *or* **option trading =** buying and selling share options

◊ **optional** *adjective* which can be added if the customer wants; *the insurance cover is optional;* **optional extras =** items (such as air-conditioning) which can be added to a car if wanted

order 1 *noun* **(a)** arrangement of records (filing cards, invoices, etc.); **alphabetical order =** arrangement by the letters of the alphabet (A, B, C, etc.); **chronological order =** arrangement by

the order of the dates; *the reports are filed in chronological order;* **numerical order =** arrangement by numbers; *put these invoices in numerical order* **(b)** working arrangement; **machine in full working order =** machine which is ready and able to work properly; **the telephone is out of order =** the telephone is not working; **is all the documentation in order? =** are all the documents valid and correct? **(c) pay to the order of Mr. Smith =** pay money directly into Mr. Smith's account **(d)** official request for goods to be supplied; *to give someone an order or to place an order with someone for twenty filing cabinets;* **to fill** *or* **to fulfill an order =** to supply items which have been ordered; *we are so understaffed we cannot fulfill any more orders before Christmas;* **to supply an order for twenty filing cabinets;** **purchase order =** official paper which places an order for something; **order fulfillment =** supplying items which have been ordered; **terms: cash with order =** the goods will be supplied only if payment in cash is made at the same time as the order is placed; **items available to order only =** items which will be manufactured only if someone orders them; **on order =** ordered but not delivered; *this item is out of stock, but is on order;* **unfulfilled orders** *or* **back orders** *or* **outstanding orders =** orders received in the past and not yet supplied; **order book =** record of orders; **the company has a full order book =** it has enough orders to work at full capacity; **telephone orders =** orders received over the telephone; *since we mailed the catalog we have had a large number of telephone orders;* **order form =** blank form on which an order is written; **a pad of order forms =** a pad of forms for orders to be written on; **order number =** number given to an order (it may be preprinted on the order form) so that the order can be identified **(e)** item which has been ordered; *the order is to be delivered to our warehouse* **(f)** instruction; **delivery order =** instructions given by the customer to the person holding his goods, telling him to deliver them **(g)** document which allows money to be paid to someone; *he sent us an order on the San Diego Bank;* **money order =** document which can be bought, usually by a person without a checking account, for sending money through the mail **2** *verb* **(a)** to ask for goods to be supplied; *to order twenty filing cabinets to be delivered to the* *warehouse; they ordered a new Rolls Royce for the company president* **(b)** to arrange in a certain way; *the address list is ordered by country; that filing cabinet contains invoices ordered by date*

ordinance *noun* statute enacted by the legislative branch of a city government

ordinary *adjective* normal *or* not special; **ordinary member =** person who pays dues to belong to a group; **ordinary shares =** normal shares in a company, which have no special bonuses or restrictions; **ordinary interest =** interest calculated on 360 days, not 365

organization *noun* **(a)** way of arranging something so that it works efficiently; *the chairman handles the organization of the annual meeting; the organization of the group is too centralized to be efficient; the organization of the head office into departments;* **study of organization and methods =** examining how an office works, and suggesting how it can be made more efficient; **organization chart =** list of people working in various departments, showing how a company *or* office is organized; **line organization =** organization of a business where each manager is responsible for doing what his superior tells him to do **(b)** group or institution which is arranged for efficient work; **the Organization of Petroleum Exporting Countries =** group of major countries who are producers and exporters of oil; **a government organization =** official body, run by the government; **a travel organization =** body representing companies in the travel business; **an employers' organization =** group of employers with similar interests

◊ **organize** *verb* to arrange something so that it works efficiently; *the company is organized into six profit centers; the group is organized by areas of sales;* **organized labor =** workers who are members of labor unions

◊ **organizational** *adjective* referring to the way in which something is organized; *the paper gives a diagram of the company's organizational structure*

◊ **organizer** *noun* person who arranges things efficiently

◊ **organizing committee** *noun* group of people who arrange something; *he is a member of the organizing committee for the conference*

QUOTE governments are coming under increasing pressure from politicians, organized labor and business to stimulate economic growth
Duns Business Month

oriented *adjective* working in a certain direction; **profit-oriented company =** company which does everything to make a profit; **export-oriented company =** company which produces goods mainly for export

origin *noun* where something comes from; *spare parts of European origin;* **certificate of origin =** document showing where goods were made; **country of origin =** country where a product is manufactured

◊ **original 1** *adjective* which was used or made first; *they sent a copy of the original invoice; he kept the original receipt for reference* **2** *noun* first copy made; *send the original and file two copies*

◊ **originally** *adverb* first *or* at the beginning

OSHA = OCCUPATIONAL SAFETY AND HEALTH ACT

o-t-c = OVER-THE-COUNTER

QUOTE traded o-t-c, it came public at 10 in 1987, moved to 13, then slid to 3. More recently it climbed back to 10 for a market value of $30 million
Forbes Magazine

ounce *noun* measure of weight (= one-sixteenth of a pound)
NOTE: usually written **oz** after figures

QUOTE trading at $365 an ounce on May 24, gold has declined $45 or 11% since the beginning of the year, and the more volatile silver has dropped 14% to $5.17 an ounce
Business Week

out *adverb* **(a)** on strike; *the workers have been out on strike for four weeks; as soon as the management made the offer, the staff came out; the shop stewards called the workforce out* **(b) to be out =** to be wrong in calculating something; *the balance is $10 out; we are $20,000 out in our calculations =* we have $20,000 too much *or* too little **(c)** to miss work because of an illness *or* injury; *two employees were out this week with flu*

◊ **outbid** *verb* to offer a better price than someone else; *we offered $100,000 for the warehouse, but another company outbid us*

NOTE: **outbidding - outbid**

◊ **outfit** *noun* small, sometimes badly run, company; *they called in a public relations outfit; he works for some finance outfit*

◊ **outflow** *noun* **outflow of capital from a country** = capital which is sent out of a country for investment abroad

◊ **outgoing** *adjective* **(a) outgoing mail** = mail which is being sent out **(b) the outgoing chairman** *or* **the outgoing president** = chairman *or* president who is about to retire

◊ **outgoings** *plural noun* money which is paid out

◊ **outlay** *noun* money spent *or* expenditure; **capital outlay** = money spent on fixed assets (such as property, machinery, furniture); **for a modest outlay** = for a small sum

◊ **outlet** *noun* place where something can be sold; **retail outlets** = stores which sell to the general public at retail prices; **factory outlets** = stores where merchandise shipped directly from the factory is sold, generally at a wholesale price; **outlet store** = store that sells cheap discontinued lines, etc.

◊ **outline 1** *noun* general description, without giving many details; *they drew up the outline of a plan or an outline plan;* **outline planning permission** = general permission to build on a piece of land, but not final because there are no details **2** *verb* to make a general description; *the chairman outlined the company's plans for the coming year*

◊ **outlook** *noun* view of what is going to happen in the future; *the economic outlook is not good; the stock market outlook is disturbing*

◊ **out of court** *adverb & adjective* **a settlement was reached out of court** = a dispute was settled between two parties privately without continuing a court case; *they are hoping to reach an out-of-court settlement*

◊ **out of date** *adjective & adverb* old-fashioned *or* no longer modern; *their computer system is years out of date; they are still using out-of-date equipment*

◊ **out of pocket** *adjective & adverb* having paid out money personally; *the deal has left me out of pocket;* **out-of-pocket costs** *or* **expenses** = amount of money to pay a worker back for his own money which he has spent on company business

◊ **out of stock** *adjective & adverb* with no stock left; *those disks are temporarily out of stock; several out-of-stock items have been on order for weeks*

◊ **out of work** *adjective & adverb* with no job; *the recession has put millions out of work; the company was set up by three out-of-work engineers*

◊ **output 1** *noun* **(a)** amount which a company or a person or a machine produces; *output has increased by 10%; 25% of our output is exported;* **output per hour** = amount produced in one hour; **output bonus** = extra payment for increased production **(b)** information which is produced by a computer **2** *verb* to produce (by a computer); *the printer will output color graphs; that is the information outputted from the computer*
NOTE: **outputting - outputted** *or* **output**

◊ **outright** *adverb & adjective* completely; **to purchase something outright** *or* **to make an outright purchase** = to buy something completely, including all rights in it

◊ **outsell** *verb* to sell more than someone; *the company is easily outselling its competitors*
NOTE: **outselling - outsold**

◊ **outside** *adjective & adverb* not in a company's office or building; **to send work to be done outside** = to send work to be done in other offices; **outside dealer** = person who is not a member of the stock exchange but is allowed to trade; **outside directors** = directors who are not executive officers of the company, but are appointed because of their experience and contacts as board members of other companies; **outside line** = line from an internal office telephone system to the main telephone exchange; *you dial 9 to get an outside line;* **outside worker** = worker who does not work in a company's offices

◊ **outstanding** *adjective* not yet paid or completed; **outstanding debts** = debts which are waiting to be paid; **outstanding orders** = orders received but not yet supplied; **what is the amount outstanding?** = how much money is still owed?; **matters outstanding from the previous meeting** = questions which were not settled at the previous meeting

◊ **out tray** *noun* basket on a desk for letters or memos which have been dealt with and are ready to be passed on *or* mailed

◊ **outturn** *noun* amount produced by a country *or* company

◊ **outvote** *verb* to defeat in a vote; **the chairman was outvoted =** the majority voted against the chairman

◊ **outward** *adjective* going away from the home country; *the ship is outward bound; on the outward voyage the ship will stop at the West Indies;* **outward cargo** *or* **outward freight =** goods which are being exported; **outward mission =** visit by a group of businessmen to a foreign country

QUOTE crude oil output plunged during the last month and is likely to remain near its present level for the near future
Wall Street Journal
QUOTE American demand has transformed the profit outlook for many European manufacturers
Duns Business Month

over 1 *preposition* **(a)** more than; *the carpet costs over $1000; packages not over two pounds; the increase in sales was over 25%* **(b)** compared with; *increase in output over last year; increase in debtors over the last quarter's figure* **(c)** during; *over the last half of the year profits doubled* **2** *adverb* **held over to the next meeting =** postponed *or* put back to the next meeting; **to carry over a balance =** to take a balance from the end of one page or period to the beginning of the next

◊ **over-** *prefix* more than; **store which caters to the over-60s =** store which has goods which appeal to people who are more than sixty years old

◊ **overall** *adjective* covering *or* including everything; *although some divisions traded profitably, the company reported an overall fall in profits =* the company reported a general fall in profits; **overall plan =** plan which covers everything

◊ **overbook** *verb* to book more people than there are seats or rooms available; *the hotel or the flight was overbooked*

◊ **overbooking** *noun* booking of more people than there are seats or rooms available

◊ **overbought** *adjective* having bought too much; **the market is overbought =** prices on the stock market are too high, because there have been too many buyers

◊ **overcapacity** *noun* unused capacity for producing something

◊ **overcharge 1** *noun* charge which is higher than it should be; *to pay back an overcharge* **2** *verb* to ask too much money; *they overcharged us for meals; we asked for a refund because we had been overcharged*

◊ **overdraft** *noun* amount of money which a person has written on a check which is more than he has in the account; **overdraft loan =** arrangement by which a bank allows a customer to write checks for more than he has in his account, the excess being temporarily loaned by the bank

◊ **overdraw** *verb* to take out more money from a bank account than there is in it

NOTE: **overdrawing - overdrew - overdrawn**

◊ **overdue** *adjective* which has not been paid on time; **interest payments are three weeks overdue =** interest payments which should have been made three weeks ago

◊ **overestimate** *verb* to think something is larger or worse than it really is; *he overestimated the amount of time needed to fit out the factory*

◊ **overextend** *verb* **the company overextended itself =** the company borrowed more money than its assets would allow

◊ **overhead 1** *adjective* **overhead costs** *or* **expenses =** costs of running a business that are not directly associated with the product *or* service sold; **overhead budget =** plan of probable overhead costs **2** *noun* costs of running a business that are not directly associated with the product *or* service sold; *the sales revenue covers the manufacturing costs but not the overhead*

◊ **overheated** *adjective* economy which is expanding rapidly and may lead to inflation

◊ **overlook** *verb* **(a)** to look out over; *the president's office overlooks the factory* **(b)** not to pay attention to; *in this instance we will overlook the delay*

◊ **overmanning** *noun* having more workers than are needed to do a company's work; *to aim to reduce overmanning*

◊ **overpaid** *adjective* paid too much; *our employees are overpaid and underworked*

◊ **overpayment** *noun* paying too much

◊ **overproduce** *verb* to produce too much

◊ **overproduction** *noun* manufacturing too much of a product

◊ **overrated** *adjective* valued more highly than it should be; *the effect of the dollar on European business cannot be overrated; their "first-class service" is very overrated*

◇ **override 1** *noun* commission which is paid to managers **2** *verb* to cancel *or* to go round; *to override the automatic computer system*

◇ **overrun** *verb* to go beyond a limit; *the company overran the time limit set to complete the factory*

NOTE: **overrunning - overran - overrun**

◇ **overseas 1** *adjective* across the sea *or* to foreign countries; **an overseas call** = phone call to another country; **the overseas division** = section of a company dealing with trade with other countries; **overseas markets** = markets in foreign countries; **overseas trade** = trade with foreign countries **2** *noun* foreign countries; *the profits from overseas are far higher than those of the home division*

◇ **overseer** *noun* person who supervises other workers

◇ **oversell** *verb* to sell more than you can produce; **he is oversold** = he has agreed to sell more product than he can produce; **the market is oversold** = stock market prices are too low, because there have been too many sellers

NOTE: **overselling - oversold**

◇ **overspend** *verb* to spend too much; **to overspend one's budget** = to spend more money than is allowed in the budget

NOTE: **overspending - overspent**

◇ **overspending** *noun* spending more than is allowed; *the board decided to limit the overspending by the production departments*

◇ **overstaffed** *adjective* with more workers than are needed to do the work of the company

◇ **overstock** *verb* to have more stock than is needed; **to be overstocked with spare parts** = to have too many spare parts in stock

◇ **overstored** *adjective* (market) which has too many stores

◇ **oversubscribe** *verb* **the share offer was oversubscribed six times** = people applied for six times as many new shares as were available

◇ **over-the-counter (o-t-c)** *adjective* **over-the-counter sales** = legal selling of shares which are not listed in an official stock exchange list; *this share is available on the over-the-counter market*

◇ **overtime 1** *noun* hours worked more than the normal working time; *to work six hours' overtime; the overtime rate is one and a half times normal pay;* **overtime ban** = order by a labor union

which forbids overtime work by its members; **overtime pay** = pay for extra time worked **2** *adverb* **to work overtime** = to work longer hours than specified in the contract of employment

◇ **overvalue** *verb* to give a higher value than is right; **these shares are overvalued at $1.25** = the shares are worth less than the $1.25 for which they are selling; **the pound is overvalued against the dollar** = the exchange rate gives too many dollars to the pound, given the strength of the two countries' economies

◇ **overweight** *adjective* **the package is two ounces overweight** = the package weighs two ounces too much

◇ **overworked** *adjective* having too much work to do; *our employees complain of being underpaid and overworked*

> QUOTE it ties up less capital in inventory and with its huge volume spreads out costs over bigger sales; add in low overhead (i.e. minimum staff, no deliveries, no credit cards) and a warehouse club can offer bargain prices
> *Duns Business Month*

owe *verb* to have to pay money; *he owes the bank $250,000; he owes the company for the stock he purchased* = he has not paid for the stock

◇ **owing** *adjective* **(a)** which is owed; *money owing to the directors; how much is still owing to the company by its debtors?* **(b) owing to** = because of; *the plane was late owing to fog; I am sorry that owing to the strike, we cannot supply your order on time*

own *verb* to have *or* to possess; *he owns 50% of the stock of the corporation;* **a wholly-owned subsidiary** = a subsidiary which belongs completely to the parent corporation; **a state-owned industry** = industry which is nationalized

◇ **own brand goods** *noun* products specially packed for a store with the store's name on them

◇ **owner** *noun* person who owns something; **sole owner** = person who owns something by himself; **owner-occupier** = person who owns and lives in a house; **goods sent at owner's risk** = situation where the owner is responsible for any damage to the goods during transportation

◇ **ownership** *noun* act of owning something; **common** *or* **collective ownership** = situation where a business is owned by the workers who work in it;

joint ownership = situation where two people own the same property; **public ownership** *or* **state ownership** = situation where an industry is nationalized; **private ownership** = situation where a company is owned by private shareholders; **the ownership of the company has passed to the banks** = the banks have become owners of the company

◊ **own label goods** *noun* goods specially produced for a store with the store's name on them

oz = OUNCE(S)

Pp

p.a. = PER ANNUM, PUBLIC ADDRESS (SYSTEM)

pack 1 *noun* **pack of items** = items put together in a container for selling; *pack of cigarettes; pack of chewing gum; pack of envelopes;* **items sold in packs of 200** = sold in boxes containing 200 items; **blister pack** = type of packing where the item for sale is covered with a stiff plastic cover sealed to a card backing; **display pack** = specially attractive box for showing goods for sale; **six-pack** = box containing six items (often bottles) **2** *verb* to put things into a container for selling *or* sending; *to pack goods into cartons; the cookies are packed in plastic wrappers; the computer is packed in expanded polystyrene before being shipped*

◊ **package 1** *noun* **(a)** goods packed and wrapped for sending by mail; *the Post Office does not accept bulky packages; the goods are to be sent in airtight packages* **(b)** box or bag of goods for selling; *a package of crackers; the instructions for assembling the toy are printed on the package* **(c)** group of different items joined together in one deal; **pay package** *or* **salary package** *or* **compensation package** = salary and other benefits offered with a job; *the job carries an attractive salary package;* **package bargaining** = negotiations between unions and employers concerning all items in a pay package **(d) package deal** = agreement where several different items are agreed

on at the same time; *we are offering a package deal which includes the whole office computer system, staff training and hardware maintenance;* **package tour** = tour where the hotel, travel and meals are all included in the price; *the travel company is arranging a package trip to the international computer exhibition* **2** *verb* **(a) to package goods** = to wrap and pack goods in an attractive way **(b) to package tours** = to sell a tour package including travel hotels and food

◊ **packaging** *noun* **(a)** the action of putting things into packages **(b)** material used to protect goods which are being packed; *airtight packaging; packaging material* **(c)** attractive material used to wrap goods for display

◊ **packager** *noun* person who creates a book for a publisher

◊ **packer** *noun* person who packs goods

◊ **packet** *noun* small package of goods; *packet of cigarettes; packet of letters; packet of file cards*

◊ **packing** *noun* **(a)** action of putting goods into boxes and wrapping them for shipping; *what is the cost of the packing? packing is included in the price;* **packing case** = large wooden box for carrying easily broken items; **packing charges** = money charged for putting goods into boxes; **packing list** *or* **packing slip** = list of goods which have been packed, sent with the goods to show they have been checked **(b)** material used to protect goods; *packed in airtight packing;* **nonreturnable packing** = packing which is to be thrown away when it has been used and not returned to the sender

> QUOTE in today's fast-growing packaged goods area many companies are discovering that a well-recognized brand name can be a priceless asset
> *Duns Business Month*

pad *noun* **(a)** pile of sheets of paper attached together on one side; **desk pad** = pad of paper kept on a desk for writing notes; **memo pad** *or* **note pad** = pad of paper for writing memos or notes; **message pad** = pad of paper kept by a telephone for noting messages **(b)** soft material like a cushion; *the machine is protected by rubber pads;* **ink pad** = cushion with ink in it, used to put ink on a rubber stamp

page *verb* to call someone over a p.a. system, asking him to come to the telephone

paid *adjective* **(a)** with money given; **paid vacation** = vacation where the worker's wages are still paid even though he is not working **(b)** which has been settled; *postage paid; tax paid; paid bills* = bills which have been settled; *the invoice is marked "paid"* **(c) paid-in capital** = all money paid for the issued capital stock; **paid-up policy** = insurance policy on which all premiums have been paid

pallet *noun* flat wooden base on which goods can be stacked for easy handling by forklifts

◊ **palletize** *verb* to put goods on pallets; *palletized cartons*

pamphlet *noun* small booklet of advertising material *or* of information

panel *noun* **(a)** flat surface standing upright; **display panel** = flat area for displaying goods in a store window **(b) panel of experts** = group of people who give advice on a problem; **consumer panel** = group of consumers who report on goods they have used so that the manufacturer can improve the goods, or use the consumers' reports in his advertising

panic *adjective* frightened; **panic buying** = rush to buy something at any price because stocks may run out or because the price may rise; *panic buying of sugar* or *of dollars;* **panic selling of stock** = rush to sell stock because of possible business collapse

paper *noun* **(a)** thin material for writing on *or* for wrapping; **brown paper** = thick paper for wrapping parcels; **carbon paper** = sheet of paper with a dark carbon coating on one side used in a typewriter to make a copy; *she put the carbon paper in the wrong way around;* **duplicating paper** = special paper to be used in a duplicating machine; **graph paper** = paper with small squares printed on it, used for drawing graphs; **lined paper** = paper with thin lines printed on it; **typing paper** = thin paper for use in a typewriter; **wrapping paper** = paper for wrapping (NOTE: no plural) **(b) papers** = documents; *he sent me the relevant papers on the case; he has lost the customs papers; the office is asking for the tax papers* **(c) paper bag** = bag made of paper; **paper feed** = device which puts paper into a printer or

photocopier; **paper money** *or* **paper currency** = money made of paper, with its value printed on it **(d) on paper** = in theory; *on paper the system is ideal, but we have to see it working before we will sign the contract;* **paper loss** = loss made when an asset has fallen in value but has not been sold; **paper profit** = profit made when an asset has increased in value but has not been sold; **paper millionaire** = person who owns shares which, if he sold them, would make him a millionaire **(e)** documents which can represent money (bills of exchange, promissory notes, etc.); **negotiable paper** = document which can be transferred from one owner to another for money **(f)** newspaper; **trade paper** = newspaper aimed at people working in a certain industry; **free paper** = newspaper which is given away free, and which relies for its income on its advertising

◊ **paperclip** *noun* piece of bent wire, used to hold pieces of paper together

◊ **paperwork** *noun* office work, especially writing memos and filling in forms; *exporting to Russia involves a large amount of paperwork*

par *adjective* equal *or* at the same price; **par value** = face value *or* the value printed on a stock certificate; **stock at par** = stock whose market price is the same as the face value; **shares above par** *or* **below par** = shares with a market price higher or lower than their par value

parachute *noun* **golden parachute** = contract which provides a large sum of money or other benefits to a top executive when the company he is working for merges with another firm and he loses his job

paragraph *noun* group of several lines of writing which makes a separate section; *the first paragraph of your letter* or *paragraph one of your letter; please refer to the paragraph in the contract on "shipping instructions"*

parameter *noun* fixed limit; *the budget parameters are fixed by the finance director; spending by each department has to fall within certain parameters*

parcel 1 *noun* **(a)** goods wrapped up in paper *or* plastic, etc., to be sent by mail; **to tie up a parcel** = to fasten a parcel with string; **parcel delivery service =** private company which delivers parcels within a certain area; **parcel post =** fourth-class mail service for sending parcels; *to send a box by parcel post;* **parcel rates =** charges for sending parcels by post **(b) parcel of shares =** group of shares (such as 50 or 100) which are sold as a group; *the shares are on offer in parcels of 50* **2** *verb* **to parcel out =** to distribute; *office supplies were parceled out to the new secretaries*

parent company *noun* company which owns more than 50% of the stock of another company

pari passu *phrase* equally; *the new shares will rank pari passu with the existing ones*

parity *noun* being equal; *the female employees want parity with the men =* they want to have the same rates of pay and benefits as the men; *the pound fell to parity with the dollar =* the pound fell to a point where one pound equaled one dollar

> QUOTE the draft report on changes in the international monetary system casts doubt about any return to fixed exchange-rate parities
> *Wall Street Journal*

park 1 *noun* open space with grass and trees; **industrial park =** area of land near a town specially set aside for factories and warehouses **2** *verb* to leave your car in a place while you are not using it; *the rep parked his car outside the store; you cannot park here during the rush hour; parking is difficult in the center of the city;* **parking lot =** area for parking cars

Parkinson's law *noun* law, based on wide experience, that in business as in government the amount of work increases to fill the time available for it

parol contract *noun* informal contract which is spoken and not written

part *noun* **(a)** piece *or* section; *part of the shipment was damaged; part of the workforce is on overtime;* **part of the expenses will be refunded =** some of the expenses, but not all **(b) in part =** not completely; *to contribute in part to the costs* *or* *to pay the costs in part* **(c) spare part =** small piece of machinery to replace a part of a machine which is

broken; *the photocopier will not work - we need to replace a part* *or* *a part needs replacing* **(d) part-owner =** person who owns something jointly with one or more other persons; *he is part-owner of the restaurant;* **part-ownership =** situation where two or more persons own the same property

◊ **part-time** *adjective & adverb* not working for the whole working day; *she works part-time; he is trying to find part-time work when the children are in school; a part-time worker; we are looking for part-time staff to work our computers;* part-time work *or* part-time **employment =** work for part of a working day

◊ **part-timer** *noun* person who works part-time

partial *adjective* not complete; **partial loss =** situation where only part of the insured property has been damaged or lost; **partial payment =** payment of part of a whole payment; **partial shipment =** shipping only some items of an order; *he got partial compensation for the damage to his house =* he was compensated for part of the damage

participation *noun* taking part; **worker participation =** situation where the workers take part in making management decisions

◊ **participative** *adjective* where both sides take part; *we do not treat management-worker relations as a participative process*

particular 1 *adjective* special *or* different from others; *the photocopier only works with a particular type of paper;* **particular average =** situation where part of a shipment is lost or damaged and the insurance costs are borne by the owner of the lost goods and not shared among all the owners of the shipment **2** *noun* **(a) particulars =** details; *sheet which gives particulars of the items for sale; the inspector asked for particulars of the missing car;* **to give full particulars of something =** to list all the known details about something **(b) in particular =** specially *or* specifically; *fragile goods, in particular glasses, need special packing*

partly *adverb* not completely; **partly-paid capital =** capital which represents partly-paid stock; **partly-secured creditors =** creditors whose debts are not fully covered by the value of the security

partner *noun* person who works in a business and has an equal share in it with other partners; **he became a partner in a law firm; active partner** *or* **working partner** = partner who works in a partnership; **junior partner** *or* **senior partner** = person who has a small or large part of the shares in a partnership; **inactive partner** = partner who has a share in a business but does not work in it

◇ **partnership** *noun* (a) business where two or more people share the risks and profits equally; *to go into partnership with someone; to join with someone to form a partnership;* to offer someone a partnership *or* to take someone into partnership with you = to have a working business and bring someone in to share it with you; **to dissolve a partnership** = to bring a partnership to an end (b) **limited partnership** = business where the liability of the partners is limited to the amount of capital they have each provided to the business and where the partners may not take part in the running of the business

party *noun* (a) company *or* person involved in a legal dispute *or* legal agreement; *one of the parties to the suit has died; the company is not a party to the agreement* (b) **third party** = any third person, in addition to the two main people involved in a contract; **third party insurance** *or* **third party policy** = insurance to cover damage to any person who is not one of the people named in the insurance contract (that is, not the insured person nor the insurance company)

pass 1 *noun* permit to allow someone to go into a building; *you need a pass to enter the headquarters building; all members of staff must show a pass 2 verb* (a) **to pass a dividend** = to pay no dividend in a certain year (b) to approve; *the finance director has to pass an invoice before it is sent out; the loan has been passed by the board;* **to pass a resolution** = to vote to agree to a resolution; *the meeting passed a proposal that salaries should be frozen* (c) to be successful; *he passed his typing test; she has passed all her exams and now is a certified accountant*

◇ **passbook** *noun* book given by a bank *or* savings and loan which shows money

which you deposit *or* withdraw from your savings account

◇ **pass off** *verb* to pass something off as something else = to pretend that it is another thing in order to cheat a customer; *he tried to pass off the wine as French, when in fact it came from California*

passage *noun* voyage by ship

passenger *noun* person who travels in a plane, bus, taxi, plane, etc., but is not the driver or member of the crew; **passenger terminal** = air terminal for people going on planes, not for cargo; **passenger train** = train which carries passengers but not freight

passport *noun* official document proving that you are a citizen of a country, which you have to show when you travel from one country to another; *we had to show our passports at the customs desk; his passport is out of date; the passport officer stamped my passport*

patent 1 *noun* (a) official document showing that a person has the exclusive right to make and sell an invention for a limited period of time; *to take out a patent for a new type of light bulb; to apply for a patent for a new invention;* **letters patent** = official document which gives someone the exclusive right to make and sell something which they have invented; **patent applied for** *or* **patent pending** = words on a product showing that the inventor has applied for a patent for it or that it has been put on the market before a patent is granted; **to forfeit a patent** = to lose a patent because payments have not been made; **to infringe a patent** = to make and sell a product which works in the same way as a patented product and not pay a royalty for it; **infringement of patent** *or* **patent infringement** = act of illegally making or selling a product which is patented (b) **patent agent** = person who advises on patents and applies for patents on behalf of clients; **to file a patent application** = to apply for a patent; **patent medicine** = medicine which is registered as a patent; **patent office** = government office which grants patents and supervises them; **patent rights** = rights which an inventor holds under a patent **2** *verb* **to patent an invention** = to register an invention with the patent office to prevent other people from copying it

◇ **patented** *adjective* which is protected by a patent

paternity *noun* **paternity leave** = permission for a man to be away from work when his wife is having a baby

pattern *noun* (a) **pattern book** = book showing examples of design (b) general way in which something usually happens; *pattern of prices* or *price pattern; pattern of sales* or *sales pattern; pattern of trade* or *trading pattern* = general way in which trade is carried on; *the company's trading pattern shows high export sales in the first quarter and high domestic sales in the third quarter*

pawn 1 *noun* (a) **to put something in pawn** = to leave a valuable object with someone in exchange for a loan which has to be repaid if you want to take back the object; **to take something out of pawn** = to repay the loan and so get back the object; **pawn ticket** = receipt given by the pawnbroker for the object left in pawn (b) person or organization with little power 2 *verb* **to pawn a watch** = to leave a watch with a pawnbroker who gives a loan against it
◇ **pawnbroker** *noun* person who lends money against the security of valuable objects
◇ **pawnshop** *noun* pawnbroker's shop

pay 1 *noun* (a) salary or wage or money given to someone for regular work; **back pay** = salary which has not been paid; **basic pay** = normal salary without extra payments; **take-home pay** = pay left after tax and social security have been deducted; **vacation with pay** = vacation which a worker is entitled to take and for which he is paid; **unemployment pay** = money given by the government to someone who is unemployed (b) **pay negotiations** or **pay talks** = discussions between management and workers about pay increases; **pay raise** = increase in pay; **pay stub** = piece of paper showing the full amount of a worker's pay, and the money deducted as tax, social security and other contributions (c) **pay phone** = telephone which works if you put coins into it 2 *verb* (a) to give money to buy an item or a service; *to pay $1,000 for a car; how much did you pay to have the office cleaned?;* **to pay in advance** = to give money before you receive the item bought or before the service has been completed; *we had to pay in advance to have the new*

telephone system installed; **to pay in installments** = to give money for an item by giving small amounts regularly; *we are paying for the computer by paying installments of $50 a month;* **to pay cash** = to pay the complete sum in cash; **to pay by check** = to pay by giving a check, not by using cash or credit card; **to pay by credit card** = to pay, using a credit card and not a check or cash (b) to give money; **to pay on demand** = to pay money when it is asked for, not after a period of credit; **please pay the sum of $10** = please give $10 in cash or by check; **to pay a dividend** = to give shareholders a part of the profits of a company; *these shares pay a dividend of 50¢;* **to pay interest** = to give money as interest on money borrowed or invested; *certificates of deposit pay an interest of 10%;* **pay-as-you-go** = system of paying for goods or services as they are used (c) to give a worker money for work done; *the workforce has not been paid for three weeks; we pay good wages for skilled workers; how much do they pay you per hour?;* **to be paid by the hour** = to get money for each hour worked; **to be paid at piecework rates** = to get money for each piece of work finished (d) to give money which is owed or which has to be paid; *to pay a bill; to pay an invoice; to pay duty on imports; to pay tax* (e) **to pay a check to an account** = to deposit money in the form of a check
NOTE: **paying - paid**

◇ **payable** *adjective* which is due to be paid; **payable in advance** = which has to be paid before the goods are delivered; **payable on delivery** = which has to be paid when the goods are delivered; **payable on demand** = which must be paid when payment is asked for; **payable at sixty days** = which has to be paid by sixty days after the date of invoice; **check made payable to bearer** = check which will be paid to the person who has it, not to any particular name written on it; **accounts payable** = money owed by a company; **bills payable** = bills which a debtor will have to pay; **electricity charges are payable by the tenant** = the tenant (and not the landlord) must pay for the electricity

◇ **pay back** *verb* to give money back to someone; *to pay back a loan; I lent him $50 and he promised to pay me back in a month; he has never paid me back for the money he borrowed*

◇ **payback** *noun* paying back money which has been borrowed; **payback clause** = clause in a contract which states the terms for repaying a loan; **payback period** = period of time over which a loan is to be repaid *or* an investment is to pay for itself

◊ **paycheck** *noun* salary check given to an employee

◊ **payday** *noun* regular day on which wages are paid to workers, such as every Friday or a certain date each month

◊ **pay down** *verb* to pay money down = to make a deposit; *he paid $50 down and the rest in monthly installments*

◊ **payee** *noun* person who receives money from someone *or* person whose name is on a check

◊ **payer** *noun* person who gives money to someone; **slow payer** = person *or* company which does not pay debts on time; *he is well known as a slow payer*

◊ **paying 1** *adjective* which makes a profit; *it is a paying business;* **it is not a paying proposition** = it is not a business which is going to make a profit **2** *noun* giving money; *paying of a debt*

◊ **payload** *noun* cargo *or* passengers carried by a ship *or* train *or* plane for which payment is made

◊ **payment** *noun* **(a)** giving money; *payment in cash or cash payment; payment by check; payment of interest or interest payment;* **payment method** = way in which a purchaser will pay for items purchased (i.e. cash, check, credit card, etc.); **payment on account** = paying part of the money owed; **full payment** *or* **payment in full** = paying all money owed; **payment on invoice** = paying money as soon as an invoice is received; **payment in kind** = paying by giving goods or food, but not money; **payment by results** = money given which increases with the amount of work done or goods produced **(b)** money paid; **back payment** = paying money which is owed; **deferred payments** = money paid later than the agreed date; *the company agreed to defer payments for three months;* **down payment** = part of a total payment made in advance; **repayable in easy payments** = repayable with small sums regularly; **incentive payments** = extra pay offered to a worker to make him work better; **balance of payments** = net amount of money paid *or* received by a country, resulting from its imports and exports

◊ **pay off** *verb* **(a)** to finish paying money which is owed; *to pay off a mortgage; to pay off a loan* **(b)** to pay all the money owed to someone and terminate his employment; *when the company was taken over the factory was closed and all the workers were paid off*

◊ **payoff** *noun* profit *or* reward from an enterprise; *one payoff of a college education is increased earning power*

◊ **pay out** *verb* to give money; *the company pays out thousands of dollars in legal fees; we have paid out half our profits in dividends*

◊ **payout** *noun* revenue from sales which covers the marketing costs (i.e., up to break-even point)

◊ **payroll** *noun* list of people employed and paid by a company *or* money paid by a company in salaries; *250 on the payroll;* **payroll deduction** = amount taken out of an employee's gross pay for taxes, social security, pension plan, etc.; **payroll tax** = tax on the salaries paid to people employed by a company

◊ **pay up** *verb* **(a)** to give money which is owed; *the company only paid up when we sent them a letter from our lawyer; he finally paid up six months late* **(b)** to pay a higher price than expected (for stock)

PC = PERSONAL COMPUTER

P/E *or* **P-E** *abbreviation* = PRICE/EARNINGS; **P/E ratio** = ratio between the market price of a share and the current dividend it produces; *the shares sell at a P/E ratio of 7*

peak 1 *noun* highest point; **peak period** *or* **peak time** = time of the day when most commuters are traveling *or* when most electricity is being used, etc.; **time of peak demand** = time when something is being used most; **peak output** = highest output; **peak year** = best year *or* year when the largest quantity of products was produced *or* when sales were highest; *the shares reached their peak in January; the share index has fallen 10% since the peak in January; see also* OFF-PEAK **2** *verb* to reach the highest point; *productivity peaked in January; shares have peaked and are beginning to slip back*

pecuniary *adjective* referring to money; *he gained no pecuniary advantage* = he made no profit

peddle *verb* to sell goods from door to door *or* in the street

peel-off label *noun* gummed label which is removed from a backing sheet and stuck to an envelope

peg *verb* to hold something at a certain point; **to peg prices =** to fix prices to stop them from rising; **to peg wage increases to the cost-of-living index =** to limit increases in wages to the increases in the cost-of-living index NOTE: **pegging - pegged**

pen *noun* thing for writing with, using ink; **felt pen =** pen with a point made of hard cloth; **light pen =** type of pen which when passed over a bar code can read it and send information back to a computer; **marker pen =** pen which makes a wide colored mark

penalty *noun* punishment (such as a fine) which is imposed if something is not done; **penalty clause =** provision which lists the penalties which will be imposed if the contract is not obeyed; *the contract contains a penalty clause which fines the company 1% for every week the completion date is late*

◊ **penalize** *verb* to punish *or* to fine; *to penalize a supplier for late deliveries; they were penalized for bad service*

pending 1 *adjective* waiting; **patent pending =** situation where an invention is put on the market before a patent is granted **2** *adverb* **pending advice from our lawyers =** while waiting for advice from our lawyers

penetrate *verb* **to penetrate a market =** to get into a market and capture a share of it

◊ **penetration** *noun* **market penetration =** percentage of a total market which the sales of a company cover

penny *noun* small coin, one cent, of which one hundred equal a dollar (NOTE: usually written ¢ after a figure: **26¢**; the plural is **pennies** for the coin, **cents** for the amount)

◊ **penny stock** *noun* very cheap share, costing less than $1

pension 1 *noun* (a) money paid regularly to someone who no longer works; *retirement pension; government pension or* **state pension =** pension paid by the state; **work pension =** pension which is paid by the company one worked for; **portable pension =** pension entitlement which can be moved from one company to another without loss (as a worker changes jobs); **pension contributions =** money paid by a company or worker into a pension fund; **pension entitlement =** amount of pension which someone has the right to receive when he retires; **pension fund =** money which provides pensions for retired members of staff (b) **pension plan =** plan used by a company or union which arranges for a worker to pay part of his salary over many years and receive a regular payment when he retires; **company pension plan =** pension which is organized by a company for its employees; *he decided to join the company's pension plan;* **contributory pension plan =** plan where the worker has to pay a proportion of his salary; **graduated pension plan =** pension plan where the benefit is calculated as a percentage of the salary of each person in the scheme; **non-contributory pension plan =** plan where the employer pays in all the money on behalf of the worker; **personal pension plan =** pension plan which applies to one worker only, usually a self-employed person, not to a group; **portable pension plan =** pension plan which a worker can carry from one company to another as he changes jobs **2** *verb* **to pension someone off =** to ask someone to retire and take a pension

◊ **pensionable** *adjective* able to receive a pension; **pensionable age =** age after which someone can take a pension

◊ **pensioner** *noun* person who receives a pension

per *preposition* (a) **as per =** according to; **as per invoice =** as stated in the invoice; **as per sample =** as shown in the sample; **as per previous order =** according to the details given in our previous order (b) at a rate of; **per hour** *or* **per day** *or* **per week** *or* **per year =** for each hour *or* day *or* week *or* year; *the rate is $5 per hour; he makes about $250 per month;* **we pay $10 per hour =** we pay $10 for each hour worked; **the car was traveling at twenty-five miles per hour =** at a speed which covered 25 miles in one hour; **the earnings per share =** dividend received by each share; **the average sales per representative =** the average sales achieved by one representative; **per head =** for each person; *allow $25 per head for expenses; representatives cost on average $55,000 per head per annum* (c) out of; *the rate of imperfect items is about twenty-five per* thousand; *the birth rate has fallen to twelve per hundred*

◊ **per annum** *adverb* in a year; *what are their sales per annum?*

◊ **per capita** *adjective & adverb* for each person; **average income per capita** *or* **per capita income** = average income of one person; **per capita expenditure** = total money spent divided by the number of people involved

◊ **per diem** *adverb* in one day *or* for one day; *expenses are $250 per diem*

QUOTE a 100,000 square-foot warehouse generates $600 in sales per square foot of space
Duns Business Month

perceived *adjective* which is seen or imagined; **perceived value** = value of an item as it appears to the purchaser

percent *adjective & adverb* out of each hundred *or* for each hundred; **10 percent** = ten in every hundred; *what is the percent of increase? fifty percent of nothing is still nothing*

◊ **percentage** *noun* amount shown as part of one hundred *or* of the entire amount; **percentage discount** = discount amounting to a certain portion of the whole amount; **percentage increase** = increase calculated on the basis of a rate for one hundred; **percentage point** = one percent

◊ **percentile** *noun* one of a series of ninety-nine figures below which a certain percentage of the total falls

QUOTE state-owned banks cut their prime rates a percentage point to 11%
Wall Street Journal

perfect 1 *adjective* completely correct *or* with no mistakes; *we check each batch to make sure it is perfect; she did a perfect typing test* **2** *verb* to make something which is completely correct; *he perfected the process for making high-grade steel*

◊ **perfectly** *adverb* with no mistakes *or* correctly; *she typed the letter perfectly*

perform *verb* to carry out an action *or* task; *how did the shares perform?* = did the shares go up or down?; *the company* *or* *the shares performed badly* = the company's market price fell

◊ **performance** *noun* way in which someone *or* something acts; **the poor performance of the shares on the stock market** = the fall in the share price on the stock market; *last year saw* a dip in the company's performance; *as a measure of the company's performance* = as a way of judging if the company's results are good or bad; **performance of personnel against objectives** = how personnel have worked, measured against the objectives set; **performance review** = yearly interview between a manager and each worker to discuss how the worker has worked during the year; **earnings performance** = way in which shares earn dividends; **job performance** = doing a job well or badly

QUOTE inflation-adjusted GNP edged up at a 1.3% annual rate, its worst performance since the economic expansion began
Fortune

period *noun* **(a)** length of time; *for a period of time* *or* *for a period of months* *or* *for a six-year period; sales over a period of three months; sales over the holiday period; to deposit money for a fixed period* **(b) accounting period** = period of time at the end of which the firm's accounts are made up

◊ **periodic** *or* **periodical 1** *adjective* from time to time; *a periodic review of the company's performance* **2** *noun* **periodical** = magazine which comes out regularly

peripherals *plural noun* items of computer hardware (such as terminals, printers, monitors, etc.) which are attached to a main computer system

perishable 1 *adjective* which can go bad *or* become rotten easily; **perishable goods** *or* **items** *or* **cargo 2** *plural noun* **perishables** = goods which can become rotten easily

perjury *noun* telling lies when you have made an oath in court to say what is true; *he was sent to prison for perjury; she appeared in court on a perjury charge*

◊ **perjure** *verb* **to perjure yourself** = to tell lies when you have made an oath to say what is true

perks *informal* = PERQUISITES

permanent *adjective* which will last for a very long time *or* forever; *he has found a permanent job; she is in permanent employment; the permanent staff and part-timers*

◊ **permanency** *noun* being permanent

◊ **permanently** *adverb* forever

permission *noun* being allowed to do something; **written permission** = document which allows someone to do something; **verbal permission** = telling someone that he is allowed to do something; **to give someone permission to do something** = to allow someone to do something; *he asked the manager's permission to take a day off*

permit 1 *noun* official document which allows someone to do something; **building permit** = official document which allows someone to build on a piece of land; **export permit** *or* **import permit** = official document which allows goods to be exported *or* imported; **work permit** = official document which allows someone who is not a citizen to work in a country **2** *verb* to allow someone to do something; *this document permits you to export twenty-five computer systems; the ticket permits three people to go into the trade show*

per pro = PER PROCURATIONEM with the authority of; *the secretary signed per pro the manager*

perquisites *plural noun* extra items given by a company to workers in addition to their salaries (such as medical insurance)

person *noun* (a) someone *or* man *or* woman; *insurance policy which covers a named person;* **the persons named in the contract** = people whose names are given in the contract; **the document should be witnessed by a third person** = someone who is not named in the document should witness it (b) **in person** = someone himself *or* herself; *this important package is to be delivered to the chairman in person* = the package has to be given to the chairman himself (and not to his secretary, assistant, etc.); **he came to see me in person** = he himself came to see me

◊ **person-to-person call** *noun* telephone call where you ask the operator to connect you with a named person

◊ **personal** *adjective* (a) referring to one person; **personal allowances** = part of a person's income which is not taxed; **personal assets** = movable assets which belong to a person; **personal computer** = small computer which can be used at home; **personal effects** *or* **personal property** = things which belong to someone; **person guarantee** *or* **personal security** = guarantee given by one person for a loan to another; **personal income** = (i) income received by an individual; (ii) total amount of income received by households in the nation; **apart from the family shares, he has a personal holding in the company** = he has stock which he owns himself; **the car is for his personal use** = the car is for him to use himself (b) private; *I want to see the director on a personal matter;* **personal call** = telephone call not related to business; *employees must limit their personal calls*

◊ **personalized** *adjective* with the name or initials of a person printed on it; *personalized checks; personalized briefcase*

◊ **personally** *adverb* in person; *he personally opened the envelope; she wrote to me personally*

personnel *noun* people who work in a certain place *or* for a certain company; *the personnel of the warehouse or the warehouse personnel;* **personnel department** = section of the company which deals with the employees; **personnel management** = organizing and training of employees so that they work well and profitably; **personnel manager** = head of the personnel department

persuade *verb* to talk to someone and get him to do what you want; *after ten hours of discussion, they persuaded the CEO to resign; we could not persuade the French company to sign the contract*

peseta *noun* money used in Spain
NOTE: usually written **ptas** after a figure: **2,000ptas**

peso *noun* money used in Mexico and many other countries

pessimism *noun* expecting that everything will turn out badly; **market pessimism** *or* **pessimism on the market** = feeling that the stock market prices will fall; *there is considerable pessimism about job opportunities*

◊ **pessimistic** *adjective* feeling sure that things will work out badly; *he takes a pessimistic view of the exchange rate* = he expects the exchange rate to fall

peter out *verb* to come to an end gradually *or* to lose momentum

Peter Principle *noun* law, based on wide experience, that people are promoted until they occupy positions for which they are incompetent

petition 1 *noun* official request; **to file a petition in bankruptcy** = to ask officially to be made bankrupt *or* to ask officially for someone else to be made bankrupt **2** *verb* to make an official request; *he petitioned the government for a special pension*

petrocurrency *or* **petrodollars** *noun* dollars earned by a country from exporting oil, then invested outside that country

petrol *noun GB* gasoline

petroleum *noun* raw natural oil, found in the ground; **crude petroleum** = raw petroleum which has not been processed; **petroleum exporting countries** = countries which produce petroleum and sell it to others; **petroleum industry** = industry which uses petroleum to make other products (gasoline, soap, etc.); **petroleum products** = products (such as gasoline, soap, paint) which are made from crude petroleum; **petroleum revenues** = income from selling oil

petty *adjective* not important; **petty cash** = small amount of money kept in an office to pay small debts; **petty cash book** = book in which petty cash payments are noted; **petty cash box** = locked metal box in an office where the petty cash is kept; **petty expenses** = small sums of money spent

phase *noun* period *or* part of something which takes place; *the first phase of the expansion program*
◊ **phase in** *verb* to bring something in gradually; *the new invoicing system will be phased in over the next two months*
◊ **phase out** *verb* to remove something gradually; *Smith Corp. will be phased out as a supplier of spare parts*

QUOTE the budget grants a tax exemption for $500,000 in capital gains, phased in over the next six years
Toronto Star

phone 1 *noun* telephone *or* machine used for speaking to someone over a long distance; *we had a new phone system installed last week;* **internal phone** = telephone for calling from one office to another; **by phone** = using the telephone; *to place an order by phone;* **to be on the phone** = to be speaking to someone on the telephone; *she has been on the phone all morning; he spoke to the manager on the phone;* **phone book** = book which lists names of people and companies with their addresses and phone numbers; *look up his address in the phone book;* **phone call** = speaking to someone on the phone; **to make a phone call** = to speak to someone on the telephone; **to answer the phone** *or* **to take a phone call** = to reply to a call on the phone; **phone number** = set of figures for a particular telephone; *he keeps a list of phone numbers in a little black book; the phone number is on the company letterhead; can you give me your phone number?* **2** *verb* to **phone someone** = to call someone by telephone; *don't phone me, I'll phone you; his secretary phoned to say he would be late; he phoned the order through to the warehouse;* **to phone for something** = to make a phone call to ask for something; *he phoned for a cab*
◊ **phone back** *verb* to reply by phone; *the chairman is in a meeting, can you phone back in about half an hour?*

photocopier *noun* machine which makes a copy of a document by photographing and printing it
◊ **photocopy 1** *noun* copy of a document (in black and white or in color) made by photographing and printing it; *make six photocopies of the contract* **2** *verb* to make a copy of a document by photographing and printing it; *she photocopied the contract*
◊ **photocopying** *noun* making photocopies; *photocopying costs are rising each year;* **there is a lot of photocopying to be done** = there are many documents waiting to be photocopied
◊ **photostat 1** *noun* trademark for a type of photocopy **2** *verb* to make a photostat of a document

pick 1 *noun* thing chosen; **take your pick** = choose what you want; **the pick of the group** = the best item in the group **2** *verb* **(a)** to choose; *the board picked a banker to succeed the retiring CEO; the Association has picked Paris for its next meeting* **(b)** to select items in a warehouse to supply an order
◊ **picking** *noun* **order picking** = collecting various items in a warehouse to make up an order to be sent to a

customer; **picking list** = list of items in an order, listed according to where they can be found in the warehouse

◊ **pick out** *verb* to choose (something *or* someone) out of a lot; *he was picked out for promotion by the chairman*

◊ **pick up** *verb* to get better *or* to improve; *business or trade is picking up*

◊ **pickup** *noun* **pickup (truck)** = type of small truck for transporting goods; **pickup and delivery service** = service which takes goods from the warehouse and delivers them to the customer *or* which picks up something for servicing and returns it to the customer when finished; *the dry cleaner has a pickup and delivery service*

picket 1 *noun* striking worker who stands at the gate of a factory to try to persuade other workers not to go to work; **picket line** = line of pickets at the gate of a factory; *to man a picket line or to be on the picket line;* **to cross a picket line** = to go into a factory to work, even though pickets are trying to prevent workers from going in **2** *verb* **to picket a factory** = to put pickets at the gate of a factory to try to prevent other workers from going to work

◊ **picketing** *noun* act of standing at the gates of a factory to prevent workers from going to work; **lawful picketing** = picketing which is allowed by law; **mass picketing** = picketing by large numbers of workers; **peaceful picketing** = picketing which does not involve fighting

piece *noun* small part of something; *to sell something by the piece; the price is 25c per piece;* **mailing piece** = leaflet suitable for sending by direct mail

◊ **piece rate** *noun* rate of pay for a product produced *or* for a piece of work done and not paid for at an hourly rate; *to earn piece rates*

◊ **piecework** *noun* work for which workers are paid for the products produced *or* the piece of work done and not at an hourly rate

QUOTE the old piecework plan · which rewarded only quantity · resulted in an extraordinary amount of bad product
Business Week

pie chart *noun* diagram where information is shown as a circle cut up into sections of different sizes

pigeonhole 1 *noun* one of a series of small spaces for filing documents *or* for putting letters for delivery to separate offices **2** *verb* to file a plan or document as the best way of forgetting about it; *the whole expansion plan was pigeonholed*

pile 1 *noun* lot of things put one on top of the other; *the president's desk is covered with piles of paper; she put the letter on the pile of letters waiting to be signed* **2** *verb* to put things on top of one another; *he piled the papers on his desk*

◊ **pile up** *verb* to put *or* get into a pile; *the invoices were piled up on the table; complaints are piling up about the poor customer service*

pilferage *or* **pilfering** *noun* stealing small amounts of money *or* small items from an office *or* store

pilot *noun* **(a)** person who flies a plane *or* guides a ship into port **(b)** used as a test, which if successful will then be expanded into a full operation; *the company set up a pilot project to see if the proposed manufacturing system was efficient; the pilot factory has been built to test the new production processes; he is directing a pilot program for training unemployed young people*

pin 1 *noun* sharp piece of metal for attaching papers to a bulletin board **2** *verb* to attach with a pin; *she pinned the papers together; please pin this notice on the bulletin board*

◊ **pinfeed holes** *noun* holes along each side of the paper in continuous forms, which allow the paper to be pulled through the printer

◊ **pin up** *verb* to attach something with pins to a wall; *they pinned the posters up at the back of the exhibition stand*

PIN = PERSONAL IDENTIFICATION NUMBER number which each person has, and which is used to access an automated teller machine

pint *noun* measure of liquids (= half of a quart)

pioneer 1 *noun* first to do a type of work; **pioneer project** *or* **pioneer development** = project or development which is new and has never been tried before **2** *verb* to be the first to do something; *the company pioneered* developments in the field of electronics

pirate 1 *noun* person who copies a patented invention or a copyright work and sells it; *a pirate copy of a book* **2** *verb* to copy a copyright work; *a pirated book* or *a pirated design; the designs for the new dress collection were pirated in the Far East*
◊ **piracy** *noun* copying of patented inventions or copyright works

pit *noun* (a) coal mine (b) circular area in the center of the floor of a stock exchange

pitch *noun* **sales pitch** = talk by a salesman to persuade someone to buy

pix *plural noun informal* pictures (used in advertising or design)

place 1 *noun* (a) where something is or where something happens; **to take place** = to happen; *the meeting will take place in our offices;* **meeting place** = room or area where people can meet; **place of work** = office or factory, etc. where people work (b) position (in a competition); *three companies are fighting for first place in the home computer market* (c) job; *he was offered a place with an insurance company; she turned down three places before accepting the one we offered* (d) position in a text; *she marked her place in the text with a red pen; I have lost my place and cannot remember where I was in my filing* **2** *verb* (a) to put; **to place money in an account** = to deposit money; **to place a block of shares** = to find a buyer for a block of shares; **to place a contract** = to decide that a certain company shall have the contract to do work; **to place something on file** = to file something (b) **to place an order** = to order something; *he placed an order for 250 cartons of paper* (c) **to place someone** = to find a job for someone
◊ **placement** *noun* finding work for someone
◊ **placing** *noun* **the placing of a line of shares** = finding a buyer for a large number of shares in a new company or a company which is going public

plain *adjective* (a) easy to understand; *we made it plain to the union that 5% was the management's final offer; the manager is a very plain-spoken man* =

the manager says exactly what he thinks (b) simple; *the design of the package is in plain blue and white squares; we want the cheaper models to have a plain design*
◊ **plain cover** *noun* **to send something under plain cover** = to send something in an ordinary envelope with no company name printed on it

plaintiff *noun* party who starts a legal action against someone

plan 1 *noun* (a) organized way of doing something; *a marketing plan; an expansion plan;* **contingency plan** = plan which will be put into action if something happens which no one expects to happen; **the government's economic plans** = the government's proposals for running the country's economy (b) way of saving or investing money; *investment plan; pension plan; savings plan* (c) drawing which shows how something is arranged or how something will be built; *the designers showed us the first plans for the new offices;* **floor plan** = drawing of a floor in a building, showing where different departments are **2** *verb* to organize carefully how something should be done; **to plan for an increase in bank interest charges** = to change a way of doing things because you think there will be an increase in bank interest charges; **to plan investments** = to propose how investments should be made
NOTE: **planning - planned**
◊ **planned** *adjective* **planned economy** = system where the government plans all business activity; **planned obsolescence** = situation where the manufacturer designs his products to become out-of-date so that the customers can be persuaded to replace them with new models
◊ **planner** *noun* (a) person who plans; **the government's economic planners** = people who plan the future economy of the country for the government (b) **desk planner** or **wall planner** = book or chart which shows days or weeks or months so that the work of an office can be shown by diagrams
◊ **planning** *noun* (a) organizing how something should be done, especially how a company should be run to make increased profits; *long-term planning* or *short-term planning;* **economic planning** = planning how the economy should be controlled; **corporate planning** = planning the future financial state of a group of companies;

manpower planning = planning to get the right number of workers in each job **(b) the planning department =** section of a local government office which deals with building development and how property in different areas of the city should be used

> QUOTE the benefits package is attractive and the compensation plan includes base, incentive and car allowance totaling $50,000+
> *Globe and Mail (Toronto)*

plane *noun* aircraft *or* machine which flies in the air, carrying passengers or cargo; *I plan to take the 5 o'clock plane to New York; he could not get a seat on Tuesday's plane, so he had to wait until Wednesday; there are ten planes a day from New York to Los Angeles*

plant *noun* **(a)** the land, buildings, machinery and equipment used for an industrial business (NOTE: no plural) **(b)** large factory; *they are planning to build a car plant near the river; to set up a new plant; they closed down six plants in the north of the country; he was appointed plant manager*

platform *noun* high paved surface in a train station, so that passengers can get on or off trains; *the train for Chicago leaves from Platform 12; the ticket office is on Platform 2*

plead *verb* to speak on behalf of a client in court

pledge 1 *noun* object given to a pawnbroker as security for money borrowed; **to redeem a pledge =** to pay back a loan and interest and so get back the security; **unredeemed pledge =** pledge which the borrower has not claimed back by paying back his loan **2** *verb* **to pledge share certificates =** to deposit share certificates with the lender as security for money borrowed

plenary *noun* entire *or* complete; **plenary meeting** *or* **plenary session =** meeting at a conference when all the delegates meet together

plow back *verb* **to plow back profits into the company =** to invest the profits in the business (and not pay them out as dividends to the shareholders) by using them to buy new equipment *or* create new products

plug 1 *noun* **(a)** device at the end of a wire for connecting a machine to the electricity supply; *the printer is supplied with a plug* **(b) to give a plug to a new product =** to publicize a new product **2** *verb* **(a) to plug in =** to attach a machine to the electricity supply; *the computer was not plugged in* **(b)** to publicize *or* to advertise, especially to mention a product favorably on a TV or radio program; *they ran six commercials plugging vacations in Spain* **(c)** to block *or* to stop; *the company is trying to plug the drain on cash reserves*
NOTE: **plugging - plugged**

plummet *or* **plunge** *verb* to fall sharply; *share prices plummeted or plunged on the news of the devaluation*

> QUOTE crude oil output plunged during the past month
> *Wall Street Journal*

plus 1 *preposition* **(a)** added to; *his salary plus commission comes to more than $35,000; production costs plus overhead are higher than revenue* **(b)** more than; *homes valued at $100,000 plus =* houses valued at over $100,000 **2** *adjective* favorable *or* good and profitable; *a plus factor for the company is that the market is much larger than they had originally thought;* **the plus side of the account =** the credit side of the account; **on the plus side =** this is a favorable point; *on the plus side, we must take into account the new product line* **3** *noun* a good *or* favorable point; *to have achieved $1m in new sales in less than six months is certainly a plus for the sales team*

p.m. *adverb* in the afternoon *or* in the evening *or* after 12 o'clock noon; *the train leaves at 6:50 p.m.; if you phone after 6 p.m. the calls are at a cheaper rate*

P.O. = POST OFFICE; **P.O. box** = LOCKBOX

pocket *noun* **pocket calculator** *or* **pocket calendar =** calculator *or* calendar which can be carried in the pocket; **to be $25 in pocket =** to have made a profit of $25; **to be $25 out of pocket =** to have lost $25; **out-of-pocket costs** *or* **expenses =** amount of money to pay back a worker for his own money which he has spent on company business

point 1 *noun* **(a)** place *or* position; **point of sale** = place where a product is sold (such as a store); **point of purchase advertising material** = display material (such as posters) to advertise a product where it is being purchased; **break-even point** = position at which sales cover costs but do not show a profit; **customs entry point** = place at a border between two countries where goods are declared to customs; **starting point** = time *or* place where something starts **(b)** **decimal point** = dot which indicates the division between a whole unit and its smaller parts (such as 4.25); **one percentage point** = 1 per cent; **half a percentage point** = 0.5 per cent; **the dollar gained two points** = the dollar increased in value against another currency by two hundredths of a cent; **the exchange fell ten points** = the stock market index fell by ten units **2** *verb* **to point out** = to show; *the report points out the mistakes made by the corporation over the last year; he pointed out that the results were better than in previous years*

poison pill *noun* method used by a corporation to make it less attractive to potential purchasers (as by borrowing huge amounts of money and paying it to stockholders in the form of dividend)

policy *noun* **(a)** decisions on the general way of doing something; *federal government policy on wages or wages policy; the government's prices policy or incomes policy; the country's economic policy; a company's trading policy;* the government made a policy statement *or* made a statement of policy = the government declared in public what its plans were; **budgetary policy** = policy of expected income and expenditure **(b)** **company policy** = the company's agreed plan of action *or* the company's way of doing things; *what is the company policy on credit? it is against company policy to give more than thirty days' credit; our policy is to submit all contracts to the legal department* **(c)** **insurance policy** = document which shows the conditions and provisions of an insurance contract; **an accident policy** = an insurance contract against accidents; **all-risks policy** = insurance policy which covers risks of any kind, with no exclusions; **a comprehensive policy** = an insurance

which covers all risks; **contingent policy** = policy which pays out only if something happens (as if the person named in the policy dies before the person due to benefit); **endowment policy** = policy where a sum of money is paid to the insured person on a certain date, or to his estate if he dies earlier; **policy holder** = person who purchased an insurance policy from an insurance company; **to take out a policy** = to sign the contract for insurance and start paying the premiums; *she took out a life insurance policy or a house insurance policy;* the insurance company made out a policy *or* drew up a policy = the company wrote the details of the contract on the policy

polite *adjective* behaving in a pleasant way; *we require that our salesgirls must be polite to customers; we had a polite letter from the finance manager* ◇ **politely** *adverb* in a pleasant way; *she politely answered the customers' questions*

political *adjective* of or concerned with government, the state and politics; **political party** = group of people who believe a country should be run in a certain way

poll 1 *noun* **opinion poll** = asking a sample group of people, taken at random, what they feel about something, so as to guess the opinion of the whole population; *opinion polls showed the public preferred butter to margarine; before starting the service the company carried out a nationwide opinion poll* **2** *verb* to poll a sample of the population = to ask a sample group of people what they feel about something; **to poll the members of the club on an issue** = to ask the members for their opinion on an issue ◇ **pollster** *noun* person who conducts polls

polybag *noun noun* bag made of transparent polythene, used for packaging goods

polystyrene *noun* **expanded polystyrene** = light solid plastic used for packing; *the computer is delivered packed in expanded polystyrene*

pool 1 *noun* **(a)** group of people, such as investors or insurers, who work together; **typing pool** = group of typists, working together in a company, offering a secretarial service to several departments **(b)** unused supply; *a pool of unemployed labor* or *of expertise* **2** *verb* **to pool resources** = to put all resources together so as to be more powerful or profitable

poor *adjective* **(a)** without much money; *the company tries to help the poorest members of the staff with soft loans; it is one of the poorest countries in the world* **(b)** not very good; *poor quality; poor service; poor turnaround time of orders* or *poor order turnaround time* ◊ **poorly** *adverb* badly; *the offices are poorly laid out; the plan was poorly presented* ; **poorly-paid staff** = staff with low wages

popular *adjective* liked by many people; *this is our most popular model; the South Coast is the most popular area for vacations;* **popular prices** = prices which are low and therefore favored by many people

population *noun* number of people who live in a country or in a town; *Detroit has a population of over one million; the working population; population statistics; population trends;* **floating population** = people who move from place to place

port *noun* **(a)** harbor or place where ships come to load or unload; *the port of Seattle;* **inland port** = port on a river or canal; **to call at a port** = to stop at a port to load or unload cargo; **port authority** = organization which runs a port; **port of call** = port at which a ship often stops; **port charges** or **port dues** = payment which a ship makes to the port authority for the right to use the port; **port of embarkation** = port at which you get on a ship; **port of entry** = port where imported goods are inspected by customs officers; **port installations** = buildings and equipment of a port; **commercial port** = port which has only goods traffic; **fishing port** = port which is used mainly by fishing boats; **free port** = port where there are no customs duties to be paid **(b)** part of a computer where a lead wire can be attached

portable **1** *adjective* which can be carried; *a portable computer* or *a portable typewriter;* **portable pension** = pension rights which a worker can take with him from one company to another as he changes jobs **2** *noun* a

portable = a computer or typewriter or appliance which can be carried

portfolio *noun* all the securities owned by someone; **portfolio management** = buying and selling shares to make profits for a person

portion *noun* small quantity, especially enough food for one person; *we serve ice cream in individual portions*

position *noun* **(a)** situation or state of affairs; **what is the cash position?** = what is the state of the company's current account?; **bargaining position** = statement of position by one group during negotiations; **to cover a position** = to have enough money to pay for a forward purchase **(b)** job or paid work in a company; *to apply for a position as manager; we have several positions vacant; all the vacant positions have been filled; she retired from her position in the accounts department;* **he is in a key position** = he has an important job

positive *adjective* meaning "yes"; *the board gave a positive reply;* **positive cash flow** = situation where more money is coming in than is being spent

possess *verb* to own; *the corporation possesses property in the center of the town; he lost all he possessed in the collapse of his business* ◊ **possession** *noun* **(a)** owning something; *the documents are in his possession* = he is holding the documents; **vacant possession** = being able to occupy a property immediately after buying it because it is empty; *the property is to be sold with vacant possession* (NOTE: no plural) **(b)** **possessions** = property or things owned; *they lost all their possessions in the fire*

possible *adjective* which might happen; *June 25 and 26 are possible dates for our next meeting; it is possible that production will be held up by industrial action;* **there are two possible candidates for the job** = two candidates are good enough to be appointed ◊ **possibility** *noun* being likely to happen; *there is a possibility that the plane will be early; there is no possibility of the chairman retiring before next Christmas*

post 1 *noun* **(a)** job *or* paid work in a company; **to apply for a post as cashier; we have three posts vacant (b)** *GB* a nation's system for handling mail **2** *verb* **(a) to post an entry** = to transfer an entry to an account **(b) to post a notice** = to put a notice on a wall *or* on a bulletin board **(c)** *GB* to mail; **to post a letter**

post- *prefix* later *or* after

postage *noun* payment for sending a letter or parcel by mail; **what is the postage to Nigeria?; postage paid** = words printed on an envelope to show that the sender has paid the postage even though there is no stamp on it; **postage stamp** = small piece of paper attached to a letter or parcel to show that you have paid for it to be sent through the mail

postal *adjective* referring to the mail services; **postal charges** *or* **postal rates** = money to be paid for sending letters or parcels by mail; **postal charges are going up by 10% in September; United States Postal Service (USPS)** = independent U.S. agency which deals with sending letters and parcels

postcard *noun* piece of cardboard for sending a message by mail (often with a picture on one side)

postdate *verb* to put a later date on a document; **he sent us a postdated check; his check was postdated to June**

poster *noun* large notice *or* advertisement to be stuck up on a billboard or directly on a wall

postmark 1 *noun* mark stamped by the Postal Service on a letter, covering the postage stamp, to show that the service has accepted it; **letter with a Boston postmark 2** *verb* to stamp a letter with a postmark; **the letter was postmarked New York**

post office *noun* **(a)** building where the postal services are based; **General Post Office; post office branch** = small post office, serving one area of a city or town **(b)** government agency which deals with sending letters and parcels; **Post Office officials** *or* **officials of the Post Office; Post Office box (P.O. Box) number** = reference number given for delivering mail to a post office, so as not to give the actual address of the person who will receive it
NOTE: in the U.S., the official name of the post office is the **U.S. Postal Service (USPS)**

postpaid *adjective* with the postage already paid; **the price is $5.95 postpaid**

postpone *verb* to arrange for something to take place later than originally planned; **he postponed the meeting to tomorrow; they asked if they could postpone payment until the cash situation was better**
◊ **postponement** *noun* arranging for something to take place later than planned; **I had to change my appointments because of the postponement of the meeting**

potential 1 *adjective* possible; **potential customers** = people who could be customers; **potential market** = market which could be exploited; **the product has potential sales of 100,000 units** = the product will possibly sell 100,000 units; **he is a potential CEO** = he is the sort of man who could become CEO **2** *noun* possibility of becoming something; **share with a growth potential** *or* **with a potential for growth** = share which is likely to increase in value; **product with considerable sales potential** = product which is likely to have very large sales; **to analyze the market potential** = to examine the market to see how large it possibly is; **earning potential** = amount of money which someone should be able to earn *or* amount of dividend which a share is capable of earning

pound *noun* **(a)** measure of weight (= 16 ounces); **to sell oranges by the pound; a pound of oranges; oranges cost 50¢ a pound** (NOTE: usually written **lb** after a figure: **25 lb) (b)** money used in the United Kingdom and many other countries; **pound sterling** = official term for the British currency NOTE: usually written **£** before a figure: **£5**
◊ **poundage** *noun* (i) rate charged per pound in weight; (ii) weight in pounds

power *noun* **(a)** strength *or* ability; **purchasing power** = quantity of goods which can be bought by a group of people *or* with a sum of money; **the purchasing power of the teenage market; the purchasing power of the dollar has fallen over the last five years; the power of a consumer group** = ability of a group to influence the government *or* manufacturers; **bargaining power =** strength of one person *or* group when discussing prices *or* wages; **earning power =** amount of money someone should be able to earn; *he is such a fine designer that his earning power is very large;* **borrowing power =** amount of money which a company can borrow **(b)** force *or* legal right; **executive power =** right to act as director *or* to put decisions into action; **power of attorney =** legal document which gives someone the right to act on someone's behalf in legal matters; **the full power of the law =** the full force of the law when applied; *we will apply the full power of the law to get possession of our property again*

p.p. *verb* = PER PROCURATIONEM on behalf of someone, used when signing a letter for someone

PR = PUBLIC RELATIONS *a PR firm is handling all our publicity; he is working in PR; the PR people gave away 100,000 balloons*

practice *noun* **(a)** way of doing things; *his practice was to arrive at work at 7:30 and start counting the cash;* **business practices** *or* **industrial practices** *or* **trade practices =** ways of managing *or* working in business, industry or trade; **sharp practice =** way of doing business which is not honest, but is not illegal; **code of practice =** rules drawn up by an association which the members must follow when doing business **(b) in practice =** when actually done; *the marketing plan seems very interesting, but what will it cost in practice?*

QUOTE the EC demanded international arbitration over the pricing practices of the provincial boards
Globe and Mail (Toronto)

pre- *prefix* before; *a prestocktaking sale; the preChristmas period is always very busy*

preaddressed envelope *noun* envelope with the address already printed on it, used to send with order forms so that the purchaser can reply more easily

precautionary *adjective* **as a precautionary measure =** in case something takes place

◊ **precautions** *plural noun* care taken to avoid something undesirable; *to take precautions to prevent thefts in the office; the company did not take proper fire precautions;* **safety precautions =** actions to try to make sure that something is safe

precinct *noun* administrative district in a city; *the Policeman was assigned to Precinct 5; the Sixth Precinct voted against the property tax increase*

predecessor *noun* person who had a job *or* position before someone else; *he took over from his predecessor last May; she is using the same office as her predecessor*

predict *verb* to say that something will certainly happen
◊ **prediction** *noun* statement of what someone believes will happen in the future

preempt *verb* to get an advantage by doing something quickly before anyone else; *they staged a management buyout to preempt a takeover bid*
◊ **preemptive** *adjective* which has an advantage by acting early; **preemptive strike against a takeover bid =** rapid action taken to prevent a takeover bid; **a preemptive right =** right of a stockholder to be first to buy a new stock issue

prefer *verb* to like something better than another thing; *we prefer the small corner store to the large supermarket; most customers prefer to choose clothes themselves, rather than take the advice of the sales clerk*
◊ **preference** *noun* thing which is preferred; *the customers' preference for small corner stores*
◊ **preferential** *adjective* showing that something is preferred more than another; **preferential duty =** special low rate of tax; **preferential terms** *or* **preferential treatment =** terms or way of dealing which is better than usual; *subsidiary companies get preferential treatment when it comes to subcontracting work*
◊ **preferred** *adjective* **preferred creditor =** creditor who must be paid first if a company is in liquidation; **preferred stock =** shares which receive their dividend before all other stock, and which are repaid first (at face value) if the corporation is in liquidation;

cumulative preferred stock = preferred stock where the dividend will be paid at a later date even if the corporation cannot pay a dividend in the current year

prejudice 1 *noun* injustice, as in the form of a biased *or* unfair judgment or action; **without prejudice** = without harming any interests (words written on a letter to indicate that the writer is not legally bound to do what he offers to do in the letter); **to act to the prejudice of a claim** = to do something which may harm a claim **2** *verb* to make biased or unfair; *to prejudice someone's claim*

preliminary *adjective* introductory *or* happening before anything else; **preliminary discussion** *or* a **preliminary meeting** = discussion *or* meeting which takes place before the main discussion *or* meeting starts; **preliminary prospectus** = document which gives information about a new stock issue

premises *plural noun* building and the land it stands on; **business premises** *or* **commercial premises** = building used for commercial use; **office premises** *or* **store premises** = building which houses an office or store; **licensed premises** = store *or* restaurant *or* bar which is licensed to sell alcohol; **on the premises** = in the building; *there is a doctor on the premises at all times*

premium *noun* (a) special gift or cash prize offered to encourage a purchaser to buy; **premium offer** = free gift offered to attract more customers (b) **insurance premium** = annual payment made by the insured person *or* a company to an insurance company; **additional premium** = payment made to cover extra items in an existing insurance; *you pay either an annual premium of $360 or twelve monthly premiums of $32* (c) extra charge for a special service; **exchange premium** = extra cost above the normal rate for buying foreign currency; *the dollar is at a premium; securities trading at a premium* = (i) stocks whose prices are higher than the face value; (ii) new stock whose market price is higher than the issue price (d) **premium product** = special product selling at a higher price than others; **premium quality** = top quality

prepack *or* **prepackage** *verb* to pack something before putting it on sale; *the fruit is prepacked or prepackaged in plastic trays; the watches are prepacked in attractive display boxes*

prepaid *adjective* paid in advance; **postage prepaid** = note showing that the mailing costs have been paid in advance; **prepaid reply card** = stamped addressed card which is sent to someone so that he can reply without paying the postage

◊ **prepay** *verb* to pay in advance
NOTE: **prepaying - prepaid**

◊ **prepayment** *noun* payment in advance; **to ask for prepayment of a fee** = to ask for the fee to be paid before the work is done

present 1 *noun* thing which is given; *these calculators make good presents; the office gave her a present when she got married* **2** *adjective* (a) happening now *or* current; *the shares are too expensive at their present price; what is the present address of the company?* (b) being there when something happens; *only six directors were present at the board meeting* **3** *verb* (a) to give someone something; *he was presented with a gold watch on completing twenty-five years' service with the company* (b) to bring *or* send and show a document; **to present a bill for acceptance** = to send a bill for payment by the person who has accepted it; **to present a bill for payment** = to send a bill to be paid

◊ **presentation** *noun* (a) showing a document; **check payable on presentation** = check which will be paid when it is presented; **free admission on presentation of the card** = you do not pay to go in if you show this card (b) demonstration *or* exhibition of a proposed plan; *the manufacturer made a presentation of his new product line to possible customers; the distribution company made a presentation of the services they could offer; we have asked two PR firms to make presentations of proposed publicity campaigns*

◊ **presently** *adverb* at the present time; *the corporation is presently revising its pricing policy*

◊ **present value** *noun* **(a)** the value something has now; *in 1974 the dollar was worth one and a half times its present value* **(b)** sum of money which if invested now at a given rate of interest would grow to a certain future value

preside *verb* to be in a position of authority; to be chairman; *to preside over a meeting; the meeting was held in the committee room, Mr. Smith presiding*
◊ **president** *noun* head of a corporation *or* a club; *he was elected president of the sports club; A.B. Smith has been appointed president of the corporation*

press *noun* newspapers and magazines; **the local press** = newspapers which are sold in a small area of the country; **the national press** = newspapers which sell in all parts of the country; *the new car has been advertised in the national press; we plan to give the product a lot of press publicity; there was no mention of the new product in the press;* **press conference** = meeting where reporters from newspapers are invited to hear news of a new product *or* of a court case *or* of a takeover bid, etc.; **press coverage** = reports about something in the press; *we were very disappointed by the press coverage of the new car ;* **press cutting** = piece cut out of a newspaper *or* magazine, which refers to an item which you find interesting; *we have kept a file of press cuttings about the new car ;* **press release** = sheet giving news about something which is sent to newspapers and TV and radio stations so that they can use the information; *the company sent out a press release about the sale of the new car*
◊ **pressing** *adjective* urgent; **pressing engagements** = meetings which have to be attended; **pressing bills** = bills which have to be paid

pressure *noun* something which forces you to do something; *he was under considerable financial pressure* = he was forced to act because he owed money; **to put pressure on someone to do something** = to try to force someone to do something; *the group tried to put pressure on the government to act; the banks put pressure on the company to reduce its borrowings ;* **working under high pressure** = working with customers asking for supplies urgently *or* with a manager telling you to work

faster; **high-pressure salesman** = salesman who forces a customer to buy something he does not really need; **pressure group** = group of people who try to influence a legislative body

prestige *noun* importance because of high quality *or* high value, etc.; **prestige advertising** = advertising in high quality magazines to increase a company's reputation; **prestige product** = expensive luxury product; **prestige offices** = expensive offices in a good area of the city

presume *verb* to assume *or* to suppose something is correct; *I presume the account has been paid; the company is presumed to be still solvent; we presume the shipment has been stolen*
◊ **presumption** *noun* thing which is assumed to be correct

pretax *adjective* before taxes have been paid *or* deducted; **pretax profit** = profit before taxes have been paid; *the dividend paid is equivalent to one quarter of the pretax profit*

> QUOTE the company's goals are a growth in sales of up to 40 per cent, a rise in pretax earnings of nearly 35 per cent and a rise in after-tax earnings of more than 25 per cent
> *Citizen (Ottawa)*

pretend *verb* to act like someone else in order to trick *or* to act as if something is true when it really is not; *he got in by pretending to be a telephone engineer; the chairman pretended he knew the final profit; she pretended she had the flu and asked to have the day off*

pretenses *plural noun* **false pretenses** = doing or saying something to cheat someone; *he was sent to prison for obtaining money under false pretenses*

prevent *verb* to stop something from happening; *we must try to prevent the takeover bid; the police prevented anyone from leaving the building; we have changed the locks on the doors to prevent the former president from getting into the building*
◊ **preventive** *adjective* which tries to stop something from happening; **to take preventive measures against theft** = to try to stop things from being stolen

previous *adjective* which happens earlier; *he could not accept the* invitation because he had a previous **engagement** = because he had earlier accepted another invitation

◊ **previously** *adverb* happening earlier

price 1 *noun* (**a**) money which has to be paid to buy something; **administered price** = price established under situations of competition, where one company has some degree of control; **asking price** = price which the seller is hoping to be paid for the item when it is sold; **bargain price** = very cheap price; **catalog price** *or* **list price** = price as marked in a catalog or list; **competitive price** = low price aimed to compete with a rival product; **cost price** = selling price which is the same as the price which the seller paid for the item (either the manufacturing price or the wholesale price); **cut price** = very cheap price; **discount price** = full price less a discount; **factory price** *or* **price ex factory** = price not including transport from the maker's factory; **fair price** = good price for both buyer and seller; **firm price** = price which will not change; *they are quoting a firm price of $1.23 a unit;* **going price** *or* **current price** *or* **usual price** = the price which is being charged now; **to sell goods off at half price** = to sell goods at half the price at which they were being sold before; **market price** = price at which a product can be sold; **net price** = price which cannot be reduced by a discount; **retail price** = price at which the retailer sells to the final customer; **retail price index** = index which shows how prices of consumer goods have increased or decreased over a period of time; **spot price** = price for immediate delivery of a commodity; *the spot price of oil on the commodity markets;* **price ceiling** = highest price which can be reached; **price control** = regulatory measures to stop prices from rising too fast; **price cutting** = sudden lowering of prices; **price war** *or* **price-cutting war** = competition between companies to get a larger market share by cutting prices; **price differential** = difference in price between products in a range; **price fixing** = illegal agreement between companies to charge the same price for competing products; **price label** *or* **price tag** = label which shows a price; *the takeover bid put a $2m price tag on the company;* **price list** = sheet giving prices of goods for sale; **price range** = series of prices for similar products from different suppliers; **cars in the $6-7,000 price range** = cars of different makes,

selling for between $6,000 and $7,000; **price-sensitive product** = product which will not sell if the price is increased (**b**) **to increase in price** = to become more expensive; *gasoline has increased in price or the price of gasoline has increased;* **to increase prices** *or* **to raise prices** = to make items more expensive; **we will try to meet your price** = we will try to offer a price which is acceptable to you; **to cut prices** = to reduce prices suddenly; **to lower prices** *or* **to reduce prices** = to sell items cheaper (**c**) *(on a Stock Exchange)* **asking price** = price which sellers are asking for shares; **closing price** = price at the end of a day's trading; **opening price** = price at the start of a day's trading; **price change** = movement in the price of a security during a trading session; **price/earnings ratio** = ratio between the market price of a share and the current earnings it produces **2** *verb* to give a price to a product; *car priced at $5,000;* **competitively priced** = sold at a low price which competes with that of similar goods from other companies; **the company has priced itself out of the market** = the company has raised its prices so high that its products do not sell

◊ **pricing** *noun* giving a price to a product; **pricing policy** = a company's policy in giving prices to its products; *our pricing policy aims at producing a 35% gross margin ;* **common pricing** = illegal fixing of prices by several businesses so that they all charge the same price; **competitive pricing** = putting a low price on a product so that it competes with similar products from other companies; **marginal pricing** = making the selling price the same as the cost of producing a single extra unit

QUOTE European manufacturers rely heavily on imported raw materials which are mostly priced in dollars
Duns Business Month

primary *adjective* basic; **primary commodities** = raw materials or food staples; **primary industry** = industry dealing with basic raw materials (such as coal, wood, farm produce); **primary products** = products (such as wood, milk, fish) which are basic raw materials

◊ **primarily** *adverb* mainly

prime *adjective* (**a**) most important; **prime time** = most expensive advertising time for TV or radio commercials, when there is the largest audience; *we are putting out a series of* prime-time commercials (b) basic; prime bills = bills of exchange which do not involve any risk; prime cost = cost involved in producing a product, excluding overhead; prime rate or prime = best rate of interest at which a bank lends to its customers

◊ prime minister noun head of a government; the Australian prime minister or the prime minister of Australia

◊ priming noun see PUMP PRIMING

QUOTE the base lending rate, or prime rate, is the rate at which banks lend to their top corporate borrowers
Wall Street Journal

principal 1 noun (a) business which is represented by an agent; the agent has come to New York to see his principals (b) money invested or borrowed on which interest is paid; to repay principal and interest 2 adjective most important; the principal stockholders asked for a meeting; the country's principal products are paper and wood

principle noun basic point or general rule; in principle = in agreement with a general rule; agreement in principle = agreement with the basic conditions of a proposal

print 1 noun words made (on paper) with a machine; to read the small print or the fine print on a contract = to read the conditions of a contract which are often printed very small so that people will not be as likely to read them 2 verb (a) to make letters on paper with a machine; printed agreement; printed regulations (b) to write in capital letters; please print your name and address on the top of the form

◊ printer noun (a) machine which prints; computer printer or line printer = machine which prints information from a computer, printing one line at a time; dot-matrix printer = machine which prints by forming letters from many tiny dots; laser printer = printing machine attached to a computer, which prints text and graphics using a laser beam (b) business which prints commercial material such as fliers, cards, letterheads, etc.

◊ print out verb to print information from a computer through a printer

◊ printout noun computer printout = printed copy of information from a computer; the sales manager asked for a printout of the agents' commissions

prior adjective earlier; prior agreement = agreement which was reached earlier; without prior knowledge = without knowing before

◊ priority noun to have priority = to have the right to be first; to have priority over or to take priority over something = to be more important than something; reducing overhead costs takes priority over increasing turnover; debenture holders have priority over ordinary shareholders ; to give something top priority = to make something the most important item

private adjective (a) belonging to a single person, not a company or the state; letter marked "private and confidential" = letter which must not be opened by anyone other than the person it is addressed to; private client or private customer = client dealt with by a salesman as a person, not as a company; private income = income from dividends or interest or rents which is not part of a salary; private investor = ordinary person with money to invest; private property = property which belongs to a particular person, not to the public (b) in private = away from other people; he asked to see the manager in private; in public he said the company would break even soon, but in private he was less optimistic (c) private company = company with a small number of shareholders, whose shares are not traded on a Stock Exchange; to take a company private = to remove a company from a Stock Exchange listing by buying most of the stock; private enterprise = businesses which are owned by private shareholders, not by the state; the project is funded by private enterprise ; the private sector = all companies which are owned by private shareholders, not by the state

◊ privately adverb not openly or not publicly; the deal was negotiated privately

◊ privatization noun selling a nationalized industry to private owners

◊ privatize verb to sell a nationalized industry to private owners

QUOTE management had offered to take the company private through a leveraged buyout for $825 million
Fortune

pro preposition for; pro tem = for the time being or temporarily; per pro = with the authority of; the secretary signed per pro the manager; pro forma =

invoice sent to a buyer before the goods are sent, so that payment can be made in advance *or* that business documents can be produced; **pro rata** = at a rate which varies according to the size or importance of something; **dividends are paid pro rata** = dividends are paid according to the number of shares held

PRO = PUBLIC RELATIONS OFFICER

probable *adjective* likely to happen; *he is trying to prevent the probable collapse of the company*

◊ **probably** *adverb* likely; *the president is probably going to retire next year; this store is probably the best in town for service*

probate *noun* proving legally that a document, especially a will, is valid; **the executor was granted probate** = the executor was told officially that the will was valid; **probate court** = court which examines wills to decide if they are valid

◊ **probation** *noun* period when a new worker is being tested before getting a permanent job; *he is on three months' probation;* **to take someone on probation**

◊ **probationary** *adjective* while someone is being tested; *a probationary period of three months; after the probationary period the company decided to offer him a permanent job*

problem *noun* thing to which it is difficult to find an answer; *the company suffers from cash flow problems or staff problems;* **to solve a problem** = to find an answer to a problem; *problem solving is a test of a good manager;* **problem area** = area of a company's work which is difficult to run; *overseas sales is one of our biggest problem areas*

QUOTE everyone blames the strong dollar for US trade problems, but they differ on what should be done

Duns Business Month

procedure *noun* way in which something is done; *to follow the proper procedure;* **this procedure is very irregular** = this is not the set way to do something; **accounting procedures** = set ways of preparing the statement of account of a company; **disciplinary procedure** = way of warning a worker that he is breaking the rules of a company; **complaints procedure** *or* **grievance procedure** = way of presenting complaints formally from a union to a management; *the union has followed the correct complaints procedure ;* **dismissal procedures** = correct way to dismiss someone, following the rules of the company

proceed *verb* to go on *or* to continue; *the negotiations are proceeding slowly;* **to proceed against someone** = to start a legal action against someone; **to proceed with something** = to go on doing something; *shall we proceed with the committee meeting?*

◊ **proceedings** *plural noun* **(a)** **conference proceedings** = written report of what has taken place at a conference **(b)** **legal proceedings** = legal action *or* lawsuit; **to take proceedings against someone;** *the court proceedings were adjourned;* **to institute proceedings against someone** = to start a legal action against someone

◊ **proceeds** *plural noun* **the proceeds of a sale** = money received from a sale after deducting expenses; *he sold his store and invested the proceeds in a computer repair business*

process 1 *noun* **(a)** **industrial processes** = processes involved in manufacturing products in factories; **decision-making processes** = ways in which decisions are reached **(b)** **work in process** = value of goods being manufactured which are not complete at the end of an accounting period **(c)** **the due process of law** = the formal work of a legal action **2** *verb* **(a)** **to process figures** = to sort out information to make it easily understood; *the sales figures are being processed by our finance department; data is being processed by our computer* **(b)** to deal with something in the usual routine way; *to process an insurance claim; orders are processed in our warehouse*

◊ **processing** *noun* **(a)** sorting of information; *processing of information or of statistics;* **batch processing** = computer system, where information is collected into batches before being loaded into the computer; **data processing** *or* **information processing** = selecting and examining data in a computer to produce information in a special form; **word processing** = working with words, using a computer to produce, check and change texts, reports, letters, etc. **(b)** **the processing of a claim for insurance** = putting a claim for insurance through the usual office routine in the insurance company; **order processing** = dealing with orders

◊ **processor** *noun* **word processor** = small computer which is used for working with words, to produce texts, reports, letters, etc.

produce 1 *noun* foodstuffs grown on the land; *home produce; agricultural produce* or *farm produce* **2** *verb* **(a)** to bring out; *he produced documents to prove his claim; the negotiators produced a new set of figures; the customs officer asked him to produce the relevant documents* **(b)** to make or to manufacture; *to produce cars* or *engines* or *books;* to mass-produce = to make large quantities of a product **(c)** to give an interest; *investments which produce about 10% per annum*

◊ **producer** *noun* person or company or country which manufactures; *country which is a producer of high quality watches; the company is a major car producer*

◊ **producing** *adjective* which produces; **producing capacity** = capacity to produce; **oil-producing country** = country which produces oil

product *noun* **(a)** thing which is made or manufactured; **basic product** = main product made from a raw material; **by-product** = secondary product made as a raw material is being processed; **end product** or **final product** or **finished product** = product made at the end of a production process **(b)** manufactured item for sale; **product advertising** = advertising a particular named product, not the company which makes it; **product analysis** = examining each separate product in a company's range to see why it sells or who buys it, etc.; **product design** = design of consumer products; **product development** = creating a new product or improving an existing product line to meet the needs of the market; **product engineer** = engineer in charge of the equipment for making a product; **product line** or **product range** = series of different products made by the same company which form a group (such as cars in different models, pens in different colors, etc.); **product management** = directing the making and selling of a product as an independent item; **product mix** = group of quite different products made by the same company **(c) gross national product (GNP)** = annual value of goods and services traded in a

country, including income from other countries

◊ **production** *noun* **(a)** showing something; **upon production of** = when something is shown; *the case will be released by the customs upon production of the relevant documents; goods can be exchanged only upon production of the sales slip* **(b)** making or manufacturing of goods for sale; *production will probably be held up by industrial action; we are hoping to speed up production by installing new machinery* ; **batch production** = production in batches; **domestic production** = production of goods within a particular country; **mass production** = manufacturing of large quantities of goods; *mass production of cars* or *of calculators;* **rate of production** or **production rate** = speed at which items are made; **production cost** = cost of making a product; **production department** = section of a company which deals with the making of the company's products; **production line** = system of making a product, where each item (such as a car) moves slowly through the factory with new sections added to it as it goes along; *he works on the production line; she is a production line worker;* **production manager** = person in charge of the production department; **production unit** = separate small group of workers producing a certain product

◊ **productive** *adjective* which produces; **productive capital** = capital which is invested to earn interest; **productive discussions** = useful discussions which lead to an agreement or decision

◊ **productively** *adverb* in a productive way

◊ **productivity** *noun* rate of output per worker or per machine in a factory; *bonus payments are linked to productivity; the company is aiming to increase productivity; productivity has fallen* or *risen since the company was taken over;* **productivity agreement** = agreement to pay a productivity bonus; **productivity bonus** = extra payments made to workers because of increased production; **productivity drive** = extra effort to increase productivity

profession *noun* **(a)** work which needs special skills learned over a period of time; *the CEO is an accountant by profession* **(b)** group of specialized workers; **the legal profession** = all lawyers; **the medical profession** = all doctors

◊ **professional** 1 *adjective* **(a)** referring to one of the professions; *the accountant sent in his bill for professional services; we had to ask our lawyer for professional advice on the contract;* a **professional person** = person who works in one of the professions (such as a lawyer, doctor, accountant); **professional qualifications** = documents showing that someone has successfully finished a course of study which allows him to work in one of the professions **(b)** expert *or* skilled; *her work is very professional; they did a very professional job in designing the new office* **(c)** doing work for money; *a professional tennis player;* he is a **professional troubleshooter** = he makes his living by helping companies to solve their problems **2** *noun* skilled person *or* person who does skilled work for money

proficiency *noun* skill *or* being capable of doing something; *she has a certificate of proficiency in English; to get the job he had to pass a proficiency test*

◊ **proficient** *adjective* capable of doing something well; *she is quite proficient in English*

profile *noun* brief description; *he asked for a company profile of the possible partners in the joint venture; the customer profile shows our average buyer to be male, aged 25-30, and employed in the service industries*

profit *noun* money gained from a sale which is more than the money spent; **clear profit** = profit after all expenses have been paid; *we made $6,000 clear profit on the deal;* **gross profit** = profit calculated as sales income less the cost of the goods sold; **net profit** = result where income from sales is larger than all expenditure; **operating profit** = result where sales from normal business activities are higher than the costs; **profit and loss statement** = statement of account for a company which shows expenditure and income balanced to show a final profit *or* loss; **profit margin** = percentage difference between sales income and the cost of sales; **profits tax** *or* **tax on profits** = tax to be paid on profits; **profit before taxes** *or* **pretax profit** = profit before any taxes have

been paid; **profit after taxes** = profit after taxes have been paid; **to take one's profit** = to sell shares at a higher price than was paid for them, rather than to keep them as an investment; **to show a profit** = to make a profit and state it in the company's statement of account; *we are showing a small profit for the first quarter;* **to make a profit** = to have more money as a result of a business deal; **to move into profit** = to start to make a profit; *the company is breaking even now, and expects to move into profit within the next two months;* **to sell at a profit** = to sell at a price which gives you a profit; **excess profit** = profit which is higher than what is thought to be normal; **excess profits tax** = tax on excess profits; **healthy profit** = large profit; **paper profit** = profit on an asset which has increased in value but has not been sold; *he is showing a paper profit of $25,000 on his investment*

◊ **profit center** *noun* person *or* department which is considered separately for the purposes of calculating a profit

◊ **profitability** *noun* **(a)** ability to make a profit **(b)** amount of profit made as a percentage of costs; **measurement of profitability** = way of calculating how profitable something is

◊ **profitable** *adjective* which makes a profit

◊ **profitably** *adverb* making a profit

◊ **profiteer** *noun* person who makes excessive profit, especially when goods are rationed *or* in short supply

◊ **profiteering** *noun* taking advantage of a situation where supply is very short in order to make excessive profit

◊ **profitsharing** *noun* arrangement where workers get a share of the profits of the company they work for; *the company offers a profitsharing plan*

◊ **profittaking** *noun* selling investments to realize the profit, rather than keeping them; *share prices fell under continued profittaking*

QUOTE because capital gains are not taxed and money taken out in profits and dividends is taxed, owners of businesses will be using accountants and tax experts to find loopholes in the law

Toronto Star

pro forma *noun* pro forma (invoice) = invoice sent to a buyer before the goods are sent, so that payment can be made or that business documents can be produced; *they sent us a pro forma*

program 1 *noun* **computer program** = instructions to a computer telling it how to do a particular piece of work; *to buy a word processing program; the finance department is running a new payroll program;* **program trading** = buying or selling stock or bonds according to a system which has been programmed into a computer **2** *verb* to write a program for a computer; **to program a computer** = to install a program in a computer; *the computer is programmed to print labels*
NOTE: **programming - programmed**

◊ **program** *noun* plan of things which will be done; *development program; research program; training program; to draw up a program of investment or an investment program*

◊ **programmable** *adjective* which can be programmed

◊ **programmer** *noun* **computer programmer** = person who writes computer programs

◊ **programming** *noun* **computer programming** = writing programs for computers; **programming engineer** = engineer in charge of programming a computer system; **programming language** = system of signs, letters and words used to instruct a computer

progress 1 *noun* movement of work forward; *to report on the progress of the work or of the negotiations;* **to make a progress report** = to report how work is going; **in progress** = which is being done but is not finished; *negotiations in progress; work in progress;* **progress payments** = payments made as each stage of a contract is completed; *the fifth progress payment is due in March* **2** *verb* to move forward or to go ahead; *the contract is progressing through various departments*

◊ **progressive** *adjective* which moves forward in stages; *progressive taxation*

prohibitive *adjective* with a price so high that you cannot afford to pay it; *the cost of redeveloping the product is prohibitive*

project *noun* (a) plan; *he has drawn up a project for developing new markets in Europe* (b) particular job which follows a plan; *we are just completing an engineering project in North Africa; the company will start work on the project next month* ; **project analysis** = examining all costs or

problems of a project before work on it is started; **project engineer** = engineer in charge of a project; **project manager** = manager in charge of a project

◊ **projected** *adjective* planned or expected; **projected sales** = forecast of sales; *projected sales in Europe next year should be over $1m*

◊ **projection** *noun* forecast of something which will happen in the future; *projection of profits for the next three years; the sales manager was asked to draw up sales projections for the next three years*

promise 1 *noun* pledge that you will do something; **to keep a promise** = to do what you said you would do; *he says he will pay next week, but he never keeps his promises;* **to go back on a promise** = not to do what you said you would do; *the management went back on its promise to increase salaries across the board;* **a promise to pay** = a promissory note **2** *verb* to pledge that you will do something; *they promised to pay the last installment next week; the personnel manager promised he would look into the grievances of the office staff*

◊ **promissory note** *noun* document stating that someone promises to pay an amount of money on a certain date

promote *verb* (a) to give someone a more important job; *he was promoted from salesman to sales manager* (b) to advertise; **to promote a new product** = to increase the sales of a new product by a sales campaign *or* TV commercials *or* free gifts (c) **to promote a new company** = to organize the setting up of a new company

◊ **promoter** *noun* **company promoter** = person who organizes the setting up of a new company or corporation

◊ **promotion** *noun* (a) moving up to a more important job; *promotion chances or promotion prospects; he ruined his chances of promotion when he argued with the CEO;* **to earn promotion** = to work hard and efficiently and so be promoted (b) **promotion of a company** = setting up a new company (c) **promotion of a product** = selling a new product by publicity *or* sales campaign *or* TV commercials *or* free gifts; *promotion budget; promotion team; sales promotion; special promotion*

◊ **promotional** *adjective* used in an advertising campaign; *the advertisers are using balloons as promotional* *material;* promotional budget = forecast cost of promoting a new product

prompt *adjective* rapid *or* done immediately; *prompt service; prompt reply to a letter;* prompt payment = payment made rapidly; **prompt supplier** = supplier who delivers orders rapidly

◊ **promptly** *adverb* rapidly; *he replied to my letter very promptly*

> QUOTE they keep shipping costs low and can take advantage of quantity discounts and other allowances for prompt payment
> *Duns Business Month*

proof *noun* evidence which shows that something is true; **documentary proof** = evidence in the form of a document; **proof of purchase** = paper (sales ticket, label from a can) which shows that a purchaser has purchased an item, and can be used to claim a refund

◊ **-proof** *suffix* which prevents something from getting in *or* getting out *or* harming; *dustproof cover; inflation-proof pension; soundproof studio*

property *noun* **(a)** personal property = things which belong to a person; *the storm caused considerable damage to personal property; the management is not responsible for property left in the hotel rooms* **(b)** land and buildings; *property tax; damage to property* or *property damage; the commercial property market is booming;* the office has been bought by a property company = by a company which buys buildings to lease them; **property developer** = person who buys old buildings *or* empty land and builds new buildings for sale or rent; **property income** = income from rents; **private property** = property which belongs to a particular person and not to the public **(c)** a building; *we have several properties for sale in the downtown area*

proportion *noun* part (of a total); *a proportion of the pretax profit is set aside for contingencies; only a small proportion of our sales comes from retail stores;* in proportion to = showing how something is related to something else; *profits went up in proportion to the fall in overhead costs; sales in Europe are small in proportion to those in the US*

◊ **proportional** *adjective* directly related; *the increase in profit is proportional to reduction in overhead*

◊ **proportionately** *adverb* in proportion

proposal *noun* suggestion *or* thing suggested; *to make a proposal or to put forward a proposal to the board;* the committee turned down the proposal = the committee refused to accept what was suggested

◊ **propose** *verb* **(a)** to suggest that something should be done; **to propose a motion** = to ask a meeting to vote for a motion and explain the reasons for this; **to propose someone as president** = to ask a group to vote for someone to become president **(b) to propose to** = to say that you intend to do something; *I propose to repay the loan at $20 a month*

◊ **proposer** *noun* person who proposes a motion at a meeting

◊ **proposition** *noun* commercial deal which is suggested; **it will never be a commercial proposition** = it is not likely to make a profit

proprietary *adjective* **(a)** product (such as a medicine) which is made and owned by a private company; **proprietary drug** = drug which is made by a particular company and marketed under a brand name, sold by retailers without a prescription from a doctor **(b)** **proprietary company** = non-operating parent company formed to invest in the securities of other companies so as to control them

◊ **proprietor** *noun* owner; *the proprietor of a hotel* or *a hotel proprietor*

pro rata *adjective & adverb* at an amount which varies according to the rate applied; *a pro rata payment; to pay someone pro rata*

prosecute *verb* to bring (someone) to court to answer a criminal charge; *he was prosecuted for embezzlement*

◊ **prosecution** *noun* **(a)** act of bringing someone to court to answer a charge; *his prosecution for embezzlement* **(b)** party who prosecutes someone; *the costs of the case will be borne by the prosecution* ; **prosecution counsel** *or* **counsel for the prosecution** = lawyer acting for the prosecution

prospect *noun* **(a)** prospects = possibilities for the future; **his job prospects are good** = he is very likely to find a job; **prospects for the market** *or* **market prospects are worse than**

those of last year = sales in the market are likely to be lower than they were last year **(b)** possibility that something will happen; *there is no prospect of negotiations coming to an end soon* **(c)** person who may become a customer; *the salesmen were looking out for possible prospects*

◊ **prospective** *adjective* which may happen in the future; *a prospective buyer* = someone who may buy in the future; *there is no shortage of prospective buyers for the computer*

◊ **prospectus** *noun* **(a)** document which gives information to attract buyers *or* customers; *the real estate company sent us a prospectus on vacation homes in Florida* **(b)** first prospectus = document which gives information about a company whose shares are being sold to the public for the first time
NOTE: plural is **prospectuses**

prosperous *adjective* successful *or* thriving; *a prosperous storekeeper; a prosperous town*

◊ **prosperity** *noun* being successful; *in times of prosperity* = when people are successful

protect *verb* to defend something against harm; *the workers are protected from unfair dismissal by government legislation; the computer is protected by a plastic cover; the cover is supposed to protect the machine from dust;* to protect an industry by imposing trade barriers = to stop a local industry from being hit by foreign competition by stopping foreign products from being imported

◊ **protection** *noun* thing which protects; *the legislation offers no protection to part-time workers*; consumer protection = protecting consumers against unfair *or* illegal traders

◊ **protective** *adjective* which protects; protective tariff = tariff which tries to ban imports to prevent foreign competition with local products; protective cover = cover which protects a machine

pro tem *adverb* temporarily *or* for a time

protest 1 *noun* **(a)** statement *or* action to show that you do not approve of something; *to make a protest against high prices;* in protest of = showing that you do not approve of something; *the workers walked off their jobs in protest of the low pay offer;* to do

something under protest = to do something, but say that you do not approve of it **(b)** official document which proves that a bill of exchange has not been paid **2** *verb* **(a)** to say that you do not approve of something; *the importers are protesting the ban on luxury goods* **(b)** to protest a bill = to draw up a document to prove that a bill of exchange has not been paid

prototype *noun* first model of a new machine before it goes into production; *prototype car or prototype plane; the company is showing the prototype of the new model at the trade show*

provide *verb* **(a)** to provide for = to allow for something which may happen in the future; *the contract provides for an annual increase in charges; $10,000 of expenses have been provided for in the budget* **(b)** to put money aside in a balance sheet to cover expenditure *or* loss in the future; *$25,000 is provided against bad debts* **(c)** to provide someone with something = to supply something to someone; *each rep is provided with a company car; staff uniforms are provided by the hotel*

◊ **provided that** *or* **providing** *conjunction* on condition that; *the goods will be delivered next week provided or providing the drivers are not on strike*

◊ **provident** *adjective* which provides benefits in case of illness *or* old age, etc.; *a provident fund; a provident society*

province *noun* **(a)** large division of a country; *the provinces of Canada* **(b)** the provinces = parts of a country away from the main capital city; *there are fewer retail outlets in the provinces than in the capital*

◊ **provincial** *adjective* referring to a province *or* to the provinces; *a provincial government; a provincial branch of a national bank*

provision *noun* **(a)** to make provision for = to see that something is allowed for in the future; *there is no provision or no provision has been made in the plans for parking at the office building* = the plans do not include space for cars to park **(b)** money put aside in a balance sheet in case it is needed in the future; *the bank has made a $2m provision for bad debts* **(c)** legal condition; *we have made provision to this effect* = we have put into the contract terms which will make this work **(d) provisions =** food

◊ **provisional** *adjective* temporary *or* not final or permanent; *provisional forecast of sales; provisional budget; they telexed their provisional acceptance of the contract*

◊ **provisionally** *adverb* temporarily; *the contract has been accepted provisionally*

proviso *noun* condition in a contract; *we are signing the contract with the proviso that the terms can be discussed again after six months*

proxy *noun* **(a)** document which gives someone the power to act on behalf of someone else; *to sign by proxy; proxy vote =* vote made by proxy; *the proxy votes were all in favor of the board's recommendation* **(b)** person who acts on behalf of someone else; *to act as proxy for someone*

P.S. *noun* = POST SCRIPTUM additional note at the end of a letter; *did you read the P.S. at the end of the letter?*

pt = PINT

ptas = PESETAS

public 1 *adjective* **(a)** referring to all the people in general; **public holiday =** day when all workers rest and enjoy themselves instead of working; **public image =** idea which the people have of a company *or* a person; *the senator is trying to improve his public image;* **public transportation =** transportation (such as buses, trains) which is used by any member of the public **(b)** referring to the federal or state government; **public expenditure =** spending of money by a local *or* national government; **public finance =** the raising of money by governments (by taxes or borrowing) and the spending of it; **public funds =** government money available for expenditure; **public ownership =** situation where an industry is nationalized **(c) the company is going public =** the company is going to place some of its shares for sale on the stock market so that anyone can buy them **2** *noun* **the public** *or* **the general public =** the people; **in public =** in front of everyone; *in public he said that the company would soon be in profit, but in private he was less optimistic*

◊ **public-address system (PA system)** *noun* microphone and loudspeaker used to broadcast information to a large audience; *they called the little girl's parents over the store's public address system*

◊ **public relations (PR)** *plural noun* keeping good relations between a company *or* a group and the public so that people know what the company is doing and can approve of it; *a public relations man; he works in public relations; a public relations firm handles all our publicity;* **a public relations exercise =** a campaign to improve public relations

◊ **public sector** *noun* nationalized industries and services; *a report on wage increases in the public sector or on public sector wage settlements*

◊ **public-service** *adjective* referring to the good of the general public; **public-service advertising =** advertising on behalf of charities, such as the Red Cross; **public-service broadcasting =** broadcasting educational programs, appeals for charities, etc.

publication *noun* **(a)** making something public; *the publication of the latest trade figures* **(b)** printed document which is to be sold *or* given to the public; *he asked the library for a list of government publications;* **the company has six business publications =** the company publishes six magazines or newspapers referring to business

publicity *noun* attracting the attention of the public to products or services by mentioning them in the media; **publicity agency =** office which organizes publicity for companies who do not have publicity departments; **publicity budget =** money allowed for expenditure on publicity; **publicity campaign =** period when planned publicity takes place; **publicity copy =** text of an advertisement before it is printed; **publicity department =** section of a company which organizes the company's publicity; **publicity expenditure =** money spent on publicity; **publicity manager =** person in charge of a publicity department; **publicity matter =** sheets *or* posters *or* leaflets used for publicity

◊ **publicize** *verb* to attract people's attention to a product for sale *or* a service *or* an entertainment; *the campaign is intended to publicize the services of the tourist board; we are trying to* *publicize our products by advertisements on buses*

publish *verb* to have a document (such as a catalog *or* book *or* magazine *or* newspaper) written and printed and then sell *or* give it to the public; *the society publishes its list of members annually; the government has not published the figures on which its proposals are based; the company publishes six magazines for the business market*
◊ **publisher** *noun* person *or* company which publishes

pull off *verb informal* to succeed in negotiating a deal
◊ **pull out** *verb* to stop being part of a deal *or* agreement; *our Australian partners pulled out of the contract*
◊ **pull ticket** *noun* list of items in an order, listed according to where they can be found in the warehouse

pump priming *noun* government investment in new projects which it hopes will benefit the economy

punched card *noun* card with coded sequences of holes in it which a computer can read and store as information

purchase 1 *noun* thing which has been bought; **to make a purchase** = to buy something; **purchase book** = records of purchases; **purchase ledger** = book in which expenditure is noted; **purchase order** = official order made out by a purchasing department for goods which a company wants to buy; *we cannot supply you without a purchase order number;* **purchase price** = price paid for something; **bulk purchase** *or* **quantity purchase** = buying of large quantities of goods at low prices; **cash purchase** = purchase made in cash **2** *verb* to buy; **to purchase something for cash** = to pay cash for something
◊ **purchaser** *noun* person *or* company which purchases; **the company is looking for a purchaser** = the company is trying to find someone who will buy it; *the company has found a buyer*
◊ **purchasing** *noun* buying; **purchasing department** = section of a company which deals with buying of stock, raw materials, equipment, etc.; **purchasing manager** = head of a purchasing department; **purchasing officer** = person in a company *or* organization who

is responsible for buying stock, raw materials, equipment, etc.; **purchasing power** = quantity of goods which can be bought by a group of people *or* with an amount of money; *the decline in the purchasing power of the dollar;* **central purchasing** = purchasing organized by the main office for all departments or branches

purpose *noun* aim *or* plan; **we need the invoice for tax purposes** = to be used in filing a tax return

put 1 *noun* **put option** = right to sell stock at a certain price at a certain date **2** *verb* to place *or* to fix; **the statement of account puts the stock value at $10,000** = it states that the value of the stock is $10,000; **to put a proposal to the vote** = to ask people to vote for *or* against a proposal; **to put a proposal to the board** = to ask the board to consider a suggestion
NOTE: **putting - put**
◊ **put down** *verb* **(a)** to make a deposit; *to put down money on a house* **(b)** to write an item in a ledger *or* an account book; *to put down a figure for expenses*
◊ **put in** *verb* **to put an ad in a paper** = to have an ad printed in a newspaper; **to put in a bid for something** = to offer (usually in writing) to buy something; **to put in an estimate for something** = to give someone a written calculation of the probable costs of carrying out a job; **to put in a claim for damage** = to ask an insurance company to pay for damage; **the union put in a 6% wage claim** = the union asked for a 6% increase in wages
◊ **put into** *verb* **to put money into a business** = to invest money in a business
◊ **put off** *verb* **(a)** to arrange for something to take place later than planned; *the meeting was put off for two weeks; he asked if we could put the visit off until tomorrow* **(b)** to fail to give attention to; *his business will fail if he continues to put off his previous debts*
◊ **put on** *verb* **to put an item on the agenda** = to list an item for discussion at a meeting; **to put an embargo on trade** = to forbid trade; **property shares put on gains of 10%-15%** = shares in property companies increased in value by 10%-15%
◊ **put out** *verb* to publish; *the company puts out a catalog twice a hear*
◊ **put up** *verb* **(a)** to provide *or* to supply; **who put up the money for the store?** = who provided the investment money for

the store to open?; **to put something up for sale** = to advertise that something is for sale; *when he retired he decided to put his big house up for sale* (b) to increase *or* to make higher; *the store has put up all its prices by 5%*

Qq

quadruplicate *noun* **in quadruplicate** = with the original and three copies; *the invoices are printed in quadruplicate*

qualification *noun* (a) proof that you have completed a specialized course of study; *to have the right qualifications for the job; professional qualifications* = necessary training and certification for working in a particular profession (b) **period of qualification** = time which has to pass before someone qualifies for something
◊ **qualify** *verb* (a) **to qualify for** = to be in the right position for *or* to be entitled to; *the company does not qualify for a government grant; she qualifies for unemployment pay* (b) **to qualify as** = to follow a specialized course and pass examinations so that you can do a certain job; *she has qualified as an accountant* (c) **the auditors have qualified their audit** = the auditors have found something in the financial statement of the company which they do not agree with, and have noted it
◊ **qualified** *adjective* (a) having passed special examinations in a subject; *she is a qualified accountant; we have appointed a qualified designer to supervise the new factory project;* **highly qualified** = with exceptional training and experience; *all our staff are highly qualified; they employ twenty-six highly qualified engineers* (b) with some reservations *or* conditions; *qualified acceptance of a contract; the plan received qualified approval from the board* (c) **qualified opinion** = auditors' report which includes description of something in the financial statement of the company that the auditors do not agree with
◊ **qualifying** *adjective* (a) **qualifying period** = time which has to pass before something becomes eligible for a grant *or* subsidy, etc.; *there is a six-month qualifying period before you can get a grant from the state government* (b)

qualifying shares = number of shares which you need to own to get a bonus issue *or* to be a director of a corporation, etc.

quality *noun* (a) what something is like *or* how good or bad something is; *good quality or bad quality;* **we sell only quality farm produce** = we sell only farm produce of the best quality; *there is a market for good quality secondhand computers;* **high quality** *or* **top quality** = very best quality; *the store specializes in high quality imported items;* **quality circles** = informal discussions on the shop floor where workers and managers discuss ways of improving product quality (b) **quality control** = checking that a certain standard of quality is maintained; **quality controller** = person who checks the quality of a product

quantify *verb* **to quantify the effect of something** = to represent the effect of something using numbers; *it is impossible to quantify the effect of the new legislation on our sales volume*
◊ **quantifiable** *adjective* which can be quantified; *the effect of the change in the discount structure is not quantifiable*

quantity *noun* (a) amount *or* number of items; *a small quantity of illegal drugs; he bought a large quantity of spare parts* (b) large amount; *the company offers a discount for quantity purchase;* **quantity discount** = discount given to a customer who buys large quantities of goods

quart *noun* measure of liquids (= 2 pints)

quarter *noun* (a) one of four equal parts; **a quarter of a gallon** *or* **a quarter gallon** = 250 milliliters; **a quarter of an hour** = 15 minutes; **three-quarters** = 75%; *three-quarters of the staff are less than thirty years old; he paid only a quarter of the list price* (b) period of three months; **first quarter** *or* **second**

quarter or **third quarter** or **fourth quarter** or **last quarter** = periods of three months from January to the end of March or from April to the end of June or from July to the end of September or from October to the end of the year; *the installments are payable at the end of each quarter; the first quarter's rent is payable in advance;* quarter day = day which begins a quarter, when rents or fees, etc. should be paid **(c)** 25-cent coin

◊ **quarterly** *adjective* & *adverb* happening every three months or happening four times a year; *there is a quarterly charge for electricity; the bank sends us a quarterly statement; we agreed to pay the rent quarterly or on a quarterly basis*

quartile *noun* one of three figures, below which 25%, 50% or 75% of a total falls

quasi- *prefix* almost or which seems like; *a quasi-official body*

quay *noun* wharf with facilities for loading and unloading ships; **price ex quay** = price of goods after they have been unloaded, not including transport from the harbor

◊ **quayage** *noun* charge made for using a quay

query 1 *noun* **(a)** question; *the chief accountant had to answer a mass of queries from the auditors* **(b)** inquiry from a potential customer about a product or service **2** *verb* to ask a question about something or to suggest that something may be wrong; *the shareholders queried the payments to the chairman's son*

question 1 *noun* **(a)** statement which needs an answer; *the CEO refused to answer questions about layoffs; the market research team prepared a series of questions to test the public's reactions to color and price* **(b)** problem; *he raised the question of moving to less expensive offices; the main question is that of cost; the board discussed the question of pension payments* **2** *verb* **(a)** to ask questions; *the police questioned the accounts staff for four hours; she questioned the chairman on the company's investment policy* **(b)** to query or to suggest that something may be wrong; *we all question how accurate the computer printout is*

◊ **questionnaire** *noun* printed list of questions, especially used in market research; *to send out a questionnaire to test the opinions of users of the system; to answer* or *to fill in a questionnaire about vacations abroad*

quick *adjective* fast or not taking any time; *the company made a quick recovery; he is looking for a quick return on his investments; we are hoping for a quick sale*

◊ **quickly** *adverb* rapidly or without taking much time; *the sale of the company went through quickly; the accountant quickly looked through the pile of invoices*

quiet *adjective* calm or not excited; *the market is very quiet; currency exchanges were quieter after the government's statement on exchange rates*

quit *verb* to resign or to leave (a job); *he quit after an argument with the vice-president; several of the managers are quitting to set up their own company* NOTE: **quitting - quit**

◊ **quitclaim** *noun* deed by which someone renounces all interest in a property

quite *adverb* **(a)** really or truly; *he is quite a good salesman; she can type quite fast; sales are quite satisfactory in the first quarter* **(b)** very or completely; *he is quite capable of running the department alone; the company is quite possibly going to be sold* **(c)** quite a few or quite a lot = many; *quite a few of our sales reps are women; quite a lot of orders come in the preChristmas period*

quorum *noun* minimum number of people who have to be present at a meeting to make it valid; **to have a quorum** = to have enough people present for a meeting to go ahead; *do we have a quorum?*

quota *noun* fixed amount of something which is required; **import quota** = fixed quantity of a particular type of goods which the government says is to be imported; *the government has imposed a quota on the importation of cars; the quota on imported cars has been lifted;* **quota system** = system where imports or supplies are regulated by fixing maximum amounts; **to arrange**

distribution through a quota system = to arrange distribution by allowing each distributor only a certain number of items

QUOTE Canada agreed to a new duty-free quota of 600,000 tons a year

Globe and Mail (Toronto)

quote 1 *verb* **(a)** to repeat precisely words used by someone else; to repeat a reference number; *he quoted figures from the annual report; in reply please quote this number; when making a complaint please quote the batch number printed on the box; he replied, quoting the number of the account* **(b)** to estimate *or* to say what costs may be; *to quote a price for supplying stationery; their prices are always quoted in dollars; he quoted me a price of $1,026; can you quote for supplying 20,000 envelopes?* **2** *noun informal* estimate of how much something will cost; *to give someone a quote for supplying computers; we have asked for quotes for remodeling the store; his quote was the lowest of three; we accepted the lowest quote*

◇ **quotation** *noun* **(a)** estimate of how much something will cost; *they sent in their quotation for the job; to ask for quotations for remodeling the store; his quotation was much lower than all the others; we accepted the lowest quotation* **(b)** quotation on a stock exchange *or* stock exchange quotation = listing of the price of a share on a stock exchange; *the corporation is going for a quotation on a stock exchange* = it has applied to a stock exchange to have its shares listed; *we are seeking a stock market quotation*

◇ **quoted** *adjective* quoted company = company whose shares can be bought *or* sold on a stock exchange; quoted shares = shares which can be bought *or* sold on a stock exchange

qty = QUANTITY

qwerty *or* **QWERTY** *noun* qwerty keyboard = English language keyboard for a typewriter *or* computer, where the first letters are Q-W-E-R-T-Y; *the computer has a normal qwerty keyboard*

Rr

R&D = RESEARCH AND DEVELOPMENT *the R&D department; the company spends millions on R&D*

rack *noun* **(a)** frame to hold items for display; *card rack; display rack; magazine rack;* rack jobber = wholesaler who sells goods by putting them on racks in retail stores **(b)** rack rent = very high rent

racket *noun* illegal deal which makes a lot of money; *he runs a cut-price ticket racket*

◇ **racketeer** *noun* person who runs a racket

◇ **racketeering** *noun* crime of carrying on an illegal business to make money

raid *noun* dawn raid = buying large quantities of a company's stock at the beginning of a day's trading; bear raid = selling large quantities of a company's stock to try to bring down prices

◇ **raider** *noun* company which buys stock of another company to try to gain a controlling interest

rail *noun* railroad *or* system of travel using trains; *six million commuters travel to work by rail each day; we ship all our goods by rail; rail travelers are complaining about rising fares; rail travel is cheaper than air travel*

◇ **railhead** *noun* end of a railroad line; *the goods will be sent to the railhead by truck*

◇ **railroad** *or* **railway** *noun* transportation system using trains to carry passengers and goods; *he works for a midwestern railroad; a railroad line*

raise 1 *noun* increase in salary; *he asked the boss for a raise; she is pleased - she got her raise* **2** *verb* **(a)** to bring to attention *or* to bring forward for consideration; *to raise a question or a point at a meeting; in answer to the questions raised by Mr. Smith; the chairman tried to prevent the question of layoffs from being raised*

(b) to increase *or* to make higher; *the government has raised the tax levels; air fares will be raised on June 1; the company raised its dividend by 10%; when the company raised its prices, it lost half of its share of the market* **(c)** to obtain (money) *or* to organize (a loan); *the company is trying to raise the capital to fund its expansion program; the government raises more money by indirect taxation than by direct; where will he raise the money from to start up his business?*

rake in *verb* to gather together; **to rake in cash** *or* **to rake it in** = to make a lot of money

◊ **rake-off** *noun* commission; *the group gets a rake-off on all the company's sales; he received a $100,000 rake-off for introducing the new business* NOTE: plural is **rake-offs**

rally 1 *noun* rise in price when the trend has been downward; *shares staged a rally on the New York Stock Exchange; after a brief rally shares fell back to a new low* **2** *verb* to rise in price, when the trend has been downward; *shares rallied with the news of the budget approval*

ramp *noun* **loading ramp** = raised platform which makes it easier to load goods onto a truck

random *adjective* done without making any special choice; **random check** = examination of items taken from a group without any special choice; **random error** = computer error which has no standard explanation; **random sample** = sample for testing taken without any pattern of choice; **random sampling** = choosing samples for testing without any standard for selection; **at random** = without special reason for choice; *the chairman picked out two salesmen's reports at random*

range 1 *noun* **(a)** series of items from which the customer can choose; *we offer a wide range of sizes or range of styles; their range of products or product range is too narrow; we have the most modern range of models on the market* **(b)** variation from small to large; *I am looking for something in the $20 - $30 price range; we make shoes in a wide range of prices* **(c)** group *or* series; *this falls within the company's range of activities* **2** *verb* to vary *or* to be different; *the company sells products*

ranging from the cheap down-market pens to imported luxury items; the corporation's salary scale ranges from $15,000 for a trainee to $500,000 for the president; their activities range from mining in the U.S. to computer servicing in Scotland

rank 1 *noun* position in a company *or* an organization; *all managers are of equal rank;* **in rank order** = in order according to position of importance **2** *verb* **(a)** to classify in order of importance; *candidates are ranked in order of appearance* **(b)** to be in a certain position; *the nonvoting shares rank equally with the voting shares;* **all managers rank equally** = all managers have the same status in the company

◊ **rank and file** *noun* ordinary people forming a large part of some group; *the rank and file of the union membership; the decision was not liked by the rank and file;* **rank-and-file members** = ordinary members, as distinguished from those in positions of leadership

◊ **ranking** *adjective* in a certain position; **high-ranking official; he is the top-ranking** *or* **the senior-ranking official in the delegation** = the member of the delegation who occupies the highest official post

rapid *adjective* fast *or* quick; **we offer 5% discount for rapid settlement** = we take 5% off the price if the customer pays quickly

◊ **rapidly** *adverb* quickly *or* fast; *the company rapidly ran up debts of over $1m; the new clothes store rapidly increased its sales*

rare *adjective* not common; *experienced salesmen are rare these days; it is rare to find a small business with good cash flow*

◊ **rarely** *adverb* not often; *the company's shares are rarely sold on the Stock Exchange; the chairman is rarely in his office on Friday afternoons*

rata *see* PRO RATA

rate 1 *noun* **(a)** money charged for time worked *or* work completed; **fixed rate** = charge which cannot be changed; **flat rate** = charge which always stays the same; *a flat-rate increase of 10%; we pay a flat rate for electricity each quarter; he is paid a flat rate of $2 per* *thousand;* **full rate =** full charge, with no reductions; **the going rate =** the usual *or* the current rate of payment; **the market rate =** normal price in the market; *we pay the going rate or the market rate for typists; the going rate for offices is $10 per square foot;* **reduced rate =** specially cheap charge; **rate card =** document showing the rates charged for advertising in a newspaper or magazine **(b) discount rate =** percentage taken by a bank when it buys bills; **insurance rates =** amount of premium which has to be paid per $1000 of insurance; **interest rate** *or* **rate of interest =** percentage charge for borrowing money; **rate of return =** amount of interest *or* dividend which comes from an investment, shown as a percentage of the money invested **(c) bank base rates =** basic rate of interest which a bank uses to calculate the actual rate of interest on loans to customers; **cross rate =** exchange rate between two currencies expressed in a third currency; **exchange rate** *or* **rate of exchange =** rate at which one currency is exchanged for another; *what is today's rate or the current rate for the dollar?;* **to calculate costs on a fixed exchange rate =** to calculate costs on an exchange rate which does not change; **forward rate =** rate for purchase of foreign currency at a fixed price for delivery at a later date; **freight rates =** charges for transporting goods; **night rate =** discounted telephone calls at night **(d)** amount *or* number *or* speed compared with something else; *the rate of increase in layoffs; the rate of absenteeism or the absenteeism rate always increases in warm weather;* **birth rate =** number of children born per 1,000 of the population; **call rate =** number of calls which a salesman makes during a certain period of time; **depreciation rate =** rate at which an asset is depreciated each year in the company statement of account; **error rate =** number of mistakes per thousand entries *or* per page, etc; **rate of sales =** speed at which units are sold **2** *verb* **to rate someone highly =** to value someone *or* to think someone is very good

ratify *verb* to approve officially; *the agreement has to be ratified by the board*

◇ **ratification** *noun* official approval; *the agreement has to go to the board for ratification*

rating *noun* **(a) credit rating =** evaluation of a customer's ability to repay a loan; **merit rating =** judging how well a worker does his work, so that he can be paid according to merit; **performance rating =** judging how well a share *or* a company has performed **(b) ratings =** estimated number of people who watch TV programs; *the show is high in the ratings, which means it will attract good publicity*

ratio *noun* proportion *or* quantity of something compared to something else; *the ratio of successes to failures; our product outsells theirs by a ratio of two to one;* **price/earnings ratio (P/E ratio) =** comparison between the market price of a share and the current dividend it produces; *the shares sell at a P/E ratio of 7*

ration *verb* to allow someone only a certain amount (of food *or* money); *to ration investment capital or to ration funds for investment;* **to ration mortgages =** to make only a certain amount of money available for house mortgages, and so restrict the number of mortgages which can be given; *mortgages are rationed for first-time buyers*

◇ **rationing** *noun* allowing only a certain amount of something to be sold; *there may be a period of food rationing this winter; there were periods of gasoline rationing in the early 1970s*

rationale *noun* set of reasons for doing something; *I do not understand the rationale behind the decision to sell the warehouse*

rationalization *noun* explanation *or* interpretation made in rational terms

◇ **rationalize** *verb* explain *or* interpret on rational grounds; *he tried to rationalize to the boss about why he had been late for work*

rat race *noun* competition for success in business *or* in a career; *he decided to get out of the rat race and buy a small farm*

raw *adjective* in the original state *or* not processed; **raw data =** data as it is put into a computer, without being analyzed; **raw materials =** substances which have not been manufactured (such as wool, wood, sand)

QUOTE it makes sense for them to produce goods for sale back home in the US from plants in Britain where raw materials are relatively cheap
Duns Business Month

re *preposition* about *or* concerning *or* referring to; *re your inquiry of May 29; re: Smith's memo of yesterday; re: the agenda for the annual meeting*

re- *prefix* again

reach *verb* (a) to arrive at a place *or* at a point; *the plane reaches Hong Kong at noon; sales reached $1m in the first four months of the year; I did not reply because your letter never reached me* (b) to come to; **to reach an agreement =** to agree; **to reach an accommodation with creditors =** to agree on terms for a settlement with creditors; **to reach a decision =** to decide; *the two parties reached an agreement over the terms for the contract; the board reached a decision about closing the factory*

react *verb* **to react to =** to do *or* to say something in reply to what someone has done *or* said; *shares reacted sharply to the fall in the exchange rate; how will the chairman react when we tell him the news?*

◊ **reaction** *noun* change *or* action in reply to something said or done; *the reaction of the shares to the news of the takeover bid*

read *verb* to look at printed words and understand them; *the terms and conditions are printed in very small letters so that they are difficult to read; has the CEO read your report on sales in India?; can the computer read this information?* = can the computer take in this information and understand it or analyze it?

◊ **readable** *adjective* which can be read; **machine-readable codes =** sets of signs or letters (such as bar codes) which can be read and understood by a computer; **the data has to be presented in computer-readable form =** in a form which a computer can read

readjust *verb* to adjust again; *to readjust prices to take account of the rise in the costs of raw materials; bond prices readjusted quickly to the news of the devaluation*

◊ **readjustment** *noun* act of readjusting; *a readjustment in pricing; after the devaluation there was a period of readjustment in the exchange rates*

readvertise *verb* to advertise again; **to readvertise a job opening =** to put in a second advertisement for a vacant position; *all the candidates failed the test, so we will just have to readvertise*

◊ **readvertisement** *noun* second advertisement for a vacant position

ready *adjective* (a) fit to be used *or* to be sold; *the order will be ready for delivery next week; the driver had to wait because the shipment was not ready;* **make-ready time =** time to get a machine ready to start production (b) **ready cash =** money which is immediately available for payment; *these items find a ready sale in the Middle East =* these items sell rapidly *or* easily in the Middle East

◊ **ready-made** *or* **ready-to-wear** *adjective* (clothes) which are mass-produced, not made for each customer personally; *the ready-to-wear trade has suffered from foreign competition*

real *adjective* (a) genuine *or* true *or* not an imitation; *his case is made of real leather or he has a real leather case; that car is a real bargain at $300;* **real income** *or* **real wages =** income which is available for spending, calculated taking inflation into account; **in real terms =** actually *or* really; *prices have gone up by 3% but with inflation running at 5% that is a fall in real terms* (b) **real time =** time when a computer is working on the processing of data while the problem to which the data refers is actually taking place; **real-time system =** computer system where data is inputted directly into the computer which automatically processes it to produce information which can be used immediately (c) **real estate =** property (in the form of land or buildings); *he made his money from real estate deals in the 1970s;* **real estate agent =** person who sells property for customers; **the real estate market =** buying and selling real estate

◊ **really** *adverb* in fact; *the company is really making an acceptable profit; the office building really belongs to the chairman's father; the store is really a general store, though it does carry some books*

◊ **realtor** *noun* real estate agent who belongs to the National Association of Realtors, an organization that promotes professional ethics in real estate sales

◊ **realty** *noun* property *or* real estate

QUOTE on top of the cost of real estate, the investment in inventory and equipment to open a typical warehouse comes to around $5 million
Duns Business Month

realize *verb* (a) to understand clearly; *he soon realized the meeting was going to vote against his proposal; the small storekeepers realized that the supermarket would take away some of their trade; when she went into the manager's office she did not realize she was going to be promoted* (b) to make something become real; **to realize a project** *or* **a plan** = to put a project *or* a plan into action (c) to sell for cash; *to realize property or assets; the sale realized $100,000*

◊ **realizable** *adjective* **realizable assets** = assets which can be sold for cash

◊ **realization** *noun* (a) gradual understanding; *the chairman's realization that he was going to be outvoted* (b) making real; *the realization of a project* = putting a project into action; *the plan moved a stage nearer realization when the contracts were signed* (c) realization of assets = selling of assets for cash

reapply *verb* to apply again; *when he saw that the job had still not been filled, he reapplied for it*

◊ **reapplication** *noun* second application

reappoint *verb* to appoint someone again; *he was reappointed chairman for another three-year period*

◊ **reappointment** *noun* being reappointed

reason *noun* explanation why something has happened; *the airline gave no reason for the plane's late arrival; the personnel manager asked him for the reason why he was late again; the chairman was asked for his reasons for closing the factory*

◊ **reasonable** *adjective* (a) sensible *or* just *or* rational; *the manager of the store was very reasonable when she tried to explain that she had left her credit cards at home;* **no reasonable offer refused** = we will accept any offer which is not extremely low (b) moderate *or* not expensive; *the restaurant offers good food at reasonable prices*

reassess *verb* to assess again

◊ **reassessment** *noun* new assessment

reassign *verb* to assign again

◊ **reassignment** *noun* new assignment

reassure *verb* (a) to make someone calm *or* less worried; *the markets were reassured by the Treasury Secretary's statement on import controls; the manager tried to reassure her that she would not lose her job* (b) to reinsure *or* to spread the risk of an insurance by asking another insurance company to cover part of it and receive part of the premium

◊ **reassurance** *noun* making someone calm

rebate *noun* (a) reduction in the amount of money to be paid; *to offer a 10% rebate on selected goods* (b) money returned to someone because he has paid too much; *he got a tax rebate at the end of the year*

rebound *verb* to go back up again quickly; *the market rebounded with the news of the government's decision*

recd = RECEIVED

receipt 1 *noun* (a) paper showing that money has been paid *or* that something has been received; *customs receipt; rent receipt; receipt for items purchased; please produce your receipt if you want to exchange items;* **receipt book** *or* **book of receipts** = book of blank receipts to be filled in when purchases are made (b) act of receiving something; **to acknowledge receipt of a letter** = to write to say that you have received a letter; *we acknowledge receipt of your letter of June 15; goods will be supplied within thirty days of receipt of order; invoices are payable within thirty days of receipt; on receipt of the notification, the company lodged an appeal* (c) receipts = money taken in sales; *to itemize receipts and expenditures; receipts*

are down against the same period of last year 2 *verb* to stamp *or* to sign a document to show that it has been received *or* to stamp an invoice to show that it has been paid

receive *verb* to get something which has been delivered; **we received the payment ten days ago; the workers have not received any salary for six months; the goods were received in good condition**

◊ **receivable** *adjective* which can be received; **accounts receivable** = money owed to a business; **bills receivable** = bills which a creditor will receive

◊ **receivables** *plural noun* money which is owed to a business

◊ **receiver** *noun* **(a)** person who receives something; **the receiver of the shipment (b)** person appointed by a court to run a business which is in financial difficulties, to pay off its debts as far as possible, and to close it down; **the court appointed a receiver for the company; the company is in the hands of the receiver**

◊ **receivership** *noun* **the company went into receivership** = the company was put into the hands of a receiver

◊ **receiving** *noun* **(a)** act of getting something which has been delivered; **receiving clerk** = official who works in a receiving office; **receiving department** = section of a company which deals with incoming goods *or* payments; **receiving office** = office where goods *or* payments are received **(b) receiving order** = order from a court appointing a receiver to a company

recent *adjective* which happened not very long ago; **the company's recent acquisition of a chain of shoe stores; his recent appointment to the board; we will mail you our most recent catalog**

◊ **recently** *adverb* not very long ago; **the company recently started on an expansion program; they recently decided to close the branch office in Australia**

reception *noun* place (in a hotel *or* office) where visitors register *or* say who they have come to see; **reception clerk** = person who works at the reception desk; **reception desk** = desk where customers *or* visitors check in

◊ **receptionist** *noun* person in a hotel *or* office who meets guests *or* clients, answers the phone, etc.

recession *noun* fall in trade *or* in the economy; **the recession has reduced profits in many companies; several firms have closed factories because of the recession**

recipient *noun* person who receives; **the recipient of an allowance from the company**

reciprocal *adjective* applying from one country *or* person *or* company to another and vice versa; **reciprocal agreement; reciprocal contract; reciprocal holdings** = situation where two corporations own shares in each other to prevent takeover bids; **reciprocal trade** = trade between two countries

◊ **reciprocate** *verb* to do the same thing to someone as he has just done to you; **they offered us an exclusive agency for their cars and we reciprocated with an offer of the agency for our buses**

◊ **reciprocity** *noun* acting in the same toward someone as he has acted toward you (such as by buying from a business which buys from your business)

QUOTE in 1934 Congress authorized President Roosevelt to seek lower tariffs with any country willing to reciprocate
Duns Business Month

reckon *verb* **(a)** to calculate; **to reckon the costs at $25,000; we reckon the loss to be over $1m; they reckon the insurance costs to be too high (b)** to **reckon on** = to depend on *or* to expect something to happen; **they reckon on being awarded the contract; he can reckon on the support of the executive vice-president**

recognize *verb* **(a)** to know someone *or* something because you have seen *or* heard them before; **I recognized his voice before he said who he was; do you recognize the handwriting on the letter? (b) to recognize a union** = to accept that a union can act on behalf of the employees; **although all the employees had joined the union, the management refused to recognize it; recognized agent** = agent who is approved by the company for which he acts

◊ **recognition** *noun* act of recognizing; **to grant a union recognition** = to recognize a labor union

recommend *verb* **(a)** to suggest that something should be done; **the**

investment adviser recommended buying shares in aircraft companies; we do not recommend junk bonds as a safe investment; **manufacturer's recommended price (MRP)** *or* **recommended retail price (RRP)** = price which a manufacturer suggests the product should be sold at on the retail market, though often reduced by the retailer **(b)** to say that someone *or* something is good; *he recommended a store on Main Street for shoes; I certainly would not recommend Miss Smith for the job; the board meeting recommended a dividend of 50 a share; can you recommend a good hotel in Amsterdam?*

◊ **recommendation** *noun* saying that someone *or* something is good; *we appointed him on the recommendation of his former employer*

reconcile *verb* to make two accounts *or* statements agree; *to reconcile one account with another; to reconcile the accounts*

◊ **reconciliation** *noun* making two accounts *or* statements agree; **reconciliation statement** = statement which explains why two accounts do not agree

reconstruction *noun* building again; *the economic reconstruction of an area after a disaster*

record 1 *noun* **(a)** report of something which has happened; *the chairman signed the minutes as a true record of the last meeting;* **for the record** *or* **to keep the record straight** = to note something which has been done; *for the record, I would like these sales figures to be noted in the minutes;* **on record** = correctly reported; *the chairman is on record as saying that profits are set to rise;* **off the record** = unofficially *or* in private; *he made some comments off the record about the disastrous home sales figures* **(b) records** = documents which contain a company's historical information; *the names of customers are kept in the company's records; we find from our records that our invoice number 1234 has not been paid* **(c)** description of what has happened in the past; *the salesman's record of service or service record; the company's record in industrial relations;* **track record** = success or failure of a company *or* salesman in the past; *he has a good*

track record as a salesman; the company has no track record in the computer market **(d)** success which is better than anything before; **record sales** *or* **record losses** *or* **record profits** = sales *or* losses *or* profits which are higher than ever before; *1988 was a record year for the company; sales for 1990 equaled the record of 1988; our top salesman has set a new record for sales per call;* **we broke our record for June** = we sold more than we have ever sold before in June **2** *verb* to note *or* to report; *the company has recorded another year of increased sales; your complaint has been recorded and will be investigated*

◊ **record-breaking** *adjective* which is better than anything which has happened before; *we are proud of our record-breaking profits in 1989*

◊ **recording** *noun* making of a note; *the recording of an order or of a complaint*

recoup *verb* **to recoup one's losses** = to get back money which you thought you had lost

recourse *noun* right to claim money from a borrower in default; **to decide to have recourse to the courts** = to decide in the end to sue someone

recover *verb* **(a)** to get back something which has been lost; *he never recovered his money; the initial investment was never recovered; to recover damages from the driver of the car; to start a court action to recover property* **(b)** to get better *or* to rise; *the market has not recovered from the rise in oil prices; the stock market fell in the morning, but recovered during the afternoon*

◊ **recoverable** *adjective* which can be got back

◊ **recovery** *noun* **(a)** getting back something which has been lost; *we are aiming for the complete recovery of the money invested; to start an action for recovery of property* **(b)** upward movement of shares *or* of the economy; *the economy staged a recovery; the recovery of the economy after a slump;* **recovery shares** = shares which are likely to go up in value because the company's performance is improving

recruit *verb* **to recruit new staff** = to get new staff to join a company; *we are recruiting sales personnel for our new store*

◊ **recruitment** or **recruiting** noun the recruitment of new staff = looking for new staff to join a company

rectify verb to correct something or to make something right; *to rectify an entry*

◊ **rectification** noun correction

recurrent adjective which happens again and again; *a recurrent item of expenditure*

recycle verb to take waste material and process it so that it can be used again; **recycled paper** = paper made from waste paper

red noun **in the red** = showing a debit or loss; *my bank account is in the red; the company went into the red in 1984; the company is out of the red for the first time since 1950*

◊ **red herring** noun first prospectus setting out details of a new issue of securities

◊ **red tape** noun official paperwork which takes a long time to complete; *the Australian joint venture has been held up by government red tape*

> QUOTE he understood that little companies disliked red tape as much as big companies did and would pay to be relieved of the burden
> *Forbes Magazine*

redeem verb **(a)** to pay off a loan or a debt; *to redeem a mortgage; to redeem a debt* **(b)** to redeem a bond = to sell a bond for cash

◊ **redeemable** adjective which can be sold for cash

redemption noun **(a)** repayment of a loan; **redemption date** = date on which a loan, etc., is due to be repaid; **redemption before due date** = paying back a loan before the date when repayment is due; **redemption value** = value of a security when redeemed; **redemption yield** = yield on a security including interest and its redemption value **(b)** repayment of a debt; *redemption of a mortgage*

redeploy verb to move workers from one place to another or to give workers totally different jobs to do; *we closed the design department and redeployed the workforce in the publicity and sales departments*

◊ **redeployment** noun moving workers from one place to another

redevelop verb to knock down the buildings on a site, and build new ones

◊ **redevelopment** noun knocking down of existing buildings to replace them with new ones; *the redevelopment plan was rejected by the planning committee*

redistribute verb to move items or work or money to different areas or people; *the government aims to redistribute wealth by taxing the rich and giving grants to the poor; the orders have been redistributed among the company's factories*

◊ **redistribution** noun **redistribution of wealth** = sharing wealth among the whole population

redraft verb to draft again; *the whole contract had to be redrafted to take in the objections from the chairman*

reduce verb to make smaller or lower; *to reduce expenditures or prices or taxes; we have laid off some workers to reduce labor costs; prices have been reduced by 15%; carpets are reduced from $100 to $50; the company reduced output because of a fall in demand; the government's policy is to reduce inflation to 5%*

◊ **reduced** adjective lower; *reduced prices have increased unit sales; prices have fallen due to a reduced demand for the goods*

reduction noun lowering (of prices, etc.); *price reductions; tax reductions; staff reductions; reduction of expenditures; reduction in demand; the company was forced to make job reductions*

redundant adjective more than is needed or useless; *redundant capital; redundant clause in a contract; the new legislation has made clause 6 redundant*

reelect verb to elect again; *he was reelected chairman*

◊ **reelection** noun being elected again; *she is eligible to stand for reelection* = it is possible for her to be reelected if she wants

reemploy verb to employ someone again

◊ **reemployment** *noun* employing someone again

reentry *noun* coming back in again; **reentry visa** *or* **permit** = visa which allows someone to leave a country and go back in again

reexamine *verb* to examine something again
◊ **reexamination** *noun* examining something which has already been examined before

reexport 1 *noun* exporting of goods which have been imported; *reexport trade; we import wool for reexport; the value of reexports has increased* **2** *verb* to export something which has been imported
◊ **reexportation** *noun* exporting goods which have been imported

ref = REFERENCE

refer *verb* (a) to mention *or* to deal with *or* to write about something; *we refer to your estimate of May 26; he referred to an article which he had seen in the "New York Times"; referring to your letter of June 4* (b) to pass a problem on to someone else to decide; *to refer a question to a committee; we have referred your complaint to our supplier*
NOTE: **referring - referred**
◊ **reference** *noun* (a) terms of reference = areas which a committee *or* an inspector can deal with; *under the terms of reference of the committee, it cannot investigate complaints from the public; the committee's terms of reference do not cover exports* (b) mentioning *or* dealing with; *with reference to your letter of May 25* (c) numbers *or* letters which make it possible to find a document which has been filed; *our reference: PC/MS 1234; thank you for your letter (reference 1234); please quote reference 1234 in all correspondence; when replying please quote reference 1234* (d) written report on someone's character *or* ability, etc.; *to write someone a reference or to give someone a reference; to ask applicants to supply references;* **to ask a company for trade references** *or* **for bank references** = to ask for reports from traders *or* a bank on the company's financial status and reputation; **letter of reference** = letter in which an employer *or* former employer recommends someone for a job; *he enclosed letters of reference from his two previous employers* (e) person who reports on someone's character *or* ability, etc.; *to give someone's name as a reference; please use me as a reference if you wish*

refinance *verb* to arrange a new loan to finance an existing mortgage or loan
◊ **refinancing** *noun* **refinancing of a loan** = floating a new loan to pay back a previous loan

refit *verb* to fit out (a store *or* factory *or* ship) again
NOTE: **refitting - refitted**
◊ **refitting** *noun* fitting out (of a store *or* factory *or* ship) again

reflate *verb* **to reflate the economy** = to stimulate the economy by increasing the money supply *or* by reducing taxes, leading to increased inflation; *the government's attempts to reflate the economy were not successful*
◊ **reflation** *noun* act of stimulating the economy by increasing the money supply *or* by reducing taxes
◊ **reflationary** *adjective* **reflationary measures** = acts which are likely to stimulate the economy

refresher course *noun* course of study to make you practice your skills again in order to improve them; *he took a refresher course in bookkeeping*

refund 1 *noun* money paid back; *to ask for a refund; a tax refund; she got a refund after she had complained to the manager;* **full refund** *or* **refund in full** = refund of all the money paid; *he got a full refund when he complained about the service* **2** *verb* to pay back money; *to refund the cost of postage; all money will be refunded if the goods are not satisfactory*
◊ **refundable** *adjective* which can be paid back; **refundable deposit;** *the entrance fee is refundable if you purchase $5 worth of goods*

refuse *verb* to say that you will not do something *or* will not accept something; *they refused to pay; the bank refused to lend the company any more money; he asked for a raise but it was refused; the loan was refused by the bank; the customer refused the goods or refused to accept the goods*

NOTE: you refuse **to do something** or refuse **something**

◊ **refusal** *noun* saying no; **his request met with a refusal =** his request was refused; **to give someone first refusal of something =** to allow someone to be the first to decide if they want something or not; **blanket refusal =** refusal to accept many different items

regard *noun* **with regard to =** concerning *or* dealing with; **with regard to your request for unpaid leave**

◊ **regarding** *preposition* concerning *or* dealing with; **instructions regarding the shipment of goods to Africa**

◊ **regardless** *adjective* **regardless of =** in spite of; **the chairman furnished his office regardless of expense =** without concern of how much it would cost

region *noun* large area of a country; **in the region of =** about *or* approximately; **he was earning a salary in the region of $25,000; the house was sold for a price in the region of $100,000**

◊ **regional** *adjective* referring to a region; **regional planning =** planning the industrial development of a region

register 1 *noun* **(a)** official list; **to enter something in a register; to keep a register up to date; register of debentures** *or* **debenture register =** list of debenture holders of a company; **register of directors =** official list of the directors of a company; **land register =** list of pieces of land, showing who owns it and what buildings are on it; **register of stockholders =** list of stockholders in a corporation, with their addresses **(b)** large book for recording details (as in a hotel, where guests sign in, or in a registry where deaths are recorded) **(c) cash register =** machine which shows and adds the prices of items bought in a store, with a drawer for keeping the cash received **2** *verb* **(a)** to write something in an official list; **to register a company; to register a sale; to register a property; to register a trademark (b)** to arrive at a hotel *or* at a conference, sign your name and write your address on a list; **they registered at the hotel under the name of Macdonald (c)** to send (a letter) by registered mail; **I registered the letter, because it contained money**

◊ **registered** *adjective* **(a)** which has been noted on an official list; *registered stock transaction; registered trademark* **(b)** **registered letter** *or*

registered parcel = letter *or* parcel which is noted by the post office before it is sent, so that compensation can be claimed if it is lost; **to send documents by registered mail**

◊ **registrar** *noun* person who keeps official records; **the company registrar**

◊ **registration** *noun* act of having something noted on an official list; **registration of a trademark** *or* **of a share transaction; certificate of registration** *or* **registration certificate =** document showing that an item has been registered; **registration fee =** money paid to have something registered *or* money paid to attend a conference; **registration number =** official number (such as the number of a car)

◊ **registry** *noun* **(a)** place where official records are kept; **registry office =** office where records of births, marriages and deaths are kept **(b) port of registry =** port where a ship is registered

regret *verb* to be sorry; **I regret having to lay off so many workers; we regret the delay in answering your letter; we regret to inform you of the death of the chairman**
NOTE: you **regret doing something** or **regret to do something** or **regret something**. Note also: **regretting - regretted**

regular *adjective* **(a)** which happens *or* comes at the same time each day *or* each week *or* each month *or* each year; **his regular train is the 12:45; the regular flight to Chicago leaves at 10:00; regular customer =** customer who always buys from the same store; **regular income =** income which comes in every week or month; **she works freelance so she does not have a regular income; regular staff =** full-time staff **(b)** ordinary *or* standard; **the regular price is $1.25, but we are offering them at 99; regular size =** ordinary size (smaller than economy size, family size, etc.)

◊ **regularly** *adverb* happening often each day *or* week *or* month *or* year; **the first train in the morning is regularly late**

◊ **regulate** *verb* **(a)** to adjust something so that it works well *or* is correct **(b)** to change *or* maintain something by law; **prices are regulated by supply and demand =** prices are increased or lowered according to supply and demand; **government-regulated price =** price which is imposed by the government

◊ **regulation** *noun* (a) act of making sure that something will work well; *the regulation of trading practices* (b) **regulations** = laws *or* rules; *the new government regulations on housing standards; fire regulations or safety regulations; regulations concerning imports and exports*

reimburse *verb* **to reimburse someone for his expenses** = to pay someone back for money which he has spent; *you will be reimbursed for your expenses or your expenses will be reimbursed*
◊ **reimbursement** *noun* paying back money; *reimbursement of expenses*

reimport 1 *noun* importing of goods which have been exported from the same country 2 *verb* to import goods which have been exported
◊ **reimportation** *noun* importing goods which have been exported

reinstate *verb* to put someone back into a job from which he was dismissed; *the union demanded that the dismissed workers be reinstated*
◊ **reinstatement** *noun* putting someone back into a job from which he was dismissed

reinsure *verb* to spread the risk of an insurance, by asking another insurance company to cover part of it and receive part of the premium
◊ **reinsurance** *noun* act of reinsuring
◊ **reinsurer** *noun* insurance company which agrees to insure part of a risk for another insurer

reinvest *verb* to invest again; *he reinvested the money in government stocks*
◊ **reinvestment** *noun* (i) investing again in the same securities; (ii) investing a company's earnings in its own business by using them to create new products for sale

reissue 1 *noun* issue of something again 2 *verb* to issue something again; *the company reissued its catalog with a new price list*

reject 1 *noun* thing which has been thrown out because it is not of the usual standard; *sale of rejects or of reject items; to sell off reject stock* 2 *verb* to refuse to accept *or* to say that something is not satisfactory; *the union rejected the management's proposals; the company rejected the takeover bid* = the directors recommended that the shareholders should not accept the bid
◊ **rejection** *noun* refusal to accept

related *adjective* connected *or* linked; *related items on the agenda;* **related company** = company which is partly owned by another company
◊ **relating to** *adverb* referring to *or* connected with; *documents relating to the agreement*
◊ **relation** *noun* (a) **in relation to** = referring to *or* connected with; *documents in relation to the agreement* (b) **relations** = links (with other people *or* other companies); *we try to maintain good relations with our customers;* **to enter into relations with a company** = to start discussing a business deal with a company; **to break off relations with someone** = to stop dealing with someone; **industrial relations** *or* **labor relations** *or* **work relations** = relations between management and workers; *the company has a history of bad labor relations* (c) **public relations (PR)** = keeping good links between a company *or* a group and the public so that people know what the company is doing and approve of it; **public relations department** = section of a company which deals with relations with the public; **public relations officer** = official who deals with relations with the public
◊ **relatively** *adverb* more or less; *we have appointed a relatively new PR firm to handle our publicity*

release 1 *noun* (a) setting free; *release from a contract; release of goods from customs* (b) **press release** = sheet giving news about something which is sent to newspapers and TV and radio stations so that they can use the information in it; *the company sent out or issued a press release about the launch of the new car* (c) **new releases** = news records put on the market 2 *verb* (a) to free; *to release goods from customs; the customs office released the goods against payment of a fine; to release someone from a debt* (b) to make something public; *the company released information about the new mine in Australia; the government has refused to release figures for the number of unemployed women* (c) to place on the market; *to release a new record*

relevant *adjective* which has to do with what is being discussed; *which is the relevant government department? can you give me the relevant papers?*

reliable *adjective* which can be trusted; *reliable company; the sales manager is completely reliable; we have reliable information about our rival's sales; the company makes a very reliable product*

◊ **reliability** *noun* being reliable; *the product has passed its reliability tests*

◊ **rely on** *verb* to depend on *or* to trust; *the chairman relies on the finance department for information on sales; we rely on part-time staff for most of our mail-order business; do not rely on the agents for accurate market reports*

relief *noun* help; **tax relief** = allowing someone to pay less tax; **there is full tax relief on mortgage interest payments** = no tax is payable on income used to pay interest on a mortgage; **mortgage relief** = allowing someone to pay no tax on mortgage interest payments; **relief shift** = shift which comes to take the place of another shift, usually the shift between the day shift and the night shift; **unemployment relief** = the creation of new jobs to try to reduce the number of people who are unemployed

remain *verb* (a) to be left; *half the stock remained unsold; we will sell off the old stock at half price and anything remaining will be thrown away* (b) to stay; *she remained behind at the office after 6:30 to finish her work*

◊ **remainder 1** *noun* (a) amount *or* proportion left behind; *the remainder of the stock will be sold off at half price* (b) **remainders** = new books sold cheaply; **remainder dealer** = book dealer who buys unsold new books from publishers at a very low price **2** *verb* to **remainder books** = to sell new books off cheaply; *the store was full of piles of remaindered books*

remember *verb* to bring back into your mind something which you have seen *or* heard *or* read before; *do you remember the name of the president of Smith Corporation? I cannot remember the make of the photocopier which he said was so good; did you remember to ask the switchboard to put my calls through to the boardroom? she*

remembered seeing the item in a supplier's catalog
NOTE: you **remember doing something** which you did in the past; you **remember to do something** in the future

remind *verb* to make someone remember; *I must remind my secretary to book the flight for New York; he reminded the chairman that the meeting had to finish at 6:30*

◊ **reminder** *noun* letter to remind a customer that he has not paid an invoice; *to send someone a reminder*

remit *verb* to send (money); *to remit by check*
NOTE: **remitting - remitted**

◊ **remittance** *noun* money which is sent; *please send remittances to the treasurer; enclosed is my remittance for the order shipped May 9*

remnant *noun* odd piece of a large item sold separately; *remnant sale* or *sale of remnants*

remodel *verb* to fit out (a store *or* factory *or* ship) again, in a more modern style

◊ **remodeling** *noun* fitting out (of a store *or* factory *or* ship) again

remove *verb* to take something away; *we can remove his name from the mailing list; the government has removed the ban on imports from Japan; the minister has removed the embargo on the sale of computer equipment;* **two directors were removed from the board at the annual meeting** = two directors were dismissed from the board

◊ **removal** *noun* firing someone from a job; *the removal of the financial manager is going to be very difficult*

remunerate *verb* to pay someone for doing something; *to remunerate someone for his services*

◊ **remuneration** *noun* payment for services; *she has a monthly remuneration of $400*

◊ **remunerative** *adjective* (job) which pays well; *he is in a very remunerative job*

renew *verb* to continue something for a further period of time; *to renew a bill of exchange* or *to renew a lease;* **to renew a subscription** = to pay a subscription for another year; **to renew an insurance policy** = to pay the premium for another year's insurance

◊ **renewal** *noun* act of renewing; *renewal of a lease* or *of a subscription* or *of a bill; the lease is up for renewal next month; when is the renewal date of the bill?;* **renewal notice** = note sent by an insurance company asking the insured person to renew the insurance; **renewal premium** = premium to be paid to renew an insurance policy

rent 1 *noun* money paid to use an office or house or factory for a period of time; **high rent** or **low rent** = expensive or cheap rent; *rents are high in the center of the town; we cannot afford to pay downtown rents; to pay three months' rent in advance;* **back rent** = rent owed; **ground rent** = rent paid by the main tenant to the ground landlord; **nominal rent** = very small rent; **rent control** = government regulation of rents; **income from rents** or **rent income** = income from letting offices or houses, etc. **2** *verb* **(a)** to pay money to use an office or house or factory or piece of equipment for a period of time; *to rent an office* or *a car; he rents an office in the center of town; they were driving a rented car when they were stopped by the police* **(b) to rent (out)** = to own a car or office, etc. and let it to someone for money; *we rented part of the building to an accounting firm*

◊ **rental** *noun* money paid to use an office or house or factory or car or piece of equipment, etc., for a period of time; *the telephone rental bill comes to over $500 a quarter;* **rental income** or **income from rentals** = income from letting offices or houses, etc.; **car rental firm** = company which specializes in offering cars for rent; **fleet rental** = renting all a company's cars from a single car company at a special price

◊ **renter** *noun* person who rents a house or apartment

renunciation *noun* act of giving up; **letter of renunciation** = form sent with new shares, which allows the person who has been allotted the shares to refuse to accept them and so sell them to someone else

reopen *verb* to open again; *the office will reopen soon after its remodeling*

◊ **reopening** *noun* opening again; *the reopening of the store after remodeling*

reorder 1 *noun* new order for something which has been ordered before; *the product has only been on the market ten days and we are already getting reorders;* **reorder level** = minimum amount of stock of an item which must be reordered **2** *verb* to place a new order for something; *we must reorder these items because stock is getting low*

reorganize *verb* to organize in a new way

◊ **reorganization** *noun* new way of organizing; *his job was downgraded in the office reorganization* or *in the reorganization of the office;* **reorganization of a company** or **a company reorganization** = restructuring the finances of a company

rep 1 *noun* = REPRESENTATIVE *to hold a reps' meeting; our reps make on average six calls a day;* **commission rep** = representative who is not paid a salary but receives a commission on sales **2** *verb informal* = REPRESENT *he reps for two firms on commission*

repack *verb* to pack again

◊ **repacking** *noun* packing again

repair 1 *noun* mending something which was broken; *to carry out repairs to the machinery; his car is in the garage for repair* **2** *verb* to mend something which is broken; *the photocopier is being repaired*

◊ **repairer** or **repairman** *noun* person who carries out repairs; *the repairman has come to fix the photocopier*

repay *verb* to pay back; *to repay money owed; the company had to cut back on expenditure in order to repay its debts;* **he repaid me in full** = he paid me back all the money he owed me
NOTE: **repaying - repaid**

◊ **repayable** *adjective* which can be paid back; *loan which is repayable over ten years*

◊ **repayment** *noun* paying back; money which is paid back; *the loan is due for repayment next year*

repeat *verb* **(a)** to say or do something again; *he repeated his address slowly so that the salesgirl could write it down; when asked what the corporation planned to do, the chairman repeated "Nothing"* **(b)** to

repeat an order = to order something again

◊ **repeat order** *noun* new order for something which has been ordered before; *the product has been on the market only ten days and we are already flooded with repeat orders*

replace *verb* to put someone *or* something in the place of something else; *the cost of replacing damaged stock is very high; the photocopier needs replacing; the company will replace any defective item free of charge; we are replacing all our salaried staff with freelancers*

◊ **replacement** *noun* (a) replacement cost *or* cost of replacement = cost to replace an existing item; **replacement value** = value of something for insurance purposes if it were to be replaced; *the computer is insured at its replacement value* (b) item which replaces something; *we are out of stock and are waiting for replacements* (c) person who replaces someone; *my secretary is leaving next week, so we are advertising for a replacement*

reply 1 *noun* answer; *there was no reply to my letter or to my phone call; I am writing in reply to your letter of July 24; the company's reply to the merger plans;* **reply coupon** = form attached to a coupon ad which must be filled in and returned to the advertiser; **reply paid card** *or* **letter** = card or letter to be sent back to the sender with a reply, the sender having already paid for the return postage **2** *verb* to answer; *to reply to a letter; the company has replied to the merger threat by offering the shareholders higher dividends*

report 1 *noun* (a) statement describing what has happened *or* describing a state of affairs; *to draft a report; to make a report or to present a report or to send in a report; the sales manager reads all the reports from the sales team; the chairman has received a report from the insurance company; the company's annual report or the chairman's report or the board of directors' report* = document sent each year by the chairman of a corporation or the board of directors to the stockholders, explaining what the corporation has done during the year; **confidential report** = secret document which must not be shown to other people; **feasibility report** = document

which says if something can be done; **financial report** = document which gives the financial position of a company *or* of a club, etc.; **progress report** = document which describes what progress has been made; **the treasurer's report** = document from the treasurer of an organization to explain the financial state of the organization to its members (b) **a report in a newspaper** *or* **a newspaper report** = article *or* news item; *can you confirm the report that the company is planning to close the factory?* (c) official document from a government committee; *the Senate has issued a report on the credit problems of exporters* **2** *verb* (a) to make a statement describing something; *the salesmen reported an increased demand for the product; he reported the damage to the insurance company; we asked the bank to report on his financial status; he reported seeing the absentee in a store* (b) to report to someone = to be responsible to *or* to be under someone; *he reports direct to the CEO; the salesmen report to the sales manager* (c) to go to a place *or* to attend; *to report for an interview; please report to our New York office for training*
NOTE: for (a), you **report something** or **report on something**

> QUOTE a draft report on changes in the international monetary system
> *Wall Street Journal*

repossess *verb* to take back an item which someone is buying under an installment plan, because the purchaser cannot continue the payments

represent *verb* (a) to work for a company, showing goods or services to possible buyers; *he represents an American car company in Europe; our French distributor represents several other competing firms* (b) to act for someone; *he sent his lawyer and accountant to represent him at the meeting; three managers represent the workforce in discussions with the directors*

◊ **re-present** *verb* to present something again; *he re-presented the check two weeks later to try to get payment from the bank*

◊ **representation** *noun* (a) act of selling goods for a company; *we offered them exclusive representation in Europe; they have no representation in the U.S.A.* (b) having someone to act on your behalf; *the minority shareholders* *want representation on the board* (c) complaint made on behalf of someone; *the managers made representations to the board on behalf of the hourly-paid members of staff*

◊ **representative 1** *adjective* which is an example of what all others are like; *we displayed a representative selection of our product range; the sample chosen was not representative of the whole batch* **2** *noun* **(a)** sales representative = person who works for a company, showing goods or services for sale; *we have six representatives in Europe; they have vacancies for representatives to handle accounts in the Northeast* **(b)** company which works for another company, selling their goods; *we have appointed Smith & Co. our exclusive representatives in Europe* **(c)** person who acts on someone's behalf; *he sent his lawyer and accountant to act as his representatives at the meeting; the board refused to meet the representatives of the workforce*

repudiate *verb* to refuse to accept; *to repudiate an agreement* = to refuse to continue with an agreement

◊ **repudiation** *noun* refusal to accept

reputable *adjective* with a good reputation; *we only use reputable carriers; a reputable firm of accountants*

◊ **reputation** *noun* opinion of someone *or* something held by other people; *company with a reputation for quality; he has a reputation for being difficult to negotiate with*

request 1 *noun* asking for something; *they put in a request for a government subsidy; his request for a loan was turned down by the bank;* on request = if asked for; *we will send samples on request* or "*samples available on request*" **2** *verb* to ask for; *to request assistance from the government; I am sending a catalog as requested*

require *verb* **(a)** to ask for *or* to demand something; *to require a full explanation of expenditure; the law requires you to report all income to the IRS* **(b)** to need; *the document requires careful study; to write the program requires a computer specialist*

◊ **requirement** *noun* what is needed; *one requirement of the job is experience with computers*

◊ **requirements** *plural noun* things which are needed; *to meet a customer's requirements;* the requirements of a market *or* market requirements = things which are needed by the market; budgetary requirements = spending or income needed to meet the budget forecasts; manpower requirements = number of workers needed

requisition 1 *noun* official order for something, usually from one department in a company to the supplies or purchasing department; *what is the number of your latest requisition?;* check requisition = official note from a department to the corporation finance department asking for a check to be written **2** *verb* to put in an official order for something; to ask for supplies to be sent

resale *noun* selling goods which have been bought; *to purchase something for resale; the contract forbids resale of the goods to Japan*

◊ **resale price maintenance** *noun* system where the price for an item is fixed by the manufacturer and the retailer agrees to sell it at that price

rescind *verb* to annul *or* to cancel; *to rescind a contract* or *an agreement*

rescue 1 *noun* saving someone *or* something from danger; rescue operation = arrangement by a group of people to save a company from collapse; *the banks planned a rescue operation for the company* **2** *verb* to save someone *or* something from danger; *the company nearly collapsed, but was rescued by the banks*

research 1 *noun* trying to find out facts *or* information; consumer research = research into why consumers buy goods and what goods they may want to buy; market research = examining the possible sales of a product and the possible customers for it before it is put on the market; research and development (R & D) = scientific investigation which leads to making new products or improving existing products; *the company spends millions on research and development; he is engaged in research into the packaging of the new product line; the company is carrying out research to find a medicine to cure colds;* research department = section of a company which does research; research institute *or* **organization** = place which exists only to carry out research; **research unit** = separate small group of research workers; **research worker** = person who works in a research department **2** *verb* to study *or* to try to find out information about something; *to research the market for a product*

◊ **researcher** *noun* person who carries out research

reservation *noun* booking a seat *or* table *or* room; *I want to make a reservation on the train to Pittsburgh tomorrow evening;* **room reservations** = department in a hotel which deals with advance arrangements for rooms; *can you put me through to reservations?*

reserve 1 *noun* **(a)** money from profits not paid as dividend, but kept back by a company in case it is needed for a special purpose; **bank reserves** = cash and securities held by a bank to cover deposits; **capital reserves** = part of capital used to supplement cash flow when needed; **capitalization of reserves** = issuing free bonus shares to shareholders; **cash reserves** = a company's reserves in cash deposits or bills kept in case of urgent need; *the company was forced to fall back on its cash reserves; to have to draw on reserves to pay the dividend;* **contingency reserve** *or* **emergency reserves** = money set aside in case it is needed urgently; **reserve for bad debts** = money kept by a company to cover debts which may not be paid; **hidden reserves** = illegal reserves which are not declared in the company's balance sheet; **sums chargeable to the reserve** = sums which can be debited to a company's reserves; **reserve fund** = profits in a business which have not been paid out as dividend but have been plowed back into the business **(b)** deposit which a commercial bank has to keep with the Federal Reserve Bank **(c)** **reserve currency** = strong currency held by other countries to support their own weaker currencies; **currency reserves** = foreign money held by a government to support its own currency and to pay its debts; **a country's foreign currency reserves** = a country's reserves in currencies of other countries; *the UK's gold and dollar reserves fell by $200 million during the quarter* **(d)** **in reserve** = kept to be used at a later date; *to keep something in reserve; we are keeping our new product in reserve until the launch date* **(e)**

reserves = supplies kept in case of need; *our reserves of fuel fell during the winter; the country's reserves of gas or gas reserves are very large* **(f)** **reserve price** = lowest price which a seller will accept at an auction; *the painting was withdrawn when it did not reach its reserve* **2** *verb* **to reserve a room** *or* **a table** *or* **a seat** = to ask for a room *or* table *or* seat to be kept free for you; *I want to reserve a table for four people; can your secretary reserve a seat for me on the train to Chicago?*

residence *noun* **(a)** house *or* apartment where someone lives; *he has a country residence where he spends his weekends* **(b)** act of living *or* operating officially in a country; **residence permit** = official document allowing a foreigner to live in a country; *he has applied for a residence permit; she was granted a residence permit for one year*

◊ **resident** *noun* person *or* company living or operating in a country; *the company is a resident in France;* **resident alien** = person who has permanent resident status in a country, but not citizenship; **nonresident** = person *or* company which is not officially resident in a country; *he has a nonresident account with a French bank; she was granted a nonresident visa*

residue *noun* money left over; *after paying various bequests the residue of his estate was split between his children*

◊ **residual** *adjective* remaining after everything else has gone

resign *verb* to give up a job; *he resigned from his post as treasurer; he has resigned effective July 1; she resigned as finance director*

◊ **resignation** *noun* act of giving up a job; *he wrote his letter of resignation to the chairman;* **to hand in** *or* **to give in** *or* **to send in one's resignation** = to resign from a job

resist *verb* to fight against something *or* not to give in to something; *the chairman resisted all attempts to make him resign; the company is resisting the takeover bid*

◊ **resistance** *noun* showing that people are opposed to something; *there was a lot of resistance from the shareholders to the new plan; the chairman's proposal met with strong*

resistance from the banks; consumer resistance = lack of interest by consumers in buying a new product; *the new product met no consumer resistance even though the price was high*

resolution *noun* decision to be reached at a meeting; **to put a resolution to a meeting** = to ask a meeting to vote on a proposal; *the meeting passed or carried or adopted a resolution to go on strike; the meeting rejected the resolution or the resolution was defeated by ten votes to twenty*

resolve *verb* to decide to do something; *the meeting resolved that a dividend should not be paid*

resources *plural noun* (a) source of supply of something; **natural resources** = supplies of gas, oil, coal, etc. which are available in the ground; *the country is rich in natural resources; we are looking for a site with good water resources* = a site with plenty of water available (b) **financial resources** = supply of money for something; *the costs of the L.A. office are a drain on the company's financial resources; the company's financial resources are not strong enough to support the cost of the research program; the cost of the new project is easily within our resources* = we have enough money to pay for the new project

respect 1 *noun* **with respect to** = concerning **2** *verb* to pay attention to; *to respect a clause in an agreement; the company has not respected the terms of the contract*

◊ **respectively** *adverb* referring to each one separately; *Mr. Smith and Mr. Jones are respectively CEO and Sales Manager of Smith Corp.*

response *noun* reply *or* reaction; *there was no response to our recent mailing; we got very little response to our complaints;* **response rate** = number of replies to a mailing, shown as a percentage of the addresses mailed

responsibility *noun* (a) being responsible *or* accountable; *there is no responsibility on the company's part for loss of customers' property; the management accepts no responsibility for loss of goods in storage* (b) **responsibilities** = duties; *he finds the responsibilities of being president too heavy*

◊ **responsible** *adjective* (a) **responsible for** = accountable for *or* in charge of; *he is responsible for all sales* (b) **responsible to someone** = being under someone's authority; *he is directly responsible to the vice-president for research* (c) **a responsible job** = job where important decisions have to be made *or* where the employee is accountable for many decisions; *he is looking for a responsible job in marketing*

rest *noun* what is left; *the chairman went home, but the rest of the directors stayed in the boardroom; we sold most of the stock before Christmas and hope to clear the rest in a sale; the rest of the money is invested in stocks*

restaurant *noun* place where you can buy a meal; *he runs a French restaurant in New York*

restitution *noun* (a) giving back (property); *the court ordered the restitution of assets to the company* (b) compensation *or* payment for damage or loss

restock *verb* to order more stock; *to restock after the Christmas sales*

◊ **restocking** *noun* ordering more stock

restraint *noun* control; **pay restraint** *or* **wage restraint** = keeping increases in wages under control; **restraint of trade** = attempt by companies to fix prices *or* create monopolies *or* reduce competition, which could affect free trade

restrict *verb* to limit *or* to impose controls on; *to restrict credit; we are restricted to a staff of 20 by the size of our offices; to restrict the flow of trade or to restrict imports;* **to sell into a restricted market** = to sell goods into a market where the supplier has agreed to limit sales to avoid competition

◊ **restriction** *noun* limit *or* control; *import restrictions or restrictions on imports;* **to impose restrictions on imports** *or* **on credit** = to start limiting imports *or* credit; **to lift credit restrictions** = to allow credit to be given freely

◊ **restrictive** *adjective* which limits; **restrictive trade practices** =

arrangement between companies to fix prices *or* to share the market, etc.

restructure *verb* to reorganize the financial basis of a company

◊ **restructuring** *noun* **the restructuring of the company =** reorganizing the financial basis of a company

result 1 *noun* **(a)** profit or loss account for a company at the end of a trading period; *the company's results for 1984* **(b)** something which happens because of something else; *what was the result of the price investigation? the company doubled its sales force with the result that the sales rose by 26%;* the expansion program has produced **results =** has produced increased sales; **payment by results =** being paid for profits *or* increased sales **2** *verb* **(a) to result in =** to produce as a result **(b) to result from =** to happen because of something; *the increase in debt resulted from the expansion program; the doubling of the sales force resulted in increased sales; the extra orders resulted in overtime work for all the factory employees*

resume *verb* to start again; *the discussions resumed after a two-hour break*

resume *or* **résumé** *noun* summary of a person's career, with details of education and work experience; *please submit a resume with your application*

resumption *noun* starting again; *we expect an early resumption of negotiations =* we expect negotiations will start again soon

retail 1 *noun* sale of small quantities of goods to ordinary customers; **retail dealer =** person who sells to the general public; **retail price =** full price paid by a customer in a store; **retail price index =** index showing how prices of retail goods have risen over a period of time; **retail store** *or* **retail outlet =** store which sells goods to the general public; **the retail trade =** all people *or* businesses selling goods retail; *the goods in stock have a retail value of $1m =* the value of the goods if sold to the public is $1m, before discounts etc. are taken into account **2** *adverb* **he sells retail and buys wholesale =** he buys goods in bulk at a wholesale discount and sells in small quantities to the public **3** *verb* **(a) to**

retail goods = to sell goods direct to the public **(b)** to sell for a price; *these items retail at or for 25¢ =* the retail price of these items is 25¢

◊ **retailer** *noun* person who runs a retail business, selling goods direct to the public

◊ **retailing** *noun* selling of full price goods to the public; *from car retailing the company branched out into car leasing*

retain *verb* **(a)** to keep; *out of the profits, the company has retained $50,000 as provision against bad debts;* **retained earnings =** profit not distributed to the shareholders as dividend; *the balance sheet has $50,000 in retained earnings* **(b) to retain a lawyer to act for a company =** to agree with a lawyer that he will act for you (and pay him a fee in advance)

◊ **retainer** *noun* money paid in advance to someone so that he will work for you, and not for someone else; *we pay him a retainer of $1,000*

retire *verb* **(a)** to stop work and take a pension; *she retired with a $6,000 pension; the founder of the company retired at the age of 85; the store is owned by a retired policeman* **(b)** to make a worker stop work and take a pension; *they decided to retire all staff over 50* **(c)** to come to the end of an elected term of office; *the treasurer retires from the council after six years; two retiring directors offer themselves for reelection*

◊ **retiree** *noun* person who has retired

◊ **retirement** *noun* act of retiring from work; **to take early retirement =** to leave work before the usual age; **retirement age =** age at which people retire (usually 65); **retirement pension =** pension which someone receives when he retires; **retirement plan =** system by which the employer and employee both contribute to a fund which will provide the retiree with a pension

retrain *verb* to train someone for a new job, or to do the same job in a more modern way

◊ **retraining** *noun* act of training again; *the store is closed for staff retraining; he had to attend a retraining session*

retrenchment *noun* reduction of expenditure *or* of new plans; *the company is in for a period of retrenchment*

retrieve *verb* to get back (something) which has been lost; to get back (information) which is stored in a computer; *the company is fighting to retrieve its market share; all of the information was accidentally wiped off the computer so we cannot retrieve our sales figures for the last month*

◊ **retrieval** *noun* getting back; **data retrieval** *or* **information retrieval** = getting information from the data stored in a computer; **retrieval system** = system which allows information to be retrieved

retroactive *adjective* which takes effect from a time in the past; *retroactive pay raise; they got a pay raise retroactive to last January*

◊ **retroactively** *adverb* going back to a time in the past

return 1 *noun* **(a)** going back *or* coming back; **return trip** = journey back to where you came from **(b)** sending back; **return address** = address to send back something; **return postcard** = card enclosed in a mailing, which can be returned to the mailing organizer; **these goods are all on sale or return** = if the retailer does not sell them, he sends them back to the supplier, and pays only for the items sold **(c)** profit *or* income from money invested; *to bring in a quick return; what is the gross return on this line?;* **return on investment (ROI)** *or* **return on capital** = profit shown as a percentage of money invested; **rate of return** = amount of interest *or* dividend produced by an investment, shown as a percentage of the original investment amount **(d)** **official return** = official report; **to file an income tax return** = to send a statement of income to the tax office; **daily** *or* **weekly** *or* **quarterly sales return** = report of sales made each day *or* week *or* quarter **2** *verb* to send back; *to return unsold stock to the wholesaler; to return a letter to sender;* **returned empties** = empty bottles *or* containers which are sent back to a supplier

◊ **returnable** *adjective* which can be returned; *these bottles are not returnable*

◊ **returns** *plural noun* **(a)** profits *or* income from investment; *the company is looking for quick returns on its investment;* **law of diminishing returns** = general rule that as more factors of production (land, labor and capital) are added to the existing factors,

so the increase in the amount they produce is proportionately smaller **(b)** unsold goods, especially books *or* newspapers *or* magazines sent back to the supplier

> QUOTE with interest rates running well above inflation, investors want something that offers a return for their money
> *Business Week*

revalue *verb* to value something again (at a higher value than before); *the company's properties have been revalued; the dollar has been revalued against all world currencies*

◊ **revaluation** *noun* act of revaluing; *the balance sheet takes into account the revaluation of the company's properties; the revaluation of the dollar against the franc*

revenue *noun* **(a)** money received; *revenue from advertising* *or* *advertising revenue; oil revenues have risen with the rise in the dollar;* **revenue statement** = statement of account of a business which records money received as sales, commission etc. **(b)** money received by a government in tax; **Internal Revenue Service** = federal government department which deals with tax; **revenue officer** = person working in the government tax offices

reversal *noun* change from being profitable to unprofitable; *the company suffered a reversal in the Far East*

reverse *verb* to change a decision to the opposite; to move in the opposite direction; *the committee reversed its decision on import quotas*

> QUOTE the trade balance sank $17 billion, reversing last fall's brief improvement
> *Fortune*

reversion *noun* return of property to an original owner; **he has the reversion of the estate** = he will receive the estate when the present lease ends

◊ **reversionary** *adjective* (property) which passes to another owner on the death of the present one

review 1 *noun* **(a)** general examination; *to conduct a review of distributors;* **financial review** = examination of an organization's finances; **wage review** *or* **salary review** = examination of salaries *or* wages in a company to see if the workers should earn more; **she had a**

salary review last April = her salary was examined (and increased) in April **(b)** magazine *or* periodic journal **2** *verb* to examine something generally; **to review salaries** = to look at all salaries in a company to decide on increases; *his salary will be reviewed at the end of the year; the company has decided to review freelance payments in the light of the rising cost of living;* **to review discounts** = to look at discounts offered to decide whether to change them

revise *verb* to change something which has been calculated *or* planned; *sales forecasts are revised annually; the chairman is revising his speech to the shareholders*

revive *verb* to make more lively; to increase (after a recession); *the government is introducing measures to revive trade; industry is reviving after the recession*
◊ **revival** *noun* **revival of trade** = increase in trade after a recession

revocable letter of credit *noun* letter of credit which can be canceled

revoke *verb* to cancel; *to revoke a clause in an agreement; the quota on luxury items has been revoked*

revolving *adjective* **revolving credit** = system where someone can borrow money at any time up to an agreed amount, and continue to borrow while still paying off the original loan; **revolving letter of credit** = letter of credit which has a total limit which is automatically renewed

rich *adjective* **(a)** having a lot of money; *a rich bond dealer; a rich oil company* **(b)** having a lot of natural resources; *the country is rich in minerals; oil-rich territory*

rid *verb* **to get rid of something** = to throw something away because it is useless; *the company is trying to get rid of all its old stock; our department has been told to get rid of twenty employees*
NOTE: **getting rid - got rid**

rider *noun* additional clause; *to add a rider to a contract*

rig 1 *noun* **oil rig** = platform which holds the equipment for taking oil out of

the earth **2** *verb* to arrange for a result to be changed; *they tried to rig the election of officers;* **to rig the market** = to make share prices go up or down so as to make a profit
NOTE: **rigging - rigged**

right 1 *adjective* **(a)** good *or* correct; *the chairman was right when he said the figures did not add up; this is not the right plane for Paris* **(b)** opposite of left; *the credits are on the right side of the page* **2** *noun* **(a)** legal title to something; *right of renewal of a contract; she has a right to the property; he has no right to the patent; the staff have a right to know how the company is doing;* **foreign rights** = legal title to sell something (especially a book) in a foreign country; **right to strike** = legal title for workers to stop working if they have a good reason for it; **right of way** = legal title to go across someone's property **(b)** **rights offering** *or* **stock rights** = giving existing stockholders the right to buy more stock at a lower price than the current market price
◊ **rightful** *adjective* legally correct; **rightful claimant** = person who has a legal claim to something; **rightful owner** = legal owner
◊ **right-hand** *adjective* belonging to the right side; *the credit side is the right-hand column in the statement; he keeps the address list in the right-hand drawer of his desk;* **right-hand man** = main assistant

rise 1 *noun* increase *or* growing high; *rise in the price of raw materials; oil price rises brought about a recession in world trade; there is a rise in sales of 10%* *or* *sales show a rise of 10%; salaries are increasing to keep up with the rises in the cost of living; the recent rise in interest rates has made mortgages more expensive* **2** *verb* to move upward *or* to become higher; *prices are rising faster than inflation; interest rates have risen to 15%*
NOTE: **rising - rose - has risen**

QUOTE the stock rose to over $20 a share, higher than the $18 bid
Fortune

risk *noun* **(a)** possible harm *or* chance of danger; **to run a risk** = to be likely to suffer harm; **to take a risk** = to do something which may make you lose money or suffer harm; **financial risk** = possibility of losing money; *there is no financial risk in selling to East European countries on credit; he is* *running the risk of overspending his promotion budget; the company is taking a considerable risk in manufacturing 25m units without doing any market research* **(b)** **risk capital =** capital for investment which may easily be lost in risky projects, but which can also provide high returns **(c)** **at owner's risk =** situation where goods shipped *or* stored are insured by the owner, not by the transport company or the storage company; *goods left here are at owner's risk; the shipment was sent at owner's risk* **(d)** loss *or* damage against which you are insured; **fire risk =** situation *or* goods which could start a fire; *that warehouse full of paper is a fire risk* **(e)** he is a good *or* bad risk = it is not likely *or* it is very likely that the insurance company will have to pay out against claims where he is concerned

◊ **risk-free** *or* **riskless** *adjective* with no risk involved; *a risk-free investment*

◊ **risky** *adjective* dangerous *or* which may cause harm; *he lost all his money in some risky ventures in South America*

QUOTE the accepted wisdom built upon for well over 100 years that government and high-grade corporate bonds were almost riskless
Forbes Magazine

rival *noun* person *or* company which competes in the same market; *a rival company; to undercut a rival; we are analyzing the rival brands on the market*

road *noun* **(a)** path used by cars *or* trucks, etc.; *to send or to ship goods by road; road transport costs have risen; the main office is on Maple Road; use the Park Road entrance to get to the buying department* **(b)** on the road = traveling; *the salesmen are on the road thirty weeks a year; we have twenty salesmen on the road*

robot *noun* machine which can be programmed to work like a person; *the car is made by robots*

◊ **robotics** *noun* study of robots *or* making of robots

rock *noun* large stone; *the company is on the rocks* = the company is in great financial difficulties

◊ **rock bottom** *noun* **rock-bottom prices =** the lowest prices possible; *sales have reached rock bottom* = sales have reached the lowest point possible

rocket *verb* to rise fast; *rocketing prices; prices have rocketed*

ROI = RETURN ON INVESTMENT

roll 1 *noun* something which has been turned over and over to wrap around itself; *the desk calculator uses a roll of paper* **2** *verb* to make something go forward by turning it over; *they rolled the computer into position*

◊ **roll over** *verb* to roll over credit *or* a debt = to make credit available over a continuing period *or* to allow a debt to stand after the repayment date; **to roll over your IRA =** to change the institution where your IRA funds are kept without penalty for withdrawal

◊ **rolling plan** *noun* plan which runs for a period of time and is updated regularly for the same period

◊ **rolling stock** *noun* property of a railroad that is on wheels, such as freight cars, passenger cars, etc.

room *noun* **(a)** part of a building, divided off from other parts by walls; *the chairman's room is at the end of the corridor;* **conference room =** room where a small meeting can take place; **mail room =** section of a building where incoming letters and packages are sorted and distributed to departments **(b)** bedroom in a hotel; *I want a room with bath for two nights;* **double room =** room with two beds, for two people; **room service =** arrangement in a hotel where food or drink can be served in a guest's bedroom **(c)** space; *the filing cabinets take up a lot of room; there is no more room in the computer file*

rotation *noun* taking turns; **to fill the position of chairman by rotation =** each member of the group is chairman for a period then gives the position to another member

rough *adjective* **(a)** approximate *or* not very accurate; **rough calculation** *or* **rough estimate =** approximate answer; *I made some rough calculations on the back of an envelope* **(b)** not finished; **rough copy =** draft of a document which will have changes made to it before it is complete; *he made a rough draft of the new design*

◊ **roughly** *adverb* more or less; *the sales volume is roughly twice last year's; the development cost of the project will be roughly $25,000*

◇ **rough out** *verb* to make a draft *or* a general design; *the financial manager roughed out a plan of investment*

round 1 *adjective* **(a) in round numbers** = not totally accurate, but correct to the nearest 10 or 100; **round lot** = fixed lot of stock or bonds for sale (usually 100) **(b) round trip** = journey from one place to another and back again; *round-trip ticket; round-trip fare*

◇ **round off** *verb* to express as the nearest whole number; *round off the amounts to the nearest dollar*

route *noun* **(a)** way which is regularly taken; **bus route** = normal way taken by a bus from one place to another; *companies were warned that normal shipping routes were dangerous because of the war* **(b) en route** = on the way; *the tanker sank when she was en route to the Gulf*

routine 1 *noun* normal *or* regular way of doing something; *he follows a daily routine - he takes the 8:15 train to New York, then the bus to his office, and returns by the same route in the evening; remodeling the conference room has disturbed the office routine* **2** *adjective* normal *or* which happens regularly; *routine work; routine call; a routine check of the fire equipment*

royalty *noun* money paid to an inventor *or* writer *or* the owner of land for the right to use his property (usually a certain percentage of sales, or a certain amount per sale); *oil royalties; he is receiving royalties from his invention*

RRP = RECOMMENDED RETAIL PRICE

RSVP = REPONDEZ S'IL VOUS PLAIT letters on an invitation showing the person to whom replies should be sent

rubber check *noun* check which cannot be cashed because the person writing it does not have enough money in the account to pay it, and so it will "bounce"

◇ **rubber stamp 1** *noun* stamp with rubber letters or figures on it to put the date *or* a note on a document; *he stamped the invoice with the rubber stamp "Paid"* **2** *verb* to agree to something without discussing it; *the board simply rubber stamped the agreement*

ruble *noun* money used in Russia

rule 1 *noun* general way of conduct; **as a rule** = usually; *as a rule, we do not give discounts over 20%;* **company rules** = general way of working in a company; *it is a company rule that smoking is not allowed in the offices* **2** *verb* **(a)** to give an official decision; *the commission of inquiry ruled that the company was in breach of contract; the judge ruled that the documents had to be deposited with the court* **(b)** to be in force *or* to be current; *prices which are ruling at the moment*

◇ **ruling 1** *adjective* in operation at the moment *or* current; *we will invoice at ruling prices* **2** *noun* decision; *the inquiry gave a ruling on the case; according to the ruling of the court, the contract was illegal*

run 1 *noun* **(a)** operation carried out using a machine, such as a computer; **a check run** = series of checks processed through a computer; **a computer run** = period of work of a computer; **test run** = trial made on a machine **(b)** rush to buy something; *the Post Office reported a run on the new stamps;* **a run on the bank** = rush by customers to take deposits out of a bank which they think may close down; **a run on the dollar** = rush to sell dollars and buy other currencies **(c)** regular route (of a plane *or* bus) **2** *verb* **(a)** to be in force; *the lease runs for twenty years; the lease has only six months to run* **(b)** to amount to; *the costs ran into thousands of dollars* **(c)** to manage *or* to organize; *she runs a mail-order business from home; they run a company sports club; he is running a multimillion-dollar company* **(d)** to work on a machine; *do not run the photocopier for more than four hours at a time; the computer was running invoices all night* **(e)** *(of buses, trains etc.)* to be working; *there is a bus running between Cleveland and Columbus; this train runs on weekdays*

NOTE: **running - ran - has run**

> QUOTE with interest rates running well above inflation, investors want something that offers a return for their money
>
> *Business Week*

runaway *adjective* **runaway inflation** = very rapid inflation, which is almost impossible to reduce

◇ **run into** *verb* **(a) to run into debt** = to start to have debts **(b)** to amount to; *costs have run into thousands of dollars; he has an income running into*

five figures = he earns more than $10,000

◊ **running** *noun* **(a) running total** = total carried from one column of figures to the next **(b) running costs** *or* **running expenses** *or* **costs of running a business** = money spent on the day-to-day cost of keeping a business going **(c) the company has made a profit for six years running** = the company has made a profit for six years one after the other

◊ **run out of** *verb* to have nothing left *or* to use up all the stock; *we have run out of letterhead stationery; the printer has run out of paper*

◊ **run up** *verb* to make debts go up quickly; *he quickly ran up a bill for $250*

rupee *noun* money used in India and some other countries

rush 1 *noun* doing something fast; **rush hour** = time when traffic is worst *or* when everyone is trying to travel to work or from work back home; *the taxi was delayed in the rush hour traffic;* **rush job** = job which has to be done fast; **rush order** = order which has to be supplied fast **2** *verb* to make something go fast; *to rush an order through the factory; to rush a shipment to Africa*

Ss

s & h = SHIPPING AND HANDLING

S&L = SAVINGS AND LOAN ASSOCIATION
NOTE: plural is **S&Ls**

sabotage *noun* illegal action to damage machinery or records, so as to prevent a business from working profitably

sack 1 *noun* large bag made of strong cloth or plastic, used for produce or for carrying mail; *a sack of potatoes; we sell onions by the sack* **2** *verb* **to sack someone** = to dismiss someone from a job; *he was sacked or he got sacked after being late for work*

safe 1 *noun* heavy metal box which cannot be opened without dialing a combination or using a special key, in

which valuable documents, money, etc. can be kept; *put the documents in the safe; we keep the petty cash in the safe;* **fireproof safe** = safe which cannot be harmed by fire; **night safe** = safe in the outside wall of a bank, where money and documents can be deposited at night, using a special door; **wall safe** = safe installed in a wall **2** *adjective* **(a)** out of danger; **keep the documents in a safe place** = in a place where they cannot be stolen or destroyed **(b) safe investments** = shares, etc., which are not likely to fall in value

◊ **safe deposit** *noun* safe where you can leave jewelry or documents

◊ **safe deposit box** *noun* box which you can rent to keep jewelry or documents in a bank's safe

◊ **safely** *adverb* without being harmed; *the cargo was unloaded safely from the sinking ship*

◊ **safeguard** *verb* to protect; *to safeguard the interests of the shareholders*

◊ **safekeeping** *noun* being looked after carefully; *we put the documents into the bank for safekeeping*

◊ **safety** *noun* **(a)** being free from danger or risk; **safety margin** = time *or* space allowed for something to be safe; **margin of safety** = sales which are above the break-even point; **to take safety precautions** *or* **safety measures** = to act to make sure something is safe; **safety regulations** = rules to make a place of work safe for the workers **(b) fire safety** = making a place of work safe for the workers in case of fire; **fire safety officer** = person in a company responsible for seeing that the workers are safe if a fire breaks out **(c) for safety** = to make something safe *or* to be safe; *put the documents in the drawer for safety; to take a copy of the disk for safety;* **safety stock** = extra inventory carried by a business to avoid the possibility of a stockout

sail *verb* (i) to travel on water; (ii) to leave harbor; *the ship sails at 12:00*

◊ **sailing** *noun* departure (of a ship); *there are no sailings from Boston to the Caribbean because of the strike*

salary *noun* payment for work, made to an employee usually as a check at the end of each month; *she got a salary increase in June; the company froze all salaries for a six-month period;* **basic salary** = normal salary without extra payments; **gross salary** = salary before tax is deducted; **net salary =** salary which is left after deducting tax and social security contributions; **starting salary =** amount of payment for an employee when starting work; *he was appointed at a starting salary of $10,000;* **salary cut =** sudden reduction in salary; **salary check =** monthly check by which an employee is paid; **salary deductions =** money which a company removes from salaries to give to the government as tax, social security contributions, etc.; **salary review =** examination of salaries in a company to decide if workers should earn more; *she had a salary review last April or her salary was reviewed last April;* **scale of salaries** *or* **salary scale =** list of salaries showing different levels of pay in different jobs in the same company; **a company's salary structure =** organization of salaries in a company, with different rates for different types of jobs

◊ **salaried** *adjective* earning a salary; *the company has 250 salaried staff members*

sale *noun* (a) act of selling, giving an item or providing a service in exchange for money; **cash sale =** selling something for cash; **credit card sale =** selling something on credit, using a credit card; **forced sale =** selling something because a court orders it *or* because it is the only thing to do to avoid a financial crisis; **sale and leaseback =** situation where a company sells a property to raise cash and then leases it back from the purchaser; **sale or return =** system where the retailer sends goods back if they are not sold, and pays the supplier only for goods sold; *we have taken 4,000 items on sale or return;* **bill of sale =** document which the seller gives to the buyer to show that a sale has taken place; **conditions of sale =** agreed ways in which a sale takes place (such as discounts and credit terms) (b) **for sale =** ready to be sold; **to offer something for sale** *or* **to put something up for sale =** to announce that something is ready to be sold; *they put the factory up for sale; his store is for sale; these items are not for sale to the general public* (c) **on sale =** ready to be sold in a store; *these items are on sale in most drugstores* (d) **sales =** (i) money received for selling something; (ii) number of items sold; *sales have risen over the first quarter;* **gross sales =** total income from sales; **net sales =** income from sales after deduction of commissions, returns, etc.;

sales analysis = examining the reports of sales to see why items have or have not sold well; **sales appeal =** quality which makes customers want to buy; **sales book =** record of sales; **book sales =** sales as recorded in the sales book; **sales budget =** plan of probable sales; **sales campaign =** planned work to achieve higher sales; **sales conference** *or* **sales meeting =** meeting of sales managers, representatives, publicity staff, etc., to discuss results and future sales plans; **cost of sales =** all the costs of a product sold, including manufacturing costs and the staff costs of the production department; **sales department =** section of a company which deals in selling the company's products or services; **domestic sales =** sales in the home market; **sales drive =** vigorous work to increase sales; **sales executive =** person in a company in charge of sales; **sales figures =** total sales, or sales broken down by category; **sales force =** group of salesmen; **sales forecast =** calculation of future sales; **forward sales =** sales (of shares, commodities, foreign exchange) for delivery at a later date; **sales ledger =** book in which income from sales is recorded; **sales ledger clerk =** office worker who deals with the sales ledger; **sales literature =** printed information (such as leaflets, prospectuses) which helps sales; **sales manager =** person in charge of a sales department; **sales people** *or* **sales staff =** employees working in the sales department, selling goods or services; **sales pitch =** talk by a salesman to persuade a customer to buy a product; **sales quota =** amount of sales that each salesman is expected to make during a certain period; **monthly sales report =** report made showing the number of items *or* amount of money received for selling stock; *in the sales reports all the European countries are bracketed together;* **sales revenue =** money received from sales; **sales tax =** tax to be paid on each sale (usually levied by states on retail sales); **sales volume** *or* **volume of sales =** number of units sold (e) selling of goods at specially low prices; *the store is having a sale to clear old stock; the sale price is 50% of the normal price;* **clearance sale =** sale of items at low prices to get rid of the stock; **half-price sale =** sale of items at half the usual price

◊ **salability** *or* **saleability** *noun* quality of an item which makes it easy to sell

◊ **salable** *or* **saleable** *adjective* which can easily be sold

◊ **salesclerk** *noun* person who sells goods to customers in a store

◊ **salesgirl** *noun* girl who sells goods to customers in a store

◊ **saleslady** *noun* woman who sells goods to customers in a store

◊ **salesman** *noun* **(a)** man who sells goods or services to members of the public; *he is the head salesman in the carpet department; a used car salesman;* door-to-door **salesman** = man who goes from one house to the next, asking people to buy something; **insurance salesman** = man who encourages clients to take out insurance policies **(b)** person who represents a company, selling its products or services to retail stores; *we have six salesmen calling on accounts in central New York*
NOTE: plural is **salesmen**

◊ **salesmanship** *noun* art of selling *or* of persuading customers to buy

◊ **salesperson** *noun* person who sells goods or services to customers

◊ **salesroom** *noun* room where an auction takes place

◊ **saleswoman** *noun* woman in a store who sells goods to customers
NOTE: plural is **saleswomen**

QUOTE the wage agreement includes sales clerks and commission sales people in stores in Toronto
Toronto Star

salvage 1 *noun* **(a)** saving a ship *or* a cargo from being destroyed; **salvage money** = payment made by the owner of a ship *or* a cargo to the person who has saved it; **salvage vessel** = ship which specializes in saving other ships and their cargoes **(b)** goods saved from a wrecked ship *or* from a fire, etc.; *a sale of flood salvage items;* **salvage value** = scrap value, the value of an item sold for scrap **2** *verb* **(a)** to save goods *or* a ship from being wrecked; *we are selling off a warehouse full of salvaged goods* **(b)** to save something from loss; *the company is trying to salvage its reputation after the CEO was sent to prison for fraud; the receiver managed to salvage something from the collapse of the company*

sample 1 *noun* **(a)** specimen, a small part of an item which is used to show what the whole item is like; *a sample of the cloth or a cloth sample;* **check sample** = sample to be used to see if a whole consignment is acceptable; **free sample** = sample given free to advertise a

product; **sample book** *or* **book of samples** = book showing samples of different types of cloth *or* paper, etc. **(b)** small group taken to show what a larger group is like; *we interviewed a sample of potential customers;* **a random sample** = a sample taken without any selection **2** *verb* **(a)** to test *or* to try something by taking a small amount; *to sample a product before buying it* **(b)** to ask a representative group of people questions to find out what the reactions of a much larger group would be; *they sampled 2,000 people at random to test the new drink*

◊ **sampling** *noun* **(a)** testing a product by taking a small amount; *sampling of California produce;* **acceptance sampling** = testing a small sample of a batch to see if the whole batch is good enough to be accepted; **free sampling** = giving a small amount of a product as a free gift, for promotional purposes **(b)** testing the reactions of a small group of people to find out the reactions of a larger group of consumers; *random sampling*

sanction 1 *noun* **(a)** permission; *you will need the sanction of the local authorities before you can knock down the office building* **(b)** economic **sanctions** = restrictions on trade with a country in order to influence its political situation *or* in order to make its government change its policy; *to impose sanctions on a country or to lift sanctions* **2** *verb* to approve; *the board sanctioned the expenditure of $1.2m on the development project*

sandwich boards *noun* printed signs carried in front of and behind a person to display advertisements

◊ **sandwich lease** *noun* lease held by someone who sublets the property he is leasing

◊ **sandwich man** *noun* man who carries sandwich boards

satisfaction *noun* feeling of being happy *or* good feeling; **customer satisfaction** = making a customer pleased with what he has bought; **job satisfaction** = a worker's feeling that he is happy in his place of work and pleased with the work he does

◊ **satisfy** *verb* **(a)** to satisfy a client = to make a client pleased with what he has purchased; **a satisfied customer** = a customer who has got what he wanted **(b)** to satisfy a demand = to fill a demand; *we cannot produce enough to satisfy the demand for the product*

saturation *noun* filling completely; **saturation of the market** *or* **market saturation =** situation where the market has taken as much of the product as it can buy; **the market has reached saturation point =** the market is at a point where it cannot buy any more of the product
◊ **saturate** *verb* to fill something completely; *to saturate the market; the market for home computers is saturated*

save *verb* (a) to keep (money) *or* not to spend (money); *he is trying to save money by walking to work; she is saving to buy a house* (b) not to waste *or* to use less; *to save time, let us continue the discussion in the taxi to the airport; the government is encouraging companies to save energy* (c) to store data on a computer disk; *do not forget to save your files when you have finished keyboarding them*
◊ **save on** *verb* not to waste *or* to use less; *by introducing shift work we find we can save on fuel*
◊ **saver** *noun* person who saves money
◊ **save up** *verb* to put money aside for a special purpose; *they are saving up for a vacation in Europe*
◊ **saving 1** *noun* using less; *we are aiming for a 10% saving in fuel 2 suffix* which uses less; *an energy-saving or labor-saving device =* machine which saves energy *or* labor; *timesaving =* which takes less time
◊ **savings** *plural noun* money saved; *he put all his savings into a money market account; savings bond =* document showing that you have invested money in a government savings plan (usually exempt from taxes); **savings account =** bank account where you can put money in regularly and which pays interest
◊ **savings bank** *noun* bank which accepts deposit of money and pays interest on it (it invests the money deposited in mortgages to homebuyers or in safe securities)
◊ **savings and loan (association) (S&L)** *noun* financial association which accepts and pays interest on deposits from investors and lends money to people who are buying property

SBA = SMALL BUSINESS ADMINISTRATION

scab *noun informal* worker who goes on working when there is a strike

scale 1 *noun* (a) system which is graded into various levels; **scale of charges** *or* **scale of prices =** list showing various prices; **fixed scale of charges =** rate of charging which does not change; **scale of salaries** *or* **salary scale =** list of salaries showing different levels of pay in different jobs in the same company; *he was appointed to the top end of the salary scale; incremental scale =* salary scale with regular annual salary increases (b) **large scale** *or* **small scale =** working with large *or* small amounts of investment *or* staff, etc.; **to start in business on a small scale =** to start in business with a small staff *or* few products *or* small investments; **economy of scale =** making a product at a lower unit cost by manufacturing it or buying it in larger quantities (c) *(also* **scales)** machine for weighing **2** *verb* **to scale down** *or* **to scale up =** to lower *or* to increase in proportion

scalper *noun* person who makes a quick profit, often by illegal means, as by buying and then reselling tickets to a popular show or sporting event

scam *noun informal* case of fraud

scarce *adjective* not easily found *or* not common; *scarce raw materials; reliable, trained employees are scarce*
◊ **scarceness** *or* **scarcity** *noun* lack *or* being scarce; *the scarceness of trained staff; there is a scarcity of trained staff; scarcity value =* value of something because it is rare and there is a large demand for it

schedule 1 *noun* (a) timetable *or* plan of time drawn up in advance; **to be ahead of schedule =** to be early; **to be on schedule =** to be on time; **to be behind schedule =** to be late; *the project is on schedule; the building was completed ahead of schedule; I am sorry to say that we are three months behind schedule; the sales manager has a busy schedule of appointments; his secretary tried to fit me into his schedule* (b) list (especially additional documents attached to a contract); *please find enclosed our schedule of charges; schedule of territories to which a contract applies; see the attached schedule or as per the attached schedule* **2** *verb* (a) to list officially; **scheduled prices** or **scheduled charges (b)** to plan the time when something will happen; **the building is scheduled for completion in May; scheduled flight** = regular flight which is in the airline timetable; **he left for Helsinki on a scheduled flight**

◊ **scheduling** noun drawing up a plan or a timetable

scheme noun plan or arrangement or way of working; **bonus scheme; profitsharing scheme**

scope noun opportunity or possibility; **there is scope for improvement in our sales performance** = the sales performance could be improved; **there is considerable scope for expansion into the export market**

scrap 1 noun waste material or pieces of metal to be melted down to make new metal ingots; **to sell a ship for scrap; its scrap value is $2,500; scrap dealer** or **scrap merchant** = person who deals in scrap **2** verb **(a)** to give up or to stop working on; **to scrap plans for expansion (b)** to throw (something) away as useless; **they had to scrap 10,000 spare parts**
NOTE: **scrapping - scrapped**

screen 1 noun glass surface on which computer information or TV pictures, etc., can be shown; **a TV screen; he brought up the information on the screen 2** verb **to screen candidates** = to examine candidates to see if they are completely suitable

◊ **screening** noun **the screening of candidates** = examining candidates to see if they are suitable

scrip noun temporary document that entitles the holder to receive stock, cash or something else of value on presentation

SDR = SPECIAL DRAWING RIGHTS

sea noun area of salt water; **to send a shipment by sea**

◊ **seaport** noun port by the sea

seal 1 noun **(a) common seal** or **company's seal** = metal stamp for stamping documents with the name of the company; **to attach the company's seal to a document (b)** piece of paper or metal or wax attached to close

something, so that it can be opened only if the paper or metal or wax is removed or broken; **customs seal** = seal attached by customs office to a box, to show that the contents have or have not passed through the customs **(c) seal of approval** = certificate showing that a product has been approved by an organization **2** verb **(a)** to close something tightly; **the computer disks were sent in a sealed container; sealed envelope** = envelope where the back has been stuck down to close it; **the information was sent in a sealed envelope; sealed bids** = bids sent in sealed envelopes, which will all be opened at a certain time; **the company has asked for sealed bids for the warehouse (b)** to attach a seal or to stamp something with a seal; **the customs office sealed the shipment**

search noun **(a)** process of looking for something; **the committee began the search for a new president** (in real estate) examination of records of a property, to make sure that the vendor has the right to sell it

season noun **(a)** one of four parts which a year is divided into (spring, summer, fall, winter) **(b)** a period of time when something usually takes place; **tourist season** = period when there are many people on vacation; **busy season** or **slack season** = period when a company is busy or not very busy; **end of season sale** = selling goods cheaply when the season in which they would be used is over (such as summer clothes sold cheaply in the fall)

◊ **seasonal** adjective which lasts for a season or which only happens during a particular season; **the demand for this item is very seasonal; seasonal variations in sales patterns; seasonal adjustments** = changes made to figures to take account of seasonal variations; **seasonal demand** = demand which exists only during part of the year; **seasonal unemployment** = unemployment which rises and falls according to the season

◊ **seasonally** adverb **seasonally adjusted figures** = statistics which are adjusted to take account of seasonal variations

◊ **season ticket** noun (i) rail or bus ticket which can be used for any number of rides over a period (as 6 or 12 months); (ii) ticket to all games or performances in a particular series

sec = SECOND, SECRETARY

SEC = SECURITIES AND EXCHANGE COMMISSION

second 1 *adjective* (thing) which comes after the first; **second mortgage** = further mortgage on a property which is already mortgaged; **second quarter** = three month period from April to the end of June **2** *verb* **to second a motion** = to be the first person to support a proposal put forward by someone else; *Mrs. Smith seconded the motion or the motion was seconded by Mrs. Smith*

◊ **secondary** *adjective* second in importance; **secondary industry** = industry which uses basic raw materials to make manufactured goods

◊ **second-class** *adjective & adverb* less expensive *or* less comfortable way of traveling; *to travel second-class; the price of a second-class ticket is half that of a first class; I find second-class hotels are just as comfortable as the best ones;* second-class mail = mail service for sending newspapers and magazines

◊ **seconder** *noun* person who seconds a proposal; *there was no seconder for the motion so it was not put to the vote*

◊ **second half** *or* **second half-year** *noun* period of six months from July 1 to end of December; *the figures for the second half are up on those for the first part of the year*

◊ **secondhand** *adjective & adverb* used *or* not new *or* which has been owned by someone before; *a secondhand car salesman; the secondhand computer market or the market in secondhand computers; to buy something secondhand; look at the prices of secondhand cars or look at secondhand car prices;* secondhand dealer = dealer who buys and sells secondhand items

◊ **second-rate** *adjective* not of good quality; *never buy anything second-rate*

◊ **seconds** *plural noun* items which have been turned down by the quality controller as not being top quality; *the store has a sale of seconds*

secret *noun & adjective* (something) hidden *or* not known by many people; *the chairman kept the contract secret from the rest of the board; they signed a secret deal with their main rivals;* to keep a secret = not to tell someone a secret which you know

◊ **secretary** *noun* (a) person who helps to organize work *or* types letters *or* files documents *or* arranges meetings, etc., for someone; *my secretary deals with incoming orders; his secretary phoned to say he would be late;* executive secretary = secretary to an executive *or* to a top-level member of an organization **(b)** official of a company *or* society; *he was elected secretary of the committee or committee secretary;* corporate secretary = person (in some corporations) who is responsible for the legal and financial affairs **(c)** U.S. government official who heads an administrative department; **Secretary of State** = head of the State Department, which deals with foreign affairs; **Secretary of the Treasury** = head of the Treasury, which deals with financial affairs

◊ **secretarial** *adjective* referring to the work of a secretary; *she is taking a secretarial course; he is looking for secretarial work; we need extra secretarial help to deal with the mailings;* secretarial college = college which teaches typing, shorthand and word processing

◊ **secretariat** *noun* administrative office of a government *or* international organization; *the United Nations secretariat*

section *noun* part of something; **legal section** = department in a business dealing with legal matters

sector *noun* **(a)** part of the economy *or* the business organization of a country; *all sectors of the economy suffered from the fall in the exchange rate; technology is a booming sector of the economy;* public sector = part of the economy that includes all government levels and public services; **private sector** = part of the economy that includes businesses and households; *the expansion is funded completely by the private sector; salaries in the private sector have increased faster than in the public* **(b)** *(on a Stock Exchange)* group of securities relating to a single industry

secure 1 *adjective* safe *or* which cannot change; **secure job** = job from which you are not likely to be dismissed or laid off; **secure investment** = investment where you are not likely to lose money **2** *verb* **(a) to secure a loan** = to pledge a property as a security for a loan **(b)** to get (something) safely into your control; *he secured the backing of an Australian group*

◊ **secured** *adjective* **secured loan** = loan which is guaranteed by the borrower giving valuable property as security; **secured creditor** = person who is owed money by someone, and can legally claim the same amount of the borrower's property if he fails to pay back the money owed; **secured debts** = debts which are guaranteed by assets

◊ **securities** *plural noun* investments in stocks and bonds; certificates to show that someone owns stock; **listed securities** = securities which can be bought or sold *or* securities which appear on an official stock exchange list; **securities analyst** = person who notes the performance of securities and offers advice to investors and brokers; **the securities market** = stock exchanges, places where stocks and shares can be bought or sold; **securities trader** = person whose business is buying and selling stocks and shares; **Securities and Exchange Commission (SEC)** = federal agency that protects investors by regulating and supervising the selling of securities

◊ **security** *noun* **(a) job security** = feeling which a worker has that he has a right to keep his job *or* that his job will never end; **security of employment** = feeling by a worker that he has the right to keep his job until he retires; **security of tenure** = right to keep a job *or* rented accommodation, provided that certain conditions are met **(b)** being protected; **airport security** = actions taken to protect aircraft and passengers against attack; **security guard** = person who protects an office *or* factory against burglars; **office security** = protecting an office against theft **(c)** being secret; *security is an important consideration for government contractors;* **security printer** = printer which prints paper money, secret government documents, etc. **(d) social security** = money *or* help provided by the government to people who need it; *he lives on social security payments* **(e)** guarantee that someone will repay money borrowed; **to stand security for someone** = to guarantee that if the person does not repay a loan, you will repay it for him; *to give something as security for a debt; to use a house as security for a loan; the bank lent him $20,000 without security*

seed money *noun* first payment of venture capital into a new business

seek *verb* to ask for; *they are seeking damages for loss of revenue;* **to seek an interview** = to ask if you can see someone; *she sought an interview with the mayor*
NOTE: **seeking - sought**

seize *verb* to take hold of something *or* to take possession of something; *the customs office seized the shipment of books; the court ordered the company's funds to be seized*

◊ **seizure** *noun* taking possession of something; *the court ordered the seizure of the shipment or of the company's funds*

select 1 *adjective* of top quality *or* specially chosen; *our customers are very select; a select range of merchandise* **2** *verb* to choose; **selected items are reduced by 25%** = some items have been reduced by 25%

◊ **selection** *noun* choice; thing which has been chosen; *the store carries a wide selection of clothing;* **selection board** *or* **selection committee** = committee which chooses a candidate for a job; **selection procedure** = general method of choosing a candidate for a job

◊ **selective** *adjective* which chooses; **selective strikes** = strikes in certain areas *or* at certain factories, but not everywhere

self *pronoun* your own person; *(on checks)* **"pay self"** = pay the person who has signed the check

◊ **self-** *prefix* referring to oneself; **self-addressed envelope** = envelope addressed by someone to himself, so that information can be sent back to him

◊ **self-contained office** *noun* office which has all facilities inside it, and its own entrance, so that it is separate from other offices in the same building

◊ **self-employed 1** *adjective* working for yourself *or* not on the payroll of a company; *a self-employed engineer; he worked for a bank for ten years but now is self-employed* **2** *noun* **the self-employed** = people who work for themselves

◊ **self-financed** *adjective* **the project is completely self-financed** = the project pays its development costs out of its own revenue, with no subsidies

◊ **self-financing 1** *noun* the financing of development costs, purchase of capital assets etc., of a company from its own resources **2** *adjective* **the company is** completely self-financing = the company finances its development costs *or* capital assets, etc., from its own resources

◊ **self-made man** *noun* man who is rich and successful because of his work, not because he inherited money or position

◊ **self-mailer** *noun* envelope or card addressed back to the mailing company, so that people can respond to a mailing

◊ **self-regulation** *noun* regulating by a body (such as a stock exchange) of its own members

◊ **self-regulatory** *adjective* (organization, such as a stock exchange) which regulates itself

◊ **self-service** *adjective* a self-service store = store where customers take goods from the shelves and pay for them at the checkout; **self-service gasoline station** = gasoline station where the customers put the gasoline in their cars themselves

◊ **self-sufficiency** *noun* being self-sufficient

◊ **self-sufficient** *adjective* producing enough food *or* raw materials for its own needs; *the country is self-sufficient in oil*

◊ **self-supporting** *adjective* which finances itself from its own resources, with no subsidies

sell 1 *noun* act of selling; **to give a product the hard sell** = to make great efforts to persuade customers to buy it; *he tried to give me the hard sell* = he put a lot of effort into trying to persuade me to buy his product; **soft sell** = persuading people to buy, by encouraging and not forcing them to do so **2** *verb* (a) to exchange goods for money; *they have decided to sell their house; they tried to sell their house for $100,000; to sell something on credit; her house is difficult to sell; their products are easy to sell;* **to sell forward** = to sell foreign currency, commodities, etc., for delivery at a later date (b) to be bought; *these items sell well in the preChristmas period; those packs sell for $25 a dozen*
NOTE: **selling - sold**

◊ **sell-by date** *noun* date on a food package which is the last date on which the food is guaranteed to be good

◊ **seller** *noun* (a) person who sells; *there were few sellers in the market, so prices remained high;* **seller's market** = market where the seller can ask high prices because there is a large demand for the product (b) thing which sells; *this*

book is a steady seller; **best-seller** = item (especially a book) which sells very well

◊ **selling 1** *noun* **direct selling** = selling a product direct to the customer without going through a store; **mail-order selling** = selling by taking orders and supplying a product by mail; **selling costs** = amount of money to be paid for advertising, reps' commissions, etc., involved in selling something; **selling price** = price at which someone is willing to sell **2** *suffix* **fast-selling items** = items which sell quickly; **best-selling car** = car which sells better than other models

◊ **sell off** *verb* to sell goods quickly to get rid of them

◊ **sell out** *verb* (a) to sell all stock; *to sell out of a product line; we have sold out of electronic typewriters; this item has sold out* (b) to sell out = to sell one's business; *he sold out and retired to Florida*

◊ **sellout** *noun* **this item has been a sellout** = all the stock of the item has been sold

◊ **sell up** *verb* to sell a business and all the stock

semi- *prefix* half *or* partial

◊ **semi-finished** *adjective* **semi-finished products** = products which are partly finished

◊ **semi-skilled** *adjective* **semi-skilled workers** = workers who have had some training

send *verb* to make someone *or* something go from one place to another; *to send a letter or an order or a shipment; the company is sending him to France to be general manager of the Paris office; send the letter airmail if you want it to arrive next week; the shipment was sent by rail*
NOTE: **sending - sent**

◊ **send away for** *verb* to write asking for something to be sent to you; *we sent away for the new catalog*

◊ **sender** *noun* person who sends; **"return to sender"** = words on an envelope *or* parcel to show that it is to be sent back to the person who sent it

◊ **send for** *verb* to write asking for something to be sent to you; *we sent for the new catalog*

◊ **send in** *verb* to send (a letter); *he sent in his resignation; to send in an application*

◊ **send off** *verb* to put (a letter) in the mail

◊ **send on** *verb* to mail a letter which you have received, and address it to someone else; *he sent the letter on to his brother*

senior *adjective* older; more important; (worker) who has been employed longer than another; **senior manager** *or* **senior executive** = manager *or* director who has been an executive longer than others; **senior partner** = person in a firm who as been a partner longer than anyone else; **John Smith, Senior** = the older John Smith (i.e., the father of John Smith, Junior)
◊ **seniority** *noun* being older; being an employee of the company longer; **the managers were listed in order of seniority** = the manager who had been an employee the longest was put at the top of the list

sensitive *adjective* able to feel something acutely; *the market is very sensitive to the result of the elections;* **price-sensitive product** = product which will sell less if the price is increased

separate 1 *adjective* not together; **to send something under separate cover** = to send something in a different envelope **2** *verb* to divide; *the personnel are separated into part-timers and full-time staff*
◊ **separately** *adverb* not together; *each job was invoiced separately*
◊ **separation** *noun* leaving a job (resigning, retiring, or being fired or laid off); **separation rate** = number of workers who have quit jobs during a certain period

sequester *or* **sequestrate** *verb* to take and keep (property) because a court has ordered it
◊ **sequestration** *noun* taking and keeping of property on the order of a court
◊ **sequestrator** *noun* person who takes and keeps property on the order of a court

serial number *noun* number in a series, used for identification; *this batch of shoes has the serial number 25-02*

series *noun* group of items following one after the other; *a series of successful takeovers made the corporation one of the largest in the trade*

NOTE: plural is **series**

serious *adjective* severe *or* important; *the storm caused serious damage; the management is making serious attempts to improve working conditions; the damage to the computer was not very serious*
◊ **seriously** *adverb* badly; *the cargo was seriously damaged by water*

servant *noun* person who is paid to work in someone's house; **civil servant** = person who works in the administrative offices of a government

serve *verb* to deal with (a customer); **to serve a customer** = to take a customer's order and provide what he wants; **to serve in a restaurant** = to fill customers' orders; **to serve someone with a writ** *or* **to serve a writ on someone** = to give someone a writ officially, so that he has to obey it

service 1 *noun* **(a)** working for a company *or* in a store, etc.; **length of service** = number of years someone has worked **(b)** the work of dealing with customers *or* payment for help for the customer; *the service in that restaurant is extremely slow; to add on 10% for service;* **the bill includes service** = includes a charge added for the work involved; *is the service included?* **(c)** keeping a machine in good working order; *the machine has been sent in for service; the routine service of equipment;* **service agreement** *or* **service contract** = contract by which a company keeps a piece of equipment in good working order; **service center** = office *or* workshop which specializes in keeping machines in good working order; **service department** = section of a company which keeps customers' machines in good working order; **service engineer** = engineer who specializes in keeping machines in good working order; **service handbook** *or* **service manual** = book which shows how to service a machine; **service station** = garage where you can buy gasoline and have small repairs done to a car **(d)** business *or* office which gives help when it is needed; **answering service** = office which answers the telephone and takes messages for a company; **24-hour service** = help which is available for the whole day; **service bureau** = business which does work for other businesses, such as preparing mailings, keyboarding address lists, etc.; **service department** =

department of a company which does not deal with production or sales (accounts, personnel, etc.); **service companies** or **service industry** = companies or industry which does not make products, but offers a service (such as banking, insurance, transportation) **(e) to put a machine into service** = to start using a machine **(f)** regular working of a public organization; *the postal service is efficient; the bus service is very irregular; we have a good train service to New York;* **the civil service** = the administrative offices of a government; *he has a job in the civil service; she had to take a civil service exam to qualify for the position* **2** verb **(a)** to keep a machine in good working order; *the car needs to be serviced every six months; the computer has gone back to the manufacturer for servicing* **(b)** to service a debt = to pay interest on a debt; *the company is having problems in servicing its debts*

◊ **service charge** noun **(a)** charge added to costs (as in a restaurant) to pay for service **(b)** charge deducted from a bank account for services provided by the bank (such as arranging a loan)

> QUOTE over the next decade, rising wage costs will force America's service companies to restructure, just as manufacturing companies have done over the past ten years
> *Forbes Magazine*

session noun meeting or period when a group of people meets; *the morning session* or *the afternoon session will be held in the conference room;* **opening session** or **closing session** = first part or last part of a conference

set 1 *noun* group of items which go together or which are used together or which are sold together; *set of tools* or *set of equipment;* **boxed set** = set of items sold together in a box **2** *adjective* fixed or which cannot be changed; *each dish on the menu has a set price; she has a set goal in life* - *to become president of the company* **3** verb to fix or to arrange; *we have to set a price for the new computer; the price of the calculator has been set low, so as to achieve maximum unit sales;* **the auction set a record for high prices** = the prices at the auction were the highest ever reached
NOTE: **setting - set**

◊ **set against** verb to balance one group of figures against another group to try to make them cancel each other out; *to set*

the costs against the invoice; can you set the expenses against tax?

◊ **set aside** verb to decide not to apply a decision; *the arbitrator's award was set aside on appeal*

◊ **set back** verb to make something late; *the project was set back six weeks by bad weather*

◊ **setback** noun stopping progress; *the company suffered a series of setbacks in 1984; the shares had a setback on the stock exchange*

◊ **set out** verb to put clearly in writing; *to set out the details in a report*

◊ **set up** verb **(a)** to begin (something) or to organize (something) new; *to set up an inquiry* or *a special committee;* **to set up a company** = to start a company legally **(b)** **to set up in business** = to start a new business; *he set up in business as an insurance broker; he set himself up as a tax consultant*

◊ **setting up costs** or **setup costs** plural noun costs of getting a machine or a factory ready to make a new product after finishing work on another one

◊ **setup** noun **(a)** arrangement or organization; **the setup in the office** = the way the office is organized **(b)** commercial firm; *he works for a PR setup*

> QUOTE a sharp setback in foreign trade accounted for most of the winter slowdown
> *Fortune*

settle verb **(a)** **to settle an account** = to pay what is owed **(b)** **to settle a claim** = to agree to pay what is asked for; *the insurance company refused to settle his claim for storm damage;* **the two parties settled out of court** = the two parties reached an agreement privately without continuing the court case

◊ **settlement** noun **(a)** payment of an account; **settlement date** = day when stock that has been bought must be paid for and transferred to the buyer; *our basic discount is 20% but we offer an extra 5% for rapid settlement* = we take a further 5% off the price if the customer pays quickly; **settlement in cash** or **cash settlement** = payment of an invoice in cash, not by check **(b)** final stage in the purchase of a property; *we go to settlement next week* **(c)** agreement after an argument; **to effect a settlement between two parties** = to bring two parties together to make them agree

◊ **settle on** verb to leave property to someone when you die; *he settled his property on his children*

several *adjective* more than a few *or* some; *several managers are retiring this year; several of our products sell well in Japan*

◊ **severally** *adverb* separately *or* not jointly; **they are jointly and severally liable =** they are liable both as a group and as individuals

severance pay *noun* money paid as compensation to someone who is losing his job

severe *adjective* bad *or* serious; *the company suffered severe losses in the European market; the government imposed severe financial restrictions*

◊ **severely** *adverb* badly *or* in a serious way; *train services have been severely affected by snow*

shady *adjective* not honest; *shady deal*

shake *verb* (a) to move something quickly from side to side (b) to surprise *or* to shock; *the markets were shaken by the company's latest figures*
NOTE: shaking - shook - has shaken

◊ **shakeout** *noun* marked change in an industry, which forces weaker companies to go out of business; *only three companies were left after the shakeout in the computer market*

◊ **shakeup** *noun* total reorganization; *the CEO ordered a shakeup of the sales departments*

◊ **shaky** *adjective* not very sure *or* not very reliable; *the year got off to a shaky start*

share 1 *noun* (a) **to have a share in =** to take part in *or* to contribute to; *to have a share in management decisions; market share* *or* **share of the market =** percentage of a total market which the sales of a company cover; *the company hopes to boost its market share; their share of the market has gone up by 10%* (b) one of many parts into which a company's capital is divided; *he bought a block of shares in IBM; shares fell on the Tokyo market; the company offered 1.8m shares on the market;* **share capital =** value of the assets of a company held as shares **2** *verb* (a) to own *or* use something together with someone else; *to share a telephone; to share an office* (b) to divide something up among several people; *three companies share the market; to share computer time; to share the profits among the senior executives;* to share information *or* to

share data = to give someone information which you have

◊ **shareholder** *noun* person who owns shares in a mutual fund *or* in a company; *to call a shareholders' meeting;* **shareholders' equity =** total assets minus total liabilities of a\ company; **majority** *or* **minority shareholder =** person who owns more *or* less than half the shares in a company; *the lawyer acting on behalf of the minority shareholders*

◊ **shareholding** *noun* group of shares in a company owned by one person; **a majority shareholding** *or* **a minority shareholding =** group of shares which are more *or* less than half the total; *he acquired a minority shareholding in the company; she has sold all her shareholdings;* **dilution of shareholding =** situation where the ordinary share capital of a company has been increased, but without an increase in the assets so that each share is worth less than before

◊ **sharing** *noun* dividing up; **profit sharing =** dividing profits among workers; *the company operates a profitsharing scheme;* **time-sharing =** (i) owning a property in part, with the right to use it for a period each year; (ii) sharing a computer system with different users working on different terminals

shark *noun* **loan shark =** person who lends money at a very high interest rate

sharp *adjective* (a) sudden; *sharp rally on the stock market; sharp drop in prices* (b) **sharp practice =** way of doing business which is not honest, but not illegal

◊ **sharply** *adverb* suddenly; *shares dipped sharply in yesterday's trading*

sheet *noun* (a) **sheet of paper =** piece of paper; **sheet feed =** device which puts one sheet at a time into a computer printer or photocopier; **sales sheet =** paper which gives details of a product and explains why it is good; **time sheet =** paper showing when a worker starts work and when he leaves work in the evening (b) **balance sheet =** statement of the financial position of a company at the end of a financial year or at the end of a period; *the company's balance sheet for 1984; the accountants prepared a balance sheet for the first half-year*

shelf *noun* flat surface attached to a wall *or* in a cupboard on which items for sale are displayed; *the shelves in the supermarket were full of items before the Christmas rush;* **shelf life of a product =** number of days or weeks when the product will stay on the shelf in the store and still be good to use; **shelf space =** amount of space on shelves in a store

NOTE: plural is **shelves**

QUOTE until recently, plastics weren't used for food that requires long shelf life because most of them didn't provide sufficient oxygen penetration to prevent food spoilage
Industrial World

shell corporation *noun* corporation which does not trade, but exists only as a name to be used to hold shares in other businesses

shelter *noun* protected place; **tax shelter =** financial arrangement (such as a pension plan) where investments can be made without tax

shelve *verb* to postpone *or* to put back to another date; *the project was shelved; discussion of the problem has been shelved*

◇ **shelving** *noun* **(a)** rows of shelves *or* space on shelves; *we installed metal shelving in the household goods department* **(b)** postponing; *the shelving of the project has resulted in six dismissals*

shift 1 *noun* **(a)** group of workers who work for a period, and then are replaced by another group; period of time worked by a group of workers; **day shift =** shift worked during the daylight hours (from early morning to late afternoon); **night shift =** shift worked during the night; **relief shift =** shift worked between the day shift and the night shift (i.e., between late afternoon and midnight); *there are 150 men on the day shift; he works the day shift or night shift; we work an 8-hour shift; the management is introducing a shift system or shift working;* **they work double shifts =** a group of workers is working twice the normal amount of time ordinarily worked **(b)** movement *or* change; *a shift in the company's marketing strategy; the company is taking advantage of a shift in the market toward higher priced goods* **2** *verb* to move *or* to sell; *we shifted 20,000 items in one week*

◇ **shift key** *noun* key on a typewriter *or* computer which makes capital letters

◇ **shift work** *noun* system of work in a factory with shifts

ship 1 *noun* large boat for carrying passengers and cargo on the sea; **cargo ship =** ship which carries cargo, not passengers; **container ship =** ship made specially to carry containers; **to jump ship =** (i) to leave the ship on which you are working and not come back; (ii) to abandon a project when it is already in progress **2** *verb* to send (goods), but not always on a ship; *to ship goods to Germany; we ship all our goods by rail; the consignment of cars was shipped abroad last week;* **to drop ship =** to deliver a large order direct to a customer's store or warehouse, without going through an agent

NOTE: **shipping - shipped**

◇ **shipment** *noun* group of goods sent; *two shipments were lost in the fire; a shipment of computers was damaged; we make two shipments a week to L.A.;* **bulk shipment =** shipments of large quantities of goods; **consolidated shipment =** goods from different companies grouped together into a single shipment; **drop shipment =** delivery of a large order from a manufacturer direct to a customer's store or warehouse, without going through an agent

◇ **shipper** *noun* person who sends goods *or* who organizes the sending of goods for other customers

◇ **shipping** *noun* sending of goods; *shipping charges or shipping costs;* **shipping agent =** company which specializes in the sending of goods; **shipping clerk =** clerk who deals with shipping documents; **shipping company** *or* **shipping line =** company which owns ships; **shipping instructions =** details of how goods are to be shipped and delivered; **shipping note =** note which gives details of goods being shipped; **shipping and handling (s&h) =** cost added to the purchase price to pay for packing and transport

NOTE: **shipping** does not always mean using a ship

◇ **shipyard** *noun* factory where ships are built or repaired

shoot up *verb* to go up fast; *prices have shot up during the strike*

NOTE: **shooting - shot**

shop 1 *noun* **(a)** small business where goods are stored and sold **(b)** place where goods are made *or* workshop; **machine**

shop = place where working machines are kept; **repair shop** = small factory where machines are repaired **(c) agency shop** = contract arrangement making it mandatory for workers who refuse to join a union to pay the union a fee; **closed shop** = arrangement where a company agrees to employ only union members in certain jobs; **union shop** = arrangement where a new nonunion employee must join a labor union within a certain time from starting his employment; *the union is asking the management to agree to a closed shop* **2** *verb* **to shop (for)** = to look for things in stores

NOTE: **shopping - shopped**

◇ **shop around** *verb* to go to various stores or offices and compare prices before making a purchase *or* before placing an order; *you should shop around before getting your car serviced; he is shopping around for a new computer; it pays to shop around when you are planning to ask for a mortgage*

◇ **shop floor** *noun* the part of the factory where the workers work

QUOTE these reforms still hadn't fundamentally changed conditions on the shop floor. Absenteeism was as high as 20% on some days

QUOTE in the early 1980s, life on the shop floor at the automotive works typified everything that was wrong with work relations in the US

Business Week

shopkeeper *noun* person who owns or runs a shop

◇ **shoplifter** *noun* person who steals goods from stores

◇ **shoplifting** *noun* stealing goods from stores

◇ **shopper** *noun* **(a)** person who buys goods in a store; *the store stays open till midnight for late-night shoppers* **(b)** free newspaper, distributed to a local community, with advertising from local stores

◇ **shopping** *noun* **(a)** buying goods in a store; goods bought in a store; *to go shopping; to do one's shopping in the local supermarket* **(b) shopping basket** = basket for carrying shopping; **shopping cart** = metal basket with wheels used by shoppers to carry goods in a supermarket; **shopping center** = group of stores, restaurants, etc., with a common parking lot; **shopping mall** = enclosed covered area for shopping, with stores, restaurants, banks and other facilities; **window shopping** = looking at goods in store windows, without buying anything; **shopping around** =

looking at prices in various stores before buying what you want

◇ **shop steward** *noun* elected union representative of workers who reports their complaints to the management

short 1 *adjective* **(a)** for a small period of time; **short credit** = terms which allow the customer only a little time to pay; **in the short term** = in the near future *or* quite soon **(b)** not as much as should be; *the shipment was three items short; when we cashed out we were $10 short* = we had $10 less than we should have had; **to give short weight** = to sell something which is lighter than it should be **(c) short of** = with less than needed *or* with not enough of; *we are short of staff* or *short of money; the company is short of new ideas* **(d) to sell short** = to agree to sell something (such as shares) which you do not possess, but which you think you will be able to buy for less; **short selling** *or* **selling short** = arranging to sell something in the future which you think you can buy for less than the agreed selling price **2** *noun* **shorts** = bonds which mature in less than one year's time

◇ **shortage** *noun* lack *or* not having enough; *a chronic shortage of skilled personnel; we employ part-timers to make up for staff shortages; import controls have resulted in the shortage of spare parts;* **manpower shortage** *or* **shortage of manpower** = lack of workers; **there is no shortage of investment advice** = there are plenty of people who want to give advice on investments

◇ **shortchange** *verb* **(a)** to give a customer less change than is right, hoping that he will not notice **(b)** to give someone less than he expected in a negotiated arrangement; *after seeing the results of the firm's negotiations, the manager felt shortchanged*

◇ **short-dated** *adjective* **short-dated bills** = bills which are payable within a few days; **short-dated securities** = government stocks which mature in less than five years time

◇ **shorten** *verb* to make shorter; *to shorten credit terms*

◇ **shortfall** *noun* amount which is missing which would make the total expected sum; *we had to borrow money to cover the shortfall between expenditure and revenue*

◇ **shorthand** *noun* rapid way of writing using a special system of signs; **shorthand secretary** = secretary who takes dictation in shorthand; **shorthand typist** = typist who can take dictation in shorthand and then type it; **to take shorthand** = to write using shorthand; *he took down the minutes in shorthand*

◊ **shorthanded** *adjective* without enough staff; *we are shorthanded this week because of staff sickness*

◊ **short-haul** *adjective* (transportation) over a short distance; **short-haul flight** = flight over a short distance (up to 500 miles)

◊ **shortlist 1** *noun* list of some of the better people who have applied for a job, who can be asked to come for a test or an interview; *to draw up a shortlist; he is on the shortlist for the job* **2** *verb* to make a shortlist; *four candidates have been shortlisted; shortlisted candidates will be asked for an interview*

◊ **short-range** *adjective* **short-range forecast** = forecast which covers a period of a few months

◊ **short-term** *adjective* for a short period; *to place money on short-term deposit; a short-term contract;* **on a short-term basis** = for a short period; **short-term debts** = debts which have to be repaid within a few weeks; **short-term forecast** = forecast which covers a period of a few months; **short-term gains** = gains made over a short period (less than 12 months); **short-term loan** = loan which has to be repaid within a few weeks

> QUOTE short-term interest rates have moved up quite a bit from year-ago levels
> *Forbes Magazine*

show 1 *noun* (a) exhibit *or* display of goods or services for sale; *auto show; computer show;* **show house** = house built and furnished so that possible buyers can see what similar houses could be like (b) **show of hands** = vote where people show how they vote by raising their hands; *the motion was carried on a show of hands* **2** *verb* to make something be seen; *to show a gain or a fall; to show a profit or a loss*
NOTE: **showing - showed - has shown**

◊ **showcase** *noun* cupboard with a glass front or top to display items

◊ **showroom** *noun* room where goods are displayed for sale; *car showroom*

shrink *verb* to get smaller; *the market has shrunk by 20%; the company is having difficulty selling into a shrinking market*

NOTE: **shrinking - shrank - has shrunk**

◊ **shrinkage** *noun* (a) amount by which something gets smaller; *to allow for shrinkage* (b) losses of inventory through theft, waste or carelessness

◊ **shrink-wrapped** *adjective* covered in tight plastic protective cover

◊ **shrink-wrapping** *noun* act of covering (a book, fruit, record, etc.) in a tight plastic cover

shut 1 *adjective* closed *or* not open; *the office is shut on Saturdays* **2** *verb* to close; *to shut a store or a warehouse*
NOTE: **shutting - shut**

◊ **shut down** *verb* to shut down a factory = to make a factory stop working for a time; *the offices will shut down for Christmas; six factories have shut down this month*

◊ **shutdown** *noun* shutting of a factory

sick *adjective* ill *or* not well; **sick leave** = time when a worker is away from work because of illness; **sick pay** = pay paid to a worker who is sick, even if he cannot work

side *noun* (a) part of something near the edge; **credit side** = right-hand side of a statement of account showing money received; **debit side** = left-hand side of a statement of account showing money owed or paid (b) one of the surfaces of a flat object; *please write on one side of the paper only* (c) **on the side** = separate from your normal work, and hidden from your employer; *he works in an accountant's office, but he runs a construction company on the side; her salary is too small to live on, so the family lives on what she can make on the side*

◊ **sideline** *noun* business which is extra to your normal work; *he runs a profitable sideline selling postcards to tourists*

sight *noun* seeing; **bill payable at sight** = bill which must be paid when it is presented; **sight bill** *or* **sight draft** = bill of exchange which is payable at sight; **to buy something sight unseen** = to buy something without having inspected it

> QUOTE if your company needed a piece of equipment priced at about $50,000, would you buy it sight unseen from a supplier you had never met?
> *Nation's Business*

sign 1 *noun* advertising board *or* notice which advertises something; *they have* asked for planning permission to put up a large red store sign; advertising signs cover most of the buildings in the center of the town **2** *verb* to write your name in a special way on a document to show that you have written it or approved it; *to sign a letter* or *a contract* or *a document* or *a check; the letter is signed by the CEO; the check is not valid if it has not been signed by the finance director;* the warehouse manager signed for the goods = the manager signed a receipt to show that the goods had been received; **he signed the goods in** or **he signed the goods out** = he signed the stock report to show that the goods had arrived or had been dispatched

◊ **signatory** *noun* person who signs a contract, etc.; *you must get the permission of all the signatories to the agreement if you want to change the terms*

◊ **signature** *noun* name written in a special way by someone; *a pile of letters waiting for the president's signature; she found a pile of checks on her desk waiting for signature; all checks need two signatures*

◊ **sign on** *verb* to start work, by signing your name in the personnel office

silent partner *noun* partner who has a share of the business but does not work in it

simple interest *noun* interest calculated on the capital only, and not added to it

sincerely *adverb* Sincerely yours or Yours sincerely = words used as an ending to a business letter addressed to a named person

sine die *phrase* to adjourn a case sine die = to postpone the hearing of a case without fixing a new date for it

single *adjective* one alone; **single premium insurance policy** = insurance policy where only one premium is paid rather than regular annual premiums; **single-entry bookkeeping** = method of bookkeeping where payments or sales are noted with only one entry; **in single figures** = less than ten; *sales are down to single figures; inflation is now in single figures;* **single-figure inflation** = inflation rising at less than 10% per annum

sink *verb* (**a**) to go to the bottom of the water; *the ship sank in the storm and all the cargo was lost* (**b**) to go down suddenly; *prices sank at the news of the closure of the factory* (**c**) to invest money (into something); *he sank all his savings into a used car business* NOTE: **sinking - sank - sunk**

◊ **sinking fund** *noun* fund built up out of amounts of money put aside regularly to meet a future need, as to redeem debentures

sir *noun* formal way of addressing a man; **Dear Sir** = way of addressing a letter to a man whom you do not know; **Dear Sirs** = way of addressing a letter to a firm

sister ship *noun* ship which is of the same design and belongs to the same company as another ship

sit-down *noun* sit-down protest or sit-down strike or sit-in strike = strike where the workers stay in their place of work and refuse to work or to leave

site 1 *noun* place where something is built; *we have chosen a site for the new factory; the supermarket is to be built on a site near the railroad station;* **building site** or **construction site** = place where a building is being constructed; *all visitors to the site must wear safety helmets;* **site engineer** = engineer in charge of a building being constructed **2** *verb* **to be sited** = to be placed; *the factory will be sited near the freeway*

situated *adjective* placed; *the factory is situated on the edge of the town; the office is situated near the railroad station*

◊ **situation** *noun* (**a**) state of affairs; *financial situation of a company; the general situation of the economy* (**b**) job; **situations vacant** or **situations wanted** = list in a newspaper of vacancies for workers or of people wanting work

size *noun* measurements of something or how big something is or how many there are of something; *what is the size of the container? the size of the staff has doubled in the last two years; this package is the maximum size allowed by the post office*

skeleton staff *noun* few staff left to carry on essential work while most of the workforce is away

skid = PALLET

skill *noun* ability to do something because you have been trained; *she has acquired some very useful office management skills; he will have to learn some new skills if he is going to direct the factory*

◊ **skilled** *adjective* having learned certain skills; **skilled workers** *or* **skilled labor** = workers who have special skills *or* who have had long training

slack *adjective* not busy; *business is slack at the end of the week; January is always a slack period*

◊ **slacken off** *verb* to become less busy; *trade has slackened off*

slander 1 *noun* untrue spoken statement which damages someone's character; **action for slander** *or* **slander action** = case in a law court where someone says that another person had slandered him **2** *verb* to **slander someone** = to damage someone's character by saying untrue things about him; *Compare* LIBEL

slash *verb* to cut *or* to reduce sharply; *to slash prices or credit terms; prices have been slashed in all departments; the bank has been forced to slash interest rates*

sleeper *noun* security which has not risen in value for some time, but which may suddenly do so in the future

◊ **sleeping partner** *noun* partner who has a share in the business but does not work in it

slide *verb* to move down steadily; *prices slid after the company reported a loss* NOTE: **sliding - slid**

◊ **sliding** *adjective* which rises in steps; **a sliding scale of charges** = list of charges which rises gradually according to value *or* quantity *or* time, etc.

slight *adjective* not very large *or* not very important; *there was a slight improvement in the balance of trade; we saw a slight increase in sales in February*

◊ **slightly** *adverb* not very much; *sales fell slightly in the second quarter; the*

Swiss bank is offering slightly better terms

slip 1 *noun* (a) small piece of paper; **compliments slip** = piece of paper with the name of the company printed on it, sent with documents, gifts, etc., instead of a letter; **deposit slip** = piece of paper stamped by the cashier to prove that you have paid money into your account; **distribution slip** = paper attached to a document *or* to a magazine, showing all the people in an office who should read it; **pay slip** = piece of paper showing the full amount of a worker's pay, and the money deducted as tax, pension and social security contributions; **sales slip** = paper showing that an article was bought at a certain store; *goods can be exchanged only if accompanied by a sales slip* (b) mistake; *he made a couple of slips in calculating the discount* **2** *verb* to go down and back; *profits slipped to $1.5m; shares slipped back at the close* NOTE: **slipping - slipped**

◊ **slip up** *verb* to make a mistake; *we slipped up badly in not signing the agreement with the Chinese company*

◊ **slipup** *noun* mistake

slogan *noun* publicity slogan = group of words which can be easily remembered, and which is used in advertising a product; *we are using the slogan "Smiths can make it" on all our publicity*

slot machine *noun* machine which people put coins in so that they can gamble to make more money

slow 1 *adjective* not going fast; *a slow start to the day's trading; the sales got off to a slow start, but picked up later; business is always slow after Christmas; they were slow to reply or slow at replying to the customer's complaints; the board is slow to come to a decision; there was a slow improvement in sales in the first half of the year* **2** *adverb* to go slow = to protest against management by working slowly

◊ **slow down** *verb* to stop rising *or* moving *or* falling; *inflation is slowing down; the fall in the exchange rate is slowing down; the management decided to slow down production*

◊ **slowdown** *noun* becoming less busy; *a slowdown in the company's expansion*

◊ **slowly** *adverb* not fast; *the company's sales slowly improved; we are slowly increasing our market share*

slump 1 *noun* **(a)** rapid fall; *slump in sales; slump in profits; slump in the value of the dollar; the dollar's slump on the foreign exchange markets* **(b)** short period of economic decline; *the economy has recovered from the slump of February and march* **2** *verb* to fall fast; *profits have slumped; the dollar slumped on the foreign exchange markets*

QUOTE when gold began rising, after a long flat period in the fall of 1986, the dollar was slumping
Business Week

slush fund *noun* money kept to one side to give to people to persuade them to do what you want

small *adjective* not large; **small businesses =** little companies with low sales and few employees; **Small Business Administration (SBA) =** federal agency that assists and advises small businesses; **small businessman =** man who runs a small business; **small change =** loose coins; **small claims court =** court which deals with disputes over small amounts of money; **the small investor =** person who has a small amount of money to invest

◊ **small-scale** *adjective* working with few staff and not much money; **a small-scale enterprise =** a small business

QUOTE running a small business, no matter how glamorous it may seem, is in many ways tougher and more disagreeable than being a top functionary in a large one
Forbes Magazine

smash *verb* to break (a record) *or* to do better than (a record); *to smash all production records; sales have smashed all records for the first half of the year*

smuggle *verb* to take goods into a country without declaring them to customs; *they had to smuggle the spare parts into the country*

◊ **smuggler** *noun* person who smuggles
◊ **smuggling** *noun* taking goods illegally into a country; *he made his money in arms smuggling*

snap *adjective* rapid *or* sudden; *the board came to a snap decision; they carried out a snap check or a snap*

inspection of the representatives' travel bills

◊ **snap up** *verb* to buy something quickly; *to snap up a bargain; he snapped up 15% of the company's shares*
NOTE: snapping - snapped

soar *verb* to go up rapidly; *food prices soared during the cold weather; stock prices soared on the news of the takeover bid* *or* *the news of the takeover bid sent stock prices soaring*

social *adjective* referring to society in general; **social costs =** ways in which something will affect people; *the report examines the social costs of building the factory in the middle of the town;* **social security =** federal government program providing old age, survivor, and unemployment benefits through contributions deducted from workers' paychecks; **Social Security Number =** number given to each person which identifies him or her for social security payments; **the social system =** the way society is organized

◊ **society** *noun* **(a)** way in which people in a country are organized; **consumer society =** type of society where consumers are encouraged to buy goods; **the affluent society =** type of society where most people are rich **(b)** club *or* group of people with the same interests; *she has joined a computer society; he belongs to the Society for Mechanical Engineers*

◊ **socio-economic** *adjective* referring to social and economic conditions; *the socio-economic system in capitalist countries;* **socio-economic groups =** groups in society divided according to income, education and position

soft *adjective* not hard; **soft currency =** currency of a country with a weak economy, which is cheap to buy and difficult to exchange for other currencies; **soft loan =** loan (from a company to an employee or from a government to another government) at very low or zero interest; **soft market =** market where prices are falling because there are few buyers; **to take the soft option =** to decide to do something which involves least risk, effort or problems; **soft sell =** persuading people to buy by encouraging them, but not forcing them to do so

◊ **software** *noun* computer programs (as opposed to machines)

QUOTE the current property market is soft, but an influx of demands for coverage likely will harden it, giving insurance companies the chance once again to bring the municipal market into the fold

American City & County

sole *adjective* only; **sole agency =** agreement to be the only person to represent a company *or* to sell a product in a certain area; *he has the sole agency for Ford cars;* **sole agent =** person who has the sole agency for a product in an area; **sole distributor =** retailer who is the only one in an area who is allowed to sell a certain product; **sole owner =** person who owns a business on his own, with no partners

solicit *verb* **to solicit orders =** to ask for orders *or* to try to get people to order goods
◊ **solicitor** *noun* **(a)** someone who seeks trade, asks for contributions, etc. **(b)** British lawyer who gives advice to members of the public and acts for them legally

solo *or* **solus** *noun* alone *or* single; **advertisement solus** *or* **solo advertisement =** advertisement which does not appear near other advertisements for similar products

solution *noun* answer to a problem; *to look for a solution to the financial problems; the programmer came up with a solution to the systems problem; we think we have found a solution to the problem of getting skilled staff*

solve *verb* **to solve a problem =** to find an answer to a problem; *the loan will solve some of our short-term problems*

solvent *adjective* having enough money to pay debts; *when he bought the company it was barely solvent*
◊ **solvency** *noun* being able to pay all debts

sort *verb* to arrange in a certain order; *she is sorting index cards into alphabetical order*
◊ **sort out** *verb* to put into order; to settle (a problem); *did you sort out the accounting problem with the auditors?*

sound *adjective* reasonable *or* which can be trusted; *the company's financial*

situation is very sound; he gave us some very sound advice
◊ **soundness** *noun* being reasonable

source *noun* place where something comes from; *source of income; you must declare income from all sources on your tax return;* **income which is taxed at source =** where the tax is removed before the income is paid

space *noun* empty place *or* empty area; **advertising space =** space in a newspaper set aside for advertisements; **to take advertising space in a newspaper =** to place a large advertisement in a newspaper; **floor space =** area of the floor in an office; **office space =** area available for offices or used by offices; *we are looking for extra office space for our new corporate finance department*
◊ **space bar** *noun* key on a typewriter *or* computer which makes a single space between letters
◊ **space out** *verb* to place things with spaces between them; *the company name is written in spaced-out letters; payments can be spaced out over a period of ten years*

spare *adjective* extra *or* not being used; *he has invested his spare capital in a computer store;* **to use up spare capacity =** to make use of time or space which has not been fully used; **spare part =** small piece of machinery used to replace part of a machine which is broken; *the photocopier will not work - it needs a spare part;* **spare time =** time when you are not at work; *he built himself a radio in his spare time*

spec *noun* **to buy something on spec =** to buy something as a speculation, without being sure of its value
◊ **specs** *plural noun* = SPECIFICATIONS

special *adjective* different *or* not normal *or* referring to one particular thing; *he offered us special terms; the car is being offered at a special price;* **special delivery =** type of rapid delivery mail service; **Special Drawing Rights (SDR) =** international money certificates issued by the International Monetary Fund to replace gold and hard currency reserves; they are based on a basket of international currencies and can be used to support weak currencies
◊ **specialist** *noun* person *or* company which deals with one particular type of

product or one subject; *you should go to a specialist in computers* or *to a computer specialist for advice*

◇ **speciality** or **specialty** *noun* particular interest or special type of product which a company deals in; *their speciality is computer programs;* **specialty store** = store selling a limited range of items of good quality

◇ **specialization** *noun* study of one particular thing, dealing with one particular type of product; *the company's area of specialization is accounting packages for small businesses*

◇ **specialize** *verb* to trade in one particular type of product or service; *the company specializes in electronic components; they have a specialized product line; he sells very specialized equipment for the electronics industry*

specie *plural noun* coins or hard money

specify *verb* to state clearly what is needed; *to specify full details of the goods ordered; do not include sales tax on the invoice unless specified*

◇ **specifications** *noun* detailed information about what is needed or about a product to be supplied; *to detail the specifications of a computer system;* **job specification** = detailed description of what is involved in a job; **to work to standard specifications** = to work to specifications which are acceptable anywhere in the industry; **the work is not up to specification** or **does not meet our specifications** = the product is not made in the way which was detailed

specimen *noun* thing which is given as a sample; **to give specimen signatures on a bank mandate** = to write the signatures of all people who can sign checks for an account so that the bank can recognize them

speculate *verb* to take a risk in business which you hope will bring you profits; **to speculate on the stock exchange** = to buy shares which you predict will rise in value

◇ **speculation** *noun* risky deal which may produce a short-term profit; *he bought the company as a speculation; she lost all her money in stock exchange speculations*

◇ **speculative** *adjective* **speculative builder** = builder who builds houses in

the hope that someone will want to buy them; **speculative share** = share which may go up or down in value

◇ **speculator** *noun* person who buys goods or shares or foreign currency on the prediction that they will rise in value; *a property speculator; a currency speculator; a speculator on the stock exchange* or *a stock exchange speculator*

speed *noun* rate at which something moves; **dictation speed** = number of words per minute which a secretary can write down in shorthand; **typing speed** = number of words per minute which a typist can type

◇ **speed up** *verb* to make something go faster; *we are aiming to speed up our delivery times*

spend *verb* (a) to pay money; *they spent all their savings on buying the store; the company spends thousands of dollars on research* (b) to use (time, etc.); *the company spends hundreds of man-hours on meetings; the chairman spent yesterday afternoon with the auditors; the company's supply of raw materials was completely spent*
NOTE: spending - spent

◇ **spending** *noun* paying money; *cash spending* or *credit card spending;* **consumer spending** = spending by consumers; **spending money** = money for ordinary personal expenses; **spending power** = having money to spend on goods; amount of goods which can be bought for a certain sum of money; *the spending power of the dollar has fallen over the last ten years; the spending power of the student market*

sphere *noun* area; *sphere of activity; sphere of influence*

spinoff *noun* **(a)** corporate reorganization in which a subsidiary becomes an independent company **(b)** useful product developed as a secondary product from a main item; *one of the spinoffs of the research program has been the development of the electric car*

spiral 1 *noun* thing which twists round and round; **the economy is in an upward-inflationary spiral** or **wage-price spiral** = the economy is in a situation where price rises encourage higher wage demands which in turn make prices rise **2** *verb* to twist round and round; *a period of downward-spiraling prices;* **upward-spiraling inflation** = inflation where price rises make workers ask for higher wages which then increase prices again

split 1 *noun* (a) dividing up; **stock split** *or* **split up** = dividing of shares of stock into smaller denominations, so as to make the unit value cheaper; **the company is proposing a five for one split** = the company is proposing that each existing share should be divided into five smaller shares (b) lack of agreement; *a split in the family shareholders* **2** *verb* (a) **to split shares** = to divide shares into smaller denominations; **the shares were split five for one** = five new shares were given for each existing share held (b) **to split the difference** = to come to an agreement over a price by dividing the difference between the amount the seller is asking and amount the buyer wants to pay and agreeing on a price between the two
NOTE: **splitting - split**

spoil *verb* to ruin *or* to make something bad; *half the shipment was spoiled by water; the company's 12-month performance was spoiled by a disastrous last quarter*

sponsor 1 *noun* (a) person who pays money to help research *or* to pay for a business venture; company which pays to help a sport, in return for advertising rights (b) company which advertises on TV **2** *verb* to pay money to help research *or* business development; *to sponsor a television program; the company has sponsored the football game; government-sponsored trade exhibition*

◊ **sponsorship** *noun* act of sponsoring; *government sponsorship of overseas selling missions*

spot *noun* (a) buying something for immediate delivery; **the spot market in oil** = the market for buying oil for immediate delivery; **spot price** *or* **spot rate** = price *or* rate for a commodity which is delivered immediately; **to be on the spot** = to be at a certain place; *we have a man on the spot to deal with any problems which happen on the building site* (c) TV **spot** = period on TV which is used for commercials; *we are running a series of TV spots over the next three weeks*

spread 1 *noun* (a) range; **he has a wide spread of investments** *or* **of interests** = he has shares in many different types of companies (b) difference between buying and selling prices of stocks **2** *verb* to space out over a period of time; *to spread payments over several months;* **to spread a risk** = to make the risk of insurance less great by asking other companies to help cover it
NOTE: **spreading - spread**

◊ **spreadsheet** *noun* computer printout showing a series of columns of figures

QUOTE dealers said markets were thin, with gaps between trades and wide spreads between bid and ask prices on the currencies
Wall Street Journal

square 1 *noun* (a) shape with four equal sides and four right angles; **graph paper is drawn with a series of small squares** (b) way of measuring area, by multiplying the length by the width; *the office is ten feet by twelve - its area is one hundred and twenty square feet;* **square measure** = area in square feet
NOTE: written with figures as **2** : $10ft^2$ = ten square feet; $6yd^2$ = six square yards **2** *verb* **to square a bill** = to pay a bill; **to square away** = to put in order; *he got all his paperwork squared away*

squeeze 1 *noun* government control carried out by reducing amounts available; **credit squeeze** = period when lending by the banks is restricted by the government; **profit squeeze** = control of the amount of profits which companies can pay out as dividend **2** *verb* to crush *or* to press; to make smaller; **to squeeze margins** *or* **profits** *or* **credit;** **our margins have been squeezed by the competition** = profits have been reduced because our margins have to be smaller for us to stay competitive

QUOTE the profit squeeze is at least helping the inflation outlook by ensuring that a wage-price spiral won't develop this year. The squeeze has already halted the acceleration in wage growth that began in 1987
Industrial World

stability *noun* resistance to change; firmness *or* not moving up or down; *price stability; a period of economic stability; the stability of the currency markets*

◊ **stabilization** *noun* making stable *or* preventing sudden changes in prices, etc.; **stabilization of the economy** = keeping the economy steady by preventing inflation from rising, cutting high interest rates and excess money supply

◊ **stabilize** *verb* to make steady; **prices have stabilized** = prices have stopped moving up or down; **to have a stabilizing effect on the economy** = to make the economy more stable

◊ **stable** *adjective* steady *or* not moving up or down; **stable prices; stable exchange rate; stable currency; stable economy**

stack 1 *noun* pile, a heap of things on top of each other; *there is a stack of replies to our advertisement* **2** *verb* to pile things on top of each other; *the boxes are stacked in the warehouse*

staff 1 *noun* people who work for a company or for an organization; **to be on the staff** *or* **a member of the staff** *or* **a staff member** = to be employed permanently by a company; **staff appointment** = a job on the staff; **sales staff** = people who work in the sales department; **clerical staff** *or* **office staff** = people who work in offices; **senior staff** *or* **junior staff** = older *or* younger members of staff; people in more important *or* less important positions in a company; members of staff with a high *or* low seniority NOTE: **staff** refers to a group of people and can be followed by a verb in the plural **2** *verb* to employ workers; *to be staffed with skilled part-timers; to have difficulty in staffing the department*

◊ **staffer** *noun* member of the permanent staff

◊ **staffing** *noun* providing workers for a company; **staffing levels** = numbers of members of staff required in a department of a company for it to work efficiently; **the company's staffing policy** = the company's views on staff - how many are needed for each department, if they should be full-time or part-time, what their salaries should be, etc.

stag 1 *noun* **(a)** person who buys securities and sells them immediately to make a profit **(b)** an outside, irregular dealer in stocks, not a member of the exchange **2** *verb* **to stag an issue** = to buy a new issue of stock not as an investment, but to sell immediately at a profit
NOTE: **stagging - stagged**

stage 1 *noun* period, one of several points of development; *the different*

stages of the production process; the **contract is still in the drafting stage** = the contract is still being drafted; **in stages** = in different steps; *the company has agreed to repay the loan in stages* **2** *verb* to put on *or* to organize (a show); *the exhibition is being staged in the conference center;* **to stage a recovery** = to recover; *the company has staged a strong recovery from a point of near bankruptcy*

stagflation *noun* rising prices and lack of economic expansion which happen at the same time

stagger *verb* to arrange (vacations, working hours) so that they do not all begin and end at the same time; *staggered vacations help the tourist industry; we have to stagger the lunch hour so that there is always someone on the switchboard*

stagnant *adjective* not active *or* not changing; *sales were stagnant for the first half of the year; a stagnant economy*

◊ **stagnate** *verb* not to change *or* not to make progress; *the economy is stagnating; after six hours the talks were stagnating*

◊ **stagnation** *noun* not increasing *or* not making any progress; *the country entered a period of stagnation;* **economic stagnation** = lack of expansion in the economy

stake 1 *noun* money invested; **to have a stake in a business** = to have money invested in a business; **to acquire a stake in a business** = to buy shares in a business; *he acquired a 25% stake in the business* **2** *verb* **to stake money on something** = to risk money on something

stamp 1 *noun* **(a)** device for making marks on documents; mark made in this way; *the invoice has the stamp "Received with thanks" on it; the customs officer looked at the stamps in his passport;* **date stamp** = stamp with rubber figures which can be moved, used for marking the date on documents; **rubber stamp** = stamp made of hard rubber cut to form words; **stamp pad** = soft pad of cloth with ink on which a stamp is pressed, before marking the paper **(b)** small piece of gummed paper which you buy from a post office and stick on a letter or parcel to pay for the postage; *a postage stamp; a 22>c< stamp* (c) **stamp tax =** tax on legal documents (such as the transfer of a property to a new owner) **2** *verb* (a) to mark a document with a stamp; *to stamp an invoice "Paid" ; the documents were stamped by the customs officials* (b) to put a postage stamp on (an envelope, etc.); **self-addressed stamped envelope =** envelope with your own address written on it and a stamp stuck on it to pay for the return postage; *send a self-addressed stamped envelope for further details and catalog*

stand 1 *noun* arrangement of shelves *or* tables, etc. for showing a company's products; **display stand =** special stand for displaying goods for sale **2** *verb* to be *or* to stay; **to stand liable for damages =** to be liable to pay damages; **the company's balance stands at $24,000 =** the balance is $24,000
NOTE: **standing - stood**

◊ **stand in for** *verb* to take someone's place; *Mr. Smith is standing in for the chairman, who is sick*

standard 1 *noun* normal quality *or* normal conditions which other things are judged against; **standard of living** *or* **living standards =** quality of personal home life (such as amount of food or clothes bought, size of family car, etc.); **production standards =** quality of production; **up to standard =** of acceptable quality; *this batch is not up to standard or does not meet our standards;* **gold standard =** linking of the value of a currency to value of a quantity of gold **2** *adjective* normal *or* usual; *a standard model car; we have a standard charge of $250 for a thirty-minute session;* **standard agreement** *or* **standard contract =** normal printed contract form; **standard deduction =** amount that can be deducted from income on a federal tax return, if deductions are not itemized; **standard letter =** letter which is sent without any change to various correspondents; **standard operating procedures (SOP) =** written rules on routine transactions carried out by a business

◊ **standardization** *noun* making sure that everything fits a standard *or* is produced in the same way; *standardization of design; standardization of measurements;* **standardization of products =** reducing a large number of different products to a series which have the same measurements *or* design *or* packaging, etc.

◊ **standardize** *verb* to make sure that everything fits a standard *or* is produced in the same way

standby *noun* (a) **standby ticket =** cheap air ticket which allows the passenger to wait until the last moment to see if there is an empty seat on the plane; **standby fare =** cheap fare for a standby ticket (b) **standby arrangements =** plans for what should be done if an emergency happens, especially money held in reserve in the International Monetary Fund for use by a country in financial difficulties; **standby credit =** credit which is available if a company needs it

standing 1 *adjective* **standing order =** order for goods which are supplied in the same amounts on a regular basis **2** *noun* (a) **long-standing customer** *or* **customer of long standing =** person who has been a customer for many years (b) good reputation; *the financial standing of a company;* **company of good standing =** very reputable company

standstill *noun* situation where work has stopped; *production is at a standstill; the strike brought the factory to a standstill*

staple 1 *adjective* (a) **staple commodity =** basic food or raw material; **staple industry =** main industry in a country; **staple product =** main product (b) small piece of bent metal for attaching papers together; *he used a pair of scissors to take the staples out of the documents* **2** *verb* to staple papers together = to attach papers with staples; *he could not take away separate pages, because the documents were stapled together*

◊ **stapler** *noun* device used to attach papers together with staples

start 1 *noun* beginning; **cold start =** beginning a new business *or* opening a new store with no previous sales to base it on; **housing starts =** number of new private houses or apartments of which construction has been started during a year **2** *verb* **to start a business from scratch =** to begin a new business, with no previous sales to base it on

◊ **starting** *noun* beginning; **starting date =** date on which something starts; **starting salary =** salary for an employee when he starts work with a company

◇ **start-up** *noun* beginning of a new company *or* new product; *start-up costs*
NOTE: plural is **start-ups**

stat = PHOTOSTAT

state 1 *noun* **(a)** independent country; semi-independent section of a federal country (such as the US); **state bank** = bank which is set up under a charter from a state, as opposed to a national bank; **state taxes** = taxes which are payable to a state, as opposed to federal taxes **(b)** government of a country; **state enterprise** = company run by the state; *the bosses of state industries are appointed by the government;* **state ownership** = situation where an industry is nationalized **(c)** condition; *in what state did he leave the business?* **2** *verb* to say clearly; *the document states that all revenue has to be declared to the tax office*

◇ **state-controlled** *adjective* run by the state; *state-controlled television*

◇ **state-of-the-art** *adjective* technically as advanced as possible

◇ **state-owned** *adjective* owned by the state or by a state

> QUOTE state-owned banks cut their prime rates a percentage point to 11%
> *Wall Street Journal*
> QUOTE each year American manufacturers increase their budget for state-of-the-art computer-based hardware and software
> *Duns Business Month*

statement *noun* **(a)** saying something clearly; **to make a false statement** = to say something which is not true; **statement of expenses** = detailed list of money spent; **bank statement** = written document from a bank showing withdrawals and deposits and balance of an account; **monthly** *or* **quarterly statement** = statement which is sent every month *or* every quarter by the bank **(b)** **financial statement** = document which shows the financial situation of a company; *the finance department has prepared a financial statement for the shareholders;* **income statement** *or* **profit and loss statement** = financial statement of a company with expenditure and income balanced to show a final profit or loss **(c)** **statement of account** = list of invoices and credits and debits sent by a supplier to a customer at the end of each month

station *noun* **(a)** place where trains stop for passengers; *the train leaves Central Station at 4:15* **(b)** TV station *or* radio

station = building where TV or radio programs are produced

stationery *noun* **(a)** office supplies for writing, such as paper, carbons, pens, etc.; **stationery supplier (b)** letter paper and matching envelopes; *the office stationery*

statistics *plural noun* study of facts in the form of figures; *to examine the sales statistics for the previous six months; government trade statistics show an increase in imports*
◇ **statistical** *adjective* based on figures; **statistical analysis; statistical information; statistical discrepancy** = amount by which sets of figures differ
◇ **statistician** *noun* person who analyzes statistics

status *noun* **(a)** importance *or* position in society; *the chairman's car is a status symbol* = the size of the car shows the chairman's level of prestige in the company; **loss of status** = becoming less important in a group **(b)** **legal status** = legal position **(c)** financial position of a person or business; **credit status** = ability of a customer to repay a loan
◇ **status quo** *noun* state of things as they are now; *the contract does not alter the status quo*

statute *noun* law made by the legislative body of a country; **statute book** = book of laws passed by a legislative body; **statute of limitations** = law which allows only a certain amount of time (a few years) for someone to claim damages or property
◇ **statutory** *adjective* fixed by law; *there is a statutory period of probation of thirteen weeks*

stay 1 *noun* **(a)** length of time spent in one place; *the tourists were in town only for a short stay* **(b)** **stay of execution** = temporary stopping of a legal order; *the court granted the company a two-week stay of execution* **2** *verb* to stop at a place; *the chairman is staying at the Ritz Hotel; profits have stayed below 10% for two years; inflation has stayed high in spite of the government's efforts to bring it down*

steady 1 *adjective* continuing in a regular way; *steady increase in profits; the market stayed steady; there is a steady demand for computers* **2** *verb* to become firm *or* to stop fluctuating; *the markets steadied after last week's fluctuations; prices steadied on the commodity markets; the government's recommendations had a steadying influence on the exchange rate*

◇ **steadily** *adverb* in a regular *or* continuous way; *output increased steadily over the last two quarters; the company has steadily increased its market share*

◇ **steadiness** *noun* being firm *or* not fluctuating; *the steadiness of the markets is due to the government's intervention*

steal *verb* to take something which does not belong to you *or* which you do not have a rightful claim to; *the rival company stole our best clients; one of our biggest problems is stealing in the wine department*
NOTE: **stealing - stole - has stolen**

steep *adjective* very sudden *or* very high (price); *a steep increase in interest charges; a steep decline in overseas sales*

stencil *noun* sheet of special paper which can be written or typed on, and used in a duplicating machine

stenographer *noun* person who can write in shorthand

step *noun* (a) action; *the first step taken by the new CEO was to analyze all the expenses;* to take steps to prevent something from happening = to act to stop something from happening (b) movement; *becoming assistant to the CEO is a step up the promotion ladder;* in step with = moving at the same rate as; *the dollar rose in step with the yen;* out of step with = not moving at the same rate as; *the dollar was out of step with European currencies; wages are out of step with the cost of living*

◇ **step up** *verb* to increase; *to step up industrial action; the company has stepped up production of the latest models*
NOTE: **stepping - stepped**

sterling *noun* standard currency used in the United Kingdom; *to quote prices in sterling or to quote sterling prices;* pound sterling = official term for the British currency

stevedore *noun* person who works in a port, loading or unloading ships

steward *noun* (a) man who serves drinks *or* food on a ship *or* plane (b) **shop steward** *or* **union steward** = elected union representative of workers, who represents their complaints to the management

◇ **stewardess** *noun* woman who serves drinks *or* food on a ship *or* plane

stick *verb* (a) to attach with glue; *to stick a stamp on a letter; they stuck a poster on the door* (b) to stay still *or* not to move; *sales have stuck at $2m for the last two years*
NOTE: **sticking - stuck**

◇ **sticker 1** *noun* small piece of gummed paper or plastic to be stuck on something as an advertisement *or* to indicate a price; **sticker price** = price as shown on a sticker; **airmail sticker** = blue sticker with the words "By air mail" which can be stuck on an envelope or parcel to show that it is being sent by air **2** *verb* to put a price sticker on an article for sale; *we had to sticker all the stock*

stiff *adjective* strong *or* difficult; *stiff competition; he had to take a stiff test before he qualified*

stimulate *verb* to encourage *or* to make (something) become more active; *to stimulate the economy; to stimulate trade with the Middle East*

◇ **stimulus** *noun* thing which encourages activity
NOTE: plural is **stimuli**

stipulate *verb* to demand that a condition be put into a contract; *to stipulate that the contract should run for five years; to pay the stipulated charges; the company failed to pay on the date stipulated in the contract; the contract stipulates that the seller pays the buyer's legal costs*

◇ **stipulation** *noun* condition in a contract

stock 1 *noun* (a) quantity of raw materials; *we have large stocks of oil or coal; the country's stocks of butter or sugar* (b) quantity of goods for sale, kept in a warehouse; **safety stock** = extra inventory carried by a business to avoid the possibility of a stockout; **stock turnover** = index of the speed with which the merchandise moves in and out of the store or department; **stock**

valuation = estimating the value of inventory at the end of an accounting period; **to buy a store with stock at valuation** = to buy the inventory as the same amount as its value as estimated by the valuer; **stock on hand** = inventory held in a store *or* warehouse; **to purchase stock at valuation** = to pay for inventory the price is valued at **(c) in stock** *or* **out of stock** = available *or* not available in the warehouse *or* store; *to hold 2,000 lines in stock; the item went out of stock just before Christmas but came back into stock in the first week of January; we are out of stock of this item;* **to take stock** = to count the items in a warehouse **(d)** shares in an ordinary company; **stock certificate** = document proving that someone owns stock in a company; **debenture stock** = capital borrowed by a company, using its fixed assets as security; **stock dividend** = dividend paid in the form of new stock; **stock index** = figure showing average prices of certain stocks on a Stock Exchange (such as the Dow Jones Industrial Average); **loan stock** = money lent to a company at a fixed rate of interest; **convertible loan stock** = money lent to a company which can be converted into shares at a later date; **stock purchase option** = (i) right to buy or sell securities at a certain price at a time in the future; (ii) right to buy shares at a cheap price given by a corporation to its employees; **stock split** = dividing of shares of stock into smaller denominations, so as to make the unit value cheaper; **common stock** = ordinary stock in a company giving the stockholders the right to vote at meetings and receive a dividend; **preferred stock** = shares which receive their dividend before all other stock, and which are repaid first (at face value) if the corporation is in liquidation; **cumulative preferred stock** = preferred stock where the dividend will be paid at a later date even if the corporation cannot pay a dividend in the current year **(e) the stock market** = place where securities are bought and sold; *stock market price or price on the stock market;* **stock market valuation** = value of a security based on the current market price **(f)** normal, usually kept in stock; *butter is a stock item for any good grocer;* **stock size** = normal size; *we only carry stock sizes of shoes* **2** *verb* to hold goods for sale in a warehouse *or* store; *to stock 200 lines*

◊ **stockbroker** *noun* person who buys or sells securities for clients; **stockbroker's commission** = payment

to a broker for a deal carried out on behalf of a client

◊ **stockbroking** *noun* trade of dealing in securities for clients; *a stockbroking firm*

◊ **stock exchange** *noun* place where securities are bought and sold; *he works on the New York Stock Exchange; shares in the company are traded on the stock exchange;* **stock exchange listing** = official list of securities which can be bought or sold on a stock exchange

◊ **stockholder** *noun* person who holds stock in a company

◊ **stockholding** *noun* shares in a company held by someone

◊ **stock-in-trade** *noun* **(a)** equipment used in a trade *or* business **(b)** goods held by a business for sale

◊ **stock jobbing** *noun* buying and selling goods from manufacturers

◊ **stocklist** *noun* list of items carried in stock

◊ **stockout** *noun* situation where a business runs out of stock of goods to sell

◊ **stockpile 1** *noun* supplies kept by a country *or* a company in case of need; *a stockpile of raw materials* **2** *verb* to buy items and keep them in case of need; *to stockpile raw materials*

◊ **stockroom** *noun* room where stores of supplies are kept

◊ **stocktaking** *noun* counting of goods in stock at the end of an accounting period; *the warehouse is closed for the annual stocktaking;* **stocktaking sale** = sale of goods at cheap prices to clear a warehouse before stocktaking

◊ **stock up** *verb* to buy supplies of something which you will need in the future; *they stocked up with computer paper*

QUOTE the stock rose to over $20 a share, higher than the $18 bid
Fortune

stop 1 *noun* **(a)** end of an action; *work came to a stop when the company could not pay the workers' wages; the new finance director put a stop to the reps' expense claims* **(b)** not supplying; **account on stop** = account which is not supplied because it has not paid its latest invoices; *to put an account on stop;* **to put a stop order on a check** *or* **to request a stop payment** = to tell the bank not to pay a check which you have written **2** *verb* **(a)** to make (something) not to move any more; *the shipment was stopped by the customs; the* *government has stopped the import of cars* (b) not to do anything any more; *the laborers stopped work when the company could not pay their wages; the office staff stop work at 5:30; we have stopped supplying Smith & Co.* (c) **to stop an account** = not to supply an account any more on credit because bills have not been paid; **to stop a check** *or* **to stop payment on a check** = to ask a bank not to pay a check you have written; **to stop payments** = not to make any further payments (d) **to stop someone's wages** = to take money out of someone's wages; *we stopped $25 from his pay because he was late* NOTE: **stopping - stopped**

◊ **stop over** *verb* to stay for a short time in a place on a long journey; *we stopped over in Hong Kong on the way to Singapore*

◊ **stopover** *noun* staying for a short time in a place on a long journey; *the ticket allows you two stopovers between New York and Tokyo*

◊ **stoppage** *noun* act of stopping; *stoppage of deliveries; stoppage of payments; deliveries will be late because of stoppages on the production line*

storage *noun* (a) keeping in store *or* in a warehouse; *we put our furniture into storage;* **storage capacity** = space available for storage; **storage company** = company which keeps items for customers; **storage facilities** = equipment and buildings suitable for storage; **storage unit** = device attached to a computer for storing information on disk or tape; **cold storage** = keeping food, etc., in a cold store to prevent it from going bad; **to put a plan into cold storage** = to postpone work on a plan, usually for a very long time (b) cost of keeping goods in store; *storage was 10% of value, so we scrapped the stock* (c) facility for storing data in a computer; *disk with a storage capacity of 10Mb*

◊ **store 1** *noun* (a) place where goods are stored and sold; *a furniture store; a big clothing store;* **chain store** = one store in a number of stores; **department store** = large store with sections for different types of goods; **discount store** = store which specializes in selling cheap goods sold at a high discount; **general store** = small country store which sells a wide range of products; **in-store demonstration** = demonstration of a device or product inside a department store (b) quantity of items *or* materials kept because they will be needed; *I always keep a store of envelopes ready in my desk* **2** *verb* (a) to keep in a warehouse; *to store goods for six months* (b) to keep for future use; *we store our pay records on computer*

◊ **storekeeper** *noun* (a) person in charge of a storeroom (b) person who owns and operates a retail store

◊ **storeroom** *noun* room where stock can be kept; small warehouse attached to a factory

straight line method *noun* depreciation calculated by dividing the cost of an asset by the number of years it is expected to be used

strategy *noun* plan of future action; *business strategy; company strategy; marketing strategy; financial strategy*

◊ **strategic** *adjective* based on a plan of action; **strategic planning** = structuring the future work of a company, according to a long-term plan

stream *noun* mass of people *or* traffic, all going in the same direction; *we had a stream of customers on the first day of the sale;* **to come on stream** = to start production

◊ **streamer** *noun* device for attaching a tape storage unit to a computer

◊ **streamline** *verb* to make (something) more efficient *or* more simple; *to streamline the accounting system; to streamline distribution services*

◊ **streamlined** *adjective* efficient *or* rapid; *streamlined production; the company introduced a streamlined system of distribution*

◊ **streamlining** *noun* making efficient

street *noun* road in a town or city; **Wall Street** = name for the business and financial district of New York; **street directory** = map of a town with all the streets listed in alphabetical order in an index

strength *noun* being strong *or* at a high level; *the company took advantage of the strength of the demand for home computers; the strength of the dollar increases the possibility of high interest rates*

stretch *verb* to extend *or* make longer; *the investment program has stretched the company's resources; he is not fully stretched* = his job does not make him work as hard as he could

strict *adjective* exact; *in strict order of seniority*

◊ **strictly** *adverb* exactly; *the company asks all staff to follow strictly the buying procedures*

strike 1 *noun* **(a)** stopping of work by the workers (because of lack of agreement with management *or* because of orders from a union); **all-out strike** = complete strike by all workers; **general strike** = strike of all the workers in an industry; **official strike** = strike which has been approved by the main office of a union; **protest strike** = strike in protest at a particular grievance; **sit-down strike** *or* **sit-in strike** = strike where workers stay in their place of work and refuse to work or leave; **sympathy strike** = strike to show that workers agree with another group of workers who are on strike; **token strike** = short strike to show that workers have a grievance; **unofficial strike** = strike by local workers, which has not been approved by the main union; **wildcat strike** = strike organized by workers without the main union office knowing about it **(b) to take strike action** = to go on strike; **strike call** = demand by a union for a strike; **no-strike agreement** *or* **no-strike clause** = (clause in an) agreement where the workers say that they will never strike; **strike fund** = money collected by a labor union from its members, used to pay strike pay; **strike pay** = wages paid to striking workers by their union; **strike ballot** *or* **strike vote** = vote by workers to decide if a strike should be held **(c) to come out on strike** *or* **to go on strike** = to stop work; *the office workers are on strike for higher pay;* **to call the workforce out on strike** = to tell the workers to stop work; *the union called its members out on strike* **2** *verb* **(a)** to stop working because there is no agreement with management; *to strike for higher wages or for shorter working hours; to strike in protest against bad working conditions;* **to strike in sympathy with the postal workers** = to strike to show that you agree with the postal workers who are on strike **(b) to strike a bargain with someone** = to come to an agreement; **a deal was struck at $25 a unit** = we agreed on the price of $25 per unit
NOTE: **striking - struck**

◊ **strikebound** *adjective* not able to work *or* to move because of a strike; *six ships are strikebound in the docks*

◊ **strikebreaker** *noun* worker who is hired by a business to work while everyone else is on strike

◊ **striker** *noun* worker who is on strike

strong *adjective* with a lot of force *or* strength; *a strong demand for home computers; the company needs a strong chairman;* **strong dollar** = dollar which is high against other currencies

◊ **strongbox** *noun* safe *or* heavy metal box which cannot be opened easily, in which valuable documents, money, etc., can be kept

◊ **strongroom** *noun* special room (in a bank) where valuable documents, money, gold, etc., can be kept

QUOTE everybody blames the strong dollar for US trade problems
Duns Business Month
QUOTE in a world of floating exchange rates the dollar is strong because of capital inflows rather than weak because of the nation's trade deficit
Duns Business Month

structure 1 *noun* way in which something is organized; *the paper gives a diagram of the company's organizational structure; the price structure in the small car market; the career structure within a corporation; the company is reorganizing its discount structure;* **capital structure of a company** = way in which a company's capital is set up; **the company's wage** *or* **salary structure** = organization of salaries in a company with different rates of pay for different types of job **2** *verb* to arrange in a certain way; *to structure a meeting*

◊ **structural** *adjective* referring to a structure; *to make structural changes in a company;* **structural unemployment** = unemployment caused by the changing structure of an industry *or* society

stub *noun* **check stub** = piece of paper left in a check book after a check has been written and taken out, indicating the amount of the check; **pay stub** = piece of paper showing the full amount of a worker's pay, and the money deducted as tax, social security and other contributions

studio *noun* place where designers, film producers, artists, etc., work; **design studio** = independent firm which specializes in creating designs for companies

study 1 *noun* examining something carefully; *the company has asked the consultants to prepare a study of new production techniques; he has read the government study on sales opportunities;* to carry out a feasibility study on a project = to examine the costs and possible profits to see if the project should be started **2** *verb* to examine (something) carefully; *we are studying the possibility of setting up an office in New York; the government studied the committee's proposals for two months; you will need to study the market carefully before deciding on the design of the product*

stuff *verb* to put papers, etc., into envelopes; *we pay casual workers $2 an hour for stuffing envelopes or for envelope stuffing*
◇ **stuffer** *noun* advertising paper to be put in an envelope for mailing

style *noun* way of doing *or* making something; *a new style of product; old-style management techniques*

sub *noun* = SUBSCRIPTION, SUBSTITUTE

sub- *prefix* under, less important
◇ **subagency** *noun* small agency which is part of a large agency
◇ **subagent** *noun* person who is in charge of a subagency
◇ **subcommittee** *noun* small committee which is part of *or* set up by a main committee; *the next item on the agenda is the report of the finance subcommittee*
◇ **subcontract 1** *noun* contract between the main contractor for a whole project and another firm that will do part of the work; *they have been awarded the subcontract for all the electrical work in the new building; we will put the electrical work out to subcontract* **2** *verb* to agree with a company that they will do part of the work for a project; *the electrical work has been subcontracted to Smith Corp.*
◇ **subcontractor** *noun* company which has a contract to do work for a main contractor
◇ **subdivision** *noun* piece of empty land to be divided up for building new houses

subject to *adjective* **(a)** depending on; *the contract is subject to government approval* = the contract will be valid only if it is approved by the government; **agreement** *or* **sale subject to contract** = agreement *or* sale which is not legal until a proper contract has been signed; **offer subject to availability** = the offer is valid only if the goods are available **(b)** *these articles are subject to import tax* = import tax has to be paid on these articles

sub judice *adverb* not decided *or* under consideration by a court; *the papers cannot report the case because it is still sub judice*

sublease 1 *noun* lease from a tenant to another tenant **2** *verb* to lease a leased property to another tenant; *they subleased part of their offices*
◇ **sublessee** *noun* party which takes a property on a sublease
◇ **sublessor** *noun* tenant who lets a leased property to another tenant
◇ **sublet** *verb* to let a leased property to another tenant; *we have sublet part of our office to a financial consultant*
NOTE: **subletting - sublet**

submit *verb* to put (something) forward to be examined; *to submit a proposal to the committee; he submitted a claim to the insurers; the reps are asked to submit their expense claims once a month*
NOTE: **submitting - submitted**

subordinate 1 *adjective* less important; **subordinate to** = governed by *or* which depends on **2** *noun* member of staff who is supervised by someone; *his subordinates find him difficult to work with*

subpoena 1 *noun* order telling someone to appear in court as a witness **2** *verb* to order someone to appear in court; *the head of corporate finance was subpoenaed by the prosecution*

subscribe *verb* **(a) to subscribe to a magazine** = to pay for a series of issues of a magazine **(b) to subscribe for shares** = to apply to buy stock in a new company
◇ **subscriber** *noun* **(a) subscriber to a magazine** *or* **magazine subscriber** = person who has paid in advance for a series of issues of a magazine; *the extra issue is sent free to subscribers* **(b) subscriber to a share issue** = person who has applied for shares in a new company

◇ **subscription** *noun* **(a)** money paid in advance for a series of issues of a magazine *or* tickets to a theater; *did you remember to pay the subscription to the computer magazine?* ; **to take out a subscription to a magazine =** to start paying for a series of issues of a magazine; **to cancel a subscription to a magazine =** to stop paying for a magazine; **subscription agent =** business that sells subscriptions to magazines for a commission; **subscription rates =** amount of money to be paid for a series of issues of a magazine **(b) subscription to a new issue of securities =** offering shares in a new company for sale; **subscription list =** list of subscribers to a new issue of securities; **the subscription lists close at 10:00 on September 24 =** no new applicants will be allowed to subscribe for the issue after that date; **subscription price =** price at which stockholders can buy new shares in a corporation

subsidiary 1 *adjective* (thing) which is less important; *they agreed to most of the conditions in the contract but queried one or two subsidiary items;* **subsidiary company =** company which is more than 50% owned by a parent company **2** *noun* company which is more than 50% owned by a parent company; *most of the group profit was contributed by the subsidiaries in the Far East*

subsidize *verb* to help by giving money; *the government has refused to subsidize the car industry; subsidized agriculture; the federal government is subsidizing the local job creation program*
◇ **subsidy** *noun* **(a)** money given to help something which is not profitable; *the industry exists on government subsidies; the government has increased its subsidy to airlines* **(b)** money given by a government to make something cheaper; *the subsidy on butter or the butter subsidy*

subsistence *noun* minimum amount of food, money, housing, etc., which a person needs; **to live at subsistence level =** to have only just enough money to live on

substantial *adjective* large *or* important; *she was awarded substantial damages =* she received a large sum of money as damages; **to**

acquire a substantial interest in a company = to buy a large number of shares in a company

substitute 1 *noun* person *or* thing which takes the place of someone *or* something else **2** *verb* to take the place of something else

subtenancy *noun* agreement to sublet a property
◇ **subtenant** *noun* person *or* company to which a property has been sublet

subtotal *noun* total of one section of a complete set of figures

subtract *verb* to take away (something) from a total; *if the profits from the Far Eastern operations are subtracted, you will see that the group has not been profitable in the North American market*

subvention *noun* subsidy

succeed *verb* **(a)** to do well *or* to be profitable; *the company has succeeded best in the overseas markets; his business has succeeded more than he had expected* **(b)** to do what was planned; *she succeeded in passing her shorthand test; they succeeded in putting their rivals out of business* **(c)** to follow (someone); *Mr. Smith was succeeded as chairman by Mr. John A. Carter*
◇ **success** *noun* **(a)** doing something well; *the launch of the new model was a great success; the company has had great success in the Japanese market* **(b)** doing what was intended; *we had no success in trying to sell the lease; he has been looking for a job for six months, but with no success*
◇ **successful** *adjective* which does well; *a successful businessman; a successful selling trip to Germany*
◇ **successfully** *adverb* done well; *he successfully negotiated a new contract with the unions; the new model was successfully launched last month*
◇ **successor** *noun* person who takes over from someone; *Mr. Smith's successor as chairman will be Mr. John A. Carter*

sue *verb* to take someone to court *or* to start legal proceedings against someone to get money as compensation; *to sue* someone for damages; *he is suing the company for $50,000 compensation*

suffer *verb* to be in a bad situation *or* to do badly; *exports have suffered during the last six months; to suffer from something =* to do badly because of something; *the company's products suffer from bad design; the group suffers from bad management*

> QUOTE the holding company has seen its earnings suffer from big write-downs in conjunction with its agricultural loan portfolio
> *Duns Business Month*

sufficient *adjective* enough; *the company has sufficient funds to pay for its expansion program*

suggest *verb* to put forward a proposal; *the chairman suggested (that) the next meeting should be held in October; we suggested Mr. Smith for the position of treasurer*

◇ **suggestion** *noun* proposal *or* idea which is put forward; **suggestion box =** place in a company where employees can put forward their ideas for making the company more efficient and profitable

suitable *adjective* convenient *or* which fits; *Wednesday is the most suitable day for board meetings; we had to readvertise the job because there were no suitable candidates*

suitcase *noun* container with a handle for carrying clothes and personal belongings when traveling; *the customs officer made him open his three suitcases*

sum *noun* (a) quantity of money; *a sum of money was stolen from the personnel office; he lost large sums on the stock exchange; she received the sum of $500 in compensation;* **lump sum =** money paid in one payment, not in several small payments (b) total of a series of figures added together

summary *noun* short account of what has happened *or* of what has been written; *the chairman gave a summary of his discussions with the German trade delegation; the sales department has given a summary of sales to Europe for the first six months*

summons *noun* official order to appear in court; *he ignored the summons and went on vacation to Mexico*

sundry *adjective* & *noun* various; **sundry items** *or* **sundries =** small items which are not listed in detail

sunrise industries *noun* technologically advanced industries, such as computers

sunset industries *noun* old style industries, such as automobile manufacture

superannuation *noun* pension paid to someone who is too old *or* ill to work any more; **superannuation plan =** pension plan designed to compensate individuals who are unable to work due to poor health *or* old age

superette *noun* small supermarket

superintend *verb* to be in charge of; *he superintends the company's overseas sales*

◇ **superintendent** *noun* person in charge

superior 1 *adjective* better *or* of better quality; *our product is superior to all competing products; their sales are higher because of their superior distribution service* **2** *noun* more important person; *each manager is responsible to his superior for accurate reporting of sales*

supermarket *noun* large grocery store, where customers serve themselves and pay at a checkout; *sales in supermarkets* or *supermarket sales account for half the company's total sales*

superstore *noun* very large self-service store which sells a wide range of goods

supertanker *noun* very large oil tanker

supervise *verb* to watch work carefully to assure that it is well done; *the move to the new offices was supervised by the administrative manager; she supervises six clerks in the finance department*

◇ **supervision** *noun* being supervised; *new employees work under supervision for the first three months;*

she is very experienced and can be left to work without any supervision; the cash was counted under the supervision of the finance manager

◊ **supervisor** *noun* person who supervises

◊ **supervisory** *adjective* as a supervisor; *supervisory staff; he works in a supervisory capacity*

supplement 1 *noun* (a) thing which is added; *the company gives him a supplement to his pension* (b) special section added to a newspaper (such as a books supplement or a sport supplement) **2** *verb* to add; *we will supplement the warehouse staff with six part-timers during the Christmas rush*

◊ **supplementary** *adjective* in addition to; **supplementary unemployment benefits** = payments made by a company to its laid-off workers, in addition to ordinary unemployment insurance

supply 1 *noun* (a) providing something which is needed; **money supply** = amount of money which exists in a country; **supply price** = price at which something is provided; **supply and demand** = amount of a product which is available and the amount which is wanted by customers; **the law of supply and demand** = general rule that the amount of a product which is available is related to the needs of the possible customer (b) **in short supply** = not available in large enough quantities to meet the demand; *spare parts are in short supply because of the strike* (c) stock of something which is needed; *the factory is running short of supplies of coal; supplies of coal have been reduced;* **office supplies** = goods needed to run an office (such as paper, pens, typewriters) **2** *verb* to provide something which is needed; *to supply a factory with spare parts; the finance department supplied the committee with the figures; details of staff addresses and phone numbers can be supplied by the personnel staff*

◊ **supply-side economics** *noun* economic theory stating that governments should encourage producers and suppliers of goods by cutting taxes, rather than encourage demand by making more money available in the economy

◊ **supplier** *noun* person *or* company which supplies *or* sells goods or services;

office equipment supplier; they are major suppliers of spare parts to the car industry

support 1 *noun* (a) giving money to help; *the government has provided support to the electronics industry; we have no financial support from the banks* (b) agreement *or* encouragement; *the chairman has the support of the committee* **2** *verb* (a) to give money to help; *the government is supporting the electronics industry to the tune of $2bn per annum; we hope the banks will support us during the expansion period* (b) to encourage *or* to agree with; *she hopes the other members of committee will support her; the market will not support another price increase*

surcharge *noun* extra charge; **import surcharge** = extra duty charged on imported goods, to try to stop them from being imported and to encourage local manufacture

surety *noun* (a) person who guarantees that someone will do something; *to stand surety for someone* (b) deeds *or* share certificates, etc., deposited as security for a loan

surface *noun* land *or* sea; **to send a package by surface mail** = to send it by land or sea, but not by air; **surface transport** = transport on land or sea

surplus *noun* extra stock *or* something which is more than is needed; *surplus government equipment; surplus butter is on sale in the stores; we are holding a sale of surplus stock; we are trying to let surplus capacity in the warehouse;* **a budget surplus** = more revenue than was planned for in the budget; **to absorb a surplus** = to take a surplus into a larger amount

surrender 1 *noun* giving up of an insurance policy before the contracted date for maturity; **cash surrender value** = money which an insurer will pay if a life insurance policy is given up before the insured person dies **2** *verb* **to surrender a policy** = to give up an insurance policy

surtax *noun* extra tax on high income

survey 1 *noun* (a) general report on a problem; *the federal government has* published a survey of population trends; we have asked the sales department to produce a survey of competing products (b) examining something to see if it is in good condition; we have asked for a survey of the house before buying it; the insurance company is carrying out a survey of the damage; damage survey = survey of damage done (c) measuring the form and position of a piece of land 2 verb to examine (something) to see if it is in good condition

◊ surveyor noun (a) person who measures land or prepares surveys (b) inspector or superintendent

suspend verb (a) to stop (something) for a time; we have suspended payments while we are waiting for news from our agent; sailing has been suspended until the weather gets better; work on the construction project has been suspended; the management decided to suspend negotiations; trading in the stock has been suspended pending an announcement about the corporation's future (b) to stop (someone) from working for a time; he was suspended on full pay while the police investigations were going on

◊ suspense account noun temporary account used to list income or payments which have not been finally allocated

◊ suspension noun stopping something for a time; suspension of payments; suspension of deliveries

swap 1 noun exchange of one thing for another 2 verb to exchange one thing for another; he swapped his old car for a new motorcycle; they swapped jobs = each of them took the other's job
NOTE: swapping - swapped

swatch noun small sample; color swatch = small sample of color which the finished product must look like

sweat noun drops of liquid which come through your skin when you are hot

◊ sweated labor noun (a) people who work hard for very little money; of course the firm makes a profit - it employs sweated labor (b) hard work which is very underpaid

◊ sweatshop noun factory using sweated labor

switch verb to change from one thing to another; to switch funds from one investment to another; the job was

switched from our Wisconsin factory to Japan

◊ switchboard noun central point in a telephone system, where all lines meet; switchboard operator = person who works the central telephone system

◊ switch over to verb to change to something quite different; we have switched over to a French supplier; the factory has switched over to gas for heating

swop = SWAP

symbol noun sign or picture or object which represents something; they use a bear as their advertising symbol

sympathy noun feeling sorry because someone else has problems; the manager had no sympathy for his secretary who complained of being overworked; sympathy strike = strike to show that workers agree with another group of workers who are on strike; to strike in sympathy = to stop work to show that you agree with another group of workers who are on strike; the postal workers went on strike and the telephone engineers came out in sympathy

◊ sympathetic adjective showing sympathy; sympathetic strike = sympathy strike

syndicate 1 noun group of people or companies working together to make money; a German finance syndicate; underwriting syndicate = (i) group of underwriters who insure a large risk; (ii) group of financial institutions that underwrite a new issue of securities 2 verb to produce an article, drawing, etc., which is published in several newspapers or magazines

◊ syndicated adjective published in several newspapers or magazines; he writes a syndicated column on personal finance

synergy noun producing greater effects by joining forces than by acting separately

synthetic adjective artificial or made by man; synthetic fibers or synthetic materials = materials made as products of a chemical process

system noun (a) arrangement or organization of things which work together; our accounting system has worked well in spite of the large increase in orders; **decimal system =** system of mathematics based on the number 10; **filing system =** way of putting documents in order for easy reference; **to operate a quota system =** to regulate supplies by fixing quantities which are allowed; *we arrange our distribution using a quota system - each agent is allowed only a certain number of units* **(b) computer system =** set of programs, commands, etc., which run a computer **(c) systems analysis =** using a computer to suggest how a company should work by analyzing the way in which it works at present; **systems analyst =** person who specializes in systems analysis

◇ **systematic** *adjective* in order *or* using some method; *he ordered a systematic report on the distribution service*

Tt

tab *noun* = TABULATOR

table 1 *noun* **(a)** piece of furniture with a flat top and legs; **typing table =** table for a typewriter **(b)** list of figures *or* facts set out in columns; **table of contents =** list of contents in a book; **actuarial tables =** lists showing how long people of certain ages are likely to live, used to calculate life insurance premiums **2** *verb (at a meeting)* to remove a proposal from consideration for an indefinite period; *the motion to hold a new election was tabled*

◇ **tabular** *adjective* in tabular form = arranged in a table

◇ **tabulate** *verb* to set out in a table

◇ **tabulation** *noun* arrangement of figures in a table

◇ **tabulator** *noun* part of a typewriter *or* computer which sets words or figures automatically in columns

tacit *adjective* agreed but not stated or implied; *tacit approval; tacit agreement to a proposal*

tactic *noun* way of doing things so as to be at an advantage; *his usual tactic is to buy shares in a company, then mount a takeover bid, and sell out at a profit; the directors planned their tactics*

before going into the meeting with the union representatives

tag *noun* label attached by a string; *price tag; name tag*

take 1 *noun* money received in a store **2** *verb* **(a)** to receive *or* to get; **the store takes $2,000 a week =** the store receives $2,000 a week in cash sales; **he takes home $250 a week =** his salary, after deductions for tax, etc., is $250 a week **(b)** to do a certain action; **to take action =** to do something; *you must take immediate action if you want to stop thefts;* **to take a call =** to answer the telephone; **to take the chair =** to be the chairperson of a meeting; *in the absence of the chairman the associate took the chair;* **to take dictation =** to write down what someone is saying; *the secretary was taking dictation from the president;* **to take stock =** to count the items in a warehouse; **to take stock of a situation =** to examine the state of things before deciding what to do **(c)** to need (a time *or* a quantity); *it took the factory six weeks or the factory took six weeks to clear the backlog of orders; it will take her all morning to do my letters; it took six men and a crane to get the computer into the office*

NOTE: **taking - took - has taken**

◇ **take away** *verb* **(a)** to remove one figure from a total; *if you take away the domestic sales, the total sales are down* **(b)** to remove; *we had to take the work away from the supplier because the quality was so bad; the police took away piles of documents from the office*

◇ **take back** *verb* **(a)** to return with something; *when the watch broke, he took it back to the store; if you do not like the color, you can take it back to change it* **(b)** to take back dismissed **workers =** to allow former workers to join the company again

◇ **take-home pay** *noun* amount of money received in wages, after tax, etc., has been deducted

◇ **take into** *verb* to take inside; *to take items into stock or into the warehouse*

◇ **take off** *verb* **(a)** to remove *or* to deduct; *he took $25 off the price* **(b)** to start to rise fast; *sales took off after the TV commercials* **(c)** she took the **day off =** she decided not to work for the day

◇ **take on** *verb* to agree to employ someone *or* to agree to do something; *she* took on the job of preparing the tax returns; *to take on more staff; he has taken on a lot of extra work*

◊ **take out** *verb* to remove; **to take out a patent for an invention** = to apply for and receive a patent; **to take out insurance against theft** = to pay a premium to an insurance company, so that if a theft takes place the company will pay compensation

◊ **take over** *verb* (a) to start to do something in place of someone else; *Miss Black took over from Mr. Jones on May 1; the new chairman takes over on July 1* (b) to take over a company = to buy (a business) by offering to buy most of its shares; *the buyer takes over the company's liabilities; the company was taken over by a large multinational*

◊ **takeover** *noun* buying a business; **takeover bid** = offer to buy all or most of the shares in a company so as to control it; **to make a takeover bid for a company** = to offer to buy most of the shares in a company; **to withdraw a takeover bid** = to say that you no longer offer to buy a company; **the company rejected the takeover bid** = the directors recommended that the shareholders should not accept the offer; *the disclosure of the takeover bid raised share prices;* **contested takeover** = takeover where the board of the company being bought does not recommend it, and tries to fight it

◊ **taker** *noun* buyer *or* person who wants to buy; *there were no takers for the new issue of securities*

◊ **take up** *verb* **to take up an option** = to accept an option which has been offered and put into action; *half the rights issue was not taken up by the shareholders;* **take up rate** = percentage of acceptances for a rights issue

◊ **takings** *plural noun* money received in a store *or* a business; *the week's takings were stolen from the cash desk*

QUOTE many takeovers result in the new managers/owners rationalizing the capital of the company through better asset management
Duns Business Month
QUOTE capital gains are not taxed, but money taken out in profits and dividends is taxed
Toronto Star

tally 1 *noun* list of things counted *or* recorded; *to keep a tally of stock movements or of expenses;* **tally clerk** = person whose job is to list quantities of cargo; **tally sheet** = sheet on which

quantities are listed **2** *verb* to correspond with *or* to be the same; *the invoices do not tally; the finance department tried to make the figures tally*

tangible *adjective* **tangible assets** = assets that can actually be appraised for value (such as furniture, jewelry, real estate, etc.)

tanker *noun* special ship for carrying liquids (especially oil)

tape *noun* (a) long, flat, narrow piece of plastic; **magnetic tape** = sensitive tape for recording information; **computer tape** = magnetic tape used in computers; **measuring tape** *or* **tape measure** = long tape with inches *or* centimeters marked on it for measuring how long something is (b) roll of narrow plastic with adhesive, used for sticking papers, etc. (c) long strip of paper on which stock exchange information is printed and sent to subscribers by wire

tare *noun* (allowance made for the) weight of a container and packing which is deducted from the total weight; (allowance made for the) weight of a vehicle in calculating transport costs; *to allow for tare*

target 1 *noun* thing to aim for; **production targets** = amount of units a factory is expected to produce; **sales targets** = amount of sales a representative is expected to achieve; **target company** = company which another company is planning to take over; **target market** = market in which a company is planning to sell its goods; **to set targets** = to fix amounts *or* quantities which workers have to produce *or* reach; **to meet a target** = to produce the quantity of goods *or* sales which are expected; **to miss a target** = not to produce the amount of goods *or* sales which are expected; *they missed the target figure of $2m in sales* **2** *verb* to aim to sell; **to target a market** = to plan to sell goods in a certain market

QUOTE in a normal leveraged buyout the acquirer raises money by borrowing against the assets of the target company
Fortune

tariff *noun* (a) rate of charging for a public utility *or* business; **freight tariffs** (b) **customs tariffs** = tax to be paid for importing *or* exporting goods; **tariff barriers** = customs duty intended to make imports more difficult; *to impose tariff barriers on* or *to lift tariff barriers from a product;* **differential tariffs** = different duties for different types of goods; **General Agreement on Tariffs and Trade** = international agreement to try to reduce restrictions in trade between countries

task *noun* **(a)** work which has to be done; *a list of tasks for the day* **(b) task force** = special group of workers *or* managers who are chosen to carry out a special job *or* to deal with a special problem

tax 1 *noun* **(a)** money taken by a government *or* by an official body to pay for government services; **airport tax** = tax included in the price of an air ticket to cover the cost of running an airport; **capital gains tax** = tax on capital gains; **capital transfer tax** = tax on gifts or bequests of money or property; **corporate tax** = tax on profits made by incorporated companies; **corporation income tax** = tax on net earnings of incorporated companies; **excess profits tax** = tax on profits which are higher than what is considered normal; **personal income tax** = tax on salaries and wages earned by individuals; **land tax** = tax on the amount of land owned; **property tax** = tax levied on real estate; **sales tax** = tax on the price of goods sold **(b) ad valorem tax** = tax calculated according to the value of the goods taxed; **back tax** = tax which is owed; **basic tax** = tax paid at the normal rate; **direct tax** = tax paid directly to the government (such as income tax); **indirect tax** = tax paid to someone who then pays it to the government (such as sales tax); **to levy a tax** *or* **to impose a tax** = to require a tax to be paid; *the government has imposed a 15% tax on gasoline;* **to lift a tax** = to remove a tax; *the tax on corporate profits has been lifted;* **exclusive of tax** = not including tax; **tax abatement** = reduction of tax; **tax adjustments** = changes made to tax; **tax adviser** *or* **tax consultant** = person who gives advice on tax problems; **tax allowance** *or* **allowances against tax** = part of the income which a person is allowed to earn and not pay tax on; **tax avoidance** = trying (legally) to minimize the amount of tax to be paid; **tax bracket** = area of taxable income (for individuals and corporations) at which a particular percentage tax is payable; **in the top tax bracket** = paying the highest level of tax; **tax concession** = allowing less tax to be

paid; **tax credit** = reduction in the amount of tax owed under certain circumstances; *investment tax credit; child care tax credit;* **tax deductions** = business expenditures which can be claimed against tax; **tax evasion** = trying illegally not to pay tax; **tax exemption** = (i) being free from payment of tax; (ii) part of income which a person is allowed to earn and not pay tax on; **tax form** = blank form to be filled in with details of income and allowances and sent to the tax office each year; **tax haven** = country where taxes are low, encouraging companies to set up their main offices there; **tax loophole** = legal means of not paying tax; **tax relief** = allowing someone not to pay tax on certain parts of his income; **tax return** = completed tax form, with details of income and allowances; **tax shelter** = financial arrangement (such as a pension plan) where investments can be made without tax; **tax year** = twelve-month period on which taxes are calculated **2** *verb* to make someone pay a tax *or* to impose a tax on something; *to tax businesses at 50%; income is taxed at 35%; luxury items are heavily taxed*

◊ **taxable** *adjective* which can be taxed; **taxable items** = items on which a tax has to be paid; **taxable income** = income on which a person has to pay tax

◊ **taxation** *noun* act of taxing; **direct taxation** = taxes (such as income tax) which are paid direct to a government; **indirect taxation** = taxes (such as sales tax) which are not paid direct to a government; *the government raises more money by indirect taxation than by direct;* **double taxation** = taxing the same income twice; **double taxation agreement** = agreement between two countries that a person living in one country will not be taxed in both countries on the income earned in the other country

◊ **tax-deductible** *adjective* which can be deducted from total income before tax is calculated; **these expenses are not tax-deductible** = tax has to be paid on these expenses

◊ **tax-exempt** *adjective* not required to pay tax; (income *or* goods) which are not subject to tax

◊ **tax-free** *adjective* on which tax does not have to be paid

◊ **taxpayer** *noun* person *or* company which has to pay tax; *basic taxpayer or taxpayer at the basic rate; corporate taxpayers*

taxi *noun* car which takes people from one place to another for money; *he took a taxi to the airport; taxi fares are very high in New York*

T bill = TREASURY BILL

team *noun* group of people who work together; **management team** = group of all the managers working in the same company; **sales team** = all representatives, salesmen and sales managers working in a company
◊ **teammate** *noun* colleague who works in the same team
◊ **teamster** *noun* truck driver
◊ **teamwork** *noun* being able to work together as a group

technical *adjective* **(a)** referring to a particular machine *or* process; *the document gives all the technical details on the new computer* **(b)** **technical correction** = situation where the price of a stock or bond or currency moves up or down because it was previously too low or too high
◊ **technician** *noun* person who specializes in industrial work; *computer technician*; **laboratory technician** = person who deals with practical work in a laboratory
◊ **technique** *noun* skilled way of doing a job; *the company has developed a new technique for processing steel; he has a special technique for answering complaints from customers;* **management techniques** = skill in managing a business; **marketing techniques** = skill in marketing a product
◊ **technology** *noun* applying scientific knowledge to industrial processes; **information technology** = working with data stored on computers; **the introduction of new technology** = putting new electronic equipment into a business or industry
◊ **technological** *adjective* referring to technology; **the technological revolution** = changing of industry by introducing new technology; **technological unemployment** = unemployment caused by the introduction of new technology

tel = TELEGRAM, TELEPHONE

telecommunications *plural noun* systems of passing messages over long distances (by cable, radio, etc.)

telegram *noun* message sent a long distance by telegraph; *to send an international telegram*
◊ **telegraph 1** *noun* system of sending messages along wires; *to send a message by telegraph;* telegraph office = office from which telegrams can be sent **2** *verb* to send a message by telegram; *to telegraph an order*
◊ **telegraphic** *adjective* referring to a telegraph system; **telegraphic address** = short address used for sending telegrams
◊ **telemarketing** *noun* marketing a product *or* service by telephone

telephone 1 *noun* machine used for speaking to someone over a long distance; *we had a new telephone system installed last week;* **to be on the telephone** = to be speaking to someone using the telephone; *the sales director is on the telephone to Hong Kong; she has been on the telephone all day;* **by telephone** = using the telephone; *to place an order by telephone; to reserve a room by telephone;* house telephone *or* internal telephone = telephone for calling from one room to another in an office or hotel; **telephone book** *or* **telephone directory** = book which lists all people and businesses in a region in alphabetical order with their telephone numbers; *he looked up the number of the company in the telephone book;* telephone call = speaking to someone on the telephone; **to make a telephone call** = to speak to someone on the telephone; **to answer the telephone** *or* **to take a telephone call** = to speak in reply to a call on the telephone; **telephone exchange** = central office where the telephones of a whole district are linked; **telephone number** = set of figures for a particular telephone customer; *can you give me your telephone number?;* **telephone operator** = person who operates a telephone switchboard; **telephone orders** = orders received by telephone; *since we mailed the catalog we have received a large number of telephone orders;* **telephone switchboard** = central point in a telephone system where all internal and external lines meet **2** *verb* **to telephone a place** *or* **a person** = to call a place *or* someone by telephone; *his secretary telephoned to say he would be late;* **he telephoned the order through to the warehouse** = he telephoned the warehouse to place an order

◊ **teleprinter** *or* **teletypewriter** *noun* machine like a typewriter, which can send messages by telegraph and print incoming messages; **teleprinter operator**

◊ **telesales** *noun* selling a product *or* service by telephone

teletype *or* **telex 1** *noun* **(a)** system of sending messages by teleprinter; **to send information by telex; the order came by telex; telex line =** wire linking a telex machine to the telex system; **we cannot communicate with our Nigerian office because of the breakdown of the telex lines; telex operator =** person who operates a telex machine; **telex subscriber =** company which has a telex **(b) a telex =** (i) a machine for sending and receiving telex messages; (ii) a message sent by telex; *he sent a telex to his head office; we received his telex this morning* **2** *verb* to send a message using a teleprinter; *can you telex the Canadian office before they open? he telexed the details of the contract to New York*

teller *noun* person who carries out a customer's transaction at a bank

tem *see* PRO TEM

temp 1 *noun* temporary secretary; *we have had two temps working in the office this week to clear the backlog of letters* **2** *verb* to work as a temporary secretary

◊ **temping** *noun* working as a temporary secretary; *she can earn more money temping than from a full-time job*

temporary *adjective* which only lasts a short time; *he was granted a temporary export license; to take temporary measures; he has a temporary post with a construction company; he has a temporary job as a filing clerk or he has a job as a temporary filing clerk;* **temporary agency =** office which deals with finding temporary help for business; **temporary employment =** full-time work which does not last for more than a few days or months; **temporary staff =** staff who are appointed for a short time

◊ **temporarily** *adverb* lasting only for a short time

tenancy *noun* (i) agreement by which a tenant can occupy a property; (ii) period

during which a tenant has an agreement to occupy a property

◊ **tenant** *noun* person *or* company which rents a house *or* apartment *or* office to live or work in; *the tenant is liable for repairs*

tend *verb* to be likely to do something; *he tends to appoint young girls to his staff*

◊ **tendency** *noun* being likely to do something; *the market showed an upward tendency; there has been a downward tendency in the market for several days;* **the market showed a tendency to stagnate =** the market seemed to stagnate rather than advance

tender 1 *noun* **(a)** offer to pay a debt in full, with evidence of ability to pay **(b) to sell shares by tender =** to ask people to offer in writing a price for shares; **tender offer =** offer to buy shares in a company at a certain price from individual shareholders **(c) legal tender =** coins or notes which can be legally used to pay a debt **2** *verb* **(a)** to put forward an offer of money to satisfy a debt **(b) to tender one's resignation =** to submit one's resignation

tentative *adjective* not certain; *they reached a tentative agreement over the proposal; we suggested Wednesday May 10 as a tentative date for the next meeting*

◊ **tentatively** *adverb* not sure; *we tentatively suggested Wednesday as the date for our next meeting*

tenure *noun* **(a)** right to hold property *or* position; **security of tenure =** right to keep a job *or* rented accommodation provided certain conditions are met **(b)** time when a position is held; *during his tenure as chairman*

term *noun* **(a)** period of time when something is legally valid; *the term of a lease; the term of the loan is fifteen years; to have a loan for a term of fifteen years; during his term of office as chairman;* **term deposit =** money invested for a fixed period at a higher rate of interest; **term life insurance =** life insurance which covers a person's life for a certain period of time; *he took out a ten-year term insurance;* **term loan =** loan for a fixed period of time; **short-term =** for a period of months; **long-term =** for a long period of time; **medium-term =** for a period of one or two years **(b) terms =** conditions *or* duties which have to be carried out as part of a contract *or* arrangements which have to be agreed on before a contract is valid; *he refused to agree to some of the terms of the contract; by or under the terms of the contract, the company is responsible for all damage to the property; to negotiate for better terms;* **terms of payment** *or* **payment terms =** conditions for paying something; **terms of sale =** conditions attached to a sale; **cash terms =** special terms which apply if the customer pays cash; **"terms: cash with order" =** terms of sale showing that payment has to be made in cash when the order is placed; **easy terms =** terms which are not difficult to accept *or* price which is easy to pay; *the building is let on very easy terms; to pay for something on easy terms;* **on favorable terms =** on especially good terms; **trade terms =** special discount for people in the same trade **(c)** part of an academic year **(d) terms of employment =** conditions set out in a contract of employment

terminal *noun* **(a) computer terminal =** keyboard and screen, by which information can be put into a computer or can be called up from a database; *computer system consisting of a microprocessor and six terminals* **(b) airport terminal** *or* **terminal building =** main building at an airport where passengers arrive and leave; **container terminal =** area of a harbor where container ships are loaded or unloaded; **ocean terminal =** building at a port where passengers arrive and depart

terminate *verb* to end (something) *or* to bring (something) to an end; *to terminate an agreement; his employment was terminated; the offer terminates on July 31; the flight from Paris terminates in New York*
◊ **terminable** *adjective* which can be terminated
◊ **termination** *noun* **(a)** bringing to an end; **termination clause =** clause which explains how and when a contract can be terminated **(b)** leaving a job (resigning, retiring, or being fired or laid off)

territory *noun* area visited by a salesman; *a rep's territory; his territory covers the northern half of the state*

tertiary *adjective* **tertiary industry =** service industry, an industry which does

not produce or manufacture but offers a service (such as banking, retailing or accountancy); **tertiary sector =** section of the economy containing the service industries

test 1 *noun* **(a)** examination to see if something works well *or* is possible; **test certificate =** certificate to show that something has passed a test; **driving test =** examination to see if someone is able to drive a car; **feasibility test =** test to see if something is possible; **market test =** examination to see if a sample of a product will sell in a market **(b) test case =** legal action where the decision will fix a principle which other cases can follow **2** *verb* to examine something to see if it is working well; *to test a computer system; to test the market for a product or to test market a product* = to show samples of a product in a market to see if it will sell well; *we are test marketing the toothpaste in Iowa*
◊ **test-drive** *verb* to test-drive a car = to drive a car (before buying it) to see if it works well
◊ **testing** *noun* examining something to see if it works well; *during the testing of the system several defects were corrected*

testimonial *noun* written report about someone's character *or* ability; *to write someone a testimonial;* **unsolicited testimonial =** letter praising someone *or* a product, without the writer having been asked to write it; **testimonial advertising =** advertising which uses favorable comments about a product made by satisfied customers

text *noun* written part of something; *he wrote notes at the side of the text of the agreement;* **text processing =** working with words, using a computer to produce, check and change documents, reports, letters, etc.

thank *verb* to tell *or* show someone that you are grateful for what has been done; *the committee thanked the retiring chairman for his work; "Thank you for your letter of June 25"*
◊ **thanks** *plural noun* word showing that someone is grateful; *"many thanks for your letter of June 25" ;* **vote of thanks =** official vote at a meeting to show that the meeting is grateful for what someone has done; *the meeting passed a vote of thanks to the*

organizing committee for their work in setting up the international conference
◊ **thanks to** *adverb* because of; *the company was able to continue trading, thanks to a loan from the bank; it was no thanks to the bank that we avoided making a loss* = we avoided making a loss in spite of the bank's actions

theft *noun* stealing; *we have brought in security guards to protect the store against theft; they are trying to cut their losses from theft; to take out insurance against theft*

theory *noun* statement of the general principle of how something should work; *in theory the plan should work* = the plan may work, but it has not been tried in practice .

thin market *noun* situation where there is little business done on a stock exchange or commodity market

think tank *noun* group of experts who advise *or* put forward plans

third *noun* part of something which is divided into three; **to sell everything at one third off** = to sell everything at a discount of 33%; **the company has two thirds of the total market** = the company has 66% of the total market; **third-class mail** = mail service for unsealed letters and advertising material; **third market** = dealings in securities by brokers who are not members of a Stock Exchange
◊ **third party** *noun* any person other than the two main parties involved in a contract; **third-party insurance** = insurance to cover damage to any person who is not one of the people named in the insurance contract; **the case is in the hands of a third party** = the case is being dealt with by someone who is not one of the main interested parties
◊ **third quarter** *noun* three months' period from July to September
◊ **Third World** *noun* countries of Africa, Asia and South America which do not have highly developed industries; *we sell tractors to Third World countries*

threshold *noun* limit *or* point at which something changes; **threshold agreement** = contract which says that if the cost of living goes up by more than a certain amount, pay will go up to match it; **pay threshold** = point at which pay

increases because of a threshold agreement

thrift *noun* **(a)** saving money by spending carefully **(b) thrifts** *or* **thrift institutions** = savings banks *or* savings and loan associations *or* credit unions, which accept and pay interest on deposits from small investors
◊ **thrifty** *adjective* careful not to spend too much money

thrive *verb* to grow well *or* to be profitable; *a thriving economy; thriving black market in car radios; the company is thriving in spite of the recession*

throughput *noun* amount of work done *or* of goods produced in a certain time; *we hope to increase our throughput by putting in two new machines; the invoice department has a throughput of 6,000 invoices a day*

throwaway *noun* handbill *or* flier

throw out *verb* **(a)** to reject *or* to refuse to accept; *the proposal was thrown out by the planning committee; the board threw out the draft contract submitted by the union* **(b)** to get rid of (something which is not wanted); *we threw out the old telephones and installed a computerized system; the shareholders threw out the old board of directors*
NOTE: **throwing - threw - has thrown**

thumbtack *noun* pin with a large flat head, used to pin papers to a bulletin board

tick 1 *noun* **(a)** mark on paper to show that something is correct *or* approved *or* chosen; *put a tick in the box marked "R"* **(b)** movement of the price of a stock up or down **2** *verb* to mark with a sign to show that something is correct; *tick the box marked "R" if you require a receipt*

◊ **ticker** *noun* machine (operated by telegraph) which prints details of share prices and transactions rapidly on paper tape; **ticker tape =** paper tape which prints information about stock exchange prices and volumes of securities sold, and which is sent to subscribers by wire

ticket *noun* (a) piece of paper *or* card which allows you to do something; **entrance ticket** *or* **admission ticket =** ticket which allows you to go in; **theater ticket =** ticket which allows you a seat in a theater (b) piece of paper *or* card which allows you to travel; *train ticket or bus ticket or plane ticket;* **season ticket =** train *or* bus ticket which can be used for any number of rides over a period (as six or twelve months); **one-way ticket =** ticket for a journey from one place to another; **round-trip ticket =** ticket for a journey from one place to another and back again (c) **ticket agency** = firm which sells tickets to theaters and other entertainment; **ticket counter =** counter where tickets are sold (d) paper which shows something; **baggage ticket** = paper showing that you have left a piece of baggage with someone; **price ticket =** piece of paper showing a price

tie *verb* to attach *or* to fasten (with string, wire, etc.); *he tied the parcel with thick string; she tied two labels onto the parcel* NOTE: **tying - tied**

◊ **tie-in promotion** *noun* special displays and gimmicks related to an advertising campaign

◊ **tie-on label** *noun* label with a piece of string attached so that it can be tied to an item

◊ **tie up** *verb* (a) to attach *or* to fasten tightly; *the package is tied up with string; the ship was tied up to the quay;* **he is rather tied up at the moment =** he is very busy (b) to invest money in one way, so that it cannot be used for other investments; *he has $100,000 tied up in long-term bonds; the company has $250,000 tied up in stock which no one wants to buy*

◊ **tie-up** *noun* link *or* connection; *the company has a tie-up with a German distributor* NOTE: plural is **tie-ups**

tight *adjective* which is controlled *or* which does not allow any movement; *the manager has a very tight schedule today - he cannot fit in any more appointments; expenses are kept*

under tight control; **tight money =** money which is borrowed at a high interest rate; **tight money policy =** government policy to restrict money supply

◊ **-tight** *suffix* which prevents something from getting in; *the computer is packed in a watertight case; send the films in an airtight container*

◊ **tighten** *verb* to make (something) tight *or* to control (something); *the finance department is tightening its control over departmental budgets*

◊ **tighten up on** *verb* to control (something) more; *the IRS is tightening up on tax evasion; we must tighten up on the reps' expenses*

till *noun* cash register, the drawer for keeping cash in a store; *there was not much money in the till at the end of the day*

time *noun* (a) period when something takes place (such as one hour, two days, fifty minutes, etc.); **computer time =** time when a computer is being used (paid for at an hourly rate); **real time =** time when a computer is working on the processing of data while the problem to which the data refers is actually taking place; **time and motion study =** study in an office *or* factory of how long it takes to do certain jobs and the movements workers make to do them; **time and motion expert =** person who analyzes time and motion studies and suggests changes in the way work is done (b) hour of the day (such as 9:00, 12:15, ten o'clock at night, etc.); *the time of arrival or the arrival time is indicated on the screen; departure times are delayed by up to fifteen minutes because of the volume of traffic;* **on time =** at the right time; *the plane was on time; you will have to hurry if you want to get to the meeting on time or if you want to be on time for the meeting;* **opening time** *or* **closing time =** time when a store or office starts or stops work (c) system of hours on the clock; **Daylight Saving Time =** system where clocks are set back one hour in the summer to take advantage of the longer hours of daylight; **Standard Time =** normal time as in the winter months (d) hours worked; **he is paid time and a half on Sundays =** he is paid the normal rate plus 50% extra when he works on Sundays; **full-time =** working for the whole normal working day; **overtime =** hours worked more than the normal working time; **part-time =** not working for a whole working day **(e)** period before something happens; **time deposit** = deposit of money for a fixed period, during which it cannot be withdrawn *or* used; **delivery time** = number of days before something will be delivered; **lead time** = time between deciding to begin a process and completing it; **time limit** = period during which something should be done; **to keep within the time limits** *or* **within the time schedule** = to complete work by the time stated

◊ **time card** *noun* card which is put into a timing machine when a worker clocks in *or* clocks out, and records the time when he starts and stops work; *the time card shows he worked five days last week*

◊ **time-keeping** *noun* being on time for work; *he was advised to be more honest about his time-keeping*

◊ **time rate** *noun* rate for work which is calculated as money per hour *or* per week, and not money for work completed

◊ **timesaving 1** *adjective* which saves time; *a timesaving device* **2** *noun* trying to save time; *the management is keen on timesaving*

◊ **time scale** *noun* time which will be taken to complete work; *our time scale is that all work should be completed by the end of August; he is working to a strict time scale*

◊ **time share** *noun* system where several people each own part of a property (such as a vacation house), each being able to use it for a certain period each year

◊ **time-sharing** *noun* **(a)** = TIME SHARE **(b)** sharing a computer system, with different users using different terminals

◊ **time sheet** *noun* document showing which hours a worker has worked for a given time period

◊ **timetable** *noun* **(a)** list showing times of arrivals *or* departures of buses *or* trains *or* planes, etc.; *according to the timetable, there should be a train to New Haven at 10:22; the bus company has brought out its winter timetable* **(b)** list of appointments *or* events; *the manager has a very full timetable, so I doubt if he will be able to see you today;* **conference timetable** = list of speakers *or* events at a conference

◊ **timework** *noun* work which is paid for at a rate per hour *or* per day, not per piece of work completed

◊ **timing** *noun* way in which something happens at a particular time; *the timing of the conference is very convenient, as it comes just before my annual vacation; his arrival ten minutes after the meeting finished was very bad timing*

tip 1 *noun* **(a)** money given to someone who has helped you; *I gave the cabdriver a 25-cent tip; the staff are not allowed to accept tips* **(b)** advice on something to buy *or* to do which could be profitable; *a stock market tip; he gave me a tip about a share which was likely to rise because of a takeover bid;* **tip sheet** = newspaper which gives information about shares which should be bought or sold **2** *verb* to give money to someone who has helped you; *he tipped the waitress $5*
NOTE: **tipping - tipped**

title *noun* **(a)** right to own a property; *she has no title to the property; he has a valid title to the property;* **title deed** = document showing who is the owner of a property; **title search** = examination of records of a property, to make sure that the vendor has the right to sell it **(b)** name given to a person in a certain job; *he has the title "Chief Executive"* **(c)** name of a book *or* film, etc.

token *noun* thing which acts as a sign *or* symbol; **token charge** = small charge which does not cover the real costs; *a token charge is made for heating;* **token payment** = small payment to show that a payment is being made; **token rent** = very low rent payment to show that a rent is being paid; **token strike** = short strike to show that workers have a grievance

◊ **tokenism** *noun* practice of hiring only a small number of minority group members to comply with affirmative action laws

toll *noun* payment for using a service (usually a bridge or a ferry); *we had to cross a toll bridge to get to the island; you have to pay a toll to cross the bridge*

◊ **toll call** *noun* long-distance telephone call

◊ **toll free** *adjective & adverb* without having to pay a charge for a long-distance telephone call; *to call someone toll free;* **toll-free numbers** *or* **800 numbers** = telephone numbers beginning with the digits 800, by which calls can be made free of charge (the supplier pays for them, not the caller)

tombstone ad *noun informal* official announcement in a newspaper showing that a loan has been subscribed

ton *noun* measure of weight; **long ton =** measure of weight (= 2,240 pounds); **short ton =** measure of weight (= 2,000 pounds); **metric ton =** 1,000 kilos

◊ **tonnage** *noun* space for cargo in a ship, measured in tons; **gross tonnage =** amount of total space in a ship; **deadweight tonnage =** largest amount of cargo which a ship can carry safely

tone *noun* **dial tone =** noise made by a telephone to show that it is ready for you to dial a number

◊ **toner** *noun* black ink powder used in photocopy machines and laser printers

tool *noun* instrument used for doing manual work (such as a hammer, screwdriver); **machine tools =** tools worked by motors, used to work on wood or metal

top 1 *adjective & noun* (a) upper surface *or* upper part; *do not put coffee cups on top of the computer;* **top copy =** first sheet of a document which is typed with several carbon copies or photocopies (b) highest point *or* rank; *the company is in the top six exporters;* **top-flight** *or* **top-ranking =** in the most important position; *top-flight managers can earn very high salaries; he is the top-ranking official in the delegation;* **top-grade =** most important *or* of the best quality; *the car only runs on top-grade gasoline;* **top management =** the main executives of a company; **to give something top priority =** to make something the most important item, so that it is done immediately; **top quality =** very best quality; *we specialize in top quality imported goods* **2** *verb* to go higher than; *sales topped $1m in the first quarter* (c) *(informal)* **top dollar =** the highest price possible; *it sold for top dollar*
NOTE: **topping - topped**

◊ **top out** *noun* peak period of demand for a product *or* of the rise in price of a security

◊ **top-selling** *adjective* which sells better than all other products; *top-selling brands of toothpaste*

tort *noun* harm done to someone *or* property which can be the basis of a civil lawsuit

total 1 *adjective* complete *or* with everything added together; *total amount; total assets; total cost; total expenditure; total income; total output; total revenue;* **the cargo was written off as a total loss =** the cargo was so badly damaged that the insurers said it had no value **2** *noun* amount which is complete *or* with everything added up; *the total of the charges comes to more than $1,000;* **grand total =** final total made by adding several subtotals **3** *verb* to add up to; *costs totaling more than $25,000*

◊ **totally** *adverb* completely; *the factory was totally destroyed in the fire; the cargo was totally ruined by water*

tour *noun* trip to various places, coming back in the end to the starting place; *the group went on a tour of Italy; the Commerce Secretary went on a fact-finding tour of the region;* **conducted tour =** tour with a guide who shows places to the tourists; **package tour =** tour where the hotel, travel, and meals are all arranged in advance and paid for in one payment; **tour operator =** person *or* company which organizes tours; **to carry out a tour of inspection =** to visit various places *or* offices *or* factories to inspect them

◊ **tourism** *noun* business of providing travel, hotel rooms, food, entertainment, etc., for tourists

◊ **tourist** *noun* person who goes on vacation to visit places away from his home; **tourist bureau** *or* **tourist information office =** office which gives information to tourists about the place where it is situated; **tourist class =** lower quality or less expensive way of traveling; *he always travels first class, because he says tourist class is too uncomfortable;* **tourist visa =** visa which allows a person to visit a country for a short time on vacation

tout *verb* to publicize extravagantly; *the car was touted as the most advanced machine in the world*

track record *noun* success or failure of a company *or* salesman in the past; *he has a good track record as a secondhand car salesman; the company has no track record in the computer market*

trade 1 *noun* **(a)** business of buying and selling; **export trade** *or* **import trade** = the business of selling to other countries *or* buying from other countries; **foreign trade** *or* **overseas trade** *or* **external trade** = trade with other countries; **domestic trade** = trade in the country where a company is based; **trade cycle** = period during which trade expands, then slows down, then expands again; **balance of trade** *or* **trade balance** = international trading position of a country, excluding invisible trade; *the country had an adverse balance of trade for the second month running;* **favorable balance of trade** = situation where a country's exports are larger than its imports; **trade surplus** = difference in value between a country's high exports and low imports **(b)** **to do a good trade in a range of products** = to sell a large number of the range of products; **fair trade** = international business system where countries agree not to charge import duties on certain items imported from their trading partners; **free trade** = system where goods can go from one country to another without any restrictions; **free trade area** = group of countries practicing free trade; **trade agreement** = international agreement between countries over general terms of trade; **trade bureau** = office which specializes in commercial enquiries; **to impose trade barriers on** = to restrict the import of certain goods by charging high duty; **trade deficit** *or* **trade gap** = difference in value between a country's high imports and low exports; **trade description** = description of a product to attract customers; **trade directory** = book which lists all the businesses and business people in a region; **trade mission** = visit to a country by a group of foreign businessmen to discuss trade; **to ask a company to supply trade references** = to ask a company to give names of traders who can report on the company's financial situation and reputation **(c)** people *or* companies dealing in the same type of product; *he is in the secondhand car trade; she is very well known in the clothing trade;* **trade association** = group which links together companies in the same trade; **trade counter** = shop in a factory *or* warehouse where goods are sold to retailers; **trade discount** = discount offered by a manufacturer to retailers if they pay within a certain period of time; **trade fair** = large exhibition and meeting for advertising and selling a certain type of product; *there were two trade fairs running in Detroit at the same time; to organize or to run a trade fair;* **trade journal** *or* **trade magazine** *or* **trade paper** *or* **trade publication** = magazine or newspaper produced for people and companies in a certain trade; **trade press** = all magazines produced for people working in a certain trade; **trade price** = special wholesale price paid by a retailer to the manufacturer or wholesaler; **trade terms** = conditions of payment for goods traded, that are agreed to by the seller and purchaser **2** *verb* to buy and sell *or* to carry on a business; *to trade with another country; to trade on the stock exchange; the company has stopped trading; the company trades under the name "Eeziphitt"; the stock is trading at $15*

◇ **trade in** *verb* **(a)** to buy and sell certain items; *the company trades in imported goods; he trades in French wine* **(b)** to give in an old item as part of the payment for a new one; *the chairman traded in his old Rolls Royce for a new model*

◇ **trade-in** *noun* old item (such as a car *or* washing machine) given as part of the payment for a new one; *to give the old car as a trade-in;* **trade-in allowance** *or* **price** = amount allowed by the seller for an old item being traded in for a new one

◇ **trademark** *or* **trade name** *noun* particular name, design, etc., which has been registered by the manufacturer and which cannot be used by other manufacturers; *you cannot call your beds "Softn'kumfi" - it is a registered trademark*

◇ **trade-off** *noun* exchanging one thing for another as part of a business deal

◇ **trader** *noun* person who does business; person who buys and sells securities as a means of making a short-term profit, as opposed to longer-term investor; **commodity trader** = person whose business is buying and selling commodities; **free trader** = person who is in favor of free trade

◇ **tradesman** *noun* **(a)** person who owns *or* runs a store **(b)** skilled craftsman

NOTE: plural is **tradesmen**

◊ **tradespeople** *plural* *noun* storekeepers

◊ **trade union** *noun* labor union which represents workers in a particular trade

◊ **trading** *noun* business of buying and selling; **trading account** = account of a company's gross profit; **trading area** = (i) district where a business does most of its trade; (ii) floor of a stock exchange; **trading company** = company which specializes in buying and selling goods; **adverse trading conditions** = bad conditions for trade; **trading loss** = situation where a company's receipts are less than its expenditure; **trading partner** = company *or* country which trades with another; **trading post** = position on the floor of a Stock Exchange where certain securities are traded; **trading profit** = situation where a company's gross receipts are more than its gross expenditure; **fair trading** = way of doing business which is reasonable and does not harm the customer; **insider trading** = illegal buying or selling of shares by staff of a company who have secret information about the company's plans

> QUOTE a sharp setback in foreign trade accounted for most of the winter slowdown. The trade balance sank $17 billion
>
> *Fortune*

traffic *noun* (a) movement of cars *or* trucks *or* trains *or* planes; movement of people *or* goods in vehicles; *there is an increase in commuter traffic on the freeway; passenger traffic on the commuter lines has decreased during the summer;* **air traffic controller** = person who controls the landing and taking off of planes at an airport; **store traffic** = number of customers who pass through a store (b) illegal trade; *drug traffic or traffic in drugs*

train 1 *noun* set of rail cars pulled by an engine along railroad tracks; *a passenger train or a freight train; to take the 09:30 train to Boston; he caught his train or he missed his train; to ship goods by train* **2** *verb* to teach (someone) to do something; to learn how to do something; *he trained as an accountant; the company has appointed a trained lawyer as its CEO*

◊ **trainee** *noun* person who is learning how to do something; *we employ a trainee accountant to help in the office at peak periods; most of the laboratory personnel are trainees;* **management trainee** = young member of staff being trained to be a manager

◊ **traineeship** *noun* position of trainee

◊ **training** *noun* being taught how to do something; *there is a ten-week training period for new staff; the store is closed for staff training;* **industrial training** = training of new workers to work in an industry; **management training** = training staff to be managers, by making them study problems and work out solutions to them; **on-the-job training** = training given to workers at their place of work; **training officer** = person who deals with the training of staff; **training unit** = special group of teachers which organizes training for companies

transact *verb* to transact business = to carry out a piece of business

◊ **transaction** *noun* **business transaction** = piece of business, such as buying or selling; **cash transaction** = transaction paid for in cash; **a transaction on the stock exchange** = purchase *or* sale of securities on the stock exchange; *the paper publishes a daily list of stock exchange transactions;* **exchange transaction** = purchase *or* sale of foreign currency; **fraudulent transaction** = transaction which aims to cheat someone

transfer 1 *noun* moving someone *or* something to a new place; *he applied for a transfer to our branch in Florida;* **transfer of property** *or* **transfer of stock** = moving the ownership of property *or* stock from one person to another; **airmail transfer** = sending money from one bank to another by airmail; **bank transfer** = moving money from a bank account to an account in another country; **credit transfer** *or* **transfer of funds** = moving money from one account to another; **stock transfer form** = form to be signed by the person transferring stock; **transfer agent** = person responsible for noting the transfer of stock from one stockholder to another **2** *verb* (a) to move someone *or* something to a new place; *the accountant was transferred to our San Francisco branch; he transferred his shares to a family trust; she transferred her money to a savings account* (b) to change from one type of travel to another; *when you get to London airport, you have to transfer onto an internal flight* NOTE: **transferring - transferred**

◊ **transferable** *adjective* which can be passed to someone else; **the season ticket is not transferable** = the ticket cannot be given or lent to someone else to use

transit *noun* **(a)** movement of passengers *or* goods on the way to a destination; **to pay compensation for damage suffered in transit** *or* **for loss in transit; some of the goods were damaged in transit; goods in transit** = goods being transported from warehouse to customer; **mass transit system** = system in a large city for moving people from one place to another (often a combination of a network of bus, tram and subway lines); **transit advertising** = advertising in buses, cabs, trains, etc. **(b) transit visa** *or* **transit permit** = document which allows someone to spend a short time in one country while traveling to another country **(c) transit number** = number printed on a check, which refers to the bank and branch which issued the check, used to speed up routing of checks through the clearing system

translate *verb* to put something which is said *or* written in one language into another language; *he asked his secretary to translate the letter from the German agent; we have had the contract translated from French into Japanese*

◊ **translation** *noun* something which has been translated; *she passed the translation of the letter to the finance department*

◊ **translator** *noun* person who translates

transmission *noun* sending; **transmission of a message**

◊ **transmit** *verb* to send (a message)
NOTE: **transmitting - transmitted**

transport 1 *noun* moving of goods or people; **air transport** *or* **transport by air; rail transport** *or* **transport by rail; road transport** *or* **transport by road; passenger transport** *or* **the transport of passengers; what means of transport will you use to get to the factory?; the visitors will be using public transport** *or* **private transport** = the visitors will be coming by bus *or* train, etc., or in their own cars **2** *verb* to move goods *or* people from one place to another in a vehicle; *the company transports millions of tons of freight*

by rail each year; the visitors will be transported to the factory by air or *by helicopter* or *by taxi*

◊ **transportable** *adjective* which can be moved

◊ **transportation** *noun* **(a)** moving goods *or* people from one place to another; **public transportation system** = system of trains, buses, etc., used by the general public **(b)** vehicles used to move goods *or* people from one place to another; *the company will provide transportation to the airport;* **ground transportation** = buses, taxis, etc., available to take passengers from an airport to the city

◊ **transporter** *noun* company which transports goods

transship *verb* to move cargo from one ship to another
NOTE: **transshipping - transshipped**

travel 1 *noun* moving of people from one place to another *or* from one country to another; *business travel is a very important part of our overhead expenditure;* **travel agent** = person in charge of a travel agency; **travel agency** = office which arranges travel for customers; **travel allowance** = money which an employee is allowed to spend on traveling; **travel magazine** = magazine with articles on vacations and travel; **the travel trade** = all businesses which organize travel for people **2** *verb* **(a)** to move from one place to another *or* from one country to another; *he travels to Europe on business twice a year; in her new job, she has to travel abroad at least ten times a year* **(b)** to go from one place to another, showing a company's goods to buyers and taking orders from them; *he travels in the northern part of the state for an insurance company*

◊ **traveler** *noun* **(a)** person who travels; **business traveler** = person who is traveling on business; **traveler's checks** = checks taken by a traveler which can be cashed in a foreign country **(b) commercial traveler** = salesman who travels around an area visiting customers on behalf of his company

◊ **traveling** *noun* **traveling expenses** = money spent on traveling and hotels for business purposes

tray *noun* **filing tray** = container kept on a desk for documents which have to be filed; **in tray** = basket on a desk for letters *or* memos which have been received and are waiting to be dealt with; **out tray** = basket on a desk for letters *or* memos which have been dealt with and are ready to be sent out; **pending tray** = basket on a desk for papers which cannot be dealt with fully immediately

treasurer *noun* **(a)** person who manages the money *or* finances of a club or society, etc.; **honorary treasurer** = treasurer who does not receive any fee **(b)** main financial officer of a company

◊ **treasury** *noun* the **Treasury** = government department which deals with the country's finance; **treasury bill** *or* **T bill** = short-term bill of exchange which does not give any interest and is sold by the U.S. Treasury at a discount; **Treasury bonds** = U.S. government long-term security, sold to the public and having a maturity of longer than five years

treaty *noun* **(a)** agreement between countries; *commercial treaty* **(b)** agreement between individual persons; **to sell a house by private treaty** = to sell a home to another person not by auction

treble *verb* to increase three times; *the company's borrowings have trebled*

trend *noun* general pattern of how things are going; *there is a trend away from small food stores; a downward trend in investment; we notice a general trend to sell to the student market; the report points to inflationary trends in the economy; an upward trend in sales;* **economic trends** = way in which a country's economy is moving; **market trends** = gradual changes taking place in a market

trial *noun* **(a)** court case to judge a person accused of a crime; *he is on trial or is standing trial for embezzlement* **(b)** test to see if something is good; **on trial** = being tested; *the product is on trial in our laboratories;* **trial period** = time when a customer can test a product before buying it; **trial size package** *or* **trial sample** = small amount *or* small piece of a product used for testing; **free trial offer** = testing of a machine *or* product by a potential customer with no payment involved **(c)** **trial balance** = draft adding of debits and credits to see if they balance

tribunal *noun* official court which examines special problems and makes judgments; **adjudication tribunal** = group which adjudicates in industrial disputes; **rent tribunal** = court which can decide if a rent is too high or low

trick *noun* clever act to make someone believe something which is not true; **confidence trick** = business where someone gains another person's confidence and then tricks him

◊ **trickster** *noun* **confidence trickster** = person who carries out a confidence trick on someone

trip *noun* journey; **business trip** = journey to discuss business matters with people who live far away

triple 1 *verb* to multiply three times; *the company's debts tripled in twelve months; the acquisition of the chain of stores has tripled the group's sales* **2** *adjective* three times as much; *the cost of airfreighting the goods is triple their manufacturing cost*

triplicate *noun* **in triplicate** = with an original and two copies; *to print an invoice in triplicate;* **invoicing in triplicate** = preparing three copies of invoices

trouble *noun* problem *or* difficult situation; *we are having some computer trouble or some trouble with the computer; there was some trouble in the warehouse after the manager was fired*

◊ **troubleshooter** *noun* person whose job is to solve problems in a company

trough *noun* low point in the economic cycle

truck *noun* large motor vehicle for carrying goods; **truck wholesaler** = wholesaler who transports goods to the retailer and sells them from a truck; **forklift truck** = type of small tractor with two metal arms in front, used for lifting and moving heavy objects

◊ **trucker** *noun* person who drives a truck

◊ **trucking** *noun* carrying goods in trucks; *trucking firm*

◊ **truckload** *noun* quantity of goods that fills a truck

true *adjective* correct *or* accurate; **true copy** = exact copy; *I certify that this is a true copy; certified as a true copy*

truly *adverb* **Yours truly** *or* **Truly yours** = ending to a letter

trust 1 *noun* **(a)** being confident that something is correct, will work, etc.; *we took his statement on trust* = we accepted his statement without examining it to see if it was correct **(b)** passing goods *or* money *or* secrets to someone who will take care of them; *he left his property in trust for his grandchildren; he was guilty of a breach of trust* = he did not act correctly *or* honestly when people expected him to; *he has a position of trust* = his job shows that people believe he will act correctly and honestly **(c)** management of money *or* property for someone; *they set up a family trust for their grandchildren;* **trust company** = organization which supervises the financial affairs of private trusts, executes wills, and acts as a bank to a limited number of customers; **trust deed** = document which sets out the details of a private trust; **trust fund** = assets (money, securities, property) held in trust for someone; **investment trust** = company whose business is to make money by buying and selling securities and bonds **(d)** small group of companies which control the supply of a product **2** *verb* **to trust someone with something** = to give something to someone to look after; *can he be trusted with all that cash?*

◊ **trustbusting** *noun* breaking up monopolies to encourage competition

◊ **trustee** *noun* person who has charge of money in trust *or* person who is responsible for a family trust; *the trustees of the pension fund*

◊ **trustworthy** *adjective* (person) who can be trusted; *our cashiers are completely trustworthy*

tune *noun* piece of music; *the bank is backing him to the tune of $10,000* = the bank is helping him with a loan of $10,000

turkey *noun* business deal which flops; stock of which the price collapses on a Stock Exchange

turn 1 *noun* **(a)** commission **(b)** stock **turn** = total value of stocks sold in a year divided by the average value of

goods in stock; *the company has a stock turn of 6.7* **2** *verb* to change direction *or* to go around in a circle

◊ **turn around** *verb* to make (a company) change from making a loss to being profitable; **he turned the company around in less than a year** = he made the company profitable in less than a year

◊ **turnaround** *noun* **(a)** value of goods sold during a year divided by the average value of goods held in stock **(b)** action of emptying a ship, plane, etc., and getting it ready for another commercial trip; **turnaround time** = time taken to complete a job **(c)** making a company profitable again

◊ **turn down** *verb* to refuse; *the board turned down their merger bid; the bank turned down their request for a loan; the application for a license was turned down*

◊ **turnkey** *noun* **turnkey operation** = deal where a company takes all responsibility for constructing, fitting and staffing a building (such as a school *or* hospital *or* factory) so that it is completely ready for the purchaser to take over

◊ **turn out** *verb* to produce; *the factory turns out fifty units per day*

◊ **turn over** *verb* to pass something on to someone

◊ **turnover** *noun* **(a)** changes in staff, when some leave and others join; *staff turnover or turnover of staff; the turnover in this office has always been high* **(b)** number of times something is used *or* sold in a period (usually one year), expressed as a percentage of a total; **inventory turnover** = number of times the inventory of a business is sold during a period of twelve months **(c)** *GB* volume of sales per annum

◊ **turnpike** *noun* large highway (formerly a toll road)

twin-pack *noun* sales package, made of two packs of the same product attached together and sold at a special discount

twisting *noun (of an insurance salesman)* persuading a client to authorize a deal on which the agent will earn commission

two-part *noun* paper (for computers *or* typewriters) with a top sheet for the original and a second sheet for a copy; *two-part invoices; two-part stationery*

tycoon *noun* important businessman

type *verb* to write with a typewriter; *he can type quite fast; all his reports are typed on his portable typewriter*
◊ **typewriter** *noun* machine which prints letters *or* figures on a piece of paper when a key is pressed; *portable typewriter; electronic typewriter*
◊ **typewritten** *adjective* written on a typewriter; *he sent in a typewritten job application*
◊ **typing** *noun* writing letters with a typewriter; **typing error** = mistake made when using a typewriter; *the secretary must have made a typing error;* **typing pool** = group of typists, working together in a company, offering a secretarial service to several departments; **copy typing** = typing documents from handwritten originals, not from dictation
◊ **typist** *noun* person whose job is to write letters using a typewriter; **copy typist** = person who types documents from handwritten originals, not from dictation; **shorthand typist** = typist who takes dictation in shorthand and then types it

Uu

ultimate *adjective* last *or* final; **ultimate consumer** = the person who actually uses the product
◊ **ultimately** *adverb* in the end; *ultimately, the management had to agree to the demands of the union*
◊ **ultimatum** *noun* statement made to someone that unless he does something within a period of time, action will be taken against him; *the union officials argued among themselves over the best way to deal with the ultimatum from the management*
NOTE: plural is **ultimatums** or **ultimata**

umbrella *noun* **umbrella liability insurance** = extra liability coverage above that of most insurance policies; **umbrella organization** = large organization which includes several smaller ones

UN = THE UNITED NATIONS

unable *adjective* not able; *the chairman was unable to come to the meeting*

unacceptable *adjective* which cannot be accepted; *the terms of the contract are quite unacceptable*

unaccounted for *adjective* lost, without any explanation; *several thousand units are unaccounted for in the inventory*

unanimous *adjective* where everyone votes in the same way; *there was a unanimous vote against the proposal; they reached unanimous agreement*
◊ **unanimously** *adverb* with everyone agreeing; *the proposals were adopted unanimously*

unaudited *adjective* which has not been audited; *unaudited statement of account*

unauthorized *adjective* not permitted; *unauthorized access to the company's records; unauthorized expenditure; no unauthorized persons are allowed into the laboratory*

unavailable *adjective* not available; *the following items on your order are temporarily unavailable*
◊ **unavailability** *noun* not being available

unavoidable *adjective* which cannot be avoided; *planes are subject to unavoidable delays*

unbalanced *adjective* (budget) which does not balance *or* which is in deficit

uncalled *adjective* (capital) which a company is authorized to raise and has been issued but is not fully paid

uncashed *adjective* which has not been cashed; *uncashed checks*

unchanged *adjective* which has not changed

unchecked *adjective* which has not been checked; **unchecked figures**

unclaimed *adjective* which has not been claimed; **unclaimed baggage** = cases which have been left with someone and have not been claimed by their owners; **unclaimed property** *or* **unclaimed baggage will be sold at auction after six months**

uncollected *adjective* which has not been collected; **uncollected subscriptions; uncollected taxes**

unconditional *adjective* with no conditions; **unconditional acceptance of the offer by the board**
◇ **unconditionally** *adverb* without imposing any conditions; **the offer was accepted unconditionally by the union**

unconfirmed *adjective* which has not been confirmed; **there are unconfirmed reports that our agent has been arrested**

unconstitutional *adjective* not allowed by the rules *or* laws of a country *or* organization; **the chairman ruled that the meeting was unconstitutional**

uncontrollable *adjective* which cannot be controlled; **uncontrollable inflation**

undated *adjective* with no date written; **he tried to cash an undated check; undated bond** = bond with no maturity date

under *preposition* **(a)** lower than *or* less than; **the interest rate is under 10%; under half of the stockholders accepted the offer (b)** controlled by *or* according to; **under the terms of the agreement, the goods should be delivered in October; he is acting under rule 23 of the union constitution**
◇ **under-** *prefix* less important than *or* lower than
◇ **underbid** *verb* to bid less than someone
NOTE: **underbidding - underbid**
◇ **underbidder** *noun* person who bids less than the person who buys at an auction
◇ **undercapitalized** *adjective* without enough capital; **the company is severely undercapitalized**

◇ **undercharge** *verb* to ask for too little money; **he undercharged us by $25**
◇ **undercut** *verb* to offer something at a lower price than someone else
◇ **underdeveloped** *adjective* which has not been developed; **Japan is an underdeveloped market for our products; underdeveloped countries** = countries which are not fully industrialized
◇ **underemployed** *adjective* **(a)** with not enough work; **the staff is underemployed because of the cutback in production; underemployed capital** = capital which is not producing enough interest **(b)** working at a job that does not use your skills and potential
◇ **underemployment** *noun* **(a)** situation where workers in a company do not have enough work to do **(b)** situation where there is not enough work for all the workers in a country **(c)** situation where a person is working at a job that does not use his skills and potential
◇ **underequipped** *adjective* with not enough equipment
◇ **underestimate 1** *noun* estimate which is less than the actual figure; **the figure of $50,000 in sales volume was a considerable underestimate 2** *verb* to think that something is smaller *or* not as bad as it really is; **they underestimated the effects of the strike on their sales; he underestimated the amount of time needed to finish the work**
◇ **undermanned** *adjective* with not enough staff to do the work
◇ **undermanning** *noun* having fewer workers than are needed to do the company's work; **the company's production is affected by undermanning on the assembly line**
◇ **undermentioned** *adjective* mentioned lower down in a document
◇ **underpaid** *adjective* not paid enough; **our employees say that they are underpaid and overworked**
◇ **underpayment** *noun* payment of less than the sum due
◇ **underrate** *verb* to value less highly than should be; **do not underrate the strength of the competition in the European market; the power of the yen is underrated**
◇ **undersell** *verb* to sell more cheaply than; **to undersell a competitor; the company is never undersold** = no other company sells goods as cheaply as this one
NOTE: **underselling - undersold**

◊ **undersigned** *noun* person who has signed a letter; **we, the undersigned =** we, the people who have signed below

◊ **underspend** *verb* to spend less; **he has underspent his budget =** he has spent less than was allowed in the budget
NOTE: **underspending - underspent**

◊ **understaffed** *adjective* with not enough staff to do the company's work

◊ **understanding** *noun* private agreement; *to come to an understanding about the divisions of the market;* **on the understanding that =** on condition that *or* provided that; *we accept the terms of the contract, on the understanding that it has to be ratified by our main board*

◊ **understate** *verb* to make something seem less than it really is; *the company statement of account understates the real profit*

◊ **undertake** *verb* to agree to do something; *to undertake an investigation of the market; they have undertaken not to sell into our territory*
NOTE: **undertaking - undertook - has undertaken**

◊ **undertaking** *noun* **(a)** business; *commercial undertaking* **(b)** (legally binding) promise; *they have given us a written undertaking not to sell their products in competition with ours*

◊ **underutilized** *adjective* not used enough

◊ **undervalued** *adjective* not valued highly enough; *the properties are undervalued on the balance sheet; the dollar is undervalued on the foreign exchanges*

◊ **undervaluation** *noun* being valued at a lower worth than should be

◊ **underweight** *adjective* **the pack is twenty grams underweight =** the pack weighs twenty grams less than it should

◊ **underworked** *adjective* not given enough work to do; *the officers of the company think our employees are overpaid and underworked*

◊ **underwrite** *verb* **(a)** to accept responsibility for; **to underwrite an issue of new securities =** to guarantee that an issue will be sold by agreeing to buy all shares which are not subscribed; *the issue was underwritten by three underwriting companies* **(b)** to insure *or* to cover (a risk); **to underwrite an insurance policy (c)** to agree to pay for costs; *the government has underwritten the development costs of the project*

NOTE: **underwriting - underwrote - has underwritten**

◊ **underwriter** *noun* person who underwrites insurance *or* an issue of new securities; **marine underwriter =** person who insures ships and their cargoes

QUOTE in the past, mortgage brokers made 1% fees by bringing apartment developers to the HUD to apply for FHA mortgages. Under the new program, the brokers themselves are allowed to underwrite mortgages and get a much higher fee
Forbes Magazine

undischarged bankrupt *noun* person who has been declared bankrupt and has not been released from that condition

undiscounted *adjective* (goods) sold at full price, without a discount

undistributed profits *noun* profits which have not been distributed as dividends to shareholders

unearned income *noun* money received from interest or dividends, not from salary or profits of one's business

uneconomic *adjective* which does not make a commercial profit; **it is an uneconomic proposition =** it will not be commercially profitable; **uneconomic rent =** rent which is not enough to cover costs

unemployed *adjective* not employed or without any work; **unemployed office workers =** office workers with no jobs; **the unemployed =** the people without any jobs

◊ **unemployment** *noun* lack of jobs; **mass unemployment =** unemployment of large numbers of workers; **unemployment compensation =** payment made to someone who is unemployed

QUOTE tax advantages directed toward small businesses will help create jobs and reduce the unemployment rate
Toronto Star

unencumbered *adjective* (property) on which there is no mortgage or other lien

unfair *adjective* **unfair competition =** trying to do better than another company by using techniques such as importing foreign goods at very low prices or by wrongly criticizing a competitor's products; **unfair dismissal**

= removing someone from a job for reasons which are not fair

unfavorable *adjective* not favorable; **unfavorable balance of trade** = situation where a country imports more than it exports; **unfavorable exchange rate** = exchange rate which gives an amount of foreign currency for the home currency which is not good for trade; *the unfavorable exchange rate hit the country's exports*

unfulfilled *adjective* (order) which has not yet been supplied

unilateral *adjective* on one side only *or* done by one party only; *they took the unilateral decision to cancel the contract*
◊ **unilaterally** *adverb* by one party only; *they canceled the contract unilaterally*

uninsured *adjective* not insured

union *noun* (a) **labor union** = organization which represents workers who are its members in discussions with management about wages and conditions of work; **union agreement** = agreement between a management and a union over wages and conditions of work; **union dues** = payment made by workers to belong to a union; **union officials** = paid organizers of a union; **union recognition** = act of agreeing that a union can act on behalf of employees in a company; **union shop** = arrangement where a new nonunion employee must join a labor union within a certain time from starting his employment (b) **customs union** = agreement between several countries that goods can go between them without paying duty, while goods from other countries have special duties charged on them
◊ **unionist** *noun* member of a labor union
◊ **unionized** *adjective* (company) where the employees belong to a union

QUOTE after three days of tough negotiations, the company reached agreement with its 1,200 unionized workers
Toronto Star

unique *adjective* special *or* with nothing like it; **unique selling proposition (USP)** = special quality of a product which makes it different from other goods and therefore attractive to customers

unissued stock *noun* capital stock which a company is authorized to issue but has not issued

unit *noun* (a) single product for sale; **unit cost** = the cost of one item (i.e total product costs divided by the number of units produced); **unit price** = the price of one item (b) separate piece of equipment or furniture; **display unit** = special stand for showing goods for sale (c) **factory unit** = single building in an industrial park (d) **production unit** = separate small group of workers which produces a certain product; **research unit** = separate small group of research workers (e) **monetary unit** *or* **unit of currency** = main item of currency of a country (a dollar, pound, yen etc.)

unite *verb* to join together; *the directors united with the managers to reject the takeover bid;* **United Nations** = organization which links the countries of the world to promote good relations between them; **United States Postal Service (USPS)** = independent U.S. agency which deals with sending letters and parcels

Universal Product Code (UPC) *noun* coding system using bar codes to identify produce sold in grocery stores

unladen *adjective* empty *or* without a cargo

unlawful *adjective* against the law *or* not legal

unlimited *adjective* with no limits; *the bank offered him unlimited credit;* **unlimited liability** = situation where a sole trader or each partner is responsible for all the firm's debts with no limit at the amount each may have to pay

unlined *adjective* **unlined paper** = paper with no lines printed on it

unlisted *adjective* **unlisted securities** = securities which are not listed on a Stock Exchange; **unlisted securities market** = market for buying and selling securities which are not listed on a Stock Exchange

unload *verb* (a) to take goods off (a ship, etc.); *the ship is unloading at Hamburg; we need a forklift to unload the truck; we unloaded the spare parts at Lagos; there are no unloading* *facilities for container ships* (b) to sell (shares which do not seem attractive); *we tried to unload our stockholding as soon as the company published its results*

unobtainable *adjective* which cannot be obtained

unofficial *adjective* not official; **unofficial strike** = strike by local workers which has not been approved by the main union
◊ **unofficially** *adverb* not officially; *the tax office told the company unofficially that it would be prosecuted*

unpaid *adjective* not paid; **unpaid vacation** = vacation where the worker does not receive any pay; **unpaid invoices** = invoices which have not been paid

unprofitable *adjective* which is not profitable

QUOTE the airline has already eliminated a number of unprofitable flights
Duns Business Month

unquoted shares *plural noun* shares which have no stock exchange quotation listed

unredeemed pledge *noun* pledge which the borrower has not claimed back by paying back his loan

unregistered *adjective* (stock) which has not been registered with the Securities and Exchange Commission

unreliable *adjective* which cannot be relied on; *the postal service is very unreliable*

unsealed envelope *noun* envelope where the flap has been pushed into the back of the envelope, not stuck down

unsecured *adjective* **unsecured creditor** = creditor who is owed money, but has no security from the debtor for it; **unsecured debt** = debt which is not guaranteed by assets; **unsecured loan** = loan made with no security

unseen *adverb* not seen; **to buy something sight unseen** = to buy something without having inspected it

unsettled *adjective* which changes often *or* which is upset; *the market was unsettled by the news of the failure of the merger bid*

unskilled *adjective* without any particular skill; *unskilled labor or unskilled workforce or unskilled workers*

unsocial *adjective* **to work unsocial hours** = to work at times (i.e., in the evening *or* at night *or* during public holidays) when most people are not at work

unsold *adjective* not sold; *unsold items will be scrapped*

unsolicited *adjective* which has not been asked for; *an unsolicited gift;* **unsolicited testimonial** = letter praising someone *or* a product without the writer having been asked to write it

unstable *adjective* not stable *or* changing frequently; *unstable exchange rates*

unsubsidized *adjective* with no subsidy

unsuccessful *adjective* not successful; *an unsuccessful businessman; the project was expensive and unsuccessful*
◊ **unsuccessfully** *adverb* with no success; *the company unsuccessfully tried to break into the South American market*

unused *adjective* which has not been used; *we are trying to sell off six unused typewriters*

unwritten agreement *noun* verbal agreement not recorded in writing

up *adverb & preposition* in a higher position *or* to a higher position; *the inflation rate is going up steadily; security prices were up slightly at the end of the day*
◊ **up to** *adverb* as far as *or* as high as; *we will buy at prices up to $25*
◊ **up to date** *adjective & adverb* current *or* recent *or* modern; *an up-to-date computer system;* **to bring something up to date** = to add the latest information or equipment to something; **to keep something up to date** = to keep adding information to something so that

it always has the latest information in it; *we spend a lot of time keeping our mailing list up to date*

UPC = UNIVERSAL PRODUCT CODE

update 1 *noun* information added to something to make it current **2** *verb* to revise something so that it is always current; *the figures are updated annually*

up front *adverb* in advance; **money up front** = payment in advance; *they are asking for $100,000 up front before they will consider the deal; he had to put money up front before he could clinch the deal*

upgrade *verb* to increase the importance of something *or* of a job; *his job has been upgraded to senior manager level; her seat was upgraded to first class*

upkeep *noun* cost of keeping a building *or* machine in good order

up market *adverb* more expensive, appealing to a wealthy section of the population; **the company has decided to move up market** = the company has decided to start to produce more luxury items

upset price *noun* lowest price which the seller will accept at an auction

up tick *noun* **to trade stock on the up tick** = to trade at a higher price than the previous transaction

upturn *noun* movement toward higher sales or profits; *an upturn in the economy; an upturn in the market*

upward 1 *adjective* toward a higher position; *an upward movement* **2** *adverb (also* **upwards)** toward a higher position; *the market moved upward after the news of the federal budget*

urgent *adjective* which has to be done quickly
◊ **urgently** *adverb* immediately

use 1 *noun* way in which something can be used; **directions for use** = instructions on how to run a machine; **to make use of something** = to use something; **in use** = being worked; *the*

computer is in use twenty-four hours a day; **items for personal use** = items which a person will use for himself, not on behalf of the company; **he has the use of a company jet** = the company owns a jet which he can use if he needs it; **land zoned for industrial use** = land where planning permission has been given to build **2** *verb* to take a machine, a company, a process, etc., and work with it; *we use airmail for all our overseas correspondence; the photocopier is being used all the time; they use freelancers for most of their work*

◊ **useful** *adjective* which can help

◊ **user** *noun* person who uses something; **end user** = person who actually uses a product; **user's guide** *or* **handbook** = book showing someone how to use something

◊ **user-friendly** *adjective* which a user finds easy to work; *these programs are really user-friendly*

USP = UNIQUE SELLING PROPOSITION

USPS = UNITED STATES POSTAL SERVICE

usual *adjective* normal *or* ordinary; *our usual terms or usual conditions are thirty days' credit; the usual practice is to have the contract signed by the CEO; the usual hours of work are from 9:30 to 5:30*

usury *noun* lending money at high interest

utility *noun* company providing a service which is used by everyone, such as electricity, water, etc.

QUOTE utilities are the standard fare of conservative investors. One of the chief attractions of utility stocks are their dividends. High-grade electric utilities currently paying 7%, now compare favorably with Treasury-bill yields
Business Week

utilize *verb* to use

◊ **utilization** *noun* making use of something; **capacity utilization** = using something as much as possible

QUOTE control permits the manufacturer to react to changing conditions on the plant floor and to keep people and machines at a high level of utilization
Duns Business Month

Vv

vacancy *noun* empty place *or* room; job which is not filled; *we advertised a vacancy in the local press; we have been unable to fill the vacancy for a skilled machinist; they have a vacancy for a secretary;* **job vacancies =** jobs which are empty and need people to do them; **vacancy rate =** percentage of all office space, apartment units, etc., that is not rented

◊ **vacant** *adjective* empty *or* not occupied; **vacant possession =** being able to occupy a property immediately after buying it because it is empty; *the house is for sale with vacant possession;* situations **vacant** *or* **appointments vacant =** list (in a newspaper) of jobs which are available

vacate *verb* **to vacate the premises =** to leave premises, so that they become empty

◊ **vacation** *noun* period when a worker does not work, but rests or goes on a trip; *the CEO is on vacation in Florida;* **vacation pay =** salary received by a worker while on vacation

valid *adjective* (a) which is acceptable because it is true; *that is not a valid argument or excuse* (b) which can be used lawfully; *the contract is not valid if it has not been witnessed; ticket which is valid for three months; he was carrying a valid passport*

◊ **validate** *verb* (a) to check to see if something is correct; *the document was validated by the bank* (b) to make (something) valid

◊ **validation** *noun* act of making something valid

◊ **validity** *noun* being valid; **period of validity =** length of time for which a document is valid

valorem *see* AD VALOREM

valuable *adjective* which is worth a lot of money; **valuable property** *or* **valuables =** personal items which are worth a lot of money

◊ **valuation** *noun* estimate of how much something is worth; *to ask for a*

valuation of a property before making an offer for it; **inventory valuation =** estimating the value of inventory at the end of an accounting period; **to buy a store with inventory at valuation =** to pay for the inventory the same amount as its value as estimated by a valuer

◊ **value 1** *noun* amount of money which something is worth; *he imported goods to the value of $250; the fall in the value of the dollar; the valuer put the value of the stock at $25,000; buy that computer now - it is a very good value;* **to rise in value** *or* **to fall in value =** to be worth more *or* less; **value added =** the difference between the purchase price of manufactured items and raw materials and the amount received by the business when it sells them; **asset value =** value of a company calculated by adding together all its assets; **book value =** value as recorded in the company's books of account; **"sample only - of no commercial value" =** not worth anything if sold; **declared value =** value of goods entered on a customs declaration form; **discounted value =** difference between the face value of a share and its lower market price; **face value =** value written on a coin *or* bill *or* share; **market value =** value of an asset *or* of a product *or* of a company, if sold today; **par value =** value written on a stock certificate; **scarcity value =** value of something which is worth more because it is rare and there is a large demand for it; **surrender value =** money which an insurer will pay if an insurance policy is given up before maturity date **2** *verb* to estimate how much money something is worth; *he valued the stock at $25,000; we are having the jewelry valued for insurance*

◊ **valuer** *noun* person who estimates how much money something is worth

van *noun* enclosed (usually small) truck for transporting goods; **delivery van =** van for delivering goods to customers

variable *adjective* which changes; **variable costs =** production costs which increase with the quantity made (such as wages, raw materials); **variable overhead =** overhead (such as commission) which varies according to the total sales volume; **variable-rate mortgage =** mortgage where the interest on the capital loan varies with national interest rates

◊ **variability** *noun* being variable

◊ **variance** *noun* difference; **budget variance =** difference between the cost as estimated for the budget, and the actual cost; **at variance with =** which does not agree with; *the actual sales are at variance with the sales reported by the reps*

◇ **variation** *noun* amount by which something changes; **seasonal variations =** changes which take place because of the seasons; *seasonal variations in buying patterns*

variety *noun* different types of things; *the store stocks a variety of goods; we had a variety of visitors at the office today;* **variety store =** store selling a wide range of usually cheap items

◇ **vary** *verb* to change *or* to differ; *the gross margin varies from quarter to quarter; we try to prevent the flow of production from varying in the factory*

VDT = VISUAL DISPLAY TERMINAL

vehicle *noun* machine with wheels, used to carry goods *or* passengers on a road; *delivery vehicles can park in the loading bay;* **commercial vehicle =** van *or* truck used for business purposes

vending *noun* selling; **vending machine =** machine which provides drinks, cigarettes, etc., when a coin is put in

◇ **vendor** *noun* **(a)** person *or* company who sells; *the lawyer acting on behalf of the vendor* **(b) street vendor =** person who sells food or small items outside along the street

venture 1 *noun* business *or* commercial deal which involves a risk; *he lost money on several import ventures; she has started a new venture - a computer store;* **joint venture =** very large business project where two or more companies, often from different countries, join together; **venture capital =** capital for investment which may easily be lost in risky projects, but can also provide high returns **2** *verb* to risk (money)

venue *noun* town *or* district where a lawsuit is brought

verbal *adjective* spoken, not written; **verbal agreement =** agreement which is spoken (such as over the telephone)

◇ **verbally** *adverb* spoken, not written; *they agreed to the terms verbally, and then started to draft the contract*

verify *verb* to check to see if something is correct

◇ **verification** *noun* checking if something is correct; *the shipment was allowed into the country after verification of the documents by customs*

vertical *adjective* upright *or* straight up or down; **vertical communication =** communication between senior managers via the middle management to the workers; **vertical integration =** joining two businesses together which deal with different stages in the production or sale of a product

vessel *noun* ship; **merchant vessel =** commercial ship which carries a cargo

vested *adjective* **vested interest =** special interest in keeping an existing state of affairs (such as an employee's interest in a company pension plan); *she has a vested interest in keeping the business working =* she wants to keep the business working because she will make more money if it does

via *preposition* using (a means *or* a route); *the shipment is going via the Suez Canal; we are sending the check via our office in New York; they sent the message via the telex line*

viable *adjective* which can work in practice; **not commercially viable =** not likely to make a profit

◇ **viability** *noun* being viable *or* being able to make a profit

vice- *prefix* deputy *or* second in command; *he is the vice-chairman of an industrial group; she was appointed to the vice-chairmanship of the committee*

◇ **vice-president** *noun* one of the executive directors of a company; **senior vice-president =** one of a small group of main executive directors of a company

view *noun* way of thinking about something; *we asked the sales manager for his views on the reorganization of the reps' territories; the vice-president takes the view that credit should never be longer than thirty days;* **in view of =** because of; *in view of the falling exchange rate, we have redrafted our sales forecasts*

vigorous *adjective* energetic *or* very active; *we are planning a vigorous publicity campaign*

VIP = VERY IMPORTANT PERSON; **VIP lounge** = special room at an airport for important travelers; **we laid on VIP treatment for our visitors** *or* **we gave our visitors a VIP reception** = we arranged for our visitors to be treated and entertained well

visa *noun* special document *or* special stamp in a passport which allows someone to enter a country; *you will need a visa before you go to China; he filled in his visa application form;* **entry visa** = visa allowing someone to enter a country; **multiple entry visa** = visa allowing someone to enter a country many times; **tourist visa** = visa which allows a person to visit a country for a short time on vacation; **transit visa** = visa which allows someone to spend a short time in one country while traveling to another country

visible *adjective* which can be seen; **visible items** = real products which are imported *or* exported

visit 1 *noun* short stay in a place; *we are expecting a visit from our German agents; he is on a business visit to Chicago; we had a visit from the IRS 2* *verb* to go to a place *or* to see someone for a short time; *he spent a week in California, visiting clients in San Francisco and the Bay area; the trade delegation visited the chief manufacturing firms in the city* ◊ **visitor** *noun* person who visits; *the chairman showed the Japanese visitors around the factory;* **visitors' bureau** *or* **visitors' information center** = office which deals with visitors' questions

visual *adjective* which can be seen; **visual display terminal (VDT)** = screen attached to a computer which shows the information stored in the computer

vivos *noun* **gift inter vivos** = gift given to another living person

vocation *noun* type of job which you feel you want to do; wanting to be in a certain type of job; *he followed his vocation and became an accountant* ◊ **vocational** *adjective* referring to a choice of job; **vocational guidance** = helping young people to choose a suitable job; **vocational training** = training for a particular job

void 1 *adjective* not legally valid; **the contract was declared null and void** = the contract was said to be no longer valid **2** *verb* **to void a contract** = to make a contract invalid

volume *noun* quantity of items; **volume discount** = discount given to customer who buys a large quantity of goods; **volume of output** = number of items produced; **volume of sales** *or* **sales volume** = value of items sold; **low** *or* **high volume of sales** = small *or* large number of items sold; **volume of trade** *or* **volume of business** = number of items sold *or* number of shares sold on a stock exchange during a day's trading; *the company has maintained the same volume of business in spite of the recession*

voluntary *adjective* **(a)** done without being forced; **voluntary bankruptcy** = situation where a business declares itself bankrupt; **voluntary liquidation** = situation where a company itself decides it must close and sell its assets **(b)** done without being paid; **voluntary organization** = organization which has no paid staff ◊ **voluntarily** *adverb* without being forced or paid

vote 1 *noun* marking a paper, holding up your hand, etc., to show your opinion *or* to show who you want to be elected; **to take a vote on a proposal** *or* **to put a proposal to the vote** = to ask people present at a meeting to say if they do or do not agree with the proposal; **casting vote** = vote used by the chairman in the case where the votes for and against a proposal are equal; *the chairman has the casting vote; he used his casting vote to block the motion* **2** *verb* to show an opinion by marking a paper *or* by holding up your hand at a meeting; *the meeting voted to close the factory; 52% of the members voted for Mr. Smith as chairman;* **to vote for a proposal** *or* **to vote against a proposal** = to say that you agree *or* do not agree with a proposal; **two directors were voted off the board at the annual meeting** = the participants in the meeting voted to dismiss two directors; **she was voted onto the committee** = she was elected a member of the committee

◊ **voter** *noun* person who votes

◊ **voting** *noun* act of making a vote; **voting rights** = rights of stockholders to vote at company meetings; **voting** *or* **nonvoting stock** = stock which carry or do not carry the right to vote at company meetings

voucher *noun* **(a)** paper which is given instead of money; **cash voucher** = paper which can be exchanged for cash; *with every $20 of purchases, the customer gets a cash voucher to the value of $2;* **gift voucher** = card, bought in a store, which is given as a present and which must be exchanged in that store for goods **(b)** written document from an auditor to show that the accounts are correct *or* that money has really been paid; **voucher system** = internal auditing system, where a voucher is used to authorize payments

voyage *noun* long journey by ship

Ww

wage *noun* money paid (usually each week) to a worker for work done; *she is earning a good wage* *or* *good wages in the supermarket;* **basic wage** = normal pay without any extra payments; *the basic wage is $110 a week, but you can expect to earn more than that with overtime;* **hourly wage** *or* **wage per hour** = amount of money paid for an hour's work; **minimum wage** = lowest hourly wage which a company can legally pay its workers; **wage adjustments** = changes made to wages; **wage claim** = asking for an increase in wages; **wage differentials** = differences in salary between workers in similar types of jobs; **wage freeze** *or* **freeze on wages** = period when wages are not allowed to increase; **wage levels** = rates of pay for different types of work; **wage negotiations** = discussions between management and workers about pay; **wages policy** = government policy on what percentage increases should be paid to workers; **wage-price spiral** = situation where price rises encourage higher wage demands which in turn make prices rise; **wage scale** = list of wages, showing different rates of pay for different jobs in the same company;

the company's **wage structure** = organization of pay in a company with different rates for different types of job

◊ **wage-earner** *noun* person who earns money paid weekly in a job

◊ **wage-earning** *adjective* the **wage-earning population** = people who have jobs and earn money

QUOTE European economies are being held back by rigid labor markets and wage structures
Duns Business Month
QUOTE the profit squeeze is at least helping the inflation outlook by ensuring that a wage-price spiral won't develop this year. The squeeze has already halted the acceleration in wage growth that began in 1987
Business Week

waiting period = COOLING-OFF PERIOD

waive *verb* to give up (a right); *he waived his claim to the estate;* **to waive a payment** = to say that payment is not necessary

◊ **waiver** *noun* giving up (a right) *or* removing the conditions (of a rule); *if you want to work without a permit, you will have to apply for a waiver;* **waiver clause** = clause in a contract giving the conditions under which the rights in the contract can be given up

walk *verb* to go on foot; *he walks to the office every morning; the visitors walked around the factory*

◊ **walk off** *verb* to go on strike *or* to stop working and leave an office *or* factory; *the builders walked off the site because they said it was too dangerous*

◊ **walk out** *verb* to go on strike *or* to stop working and leave an office *or* factory; *the whole workforce walked out in protest*

◊ **walk-out** *noun* strike *or* stopping work; *production has been held up by the walk-out of the workers*
NOTE: plural is **walk-outs**

Wall Street *noun* name for the business and financial district of New York City; the American financial center; *a Wall Street analyst; she writes the Wall Street column in the newspaper*

want *noun* thing which is desired; **want ads** = advertisements listed in a newspaper under special headings (such as "property for sale" , or "jobs wanted"; **to draw up a wants list** = to make a list of things which you desire

war *noun* battle *or* fight *or* argument between countries *or* companies; **price war; tariff war**

warehouse 1 *noun* large building where goods are stored; **bonded warehouse =** warehouse where goods are stored until excise duty has been paid; **warehouse capacity =** space available in a warehouse; **price ex warehouse =** price for a product which is to be collected from the manufacturer's or agent's warehouse and so does not include delivery **2** *verb* to store (goods) in a warehouse

◊ **warehousing** *noun* act of storing goods; **warehousing costs are rising rapidly**

◊ **warehouseman** *noun* person who works in a warehouse

warn *verb* to say that there is a possible danger; **he warned the shareholders that the dividend might be cut; the government warned of possible import duties**

◊ **warning** *noun* notice of possible danger; **to issue a warning; warning notices were put up around the construction site**

warrant 1 *noun* official document which allows someone to do something; **dividend warrant =** check which makes payment of a dividend; **stock warrant =** document which says that someone has the right to a number of shares in a company **2** *verb* (a) to guarantee; **all the spare parts are warranted (b)** to show that something is reasonable; **the company's volume of trade with France does not warrant six trips a year to Paris by the vice-president, sales**

◊ **warrantee** *noun* person who is given a warranty

◊ **warrantor** *noun* person who gives a warranty

◊ **warranty** *noun* **(a)** guarantee *or* legal document by which the seller promises that a machine will work properly *or* that an item is of good quality; **the car is sold with a twelve-month warranty; the warranty covers spare parts but not labor costs (b)** promise in a contract; **breach of warranty =** failing to do something which is a part of a contract **(c)** statement made by an insured person which declares that the facts stated by him are true

wash sale *noun* buying stock and selling it almost immediately, to give the impression that business is good

wastage *noun* amount lost by being wasted; **allow 10% extra material for wastage**

◊ **waste 1** *noun* garbage, things which are not used; **the company was fined for putting industrial waste into the river; it is a waste of time asking the chairman for a raise; that computer is a waste of money - there are plenty of cheaper models which would do the work just as well 2** *adjective* not used; **waste materials; cardboard is made from recycled waste paper 3** *verb* to use more than is needed; **to waste money** *or* **paper** *or* **electricity** *or* **time; the CEO does not like people wasting his time with minor details; we turned off all the heating so as not to waste energy; wasting asset =** asset (such as a machine) that has a fixed life and is depreciated in a business' books of account

◊ **wastebasket** *noun* container near an office desk into which garbage can be put

◊ **wasteful** *adjective* which wastes a lot of something; **this photocopier is very wasteful of paper**

waterproof *or* **watertight** *adjective* which will not let water through; **the parts are sent in waterproof packing**

waybill *noun* description of goods carried and shipping instructions, made out by the carrier

weak *adjective* not strong *or* not active; **weak market =** market where prices tend to fall because there are no buyers; **prices remained weak on the New York Stock Exchange =** prices of securities did not rise

◊ **weaken** *verb* to become weak; **the market weakened =** share prices fell

◊ **weakness** *noun* being weak

wealth *noun* large quantity of money owned by someone; **wealth tax =** tax on money *or* property *or* investments owned by someone

◊ **wealthy** *adjective* very rich

wear and tear *noun* **normal wear and tear =** acceptable damage caused by normal use; **the insurance policy**

covers most damage but not normal wear and tear to the machine

week *noun* period of seven days (from Monday to Sunday); **to be paid by the week =** to be paid a certain amount of money each week; *he earns $500 a week or per week; she works thirty-five hours per week or she works a thirty-five-hour week*
◊ **weekday** *noun* normal working day (not Saturday or Sunday)
◊ **weekly** *adjective* done every week; *the weekly rate for the job is $250;* **a weekly magazine** *or* **a weekly =** magazine which is published each week

weigh *verb* (a) to measure how heavy something is; *he weighed the package at the post office* (b) to have a certain weight; *the package weighs five ounces*
◊ **weighbridge** *noun* platform for weighing a truck and its load
◊ **weighing machine** *noun* machine which measures how heavy a thing *or* a person is
◊ **weight** *noun* measurement of how heavy something is; **to sell fruit by weight =** the price is per pound of the fruit; **false weight =** weight on a store scale which is wrong and so cheats customers; **gross weight =** weight of both the container and its contents; **net weight =** weight of goods after deducting the packing material and container; **to give short weight =** to sell something which is lighter than it should be
◊ **weighted** *adjective* **weighted average =** average which is calculated taking several factors into account, giving some more value than others; **weighted index =** index where some important items are given more value than less important ones

welfare *noun* (a) well-being; *the chairman is interested in the welfare of the workers' families* (b) money paid by the government to people who need it; **welfare state =** country which provides many services for the health, education, etc., of the people

QUOTE California became the latest state to enact a program forcing welfare recipients to work for their benefits
Fortune

well-known *adjective* known by many people

◊ **well-paid** *adjective* earning a high salary

wharf *noun* place on a dock where a ship can tie up to load or unload
NOTE: plural is **wharfs** or **wharves**
◊ **wharfage** *noun* charge for tying up at a wharf
◊ **wharfinger** *noun* person who operates *or* manages a wharf

wheeler-dealer *noun* person who lives on money from a series of profitable business deals

whereof *adverb* *(formal)* **in witness whereof I sign my hand =** I sign as a witness that this is correct

white-collar union *noun* union made up of white-collar workers
◊ **white-collar worker** *noun* worker in an office, not in a factory
◊ **white goods** *plural noun* (a) large household appliances (such as refrigerators, washing machines) (b) sheets *or* towels, etc.
◊ **white knight** *noun* person *or* company which rescues a firm in financial difficulties, especially which saves a firm from being taken over by an unacceptable purchaser
◊ **white paper** *noun* report from the government on a particular problem
◊ **white sale** *noun* sale of sheets *or* towels, etc.

whole life insurance *noun* insurance where the insured person pays a fixed premium each year and the insurance company pays a sum when he dies, or a cash value payment when the policy is surrendered

wholesale *noun & adverb* buying goods from manufacturers and selling in large quantities to traders who then sell in smaller quantities to the general public; *wholesale discount; wholesale store;* **wholesale dealer =** person who buys in bulk from manufacturers and sells to retailers; **wholesale price index =** index showing the rises and falls of prices of manufactured goods as they leave the factory; *he buys wholesale and sells retail =* he buys goods in bulk at a wholesale discount and then sells in small quantities to the public
◊ **wholesaler** *noun* person who buys goods in bulk from manufacturers and sells them to retailers; **cash-and-carry**

wholesaler = wholesaler who runs a warehouse where retailers can come to buy items for cash

wholly-owned subsidiary *noun* company which is owned completely by one company and not partially by another

wildcat strike *noun* strike organized suddenly by workers without the main union office knowing about it

will *noun* legal document where someone says what should happen to their property when they die; *he wrote his will in 1964; according to her will, all her property is left to her children*

win *verb* to be successful; **to win a contract** = to be successful in bidding for a contract; *the company announced that it had won a contract worth $25m to supply buses and trucks*
NOTE: winning - won

windfall *noun* sudden winning of money *or* sudden profit which is not expected; **windfall profits tax** = tax on sudden profits

wind up *verb* (a) to end (a meeting); *he wound up the meeting with a vote of thanks to the committee* (b) to wind up a company = to put a company into liquidation; *the court ordered the company to be wound up*
NOTE: winding - wound

◊ **winding up** *noun* liquidation *or* closing of a company and selling its assets

window *noun* opening in a wall, with glass in it; **store window** = large window in a store front, where customers can see goods displayed; **window display** = display of goods in a store window; **window envelope** = envelope with a hole in it covered with plastic like a window, so that the address on the letter inside can be seen; **window of opportunity** = period of time when action should be taken, as it will no longer be possible later; **window shopping** = looking at goods in store windows, without buying anything

◊ **window dressing** *noun* (a) putting goods on display in a store window, so that they attract customers (b) putting on a display to make a business seem better *or* more profitable *or* more efficient than it really is

wire 1 *noun* telegram; **to send someone a wire 2** *verb* to send a telegram to (someone); *he wired the head office to say that the deal had been signed*

◊ **wire transfer** *noun* sending money by telegram

witching hour *noun* date (the last Friday of a month) when options based on Stock Exchange indexes expire, and heavy trading in securities takes place

withdraw *verb* (a) to take (money) out of an account; **to withdraw money from the bank** *or* **from your account; you can withdraw up to $50 from any bank on presentation of a banker's card** (b) to take back (an offer); **one of the company's backers has withdrawn** = he stopped supporting the company financially; **to withdraw a takeover bid; the chairman asked him to withdraw the remarks he has made about the finance manager**
NOTE: withdrawing - withdrew - has withdrawn

◊ **withdrawal** *noun* removing money from an account; **withdrawal without penalty at seven days' notice** = money can be taken out of a bank account, without losing any interest, provided that seven days' notice has been given; *to give seven days' notice of withdrawal*

withholding tax *noun* income tax deducted from the paycheck of a worker before he is paid

witness 1 *noun* person who sees something happen; **to act as a witness to a document** *or* **a signature** = to sign a document to show that you have watched the main signatory sign it; *the CEO signed as a witness; the contract has to be signed in front of two witnesses* **2** *verb* to sign (a document) to show that you guarantee that the other signatures on it are genuine; **to witness an agreement** *or* **a signature**

wording *noun* series of words; *did you read the wording on the contract?*

word processing *noun* working with words, using a computer to produce, check and change texts, reports, letters, etc.; **load the word processing program before you start typing; word processing bureau** = office which specializes in word processing for other companies

◊ **word processor** *noun* small computer *or* typewriter with a computer in it, used for working with words to produce texts, reports, letters, etc.

work 1 *noun* (a) things done using the hands *or* brain; **casual work =** work where the workers are hired for a short period; **clerical work =** work done in an office; **manual work =** work done by hand; **work in process =** value of goods being manufactured which are not complete at the end of an accounting period; **work team =** group of workers who work together as a team (b) job *or* something done to earn money; *he goes to work by bus; she never gets home from work before 8:00 p.m.; his work involves a lot of traveling; he is still looking for work; she has been out of work for six months;* **work permit =** official document which allows someone who is not a citizen to work in a country **2** *verb* (a) to do things with your hands *or* brain, for money; *the factory is working hard to complete the order; she works better now that she has been promoted;* **to work a machine =** to make a machine function (b) to have a paid job; *she works in an office; he works at Smith's; he is working as a cashier in a supermarket*

◊ **worker** *noun* (a) person who is employed; **blue-collar worker =** manual worker in a factory; **casual worker =** worker who can be hired for a short period; **clerical worker =** person who works in an office; **factory worker =** person who works in a factory; **manual worker =** worker who works with his hands; **white-collar worker =** office worker; **worker representation on the board =** having a representative of the workers as a member of the board of the company; **workers' compensation insurance** *or* **workers' comp =** system of insurance, varying among states, for paying workers who are injured or disabled on the job (b) person who works hard; *she's a real worker*

◊ **working** *adjective* (a) (person) who works; *the working population of a country;* **working partner =** partner who works in a partnership (b) referring to work; **working capital =** capital in cash and stocks needed for a company to be able to work; **working conditions =** general state of the place where people work (if it is hot, noisy, dark, dangerous, etc.); **working papers =** documents (drafts, notes, calculations) used in preparing a final document, such as a company's books of account

◊ **workforce** *noun* all the workers (in an office *or* factory)

◊ **workload** *noun* amount of work which a person has to do; *he has difficulty in coping with his heavy workload*

◊ **workman** *noun* man who works with his hands; **workmen's compensation =** WORKERS' COMPENSATION
NOTE: plural is **workmen**

◊ **work out** *verb* (a) to calculate; *he worked out the costs on the back of an envelope; he worked out the discount at 15%; she worked out the discount on her calculator* (b) to turn out well; *we are hoping the new flextime arrangements work out* (c) to exercise vigorously; *he always works out on his lunch hour*

◊ **workplace** *noun* place where you work

◊ **works** *noun* factory; *the steel works is expanding*

◊ **workshop** *noun* small factory

◊ **workspace** *noun* (a) area where a worker performs his work (b) memory *or* space available on a computer for temporary work

◊ **workstation** *noun* desk with a computer terminal, printer, telephone, etc., where a computer operator works

◊ **workweek** *noun* the normal **workweek =** the usual number of hours worked per week; *even though he is a freelance, he works a normal workweek*

QUOTE the control of materials from purchased parts through work in progress to finished goods provides manufacturers with an opportunity to reduce the amount of money tied up in materials
Duns Business Month

QUOTE the work teams consist of five to seven workers who rotate from job to job. The members elect team leaders who assume managerial duties such as scheduling production and overtime, ordering maintenance work and stopping the line to correct defects
Business Week

QUOTE last year he paid $22,000 for workers' compensation insurance, a sum that equaled about one-fourth of the total payroll for his small band of employees
Nation's Business

QUOTE workers' compensation costs in Texas have surged 123 percent since 1985 and are now among the highest in the nation, yet injured workers receive benefits lower than those in 46 states
Nation's Business

world *noun* (a) the earth; **the world market for steel =** the possible sales of steel in the whole world; **he has world rights to a product =** he has the right to sell the product anywhere in the world

(b) people in a particular business *or* people with a special interest; *the world of big business; the world of publishing* or *the publishing world; the world of lawyers* or *the legal world*

◇ **World Bank** *noun* central bank, controlled by the United Nations, whose funds come from the member states of the UN and which lends money to member states

◇ **worldwide** *adjective* & *adverb* everywhere in the world; *the company has a worldwide network of distributors; worldwide sales* or *sales worldwide have topped two million units; this make of computer is available worldwide*

QUOTE the EC pays farmers 27 cents a pound for sugar and sells it on the world market for 5 cents
Duns Business Month

worth 1 *adjective* having a value *or* a price; *do not get it repaired - it is worth only $25; the car is worth $6,000 on the secondhand market; he is worth $10m* = his property *or* investments, etc., would sell for $10m; *what are ten pesos worth in dollars?* = what is the equivalent of ten pesos in dollars? **2** *noun* value; *give me ten dollars' worth of gas* = give me as much gas as $10 will buy

◇ **worthless** *adjective* having no value; *the check is worthless if it is not signed*

wrap (up) *verb* to cover something all over (in paper); *he wrapped (up) the parcel in green paper; to gift-wrap a present* = to wrap a present in special colored paper
NOTE: wrapping - wrapped

◇ **wrapper** *noun* material which wraps something; *the cookies are packed in plastic wrappers*

◇ **wrapping** *noun* wrapping paper = special colored paper for wrapping presents; **gift-wrapping** = (i) service in a store for wrapping presents for customers; (ii) colored paper for wrapping presents

wreck 1 *noun* **(a)** ship which has sunk *or* which has been badly damaged and cannot float; *they saved the cargo from the wreck; oil poured out of the wreck of the tanker* **(b)** company which has collapsed; *investors lost thousands of dollars in the wreck of the investment company* **2** *verb* to damage badly *or* to ruin; *they are trying to salvage the*

wrecked tanker; the negotiations were wrecked by the unions

writ *noun* legal document ordering someone to do something *or* not to do something; *the court issued a writ to prevent the union members from going on strike; to serve someone with a writ* or *to serve a writ on someone* = to give someone a writ officially, so that they have to obey it

write *verb* to put words *or* figures on to paper; *she wrote a letter of complaint to the manager; the telephone number is written at the bottom of the letter*
NOTE: writing - wrote - has written

◇ **write down** *verb* to note an asset at a lower value than previously; *written-down value; the truck is written down in the company's books*

◇ **write-down** *noun* noting of an asset at a lower value

◇ **write off** *verb* to cancel (a debt) *or* to remove an asset from the books of account as having no value; *to write off bad debts; two cars were written off after the accident* = the insurance company determined that both cars were a total loss; *the cargo was written off as a total loss* = the cargo was so badly damaged that the insurers said it had no value

◇ **write-off** *noun* total loss *or* cancellation of a bad debt *or* removal of an asset's value in a company's books of account; *the car was a write-off; to allow for write-offs in the yearly statement*

◇ **write out** *verb* to write in full; *she wrote out the minutes of the meeting from her notes; to write out a check* = to write the words and figures on a check and then sign it

◇ **writing** *noun* something which has been written; *to put the agreement in writing; he has difficulty in reading my writing*

QUOTE the holding company has seen its earnings suffer from big write-downs in conjunction with its $1 billion loan portfolio
Duns Business Month
QUOTE the company car has been around longer than the Internal Revenue Code. So you would think that by now the rules governing write-offs for business cars would be easy to understand. Well, think again
Nation's Business

wrong *adjective* not right *or* not correct; *the total in the last column is wrong; the sales manager reported the wrong figures to the meeting*

◊ **wrongful** *adjective* unlawful; **wrongful dismissal** = removing someone from a job for reasons which are wrong

◊ **wrongly** *adverb* not correctly *or* badly; *he wrongly invoiced Smith Corp. for $250, when he should have credited them with the same amount*

W-2 form *noun* form given by an employer to each employee, showing tax and social security insurance paid

Xx Yy Zz

X = EXTENSION

Xerox 1 *noun* trade mark for a type of photocopier; *to make a xerox copy of a letter; we must order some more xerox paper for the copier; we are having a new xerox machine installed tomorrow* **2** *verb* to make a photocopy with a xerox machine; *to xerox a document; she xeroxed the whole file*

yard *noun* **(a)** measure of length (= 36 inches) (NOTE: can be written **yd** after figures: **10 yds**) **(b)** factory which builds ships

yd = YARD

year *noun* period of twelve months; **calendar year** = year from January 1 to December 31; **fiscal year** = twelve-month period for a business's or a government's financial statement; **year-end** = the end of the fiscal year, when a company's books of account are prepared; *the finance department has started work on the year-end accounts*

◊ **yearbook** *noun* reference book which is published each year with updated or new information

◊ **yearly** *adjective* happening once a year; *yearly payment; yearly premium of $250*

yellow pages *plural noun* section of a telephone directory (printed on yellow paper) which lists businesses under various headings (such as computer stores or banks, etc.)

yen *noun* money used in Japan

NOTE: usually written as **Y** before a figure: **Y2,700** (say "two thousand seven hundred yen")

yield 1 *noun* money produced as a return on an investment; **current yield** = dividend calculated as a percentage of the price paid per share; *share with a current yield of 5%;* **dividend yield** = dividend expressed as a percentage of the price of a share; **earnings yield** = money earned in dividends per share as a percentage of the market price of the share; **effective yield** = actual yield shown as a percentage of the market price, as distinct from the price paid; **fixed yield** = fixed percentage return which does not change; **gross yield** = profit from investments before tax is deducted **2** *verb* to produce (as interest *or* dividend, etc.); *government stocks which yield a small interest; shares which yield 10%*

zero *noun* no quantity; number 0; *the code for international calls is zero one one (011);* **zero inflation** = inflation at 0%

◊ **zero-base budgeting** *noun* system of budgeting where all expenditures are revalued every time a new budget is prepared

◊ **zero-coupon bond** *noun* bond which does not carry any interest *or* where the interest is contained in the capital gain

◊ **zero proof** *noun* mechanical method for posting records in a manner which proves that the previous balance on each line of posting was made accurately

ZIP code *noun* series of numbers used to represent the area or part of a city or town where an address is situated

zipper clause *noun* standard clause in a negotiated contract, representing an attempt to prevent or bar any discussion of employment conditions during the life of the agreement

zone 1 *noun* area of a city *or* country (for administrative purposes); **development zone** *or* **enterprise zone** = area which has been given special help from the government to encourage businesses and factories to set up there; **free trade zone** = area where there are no customs duties **2** *verb* to divide (a city) into different areas for planning purposes; **land zoned for light industrial use** = land where planning permission has been given to build small factories for light industry; **zoning ordinance** = local law that regulates the types of buildings and their uses in various sections of a city

◇ **zone pricing** *noun* pricing policy under which the seller divides the market into a number of zones, quoting different prices in each different zone zone

SUPPLEMENT

Abbreviations

acc *or* acct	account
ack	acknowledge
a.m.	in the morning, before noon
amt	amount
ans	answer
approx	approximate(ly)
Apr	April
apt	apartment
arr	arrive *or* arrival
asst	assistant
att	attorney
Aug	August
ave	avenue
blvd	boulevard
canc	canceled
cc	carbon copy
CIF	cost, insurance and freight
co	company *or* county
c/o	care of (put on an address)
COD	collect on delivery
cont *or* contd	continued
corr	correspondence
cr	credit
Dec	December
dely	delivery
dept	department
disc	discount
div	dividend
do	ditto (the same)
doc	document
dol	dollar
e.g.	for example
enc *or* encl	enclosure
equiv	equivalent
esp	especially
est	estimated
et al	and others
etc	etcetera (and so on)
exch	exchange
ext	extension
Feb	February
fed	federal
fig	figure *or* figuratively
FOB	free on board
FOR	free on rail
Fri	Friday
frwy	freeway
fwd	forward
gal	gallon
gds	goods
gov	governor
govt	government
HQ	headquarters
hr	hour

i.e.	that is, in other words
int	interest
inv	invoice
Jan	January
L/C	letter of credit
Mar	March
max	maximum
mfg	manufacturing
mgr	manager
min	minimum
misc	miscellaneous
mo	month
Mon	Monday
mtge	mortgage
natl	national
NB	Nota Bene, take special note that . . .
no	number
Nov	November
NSF	not sufficient funds
o/a	on account
o.b.o.	or best offer
Oct	October
o/s	out of stock
pa	per annum
P and L	profit and loss
pc	per cent *or* postcard
per	period
pfd	preferred
pkg	package
pkt	packet
p.m.	in the afternoon, in the evening, after 12 noon
prev	previous
PS *or* P.S.	post script (on a letter)
qty	quantity
qy	query
rd	road
re	with regard to
recd *or* rec'd	received
ref	with reference to
rte	route
Sat	Saturday
sec	secretary
Sep	September
shpt	shipment
st	street
Sun	Sunday
tel	telegram *or* telephone
Thur *or* Thurs	Thursday
tot	total
Tues	Tuesday
VP	vice-president
vs	versus
Wed	Wednesday
whse	warehouse
wk	week
w/o	without

USA—states

State		Capital
Alabama	(AL)	Montgomery
Alaska	(AK)	Juneau
Arizona	(AZ)	Phoenix
Arkansas	(AR)	Little Rock
California	(CA)	Sacramento
Colorado	(CO)	Denver
Connecticut	(CT)	Hartford
Delaware	(DE)	Dover
Florida	(FL)	Tallahassee
Georgia	(GA)	Atlanta
Hawaii	(HI)	Honolulu
Idaho	(ID)	Boise
Illinois	(IL)	Springfield
Indiana	(IN)	Indianapolis
Iowa	(IA)	Des Moines
Kansas	(KS)	Topeka
Kentucky	(KY)	Frankfort
Louisiana	(LA)	Baton Rouge
Maine	(ME)	Augusta
Maryland	(MD)	Annapolis
Massachusetts	(MA)	Boston
Michigan	(MI)	Lansing
Minnesota	(MN)	St Paul
Mississippi	(MS)	Jackson
Missouri	(MO)	Jefferson City
Montana	(MT)	Helena
Nebraska	(NE)	Lincoln
Nevada	(NV)	Carson City
New Hampshire	(NH)	Concord
New Jersey	(NJ)	Trenton
New Mexico	(NM)	Santa Fe
New York	(NY)	Albany
North Carolina	(NC)	Raleigh
North Dakota	(ND)	Bismarck
Ohio	(OH)	Columbus
Oklahoma	(OK)	Oklahoma City
Oregon	(OR)	Salem
Pennsylvania	(PA)	Harrisburg
Rhode Island	(RI)	Providence
South Carolina	(SC)	Columbia
South Dakota	(SD)	Pierre
Tennessee	(TN)	Nashville
Texas	(TX)	Austin
Utah	(UT)	Salt Lake City
Vermont	(VT)	Montpelier
Virginia	(VA)	Richmond
Washington	(WA)	Olympia
West Virginia	(WV)	Charleston
Wisconsin	(WI)	Madison
Wyoming	(WY)	Cheyenne
District of Columbia	(DC)	Washington

Canada—provinces

Province		*Capital*
Alberta	(Alta.)	Edmonton
British Columbia	(BC)	Victoria
Manitoba	(Man.)	Winnipeg
New Brunswick	(NB)	Frederictn
Newfoundland	(Nfld.)	St John's
Nova Scotia	(NS)	Halifax
Ontario	(Ont.)	Toronto
Prince Edward Island	(PEI)	Charlottetown
Québec	(Qué.)	Québec
Saskatchewan	(Sask.)	Regina

The Territories

Yukon Territory	(YT)	Whitehorse
Northwest Territories	(NWT)	Yellowknife

Money

In the list of world currencies that follows, words marked (*) usually have no plural e.g. 1 kyat, 'one kyat', 200 kyat, 'two hundred kyat'.

Country	Currency	Divided into	Abbreviation
Afganistan	Afghani*	puli	Af or Afs
Albania	Lek*	quindars	Lk
Algeria	Algerian dinar	centimes	AD or DA
Andorra	French Franc	centimes	
Angola	Kwanza*	cents	KW
Antigua	East Caribbean Dollar	cents	ECar$ or EC$
Argentina	Austral	centavos	
Australia	Australian Dollar	cents	A$
Austria	Schilling	groschen	Sch or ASch
Bahamas	Bahamian Dollar	cents	Ba$
Bahrein	Bahreini Dinar	fils	BD
Bangladesh	Taka*	poisha	Tk
Barbados	Barbados Dollar	cents	Bd$ BD$
Belgium	Belgian Franc	centimes	Bfr or Bf or FB
Belize	Belize Dollar	cents	B$ or $B
Benin	CFA Franc	centimes	CFA Fr
Bermuda	Bermuda Dollar	cents	Bda$
Bhutan	Ngultrum*	tikchung	N
Bolivia	Bolivian peso	centavos	B$ or $b
Botswana	Pula	cents	Pu or P
Brazil	Cruzeiro	centavos	Cr or Cr$
Brunei	Brunei Dollar	cents	Br$ or B$
Bulgaria	Lev*	stotinki	Lv
Burkina Faso	CFA Franc	centimes	CFA Fr
Burma	Kyat*	pyas	Kt
Brundi	Burundi Franc	centimes	Bur Fr or FrBr
Cambodia (see Kampuchea)			
Cameroon	CFA Franc	centimes	CFA Fr
Canada	Canadian Dollar	cents	Can$ or C$
Cape Verde Islands	Escudo Caboverdianos	centavos	CV esc
Cayman Islands	Cayman Island Dollar	cents	CayI$
Central African Republic	CFA Franc	centimes	CFA Fr
Chad	Cfa Franc	centimes	CFA Fr
Chile	Chilean Peso	centavos	Ch$
China	Yuan* or renminbi*	fen	Y
Colombia	Colombian Peso	centavos	Col$
Comoros	CFA Franc	centimes	CFA Fr
Congo	CFA Franc	centimes	CFA Fr
Costa Rica	Colón*	centimos	CR¢ or ¢
Cuba	Cuban Peso	centavos	Cub$
Cyprus	Cyprus Pound	Mils	£C or C£
Czechoslovakia	Crown or Koruna	hellers, halern	Kčs
Dahomey (see Benin)			
Denmark	Krone	örer	DKr or DKK
Djibouti	Djibouti Franc	centimes	Dj Fr
Dominica	East Caribbean Dollar	cents	ECar$ or EC$
Dominican Republic	Dominican Peso	centavos	DR$
Ecuador	Sucre*	centavos	Su
Egypt	Egyptian Pound	piastres	£E or E£
Eire (see Irisn Republic)			
El Salvador	Colón*	centavos	ES¢ or ¢
Equatorial Guinea	Ekuele* or ekpwele or peseta Guineana	cetimos	E

Country	Currency	Divided into	Abbreviation
Ethiopia	Birr* or Ethiopian Dollar	cents	Br
Fiji	Fijian Dollar	cents	$F or F$
Finland	Markka*	pennia	Fmk
France	French Franc	centimes	Fr or F or FF
French Guiana	French Franc	centimes	Fr or F or FF
Gabon	CFA Franc	centimes	CFA Fr
Gambia, The	Dalasi*	butut	Di
Germany	Deutsche Mark	pfennig	DM
Ghana	Cedi*	pesewas	¢
Great Britain (see United Kingdom)			
Greece	Drachma	lepta	Dr
Grenada	East Caribbean Dollar	cents	ECar$ or EC$
Guatamala	Quetzal	centavos	Q
Guinea	Syli*	cauris	Sy
Guinea—Bissau	Guinea—Bassau Peso	centavos	GB P
Guyana	Guyana Dollar	cents	G$ or Guy$
Haiti	Gourde*	centimes	Gde
Holland (see Netherlands)			
Honduras	Lempira*	centavos	La
Hong Kong	Hong Kong Dollar	cents	HK$
Hungary	Forint	filler	Ft
Iceland	Króna	aurar	IKr
India	Rupee	paise	R or Re or Rs
Indonesia	Rupiah*	sen	Rp
Iran	Rial*	dinars	RI
Iraq	Iragui Dinar	fils	ID
Irish Republic	Irish Pound or Punt	pence	IR£ or £
Israel	Shekel	agorot	IS
Italy	Lira	centesimi	L
Ivory Coast	CFA Franc	centimes	CFA Fr
Jamaica	Jamaican Dollar	cents	J$ or Jam$
Japan	Yen*	sen	Y or ¥
Jordan	Jordanian Dinar	fils	JD
Kampuchea	Riel*	sen	RI
Kenya	Kenyan Shilling	cents	KSh or Sh
Korea:			
North Korea	North Korean Won*	jon	NK W
South Korea	South Korean Won*	chon	SK W
Kuwait	Kuwaiti Dinar	fils	KD
Laos	Kip*	at	K or Kp
Lebanon	Lebanese Pound	piastres	£Leb or L£
Lesotho	Loti*	lisente	L
Liberia	Liberian Dollar	cents	L$
Libya	Libyan dinar	dirhams	LD
Liechtenstein	Swiss Franc	centimes	SFr or FS
Luxembourg	Luxembourg Franc	centimes	LFr
Macau	Pataca*	avos	P or $
Madeira	Portuguese Escudo	centavos	Esc
Malagasy Republic	Malagasy Franc	centimes	FMG or Mal Fr
Malawi	Kwacha*	tambala	K or MK
Malaysia	Ringgit* or Malaysian Dollar	cents	M$
Maldives	Maldivian Rupee	paise	MvRe
Mali	Mali Franc	centimes	MFr or MF
Malta	Maltese Pound	cents	£M or M£
Mauritania	Ouguiya*	khoums	U
Mauritius	Mauritian Rupee	cents	Mau Rs or R
Mexico	Peso	centavos	Mex$
Monaco	French Franc	centimes	Fr or F or FF

Country	Currency	Divided into	Abbreviation
Mongolian Republic	Tugrik*	möngös	Tug
Montserrat	E. Caribbean Dollar	cents	ECar$ or EC$
Morocco	Dirham	centimes	Dh or DH
Mozambique	Metical*	centavos	M
Namibia	South African Rand	cents	R
Nauru	Australian Dollar	cents	A$
Nepal	Nepalese Rupee	Paise	NR or NRe
Netherlands, The	Guilder or Gulden or Florin	cents	HFl or DFl or Gld or Fl
New Hebrides (see Vanuatu)			
New Zealand	New Zealand Dollar	cents	NZ$
Nicaragua	Córdoba	centavos	C$ or C
Niger	CFA Franc	centimes	CFA Fr
Nigeria	Naira*	kobo	N or ₦
Norway	Krone	örer	NKr
Oman	Omani Ryal or Rial	baizas	RO
Pakistan	Pakistan Rupee	paise	R or Pak Re
Panama	Balboa	centesimos	Ba
Papua New Guinea	Kina*	toea	Ka or K
Paraguay	Guarani*	centimos	G
Peru	Inti*	centavos	S
Philippines	Philippine Peso	centavos	P or PP
Poland	Zloty	groszy	Zl
Portugal	Escudo	centavos	Esc
Puerto Rico	US Dollar	cents	$ or US$
Qatar	Qatar Riyal	dirhams	QR
Reunion	CFA Franc	centimes	CFA Fr
Romania	Leu*	bani	L or l
Rwanda	Rwanda Franc	centimes	Bw Fr
St. Lucia	E. Caribbean Dollar	cents	ECar$ or EC$
St. Vincent	E. Caribbean Dollar	cents	ECar$ or EC$
Saudi Arabia	Saudi Riyal or Rial	halalah	SA R
Senegal	CFA Franc	centimes	CFA Fr
Seychelles	Seychelles Rupee	cents	SRe or R
Sierra Leone	Leone	cents	Le
Singapore	Singapore Dollar	cents	S$ or Sing$
Solomon Islands	Solomon Island Dollar	cents	SI$
Somalia	Somali Schilling	cents	Som Sh or So Sh
South Africa	Rand*	cents	R
Spain	Peseta	centimos	Pta
Sri Lanka	Sri Lanka Rupee	cents	SC Re
Sudan	Sudanese Pound	piastres	Sud£ or £S
Surinam	Surinam Guilder	cents	S Gld
Swaziland	Lilangeni*	cents	Li or E
Sweden	Krona	örer	SKr
Switzerland	Swiss Franc	centimes	SFr or SWFr
Syria	Syrian Pound	piastres	£Syr or S£
Taiwan	New Taiwan Dollar	cents	T$ or NT$
Tanzania	Tanzanian Shilling	cents	TSh
Thailand	Baht*	satang	Bt
Tonga	Pa'anga*	senik	
Togo	CFA Franc	centimes	CFA Fr
Trinidad & Tobago	Trinidad & Tobago Dollar	cents	TT$
Tunisia	Tunisian Dinar	millimes	TD
Turkey	Turkish Lira	kurus	TL
Tuvalu	Australian Dollar	cents	$A
Uganda	Uganda Shilling	cents	USh

Country	Currency	Divided into	Abbreviation
U.S.S.R.	Ruble	kopecks	Rub
United Arab Emirates	UAE Dirham	fils	UAE Dh *or* UD
United Kingdom	Pound (Sterling)	pence	£ *or* £Stg
United States of America	Dollar	cents	$ *or* US$
Upper Volta (see Burkina Faso)			
Uruguay	Uruguayan New Peso	centesimos	N$
Vanuatu			
Venezuela		vatu	
Vietnam	Bolívar	centimos	B
Virgin Islands	Dong*	xu	D
Western Samoa	US Dollar	cents	$ *or* US$
	Tala *or* Dollar *or* Western Samoan Dollar	cents *or* sene	WS$ *or* $WS
South Yemen	South Yemen Dinar	fils	YD
Northern Yemen	Yemeni Riyal	fils	YR
Yugoslavia	Dinar	paras	Din *or* DN
Zaire	Zaire	makata	Z
Zambia	Kwacha*	ngwee	K
Zimbabwe	Zimbabwe Dollar	cents	Z$

Measurement

U.S.				Metric	
Length					
inch	in or "	25.400	0.039	millimeter	mm
inch		2.540	0.39	centimeter	cm
foot	ft or '	0.305	3.28	meter	m
yard	yd	0.914	1.094	meter	m
mile	m or mi	1.609	0.621	kilometer	km
Weight					
ounce	oz	28.350	0.035	gram	gm
pound	lb	0.454	2.205	kilogram	kg
hundredweight	cwt	45.360	0.022	kilogram	kg
ton		0.907	1.102	metric ton	
Capacity					
pint	pt	0.473	2.113	liter	l
gallon	gal	3.785	0.264	liter	l
Area					
square inch	sq in or in^2	6.452	0.155	square centimeter	cm^2
square foot	sq ft or ft^2	0.093	10.764	square meter	m^2
square yard	sq yd or yd^2	0.836	1.196	square meter	m^2
acre		0.4047	2.471	hectare	ha^2
square mile	sq m or mi^2	2.590	0.386	square kilometer	km^2
Volume					
cubic inch	cu in or in^3	16.38	0.061	cubic centimeter	cm^3 or cc
cubic foot	cu ft or ft^3	0.028	35.315	cubic meter	m^3
cubic yard	cu yd or yd^3	0.765	1.308	cubic meter	m^3